Transaction Cost Economics
Volume II

The International Library of Critical Writings in Economics

Series Editor: Mark Blaug

Professor Emeritus, University of London
Professor Emeritus, University of Buckingham
Visiting Professor, University of Exeter

This series is an essential reference source for students, researchers and lecturers in economics. It presents by theme an authoritative selection of the most important articles across the entire spectrum of economics. Each volume has been prepared by a leading specialist who has written an authoritative introduction to the literature included.

A full list of published and future titles in this series is printed at the end of this volume.

Transaction Cost Economics Volume II

Policy and Applications

Edited by

Oliver E. Williamson

Edgar F. Kaiser Professor of Business Administration
Professor of Economics, Professor of Law
University of California at Berkeley, US

and

Scott E. Masten

Associate Professor of Business Economics and Public Policy
Graduate School of Business Administration
University of Michigan, US

THE INTERNATIONAL LIBRARY OF CRITICAL WRITINGS IN ECONOMICS

An Elgar Reference Collection

Published by
Edward Elgar Publishing Limited
Gower House
Croft Road
Aldershot
Hants GU11 3HR
England

Edward Elgar Publishing Company
Old Post Road
Brookfield
Vermont 05036
USA

British Library Cataloguing in Publication Data
Transaction Cost Economics. –
(International Library of Critical
Writings in Economics; Vol. 54)
I. Williamson, Oliver E. II. Masten,
Scott E. III. Series
338.5

Library of Congress Cataloguing in Publication Data
Transaction cost economics / edited by Oliver E. Williamson and Scott E. Masten.
p. cm. — (The International library of critical writings in economics; 54)
Includes bibliographical references and index.
Contents: 1. Theory and concepts — 2. Policy and applications
1. Transaction costs. 2. Industrial organization (Economic theory) 3. Institutional economics. I. Williamson, Oliver E.
II. Masten, Scott E., 1955– . III. Series.
HB846.3.T72 1995
338.5—dc20 95–5632
CIP

ISBN 1 85278 952 2 (2 volume set)

Printed in Great Britain by Galliard (Printers) Ltd, Great Yarmouth

Contents

Acknowledgements

The editors and publishers wish to thank the following who have kindly given permission for the use of copyright material.

American Economic Association for articles: Scott E. Masten and Keith J. Crocker (1985), 'Efficient Adaptation in Long-Term Contracts: Take-or-Pay Provisions for Natural Gas', *American Economic Review*, **75** (5), December, 1083–93; Paul L. Joskow (1987), 'Contract Duration and Relationship-Specific Investments: Empirical Evidence from Coal Markets', *American Economic Review*, **77** (1), March, 168–85.

Oxford University Press Inc. for articles: Paul L. Joskow (1985), 'Vertical Integration and Long-term Contracts: The Case of Coal-burning Electric Generating Plants', *Journal of Law, Economics, and Organization*, **1** (1), Fall, 33–80; J. Harold Mulherin (1986), 'Complexity in Long-term Contracts: An Analysis of Natural Gas Contractual Provisions', *Journal of Law, Economics, and Organization*, **2** (1), Spring, 105–17; Benjamin Klein (1988), 'Vertical Integration as Organizational Ownership: The Fisher Body–General Motors Relationship Revisited', *Journal of Law, Economics, and Organization*, **4** (1), Spring, 199–213; George John and Barton A. Weitz (1988), 'Forward Integration into Distribution: An Empirical Test of Transaction Cost Analysis', *Journal of Law, Economics, and Organization*, **4** (2), Fall, 337–55; Rafael Gely and Pablo T. Spiller (1990), 'A Rational Choice Theory of Supreme Court Statutory Decisions with Applications to the *State Farm* and *Grove City* Cases', *Journal of Law, Economics, and Organization*, **6** (2), Fall, 263–300; Scott E. Masten, James W. Meehan, Jr. and Edward A. Snyder (1991), 'The Costs of Organization', *Journal of Law, Economics, and Organization*, **7** (1), Spring, 1 25; Brian Levy and Pablo T. Spiller, 'The Institutional Foundations of Regulatory Commitment: A Comparative Analysis of Telecommunication Regulation', now published in *Journal of Law, Economics, and Organization*, **10** (2), Fall, 1994, 201–46.

RAND for articles: Victor P. Goldberg (1976), 'Regulation and Administered Contracts', *Bell Journal of Economics*, **7** (2), Autumn, 426–48; Oliver E. Williamson (1976), 'Franchise Bidding for Natural Monopolies – In General and with Respect to CATV', *Bell Journal of Economics*, **7** (1), Spring, 73–104; Kirk Monteverde and David J. Teece (1982), 'Supplier Switching Costs and Vertical Integration in the Automobile Industry', *Bell Journal of Economics*, **13** (1), Spring, 206–13; Erin Anderson and David C. Schmittlein (1984), 'Integration of the Sales Force: An Empirical Examination', *Rand Journal of Economics*, **15** (3), Autumn, 385–95.

University of Chicago Press for articles: Keith B. Leffler and Randal R. Rucker (1991), 'Transactions Costs and the Efficient Organization of Production: A Study of Timber-Harvesting Contracts', *Journal of Political Economy*, **99** (5), October, 1060–87; Barry R. Weingast and William J. Marshall (1988), 'The Industrial Organization of Congress; or, Why Legislatures, Like Firms Are Not Organized as Markets', *Journal of Political Economy*, **96** (1), 132–63.

University of Chicago Law School for articles: Roy W. Kenney and Benjamin Klein (1983), 'The Economics of Block Booking', *Journal of Law and Economics*, **XXVI** (3), October, 497–540; Thomas M. Palay (1984), 'Comparative Institutional Economics: The Governance of Rail Freight Contracting', *Journal of Legal Studies*, **XIII** (2), June, 265–87; Scott E. Masten (1984), 'The Organization of Production: Evidence from the Aerospace Industry', *Journal of Law and Economics*, **XXVII** (2), October, 403–17; Victor P. Goldberg and John R. Erickson (1987), 'Quantity and Price Adjustment in Long-Term Contracts: A Case Study of Petroleum Coke', *Journal of Law and Economics*, **XXX** (2), October, 369–98; Keith J. Crocker and Scott E. Masten (1991), 'Pretia ex Machina? Prices and Process in Long-Term Contracts', *Journal of Law and Economics*, **XXXIV** (1), April, 69–99; George L. Priest (1993), 'The Origins of Utility Regulation and the "Theories of Regulation" Debate', *Journal of Law and Economics*, **XXXVI** (1), Part 2, April, 289–323; Scott E. Masten and Edward A. Snyder (1993), '*United States versus United Shoe Machinery Corporation*: On the Merits', *Journal of Law and Economics*, **XXXVI** (1), Part 1, April, 33–70.

University of Pennsylvania Law Review for article: Oliver E. Williamson (1979), 'Assessing Vertical Market Restrictions: Antitrust Ramifications of the Transaction Cost Approach', *University of Pennsylvania Law Review*, **127**, April, 953–93.

Every effort has been made to trace all the copyright holders but if any have been inadvertently overlooked the publishers will be pleased to make the necessary arrangement at the first opportunity.

In addition the publishers wish to thank the Library of the London School of Economics and Political Science, and the Marshall Library of Economics, Cambridge University for their assistance in obtaining these articles.

Introduction

Progress in the application and testing of transaction cost economics can only be described as phenomenal. While Ronald Coase could justifiably lament the dearth of research on the organization of industry in 1972 (see the opening article in Volume I), the transaction cost literature today contains scores of empirical studies on the topics Coase viewed as central to our understanding of industrial organization – studies of the allocation of activities among firms, of the structure of contractual arrangements between firms, and of the role and extent of participation by government agencies in industry. That progress was stimulated by – indeed owes its very existence to – conceptual developments in the theory of transaction costs taking place virtually as Coase spoke. The 'operationalization' of transaction cost reasoning, which seeks to relate the relative merits of alternative institutional arrangements to observable attributes of transactions, generated an array of refutable implications regarding the institutions and organizational forms used to govern production and exchange. Efforts to collect the necessary data and subject the theory to empirical testing began very shortly thereafter.

The readings in this volume provide an overview of developments over the last two decades in the application of transaction cost reasoning to a range of organizational and public policy issues. The topics represented include both forward and backward integration decisions, the duration and structure of contracts, the merits of franchise contracting in relation to regulation, antitrust policy toward nonstandard business practices, and the design of political institutions and their interactions with private governance. The list of industries covered includes aerospace, automotive components, cable television, coal, wholesale diamonds, electrical components, movie distribution, natural gas, rail freight, shipbuilding, shoe machinery, telecommunications, and timber harvesting. At that, Volume II only scratches the surface of what is a rapidly expanding body of research. Among the applications not represented are analyses of vertical relations in aluminium, agriculture, biotechnology, education and ocean shipping as well as extensions to labour organization, corporate finance and corporate governance, multinational corporations, franchising and nonprofit organization.

The success of transaction cost economics in explaining observed patterns of organization was by no means inevitable. Not the least of the hurdles along the path was the need to assemble data of sufficiently microanalytic detail to meet the demands of the theory. By and large, economic data series, following the interests of mainstream economics, focus on prices and quantities. Transaction cost economics, in contrast, requires detailed information on organizational form as well as on attributes of transactions such as the level of uncertainty associated with exchange, the complexity of products and processes, and the extent to which assets needed for production are specific to a particular relationship. For the most part, transaction cost economists have had to develop their own data using surveys, interviews and legal, regulatory and business archives.

Nor was there any guarantee that transaction cost theory, being refutable, would be supported by the evidence. As the articles in this collection and in broader surveys of the empirical transaction cost literature attest (see Klein and Shelanski, 1994; and Crocker and Masten, forthcoming), however, the theory and evidence have displayed remarkable congruity. The effect has been to alter irreversibly the way in which economists perceive and analyse the problem of economic organization.

Despite the depth and scope of this research, the successful operationalization and application of transaction cost arguments have not gained universal recognition. Thus, even as interested a student of organization as Herbert Simon could as recently as 1991 complain that transaction costs 'are typically introduced into the analysis in a casual way, with no empirical support except to appeal to introspection and common sense .... Until [the empirical research that must be performed to estimate the exogenous parameters and to test the theory empirically] has been carried out ..., the new institutional economics and related approaches are acts of faith, or perhaps of piety' (Simon, 1991, p. 27). The articles reprinted herein should help to dispel any lingering misperceptions.

The readings in this volume are divided into four Parts: vertical integration; contracting; regulation and positive political economy; and antitrust. In the remainder of this introduction, I describe the articles, their principal findings and contributions, and conclude with some final observations on the state of and prospects for empirical and public policy research in transaction cost economics.

1. Vertical Integration

Following developments on the theoretical side, the earliest applications and most extensive testing of transaction cost propositions have focused on the choice between internal and market organization and especially the role of asset specificity in those decisions. In 'Vertical Integration as Organizational Ownership: The Fisher Body–General Motors Relationship Revisited' (reprinted as Chapter 1 pp. 3–17), Benjamin Klein elaborates on what has become a classic illustration (originally sketched in Klein, Crawford and Alchian, 1978) of the role of relationship-specific investments in the decision to integrate. In response partly to Ronald Coase's scepticism about the importance of asset specificity for economic organization (Coase, 1988), Klein describes the limits of reputation and contracting in constraining opportunism and how, as in GM's experience with Fisher Body, 'contracts may actually create, rather than solve, hold-up problems' (203). His description of the evolution of that relationship – especially the adoption of a long-term, exclusive dealing contract following the introduction of capital-intensive metal auto bodies around 1919 and the conflicts that arose when demand for metal bodies soared unexpectedly in the early years of the contract – provides a rare look at the dynamics of the transformation process and the hazards of choosing the wrong form of organization. Klein also contributes to the longstanding debate over the advantages accruing to internal organization, using GM's subsequent integration of Fisher Body to illustrate how the acquisition of 'organizational capital' through vertical integration reduces the potential for hold ups associated with relationship-specific human assets.

The role of specific assets in the decision to integrate is also the central theme in Paul Joskow's 1985 examination of the relations between coal mines and electric utilities (reprinted as Chapter 2 pp. 18–65). As predicted by the theory, Joskow found that vertical integration of coal supplies was much more prevalent among mine-mouth electric generators than for other coal-fired generating stations, reflecting the greater site specificity of the plants located adjacent to a coal mine. Furthermore, for those mine-mouth plants that were not vertically integrated, coal supplies were governed under very long-term contracts often accompanied by added supports. Joskow's detailed description of the complex yet incomplete nature of those contracts accelerated the shift in attention in economic theory from complete to incomplete contracting.

Even before Joskow's careful and revealing examination of the arrangements utilities and mines used to safeguard their relations, researchers had begun to produce and publish formal statistical tests of transaction cost arguments. The earliest of those studies was Kirk Monteverde and David Teece's (1982, reprinted as Chapter 3 pp. 66–73) analysis of the role of asset specificity in the procurement decisions of automobile manufacturers. Monteverde and Teece argue that the specialized know-how arising in the development of new automotive components and the difficulty of transferring that know-how make it costly to switch suppliers once applications engineering has been completed. Their statistical analysis, employing qualitative measures of the level of engineering effort and of the specificity of automotive components, provided the first formal evidence of the role of specific investments in the decision to integrate vertically and complements Klein's case analysis of the factors underlying organization in the automotive industry.

My 1984 article (reprinted as Chapter 4 pp. 74–88) examining the determinants of make-or-buy decisions in an aerospace programme provided additional support for the importance of relationship-specific investments in the governance of vertical relations and also offered early evidence that complexity influences the differential efficiency of contracting and internal administration. In particular, the finding that component specificity had its greatest effect on the probability of integration for relatively complex components supports the prediction that the hazards of contracting relative to internal administration rise as the obligations of the parties become more difficult to define. By formulating the make-or-buy choice as an expected cost-minimization problem, this paper also illuminates the relation between the parameters of the qualitative choice models used to test transaction cost hypotheses and the differential costs of transacting. The connection between the empirical tests and comparative institutional orientation of the theory was thus brought into sharper focus.

Although the empirical research on integration decisions has emphasized the upstream integration of suppliers, the theory underlying that research extends as well to integration downstream into distribution and marketing acivities. Given the longstanding concern in marketing with the structure of distribution channels, it is perhaps natural that marketing scholars have taken the lead in applying transaction cost insights to forward integration. The now substantial body of research on forward integration is represented here by two studies. The first, Erin Anderson and David Schmittlein's examination of distribution practices in the electronic components industry, (reprinted as Chapter 5 pp. 89–99), was the earliest study in this category. Their findings that manufacturers were significantly more likely to use direct, employee salespeople, rather than independent sales representatives when effective sales required the sales force to develop company-specific human capital and as a salesperson's performance became more difficult to measure, demonstrated for the first time that the same considerations that motivate integration upstream influence governance of downstream relations as well.

George John and Barton Weitz (1988, reprinted as Chapter 6 pp. 100–118) provide additional evidence of the importance of transaction cost considerations in forward integration decisions using a sample of industrial goods manufacturers. They analyse the decision to use direct versus indirect distribution channels, where direct channels involve sales directly to end-users and indirect channels involve sales through independent resellers such as wholesalers and retailers who, unlike Anderson and Schmittlein's independent sales representatives, actually purchase the firm's product for resale. Consistent with transaction cost hypotheses, John and Weitz find that the proportion of sales made directly to end-users increases with the time required for a new hire with prior experience in the industry to become familiar with a particular firm's products and with the amount of uncertainty associated with the transaction. The variety of indirect channels firms employ to distribute products to end-users suggests a range of additional research opportunities.

As noted previously, the progress testing transaction cost theories represented by these studies was made possible by the successful operationalization of the theory in which the differential efficiency of organizational arrangements were related to observable attributes of transactions (see especially, Williamson 1975, 1979; Klein, Crawford and Alchian, 1978). This development circumvented the need to measure and compare transaction costs directly and permitted researchers to test transaction cost hypotheses in reduced form. Such indirect tests, however, cannot disclose the magnitude of transaction cost differentials and, hence, leave open the question, what are the costs of mistaken organization? In 'The Costs of Organization' (reprinted as Chapter 7 pp. 119–43) James Meehan, Edward Snyder and I sought to estimate the effects of transactional attributes on the costs of transacting as well as on the choice of organizational mode. Using censored regression techniques and a measure of internal organization costs, we estimated the costs of internal and market organization for a sample of components and tasks involved in the construction of a ship. The results showed that the costs of mistaken organization can be large and, in general, vary with the attributes of transactions in ways predicted by transaction cost theory. The findings also suggest, however, that variations in the costs of internal organization may play a more important role in determining the boundaries of the firm than the theory usually contemplates.

The results of the empirical research on the determinants of vertical integration decisions have been remarkably consistent across studies. Among those results, the role of asset specificity in its various forms has been shown to be particularly important. Because of these efforts, the earliest and most central proposition to emerge from the conceptual developments of the 1970s now boasts a substantial empirical foundation.

2. Contracting

One of the accomplishments of transaction cost economics has been to give prominence to and display the importance of private ordering: parties entering a contract have considerable latitude to structure their relation to suit their particular circumstances. Transaction cost research on contracting has expanded our knowledge of the variety of contractual solutions transactors have devised and has shown those arrangements to vary systematically with the nature of the transaction. A recurrent theme is the desire of transactors to craft agreements that foster adaptation without having to resort to third-party enforcement.

Thomas Palay's study of rail freight contracting (1984, reprinted as Chapter 8 pp. 147–69) represents the earliest attempt to relate variations in the governance of contractual relations to the nature of the transaction. At the time of Palay's study, the nondiscrimination requirements of the Interstate Commerce Act restricted the ability of shippers and railroads to negotiate special prices for special services and made contractual protections such as minimum shipping requirements unenforceable. Palay documents how railroads and shippers developed private orderings to accommodate the special needs of shippers and to respond to carrier reluctance to invest in specialized or cargo-specific rail cars. In particular, Palay found that relations supported by specific investments, in contrast to those employing only standardized assets, tended to be characterized by the development of informal rules and procedures for handling disputes, the exchange of information for both long-term and structural planning, and a greater willingness of the parties to accommodate requests for adjustments and negotiate adaptations. For the most shipper-specific cars, vertical integration in the form of shipper ownership of cars was also employed. Palay's study thus demonstrates how, even in the absence of court ordering, transactors often manage to structure their relations to protect specific investments and accommodate necessary adaptations.

Like Joskow's description of the provisions contained in long-term coal agreements, an important contribution of Goldberg and Erickson's study of petroleum coke contracts is in portraying the variety and complexity of long-term agreements and in exposing economists to 'the way in which reasonably clever businessmen and lawyers cope with problems scholars might consider intractable' (Goldberg and Erickson, p. 369, reprinted as Chapter 9 pp. 170–99). Goldberg and Erickson trace the duration and quantity requirements of petroleum coke contracts to (1) the site specificity of production and processing facilities and (2) the need, owing to petroleum coke's bulky and hazardous nature, for its timely removal from the refinery. They interpret the pricing provisions, moreover, as operating principally to mitigate relational frictions rather than to attenuate moral hazard. Since petroleum coke contracts left the parties little discretion over quantity, Goldberg and Erickson reject incentive alignment as the motive for price adjustment and attribute the inclusion of price adjustment provisions instead to the goal of reducing precontract search and postagreement jockeying over the terms of trade.

An aspect of contracting stressed by Goldberg and Erickson is the interaction among contract terms that makes interpretation of particular provisions dependent on the rest of the agreement – detail that is often accessible only through intensive case analysis. Overcoming the vulnerability of case studies to charges of ex post rationalization, however, calls for more formal statistical analyses of larger populations. In parallel with the progress made testing transaction cost hypotheses regarding integration decisions, transaction cost economists have made substantial headway relating the incidence of particular contract provisions to attributes of transactions. An early and prominent example of that progress is Paul Joskow's econometric analysis of the duration of nearly 300 coal contracts (reprinted as Chapter 10 pp. 200–217). Building on his earlier case study, Joskow exploited regional differences in the characteristics of coal and transportation alternatives and variations in the volume of coal contracted for to construct proxies for physical- and site-specificity and dedicated assets. His findings offered the first formal evidence that the specificity of investments raises the cost of repeated ex post bargaining relative to designing and administering long-term contracts.

While coal contracts exhibit relatively little variation in terms other than duration (see Joskow, 1987, pp. 169–70), contracts in other settings often exhibit considerable diversity. Harold Mulherin (1986, reprinted as Chapter 11 pp. 218–30) and Scott Masten and Keith

Crocker (1985, reprinted as Chapter 12 pp. 231–41) analyse some of the diversity in contract provisions found in natural gas contracts. Employing a large set of producer-pipeline contracts written during the preregulatory 1940–54 period, Mulherin analyses the magnitude of take-or-pay provisions, the use of most-favoured-nation clauses to adjust price and the ownership of gathering lines between the well and pipeline, and concludes that transaction cost considerations better account for variations in each of these provisions than either risk-allocation or market-power explanations.

My 1985 article with Keith Crocker also examined take-or-pay provisions, which we interpreted as a private-ordering response to the limitations of courts in determining damages for breach of contract in natural gas transactions. Our analysis indicated that, if the purpose of take-or-pay provisions is to encourage pipelines to adapt efficiently to changing circumstances, then the magnitude of take requirements should be inversely related to the alternative value of the gas covered by each contract. We found that take-or-pay percentages in gas contracts existing in 1981 varied with the characteristics of transactions as predicted. Nonprice competition for gas, however, distorted contract incentives in those contracts subject to regulatory price ceilings.[1]

The trade-off between presale measurement (precontract search, in Goldberg and Erickson's terminology) and postagreement enforcement costs is the focus of Keith Leffler and Randall Rucker's study of pricing arrangements in timber harvesting contracts (reprinted as Chapter 13 pp. 242–69). Seeking to explain the exclusive use of either lump-sum or per-unit payment provisions in North Carolina timber contracts, Leffler and Rucker note that lump-sum contracts give harvesters an incentive to engage in privately profitable but socially unproductive appraisals of the value of timber in a tract. By making payments contingent on the quantity and quality of timber actually harvested, per-unit contracts attenuate the motive for presale measurement but demand greater monitoring and enforcement to counteract the reduction in incentives to harvest marginal timber. Leffler and Rucker present evidence that variables such as the heterogeneity and accessibility of a tract influence the choice of pricing arrangement consistent with this trade-off.

My study with Keith Crocker of price adjustment processes in long-term contracts (1991, reprinted as Chapter 14 pp. 270–300) explores how the contractual framework parties adopt to govern adaptations varies with the nature of the transaction. Crocker and I cite the prevalence of contracts in which the obligations of the parties are only vaguely circumscribed by the agreement as support for the relational view that contracts serve less as a mechanism for defining the terms of trade and aligning incentives than as a means for establishing the process through which transactors adapt exchange and resolve disputes over the course of the relationship. Applying this perspective to price adjustment provisions in natural gas contracts, we find that circumstances favouring the use of long-term, fixed-quantity agreements increased the adoption of relatively flexible renegotiation provisions over formulaic (rule-based) adjustment mechanisms that, while less costly to implement, were more likely to induce efforts to evade performance obligations in extreme situations.

Transaction cost economics has begun to address the oft-noted shortage of empirical research on contracting, shedding light on a range of common but unexplained contracting practices. While it is too soon to know the ultimate extent of its impact on the analysis and interpretation of contracts, courts have already begun to cite this research in resolving contract disputes (see, for instance, *PSI Energy v. Exxon Coal, USA*, 991 F. 2d. 1265 (1993)). Further research on the interactions between court and private ordering informed by transaction cost reasoning is likely to follow.

3. Regulation and Positive Political Economy

Although transaction cost economics has had its greatest influence on the analysis of vertical integration and contracting, one of the earliest applications of modern transaction cost reasoning concerned the relative merits of regulation and franchise contracting for public utility services. Spurred by Harold Demsetz's (1968) franchise-bidding solution to the natural monopoly problem, Oliver Williamson (1976, reprinted as Chapter 15 pp. 303–34) and Victor Goldberg (1976, reprinted as Chapter 16 pp. 335–58) set out the first detailed, comparative analyses of the roles and limitations of contracting and regulation as alternative institutions for the governance of public utility transactions. Williamson and Goldberg make the case that, far from avoiding the problems commonly ascribed to regulation, allowing for and effecting adjustments in franchise agreements given the durability and specialized nature of investments and the complexity of and uncertainty associated with public utility transactions is likely to entail contract terms and administrative machinery – cost-plus price adjustment, auditing procedures, elaborate and formal dispute resolution processes – that mirror both in character and in costs the administrative apparatus traditionally identified with rate-of-return regulation. As Goldberg puts it, 'The problems are intrinsic to the service, not to the act of regulation itself' (1976, p. 441). The 'administered contracts' perspective that focuses on the processes by which adaptations are realized contrasts sharply with the orthodox approach that views the problem of regulation principally as one of discovering and implementing competitive prices.[2]

In support of his theoretical analysis of the potential hazards of franchise contracting, Williamson provides an account of the experience of the city of Oakland, California, with franchise bidding for cable television. His review discloses that, despite attempts to build safeguards into the agreement, Oakland suffered many of the problems he and Goldberg had anticipated. Undoubtedly the most striking confirmation of Williamson's and Goldberg's interpretation and evaluation of the role and merits of franchise contracting relative to regulation, however, is George Priest's examination of the origins of public utility regulation in the late 19th and early 20th centuries. According to Priest, municipalities throughout most of the 19th century and the beginning of the 20th century arranged for public utility services – including gas, electricity, water, sewer, street railways and telegraph – using a method of franchise contracting similar to what Demsetz later envisioned. To induce the utilities to make the large investments necessary to serve a community, communities offered contracts that were typically 20 to 30, and sometimes 50, years in duration. Franchise contracting, though, 'suffered many problems ... relating to specifying the franchise contract, adapting it over time to new conditions, and monitoring compliance with the contract for the benefit of the citizenry' (p. 302). Over time, communities responded to the difficulties they were experiencing defining and enforcing more precise agreements by moving toward more flexible, relational agreements that left performance details to be administered by council subcommittees and boards of arbitrators. By the time state commissions began to take over the regulation of public utilities, franchise agreements between cities and utilities had already evolved into charters for governing adaptations that exhibited many of the properties commonly associated with rate-of-return regulation.

Yet despite parallels, regulation and franchise contracting are not identical. In particular, 'regulation by commission' and 'regulation by contract' offer different levels of commitment and flexibility. Brian Levy and Pablo Spiller exploit the differential commitment offered by contracting to analyse the merits of regulation relative to licensing as alternative modes of governance of telecommunication services. The relative efficiency of regulation and licensing, they argue, depends on the character of a country's political and legal institutions. Regulation by commission (like organization within the firm) offers greater flexibility but is more susceptible to political manipulation (opportunistic intervention). Out of fear that their investments will be appropriated through administrative price adjustments, regulated utilities will resist making ongoing investments in facilities (or will demand compensating risk premia) unless both (i) substantive restraints on regulator discretion and (ii) institutional constraints on political manipulation of the regulatory system are in place. Comparing performance across countries and time periods, Levy and Spiller (reprinted as Chapter 18 pp. 393–430) find that investments by telecommunication utilities were highest in those countries like the United States that possessed well-developed regulatory processes, constitutional protections and separation of political powers. Where those institutional conditions were lacking, countries were better off relying on licensing to foster investment. In the worst case, where institutional protections are weakest, countries have no choice but to nationalize.

Levy and Spiller's analysis illustrates the role of political and legal institutions – what Douglas North calls the institutional environment – in the discriminating alignment of governance structures and transactions. The study of political and legal institutions thus becomes important to our understanding of private governance as well as for its own purposes. At the same time, the economic theory of organization stands to enhance our understanding of the organization and operation of institutions at the environmental level. An extraordinary example of the latter is Barry Weingast and William Marshall's application of transaction cost logic to the design of legislative institutions.[3] Gains from trade among legislators arise because individual legislators need the support of a majority to pass legislation beneficial to their constituents. But because legislators cannot contract over votes or outcomes, legislative bargains are exposed to the risk of opportunistic reneging whenever legislation is voted on sequentially or constituents realize benefits over different time periods. Weingast and Marshall reason that legislatures, like other organizations, should develop rules that facilitate trade by economizing on transaction costs and describe how the committee system in the US Congress allocates decision rights in a way that supports the enforcement of legislative bargains.

Rafael Gely and Pablo Spiller's analysis (reprinted as Chapter 20 pp. 462–99) of Supreme Court decision making exemplifies another dimension of the growing field of positive political economy. Gely and Spiller argue that the behaviour of the Supreme Court can be understood as that of a self-interested, ideologically motivated actor whose ability to effect policy outcomes is constrained by the ability of other political actors, particularly Congress, to reverse Supreme Court decisions. In contrast to the legal centralist perspective that emphasizes the role of constitutional interpretation and precedent on Supreme Court decisions, Gely and Spiller focus on how the institutional structure of government, such as bicameralism and presidential veto power, constrain the Court's interpretation of statutes. Although this study, unlike others in this collection, analyses behaviour within an existing institutional structure rather than the choice or design of institutions, it illustrates that 'institutions matter in the design of public policy' (p. 264) and portends further extension of comparative institutional analysis at the level of the institutional environment.

4. Antitrust

Transaction cost economics has contributed, along with the Chicago School, to the erosion of the inhospitality tradition in antitrust policy that viewed all nonstandard contractual arrangements with hostility. Much of transaction cost economics' influence on that shift has been indirect, however. The success of transaction cost research in explaining vertical integration and contracting practices has enhanced economists' and policy makers' general appreciation of the potential efficiencies associated with the selective use of vertical arrangements, direct incorporation of transaction cost logic in the reasoning of antitrust courts has so far been limited (see Joskow, 1991).

The three articles in this section illustrate the potential advantages of expressly adopting the more 'direct approach' to assessing organization that a transaction cost orientation provides (Coase, 1972). Though each focuses on a specific case, their implications for antitrust policy and our understanding of economic organization are far broader.

In 'Assessing Vertical Market Restrictions: Antitrust Ramifications of the Transaction Cost Approach' (reprinted as Chapter 21 pp. 503–43) Oliver Williamson argues that, contrary to the inhospitality perspective prevailing at the time of the Supreme Court's 1967 decision in *United States v. Arnold, Schwinn & Co.*, contractual restraints can and often do serve legitimate efficiency purposes and that, as with vertical integration, vertical restrictions between manufacturers and distributors are primarily to be understood in transaction cost terms. Instead of hostility, Williamson argues that the presumption should be that vertical restrictions enhance efficiency; antitrust enforcement efforts should be reserved for those limited cases where market structure could conceivably support strategic objectives and, then, should entertain affirmative economies-based defences. Williamson also points out that, although Chicago School scholars such as Robert Bork have also been critical of the *Schwinn* decision, Chicago School arguments have focused on why vertical integration and restrictions could not be used to create or enhance market power, while transaction cost economics offers affirmative arguments for the use of vertical arrangements as means of economizing on the costs of governing exchange. Citing the subsequent reversal of *Schwinn* in *Continental T.V., Inc. v. GTE Sylvania Inc.* (1977) as a welcome development, Williamson nevertheless maintains that a more explicit incorporation of transaction cost principles in antitrust would foster still more sensible policy outcomes.

The two remaining studies reinforce Williamson's contention and further underscore the differences in orientation and approach between traditional antitrust, Chicago-style applied price theory and transaction cost economics. Roy Kenney and Benjamin Klein's 'The Economics of Block Booking' (reprinted as Chapter 22 pp. 544–87) analyses the practice of bundling or tying. The traditional antitrust objection to product bundling, formalized in two Supreme Court decisions outlawing the block booking of movies, was that the practice allowed monopolists to 'extend' monopoly power to nonmonopolized goods. Chicago scholars challenged the logic of monopoly extension and offered a price discrimination rationale for the bundling of movies. Although the Chicago interpretation has become the conventional wisdom, Kenney and Klein show that price discrimination as a motive is inconsistent with the facts. Instead, they interpret the block booking of movies and the bundling of uncut diamonds in terms of economizing on measurement costs. Both movies and diamonds (among other products) have the property that their values are heterogeneous and difficult for the purchaser to determine and for the producer to control. Bundling prevents buyers from sorting through and rejecting individual items from a parcel that has been average priced and thus reduces the time and resources expended in redundant sorting and repricing. Purportedly monopolistic practices are thus shown, upon closer scrutiny, to have efficiency purpose and effect in these two cases – and presumably more generally.

The final application (reprinted as Chapter 23 pp. 588–625) is a study of the government's successful challenge to United Shoe Machinery Corp.'s leasing practices in *United States v. United Shoe Machinery Corp.* (1953). United had been charged with using its long-term leases to exclude competitors from the shoe machinery business. Although Chicago School scholars had questioned the logic of exclusion, recent theoretical models have established the possibility of profitably excluding competitors despite the need to compensate customers for the loss of competition. If exclusion cannot be ruled out *a priori*, allegations of exclusionary practices will have to be assessed on their merits.

Edward Snyder and I approached the issue of United's distribution practices as a problem of comparative economic organization. Treating leasing and sales with contractual warranties as alternative means of resolving organizational problems inherent in the supply of complex, durable equipment, we showed that United's selective use of leasing was consistent with the aim of economizing on the costs of resolving disputes over culpability for product failures and that the deterrents to adopting competitor machines contained in the leases created appropriate incentives for lessees to retain and use United equipment.

Although a price theoretic orientation serves as a valuable check on allegations of anti-competitive behaviour, these three studies demonstrate that the affirmative purposes of nonstandard business practices often have transaction cost origins. Failure to appreciate the efficiency consequences of governance risks misconstruing those purposes. It was thus possible for the judge in the *United Shoe* litigation to lavish praise on United for its 'efficiency, intelligence, and vision' while denying a link between United's leasing practices and its universally acclaimed performance. By expanding our understanding of the relation between governance and economic performance, transaction cost economics has contributed to a policy environment in which failures to recognize the potential for such linkages are less likely to occur.

5. Assessment and Directions

Transaction cost economics has contributed substantially to our understanding of observed patterns of organization. Despite what fifteen years ago might have appeared to be insurmountable obstacles to acquiring the relevant data, transaction cost economics today stands on a remarkably broad empirical foundation. This is not to suggest that empirical research in transaction cost economics does not have its weaknesses. High on the list of priorities is the development of quantitative measures of the theory's explanatory variables to replace the qualitative rankings and imprecise proxies employed in much of the existing literature. Additional efforts to quantify the effects of organizational form on performance would also serve to strengthen tests of transaction cost hypotheses and provide better guidance to decision makers, both public and private. Such considerations notwithstanding, no other theory of organization possesses empirical support comparable in number, range, consistency and rigour.

In retrospect, probably the biggest surprise in the development of the economics of transaction costs has been the variety of governance arrangements that have been shown to align with transaction cost principles. Tenets developed to explain the boundaries of the firm have been successfully applied to illuminate such apparently disparate phenomena as the organization of Congress and indentured prostitution in Imperial Japan (Ramseyer, 1991). If there has been a disappointment, it may be that, despite its numerous policy ramifications, transaction cost reasoning has not had a more direct impact on public policy, especially in antitrust and regulation. But that too shows signs of changing.

Yet for all its depth and scope, transaction cost economics has only begun to explore the variety and complexity of organizational forms. There is still much to learn. The value of a comparative institutional orientation in assessing the broader political and legal institutions of society is only starting to be realized. Deeper scrutiny of the sources and parameters of bureaucratic inefficiencies is also gravely needed. If the past is any indication, application of transaction cost reasoning to these and other topics will inform as well as respond to developments in the theory. Awaiting the arrival of a theory of organization to challenge transaction cost economics, students of organization will not want for lack of things to do.

Scott E. Masten

Notes

1. In related research, Crocker and Masten (1988) examined the duration of natural gas contracts and found that the prospect of inefficient adaptation associated with distortions in take-or-pay provisions significantly reduced the willingness of parties to engage in long-term contracting.
2. A recent example of the orthodox approach is Baumol and Sidak's analysis of telecommunications regulation, which they ground 'on the premise – almost universally accepted in principle, although widely violated in practice – that the proper role of regulation is that of a substitute for competitive market forces where those forces are weak or absent' (1994, p. 5). 'The regulator's task', they continue, 'then becomes a two-part undertaking: first, to determine the rules of behavior that the regulated firm could have been expected to follow if it had operated free of regulation in a market with fully effective competitive forces; second, to constrain the regulated firm to behave as it would in such a competitive market, and to circumscribe its behavior *no less and no more than this*' (1994, p. 5; emphasis in original).
3. North and Weingast's analysis of the evolution of constitutional constraints in Volume I is another example.

References

Baumol, William J. and J. Gregory Sidak (1994) *Toward Competition in Local Telephony*. Cambridge, MA: The MIT Press.

Coase, Ronald H. (1972) 'Industrial Organization: A Proposal for Research', in V.R. Fuchs (ed.), *Policy Issues and Research Opportunities in Industrial Organization*. New York: National Bureau of Economic Research. Reprinted in *The Economics of Transaction Costs*, Vol. 1.

Coase, Ronald H. (1988) 'The Nature of the Firm: Origin, Meaning, Influence', *Journal of Law, Economics, and Organization*, **4**, 3–47. Reprinted in O.E. Williamson and S.G. Winter (eds) (1991) *The Nature of the Firm: Origins, Evolution, and Development*. New York: Oxford University Press.

Crocker, K.J. and S.E. Masten (1988) 'Mitigating Contractual Hazards: Unilateral Options and Contract Length', *Rand Journal of Economics* **19**, Autumn, 327–43.

Crocker, Keith J. and Scott E. Masten (Forthcoming) 'Regulation and Administered Contracts Revisited: Lessons from Transaction Cost Economics for Public Utility Regulation', *Journal of Regulatory Economics*.

Demsetz, Harold (1968) 'Why Regulate Utilities?', *Journal of Law and Economics* **11**, 55–66.

Joskow, Paul (1991) 'The Role of Transaction Costs Economics in Antitrust and Public Utility Regulatory Policies', *Journal of Law, Economics, and Organization* (Spring), 53–83.

Klein, Benjamin, Robert Crawford and Armen Alchian (1978) 'Vertical Integration, Appropriable Rents, and the Competitive Contracting Process', *Journal of Law and Economics*, **21**, 297–326.

Klein, Peter G. and Howard A. Shelanski (1994) *Empirical Research in Transaction Cost Economics: A Survey and Assessment*, University of California, Berkeley, Department of Economics, December (mimeo).

North, Douglas C. and Barry R. Weingast (1989) 'Constitutions and Commitment: The Evolution of Institutions Governing Public Choice in Seventeenth Century England', *Journal of Economic History*, **49** (December), 803–32.

Ramseyer, J. Mark (1991) 'Indentured Prostitution in Imperial Japan: Credible Commitments in the Commercial Sex Industry', *Journal of Law, Economics, and Organization* **7** (Spring), 89–116.

Simon, Herbert (1991) 'Organizations and Markets', *Journal of Economic Perspectives* **5** (Spring), 25–44.

Williamson, Oliver E. (1971) 'The Vertical Integration of Production: Market Failure Considerations', *American Economic Review*, **61**, 112–23.

Williamson, Oliver E. (1975) *Markets and Hierarchies: Analysis and Antitrust Implications*. New York: Free Press.

Williamson, Oliver E. (1979) 'Transaction-Cost Economics: The Governance of Contractual Relations', *Journal of Law and Economics*, **22**, 233–61.

Part I
Vertical Integration

[1]

Vertical Integration as Organizational Ownership: The Fisher Body–General Motors Relationship Revisited

BENJAMIN KLEIN
University of California, Los Angeles

I have always considered my work with Armen Alchian and Robert Crawford (1978) on vertical integration to represent an extension of Coase's classic article on "The Nature of the Firm." By focusing on the "hold-up" potential that is created when firm-specific investments are made by transactors, or what we called the appropriation of quasi-rents, I believed we had elucidated one aspect of the Coasian concept of transaction costs associated with market exchange. We hypothesized that an increase in firm-specific investments, by increasing the market transaction costs associated with a hold-up, increased the likelihood of vertical integration. This relationship between firm-specific investments, market transaction costs, and vertical integration was illustrated by examining the contractual difficulties that existed when General Motors purchased automobile bodies from Fisher Body and the corresponding benefits that were created when the parties vertically integrated.

It is clear from Coase's lectures that he considers our analysis not to represent an extension of his earlier work, but rather to be an alternative, incorrect explanation for vertical integration (1988: lecture 3). Coase recognizes that an increase in the quasi-rents yielded by firm-specific investments creates a hold-up potential. However, he argues that there is no reason to believe that this situation is more likely to lead to vertical integration than to a long-term contract. Although long-term contracts are imperfect, oppor-

I am grateful to Harold Demsetz, Kevin James, Timothy Opler, and Oliver Williamson for useful comments.

Journal of Law, Economics, and Organization vol. 4, no. 1 Spring 1988
 ISSN 8756-6222

tunistic behavior is usually effectively handled in the marketplace, according to Coase, by a firm's need to take account of the effect of its actions on future business. Coase claims that before writing his classic paper he explicitly considered opportunistic behavior as a motive for vertical integration, in particular as it applied to the General Motors–Fisher Body case, and explicitly rejected it.

Unfortunately, Coase's rejection of the opportunism analysis is based upon too simplified a view of the market contracting process and too narrow a view of the transaction costs associated with that process. A more complete analysis of how vertical integration solved the opportunistic behavior problem in the Fisher Body–General Motors case provides insight into the nature of the transaction costs that are associated with the market contracting process and how vertical integration reduces these costs. The primary transaction costs saved by vertical integration are not the "ink costs" associated with the number of contracts written and executed but, rather, are the costs associated with contractually induced hold-ups. The analysis indicates that hold-up potentials are created not solely from the existence of firm-specific investments, but also from the existence of the rigidly set long-term contract terms that are used in the presence of specific investments. Vertical integration, by shifting ownership of the firm's organizational asset, creates a degree of flexibility and avoids this contractually created hold-up potential, thereby resulting in significant transaction cost savings.

1. LONG-TERM CONTRACTS AS SOLUTIONS TO AND CAUSES OF HOLD-UP PROBLEMS

Coase is correct in believing that in many cases contractual arrangements, rather than vertical integration, can be and are used to solve hold-up problems. For example, consider the case of building a house on a piece of land. It is obvious that you would not build the house on land you had only rented for a short term. After the land lease expired the landowner could hold you up for the quasi-rents on your house investment. However, this does not mean that you need necessarily own the land, that is, vertically integrate, to solve this problem. The hold-up problem potentially could be solved by the use of a long-term rental contract on the land negotiated before the house was constructed. Since land is the type of input where anticipated quality variations are very small or nonexistent, a long-term rental contract is certainly a feasible way to minimize the hold-up potential without vertical integration.

The long-term exclusive dealing contract adopted by Fisher Body and General Motors in 1919 can be explained as an analogous contractual means to avoid a hold-up potential without vertical integration.[1] Since Fisher Body

1. The contractual agreement between Fisher Body and General Motors can be found in the minutes of the Board of Directors of Fisher Body Corporation for November 7, 1919. Analysis of this case is taken in part from Klein, Crawford, and Alchian (308–10).

had to make an investment highly specific to General Motors in the stamping machines and dies necessary to produce the automobile bodies demanded by General Motors, a significant hold-up potential was created. After Fisher made the investment, General Motors could have attempted to appropriate the quasi-rents from the investment by threatening to reduce their demand for Fisher-produced bodies, or even to terminate Fisher completely, if price were not adjusted downward. The exclusive dealing clause, which required General Motors over a ten-year period to buy all their closed metal bodies from Fisher Body, limited the ability of General Motors to opportunistically threaten Fisher Body in this manner. The contractual arrangement thereby reduced Fisher Body's reliance on General Motors' reputation and encouraged Fisher Body to make the specific investment.

Although the ten-year exclusive dealing contractual arrangement protected Fisher against a General Motors hold-up, it created a potential for Fisher to hold up General Motors. Fisher could take advantage of the requirement that General Motors could not purchase elsewhere by increasing price or decreasing quality. The contract attempted to protect General Motors against this reverse hold-up potential by specifying a formula by which price would be set over the ten-year period at a competitive level. In addition, in a further attempt to minimize the potential Fisher hold-up of General Motors, the contract also included most-favored nation provisions so that the price could not be greater than what Fisher Body charged other automobile manufacturers for "similar" bodies. Such a "price protection" clause prevents a hold-up because a price increase or decrease to any buyer is guaranteed to be given to all buyers. Hence, established buyers that are "locked-in" by a specific investment or a contractual commitment are protected by the seller's desire to make profitable new sales.

In spite of the existence of a long-term contractual arrangement with explicitly set price and price protection clauses, there is still some probability that a hold-up may occur. This is because not all elements of future performance are specified in the contract. Due to uncertainty and the difficulty of specifying all elements of performance in a contractually enforceable way, contracts will necessarily be incomplete to one degree or another. This creates the possibility for transactors to take advantage of the contract to hold-up their transacting partner. For example, the long-term land rental contract in the house construction example may permit the landowner to hold-up the house owner by opportunistically controlling the water supply to the house, or by failing to build a wall to prevent erosion of the land under the house, or by closing a road on the land for claimed repairs and thereby threatening to restrict access to the house.

Even though contracts are incomplete, the reputations of the transacting parties limit the economic feasibility of hold-up threats. It is the magnitude of these reputations and the corresponding costs that can be imposed on a transactor that attempts a hold-up that define what can be called the "self-enforcing range" of the contractual relationship. Transacting parties enter contractual arrangements by making specific investments and setting contract terms in such a way so that they are likely to be within this self-enforcing range where a hold-up will not occur. However, there is some probability that market conditions may change (for example, the value of the quasi-rents accruing to one of the parties unexpectedly increases) so that it pays for one transactor to hold-up the other in spite of the loss of reputation.[2]

For example, in the General Motors–Fisher Body case demand for the closed metal bodies manufactured by Fisher increased dramatically. When the contract was entered into in 1919 the dominant production process for automobiles consisted of individually constructed, largely wooden, open bodies; closed metal bodies were essentially a novelty. Demand for closed metal bodies grew extremely rapidly and by 1924 accounted for more than 65 percent of General Motors' automobile production.[3] This shift in demand moved the contractual arrangement outside of the self-enforcing range and made it profitable for Fisher to hold up General Motors.

Although Fisher could have taken advantage of many imperfectly specified terms of the contractual arrangement, such as delivery times or quality characteristics, Fisher effectively held up General Motors by adopting a relatively inefficient, highly labor-intensive technology and by refusing to locate the body-producing plants adjacent to General Motors assembly plant.[4] This hold-up mechanism had the advantage, from Fisher's viewpoint, of increasing profitability since the contractually specified price formula set price equal to Fisher's "variable cost" plus 17.6 percent, placing a 17.6 percent profit upcharge on Fisher's labor and transportation costs. The profit upcharge presumably was designed to cover Fisher's anticipated capital costs, which may have been difficult to isolate and measure for General Motors shipments and, therefore, were unreimbursable under the contract formula. The contract may appear to be imperfect, but it was only deficient ex post. If demand had not grown so rapidly, Fisher's reputation (that is, loss of future business with General Motors and possibly other automobile manufacturers) combined with the most favored nation clause may have been an effective constraint on Fisher Body behavior. However, the large increase in demand placed Fisher's short-run hold-up potential of General Motors, even with Fisher being forced to give up new and future sales, outside the self-enforcing range.

The Fisher Body–General Motors case illustrates that while long-term

2. This probabilistic equilibrium differs from the analysis in Klein, Crawford, and Alchian, where hold-ups were assumed not to be present in long-run equilibrium and existed solely because of transactor myopia or ignorance. Kenney and Klein presents a discussion of the "self-enforcing range" and this equilibrium, together with the implications of the analysis for contract law.

3. *Sixteenth Annual Report*, General Motors Corporation, year ended December 31, 1924.

4. See deposition testimony of Alfred P. Sloan, Jr. in United States *v.* Dupont & Co., 366 U.S. 316 (1961), 186–90 (April 28, 1952) and 2908–14 (March 14, 1953).

contract terms and transactor reputations may prevent hold-ups and encourage specific investments by tying the hands of the transacting parties, long-term contract terms may also create hold-up problems. Therefore, it is misleading to assert, as Coase does, that "opportunistic behavior is usually effectively checked" in the market by long-term contracts and the existence of transactor reputations. Although the assertion is true, a more complete analysis must recognize that transactor reputations are limited and that contracts may actually create, rather than solve, hold-up problems. It was the long-term, fixed price formula, exclusive dealing contract adopted by the transactors in response to the potential General Motors hold-up of Fisher that created the enormous Fisher hold-up potential of General Motors. The magnitude of this contractually caused hold-up was likely much greater than the quasi-rents on the General Motors–specific investments made by Fisher which the contract was attempting to protect in the first place. Although writing down binding contract terms may economize on limited brand name capital and reduce the probability of being outside the self-enforcing range, the rigidity of long-term contract terms may create a much larger hold-up potential if events actually place the parties outside the self-enforcing range. To avoid this rigidity transactors may intentionally leave their contracts incomplete and thereby give themselves "an out" if market conditions get "out of line."

It is this contractually induced hold-up potential and the costs associated with rigid ex-post incorrect contract terms, illustrated so forcefully in the Fisher–General Motors case, that represent the major transaction costs of using the market mechanism to solve the hold-up problem. These transaction costs include the real resources transactors dissipate in the contractual negotiation and renegotiation process in the attempt to create and execute a hold-up. Transactors will search for an informational advantage over their transacting partners and attempt to negotiate ex-ante contract terms that create hold-up potentials, that is, that are more likely to imply ex-post situations where contract terms are favorably incorrect. Once such a favorably incorrect situation arises, transactors will dissipate real resources during the renegotiation process in the attempt to convince their transacting partner that a hold-up potential does exist. In the Fisher–General Motors case these renegotiation transaction costs consisted of the costs associated with improper plant placement and low capital intensity of production before vertical integration occurred.[5]

5. In addition to the transaction costs associated with negotiating contractual arrangements and the transitional transaction costs associated with the renegotiating process when these arrangements do not work out in practice, there are the social costs associated with transactors not making specific investments and entering contractual arrangements to begin with. Transactors anticipate the rent-dissipating transaction costs associated with contractual negotiation and renegotiation because they recognize the limits to their reputation capital, the uncertainty of the world, and the necessary imperfections of contracts. Therefore, independent of any risk

These transaction costs associated with the use of a long-term contract represent the theoretical reason why the presence of firm-specific investments are more likely to lead to vertical integration. Specific investments create the necessity for long-term contractual terms which, in turn, imply the rent-dissipating transaction costs associated with the possibility of contractually created hold-ups. In the absence of specific investments, long-term contract terms are unnecessary and spot contracts can be used. Since the costs associated with vertical integration are generally incentive-type costs that are unrelated to the level of specific investments, vertical integration will be more likely the greater the level of specific investments. The greater the level of specific investments and hence the greater the potential costs of using the market (as more explicit and rigid contractual mechanisms must be devised to protect the specific investment), the greater the likelihood that vertical integration will be the solution.

2. PHYSICAL CAPITAL VS HUMAN CAPITAL

Vertical integration is the form in which the hold-up of General Motors by Fisher Body eventually took place, with General Motors acquiring the Fisher Body stock owned by Fisher at terms that were highly favorable to Fisher. Why did not General Motors merely make a lump sum cash payment to Fisher and renegotiate the contract, fixing ambiguous terms and hoping that another large unanticipated event would not occur in the future to shock the relationship out of the self-enforcing range? One reason is that the change in demand to closed metal bodies made Fisher a much more important specialized input supplier to General Motors, with the Fisher hold-up potential reaching essentially the entire General Motors industry-specific investment. In principle, with an ex-post incorrect contract, Fisher could potentially hold up General Motors for their entire automobile manufacturing and distribution organization. This enormous hold-up potential would imply extremely large rent-dissipating transaction costs during the contractual negotiation and renegotiaton process as General Motors attempted to protect against and Fisher attempted to take advantage of the hold-up possibilities.

Vertical integration appears to avoid these transaction costs by eliminating the second transactor. This is obvious for cases of physical capital, such as the house construction–land ownership example, where a hold-up, by definition, becomes impossible with vertical integration. It is cases like these

aversion, transactors will avoid entering contractual arrangements where there is a significant probability that the arrangement will not work out. The equilibrium contractual arrangements that transactors voluntarily adopt in the marketplace may appear, consistent with Coase's assertion, to handle opportunistic behavior—in the sense that we are unlikely to observe opportunism occurring very frequently. However, we do not see all the specific investments not made and the contractual arrangements not adopted when transactors anticipate a significant probability of being outside the self-enforcing range.

that lead to the obvious conclusion that vertical integration will more likely be used when the hold-up potential, that is, the quasi-rents from firm-specific investments, are large. As Joskow (1988) convincingly demonstrates, this insight regarding the economic motivation for ownership of firm-specific physical capital has significant empirical relevance.

However, many real-world examples involve human capital and not merely physical capital as the important firm-specific asset.[6] Since the specific human capital is embodied in individuals who by law cannot be owned and who have the potential to behave opportunistically under any alternative organizational arrangement, vertical integration does not eliminate the other transactor and the hold-up problem. In such cases it is unclear exactly what gains are entailed by vertical integration.

To understand the gains from vertical integration in the context of human capital, the economic question should be phrased not (as we have done in the house construction–land ownership case) as whether to own or rent an asset, but, as Coase essentially phrased it, as whether to make or buy an input. The former question applies only to physical capital while the latter question applies to human capital. When a firm buys an input in the marketplace, it generally does not own the physical capital associated with its production. A firm that produces an input itself also may not own the physical capital associated with its production (for example, the building where the firm has its offices). However, as we shall see, a firm that makes rather than buys an input generally has a particular relationship with the firm-specific human capital.

These issues can be focused by considering the Fisher Body–General Motors case again. If the hold-up problem were based solely on the General Motors–specific physical capital investments made by Fisher Body and had nothing to do with Fisher Body human capital, General Motors could have solved the problem by owning the physical capital. General Motors could have owned their own dies and stamping machines and let Fisher use this capital to make auto bodies for them, avoiding the hold-up problem while taking advantage of whatever cost advantage Fisher possessed in producing bodies.[7]

6. See, for example, the discussion in Klein, Crawford, and Alchian (313–19) and Williamson (240–45).

7. Coase discusses this as a particular contractual solution to the hold-up problem (1988: lecture 1). See also Monteverde and Teece. Fisher's cost advantage was unlikely due to economies of scale in the production process. Evidence for this is the fact that, after demand growth and integration, Fisher supplied bodies solely to General Motors. This is one difference between the Fisher Body case and the A. O. Smith case discussed by Coase (1988: lecture 3). There appears to be significantly greater economies of scale in producing automobile frames than producing automobile bodies, with Smith supplying frames then and now to multiple automobile manufacturers, thereby raising the cost of vertical integration as a solution to the hold-up problem (see Stigler). It is also important to note that the investment in automobile frame production is, apparently, less buyer-specific than the investment in automobile body production.

One problem with this solution is that the extent of the General Motors-specific physical capital investments is likely to be much greater than merely the dies and stamping equipment. There are, for example, complementary physical capital investments that must be made by Fisher in plant, with the associated questions of plant location and the assurance to Fisher of continued General Motors demand for the facility. These questions presumably would have to be handled by contract. To avoid contractual rigidity and the induced hold-up problems associated with ex-post incorrect contract terms General Motors could own all the physical capital and merely contract with Fisher to run the operation. While such an arrangement would create marginal distortions regarding the use of the General Motors capital equipment by Fisher, it would appear to solve the hold-up problem if the problem were based solely on specific physical capital investments.

However, much of the specific investment necessary to produce automobile bodies consists of Fisher human capital investments that, by definition, cannot be owned by General Motors. General Motors can finance Fisher's human capital investments but would require some long-term fixed price contractual commitment to prevent Fisher from threatening to terminate the relationship if General Motors did not make a lump sum payment to them equal to the quasi-rents from the human capital investment. Vertical integration, in the sense of making Fisher an employee, rather than an independent contractor, does not eliminate the potential hold-up. As opposed to physical capital, the specialized human capital would presumably still be owned by Fisher even after General Motors' vertical integration. Rather than ownership, a long-term contractual arrangement, with its associated rigidities and potential hold-up problems, must be used by the transactors.[8]

Since, by definition, one cannot own human capital, how did the vertical integration of General Motors with Fisher reduce the hold-up problem? As opposed to the case of physical capital, vertical integration did not eliminate the Fisher brothers. After vertical integration General Motors no longer bought bodies from Fisher Body Corporation. After vertical integration General Motors "made" bodies with the assistance of Fisher. However, did making the Fisher brothers employees compared to being independent contractors change things in any essential way? Although General Motors would now own the plants and presumably be able to tell the Fisher brothers where to locate them, the Fisher brothers became employee managers with the ability to hold up General Motors for their human capital–specific investments by threatening modification on some other dimension.

8. For example, one contract term that is used in employment arrangements in the entertainment industry, where the employer may make a substantial transactor-specific investment, is a right of first refusal clause. This clause reduces the credibility of hold-up threats since it requires the employee attempting to increase his wage by the amount of the quasi-rents from the employer's investment to threaten to quit working completely, rather than merely to threaten to quit the firm and work elsewhere.

3. VERTICAL INTEGRATION AS ORGANIZATIONAL OWNERSHIP

Although the use of an employee rather than an independent contractor arrangement may imply important legal differences and hence different constraints on the contracting process, such as the ease of termination by the employer and the required loyalty of the employee, I agree with Coase that the employer-employee contract does not represent the essence of a firm.[9] The transition of the Fisher brothers from independent contractors to employees does not explain what General Motors gained through vertical integration.

Vertical integration not only made the Fisher brothers employees of General Motors, but also converted all the employees of Fisher Body Corporation into employees of General Motors. General Motors moved from "buying" automobile bodies to "making" automobile bodies by obtaining ownership of the Fisher Body organization, including all the labor contracts of the cooperating workers in that organization and all the knowledge of how to make automobiles contained in that organization. It is in this sense of owning a firm's set of interdependent labor contracts and the firm-specific knowledge embodied in the organization's team of employees that an owner of a firm can own the firm's human capital.[10]

Vertical integration may solve a hold-up potential even when it hinges on human capital and, hence, the number of transactors are not reduced by the integration because it involves transferring ownership of a productive team. For example, if we consider the Fisher Body–General Motors case it is unlikely that it was the Fisher brothers themselves who possessed all the relevant firm-specific human capital information. It was much more likely that this information was possessed by the entire group of Fisher employees and was embedded in the Fisher organizational structure. Vertical integration did not merely transfer the Fisher brothers from independent contractor to employee status, but also transferred ownership of the Fisher organization and the set of interdependent labor contracts to General Motors.

The primary reason a hold-up cannot occur after such a transfer of rights

9. See Coase (1988: lecture 3) where he identifies this as the main weakness of his 1937 article.

10. The concept of specific knowledge which affects a firm's production technology and which is vested in and transferable with the firm has been discussed by numerous authors. Rosen notes that such a firm-specific information asset may be created over time by the discovery of trade connections and the assembly of an efficient "production team" and presents a model where specific knowledge is acquired through (or as a by-product of) a firm's production experience. A similar concept is developed in Prescott and Visscher and is related to the evolutionary theory of the firm presented by Nelson and Winter. The importance of information accumulation within the firm as a kind of progress function was originally discussed by Alchian (1959) and Arrow. This concept may explain why bankruptcy law provisions, which are designed to prevent the production team from disbanding, make economic sense. While physical assets generally may be salvageable, bankruptcy, accompanied by the discontinuance of a firm's operations, may destroy the organizational assets of the firm. The analysis also provides an economic justification for the "failing firm" defense in merger law.

is because collusion is difficult with a large number of entities. If there were only one employee or a few key employees, they could threaten to leave and (subject to legal constraints on trade secret or goodwill theft) take the organization with them. However, with many key individuals involved, the organization will generally be secure. A threat that all the individuals will simultaneously shirk or leave if their wages were not increased to reflect the quasi-rents on the organizational capital generally will not be credible. After vertical integration the Fisher brothers will not be able to hold up General Motors by telling all the employees to leave General Motors and show up on Monday morning at a new address. This is, in general, not economically feasible or, more important, legally possible. It is in this sense of large team organizations that vertical integration can imply ownership of human capital assets in a manner quite similar to ownership of physical capital assets.

Our analysis implies that the General Motors integration with Fisher Body is analytically quite similar to the land–house example. By integrating with Fisher, General Motors acquired the Fisher Body organizational capital. This organization is embedded in the human capital of the employees at Fisher but is in some sense greater than the sum of its parts. The employees come and go but the organization maintains the memory of past trials and the knowledge of how to best do something (that is, how to make automobile bodies). This organizational asset can be thought of as a big machine called the Fisher Corporation. When this machine was owned by the Fisher brothers, it was necessary to write an explicit automobile body supply contract which ex post turned out to create significant hold-up problems. With vertical integration General Motors avoided these contractual difficulties by buying the machine (the Fisher Corporation) and, in the sense of eliminating the need for an automobile body supply contract, eliminating the second transactor (the Fisher brothers).[11]

4. ORGANIZATIONAL OWNERSHIP VS INPUT COORDINATION

Coase would likely agree that it is useful to consider the firm as an organization. He recognizes that it is the existence of cooperating labor inputs, and not merely a single employee, that represents a firm relationship. "The em-

11. In contrast, the Grossman and Hart model of vertical integration consists of single person firms where, by definition, ownership of organizational assets cannot be transferred or consolidated. Grossman and Hart concentrate solely on physical assets and the question of which particular physical assets firms own. However, the essential question of vertical integration is not asset ownership but the make-or-buy decisions of firms. General Motors may own all the physical capital in the Fisher plant yet buy the bodies from an independent Fisher Body Corporation. The Grossman and Hart answer to the question of the distribution of physical asset ownership, which relies on employee incentive effects, cannot explain the incidence of vertical integration. Although vertical integration of Fisher and General Motors may lead to increased monitoring of the Fisher brothers because they no longer bear the full value consequences of their behavior, most of the managers at Fisher Body, both before and after integration with General Motors, are employees and not owners of Fisher physical capital.

ployer-employee contract approaches the firm relationship but . . . the full firm relationship will not come about unless several such contracts are made with people and for things that cooperate with one another" (1988: lecture 3). However, Coase emphasizes the role of the firm not as an owner of organizational assets, but as a coordinator and controller of cooperating inputs. One must consider the firm, Coase says, as "running a business." And the economic question regarding institutional form involves a "comparison of the costs of coordinating the activities of factors of production within the firm with the costs of bringing about the same result by market transactions or by means of operations undertaken within some other firm" (1988: lecture 3). It is this concept of coordination of a team of inputs that Coase attributes as the essence of a firm.

The concept of a central contracting agent that serves as a hub of a group of interdependent contracts and by coordination eliminates the necessity of contracts between those individuals assumed to be at the end of each of the spokes may appear to provide some insight into the nature of the firm. It is in the sense of coordinating control of a team that the number of market relationships is reduced and substituted for administrative decisions. This concept corresponds to Coase's notion of a reduction in the number of market transactions when vertical integration occurs (1988: lecture 3). However, every transactor in the marketplace purchasing inputs that are assembled into a final product can be considered as a hub of a series of contractual arrangements. The suppliers of the separate inputs need not have any contractual arrangement with one another. Although vertical integration may appear to eliminate the necessity for contractual arrangements between cooperating inputs, it does not.

Unfortunately, in considering whether transactors will adopt a firm or market arrangement, Coase in 1937 and again now has incorrectly identified the costs of using the market mechanism with the narrow transaction costs of discovering prices and executing contracts (1937: 390–391; 1988: lecture 3). However, vertical integration implies small, if any, savings in terms of these shopping and contract execution costs. Ownership of an organization essentially reduces the number of contracts that must be executed by, at most, one. General Motors must still have separate contracts with all the employees of Fisher Body. If the Fisher brothers remain, two new employee contracts must now be written to replace the old independent contractor body supply contract. If the Fisher brothers leave, there will be one less contract.

Rather than a decrease in the number of contracts, what vertical integration alters is the nature of the contractual arrangement. The one contract that is eliminated creates a new relationship between the transacting parties. It is no longer necessary for General Motors to prespecify production conditions (such as body plant locations, capital intensity, delivery times, and so forth) or prices. Although General Motors may actually write many of these conditions down in their internal interdivisional communications and, therefore, not save any "ink costs," these documents no longer have the force of contract law.

The absence of a legal constraint creates increased flexibility and a decreased possibility of a contractual hold-up. General Motors and Fisher no longer need to expend real resources in the attempt to determine all of the many events that might occur during the life of the production relationship and write a prespecified response to each event. Most of these events are highly unlikely and, by integrating, General Motors can wait until future conditions emerge before determining what should be done. As discussed above, not only do General Motors and Fisher save the allocatively wasteful transaction costs involved in searching for informational advantages in negotiating prespecified contractual responses, but they also avoid the real resource costs during the renegotiation process once ex-post market conditions turn out to be substantially different from the prespecified contract terms. Instead of contractual rigidity and the associated hold-up potential, the relationship becomes flexible to unanticipated market conditions.

While some commentators, including Coase, may identify this increased flexibility associated with vertical integration with the ability to coordinate or "direct" inputs, I do not believe that it is useful to focus on this ability as the central characteristic of a firm. Direction of inputs is neither a necessary nor a sufficient condition for defining a firm. For example, a conglomerate firm may merely own another firm (the organizational asset of another firm) without directing the firm's team of inputs. Alternatively, I may direct my gardener every weekend regarding what I want him to do for me, but I do not own a gardening firm. If the gardener has a group of workers that he uses to carry out my instructions, it is he who owns a gardening firm in the sense of an organization. By my direction I am specifying the particular services I desire. However, I am merely buying the particular services in the marketplace; it is the gardener who is "making" the particular services.

Direction of inputs can be accomplished in the marketplace as long as there are no specific investments made by the transacting parties and, therefore, no need for long-term contracts. Spot contracts in a competitive market can provide, in principle, a mechanism for perfect coordination and direction of cooperating inputs. A miller of flour, for example, may be able to contract in the spot market for supplies of wheat and have complete flexibility to alter quantities and qualities as required by shifts in his demand. The miller may demand in the market (that is, "direct" producers to supply) increased quantities or different qualities of wheat without any fear of a hold-up.

However, most market relationships entail transaction-specific investments and, therefore, the possibility of a hold-up. A magazine publisher, for example, may want to shift production of an issue (say, delay and increase the quantity of a press run to take account of a late-breaking story). Because of transaction-specific investments magazine printing services cannot be purchased in a perfectly competitive spot market. If the publisher purchased printing services from an independent printing firm, the printer may refuse to be "directed" in this manner without some side payment. Because of this hold-up potential, long-term contractual arrangements specifying particular contingencies and payment arrangements will be used. But these contract terms are necessarily imperfect and, as we have seen in the General Motors–Fisher Body case, may lead to the possibility of an even greater hold-up potential.

Transaction-specific investments are pervasive and exist in cases where there are no obvious specific physical capital investments. Even with regard to, say, wheat it may be costly to switch suppliers. It takes time to find new suppliers and to check product qualities and services (delivery times, reliability, and the like). Similarly, wheat suppliers must learn about particular millers' payment practices, delivery requirements, working schedules, and so on. It is because transactors make these specific investments in particular suppliers that real-world demand curves are never perfectly elastic. However, it is important to recognize that if transactor-specific investments were unimportant, spot contracts could be used and transactors would have the full ability to "direct" cooperating inputs in the marketplace. From an analytical point of view, vertical integration is not necessary in order to coordinate or "direct" cooperating inputs in the production process.

5. CONCLUSION

Given the presence of specific investments in an exchange relationship, transactors will have to decide whether to use a long-term contract or vertical integration to solve the hold-up problem. Vertical integration entails the widely recognized possibility of increased costs associated with somewhat reduced incentives and increased bureaucracy. I have discussed here the other side of the equation—the transaction costs associated with long-term contracts. The important element of these transaction costs are not the "ink costs" of writing contract terms emphasized by Coase, but the significant rent-dissipating costs borne during the negotiation and renegotiation contracting process as transactors attempt to create, avoid, and execute the hold-ups implied by necessarily imperfect long-term contractual arrangements.

While vertical integration may imply an increased ability to direct cooperating inputs compared to a long-term contractual arrangement, one must not confuse what an integrated firm may do with the basic economic motivation for the integration. Vertical integration, by shifting ownership of an organizational asset, permits transactors to avoid the transaction costs associated with a hold-up potential in the presence of specific investments. Whether transactors adopt vertical integration as a solution to a particular hold-up potential depends upon the magnitude of these specific investments, combined with the ability to write long-term contracts that flexibly track market conditions without creating an alternative hold-up potential. Since the ability to write and use long-term contracts depends, in part, upon the underlying market uncertainty and on the level of transactor reputations, these factors will also influence the likelihood of vertical integration.

This analysis of the motivation for vertical integration is consistent with the fundamental point recognized by Coase fifty years ago—that a transaction within the firm is something that is inherently different from a transaction in the marketplace. The view of the firm as merely a "nexus of contracts" that has developed in reaction to Coase's fundamental distinction between the firm and the market[12] is incomplete and misleading. I now agree with Coase that there is a useful analytical and not merely legal distinction to make between interfirm and intrafirm transactions. Firms are more than particular groups of explicit and implicit contracts. They consist of valuable team assets and developed mechanisms of handling information and control. By consolidating ownership of these organizational assets in the hands of one firm, vertical integration eliminates the need for one fundamental contract and creates an increased ability to flexibly direct production. As a consequence, a significant hold-up potential is reduced, along with an important range of transaction costs.

REFERENCES

Alchian, Armen A. 1959. "Costs and Outputs." In M. Abramovitz, ed., *The Allocation of Economic Resources*. Stanford: Stanford University Press.

———, and Harold Demsetz. 1972. "Production, Information Costs, and Economic Organization," 62 *American Economic Review* 777.

Arrow, Kenneth J. 1962. "The Economic Implications of Learning by Doing," 29 *Review of Economic Studies* 155.

Coase, Ronald H. 1937. "The Nature of the Firm," 4 *Economica* n.s. 386.

———. 1988. "The Nature of the Firm: Origin, Meaning, Influence," 4 *Journal of Law, Economics, and Organization*.

Grossman, Sanford, and Oliver Hart. 1986. "The Costs and Benefits of Ownership: A Theory of Vertical and Lateral Organization," 94 *Journal of Political Economy* 691.

Joskow, Paul L. 1988. "Asset Specificity and the Structure of Vertical Relationships: Empirical Evidence," 4 *Journal of Law, Economics, and Organization*.

Kenney, Roy, and Benjamin Klein. 1985. "The Law and Economics of Contractual Flexibility," UCLA Department of Economics working paper no. 388.

Klein, Benjamin. 1983. "Contracting Costs and Residual Claims: The Separation of Ownership and Control," 26 *Journal of Law and Economics* 367.

———, Robert Crawford, and Armen Alchian. 1978. "Vertical Integration, Appropriable Rents and the Competitive Contracting Process," 21 *Journal of Law and Economics* 297.

12. See, for example, Alchian and Demsetz, and Klein (1983).

Monteverde, K. M., and David J. Teece. 1982. "Appropriable Rents and Quasi-Vertical Integration," 25 *Journal of Law and Economics* 321.

Nelson, Richard R., and Sidney G. Winter. 1982. *An Evolutionary Theory of Economic Change*. Cambridge: Harvard University Press.

Prescott, Edward C., and Michael Visscher. 1980. "Organizational Capital," 88 *Journal of Political Economy* 466.

Rosen, Sherwin. 1972. "Learning by Experience as Joint Production," 86 *Quarterly Journal of Economics* 366.

Stigler, George. 1951. "The Division of Labor Is Limited by the Extent of the Market," 59 *Journal of Political Economy* 185.

Williamson, Oliver E. 1979. "Transaction Cost Economics: The Governance of Contractual Relations," 22 *Journal of Law and Economics* 233.

[2]

Vertical Integration and Long-term Contracts: The Case of Coal-burning Electric Generating Plants

PAUL L. JOSKOW
Massachusetts Institute of Technology

1. INTRODUCTION

What factors determine the institutional arrangements that govern supply relationships between input suppliers and their customers? Why are some transactions internalized through vertical integration? Why are many market transactions governed by complex long-term contracts? What determines the structure of such contracts and why are they used instead of simple spot market transactions? Over the past several years, a substantial amount of theoretical work has attempted to answer these questions. A much smaller quantity of empirical work devoted to testing alternative theories and expanding our understanding of vertical integration and contracting has appeared. Most of the empirical work has focused on examining the choice between vertical integration and "the market."[1] Empirical analysis of contracts has been minimal. Aside from Macaulay's classic paper and a recent paper by Goldberg and Erickson, most of the empirical analysis of contracts has been limited to examples based on interpretations of facts obtained from court decisions or secondary sources.[2] In this paper I provide a theoretical

I am grateful to Fred Dunbar, Victor Goldberg, Edmund Kitch, Oliver Williamson, Dick Schmalensee, Oliver Hart, and Steve Shavell for help and comments. I also want to thank National Economic Research Associates, Inc. for giving me access to its coal contract library.

1. Monteverde and Teece is an excellent example of this type of empirical work.
2. This is not to say that the examples have not been useful. The example presented by

Journal of Law, Economics, and Organization vol. 1, no. 1, Fall 1985
 ISSN 8756–6222

and empirical analysis of the structure of vertical arrangements governing coal supply transactions between electric utilities and coal suppliers.[3] I examine coal supply arrangements between electric utilities and coal suppliers in general but focus on the structure of these vertical relationships for mine-mouth coal plants.

Theoretical work devoted to the analysis of vertical arrangements has taken a number of different approaches.[4] I am particularly interested in what has been called the "transactions cost approach," which I attribute to Coase, Williamson, Klein, Goldberg, and others working in their tradition.[5] My plan in this paper is to use the transactions cost framework developed by these authors as the theoretical basis for analyzing coal supply arrangements and to make use of the empirical results to "test" the validity of the theory as a framework for understanding the structure of vertical relationships.

1.1. Potential Biases

Before proceeding further it is useful to answer a question likely to be in the reader's mind. Why study coal supply arrangements involving electric utilities? Since the buyers in this case are subject to economic regulation by state and federal regulatory agencies, we are confronted with a potentially complicating set of incentives that would not arise in studying the supply arrangements of unregulated firms. My reasons are quite simple. Detailed knowledge of a variety of characteristics of buyers and sellers seems essential for applying and testing transactions cost theory empirically. I already possess considerable information about electric utilities, power plants, and coal markets as a result of earlier research. Furthermore, in part because they are regulated, there is a lot of information available about particular utilities, their power plants, and their coal supply arrangements. It is even possible to obtain a large set of actual coal supply contracts and related documents. The opportunity to analyze data at this level of microeconomic detail is extremely rare.

Nevertheless, it is necessary to be sensitive to potential biases in supply arrangements that may be caused by economic regulation. It is my belief that economic regulation of electric utilities (including both the incentive created by price regulation and the direct restrictions on mergers and acqui-

---

Klein Crawford, and Alchian of the evolution of the supply relationship between General Motors and Fisher Body was instrumental in getting me interested in pursuing this project. Empirical studies of contract by Palay and by Masten have been published while this paper was in progress.

3 This is part of a larger project examining vertical relationships between electric utilities and input suppliers.

4. Some of the alternative approaches are discussed in Williamson (1983; 520–21) and Williamson (1984).

5. These papers include Coase (1937, 1972); Williamson (1971, 1975, 1979, 1983, and 1984); Klein, Crawford, and Alchian; Klein; Monteverde and Teece; and Goldberg.

sitions imposed by state and federal law) tends to discourage vertical integration. State regulators tend to be hostile to vertical integration and both state and federal regulators have, especially in recent years, treated the recovery of costs from captive (integrated) mines quite harshly.[6] There may be a similar bias against long-term contracts. The prospect of "automatic" pass-through of fuel costs through fuel adjustment clauses may also make electric utilities less responsive to the kinds of costs that motivate unregulated firms to adopt vertical arrangements that minimize costs.

I argue below that, particularly for mine-mouth plants, transaction cost theory implies that vertical integration or complex long-term contracts will be used to support exchange. Thus, data involving electric utilities are more likely to lead to rejection of the transactions cost theory than might otherwise be the case if one side of the transaction were not regulated. In an effort to at least partially control for any regulatory biases, I try to make comparisons between different types of electric generating plants. By making comparisons between supply arrangements for different types of plants with different transaction characteristics but subject to the same types of regulatory restrictions, I should be able to get a feeling for whether regulation is driving the results (in which case there should be no differences) or whether the transaction cost considerations hypothesized are important.

2. VERTICAL SUPPLY ARRANGEMENTS: AN OVERVIEW OF THE TRANSACTIONS COST APPROACH

In this section I provide a synthesis of what I take to be the primary theoretical foundations and implications of the transaction cost literature that I attribute to Coase, Williamson, Klein, Goldberg, and others. I have integrated ideas developed over time and across commentators and added my own interpretations.[7]

2.1. The Basic Theory

Economic institutions (or governance structures) emerge to minimize the costs of making transactions. These costs include both ordinary production costs (land, labor, capital, materials, and supplies) that make up the components of a neoclassical cost function and certain transactions costs associated with establishing and administering an ongoing business relationship. These transactions costs (which are identified more completely below) are real economic costs that must be taken into account along with ordinary production costs in structuring cost-minimizing economic institutions.

6. See McGraw-Hilll (1981: 371–73), *Electrical Week*, August 23, 1982, and *Electrical Week*, April 5, 1982. Some state commissions and FERC have been paying increasing attention to purchases made from subsidiaries and purchases made under long-term contracts.

7. The primary references are contained in n. 5.

There exists a continuum of *potential* governance structures for vertical relationships. At one extreme we have vertical integration. At the other extreme we have Walrasian auction markets. In between we have a wide array of potential contracting institutions that mediate transactions through the market but involve the use of a variety of specialized contractual provisions that arise as a consequence of efforts by firms to minimize the total cost of transactions over time. The nature, magnitude, and institutional response to transactions costs depends upon particular identifiable characteristics of the transactions involved. Thus, specific combinations of transactional characteristics, as they interact with more conventional production opportunities, lead to predictable cost-minimizing organizational and contractual responses.

2.2. Transactions Costs and Transaction Characteristics

Transactions costs include the following: costs of negotiating and writing contingent contracts; costs of monitoring contractual performance; costs of enforcing contractual promises; and costs associated with breaches of contractual promises. In each case these costs may include the costs of acquiring and processing information, legal costs, organizational costs, and costs associated with inefficient (in the neoclassical sense) pricing and production behavior.

There appear to be four important characteristics of transactions that have been identified as affecting the nature and magnitude of these transactions costs in important ways.[8] These include:

a. the extent to which the contemplated transactions are characterized by uncertainty and complexity;

b. the extent to which cost-minimizing transactions (in the neoclassical cost function sense) require one or both parties to a transaction to make durable transaction-specific (idiosyncratic) sunk investments;

c. the extent to which there are diseconomies associated with vertical integration that must be traded off against transactions costs that arise when market transactions are relied upon (these may include economics of scale, scope, or learning associated with supplying similar inputs in multiple vertical supply relationships; they also include incentive and command and control costs associated with bringing additional activities

8. I believe that information asymmetries can and should be further integrated into this literature and added to the list. The transactions cost literature I focus on here has either ignored or placed in the background both information asymmetries and differences between agents in the costs of bearing risks. The principle-agent literature, which is concerned with related problems, relies on assumptions about information asymmetries and risk aversion, but ignores transaction-specific investments. See Holmstrom, Shavell, and Hart. It would be productive to integrate the two approaches, but this is well beyond the scope of this paper.

inside a firm that would not arise when "market" transactions are relied upon);[9]

d. the "frequency" of transactions or more generally reputational constraints.

As uncertainty and complexity become more important in a vertical relationship the expected costs of writing, administering, and enforcing full contingent contracts increases. When uncertainty and complexity are important it becomes uneconomical to write full contingent contracts, and "market contracts" will tend to be incomplete. A contract is incomplete in the sense that it does not specify unambiguously the obligations of each party in every possible state of nature.

Contractual incompleteness sets the stage for ex post performance problems. When contingencies arise that are not fully and unambiguously covered by formal contractual provisions, one or both parties to the transaction may have incentives to "behave badly" by taking actions that increase the costs or reduce the revenues that will be obtained by the other party. The anticipation at the contract formation stage that "bad behavior" will occur when certain contingencies arise affects the cost-minimizing structure of the initial vertical relationship.

The "bad behavior" that may occur has been termed "opportunism" by Williamson. As I understand it, opportunism refers both to behavior that does not maximize joint profits (and is inefficient) when a particular contingency arises and also behavior that involves the appropriation of wealth of one party by the other in some states of nature without necessarily inducing distortions in supply or demand. In either case, upon realization that opportunistic behavior may occur, the governance structure and the terms and conditions of any arrangement chosen are adjusted ex ante. Contracts that pose more serious hazards are provided with greater safeguards.

The theory generally assumes that markets are competitive ex ante (many buyers and sellers). Opportunism can emerge ex post because certain characteristics of the supply relationship give one or both parties to the transaction some monopoly power when certain contingencies arise. In most of the recent work in this tradition, the primary source of monopoly power is the presence of durable transaction-specific sunk investments (see below). However, there appears to be a natural relationship between opportunism in this sense and more conventional notions of moral hazard that arise because of information asymmetries.[10] In the latter case, incentive problems arise because one party to the transaction both can affect (uncertain) outcomes by his own behavior and has better (less costly) access to information about the

9. Thus there are both costs and benefits associated with internal production. Grossman and Hart provide an interesting analysis of this issue.

10. Holmstrom, Shavell, and Hart are excellent examples of the approach taken in this growing literature.

causes of observed outcomes. The agent can exploit an information monopoly to its advantage.

Following the theoretical and empirical work in this tradition, I focus on durable transaction-specific sunk investments and largely ignore problems associated with information asymmetries and differences in the costs of bearing risk. Williamson (1983: 526) identifies four different types of transaction-specific sunk investments:

a. *Site specificity*: buyer and seller are in a "cheek-by-jowl" relation with one another, reflecting ex ante decisions to minimize inventory and transportation expense.

b. *Physical asset specificity*: when one or both parties to the transaction make investments in equipment and machinery that involves design characteristics specific to the transaction and which have lower values in alternative uses.

c. *Human-capital specificity*: arising as a consequence of learning-by-doing, investment, and transfer of skills (specific human capital) specific to a particular relationship.

d. *Dedicated assets*: general investments that would not take place but for the prospect of selling a significant amount of product to a particular customer. If the contract is terminated prematurely, it would leave the supplier with significant excess capacity.

Given contractual incompleteness due to uncertainty and complexity, as durable transaction-specific investments become more important, the transactions costs associated with mediating vertical relationships using conventional "spot markets" increase. Very simply, the argument is that transaction-specific sunk investments generate a stream of potentially appropriable quasi-rents equal to the difference between the anticipated value in the use to which the investments were committed and the next best use. The presence of transaction-specific investments creates incentives for one party to "hold up" the other ex post and can lead to costly haggling. When transaction-specific investments are important, governance structures will emerge ex ante to reduce the incentives either party has to exploit them ex post. Considerable emphasis has been placed on the proposition that vertical integraion is more likely to emerge when cost-minimizing (in the neoclassical sense) transactions involve durable transaction-specific sunk investments. Williamson's recent work and a great deal of Klein's work, however, consider contractual alternatives to vertical integration where transactions costs are important. If vertical integration is not economical because of diseconomies associated with internal production, contractual arrangements to govern exchange between independent agents will emerge to economize on these transactions costs. The structure of these market contracts will reflect efforts to create incentives and restrictions that reflect anticipted performance problems so that agents will perform as initially promised when different contingencies arise.

The theory also assumes that there is a strong incentive to structure contracts to minimize reliance on the legal system (which is costly and confronts grave difficulties in distinguishing promised behavior from "bad behavior") and therefore to structure vertical arrangements to achieve a "private ordering" that does not rely on legal enforcement. Nevertheless, people do sue one another for breach of contract, and various rules for defining breach and calculating damages exist (Muris). Thus, contractual arrangements should at least evolve in the shadow of the law, with recognition that court enforcement remains an option. Opportunities to specify contractual agreements in a clear and unambiguous way so as to strengthen the credibility and reduce the costs and uncertainty of legal sanctions should be taken advantage of.

The reliance of vertical integration is constrained by any diseconomies that may be associated with it. A supplier of some input that involves transaction-specific investments, for example, may achieve economies as a consequence of engaging in similar types of transactions with other buyers. There may be economies of scale associated with shared inputs across transactions or learning economies associated with repetitive production in many separate relationships. Internal incentive and command and control problems may limit the economic desirability of vertical integration.

Finally, the market may provide a natural deterrent to agents behaving badly and eliminate the need to rely on either vertical integration or complex "non-standard" contracts. There is a potential cost to breaches of written or implied contractual promises: the loss of future business from either this buyer or other buyers. In markets where buyers and sellers frequently engage in similar types of transactions, and where it is possible at low cost to distinguish "bad behavior" from "promised behavior" (perhaps combined with bad luck), reputational constraints will mitigate hold-up incentives and allow agents to more comfortably use simple auction markets, recognizing that the market provides penalties for inefficient behavior. These considerations may help to explain Macaulay's findings regarding the informality of contracts in business.

3. OVERVIEW OF U.S. COAL MARKETS

The primary market for coal today is the electric power industry, which accounts for more than 80 percent of domestic coal consumption. The second most important source of coal demand is coke plants (about 10 percent), which produce coke for the iron and steel industry. All other industrial consumers in the aggregate account for most of the remainder, with a small amount of coal continuing to be used in the residential/commercial sectors (see table 1). Coal is used to generate more than 50 percent of the electricity produced in the U.S. and accounts for more than 70 percent of fossil fuel utilization.

Coal reserves are not distributed uniformly across the country in terms of either quantity or quality. The Bureau of Land Management divides the

Table 1. U.S. Coal Consumption by Sector, 1980 and 1982

	1980		1982	
Sector	Tons (millions)	%	Tons (millions)	%
Electric utilities	569	81	594	84
Coke plants	67	10	41	6
Other industrial	60	9	64	9
Residential/commercial	6	1	8	1
	702		707	

SOURCE: *Quarterly Coal Report*, U.S. Department of Energy (DOE/EIA-0121), September 1983.

country into more than twenty coal-producing districts, but the bulk of the coal supplies are conveniently grouped into a handful of areas: the Appalachian region, the Interior (Midwestern) region, the Western region (often divided into the North Plains and Mountain regions), and Texas. Historically, most of the coal produced came from the Appalachian and Midwestern regions. Coal production in the Western region has increased dramatically in the past decade, reflecting the attractive economics of large strip-mining operations, declining productivity and labor problems in the East that increased costs, and an increasing demand for low-sulfur coal to meet air pollution restrictions.

There are substantial differences between the regions in terms of coal quality and optimal mining techniques and scale. Coal in the Appalachian region generally has a high BTU content, a sulfur content that varies from 1 to 3 percent, and ash content that varies from 10 to 15 percent (see table 2). The coal in the Interior region generally has a lower BTU content and a higher sulfur content. There is relatively little low-sulfur (1 percent or less) coal in the Midwest. Coal in the Western region varies widely in BTU content and ash content, with average BTU content significantly lower than the other regions. But Western coal generally has a very low sulfur content and relatively low mining costs (see below), making it especially attractive in midwestern states subject to sulfur emissions restrictions despite high transport costs. The coal being produced in Texas is almost all lignite, with low BTU content, low sulfur, and high ash content.

Topography and the nature of coal deposits affect the optimal type and scale of mining, and these characteristics also vary significantly among the regions. In Appalachia, underground mining accounts for about 60 percent of production and underground mines are relatively small (see table 3). Underground mines in the East appear to have relatively small minimum efficient scales (MES) (Zimmerman: 17–36), although the observed size distribution is somewhat misleading since it contains a large number of old and marginal mines which are very small. The topography of the Appalachian region makes necessary the use of relatively small mobile machinery for surface mining (Zimmerman: 26) and the MES of a strip-mining operation here is also relatively small.

In the Midwest, surface mining accounts for about 70 percent of coal production and both underground and surface mines are much larger than in the Appalachian area. The topography of the Interior region makes it eco-

Table 2. Regional Coal Characteristics, 1982 Production

Region/state/BLM district	BTU/lb	% sulfur	% ash
Appalachian			
Alabama	12,154	1.3	11.8
Georgia	12,338	1.5	11.7
Ohio	11,565	3.3	12.5
Pennsylvania			
1	12,228	1.9	14.5
2	12,233	2.0	12.1
Tennessee			
8	12,349	1.5	10.9
13	12,293	0.9	12.3
Virginia			
8	12,592	1.0	10.9
West Virginia			
3	12,708	2.3	10.7
6	12,109	3.9	11.4
8	12,213	0.9	11.8
Kentucky/East	12,184	1.1	10.6
Interior			
Illinois	10,959	2.7	10.2
Indiana	10,942	2.6	10.2
Kentucky/West	11,446	3.2	11.2
Missouri	10,276	4.8	17.1
Kansas	10,463	4.7	20.7
Texas	6,445	0.8	15.5
Western			
Wyoming	8,686	0.4	6.2
Montana	8,958	0.6	6.8
New Mexico	9,342	0.7	19.0
North Dakota	6,590	0.6	8.2
Utah	11,643	0.5	10.3
Washington	8,100	0.8	15.7

SOURCE: *Cost and Quality of Fuels for Electric Utility Plants*, U.S. Department of Energy (DOE/EIA-0191(82). August 1983, table 53.

Table 3. Underground and Surface Mining by Region, 1982

Region	% Underground	Annual output per mine	
		Underground	Surface
Appalachian	60	138,900	100,003
Interior	30	760,590	411,650
Western	11	441,810	2,646,040
U.S. total	40	170,040	242,540

SOURCE: Calculated from *Coal Data (1981/82)*, National Coal Association, II–11 and II–12.

nomical to use larger equipment and to better exploit economies of scale in strip mining than in the East. The MES of surface mines is larger in the Midwest as a result. In the Western region almost all of the coal comes from large strip mines (most of the underground mining takes place in Utah and Colorado). The topography and the nature of the deposits permits the use of large draglines and shovels, allowing fuller exploitation of surface-mining scale economies and larger MES (Zimmerman: 24–35). Surface mines are generally substantially more capital intensive than underground mines, and surface-mining technology seems to be characterized by substantial scale economies.

The bulk of the coal produced (about 75 percent) is carried by railroad (sometimes in conjunction with barge transport) (National Coal Association, 1984: 28). Transportation costs account for a large part of the delivered costs of coal on average. About half of the coal transported by rail is shipped by unit trains consisting of 100 or more specialized cars (often owned or leased by the utility buying the coal). Unit train shipments are generally acknowledged to be the most economical way of moving large volumes of coal by train. About 20 percent of the coal transported is carried by inland barges for at least part of the trip. Trucks account for a small part of the "mine-to-market" transportation but are used at both the loading end and the receiving end of the trip to collect and distribute coal (National Coal Association, 1984: 29). Coal slurry pipelines are a fourth transport option, but only one is currently operating.

Transportation opportunities vary from region to region. There appears to be more inter- and intra-mode competition in the East than in the West. For coal produced in the Interior and Western regions, rail transportation is essentially the only alternative to mine-mouth operations. Many of these producing areas must rely on one or perhaps two railroads to move coal out of these areas, and direct rail linkages between coal fields and potential load centers often do not exist.

Overall, most analysts have concluded that the coal supply market is quite competitive in the ex ante bidding sense used by Williamson (Gordon: 67–69). Concentration in mining and reserve ownership is low and entry appears to be relatively easy. Any monopoly problems are generally attributed to the railroads.

4. COAL SUPPLY ARRANGEMENTS FOR ELECTRIC GENERATING PLANTS AND TRANSACTION-SPECIFIC INVESTMENTS

When a utility considers building a new base-load generating plant it must make a number of interrelated decisions.[11] The most important decisions that must be made concern the following:

1. How large should the generating unit(s) be?
2. What type of fuel should they burn?
3. Where should the plant be located?
4. How should the generating unit's boiler be designed to minimize expected fuel costs over the life of the unit?
5. If a coal burning plant is built, what types of coal will the plant utilize, what is it likely to cost, and where is this type of coal likely to come from?
6. How will the coal be transported from the mine to the plant and what are the expected costs of transportation?

For purposes of discussion here we will assume that the optimal size of the generating units has been determined and that a decision has been made to utilize coal as the primary fuel for generating electricity in the plants that are built. In the spirit of transaction cost theory we first consider the cost minimizing options that utilities have in each of the remaining dimensions given the "ordinary" or neoclassical cost opportunities they face. We then discuss the importance of transaction-specific investments associated with four "stylized" cost minimizing investment/coal procurement strategies and the associated implications for the choice of governance structure to support cost minimizing exchange in each case.

A utility considering building a new coal plant can choose between two primary locational strategies. It can build a plant (independently or jointly with other utilities) in or near its own service territory, reflecting the electrical requirements of its system, land and cooling water availability, transportation facilities, etc., and arrange for transportation of the coal from one or more mines to the plant. This has been the approach taken for most operating coal plants. Alternatively, the utility can build (itself or jointly with other utilities) a plant adjacent to coal reserves from which coal will be mined for that plant, with effectively zero coal transportation costs, and then use a high

11. A base-load unit is a unit that is designed to operate at full capacity throughout the year, regardless of variations in total system demand. Demand variations are accommodated with "cycling" or "peaking" units. Almost all coal-burning units are designed to operate as base-load units for a substantial fraction of their useful lives, on the order of twenty years.

voltage transmission system to transport the power from the supply point to load centers. Such plants are referred to as mine-mouth plants. For utilities whose service territories are far from coal-mining areas, the choice between these two alternatives is quite discrete. Obviously, however, a utility whose electric loads are also close to coal-producing areas can take advantage of the best of both alternatives.

The decision to choose one locational strategy rather than another (ignoring transactions costs) depends on the prices of coal at the mine in different locations, the availability and costs of coal transport alternatives, the costs and institutional constraints associated with the transmission of electricity, and any institutional constraints affecting the ownership and operation of coal units in states other than those in which the utility is chartered to provide service.

A generating unit is typically designed optimally to burn coal with particular characteristics (BTU content, sulfur content, ash content, chemical composition, grindability, etc.). The use of coal that differs from the design specifications of a plant can lead to a loss in thermal efficiency or to increases in plant outages and maintenance costs. Exactly how tightly a plant is designed is, within some range, a variable of choice for the utility. The design decision depends on a utility's anticipated fuel procurement strategy, the variation in coal quality in the areas from which the utility is likely to purchase coal, the quantities of different types of coal available in these areas and the number of suppliers producing it, and the costs of building more fuel flexibility into the plant. For a mine-mouth plant, the design is necessarily governed by the characteristics of the coal in the areas adjacent to the plant.

In general, cost-minimizing coal procurement strategies and plant design are intimately related. A utility could plan to buy coal for a plant through spot market purchases or short-term contracts from a wide variety of different suppliers. If this strategy is chosen, boiler design flexibility is likely to be an important consideration, unless coal in the areas where the utility anticipates buying in this way is of fairly uniform quality. At the other extreme a utility could plan to purchase all of its coal requirements from one specific mine over the life of the plant. In this case, the plant could be designed optimally to burn coal with the characteristics expected to be available from this mine. Intermediate strategies involving more or less burning flexibility and more or less flexibility in procurement can also be pursued. A utility can choose to purchase from existing mines that are already supplying coal for other utilities and plants or contract in advance from a mine that has not yet been developed.

The cost-minimizing coal procurement strategy will depend on a number of factors. The expected f.o.b. price of coal in various areas is a primary consideration, along with the expected costs of transporting coal from the mines to the plant. Air pollution restrictions are likely to sharply constrain the kinds of coal that some utilities can burn economically. The economics of mining is likely to affect coal procurement strategies as well. If there are substantial economies of scale in mining, a utility may be able to reduce its coal costs by committing itself to purchase all of its coal from one large mine.[12] If economies of scale in mining are not important, there is little advantage to doing so. The availability of alternative transportation opportunities may also affect the strategy.

If the decision is made to build a mine-mouth plant, the location, design, and coal procurement strategy generally go hand in hand with one another. The plant is consciously located near specific coal reserves, is designed to optimally burn coal of the quality that will be mined there, and the utility expects to acquire coal for the plant from one or more adjacent mines over a large portion of the expected life of the plant.

There are numerous possible combinations of plant design strategies, coal procurement strategies, and transportation strategies that are possible. Let me identify four stylized cases for further discussion.

Case 1: The utility expects to purchase coal from a large number of existing suppliers located at different points in a fairly large geographical area through spot market purchases and simple short-term contracts. The elasticity of supply of coal of like quality from this general area is fairly high and numerous utilities are active in purchasing coal there. The identity of the particular mines from which coal is purchased is not of any importance to the utility. It anticipates making transportation arrangement with a variety of railroads and barge companies, contracting for delivery as it contracts for coal. It designs its plant with enough flexibility to accept coal of the variable quality that would be available from any of the mines in the general area.

Case 2: The utility expects to purchase coal from a relatively small number of existing mines located close to one another and producing similar types of coal. The mines currently supply coal to other utilities. To economically meet the anticipated demand the mines must make modest investments to increase their capacity. The utility expects to rely on these mines for several years but anticipates the possibility of switching suppliers, sub-

12. My reasoning here is related to Williamson's notion of dedicated assets. The development of a mine requires durable investments. The mine operator chooses both an optimal level of capacity and an optimal mining technique to meet expected demand. Mining techniques vary in capital intensity. More capital-intensive techniques are optimal at larger scales, other things equal. Without a long-term commitment by buyers to take specific quantities, the mine operator will treat nominal contract demand as being uncertain with an expected value that is less than the nominal contract demand. Mine capacity and mining technique will be chosen to reflect this expected demand and the unit cost of coal and prices determined based on this expected demand. If a buyer can commit itself to a firm demand equal to the nominal demand, it can induce the mine operator to expand capacity, reducing unit costs. Some of the savings can be passed along as a lower price than would otherwise prevail if the contract demand were treated as being uncertain. The more significant the scale economies, the greater the associated price reduction.

ject to contractual restrictions, if economic opportunities arise to do so. It anticipates relying on two different railroads to transport the coal, but alternative transportation arrangements can be made at a small cost penalty. Other suppliers of coal of this quality in proximate areas exist, but the elasticity of supply in the short run is very low. The longer-run supply elasticity is fairly large, however. The utility designs its boiler to burn coal of the type available from these two mines, applying tighter design specifications than in the case above. It recognizes that switching suppliers may make it difficult to obtain coal with the same characteristics as its initial suppliers but coal quality is sufficiently uniform in the areas where alternative suppliers are likely to be located that coal quality deviations can be accommodated with only small increases in costs.

Case 3: The utility anticipates obtaining supplies from one or two specific mines for the life of the plant. The mines are currently in operation but will make substantial investments to increase capacity in anticipation of these purchases. The quantities of coal that the utility expects to purchase do not exhaust the economic capacity of these mines, and the mine owners eventually anticipate making sales to other utilities at similar prices. There are very limited supplies available in the short run from other mines in this area, and coal quality varies widely from mine to mine in the same general geographical area. The utility anticipates relying on a single railroad to transport the coal and plans to invest in unit trains to carry the coal on this railroad's tracks. The plant is designed with tight specifications to optimally burn the coal from these mines including specific investments in pollution control equipment.

Case 4: The utility builds a mine-mouth plant and anticipates obtaining all supplies from one or two adjacent mines. The plant is designed specifically to optimally burn coal from these mines. The mine would not be built but for the existence of the plant, and opportunities to sell coal at the same price to other buyers is uncertain. The utility makes extensive investments in transmission capacity to move the power from mine to load centers.

These four cases involve very different degrees of transaction-specific investments. In the first case, the buyer makes specific investments to design its plant to burn coal of the quality produced in a fairly large geographical area, but the value of the investments would not be reduced by shifting suppliers on short notice since there is an elastic supply of coal of similar quality available from this area. Multiple transport options combined with ease of shifting suppliers does not make the value of the plant economically dependent on the behavior of a particular railroad. Suppliers have not made investments specific to the purchases of this particular plant or utility. None of the four potential types of transaction-specific sunk investments seem to be important.

In the second case, transaction-specific investments are likely to be somewhat more important. The plant has tighter design specifications. Sudden switching of suppliers could be costly because the elasticity of supply is small, although if appropriate notice is given additional mining capacity can be brought into production to satisfy additional demand at approximately the same price. Only two railroads are utilized, but alternative transport options are available at a small increase in cost. The suppliers have made some investments in direct response to the anticipated demand of this utility, but the associated mines are already operating, and alternative purchasers of the coal would probably emerge with some lag. Thus, the power plant investment is characterized by some physical asset specificity and some of the mining investments may fall into the dedicated assets category.

In the third case, transaction specific investments are much more important. The utility has designed its plant to burn coal from a particular mine. It has invested in unit trains to transport that coal. The mine owners will make investments to increase the capacity of the mine almost completely as a response to the expected demand by this utility. The utility effectively ties itself to a single transport option, although by owning the rail cars that will carry the coal it has some control over the availability of transportation and simplifies the problem of writing a contract for transport services with the railroad. In this case the investment in the plant is characterized by a greater degree of physical asset specificity. The mining investment has the character of a dedicated asset. Although the vertical relationship is not of the "cheek-by-jowl" nature implied by the concept of site specificity, the existence of a single railroad and utility investments in rolling stock to be used on that railroad seem to lead to a similar result.

The fourth case is a mine-mouth plant and is characterized by at least three of the four types of asset specificity identified by Williamson: (a) site specificity—the plant and mine are deliberately located next to one another to minimize costs; (b) physical asset specificity—the plant is designed to burn the particular types of coal located in the adjacent reserves; and (c) dedicated assets—the mine would not be built but for the promise of purchases from the adjacent plant, and the plant would not be built but for the availability of coal from the adjacent mine.[13] Human (or organizational) asset specificity "that arise in a learning-by-doing fashion" as identified by

13. The importance of dedicated assets is made clearly by one of the contracts for a mine-mouth plant that is analyzed below.

> Buyers will construct, own and operate a coal fired steam-electric generating plant . . . adjoining coal lands of Seller, based upon the assurance of a dependable supply of coal of specified quality and characteristics for the useful life of the plant.
>
> The Buyers would not design and construct a plant of this type [at this site] . . . but for the availability of a dependable supply of coal from seller through December 31, 2019. . . .
>
> It is essential to the Seller, because of the substantial capital investment it must make in order to have the capability to supply Buyers' requirements, that buyers purchase all of their coal requirements for said plant from Seller. (From the coal supply agreement between the five joint owners of units 3 and 4 of the Colstrip generating plant in Montana and Western Energy Company, dated July 2, 1980.)

Williamson may also be important especially with regard to coordination between the plant operator and the mine operator, but I will not treat this fourth form of asset specificity in this discussion.

Let us consider the implications of asset specificity for the optimal choice of governance structure in each case, assuming for now that contracts will be incomplete and reputational constraints are not important (we look at these issues in more detail below as part of the detailed analysis of mine-mouth plants). According to transaction cost theory, other things being equal, the potential for opportunism should vary directly with the importance of transaction specific investments. These problems of opportunism should in turn affect the nature of the contractual relationships between buyers and sellers. In case 1 opportunism should be minimal and reliance on spot market purchases and simple contracts should be adequate. In case 2, there is a potential for opportunistic behavior by the buyer and the seller, but this is sharply constrained since transaction-specific investments are modest. Alternatives to spot market transactions and simple short-term contracts are likely to be desirable to provide some protection for buyers and sellers from ex-post hold-up problems. Vertical integration is not a viable option, however, given the procurement strategy of the utility. In case 3, both the buyer and the seller make transaction-specific investments and opportunism is potentially quite serious. The potential for the railroad to act opportunistically is another real complication. Long-term contracts with extensive protection for both the buyer and the seller from opportunistic behavior is suggested. Vertical integration is a possibility, although if the utility also sinks investments in the mine the railroad's incentives to hold it up may be even greater. Long-term coal supply contracts with utility performance contingent on performance of the railroad may be desirable.

Asset specificity appears to be most important for mine-mouth plants and opportunism potentially the most severe. Such plants appear to be prime candidates for the use of complex long-term contracts or vertical integration to support exchange.

In the case of mine-mouth plants we can assume that neoclassical cost considerations led to this locational choice, and we can examine the choice of governance structures that have been made in response to the associated transaction cost considerations. For other plants, we have no easy way of identifying directly the underlying neoclassical cost conditions that might make one of the other strategies economical for particular plants. However, in light of the general characteristics of coal supply and transportation discussed above, we can make at least some qualitative statements about the likely incidence of each of the three cases.

For the strategy covered by case 1 to be economical (transaction cost considerations aside), several characteristics of supply and transportation must prevail. The supply areas where the utility can most economically obtain coal should have coal of fairly uniform quality, should have numerous producing mines, and should be supplying quantities of coal that are very large relative to the demands of any particular plant. Economies of scale in coal mining should not be important, so that it is not advantageous for a plant to commit itself to long-term supplies with a single supplier. In addition, transport cost savings associated with the use of several competing transport alternatives should be greater than the savings associated with the use of unit trains to transport large quantities of coal from a single point to the plant. Alternatively, the mines must be close enough together to economically move the coal to a local point for onward transport by unit trains.

These characteristics of coal supply and transportation do not appear to be satisfied in most areas of the country. To the extent that this extreme case would be an economical coal procurement strategy anywhere, it is likely to be so for some plants located in the East which utilize coal from certain areas in Appalachia and for one reason or another cannot make efficient use of unit trains.[14]

The second case is likely to be more consistent with the supply and transportation opportunities faced by many plants located in the East and especially in the eastern half of the Midwest which secure supplies from Appalachia and the eastern Interior region. This reflects potential benefits associated with making at least limited commitments to particular mines, the costs of efficiently operating plants with variable coal quality, and economies associated with concentrating coal transportation and investments in unit trains. Longer-term contracts with some protection from opportunism would be more likely in this case, although there seems to be little reason for vertical integration.

As we move further west, the advantages of reliance on a small number of mines because of scale economies, transport economies, and variations in coal quality become more important. Potential opportunism becomes more severe and reliance on spot markets or simple contracts more problematical. Long-term contracts with appropriate protective provisions become more likely. Utilities in the Midwest and West that rely on supplies of coal from the West to satisfy air pollution requirements or which take advantage of cheap lignite and subbituminous coal—and must make very specific plant investments to burn it effectively—are likely to have arrangements similar to those suggested in case 3. Procurement strategies that lie between cases 2 and 3 are likely to reflect opportunities faced by other plants in the Midwest.

Overall, this suggests that (excluding mine-mouth plants) as we move

14. The age of the plant is also likely to be relevant. Over time, technological change has made it possible to build more efficient plants that produce steam at higher temperatures and pressures. The newer high-pressure units, especially supercritical units, tend to be more sensitive to variations in coal quality. See Joskow and Rose for a discussion of changes in generating-unit technology over time.

from East to West, we should see less reliance on spot market purchases and more reliance on long-term contracts. There should be relatively little reliance on spot market purchases generally since the supply, transportation, and generating technology conditions conducive to cost-minimizing supply strategies that do not involve at least some asset specificity by either the buyer or the seller are likely to exist for a relatively small fraction of all coal-burning power plants. Mine-mouth plants are the prime candidates for complex long-term contracts or vertical integration.

5. VERTICAL INTEGRATION, SPOT MARKETS, AND CONTRACT SALES

The previous discussion suggests that we should observe considerable variation in coal supply arrangements. Spot market transactions and simple short-term contracts will be economical choices for some plants, tending to be older plants located in the East. Vertical integration is most likely for mine-mouth plants, but such plants account for a relatively small fraction of total coal utilization (on the order of 15 percent—see below). If vertical integration is not chosen to govern supply for mine-mouth plants, contracts will have to be structured to mitigate opportunism in the context of a supply relationship governed by complex long-term contracts. Most coal-burning plants are likely to face economic opportunities that fall somewhere between these two extremes and will not rely extensively on either spot markets or vertical integration or the very long and tight contracts that simulate the opportunism-mitigating features of vertical integration.

We now turn to an examination of the extent to which vertical integration, spot markets, and other contractual arrangements are utilized to support exchange between coal-generating plants and their suppliers for the industry as a whole.

Table 4 lists the utilities that are integrated into coal production in one way or another and their coal subsidiaries (where the latter information is available).[15] The table also provides information on the extent of vertical integration (percent of coal requirements provided by coal subsidiaries) for each of these companies. Less than 15 percent of coal consumed by utilities is supplied to plants by a coal company owned by the owner of the plant (or one of the owners in the case of jointly owned plants). Another 3 percent or

15. Exactly what constitutes vertical integration is far from obvious. Some utilities own a plant themselves and have a mining division or subsidiary that operates the mines. Other utilities own plants themselves, own both coal reserves and the mines, but contract with independent operators to produce the coal. Still other utilities own the reserves, but contract with independent contractors to both develop and operate the mines. In other cases, the plant is jointly owned by several utilities, only one of which has an ownership interest in the mines serving the plant. I classify any of these cases as vertical integration and make finer distinctions in the discussion of mine-mouth plants below.

so of U.S. coal consumption is produced by coal companies owned by utilities but supplied to plants not owned by the integrated utility in question. The extent of vertical integration into coal production in the electric utility industry is substantally less than in the coking (iron and steel) industry, where about 65 percent of requirements come from integrated coal suppliers.

About half of the utilities owning coal-producing subsidiaries are fully integrated, supplying all of their coal requirements (and often supplying coal to other utilities as well). The others generally supply only a small fraction of their coal needs. Those utilities that are integrated tend to be relatively large consumers of coal, but more than half of the twenty largest utility consumers of coal are not integrated. A few utilities are currently attempting to divest

Table 4. Vertical Integration into Coal Mining by Electric Utilities

Utility/subsidiaries	1980 production (tons)	(state)	Extent
Texas Utilities	27,590,768	(TX)	100% requirements
Pacific P&L/NERCO			
Bridger Coal (joint owner)	6,453,302	(WY)	100% requirements by
Decker Coal (joint owner)	5,534,429	(MT)	company-owned mines or
Glenrock Coal	3,800,000	(WY)	mines owned by joint-
Sond Mountains Minerals	500,000	(AL)	owners of plants + substan-
Spring Creek Coal	100,000	(MT)	tial third-party sales.
Bankhead Coal	390,000	(AL)	
Total	16,777,331		
American Electric Power			~30% of requirements
Windsor Power House			
Southern Ohio Coal			
Central Ohio Coal			
Southern Appalachian Coal			
Cedar Coal			
Central Appalachian			
Simco/Peabody (joint owner)			
Price River Coal		(UT)	
Total	16,057,181		
Montana Power			
Western Energy	10,448,000	(MT)	100% of requirements + third-party sales.
Washington Water Power	5,140,000	(WA)	Requirements of Centralia, system's only coal plant.
Utah P&L	4,600,000	(UT)	~65% of requirements; mines operated by contractor.
Montana/Dakota Utilities			100% of requirements +
Knife River Coal	4,788,967	(MT, ND)	third-party sales.

Table 4. Vertical Integration into Coal Mining by Electric Utilities, *continued*

Utility/subsidiaries	1980 production (tons)	(state)	Extent
Pennsylvania P&L			
Pennsylvania Mines	2,928,211	(PA)	~50% of requirements
Greenwich Collieries	1,528,807	(PA)	
Lady Jane Collieries	200,963	(PA)	
Total	4,657,981		
Black Hills P&L			100% of requirements incl.
Wyodak Resources	2,500,000	(WY)	all of Wyodak plant.
Duke Power			
Eastover Mining Co.	2,084,000	(PA)	~15% of requirements. Subsid. up for sale in 1983.
Duquesne L&P	900,000	(PA)	~20% of requirements
Iowa PS Co.			
Energy Dev. Co.	877,631	(WY)	NA
VEPCO			~15% requirements
Laurel Run Mining	619,981	(WV)	(Mt. Storm plant)
Tampa Electric			
Cal-Glo Coal	388,000	(KY)	~10% of requirements
Ohio Edison	188,439	(OH)	~5% of requirements
Carolina P&L			
Leslie Coal (80%)	545,800	(KY)	~5% of requirements
McInnes Coal (80%)	—		
Total production by utility-controlled mines			83,000,000 tons
Sales to third parties (excl. joint plant owners)			13,000,000
Net integrated production			70,000,000
% of total utility coal use (tons):	14		
% of total utility coal use (BTUs):	12		

SOURCE: Compiled from data in 1982 *Keystone Coal Manual, Moody's Public Utility Manual* (various years), annual reports, and 10-K filings.

themselves of coal subsidiaries, largely as a consequence of unfavorable regulatory treatment of coal obtained from captive mines.[16]

Thus, about 85 percent of the coal used to generate electricity is supplied through some type of market transaction mechanism. Readily available data on coal supply arrangements breaks utility coal transactions down into spot transactions and contract transactions (see table 5). Generally, spot transactions involve coal supply agreements for relatively small fixed quantities of coal with delivery schedules extending for less than a year. Transactions that involve deliveries extending over a period of more than a year generally fall in the contract category. The proportion of spot transactions varies consider-

16. Duke Power has been actively seeking a buyer for its coal subsidiary. Carolina Power and Light and Pennsylvania Power and Light are also considering selling their coal subsidiares. See, for example, *Electrical Week*, August 23, 1982.

Table 5. Spot and Contract Transactions

Year	% spot	% contract
1974	23.8	76.2
1975	18.2	81.8
1976	14.0	86.0
1977	19.4	80.6
1978	21.2	78.8
1979	12.8	87.2
1980	11.5	88.5
1981	13.1	86.9
1982	9.6	90.4

Regional Breakdown: 1982

Region	% spot
Appalachian	17.4
Interior	7.4
Texas	8.1
Western	1.6
Total	9.6

SOURCE: Calculated from *Cost and Quality of Fuels for Electric Utility Plants*, U.S. Department of Energy (DOE/EIA-0191(82)). August 1983, table 53.

ably from year to year. The relatively high values from 1974–75 and 1977–78 appear to reflect coal strikes that took place during portions of these periods. There is also substantial regional variation in the volume of coal made available through spot market transactions. The spot market accounts for a much larger fraction of transactions in the East than elsewhere, and there is essentially no spot market for coal in the West.

The contract category includes everything from one-year contracts to fifty-year contracts, and individual contracts vary widely in the annual tonnage provided for. There is probably relatively little difference from a transactional perspective between spot sales and contract sales with deliveries spread over one or two years, so it would be useful to break down the contract category further by duration and volume. Additional information on contract deliveries by duration and annual quantities is not as easily obtained from standard government sources as the initial breakdown between spot and contract. However, I have analyzed a sample of more than 200 coal contracts that accounted for more than 30 percent of contract coal deliveries in 1979 (see table 6).[17] Over 80 percent of the coal sold under these contracts involved delivery commitments for more than five years and more than 70 percent involved commitments extending over a period of more than ten

17. The contract information was obtained from Pasha Publications, *1980 Guide to Coal Contracts*, for another project. Data on 270 contracts was collected but only 205 contained both information on duration and delivered quantities for 1979.

years. This breakdown is roughly equivalent to the survey information Gordon (55–58) obtained for 1969. Longer contract periods are generally associated with larger annual volumes of coal as well.

These results are broadly consistent with the previous discussion. About 60 percent of the coal supplied to electric utilities involves relatively long-term contracts (more than five years). The spot market is not a significant governance mechanism for coal supply arrangements between utilities and coal producers. It is most important in the East and essentially nonexistent in the West. Vertical integration is not particularly important either, accounting for a somewhat smaller fraction of coal supplied.

Table 6. Distribution of 205 Contracts by Duration and Annual Tonnage

Duration	% of coal deliveries	Tons/year/contract
less than or 5 years	17	267,000
6-10 years	12	556,000
11-20 years	37	885,000
21–30 years	17	1,309,000
more than 30 years	17	2,411,000

SOURCE: See text and n. 17.

6. COAL SUPPLY ARRANGEMENTS FOR MINE-MOUTH PLANTS IMPLIED BY TRANSACTION COST CONSIDERATIONS

I argued above that coal supply transactions for mine-mouth plants are characterized by at least three of the four types of asset specificity identified by Williamson (1983: 26). From a transactional perspective, these plants are distinguished from the "typical" coal plant primarily by the unusual importance of durable transaction-specific investments. Transaction cost theory suggests that mine-mouth plants should be much more likely to be integrated or make use of complex long-term contracts than the typical generating plant. Before proceeding further it is worth considering briefly the other characteristics of transactions that are likely to affect the governance structure for coal plants generally and mine-mouth coal plants in particular:

Uncertainty/complexity: There is no easy way to measure the extent to which a particular type of transaction is subject to uncertainty or complexity. Indeed, it is not at all obvious from the literature how one even would conceptualize either a cardinal or ordinal measurement procedure. Precise measurement is not critical, however. Uncertainty and complexity are important to the extent that buyers and sellers cannot write unambiguous and easily enforceable full contingent claims contracts. When full contingent claims contracts cannot be written, contracts are necessarily incomplete. Contractual incompleteness is not the source of transactional difficulties, but rather sets the stage for contractual difficulties in the presence of transaction-specific investments or information asymmetries.

From the perspective of a utility considering investment in a coal plant with an expected life of thirty-five years or more, it is certainly reasonable to assume that there is enough uncertainty about coal demand in the short run and over the life of the plant to make it difficult to write a full contingent claims contract. Coal demand will vary with the utilization rate of the plant and the thermal efficiency of the plant. Both of these vary over time in a nondeterministic way. As a plant ages and moves higher in the dispatch profile, plant utilization will also vary with total electrical load and with the prices of fuels burned by other plants on a utility's system. Air pollution restrictions and cooling water availability may limit plant utilization and affect both the quantity and the types of coal required. Furthermore, because coal quality is very important and numerous coal characteristics are relevant for plant design and plant performance, the "simple" product *coal* is a much more complex product than first appears.

From the perspective of a mine owner considering investing in a new mine or expanding an existing mine, there is also likely to be considerable uncertainty about mining costs and coal quality over the life of the mine. Ex ante, there is at least some uncertainty about mining costs, cleaning requirements, and reserves given prevailing input prices. Over time, the nominal and real costs of mining are inherently uncertain, depending not only on the physical characteristics of the reserves, but also on changes in input prices, contract work rules, government regulations affecting mining costs, and technologies.

For the purposes of examining governance structures for coal supplied to electric utilities, I think that it is fair to assume that contracts will necessarily be incomplete. This is especially true for mine-mouth plants, where both parties make long-term reliance investments contingent on the performance of the other over many years.

Reputational constraints: Is it likely that the threat of losing future purchases (in the case of the mining company) or the prospect that buyers will have to pay higher transactions prices in future contracts (reflecting a price for anticipated breaches on the part of the buyer) will deter the kinds of "bad behavior" that the transactions cost literature is concerned with? Reputational constraints depend primarily on the importance of repeat purchase activity and the ability to distinguish bad (good) outcomes (such as high mining costs or failures to deliver promised quantities) that arise because of inefficient (efficient) behavior from bad (good) outcomes that arise simply because of bad (good) luck. Reputational constraints are likely to be most important when utilities find it economical (in the neoclassical sense) to adopt procurement strategies such as those outlined in case 1 and case 2 above. There is extensive repeat purchase activity, sales are made to many sellers from the same mines, and the utility buys from several different sellers. These constraints are not likely to be significant in the case of mine-mouth operations, however.

Individual mine-mouth operations have many idiosyncrasies that make it difficult for third parties to distinguish poor performance due to actions by either party from poor performance resulting from exogenous factors that are not subject to control by either party. Especially in the last ten or fifteen years, regulatory changes and labor problems have had profound effects on mining costs and production. Many generating units built over the past twenty years have experienced much poorer heat rates and availabilities than had been anticipated. It is likely to be difficult to determine how much of this change was due to exogenous factors and how much can be associated with suboptimal levels of effort by either party. Overall, it seems unlikely that reputational constraints can provide protection from opportunistic behavior in the case of mine-mouth plants.

Diseconomies of internal production: I have no way of evaluating objectively whether there are important economies that a large coal producer with production activity and experience from other supply arrangements would bring to a transaction that a utility embarking on coal production itself would not be able to take advantage of. I suspect that there are some economies of scale or experience in this sense that utilities would not be able to take advantage of, but I have seen no evidence that would allow me to make a definitive statement.[18] Nor is there any way to estimate empirically internal incentive and command and control problems that might increase costs from integrated production compared to the costs of market procurement and necessarily limit the economic extent of vertical integration. There is little reason to believe, however, that these considerations are more important for mine-mouth plants than they are for other types of plants.

In summary, these observations suggest the following. The assumption of incomplete contracts is probably a good one for all types of generating plants. This sets the stage for opportunism if transaction-specific investments are necessary for structuring a minimum cost supply relationship. Transaction-specific sunk investments are considerably more important for mine-mouth plants than for other types of plants. Reputational constraints are not likely to be particularly effective in the case of mine-mouth plants. Diseconomies of internal production are likely to affect the economics of vertical integration equally, regardless of the particular type of plant involved.

18. The utility owners of Western Coal (formed to supply the San Juan plant) did apparently consider taking over mining responsibilities from Utah-International, the developer and operator of the adjacent mine. Among other things they concluded that Utah could take advantage of some economies associated with its mining operations at Four Corners. See letter from Western Coal Co. to Tucson Gas and Electric and Public Service of New Mexico regarding negotiations between Western (jointly owned by the two utilities) and Utah-International (dated February 21, 1978, on file).

This all implies that coal supply transactions for a mine-mouth operation are prime candidates for the choice of vertical integration as a transaction cost-minimizing governance structure. Regulatory considerations, coal supplier economies, and other diseconomies of vertical integration may make vertical integration less attractive than alternative contractual governance structure, or even impossible. If vertical integration is not chosen, some type of long-term contractual arrangement containing provisions that anticipate performance difficulties and designed to effectuate a smooth and efficient relationship between the buyer and the seller should be forthcoming. Reliance on a spot market or even relatively short-term contracts are not likely to prove to be a cost-minimizing alternative.

Let's assume that for one reason or another a mine-mouth plant operator chooses to secure supplies through contract rather than vertical integration. What are the characteristics of an efficient contractual relationship? What contractual provisions will emerge as the parties negotiate a mutually acceptable supply agreement in response to anticipated transactions costs and contract execution difficulties? Are the resulting arrangements efficient?

From a normative (efficiency) perspective we would expect a coal supply arrangement to emerge with these desirable features:

a. The contemplated mine-mouth operation will go forward if it is the cost-minimizing way for the utility to generate electricity; the parties will be able to strike a deal.

b. Once a plant and mine are built, the plant operator will continue to take supplies from the adjacent mine as long as this is the least cost source of supply, without the buyer switching to a (socially) uneconomical supplier.

c. The seller will produce coal efficiently.

d. The seller will continue to supply the quantities and quality of coal promised as long as it represents the least cost source of supply for the plant. The seller will not uneconomically shift supplies to other buyers.

e. The agreement will be flexible enough to allow supply and demand by the supplier/purchaser to adjust to changes in economic conditions. If the current supplier is not the minimum cost producer, the agreement should provide a mechanism to shift suppliers, reduce production, etc.

f. Minimization of haggling over price and production levels that may disrupt efficient supply arrangements but may be a natural outcome of the bilateral monopoly situation that emerges once each party sinks costs in reliance on the agreement.

g. Avoidance of litigation and litigation costs.

The actual provisions that emerge will reflect efforts by each party to maximize profits with due recognition of the costs of writing, monitoring, and enforcing contractual promises. A variety of price and nonprice provisions are potentially available to support exchange and mitigate opportunism. The optimal price and nonprice provisions are likely to be related to one another and it is difficult to discuss them independently. It is even more difficult to discuss them together.

Let me assume, to begin, that the costs of producing coal do not change over time due to changes in input prices, technological change, government regulation, contractual changes in work rules, and so on, and that a price (level and structure) is negotiated at the start of the contract and is *anticipated* to be fixed over the term of the contract, although either party is free to try to exploit any ex post monopoly power to force the other to agree to a higher or lower price after production begins. I assume that other changes in market conditions may take place over time which affect the value of the coal to the buyer and the opportunity cost to the seller of supplying to the adjacent plant. Given these assumptions, I can suggest the kinds of nonprice terms that we should expect to find in these contracts to mitigate opportunism and then relax the assumptions about the costs of producing coal to examine alternative patterns for determining prices over the life of the contract.

6.1. Nonprice Provisions

Given the three types of investment specificity that characterizes this type of production, neither the utility nor the coal supplier will want to be the first mover. The utility is not going to start building a power plant on this site without some supply agreement because it would be subject to hold-up by the owner(s) of adjacent reserves. The same is true of the coal supplier vis-à-vis the utility. Furthermore, effective design of the mine-mouth operation requires cooperation between both the utility and the coal supplier. Thus, a firm governance structure is likely to be in place before any substantial plant investments are made by either party.

I expect to see very long term contracts negotiated which specify purchasing (take) and supply obligations for the plant and the mine over a substantial fraction of the life of the plant—at least twenty years. Neither the power plant owner nor the supplier is likely to want to enter into a relationship which involves frequent renegotiation of terms after each incurs transaction-specific sunk investments.

I would expect to see extensive use of requirements contracts. The quantity of coal to be delivered under the contract must be specified somehow. Coal requirements will vary from month to month and year to year. Some of this variation can be dealt with through a coal inventory accumulation, although one of the desirable features of a mine-mouth plant is the ability to minimize inventories that might otherwise be necessary to insure against transportation problems. Ideally, the power plant owner would simply like the mine to deliver enough coal to satisfy the requirements of the plant. Since requirements vary, the easiest way to specify quantities from the viewpoint of the plant operator is simply to write the contract as a requirements contract.

There are strategic reasons for the utility to write the contract as a requirements contract as well and to include provisions to restrict sales to third parties. Reducing promised deliveries during the anticipated term of the contract may be perceived as a supplier-credible threat as part of an effort to hold up the utility, because the utility's initial investment is larger, longer-lived, and less easily redeployed than those of the mining company. The mine operator could credibly reduce supplies over time by ceasing to make replacement and expansion investments and use this threat to extract better terms from the utility. Furthermore, depending on the pricing provisions in the contract, changing market conditions could make it profitable for the mining company to breach the contract to supply even if it is not efficient to do so. Clear language that the contract is for plant requirements over a specified period of time makes court enforcement easier if disputes arise between the plant owner and the mine owner that cannot be resolved otherwise. It also suggests that provisions for dealing with sales to third parties and the dedication of specific reserves to the agreement along with the requirements provisions will protect the utility from the threat and potential costs of diverting supplies to other buyers.[19]

A requirements contract serves to protect the seller in similar ways. Threats by the buyer to switch to alternative suppliers are made less credible both because comparable suppliers will not be waiting in the wings to take up the slack and because breach is easier to detect and penalize through legal sanctions.

Coal quality is of particular importance to the utility, and the mining company is in a position to affect coal quality by its mining practices. The mining company may be able to reduce its costs by mining low-quality deposits, shirking on cleaning, and increase effective prices (especially in per ton priced contracts) by increasing the quantity of "junk" in the coal. The utility may have difficulty distinguishing coal quality problems that arise because of poor mining practices and coal quality problems that arise because the reserves are of generally lower quality than had been anticipated when the contract was negotiated. The supplier may also have an interest in the precise definition of the expectations about coal quality ex ante since claims of poor coal quality may be used by a utility as an excuse to breach the contract. One would expect substantial ex ante investigation of reserve characteristics to verify that the promised quality specifications can be achieved. I would also expect the contract itself not only to specify minimum acceptable coal quality but also to define clearly the specific reserves on which ex ante

19. This is especially true if the pricing provisions of the contract have a significant cost plus component.

quantity/quality evaluations were made and to provide for the dedication of these reserves to production for this plant. To the extent that variations in coal quality can be easily "priced," I would expect pricing provisions expanded to do so.

Williamson (1983) discusses the desirability of "protective governance structures" to deal with potential hold-up problems when "hostage arrangements" cannot be structured to eliminate expropriation incentives possessed by one or both parties. Contractual incompleteness and the potential for haggling are a serious potential problem in unintegrated mine-mouth operations. While court enforcement remains an option and coal contract disputes do occasionally lead to litigation, arbitration clearly represents an opportunity to provide a dispute resolution system that does not entail the costs (broadly defined) of litigation. Thus, I expect to see arbitration provision contained in these contracts as well as other cooperative arrangements that allow for the smooth functioning of a complex agreement and the settlement of disputes without resorting to litigation.

6.2. Pricing Provisions

Establishing a pricing formula to govern compensation arrangements for contracts lasting many years that provide incentives to both the buyer and the seller to perform as promised without leading to serious inefficiencies itself is not an easy task. Dealing with the kinds of ex post performance problems addressed in the transactions cost literature and providing mechanisms for smooth adjustments in obligations as various contingencies arise is complicated by the uncertainty governing future costs and market conditions that are inherent in this relationship. Input prices are likely to change over time, technological developments may reduce the current and expected future costs of mining from similar reserves, labor agreements may change work rules and increase or decrease productivity, new government regulations may increase mining costs, unanticipated mining problems may emerge, new property and severence taxes may be applied, and so on. General changes in supply and demand are likely to lead to changes in the value of the coal at the mine-mouth operation both from the buyer's perspective and the seller's perspective.

The compensation arrangements should reflect two interrelated objectives. First, they should be structured to eliminate the incentives either party has to behave opportunistically. Second, the pricing provisions should be structured in such a way that efficient demand and supply decisions are made by both the buyer and the seller. It would, for example, be undesirable if a pricing formula gave one or both parties the incentive to reach their purchase and supply promises if this would increase the social costs of supplying coal or producing electricity. Let us examine four different methods for establishing prices over time.

1. *Market price contracts.* If the product under consideration were a homogeneous product sold in a competitive auction market and carrying a clear market price, the simplest way of determining prices might be just to stipulate that payments would be made at some fraction of an appropriate market price indicator. This is not likely to be a particularly attractive alternative as the sole determinant of prices for coal supplied for a mine-mouth operation, however.

Coal is not a homogeneous commodity with regard to the characteristics of the coal or the location of the coal. The mine-mouth supply price includes both the cost of coal and (implicitly) the cost of transportation. There simply will not be any meaningful market price for coal of this particular type delivered to the plant. This is especially problematical in the West, where there is essentially no spot market to tie anything to. Market price contracts may make a lot of sense for a homogeneous commodity like uranium, or even for coal in some areas of the country and when other types of plants are involved, but not for mine-mouth plants.

2. *Fixed price contracts:* An alternative to a market price contract is a simple fixed price contract (as I assumed above). Risk allocation problems aside, this contract has poor incentive properties with regard to continuing performance. The primary problem is that if the supplier's actual costs rise significantly above the fixed price when certain contingencies arise, the supplier will have strong incentives to breach (reduce quantities provided in the short run, cease making investments to expand its capacity to continue to supply, run down the value of the equipment, etc.) even if such behavior is inefficient. Similarly, if the expected price of coal available from alternative suppliers falls below the fixed price (due to cost reductions generally, changing market conditions, etc.) the plant operator may find it profitable to breach even if it is inefficient to do so.

Expectations of secular increases in input prices, reserve depletion, and changes in work rules and government regulations that are likely to reduce productivity make these problems worse. A long-term fixed price contract must assure that the present discounted value (PDV) of expected revenues is greater than or equal to the PDV of expected costs or the supplier will not agree to enter into the supply arrangement. Given expectations of nominal cost increases over time, this implies a fixed price that will "front load" the cash flow so that in early years the supplier is getting revenues substantially above current costs, while in later years he may receive revenues substantially below the then current cost. At some point the fixed contract price may fall below current incremental costs, and the supplier will have an incentive to abandon the mine, substantially reduce production, cease making investments, and so on.[20] Fixed prices in long-term contracts do not appear to me

20. This depends on the length of the contract, the capital output ratio, the durability of the investments, the expected rate of inflation, and the discount rate used. I have performed some simulations of the relationship between the fixed price and the incremental costs for a variety of

to be credible because the specification of a fixed price is so likely to provide incentives to one or both parties to threaten to breach and to trigger renegotiation.

3. *Cost plus profit contracts:* A third alternative is to negotiate a cost plus profit contract in which the supplier is compensated for all of the costs incurred in production, including the cost of capital. Risk allocation considerations aside, if it could be assured that the supplier would produce efficiently, such a contract has some desirable properties. It is unlikely that the buyer would have a strong incentive to breach, because it is unlikely that he could get the coal more cheaply elsewhere over the duration of the contract, unless the market value of the coal increases or decreases faster than production costs, since the mine-mouth supplier is presumably facing the same changes in input prices, regulations, technological change, etc., as are other comparable suppliers.

A cost-based price also ensures that prices are high enough so that the supplier does not have an incentive to walk away from the supply arrangement when costs increase due to input price changes, productivity changes due to changes in health and safety regulation, land reclamation costs, and so on, as might occur with a fixed price contract. A cost-based price of course does not eliminate the incentives a supplier might have to ship supplies to buyers if there is a large unanticipated increase in the value of the coal, for example, as a result of an increase in the demand for low-sulfur coal, making it more valuable in the market than it is under the contract (i.e., the long-run supply function for low-sulfur coal is upward sloping and the economic rent associated with an assumed inframarginal reserve rises). And it is unlikely that it would be efficient for the supplier to shift to another buyer if such a contingency arose. Similar inefficient responses by buyers can be expected if the value of coal falls and the "costs" used in the pricing formula reflect generated rents based on ex ante expectations.

An important problem with a cost plus contract is that it has poor incentive properties with regard to the supplier's incentives to minimize costs. Without more, the supplier has little incentive to produce efficiently. If costs rose high enough the buyer would have incentives to switch to other suppliers, but there is likely to be a potentially large wedge for inefficiency, since the next best alternative would on average be more costly to the buyer than an efficiently operated mine-mouth facility.

4. *Indexed contracts*: The fourth and final type of contract that I consider is an indexed contract. This is a natural alternative to a fixed price contract. Rather than try to set a fixed price that rolls in revenues for anticipated fu-

---

reasonable assumptions. Reasonable assumptions about expected input price inflation suggests that the abandonment problem becomes serious for contracts that are longer than fifteen or twenty years. The mines at mine-mouth plants are often organized as separate subsidiaries of larger coal companies and it is possible that a utility would have difficulty making a claim against the parent company.

ture changes in input prices, costs of government regulations, changes in union work rules, and so on, we can set a base price that is adjusted over time as input prices rise. For example, the base price can be broken down into components (labor, materials and supplies, depreciation, profit, property taxes) and then each component escalated according to an appropriate input price and productivity index. This type of contract seems to deal with some of the undesirable properties of both the fixed price and cost plus contracts. Prices now rise over time as input prices rise and productivity opportunities change, and we do not have to front-load cash flow. Prices rise as the supplier's input prices rise and production opportunities change but are independent of the actual production decisions made by the supplier. If the supplier can increase productivity more than provided for by the index, his actual costs will rise by less than the indexed price. If his costs rise—because of bad mining practices, for example—his net revenues are reduced as a result. This type of contract provides incentives for the supplier to minimize costs (given coal quantity and quality). Furthermore, the increases in input prices, technological change, and so forth will have similar effects on the costs of proximate alternative suppliers as well. Although this type of pricing provision cannot guarantee that contract prices will move in lockstep with the prices that might be charged by competing suppliers over time, it does account for several important causes of changing supply prices. An indexed contract therefore appears to dominate either a fixed price or cost plus contract.

An indexed contract is not without problems, however. It may be difficult to index some components of mining cost that will affect the costs of producing from this mine and "comparable" mines (actual and potential). New labor contracts may change work rules, increasing labor costs. New mining regulations may increase costs substantially. Technological change may reduce costs and substantially alter the cost-minimizing weights used to index the price. This kind of adjustment mechanism can also get very complicated if we try to break down the base price into numerous components. The indexed price could move far away from the economic costs of production, giving either the buyer or the seller increased incentives to breach the agreement. Complexity would encourage haggling and litigation.

In addition to general provisions for adjusting the *level* of prices, the price *structure* could be adapted to provide additional financial protection against expropriation and uneconomic buyer/supplier switching. For example, Williamson (1983) and Goldberg and Erickson suggest that nonlinear prices may be used as a device to help to insure that the buyer performs. A seller concerned that a buyer will shift to other suppliers might find a fixed annual payment (to cover sunk costs) plus a commodity charge attractive or include minimum take or pay provisions in the contract. We should recognize, however, that optimally adjusting nonlinear price schedules over time may be even more complicated than adjusting simple (linear) unit prices.

None of the price adjustment mechanisms is ideal, in the sense that the method of setting the level and structure of prices alone can deal effectively with all of the performance problems that can arise in a long-term coal supply arrangement. Thus, whatever method is used to determine prices, I also expect to see substantial reliance for protection on the kinds of nonprice provisions discussed above.

Finally, there is the problem of "surprises" that affect either the price or nonprice terms of a contract, events that were not anticipated with positive probability by either party to the contract when the contract was negotiated. The expected effects of surprises are not reflected in the terms of the contract. As I have argued elsewhere (1977: 157), "bounded rationality" suggests that there are some contingencies that are simply not contemplated by the parties when they negotiate a supply arrangement. These contingencies may involve the effects of unexpected changes in government regulation, dramatic changes in supply or demand in the market, or other changes that would impose a large financial burden on one of the parties if it performed as required by literal interpretation of the contract—a burden that was not reflected, for example, in the base price or adjustment provisions. Both parties to the contract should recognize ex ante that surprises will occur and I would expect to find general provisions in contracts, such as force majeur or gross inequity clauses, that specify a process for dealing with such unspecified contingencies if they arise.

7. COAL SUPPLY ARRANGEMENTS FOR MINE-MOUTH COAL PLANTS: GENERAL CHARACTERISTICS

Table 7 lists all of the mine-mouth coal plants with first units that began operating no earlier than 1960 (with one exception) that I was able to identify.[21] The method used to identify these plants is discussed in the appendix. There are twenty-one plants, which accounted for about 15 percent of electric utility coal deliveries. Most of the plants are multiunit facilities and more than half are jointly owned by at least two utilities. Only two of the plants used any coal purchased on the spot market and in both cases spot sales accounted for only a small fraction of total consumption.

Table 8 provides general information on the coal supply arrangements that have been made for each plant. In 1982, ten of the plants obtained all of their coal supplies from either a coal-mining division or a subsidiary of one of the utilities owning the plant (i.e., coal supply arrangements involved some form of vertical integration). One plant (Mt. Storm) obtained part of its supplies from a coal-mining subsidiary of the utility (but this accounted for 100

21. The initial source I used to date the units at different plant sites gave the wrong date for the first unit of the Montrose plant (1960 rather than 1958). I decided to leave it on the list. There are two or three other utilities with mine-mouth plants which predate the sample period.

Table 7. Mine-Mouth Coal Plants

Unit names	Utility/state	Joint owners	Units (yrs)	Capacity (MWE) 1982	Coal deliveries (tons)
Big Brown	Texas Util. (TX)	No	71, 72	1186	5,963,000
Martin Lake	Texas Util. (TX)	No	77, 78, 79	2379	11,413,000
Monticello	Texas Util. (TX)	No	74, 75	1980	9,797,000
Hunter	Utah P&L (UT)	No	78, 80 (83, 85)	892	2,525,000
Huntington	Utah P&L (UT)	No	74, 77	892	2,492,000
Naughton	Utah P&L (WY)	No	63, 68, 71	707	2,040,000
Wyodak	Pacific P&L (WY)	Yes	78	331	1,812,000
Centralia	Pacific P&L (WA)	Yes	72, 72	1329	4,400,000
Bridger	Pacific P&L (WY)	Yes	74, 75, 76, 77	2034	6,025,000
San Juan	Pub. Serv. NM (NM)	Yes	73, 76, 79, 82	1708	5,071,000
Colstrip	Montana Power (MT)	Yes	75, 76 (84, 85)	716	2,103,000
Four Corners[a]	Arizona PS (NM)	Yes	63, 63, 64, 69, 70	2269	7,291,000
Young	Minkotta Coop (ND)	Yes	70, 77	673	2,983,850
Coyote	Mont./Dakota (ND)	Yes	81	450	1,669,000
Montrose	Kan. City P&L (MO)	No	58, 60, 64	536	1,326,700
Craig	Col.-Ute Coop (CO)	Yes	79, 80 (83)	894	2,303,000
Asbury	Emp. Dist. (MO)	No	70	212	707,000
Keystone[b]	Penn. Elec (PA)	Yes	67, 68	1872	3,543,000
Homer City	Penn. Elec (PA)	Yes	69, 71, 77	2012	3,811,000
Conemaugh[b]	Penn. Elec (PA)	Yes	70, 71	1872	2,668,000
Mt. Storm	VEPCO (WV)	No	65, 66, 73	1662	3,100,000

a. Units 4 and 5 jointly owned.

b. Pennsylvania Electric operates plant for joint owners but has no direct ownershhip interest. Other GPU subsidiaries own part of the plants along with other utilities.

SOURCE: See appendix.

percent of mine's capacity). In the case of jointly owned plants with coal supplied by a coal subsidiary of one of the plant owners, there is typically a formal contract written between the owners of the plant and the coal subsidiary. I have noted these in table 8 by using the term *integrated/contract* to reflect this state of affairs.

Together, mine-mouth power plants account for about 50 million tons of "integrated" coal supplies per year. This is about 60 percent of all coal supplied to utilities by coal companies owned by one of the owners of a plant. In other words, mine-mouth plants account for about 15 percent of total coal utilization but 60 percent of all coal supply arrangements governed by some form of vertical integration. A mine-mouth plant is thus about six times more likely to rely on vertical integration to support exchange than is any other type of coal-burning power plant.

The remaining ten plants all rely primarily on long-term contracts for the supply of coal.[22] The contracts vary in duration from twenty years to fifty years, with thirty-five years being typical. The "integrated/contract" supply

22. Note that the Huntington and Hunter plants were initially supplied under long-term contracts, but the utility eventually acquired the mines. Coal supply arrangements for the San Juan plant moved in the opposite direction.

arrangements generally involve long-term contracts with thirty-five-year durations as well. Referring back to table 6 it is clear that very long contracts are far more likely to emerge to govern coal supply arrangemenuts for mine-mouth plants than they are to govern supply arrangements generally in the electric utility industry. On average less than 20 percent of the coal supplied under the 200 sample contracts had durations of greater than thirty years (and most of this is accounted for by mine-mouth plants). Both the extensive reliance on vertical integration and very long-term contracts are quite consistent with the predictions of transaction cost theory.

8. NONPRICE PROVISIONS OF LONG-TERM CONTRACTS FOR MINE-MOUTH PLANTS

I was able to obtain the actual contracts governing transactions between the coal supplier and the power plant owners for sixteen of the twenty-one mine-mouth plants on the list.[23] Since some plants have more than one contract, either because separate contracts were written for different units or (in one case) contracts were written with two adjacent mining companies, I have twenty-one contracts in all, plus amendments and revisions, covering sixteen plants. These contracts may be "incomplete," but many of them are very complicated. These were not just documents dashed off because the companys' lawyers said they should have a legal document to "confirm their orders."

Table 9 summarizes the incidence of various nonprice provisions of the coal supply contracts reflecting the discussion above.

Duration: As indicated above, most of the contracts have durations of thirty years or more, with thirty-five years being most typical. And these are real long-term contracts. Sixteen of the contracts have no scheduled renegotiation provisions. Three contracts provide for price renegotiation (subject to certain constraints) after twenty years. One provides for renegotiation of the escalation weights only. One contract allows the buyer to terminate after six years but obligates him to reimburse the mining company for all fixed costs. Short-term renegotiation provisions and options to terminate on short notice are generally not provided for, as they sometimes are in other coal contracts (McGraw-Hill, 1981: 352–53). It is also clear from reading the contracts that are available that these supply agreements are generally negotiated several years before the initial units for which the coal is to be supplied are placed in service. Neither party moves first; they move together.

Requirements contracts/dedication of reserves: Almost all of the contracts are full requirements contracts. Of those that are not, one contract simply

23. This includes the initial contracts and amendments for Hunter and Huntington.

Table 8. Coal Supply Arrangements for Mine-Mouth Plants

Unit	Supply Arrangements	Initial contract	Duration
Big Brown	Integrated	None	NA
Martin Lake	Integrated	None	NA
Monticello	Integrated	None	NA
Huntington	Initially long-term contract; util. acquired mines in 1977	1971	35 yrs
Hunter	Initially long-term contract; util. acquired mines in 1977	1974	35 yrs
Naughton	Long-term contract	1957	40 yrs
Wyodak	Integrated/contract	1977	35 yrs
Centralia	Integrated/contract	1970	35 yrs
Bridger	Integrated/contract	1974	35 yrs
San Juan	Initially coal subsidiary contracted with mining co. to build and operate mine on util. sub. reserves. Reserves later sold to mining co. and supplies now provided under long-term contract.	1972, 1980	37 yrs
Colstrip	Integrated/contract (units 1, 2)	1971	35 yrs
	(unit 3)	1980	36 yrs
Four Corners	Long-term contracts (units 1, 2, 3)	1960, 1963	35 yrs
	(units 4, 5)	1966	35 yrs
Young	Long-term contract	1966	50 yrs
Coyote	Integrated contract	1978	35 yrs
Montrose	Long-term contracts (units 1, 2)	1956	~30 yrs
	(unit 3, different mine)	1959	~35 yrs
Craig	Long-term contract	1973	35 yrs
Asbury	Long-term contract + some spot	1966	20 yrs
Keystone	Long-term contract	1964	~30 yrs
Homer City	Long-term contracts (2)	1966	~30 yrs
Conemaugh	Long-term contracts	196?	~30 yrs
Mt. Storm	Initial supply arrangements unknown; currently coal comes from adjacent company-owned mine (100% of output plus contract purchases from other suppliers with different durations, plus some spot purchases.	NA	NA

SOURCE: See appendix.

specifies annual supplies for each of twenty years, one contract specifies annual quantities (plus or minus 10 percent) for each of thirty-five years, one 90 percent requirements contract, and one plant that has two contracts each for 50 percent of requirements (with flexibility to go down to 40 percent). In all but one case specific reserves are dedicated to fulfilling the contract as well. Most of the contracts also have explicit restrictions on sales to third parties which require the approval of the plant operator, or most favored nations clauses.

Coal quality: Coal quality is handled in one or both of two ways. Most of the contracts include "contract" coal quality characteristics and "minimum" coal quality characteristics, often along with various bonus/penalty provisions if certain coal quality specs (usually BTU content) fall above or below those specified in the contract. BTU content of coal, sulfur content, size, moisture, and ash content are the most frequently specified characteristics. If coal quality specifications are not included, the contract provides for "run-of-mine" deliveries free of certain impurities from specified reserves. Some contracts have as many as sixteen coal quality characteristics specified.

Maximum delivery commitments: In addition to providing requirements obligations for the buyer and seller, the contracts typically specify maximum monthly and annual quantities that the suppliers are committed to deliver. These are often adjustable within some range if the purchasers give adequate notice to the supplier. These provisions sometimes get very complicated, especially when a sequence of generating units is planned. Even if a utility claims its requirements are greater than the maximum, the supplier has no contractual obligation to supply more than the maximum.

Arbitration: All but three of the contracts have specific arbitration provisions to deal with disputes arising under the contracts. Two of the

Table 9. Summary of Selected Nonprice Provisions of Contracts (21 contracts)

Duration	
Mean:	35 yrs
Median:	35 yrs
Mode:	35 yrs
Min:	20 yrs
Max:	50 yrs
Requirements contracts	
Full requirements:	16
Partial (%) req.:	3
Annual quantities:	2
Min take/min payment	
Yes:	16
Not mentioned:	5 (2, cost plus or two-part tariff; 1, added by amendment)
Arbitration	
Yes:	18
Not mentioned:	3
Scheduled renegotiation	
Yes:	5 (3, after 20 years, 1, escal. weights only; 1, buyer pays fixed costs on termination)
No:	16
Coal quality specs	
Yes:	14
No:	7 (run of mine for specified reserves)
Specification/dedication of reserves	
Yes:	20
Not mentioned:	1
Specific restrictions on third-party sales	
Yes:	13
Not mentioned:	8
Gross inequity	
Yes:	12
Not mentioned:	9 (3, cost plus; 3, integrated/contract; 1, "fair profit" provision)

SOURCE: See appendix.

three contracts without these provisions were eventually terminated after utility acquisition of the mines. A few of the contracts also provide for a joint utility/supplier committee to facilitate the smooth operation of the coal supply arrangements and to avoid disputes.

9. PRICING PROVISIONS IN LONG-TERM CONTRACTS

There are two general types of formulas used to determine prices in the actual coal contracts that I have reviewed. The predominant form (fourteen of twenty-one contracts) of pricing involves the specification of a base price (either per ton or per million BTUs) which is broken down into several different components (labor, materials, depreciation, profit, taxes, etc.) with an escalation provision specified for each. Usually some of the components are indexed in some way, while other components are adjusted for changes in actual cases. There is some variation among contracts in this regard. These contracts thus represent a mixture of the indexed and cost plus contracts discussed above. They recognize explicitly that prices will have to be adjusted over time (up or down) to reflect changes in input prices and several categories of real cost changes that are not subject to the control of the mining company. Prices are not, however, formally tied to market prices, nor do changes in the relationship between contract prices and market prices automatically trigger renegotiation. The older contracts tend to have a fraction of the price which is not escalated, and it is quite clear that uncertainty due to inflation and unanticipated exogenous events affecting real mining costs have been of increasing importance in structuring long-term contracts between utilities and independent suppliers over time.

The second primary type of compensation arrangement (seven contracts plus one indexed contract with a cost plus option) is a cost plus profit contract. These contracts normally specify that the buyer will pay all operating costs, depreciation, amortization, property and severence taxes, plus an allowance for profit (normally per ton or per BTU with a couple of exceptions). These contracts generally recognize explicitly that pure cost plus arrangements raise incentive problems and include specific incentive provisions.

Table 10 summarizes a number of the key provisions governing price adjustments over time.

9.1. Base Price Escalation Contracts (14 contracts)

Wages and benefits: Labor costs are normally broken down into several categories to reflect wages, benefits, employment taxes, etc. A base hourly wage rate is typically indexed to changes in wage rates (including benefits, taxes, etc.) as specified in collective bargaining agreements applicable to the area in which the mine is located (if it is unionized and sometimes if it is not) or

Table 10. Summary of Pricing Provisions in Contracts

General pricing provisions: Base price plus escalation: 14
Cost plus profit: 7 and 1 with option

ESCALATION PROVISIONS IN BASE PRICE PLUS ESCALATION CONTRACTS

- Components of base price
- Wages/benefits
  - Indexed: 11
  - Actual costs: 3
- Materials and supplies
  - Indexed: 13
  - Actual costs: 1
- Depreciation/amortization
  - Indexed: 4 (2 partial, 1 full)
  - Actual costs: 3
  - Fixed: 2
  - Aggregated with other components: 4
  - Other: 1
- Profit
  - Indexed: 5
  - ROI: 1
  - Fixed: 3
  - Aggregated with other components: 4
  - Other: 1
- Residual aggregate
  - Indexed: 4
  - Fixed: 2
  - None: 8
- Taxes/royalties
  - Actual costs: 14
- Costs due to changes in gov't regulations
  - Actual costs: 12
  - Not mentioned: 2 (subsequently added by amendement)
- Changes in contract/union work rules
  - Actual costs: 13
  - Fixed: 1 (contract has cost plus option)

COST PLUS PROFIT CONTRACTS

- Treatment of base profit per unit
  - Indexed: 6
  - ROI: 2 (includes contract with cost plus option)
- Incentive Provisions
  - Bonus/penalty based on "standard cost" comparisons: 3
  - Bonus/penalty based on market price comparions: 3
  - Option to rebid mining agreement: 1
  - Contractual promise to develop incentive provision: 1

NONLINEAR RATE STRUCTURE (in addition to/along with minimum take): 5 of 21

to the average wage rate actually paid to workers at the mine, including changes in government-mandated tax and benefit payments. I have identified the treatment of wages and benefits as indexed if the wage component had a fixed weight in the base price, excluding adjustments for contractual or legal changes in work rules, and was adjusted only for changes in prevailing wage rates. Several contracts have manning tables attached to indicate how the average wage rate is to be determined. In three of the contracts all increases in labor costs per unit output were passed through, so that changes in labor costs due to both input price changes and changes in realized productivity were reflected in transactions prices. These are denoted as adjustments based on "actual cost."

Materials and supplies (M&S): The M&S component of the base price is almost always indexed using a weighted average of several components of the wholesale price index (WPI). As many as nine separate components of the WPI are sometimes used. One contract contains a pass-through for changes in actual M&S costs. Two contracts adjust M&S costs using the same index used to adjust wages (one contract was written in 1957 and the other has an unusual cost plus option). Explosives and electricity are often indexed separately.

The fraction of the base price attributable to labor costs and materials and supplies varies considerably but generally falls within the range of 50 to 70 percent of the base price.

Depreciation/amortization: This capital cost component is treated in a variety of ways. In about half the cases it is indexed directly (one case partially indexed and one case fully indexed), using either the WPI or the consumer price index (CPI), or aggregated with a profit component and residual costs and then indexed. In three cases actual costs were passed through and in two cases this component was fixed. One contract had a more complicated treatment of depreciation and profits, which used a fixed component unless profits fell below some lower boundary, in which case prices would be adjusted upward.

Profit: In five cases a specific profit component was indexed either by the WPI or the CPI. In one case prices were adjusted upward or downward if the rate of return on sales fell above or below some range specified in the contract. In three cases the profit component was fixed. In four cases it was aggregated with depreciation and other residual costs and then indexed in three cases and was fixed in the other.

Costs due to changes in government regulations: Costs associated with complying with new government regulaions are generally treated as a cost to be passed on to the buyer. The provisions for calculating these costs are sometimes quite vague and are often subject to arbitration. The two contracts which did not contain such a provision were subsequently amended to include it. Both of these contracts were written in the 1960s.

Changes in taxes (excluding income) and royalties: These cost changes are generally simply passed through. Since they are usually changes in tax rates it is as if they were indexed.

Changes in contract/union work rules: In all but one of the contracts, provisions were made to adjust the labor component for changes in contract working hours, overtime pay, vacation time, etc. Several contracts contain detailed examples of the computations that should be made to implement this provision.

9.2. COST PLUS CONTRACTS (8 contracts)

Seven of the twenty-one contracts were primarily cost plus contracts and an additional contract gave the seller the option to switch from an indexed contract to a cost plus arrangement on six months' notice (it is counted twice in the totals). In six of these contracts the profit component is indexed to the CPI or the WPI. In two contracts the profit is based on a fair rate of return on investment.

Seven of the eight contracts (including the contract with the cost plus option) have formal incentive provisions. The eighth has vague language in the contract indicating that an incentive plan would be developed through negotiation after three years (the mine involved was subsequently acquired by the utility, before the date which would have triggered this provision). In three of the contracts there is a bonus/penalty provided for, in the form of an adjustment to the profit component based on a comparison with market prices. In one of these contracts the incentive payment is tied to a comparison between the unit cost increase under the contract and the increase in a weighted average of local, regional, and national coal prices. The other two contracts provide for a reward if the coal produced is the lowest cost of any comparable mine in the state.

Three of the contracts provide for a bonus/penalty based on the relationship between the actual costs and an indexed "standard cost." The indexed standard cost is constructed in a way similar to the construction of the base price plus escalation prices in the first set of contracts. Components are specified and then either indexed (mostly) or adjusted for some actual cost changes. The indexed standard cost is then compared to the actual cost per ton. There is a sliding scale that adjusts the profit component upward if the actual cost is below the standard cost and vice versa. The sliding scale bonus/penalty adjustment has a minimum and maximum. In each of these contracts explicit provisions are made as well for the utility to acquire the assets of the mines at net book value. In at least two of the three contracts, the utilities financed the initial development of the mines and hold mortgages on the property.[24]

The contract which gives the mining company the option to change from an indexed contract to a cost plus contract also gives the buyers the option to put the mining contract up for competitive bids if the cost plus option is exercised. The contract provides that a new mining company can acquire the assets at depreciated book cost or fair market value, whichever is lower.

24. This is probably true of Keystone as well, although I was unable to find documents indicating that utility financing had been provided.

In these cost plus contracts, the utility frequently has the contractual right not only to audit the books and submit the reasonableness of costs incurred to arbitration, but also to approve mining plans, capital expenditures, and budgets. Indeed, the distinction between vertical integration and "contract" in several of these cost plus contracts becomes almost a matter of semantics rather than a sharp distinction given the joint control, the presence of utility financing, and the cost plus nature of the pricing provisions.

9.3. Other Provisions

Nonlinear pricing/minimum take or pay: five of the contracts had nonlinear price schedules (although one had ten components with prices *increasing* as aggregate production increased). Most of the contracts have minimum take or pay provisions. Of the five contracts without minimum take or pay provisions, one was a cost plus contract, one had a two-part tariff, and one had a minimum take or pay provision added by amendment.

Gross inequity/force majeur: Many of the contracts recognize explicitly that the pricing provisions specified can track the "prudent" costs incurred by the mining company only imperfectly. While the contracts intend both parties to bear some price/cost risk, it is not the intent of the contract to impose inequitable losses on the mining company or (in fewer cases) allow it to earn inequitable profits as a result of "surprises." These contracts contain a fairly vague provision that allows one or both parties to reopen the contract by asserting that its continuance constitutes a gross inequity. Thirteen of the contracts have gross inequity provisions and in at least a few cases these provisions were used to reopen the contracts. All of the contracts recognize that certain contingencies may arise that make it impossible for the plant to continue to operate or that make it impossible for it to continue to burn coal from this mine. Fairly standard force majeur provisions are included in all of the contracts. In a few cases considerable detail regarding what does and what does not constitute force majeur and how compensation will be made during force majeur periods is contained in the contracts.

10. EXPERIENCE WITH CONTRACT EXECUTION OVER TIME

A complete analysis of coal supply arrangements for mine-mouth plants would ideally include a detailed discussion of how these supply arrangements worked out over time. Did one party to the contract try to hold up the other? Were there haggling problems? Was there uneconomical supplier switching? Did the contractual provisions allow for smooth adjustments in obligatons? Did the parties continue to perform as economic conditions changed? Did the parties resort to litigation to get contractual promises enforced?

Most of the information that one would need to do such an in-depth analysis is not publicly available. I will discuss the fragments of evidence that I have been able to put together, however.

Most of the initial supply arrangements that were made at the time the construction of a mine-mouth plant was planned have continued to govern supply arrangements up until the present time, despite fairly dramatic changes in coal prices, mining costs, and air pollution restrictions. However, many of the contracts have been amended, in several cases numerous times, for a variety of reasons. The contracts negotiated in the 1960s and early 1970s often had pricing provisions that did not provide adequate protection to the mining company for the kinds of cost increases that occurred in the 1970s. Amendments revising the base price and escalation provisions appear to be quite common. Sometimes these amendments are made in the course of negotiating a new supply agreement to accommodate additional generating units on the site. The gross inequity provisions have also been used to adjust prices. In several cases initial provisions for annual price adjustments were amended to provide for semi-annual, quarterly, or monthly base price adjustments as the inflation rate increased in the 1970s. In a few cases there were amendments clarifying the operation of the pricing provisions contained in the contracts, no doubt following a dispute between the parties. I was surprised at how enduring these relationships have been and how few modifications there have been made to the initial supply arrangements, given the many changes that have occurred in coal markets over the last twenty years.

Two of the twenty-one plants identified experienced significant changes in their initial supply arrangements. The owners of the San Juan plant initially created a jointly owned coal subsidiary (Western Coal Company), which owned the reserves and coal cleaning facilities.[25] They contracted with a subsidiary of Utah-International to build and operate a mine to produce coal from these reserves in 1972. The mining contract gave either party the option to terminate the agreement after six years, in which case the plant owners would have to acquire the mining assets. The contract price (apparently) contained a large fixed component. Utah notified the owners that it would exercise its option to terminate after six years since it was losing money. It offered to renegotiate the supply arrangement and preferred a cost plus contract. After determining that they could not produce the coal any cheaper and that an alternative fixed price contract offered by Utah was too expensive, the joint owners of the plant signed a new mining agreement with a cost plus profit pricing formula. Subsequently, Western Coal sold the

25. See letter from Western Coal Co. to Tucson Gas and Electric and Public Service of New Mexico regarding negotiations with Utah-International (dated February 21, 1978, on file).

reserves to the mine operator as well, and the utilities signed a revised thirty-seven year cost plus contract with Utah-International.

Utah Power & Light initially secured coal supplies for the Hunter and Huntington units under two long-term contracts with Peabody Coal. The first contract signed in 1971 provided for the requirements of the first two units of the Huntington plant. The second contract signed in 1974 (involving a second mine) provided for supplying the requirements of the first two units of the Hunter plant. Both contracts were for thirty-five years. The first used a base price plus escalation formula. The second used a cost plus formula with no explicit incentive provision. They both also contain unusually wide ranges in acceptable coal quality and no bonus/penalty payments tied to coal quality. Both mines were acquired by Utah Power & Light in 1977 and are operated by an independent operator under a thirty-year agreement.[26] The mining agreement does not contain coal quality specs or a bonus/penalty system. The plants encountered serious operating problems due to poor coal quality and wide variations in coal quality both before *and* after the acquisition of the mines. The utility never rejected any coal under the agreements.

I could find only one supply arrangement in the group where a dispute led to litigation. In 1973 Colorado-Ute Electric Cooperative signed a long-term requirements contract with Utah-International to supply coal for the first two units of the Craig generating station. The contract specified that the units would each have a capacity of 350 MWE. The requirements contract specified both a minimum take (and associated minimum payments) by the utility and a maximum monthly and yearly delivery obligation by the supplier. Deliveries above the maximum were at the discretion of the seller. Without telling the supplier, Colorado-Ute subsequently increased the actual size of each generating unit by about 20 percent. The year before deliveries were to commence the supplier sued for breach of contract, requesting that it be obligated only to deliver the minimum takes specified in the contract. Colorado-Ute argued that it was entitled to deliveries up to the maximum specified in the contract. The federal district court (425 F.Supp. 1093 [D. Colo. 1976]) found for the supplier, allowing him to rescind part of the agreement. Deliveries are being made under the contract, but only at the minimum take levels. A commentary on the case suggests that market conditions had changed after the contract was negotiated, that the seller could get higher prices by selling the additional coal to others, and perhaps that it could extract a higher price from Colorado-Ute.[27]

26. McGraw-Hill (1981: 392). This publication does not identify the utility and plants by name, but it is clear from the information provided that the utility is Utah Power and Light and the plants are Hunter and Huntington.

27. McGraw-Hill (1981: 486). Additional coal was eventually purchased from another supplier.

11. DISCUSSION

The empirical results are quite consistent with the predictions of the transactions cost theory. Spot markets and short-term contracts account for a relatively small fraction of coal supply transactions for electric utilities. For the utility industry as a whole, long-term contracts rather than vertical integration is the preferred governance structure. Vertical integration is much more prevalent for mine-mouth plants than it is for other coal-fired generating stations, however. Although mine-mouth plants account for only 15 percent of total coal consumption by electric utilities, they account for more than half of the supplies governed by some form of vertical integration. When contracts are chosen in lieu of vertical integration (or, in a sense, in addition to it for jointly owned generating plants) for mine-mouth plants, the parties rely on very long-term contracts to support exchange. These contracts, while certainly "incomplete," are often quite complex, containing numerous price and nonprice provisions to protect both parties from breach and to help ensure the smooth operation of the supply relationship over time.

Although my research examining coal supply arrangements for non-mine-mouth generating plants is not yet complete, preliminary results suggest that there are important differences, on average, between contracts governing exchange for mine-mouth plants compared to other types of generating plants. The contractual duration of coal supply agreements for mine-mouth plants is substantially longer than for other types of plants and involves substantially larger annual delivery commitments (compare table 6 and table 8). Preliminary analysis of about sixty contracts for other coal plants suggests that these figures may understate the differences in length of commitment. Several of the non–mine-mouth contracts contain renegotiation and termination provisions that specifically allow one or both parties to terminate the agreement without paying damages long before the stated term of the contract is reached. This is not generally the case for mine-mouth plants. Contracts for mine-mouth plants are generally written as requirements contracts. This is rarely the case for the other contracts that I have examined.[28]

Although long-term contracts establish pricing provisions ex ante, this does not mean that prices are rigid. The pricing formulas used allow for frequent price adjustments based on input price changes and other cost changes that are attributable to exogenous events. While prices will not gen-

28. I have performed a preliminary analysis of 60 contracts that do not involve mine-mouth plants. The average duration of the contracts is about thirteen years. Only four are requirements contracts. Only three involved mines that had not been developed at the time the contract was signed. Eighteen of these contracts provide for scheduled price renegotiation during the term of the contract.

erally track short-term movements in market prices, they do respond in the long run to changes in the costs of producing coal. Recent contracts often provide for quarterly or monthly adjustments, and some older contracts have been amended to do so.

The pricing provisions, along with certain nonprice provisions, also reflect an interest by buyers that their suppliers produce efficiently. Two-thirds of the contracts make extensive use of indexing provisions to adjust prices so that the price the seller receives is partially independent of his production decisions. If the seller can beat the index he can increase his profits, and if the seller does not mine efficiently his profits will fall. All of the cost plus profit contracts recognize explicitly that pure cost plus pricing has bad incentive properties with regard to efficient production. All but one of these contracts contains additional provisions to give suppliers incentives to produce efficiently.

Overall, I have found the transactions cost framework to be an extremely powerful vehicle for gaining a better understanding of the nature of vertical supply relationships between power plant owners and their coal suppliers.

APPENDIX

This appendix summarizes the methods used for collecting the information on vertical integration and contracts that is discussed in the text.

Vertical Integration

I started with lists of captive coal mines contained in the McGraw-Hill *Keystone Coal Manual* and Gordon. Individual utility entries in *Moody's Public Utilities Manual* were reviewed to verify the information provided there and to resolve differences between the two lists. Next, Pasha Publications' *Guide to Coal Contracts* was searched for additional information on utility ownership of mines. Then, the entries for the 25 largest utility consumers of coal in *Moody's* were reviewed in an effort to identify additional utility-owned mines. Finally, the ownership of all suppliers identified in the contracts with mine-mouth plants was determined from another listing in the *Keystone Coal Manual*.

Annual production figures by mines and consumption figures for utilities were obtained from the *Keystone Coal Manual*, the Department of Energy's *Cost and Quality of Fuels for Electric Utilities*, *Moody's* and annual reports.

Mine-Mouth Plants

The definition of a mine-mouth plant is at least partially subjective and no general list of such plants appears to exist. I searched for plants that were deliberately located adjacent to specific coal reserves in order to exploit these reserves to generate electricity and where the adjacent mining facilities were built in reliance on these plants. The *Guide to Coal Contracts* has extensive information on coal transportation modes used to serve many plants. Mine-mouth plants are frequently noted explicitly. In a few cases, mine-mouth plants were identified when conveyor belts or short-haul rail spurs were designated as the coal transportation mode. Gordon contains a discussion of mine-mouth plants and identifies a few. The *Keystone Coal Manual* also provides information to identify mine-mouth plants. These sources were supplemented by searches of annual reports and various government publications. I identified more plants than appear on the list but eliminated plants which had first units which began operating before 1960, since I thought that it would be difficult to obtain information on initial supply arrangements for plants that began operating so long ago. One plant (Montrose) that began supplying electricity before 1960 is on the list because the start-date that I initially identified turned out to be incorrect. I left it on the list since I had already collected the information on coal supply arrangements. Almost all of the older plants that were dropped from the list obtain at least some of their coal from utility-owned coal subsidiaries. In several cases these plants were greatly expanded with large units built in the 1960s or 1970s and rely on contracts for a large fraction of their supplies. It is possible that this selection process did not capture all mine-mouth plants in existence.

CONTRACTS

General information on the contract characteristics for each plant was obtained from the *Guide to Coal Contracts*. Individual contracts, amendments, etc., were obtained from the *Washington Service Bureau*. These contracts in turn were obtained primarily from SEC files. National Economic Research Associates gave me access to their coal contract library, where these contracts are filed. In a few cases I was able to obtain additional information by making telephone calls to individual utilities and reviewing 10-K filings.

The contracts are sometimes long and complicated. Just reading them is not very productive. I used a coding sheet which contained entries for a variety of contract characteristics based on the discussion of the implications of transactions cost theory contained in the text. Each contract was read to fill in the relevant characteristics that had been identified. In several cases it is necessary to make interpretations of provisions which are unclear or ambiguous, so the coding of the contracts involves some subjective evaluations as well. I read every contract, amendment, and any associated correspondence myself.

REFERENCES

Coase, Ronald H. 1937. "The Nature of the Firm," 4 *Economica* 386–405.

———. 1972. "Industrial Organization: A Proposal for Research," in Victor R. Fuchs, ed., *Policy Issues and Research Opportunities in Industrial Organization*, vol. 3. New York: National Bureau of Economic Research.

Goldberg, Victor P. 1976. "Regulation and Administered Conracts," 7 *Bell Journal of Economics* 426–48.

——— and John E. Erickson. Undated. "The Law and Economics of Long-Term Contracts: A Case Study of Petroleum Coke," mimeo.

Gordon, Richard L. 1975. *U.S. Coal and the Electric Power Industry*. Washington, D.C.: Resources for the Future, Johns Hopkins University Press.

Grossman, Sanford J., and Oliver Hart. 1984. "The Cost and Benefits of Ownership: A Theory of Vertical Integration," London: London School of Economics, mimeo.

Hart, Oliver D. 1983. "Optimal Labour Contracts under Asymmetric Information: An Introduction," 50 *Review of Economic Studies* 3–36.

Holmstrom, Bengt. 1979. "Moral Hazard and Observability," 10 *Bell Journal of Economics* 74–91.

Joskow, Paul L. 1977. "Commercial Impossibility, The Uranium Market and the Westinghouse Case," 6 *Journal of Legal Studies* 119–76.

———and Nancy Rose. 1984. "The Effects of Technological Change, Experience and Environmental Regulation on the Construction Costs of Coal-Burning Generating Units," MIT Department of Economics Discussion, paper.

Klein, Benjamin. 1980. "Transaction Cost Determinants of 'Unfair' Contractual Relations," 70 *American Economic Review* 356–62.

———, R. A. Crawford and A. A. Alchian. 1979. "Vertical Integration, Appropriable Rents, and the Competitive Contracting Process," 21 *Journal of Law and Economics* 297–326.

Macaulay, Stewart. 1963. "Non-Contractual Relations in Business," 28 *American Sociological Review* 55–70.

Masten, Scott E., 1984. "The Organization of Production: Evidence from the Aerospace Industry," 23 *Journal of Law and Economics* 403–19.

McGraw-Hill, Inc. 1981. *How to Negotiate and Administer a Coal Supply Agreement*. New York.

———. 1982. *Keystone Coal Industry Manual*. New York.

Monteverde, Kirk, and David J. Teece 1982. "Supplier Switching Costs and Vertical Integration in the Automobile Industry," 13 *Bell Journal of Economics* 206–13.

Moody's Investors Services. (Various Years.) *Moody's Public Utility Manual*, New York.

Muris, Timothy J. 1981. "Opportunistic Behavior and the Law of Contracts," 65 *Minnesota Law Review* 521–90.

National Coal Association. 1983. *Coal Data (1981/82)*. Washington, D.C.

———. 1984. *Facts about Coal (1984/85)*. Washington, D.C.

———. (Various years.) *Steam Electric Plant Factors*. Washington, D.C.

Palay, Thomas M. 1984. "Comparative Institutional Economics: The Governance of Freight Rail Contracting," 13 *Journal of Legal Studies* 265–88.

Pasha Publications. (1981, 1983). *Guide to Coal Contracts*. Arlington, VA.

Shavell, Steven. 1979. "Risk Sharing and Incentives in the Principal and Agent Relationship," 10 *Bell Journal of Economics* 55–73.

U.S. Department of Energy. (Various years.) *Inventory of Power Plants in the United States*, DOE/EIA-0095. Washington, D.C.: Government Printing Office.

———. (Various years.) *Cost and Quality of Fuels for Electric Utility Plants*, DOE/EIA-0191. Washington, D.C.: Government Printing Office.

———. (Various issues.) *Quarterly Coal Report*, DOE/EIA-0121. Washington, D.C.: Government Printing Office.

———. 1983. *Coal Production–1982*, DOE/EIA-0118(82). Washington, D.C.: Government Printing Office.

Williamson, Oliver E. 1971. "The Vertical Integration of Production: Market Failure Considerations," 61 *American Economic Review* 112–23.

———. 1975. *Markets and Hierarchies: Analysis and Antitrust Implications*, New York: Free Press.

———. 1979. "Transaction Cost Economics: The Governance of Contractual Relations," 22 *Journal of Law and Economics* 233–61.

———. 1983. "Credible Commitments: Using Hostages to Support Exchange," 73 *American Economic Review* 519–40.
———. 1984. *The Economic Institutions of Capitalism*. Draft manuscript.
Zimmerman, Martin. 1981. *The U.S. Coal Industry: The Economics of Policy Choice*. Cambridge: MIT Press.

[3]

Supplier switching costs and vertical integration in the automobile industry

Kirk Monteverde*

and

David J. Teece**

This article tests a transactions cost theory of vertical integration with data from the U.S. automobile industry. Existing theory is first refined to take into account industrial know-how and the cost of transferring such know-how. A testable model is then developed, which is estimated by using probit techniques. The results support the view that transactions cost considerations surrounding the development and deepening of human skills have important ramifications for delineating efficient organizational boundaries.

1. Introduction

■ In recent years, economists have begun the systematic exploration of transactions cost issues, for example, see Williamson (1975, 1979). Research has also been initiated on know-how and its relationship to the nature of the firm. Although commonly ignored in economic theory, specialized know-how has important ramifications for organizational design. In particular, vertical integration issues arise when industrial know-how, including skills, becomes deepened and specialized to a particular firm. This article attempts to draw together the literatures on transactions cost and industrial know-how, and it brings them to bear on the analysis of efficiency incentives for backward vertical integration in the U.S. automobile industry.

2. Vertical integration by U.S. automakers

■ In the context of the U.S. automobile industry, we are interested in explaining why firms take parts production in-house. We hypothesize that assemblers will vertically integrate when the production process, broadly defined, generates specialized, nonpatentable know-how. When production processes are of this kind, both assembler and supplier are exposed to the possibility of opportunistic recontracting. Even if the title to specialized equipment used by the supplier is held by the assembler, this need not provide protection against rent appropriation if transaction-specific know-how has been generated. The existence of transaction-specific know-how and skills and the difficulties of skill transfer mean that it will be costly to switch to an alternative supplier. (Teece, 1977, 1980). An assembler will tend to choose vertically integrated component production

* Stanford University.

** Stanford University.

We would like to thank Charles Holloway, Paul Kleindorfer, and the referees and editors for many useful comments.

when high switching costs would otherwise lock the assembler into dependence upon a supplier and thereby expose that assembler to opportunistic recontracting or to the loss of transaction-specific know-how.

Within the vehicle manufacturing industry, supplier switching costs appear to be associated principally with development activities for new automotive parts. The design of a new vehicle model is a complex, five-year-long undertaking. Some components cannot be procured by simply announcing to suppliers performance and design requirements. The "specs" are often unknown *ex ante*. Consequently, preproduction heuristic development is critically important to the evolution of many vehicle parts. This process generates production as well as design knowledge. A suppler working in cooperation with the assembler on preproduction development gains a first-mover advantage because of knowledge acquired during development. This suggests the following testable hypothesis:

> The greater is the applications engineering effort associated with the development of any given automobile component, the higher are the expected appropriable quasi rents and, therefore, the greater is the likelihood of vertical integration of production for that component.

We shall test this hypothesis. The dependent variable we construct is dichotomous: each sample component is coded as being predominantly manufactured either in-house or by an external supplier. We next define a set of independent variables that may be expected to influence the choice between in-house production and external purchase, with our primary interest centering upon the influence of applications engineering. We then employ probit analysis to estimate the relationship between the independent variables and our measure of vertical integration.

To form the dependent variable, a list of 133 automotive components was obtained from an assembler. For each of the components, we ascertained the extent of vertical integration by General Motors and Ford for U.S. production in 1976. Each of the 133 components was recorded as either produced internally or sourced externally. For proprietary reasons, data about the exact percentage of each item in our sample that was manufactured in-house were not divulged. Hence, we took internal production of 80 percent or more of a component as an operational definition of integrated production. Taken together, the 133 component groupings include most of the major items that go into a complete vehicle.[1] Thus, the sample provides a representative picture of vertically integrated production for Ford and General Motors in 1976. The data are presented in Table 1.

Consider the independent variables. An excellent operational measure of applications engineering effort is the cost of developing a given component. Firms in the industry have these data on a component-by-component basis, but because of the data's proprietary nature, we were not able to gain direct access to them. However, a source within the industry who is privy to the data provided an engineering cost rating for our sample of automotive components.[2] This yielded a surrogate measure of relative engineering

---

[1] One conspicuous absence, however, is that of tires, none of which are produced by either Ford or General Motors. It should also be noted that two items, steel and vinyl, which are included in the sample, might better be classed as "basic materials" rather than components, as both are further upstream in the production process than most of the other items in the sample. However, the list submitted by our sources was accepted without alteration except for the elimination of "miscellaneous" categories and unidentifiable part names.

[2] The source was the design engineer for one of the major U.S. automakers who had responsibility for supervising development of a new generation of small, fuel-efficient vehicles to be manufactured in the United States. The reliability of his ratings was tested by obtaining a separate set of ratings from another automotive engineer. The two sets of ratings shared a correlation coefficient of .8, adding confidence that our ratings were a meaningful surrogate for the underlying construct.

TABLE 1 The Backward Vertical Integration of Ford and General Motors
("1" denotes 80 percent or more of component requirements produced in-house as of 1976.)

Part Category	Ford	GM
• BODY		
Body Sheet Metal	1	1
Exterior Ornamentation		
Paint (Topcoat)		
Primer		
Bumpers	1	1
Body Lamps	1	1
Sealed Beam Bulbs		1
Weatherstrip		
Mirrors—Outside		
Mirrors—Inside		1
Interior Trim	1	1
Interior Ornamentation		1
Carpeting & Mats		
Headlining	1	1
Safety Belts		
Inertia Locks		
Lock—Cylinders		
Door Handles		1
Hinges (Door, Hood, Decklid)	1	1
Window Regulator (Power)		1
Window Regulator (Manual)	1	1
Glass	1	
Windshield Wiper Motor	1	1
Windshield Washer System	1	1
Crash Pad		1
Seat Frame & Springs		
Seat Pad		1
Seat Tracks (Man. & Elec.)		1
Lamp Bulbs		1
Head Restraints	1	1
Headlamp Assembly	1	1
Sealers & Insulation		
Armrests		1
Grill		
Frame		
Jack & Wrench		
Engine Mounts		
• ENGINE		
Engine Stampings	1	1
Cylinder Head	1	1
Block	1	1
Manifold (Intake & Exhaust)	1	1
Crankshaft	1	1
Camshaft	1	1
Piston	1	N/A
Piston Ring		
Valves (Intake & Exhaust)	1	N/A
Radiator	1	1
Fan		
Air Cleaner	1	1
Air Cleaner Element		1
Carburetor		1
Fuel Pump		1
Starter	1	1
Distributor	1	1
Spark Plug		1
Ignition Coil	1	1
Oil Filter	1	1
• EMISSION COMPONENTS		
Catalytic Converter		1
Air Pump		1
Carbon Cannister	1	1
Substrate & Coating		
PCV, EGR, etc. Valves		
• CHASSIS		
W.C., H.C. (Optional)		
Wheel Covers & Hub Caps (Std.)		1
Coil Springs	1	1
Leaf Springs		1
Shock Absorbers	1	1
Upper & Lower Arms	1	1
Spindle Assembly	1	1
Driveshaft Assembly	1	1
Wheels	1	
Wires		
Rear Axle	1	1
Drums		
Master Brake Cylinder		
Power Brake Booster		1
Parking Brake		
Muffler		
Tailpipe/Inletpipe		
Brakes		
Disc Caliper & Rotor		1
Front Suspension	1	1
Rear Suspension	1	1
• TRANSMISSION		
Auto. Transmission Assy.	1	1
Auto. Transmission Cases	1	1
Manual Trans. Assembly		1
• STEERING		
Manual Steering Gear	1	1
Power Steering Gear	1	1
Steering Linkage		1
Steering Column	1	1
Steering Wheel		1
Power Steering Pump		1
Steering Assembly	1	1
• FUEL		
Fuel Tank	1	1
Gas Cap		
• VENTILATION		
A/C Assembly	1	1
Evaporator	1	1
Expansion Valve		1
Vacuum Motors		1
Blower Wheels		
Blower Motors	1	1
Heater Assembly	1	1
Heater Core	1	1
Compressor		1
Clutch		1
ATC Components		1
Condensor	1	1
Dehydrator/Receiver		N/A
Hose Assemblies		N/A

TABLE 1 *(Continued)*

Part Category	Ford	GM	Part Category	Ford	GM
• ELECTRICAL			Antenna		1
Instrument Cluster & Panel	1	1	Speed Control System	1	1
Speedometer Cable Assembly		1	Clock		
Fuel Sender	1	1	Switches		
Alternator	1	1	• OTHER		
Regulator	1	1	Tubing (Brake/Fuel Lines)		
Battery		1	Antifreeze		
Horn	1	1	Oils & Grease		
Battery Cables		1	Steel		
Wiring Harness		1	Standard Parts, Fasteners		
Radio	1	1	Vinyl	1	
Tape Player		1	Water Pump Assembly	1	1
Speakers		1	Oil Pump	1	

effort. The rating was done on a 10-point scale with each component considered to require from "none" to "a lot" of engineering investment. We assume that such a rating scale provides a reasonable enough approximation to interval scaled data to allow use of parametric procedures.

To avoid misspecifications of the model, three sets of control variables are introduced. The first control variable distinguishes components that are specific to a company from those that are generic. Some of the components included in the sample (e.g., fasteners) are not designed specifically for any single automaker. These are items for which traditional spot market contracting may be expected to operate quite well; and for these components there would appear to be no incentive to integrate. However, components that are not specific to a single assembler's product may be expected to be among those rated as requiring the least applications engineering. To ensure that the engineering variable does not indicate a statistical relationship with integration that actually arises because nonspecific components will not be attractive integration candidates, a "component specificity" variable is introduced into the model.

The determination as to which sample components represent assembler-specific parts and which do not was accomplished with the cooperation of a replacement parts wholesaler. Company officials were asked to isolate those components for which identification of the manufacturer, make, and model of the automobile was not necessary to procure a replacement unit.[3] We assume that those components for which make and model information is not critical are not company-specific in original assembly. Using this procedure, a group of 30 items was identified as non-company-specific.

The second control variable relates to the identity of the sample firms. Because we developed a combined cross sectional model aggregating both Ford and General Motor's data, we include a dummy variable to control for systematic differences between these two firms with regard to vertical integration.

The third set of control variables relate to systems effects. The automobile represents not simply an assemblage of parts, but a "system"—a set of objects with relationships between the objects and their attributes (Hall, 1973, p. 103). In the vehicle "system," the "objects" are the individual components, and the relationships between components

[3] The actual question was: "Please examine the following list of 133 automotive components and indicate which of the noncaptive items on the list could be procured as replacement units without necessarily having to know the manufacturer, make, and model of the vehicle for which the replacement is sought. That is, which of the following categories of parts may be expected to be largely common across several manufacturers' vehicles."

consist principally of their mechanical or electrical interrelations and their "packaging"—the latter being the industry's term for physically fitting all components within the dimensions of the body. Clearly, design and implementation for any system as complex as an automobile must be tightly coordinated.[4] Because of the superior coordinating properties of vertical integration,[5] the degree to which any given component's design affects the performance or packaging of other components is a potentially important consideration in explaining the likelihood of vertically integrated production of the given component (Armour and Teece, 1980).

As shown in Table 1, the components were first grouped into nine categories (body, engine, emission components, chassis, transmission, steering, fuel, ventilation, electrical) and a tenth miscellaneous category. These categories were subsequently collapsed into six subsystems by merging emissions with engine, transmission and steering with chassis, and fuel tank and cap with body. The aggregation was based on expert evaluation of the degree of technical interrelatedness among the components. Vertical integration is predicted for components with large systems effects. Since we are unable to rank the subsystems according to the degree of interrelatedness, we simply posit that different subsystems will display different levels of vertical integration. Thus, a set of dummy variables was introduced into the model to represent each component's membership in a subsystem.

The predictor variables were combined into a single model estimated by probit techniques. A vector of parameter estimates for β was derived to maximize the log likelihood function:

$$L = \sum_{i=1}^{n} y_i \ln F(x_i'\beta) + \sum_{i=1}^{n} (1 - y_i) \ln [1 - F(x_i'\beta)],$$

where y_i is 1 if the ith component is integrated in production and zero otherwise; x_i is the vector of values of the independent variables for the ith observation; and $F(x_i'\beta)$ takes the specific form:

$$F(x_i'\beta) = \frac{1}{\sqrt{2\pi}} \int_{-\infty}^{x_i\beta} e^{-u^2/2} du.$$

The x_i vector contains, for each sample point i, the values of the eight independent variables defined below:

$ENGINEERING_i$ = rating of the ith observation on the amount of engineering effort required in designing the part;

$SPECIFIC_i$ = 1 if the ith observation corresponds to a part specific to a single assembler; 0 otherwise;

$COMPANY_i$ = 1 if the ith observation was from General Motors; 0 if the ith observation was from Ford;

[4] White observes that: "The complex process of designing, producing, testing, and modifying an automobile requires a high degree of coordination. Engine, transmission, frame, body, brakes, windshield, and other components all have to perform well with each other and have to be in the right place at the right time in the right quantities" (White, 1971, p. 78).

[5] Vertical integration permits executive fiat to be used to achieve the requisite coordination in a timely fashion (Williamson, 1975). Scherer also notes the coordination benefits of integration and offers an example from the auto industry: "The benefits from integration also increase with the complexity of product component interrelationships. It is easier to make the various parts of an automobile fit together when all parties to the coordination effort work for the same boss than when design changes must be processed through a purchasing office" (Scherer, 1980, p. 90).

$$ENGINE_i = \begin{cases} 1 & \text{if the } i\text{th observation corresponds to an engine and emissions subsystem part;} \\ 0 & \text{otherwise;} \end{cases}$$

$$CHASSIS_i = \begin{cases} 1 & \text{if the } i\text{th observation corresponds to a chassis, transmission, and steering subsystem part;} \\ 0 & \text{otherwise;} \end{cases}$$

$$VENTILATION_i = \begin{cases} 1 & \text{if the } i\text{th observation corresponds to a ventilation subsystem part;} \\ 0 & \text{otherwise.} \end{cases}$$

$$ELECTRICAL_i = \begin{cases} 1 & \text{if the } i\text{th observation corresponds to an electrical subsystem part;} \\ 0 & \text{otherwise;} \end{cases}$$

$$BODY_i = \begin{cases} 1 & \text{if the } i\text{th observation corresponds to a body, fuel tank and cap subsystem part;} \\ 0 & \text{otherwise.} \end{cases}$$

The parameter estimates for β_1 through β_8, the asymptotic t-statistics corresponding to these eight predictor variables, and the model summary statistic are given in Table 2.

Recall that in-house production of 80% or more of a component's output was selected as the operational definition of vertical integration. To establish the robustness of the

TABLE 2 **Probit Coefficients, Asymptotic t-Statistics (in parentheses), and χ^2-Statistic in Equation to Explain Vertical Integration**
(Defined upon three thresholds for percentage of in-house parts production.)

Coefficient Estimated	Related Variable	Vertical Integration Defined as In-house Production of: ≥70%	≥80%	≥90%
β_1	*ENGINEERING*	0.1319 (3.24)*	0.1461 (3.57)*	0.1453 (3.54)*
β_2	*SPECIFIC*	0.8773 (3.64)*	0.8186 (3.33)*	0.7902 (3.15)*
β_3	*COMPANY*	0.7388 (4.22)*	0.7125 (4.05)*	0.9010 (5.08)*
β_4	*ENGINE*	0.5521 (1.21)	0.5348 (1.17)	0.7168 (1.47)
β_5	*CHASSIS*	0.0615 (0.138)	0.0003 (0.001)	0.03051 (0.637)
β_6	*VENTILATION*	0.3620 (0.733)	0.4903 (0.983)	0.6552 (1.25)
β_7	*ELECTRICAL*	0.6861 (1.48)	0.6905 (1.49)	1.085 (2.18)†
β_8	*BODY*	0.0857 (0.201)	−0.2293 (−0.532)	0.1152 (0.248)
χ^2 Value		110.064*	111.291*	126.676*

* Indicates significance beyond the .001 level.
† Indicates significance beyond the .05 level.

results, we also obtained a listing of those items which would be considered integrated were the cutoff changed to 70% and then to 90%.

The principal point to note about the results in Table 2 is that regardless of the threshold chosen, the variable used as a proxy for transaction-specific skills ("engineering") is highly significant. The development effort associated with the design of any given automotive component is shown to be positively related to the likelihood of vertically integrated production of that component, thereby confirming the central hypothesis of this article.

Second, the coefficient on the "*SPECIFIC*" variable is also positive and statistically significant, which lends support to the hypothesis that only components specific to a single assembler will be candidates for vertical integration. It can also be seen that the coefficient for the "*COMPANY*" variable is positive and statistically significant, thereby indicating that General Motors is more integrated into component production than is Ford.

Finally, the systems-effects hypothesis is only mildly supported by the probit analysis. With the exception of the "*ELECTRICAL*" variable in the ≥90% integration threshold case, none of the coefficients on the five dummy variables taken alone indicates a significant relationship with backward integration. Nevertheless, the set of five systems effect dummies, taken together, significantly contributed to the explanatory power of the model.

In general, the change in magnitude of the coefficients was minor as the definition of vertical integration was altered. The variation was the greatest among the individual subsystem variables that, with the one exception of the electrical subsystem variable, were not found to be significantly different from zero.

3. Conclusion

■ Transactions cost considerations surrounding the development and deepening of human skills appear to have important ramifications for vertical integration in the automobile industry, thereby supporting the transactions cost paradigm advanced by Williamson. GM and Ford are more likely to bring component design and manufacturing in-house if relying on suppliers for preproduction development service will provide suppliers with an exploitable first-mover advantage. We posit that this is a result of the high switching costs entailed if the supplier acquires transaction specific know-how at the assembler's expense. Since know-how cannot simply be transferred from supplier to supplier like a book of blueprints (Winter, 1980), backward integration is the more prudent course of action. General Motors and Ford also have a preference for backward vertical integration when the components are firm-specific and their design must be highly coordinated with other parts of the automobile system.

Hence, the vertical structure of GM and Ford appears to be based at least in part on efficiency considerations. Specifically, the structure appears to be designed to take advantage of the coordinating properties of hierarchies as well as the ability of internal organization to reduce the exposure of the automakers to opportunism from suppliers—a hazard which is apparently absent in the less integrated Japanese industry[6] where "the relationship between the major auto firm and its satellite suppliers is one of total cooperation" (Ouchi, 1981, p. 19).

References

ARMOUR, H.O. AND TEECE, D.J., "Vertical Integration and Technological Innovation." *Review of Economics and Statistics* (August 1980), pp. 470–474.

[6] We posit that cooperation between the auto companies and remaining suppliers will also characterize the U.S. industry because the integrated and "quasi-integrated" (Monteverde and Teece, 1982) structure of the industry has eliminated most occasions for opportunistic rent appropriation.

FINNEY, D.J. *Probit Analysis*. Cambridge, England: The University Press, 1952.

HALL, A.D. "Some Fundamental Concepts of Systems Engineering" in S.L. Optner, ed., *Systems Analysis*: Middlesex, U.K.: Penguin, 1973.

MONTEVERDE, K.A. AND TEECE, D.J. "Appropriable Rents and Quasi-Vertical Integration." *Journal of Law and Economics* (forthcoming, 1982).

OUCHI, W. *Theory Z: How American Business Can Meet the Japanese Challenge*. Reading, Ma.: Addison-Wesley, 1981.

SCHERER, F.M. *Industrial Market Structure and Economic Performance*, 2nd ed. Chicago: Rand McNally, 1980.

TEECE, D.J. "Technology Transfer by Multinational Firms: The Resource Costs of Transferring Technological Know-How." *Economic Journal* (June 1977), pp. 242–261.

———. "Economies of Scope and the Scope of the Enterprise." *Journal of Economic Behavior and Organization* (September 1980), pp. 223–247.

WHITE, L.J. *The Automobile Industry since 1945*. Cambridge: Harvard University Press, 1971.

WILLIAMSON, O.E. *Markets and Hierarchies: Analysis and Antitrust Implications*. New York: Free Press, 1975.

———. "Transactions-Cost Economics: The Governance of Contractual Relations." *Journal of Law and Economics* (October 1979), pp. 233–261.

WINTER, S.G. "An Essay on the Theory of Production." Yale School of Organization and Management, Working Paper Series A #39, June 1980.

[4]

THE ORGANIZATION OF PRODUCTION: EVIDENCE FROM THE AEROSPACE INDUSTRY*

SCOTT E. MASTEN
University of Michigan

THE interface between successive stages of production is frequently governed by contractual agreements, and the efficiency of such arrangements has been the subject of considerable attention in the economic literature. But production is organized administratively within firms as well as contractually between them, and given the practical limitations of bureaucratic organization, the relevant question can be seen to be not merely whether contractual deficiencies exist but how severe such deficiencies may be relative to the alternative costs of organizing production internally. The important issue from an institutional choice perspective thus becomes how the particular details of a transaction affect the *differential* efficiency of alternative organizational forms.

Recent theoretical work has sought to identify such relationships.[1] In particular, the choice between internal and external organization and, in the event of the latter, the choice of contract terms have been related to several critical parameters of the transaction. This paper presents some

* I would like to thank Oliver Williamson and Roger Sherman for helpful comments. The cooperation of the General Electric Company is also gratefully acknowledged. Support for this research was received from the Center for the Study of Organizational Innovation and from Sloan and National Science Foundation grants for the study of Transaction Cost Economics at the University of Pennsylvania. The paper was completed while I was at the University of Virginia.

[1] See, in particular, Benjamin Klein, Robert G. Crawford, & Armen A. Alchian, Vertical Integration, Appropriable Rents, and the Competitive Contracting Process, 21 J. Law & Econ. 297 (1978); and Oliver E. Williamson, Transaction-Cost Economics: The Governance of Contractual Relations, 22 J. Law & Econ. 233 (1979). A formal model treating the make-or-buy decision as part of a producer's overall optimization problem may be found in Scott E. Masten, Transaction Costs, Institutional Choice and the Theory of the Firm (1982) (unpublished Ph.D. dissertation, Univ. Pennsylvania); *id.*, Institutional Choice and the Organization of Production: the Make-or-Buy Decision (January 1984) (unpublished manuscript Univ. Virginia, Dept. Economics).

[*Journal of Law & Economics*, vol. XXVII (October 1984)]
 0022-2186/84/2702-0006$01.50

evidence of the practical import of those relationships, based on a study of input procurement practices in the aerospace industry.

The administration of procurement in this industry is two tiered. On the first level, the government chooses a prime contractor who is assigned overall responsibility for a particular program; and on the second, the contractor manages the production of the system itself, including what is of particular interest here—the administration of subcontracts. This paper considers procurement practices at both levels. To begin, the essential elements of the theory will be briefly reviewed in Section I. Section II then presents the results of an examination of input procurement for an aerospace system containing nearly two thousand component specifications. Tests are based on a probit model of the dichotomous choice between internal and external procurement of supplies. The estimated coefficients provide indirect measures of the relative costs of internal and external procurement with respect to several qualitative variables. Following this, the procurement policies of the federal government are reviewed and interpreted in light of the theory, with particular emphasis on the form of the relationship between the government and the prime contractor. Conclusion and additional comments appear in the final section.

I. The Make-or-Buy Decision

Having selected an end-product line, a producer must decide which in the stream of intermediate products and processes successively combining to form his eventual output he will administer within the organization and which he will delegate to outside suppliers, along with the terms under which any external procurements would take place. In practice, this series of procurement decisions—sometimes referred to as a producer's make-or-buy program—involves a large number of considerations including design requirements; inventory needs; quality control; production, overhead, and transportation costs; and the capabilities, capacities, and negotiating strength of potential suppliers relative to those of the producer himself.[2]

Transaction cost economics has sought to place these concerns within an economic context and relate the outcome of individual make-or-buy decisions to details of the transaction. According to that view, the choice among alternative organizational arrangements is part of an agent's over-

[2] These concerns and many others are evident in E. Raymond Corey, Procurement Management: Strategy, Organization, and Decision-Making (1978), and were also present in internal memoranda and discussions with company representatives.

all optimization problem, and the net value of a transaction organized in a particular manner depends not only on the losses due to potential misallocations of resources but also on the costs of conducting the transaction itself. Hence, a manager choosing a procurement mode will consider, in addition to the value of the goods and services actually procured, both the opportunity costs of the additional demands that would be placed on his time and attention by internalizing a transaction and the various "organizational" expenses that would be involved in dealing with outside suppliers. The latter include the costs of negotiating the terms under which exchange is to take place and, oftentimes, the various expenses associated with adopting and upholding formal contractual agreements.

In general, the organizational costs associated with market exchange increase, the more specialized, profitable, and durable are the investments associated with a given transaction. Idiosyncratic assets, because of their specialized and durable nature, imply that parties to a transaction face only imperfect exchange alternatives for an extended period. The more specialized those assets, the larger will be the quasi-rents at stake over that period and hence the greater the incentive for agents to attempt to influence the terms of trade through bargaining or other rent-seeking activities once the investments are in place.

The role of contracts is to prevent such activities from dissipating too large a portion of the gains from trade by stipulating acceptable behavior at the outset of a transaction-specific relationship. But contracts incur expenses in both specification and enforcement that limit their usefulness. First, because contingent performance is costly to stipulate and even more difficult for courts to administer, contracts typically contain few provisions and, as a result, tend to be inflexible mechanisms for governing exchange. The greater the complexity of the transaction and the level of uncertainty associated with it, the greater the likelihood of being bound to an inappropriate action, and hence the greater the implicit costs of contractual organization. This inflexibility, in turn, tends to constrict the time span of contractual agreements. Because confidence that any given state of the world will obtain decreases the more distant the relevant horizon, committing yourself to a particular activity becomes less desirable the more remote the specified date of performance. A trade-off therefore exists between the opportunity costs of being bound to an inflexible agreement and the hazards of negotiating follow-on procurements in a condition of bilateral monopoly. In sum, the more idiosyncratic are the investments associated with a particular transaction, the greater are the incentives to incur the costs of writing more detailed and longer term contracts. Greater uncertainty or complexity of a transaction, however, implies, on the one hand, an incentive to write more detailed agreements and, on the other, a disincentive to commit to long term contractual relationships.[3]

Greater complexity would also, of course, put additional strain on decision makers under internal organization, which is intended to eliminate rent seeking by internalizing the quasi-rents that are the object of that behavior.[4] But the possibility of rendering decisions in an adaptive, sequential fashion under internal organization reduces the need relative to contracting of exploring and enumerating the full contingency tree ex ante.[5] Nevertheless, the expediency of internalizing successive transactions is limited by the bureaucratic inefficiencies that inevitably develop as organizations get large.

II. Input Procurement in the Aerospace Industry

There is an abundance of supportive, if informal, evidence illustrating the relationships discussed above. A recent article on the semiconductor industry, for example, revealed the existence of a correlation between design specificity and the internal procurement of supplies in the production of electronic components: "Most major chip buyers, after trying but failing to get the big producers to serve their needs for low volumes of custom circuits, have launched chip-production lines of their own and today turn out almost all of the custom chips made as well as two-thirds of such semi-custom products as gate arrays."[6]

In addition, the article contended that the reason that downstream producers found it necessary to develop in-house production capabilities for these products, despite the expertise of the established chip manufacturers and "the high cost of maintaining internal production," was to avoid the "frictions between vendors and customers" encountered in a market where specialized designs are highly profitable and increasingly complex.[7]

Although accounts of this type can be illuminating, they lack the au-

[3] The trade-offs involved here are discussed at greater length in Masten, Transaction Costs, Institutional Choice and the Theory of the Firm, *supra* note 1.

[4] In the case of specialized human capital, quasi-rents cannot be eliminated by internalization in the same way that they can with physical capital. Rather, hierarchical organization seeks to substitute internal for third-party adjudication of conflicting interests. Thus, from this perspective, the firm becomes a quasi-judicial body entrusted by its members to resolve disputes and enforce cooperative behavior.

[5] Oliver E. Williamson, Markets and Hierarchies: Analysis and Antitrust Implications 25 (1975).

[6] The 80's Look in Chips: Custom, Not Standard, Business Week, January 18, 1982, at 36H.

[7] *Id.* at 36D-L.

thority often accorded formal tests of hypotheses. Unfortunately, the level of detail at which the theory operates has made rigorous applications difficult. One way in which the information requirements can be moderated, however, is to restrict attention to a single industry. This reduces the need for absolute measures for such variables as design specificity and complexity and permits qualitative tests based on ordinal rankings of inputs by their characteristics. Recently, this strategy has been employed by Kirk Monteverde and David Teece to analyze vertical integration in the automobile industry and by Thomas Palay in a study of railroads.[8] The present paper examines related issues in the context of defense-related production, an area in which specialized designs are common and the alternative values of investments often limited.

The model I wish to test is the following: Let G_i be the institution chosen by the producer to govern the acquisition of product or process i, and let G_i^* represent internal organization of that activity and $\tilde{G}_i$ external or "market" procurement. Then the outcome of the producer's make-or-buy decision can be summarized as

$$G_i = G_i^* \quad \text{if } L_i^*(\omega_i) < \tilde{L}(\lambda_i, \omega_i),$$

and

$$G_i = \tilde{G}_i \quad \text{if } L_i^*(\omega_i) \geqslant \tilde{L}(\lambda_i, \omega_i),$$

where L_i^* is the cost of maintaining production internally and $\tilde{L}_i$ is the cost of market-mediated exchange, depicted as a function of the specificity (λ) and complexity (ω) of the transaction.

The aerospace system studied contained 1,887 component specifications, each of which was identified as either a "make" or "buy" item by a team of company representatives made up of the managers of the material systems and manufacturing engineering departments and members of their staffs. The disposition of the entire make-or-buy program is summarized by generic category in Table 1.

The procurement team was asked to complete questionnaires designed to elicit information about the attributes of the items and associated investments. Each of the items within several of the cells in Table 1 shared similar characteristics, permitting completion of a single questionnaire for the entire cell. The remaining cells were randomly sampled in approximate proportion to the ratio between the size of the cell and the total

[8] Kirk Monteverde & David J. Teece, Supplier Switching Costs and Vertical Integration in the Automobile Industry, 13 Bell J. Econ. 206 (1982); Thomas Palay, Comparative Institutional Economics: The Governance of Rail-Freight Contracting, 13 J. Legal Stud. 265 (1984).

TABLE 1
THE MAKE-OR-BUY PROGRAM

Category	Quantity	Make	Buy
Top and major subassemblies	17	17	. . .
Components assembly	185	114	71
Structure machining	11	5	6
Structure forgings	8	. . .	8
Mechanical detail parts	138	53	85
Connectors	180	. . .	180
Printed wire board assembly	80	80	. . .
Flexible/hard printed wire boards	151	147	4
Electrical piece parts	971	11	960
Heat shields	4	. . .	4
Insulating materials	62	10	52
Harness/coax	80	80	. . .

number of components in the system. The result was thirty-four individual observations, which can be statistically weighted to reflect their actual distribution in the program.[9]

From this information, two measures of specificity were developed. The first, corresponding to design specificity, was based on whether an item was identified as used exclusively by this company (highly specialized), used or easily adaptable for use by other aerospace firms (somewhat specialized), or used in other industries (relatively standard). "Electrical piece parts" such as transistors and resistors, for example, would be standard items, while hybrid circuits designed to individual specifications would be considered highly specialized.[10]

A second variable was created to reflect site specificity based on whether colocation or grouping of facilities or processes was considered to be an important factor in production. Various economies may arise from positioning successive operations side by side. But if associated assets are costly to reposition, their alternative use value may be low. Such was the case in this system with the computerized lathes and other machinery used to bore and mill nose cones. The machinery itself has a

[9] Since the data for this study were generated from a choice based sample, weighted exogenous sampling maximum likelihood estimation was employed. For a discussion of the properties of these estimators see Charles F. Manski & Steven R. Lerman, Estimation of Choice Probabilities from Choice Based Samples, 45 Econometrica 1977 (1977).

[10] Although *asset* design would be preferable to *input* design as a measure of specificity, it is difficult, even at this level of disaggregation, to separate the specialized from standard assets used in the manufacture of a given input. The fact that specialized inputs may at times be produced using standardized assets, however, merely implies that input design measures will have lower *t*-statistics than would asset design; hence, information on the latter would only improve the explanatory power of the model. See *infra*.

number of uses. However, because of transfer and control costs between operations, the configuration and geographical location of the equipment is important. Meanwhile, installation and removal costs make relocation impractical. Consequently, once the assets have been positioned, they are more or less committed to a particular use.

Since this study focused on a single system, it was not possible to test the effects of demand uncertainty on the internalization decision using these data alone. Complexity, however, may be used as a proxy for the degree of uncertainty on the production side; the more complex a component, the more details to be accounted for and the more dimensions in which something can go wrong. To determine the relative complexity of the components, a ranking system used internally by the company was adopted. In that three-way classification scheme, "A-items" were the most and "C-items" the least complex.

For estimation purposes, the following specification of the model was employed:

$$L_i^* = \bar{B} + b \cdot \omega_i + u_i,$$

and

$$\tilde{L}_i = a \cdot \lambda_i + c \cdot \omega_i + v_i,$$

where u_i and v_i are random errors assumed to have independent normal distributions, and a, b, and c are coefficients. $\bar{B}$ represents the "administrative burden" of internalizing a transaction and would be expected to be positive. Since complexity increases the costs associated with organizing production both administratively within firms and contractually between them, both b and c should be positive. But because flexibility in contracting demands prior anticipation of potential problems while internal organization permits adaptation to changing circumstances in a sequential fashion, the differential effect of complexity on the costs of alternative organizational arrangements favors internal organization over contractual exchange.[11] Hence, we would expect $c - b > 0$. Finally, the coefficient on item specificity, a, is also expected to be positive reflecting the greater potential for opportunistic behavior in idiosyncratic transactions.

Since L^* and $\tilde{L}$ are not actually observed, the estimation is based on the disposition of the dichotomous make-or-buy choice. The probability that input j will be produced inside the firm is

$$\begin{aligned} \text{pr}(L_j^* < \tilde{L}_j) &= \text{pr}(u_j - v_j < a\lambda_j + (c - b)\omega_j - \bar{B}) \\ &= F(a\lambda_j + (c - b)\omega_j - \bar{B}), \end{aligned}$$

[11] See Williamson, *supra* note 5.

TABLE 2
ESTIMATED COEFFICIENTS FOR THE MAKE-OR-BUY DECISION

Variable	Coefficient	t-Ratio	Mean of Variable
CONSTANT	−3.8657	−6.8064	1.00000
COMPLEX	1.8865	5.4444	.84208
SPECI	3.3696	6.5486	.34605
STANDARD	−2.7775	−.1724	.50874
COLOC	5.1120	.1269	.09433

χ^2: 32.0788, 4 *df**
Pseudo R^2: .610734†
Proportion of observations for which $y = 1$: .2729.

*Indicates that the equation is significant beyond the .001 level.
†This measure is analogous to standard R^2s. Its properties are discussed in Takeshi Amemiya, Qualitative Response Models: A Survey, 19 J. Econ. Literature 1483 (1981).

where $F(\cdot)$ is the normal distribution. The likelihood function of the model is

$$\Lambda = \prod_{i=1}^{n} F(a\lambda_i + (c - b)\omega_i - \bar{B})^{y_i} [1 - F(a\lambda_i + (c - b)\omega_i - \bar{B})]^{(1 - y_i)},$$

where $y_i = 1$ if item i is produced internally and zero if acquired outside the firm. The actual explanatory variables used in the estimations were

$$\begin{aligned}
\text{COMPLEX}_i &= 1 && \text{if the item is rated as complex (A- and B-items),}^{12} \\
&= 0 && \text{otherwise (C-items);} \\
\text{SPECI}_i &= 1 && \text{if the item is highly specialized,} \\
&= 0 && \text{otherwise;} \\
\text{STANDARD}_i &= 1 && \text{if the item is relatively standard,} \\
&= 0 && \text{otherwise;}^{13} \\
\text{COLOC}_i &= 1 && \text{if colocation of assets or processes is considered important,} \\
&= 0 && \text{otherwise.}
\end{aligned}$$

Maximum likelihood estimates for the weighted observations and corresponding statistics are presented in Table 2. The column on the far

[12] No significant difference was found in the coefficients on A- and B-items in any of the various specifications of the model experimented with.

[13] The variables SPECI, and STANDARD$_i$ were derived from the same ordinally measured construct; see text at note 10 *supra*. "Somewhat specialized" items are the omitted category.

		SPECI 0	SPECI 1
COMPLEX	0	< .01	.31
	1	.02	.92

FIGURE 1

right-hand side of the table, "mean of variable," indicates the proportion of inputs possessing that characteristic.

The coefficients on both COMPLEX and SPECI are highly significant and positive as expected, indicating that the probability of internalization is higher for complex and highly specialized inputs. But although the coefficients for COLOC and STANDARD have the expected signs, statistical confidence in these estimates is low.[14]

Note also that the constant term in this equation has a large effect on the probability of internalization. This coefficient reflects the predisposition of management toward external procurement and, given the specification of the model, can be interpreted as an indirect measure of the administrative burden incurred by internalizing an additional transaction. Each of the remaining coefficients provides an estimate of the implicit costs of contracting *relative* to this burden for transactions possessing the corresponding characteristic.

The matrix in Figure 1 presents the estimated probabilities that components possessing the corresponding characteristics will be produced internally.[15] As is apparent from these estimates, the degree of specialization is by far the most important determinant of organizational form in this system. The lack of alternative uses for a component increases the probability that it will be procured internally from less than 1 percent to 31 percent for relatively uncomplex items and from 2 percent to 92 percent for more complex components. Since the omitted category includes those inputs

[14] The insignificant coefficient on STANDARD implies that there is no significant difference between the effects of "standard" items and the omitted category, "somewhat specialized" items, on the internalization decision. In other words, "standard" items are at least as likely to be procured externally as are "somewhat specialized" components.

[15] Specifically, the probability that component *i* will be procured internally is $F(-3.8657 + 1.8865\text{COMPLEX}_i + 3.3696\text{SPECI}_i)$ where *F* is the cumulative normal distribution.

used only in other aerospace applications, these estimates suggest that the existence of alternative uses for a component, even in a fairly highly concentrated industry such as this, warrants reliance on external procurement.

The complexity of an item also increases the probability that it will be "sourced in-house." Moreover, as expected, the hazards of incomplete contracts in complex environments appear to be much greater when specialized designs are involved, increasing the likelihood of internalization from 31 percent to 92 percent (as compared with less than 1 percent to only about 2 percent for items which are only "somewhat specialized"). Thus, as predicted by the theory, the need to employ specialized designs appears to be a necessary condition for the breakdown of market-mediated exchange and the subsequent internalization of production, especially where fairly complex products are involved.

Additional detail missed in the surveys but obtainable case by case further supports the hypothesized relationships. For instance, the system design called for both rigid and flexible printed wire boards. Although both types involved specialized designs, the flexible boards could be produced using standard equipment and were procured externally. The hard boards, on the other hand, were unique items that could not be produced using existing facilities. Not having an expertise in this area, the company sought to establish outside sources but found that manufacturers were "unwilling" to take on the business. The fact that the company was obliged to develop its own production capability suggests that the "organizational savings" from sourcing outside the company were not adequate to compensate potential suppliers for the hazards to which they would be exposed by incurring such specialized costs. However, the components that, although specially designed, could be produced with standard assets were not subject to those hazards. Such evidence supports the contention that asset design is a more powerful predictor of organization form than is input design.

The survey also indicated other factors of concern to procurement managers in deciding whether to internalize production. Among the more important were the existence of preexisting production capability or capacity and the perception of a need for "control" over the production process. But each of these concerns is itself explained in large part by the degree of complexity and specificity of the item: the company was more likely to have previously developed a capability or capacity for the production of more specialized and complex components, and the perception of a need for control arose primarily in those cases in which the market or the courts were least likely to regulate transactions effectively, again when production was highly specialized and complex.

III. Government Procurement Policies

Although data sufficiently detailed to permit evaluation of all the hypotheses of the transaction-cost paradigm are not yet available, it is possible at least to compare the concerns identified in these theories with the procedures adopted by procurement managers. This section selectively examines several of the federal government's procurement policies to see how well they conform to the theory presented in Section I.

A. *Make-or-Buy Policies*

Although in defense-related production the basic responsibility for procurement decisions, as with all management functions, remains with the firm, the government reserves the right to review a prospective contractor's make-or-buy program.[16] Of particular interest from the standpoint of the present analysis is that proposed make-or-buy programs need only be submitted for review "where the work is complex, the dollar value substantial, and there is not adequate price competition."[17] More specifically, information on a prospective contractor's make-or-buy program is *not* required by the government:

> i) when a proposed contract has total estimated value of less than $1,000,000 . . . ;
> ii) in research and development contracts, unless the contract is for prototypes or hardware and it can reasonably be anticipated that significant follow-up quantitites of the product will be procured;
> iii) when the contracting officer determines that the price is based on adequate price competition, or established catalog or market prices of commercial items sold in substantial quantities to the general public . . . ; or
> iv) when the contracting officer determines that the work is not complex.[18]

What is notable about this passage is that each of the stipulations contained in it has a direct correlate in transaction-cost theory: special attention or precautions are unnecessary for transactions which (i) are low in value, (ii) are not likely to generate first-mover advantages in follow-on production, (iii) are accompanied by price competition or involve standard products, or (iv) are not complex. If the value of the contract is

[16] The government defines a contractor's make-or-buy program as "that part of a contractor's written plan which identifies the major subsystems, assemblies, subassemblies, and components to be manufactured, developed, or assembled in his own facilities, and those which will be obtained elsewhere by subcontract." Defense Acquisition Regulations, Gov't Cont. Rep. (CCH) ¶ 32,888. The objective of such reviews is to assure that the contractor has applied "sound business and technical judgement" and that his decisions will not "adversely affect the government's interests," *id.* ¶ 32,888.15.

[17] *Id.* ¶ 32,887.

[18] *Id.* ¶ 32,888.

small, the potential losses to an inappropriate make-or-buy program will also be small and therefore will not generally justify the cost of review. Where large amounts are at stake, however, an improper make-or-buy decision can have more serious consequences. Review is also desirable where research and development activities will bestow extended advantages on the agent; a contractor's decision to subcontract some part of this work to another firm may leave both the prime contractor and the government open to extortion in subsequent dealings. In contrast, items which are generally available pose relatively few such hazards. Finally, when work is not complex, an agent has fewer opportunities to deceive the government about his costs and is therefore less likely to be successful in obtaining unwarranted price adjustments.

B. Procurement Hazards and Remedies

The government's policies for administering its own acquisitions further reveal its awareness of the potential for opportunistic behavior on the part of contractors and of the conditions under which such behavior is most likely to emerge. "Buying in" is one manifestation explicitly recognized as a potential hazard. " 'Buying in' refers to the practice of attempting to obtain a contract award by knowingly offering a price or cost estimate less than anticipated costs with the expectation of either (i) increasing contract price or estimated cost during the period of performance through change orders or other means, or (ii) receiving future 'follow-on' contracts at prices high enough to recover any losses on the original 'buy-in' contract."[19]

Contracting officers are advised to be particularly alert to this possibility when performance of the contract involves substantial "preproduction engineering, special tooling, special plant rearrangement, training programs and such nonrecurring costs as initial rework, initial spoilage, and pilot runs,"[20] all of which represent specialized investments in the transaction. Where such investments are at stake, the government provides several policy options directed at preventing the incidence of buying in at the outset of the relationship.

1. *Acquisition of Special Tooling.* One option, applicable at least in cases where first-mover advantages are embedded in specialized physical capital, is for the government to take title to specialized assets.[21] Oppor-

[19] *Id.* ¶ 32,069.

[20] *Id.* ¶ 32,866.

[21] This alternative is referred to as quasi-vertical integration by Kirk Monteverde & David J. Teece, Appropriable Rents and Quasi-Vertical Integration, 25 J. Law & Econ. 321 (1982).

tunism by the original contractor can then be countered by transferring the assets to more cooperative suppliers. The government's policies covering the acquisition of special tooling and special test equipment address this alternative in detail, clearly indicating a sensitivity to the trade-offs between the hazards of leaving title to specialized tooling with contractors and the costs of internal administration.

Policy. It is the policy of the Department of Defense that contractors provide and retain title to special tooling required for the performance of defense contracts to the maximum extent consistent with sound procurement objectives. Government acquisition of title or the right to title in special tooling creates substantial administrative burden, encumbers the competitive procurement process and frequently results in the retention of special tooling without advantage commensurate with such burden. In certain instances, however, the acquisition of special tooling or rights thereto may help the Government obtain fair prices, recover the residual value of special tooling paid for by the Government, and increase competition in subsequent procurements by increasing the number of sources, where tooling is susceptible of use by more than one contractor, considering its adaptability and all costs of movement.[22]

The instances in which acquisition is likely to be beneficial are precisely those in which buying in is apt to be a problem, namely, where because of "start-up costs or other nonrecurring costs, . . . the successful offeror is likely to become, in effect, a sole source for follow-on procurements."[23]

The data accumulated on the aerospace system discussed in the preceding section indicates that the government frequently employs the option to acquire special tooling. Of the fifty-four investments in special tooling or test equipment covered by the surveys, the government retained title in all but seven instances. Moreover, with one exception involving proprietary technology, each of the latter either was ranked as having a high alternative use value or had a shorter use life than the average for the forty-seven to which the government acquired title.

The expediency of this policy toward special tooling depends heavily on the mobility and adaptability of the assets in question; rents will still accrue to equipment unless it can be removed and reassigned to other uses or users at low cost. In addition, the policy cannot eliminate advantages that arise from specialized know-how acquired through performance of the contract.

[22] Defense Acquisition Regulations, supra note 16, ¶ 34,705. See also the criteria in *id.* ¶ 34,705.10. "*Special tooling* means all jigs, dies, fixtures, molds, patterns, taps, gauges, other equipment and manufacturing aids . . . which are of such a specialized nature that, without substantial modification, their use is limited to the development or production of particular supplies or parts thereof, or the performance of particular services." *Id.* ¶ 34,657. A similar definition applies to special test equipment, ¶ 34,657.35.

[23] *Id.* ¶ 32,866.

2. *Extended Contracting.* Because the latter policy option applies only where specialized investments are easily transferable, the government provides other methods to attempt to forestall buying in. In particular, where specialized investments cannot be internalized for adaptability or administrative reasons, government policy calls for the use of more extensive contracting: "To avoid or minimize the opportunity for 'buying in' on a procurement which is likely to be succeeded by one or more 'follow-on' procurements, the Government should obtain from the contractor a binding price commitment covering as much of the entire program as is practicable. Such a commitment may be secured through employment of one of the following procurement techniques: (i) multi-year procurement . . . ; or (ii) price options for additional quantities. . . ."[24]

Quantity options are intended for use in contracts where "additional requirements are foreseeable but not known and . . . realistic competition for the option is impracticable once the initial contract is awarded."[25] Similarly, multiyear contracting and subcontracting are encouraged where "the item is expected to be obtained only from a sole source during the entire multi-year period."[26] But because of the rigidity of contracting in general, multiyear agreements should only be adopted if "(i) the contract or service is of stable design and specification [and] (ii) the quantity required is reasonably firm and continuing,"[27] that is, where the degree of uncertainty is moderate. Thus, the terms and conditions under which extended contracting is to be employed indicate a perception of the benefits and hazards of the institution that coincide with the arguments outlined in Section I.

IV. Conclusions

Evidence from both stages of the defense procurement process indicates a general reluctance on the part of administrators to internalize transactions: government procurement policies refer explicitly to the "substantial administrative burden" incurred in acquiring and managing equipment and facilities, and estimations of actual contractor procurement practices indicate a strong "predisposition" toward external sourcing. But it is a reluctance that can be overcome by exposure to the hazards of market exchange when components are specialized and complex, as the evidence also attests.

[24] *Id.* ¶ 32,069.

[25] *Id.* ¶ 32,423; also see Use of Options, *id.* ¶ 32,081.

[26] *Id.* ¶ 32,082.

[27] *Id.* ¶ 32,081.

Overall, the data on the aerospace system support the contention that design specificity and complexity are necessary, if not sufficient, conditions for the breakdown of cooperation in market-mediated exchanges and the subsequent integration of production within the firm. In addition, the procurement policies professed by the government provide supportive detail not yet available in the formal analysis, such as the effects of uncertainty on the scope of contractual agreements and the relevance of the absolute value of investments on the need for specialized governance structures. How one views this evidence depends on one's prior assumptions. In a descriptive sense, these excerpts suggest that agents engaged in procurement activities are concerned with the sorts of issues addressed in the transaction-cost paradigm. From a prescriptive standpoint, the model indicates that the government's policies in this regard are appropriate and sensible. Whether or not these policies are actually carried out is, of course, another matter.[28]

Finally, the estimations reported here provide an indication of the relative efficiency of contractual and hierarchical organizational forms. While at a rudimentary level at present, this sort of analysis may eventually permit economists to assess the value of particular contractual arrangements to the parties involved and, subsequently, to evaluate the desirability of adopting alternative legal conventions or of government interference in contractual relationships.

[28] See, for example, Oliver E. Williamson, The Economics of Defense Contracting: Incentives and Performance, in Issues in Defense Economics 229–32 (Roland N. McKean ed. 1979).

[5]

Rand Journal of Economics
Vol. 15, No. 3, Autumn 1984

Integration of the sales force: an empirical examination

Erin Anderson*

and

David C. Schmittlein*

This article develops and tests a model of integration of a marketing function, personal selling. The model, derived from transaction cost analysis as developed principally by Williamson, is formulated as a logistic function, which is estimated with data from the electronic components industry. As expected, integration is associated with increasing levels of asset specificity, difficulty of performance evaluation, and the combination of these two factors. Contrary to the transaction cost model, neither frequency of transactions nor interaction of specificity and environmental uncertainty is significantly related to integration. The transaction cost model improves significantly upon the fit of a simple model relating integration to company size alone. These results suggest that for studying transactions of this kind, it is fruitful to view the firm as a governance structure.

1. Introduction

■ In recent years considerable attention has been paid to the question of when vertical integration takes place (Williamson, 1979; Klein, Crawford, and Alchian, 1978; Holmstrom, 1979). These approaches consider contracts in far more detail than their predecessors did; and, at least implicitly, they recognize the behavioral phenomena of bounded rationality and opportunism and make allowances for the environmental phenomenon of uncertainty. But these and other recent treatments have been subject to little empirical testing other than by selected case studies.[1]

Discussions of vertical integration typically focus on manufacturing. This leads to emphasis on the valuation of physical assets, which may or may not be specialized to the user. Although it has been recognized that human assets are also relevant (Williamson, 1981b; Monteverde and Teece, 1982), less attention has been paid to their role. We focus on the integration of a particular marketing function, personal selling (as opposed to

* University of Pennsylvania.

This research was supported by the Marketing Science Institute, the Wharton Center for Marketing Strategy Research, and the University of California, Los Angeles.

The authors would like to thank Oliver Williamson, Barton Weitz, Stanley Ornstein, and Vijay Mahajan for helpful comments. We also appreciate the detailed and insightful comments of an anonymous reviewer and of Alvin Klevorick.

[1] Two exceptions are Monteverde and Teece (1982) and Teece (1980).

mass communications). The issue is whether to use a manufacturers' representative or a "direct" (employee) salesperson to sell a product line. The resolution of this issue turns on human assets, if only because differences in physical assets are negligible in this setting.

Section 2 further develops this issue and presents a transaction-cost explanation based on the work of Williamson (1975, 1979, 1981a,b), from which we develop a theoretical model. Section 3 discusses collection of field data from 172 sales managers for 16 electronic component manufacturers. Estimation of the logistic function is the subject of Section 4, and the results are presented in Section 5. Section 6 discusses the implications of these exploratory findings.

2. Relevant transaction costs

■ A manufacturers' representative ("rep") is an independent business entity that offers selling services to a manufacturer ("principal") in return for a commission on any sales realized. A typical rep agency consists of several salespeople and office staff and operates like the sales department of a firm. The agency, however, represents a number of noncompeting manufacturers whose products fit to form a sales package (e.g., office supplies from one maker, typewriters from another). Reps usually bear all sales expenses and are the principal's exclusive salespeople for a defined set of customers (e.g., office products stores in Southern California). Thus, reps are what we shall refer to as the market governance mode. In contrast, "direct" sales people are employees of one manufacturer, typically paid by salary or salary plus incentives. Hence, direct salespeople are the integrated (hierarchical) governance mode.[2]

As of 1974, 50% of all U.S. manufacturers used reps, either alone or in conjunction with a direct sales force (Research Institute of America, 1975). Yet, as of 1977, only 10% of U.S. dollar volume in 15 major industrial categories was conducted through reps (Taylor, 1981). Apparently, the market mode is less often used than the integrated mode, although this varies considerably across product categories.

Williamson (1975, 1979, 1981a,b) has developed a transaction-cost theory of integration. Klein, Crawford, and Alchian (1978) offer a closely related treatment. The logic and concepts of Williamson's approach are readily transferable to the rep/direct choice and provide a framework for our exploratory analysis of this issue.

Asset specificity arises when durable assets become customized to the user. When assets are fungible, market contracting is preferable since the agent pooling several firms' demands more fully exhausts scale economies and risk-pooling benefits. At the same time, the threat of ready replacement disciplines performance. In contrast, if assets become specialized to a relationship, the parties are locked into bilateral exchange. The result is that opportunism and maladaptation are unchecked by market forces.[3] In such circumstances, integration enables the firm to dampen opportunism and inflexibility because integration carries with it access, audit, and incentive advantages. Other things equal, reps should be more efficient (and presumably chosen more often) when assets are nonspecific and direct salespeople should be more efficient and chosen more often when assets are highly specific.

A salesperson or sales force possesses physical and human assets. Physical assets (cars, offices, etc.) are unspecialized, and hence may be disregarded in our analysis. Of

---

[2] Markets and hierarchies are really endpoints on a continuum from a completely independent external entity to a completely dependent internal entity. Rep and direct sales forces may fall at different points along the continuum; however, for purposes of exploratory analysis, we simplify into rep (external) and direct (internal).

[3] Although in theory a sufficiently complex contingent claims contract might produce the same effect, in practice bounded rationality, uncertainty, and the derivative condition of information impactedness render this solution infeasible.

the human assets (knowledge/ability and relationships), those which are specialized relate to the principal (company) and the customer. The relevant specialized knowledge and relationships can be described as follows.

Consider the salesperson experienced in a given industry who begins to represent Company *A*. The salesperson's industry skills are all that is necessary—unless *A* is a distinctive firm. Suppose that Company *A* has its own particular operating procedures, formal and informal, which our salesperson must learn. To get Company *A* to act effectively (e.g., to rectify a customer complaint quickly), our salesperson must have built relationships within the firm (e.g., with production personnel or design engineers). Further, if *A*'s products are not standard, it is necessary to learn their distinctive features and applications. Finally, our salesperson may acquire sensitive information to perform his tasks. The knowledge and relationships our salesperson eventually acquires about *A* are assets specific to *A*. The more these assets affect the salesperson's performance, the higher their value and the more the selling task is characterized by asset specificity.

This scenario may be repeated on the customer side. *A*'s customers may be distinctive in their ways of doing things and in their orientations and needs. The importance of these features is magnified when *A*'s sales are concentrated in critical "key" accounts: for these accounts it pays to learn every customer idiosyncracy. Further, with some accounts relationships cultivated may become so important that the customer exhibits loyalty to the salesperson—not to the principal.[4] Thus, where customers are distinctive, where sales are concentrated in key accounts, and where relationships matter (especially where loyalty to the salesperson may arise), asset specificity is high.

A major proposition follows: the greater the total value of company-specific assets (on the company and customer sides), the greater the likelihood of vertical integration in the form of a direct sales force.

□ **Uncertainty.** Williamson (1979) highlights one form of environmental uncertainty, that of environmental unpredictability. This complicates writing and enforcing contingent claims contracts since the environment shifts in unforeseen ways. The market mode is still advantageous, but transactions will be completed less smoothly than in more certain environments. Thus, the presumption of market superiority is undisturbed—*unless* assets are specific to a nontrivial degree.

The shifting environment forces renegotiation, which may lead to delays. This poses a fundamental problem under the market mode because even the best contracts are incomplete. The integrated firm is better able to cope because adaptations can be made as needed without revising formal agreements between independent parties (Williamson, 1979). Hence, the likelihood of integration is expected to increase, given nontrivial asset specificity, with increasing uncertainty.

Williamson's later writings (1981a) recognize a second form of uncertainty, which he calls "internal." Alchian and Demsetz (1972) highlight the same concept, which they call the difficulty with which individual productivity can be metered. We refer to this second form of uncertainty as the difficulty of evaluating performance. It occurs in the selling function for three reasons. First, it may be infeasible to record each salesperson's results accurately. For example, in selling air freight services, records are kept at the warehouse level, while salespeople operate at the customer level. Second, responsibility for a sale may not be assignable to an individual. This occurs when team sales are involved or when customers may place an order with someone other than the salesperson

[4] This asset is especially potent. It is specific in that it grows while the salesperson represents that principal and is particularly beneficial to the principal while the transaction continues. But this asset may be transferred to another principal should the transaction end, which makes the threat of opportunism acute.

who makes the presentation. Third, "performance" may not be a simple, readily measurable scalar. It may be a vector of indicators, the relative importance of each being hard to ascertain and the value of each being difficult to measure (e.g., satisfaction of prospects approached, value of market intelligence provided).

When performance is difficult to evaluate, imperfect input measures and a manager's subjective judgment are preferable to defective (simple, observable) output measures. Integration is not essential, since monitoring and judgmental evaluation of individual performance can be done by managers of a firm that contracts to provide service to another. Nevertheless, the evaluators must be evaluated themselves, and simple output measures of the contractor's performance are often inadequate when underlying individual results are difficult to assess.

Accordingly, the likelihood of integration should increase with the difficulty of monitoring performance.

□ **Making the tradeoff: frequency.** The transaction costs imposed by specific assets (especially in combination with environmental unpredictability) and by monitoring difficulty make vertical integration more appealing. But a specialized governance mechanism involves significant setup and maintenance costs. For rarely occurring transactions, losses from opportunism and inflexibility are likely to be lower than the integrated firm's incremental overhead. As a transaction recurs more frequently, however, integration becomes more desirable since potential losses from not integrating outweigh the overhead costs of integration.

The issue is whether a firm can at least break even on the fixed cost of an integrated function. Although the idea is logically appealing, it is difficult to express empirically. Fixed costs are difficult to estimate and the breakeven point (over an arbitrary time span) is unclear. Nonetheless, one does see rules of thumb used to approximate this minimum scale notion. For example, we were told by two sales managers in the electronic components industry that a common heuristic involves drawing a geographical territory that a salesperson could physically cover and estimating its maximum attainable sales potential. If less than $1,000,000 is at stake, the territory is too "sparse" or "thin" to be covered by a direct salesperson. Density, then, is an analogue of frequency in the selling setting and may be thought of as the ratio of attainable potential to required travel in a territory. Since the desirability of integration increases as density increases (though the breakeven point is unascertainable), we expect to see more use of a direct sales force as density increases.

Scherer (1980, p. 84) suggests that firm size is also a very important factor. Since large firms achieve economies of scale in finding, holding, and utilizing management skills, a large firm "may be able to get more mileage out of its expenditures on a field sales force and other marketing instruments." Scale economies are likely to play an important role in virtually all integration decisions. More generally, size is widely regarded as a pervasive influence on firm behavior (Miles, 1980) and on firm and industry performance for reasons of scale and scope economy, market power aspirations, and the ability to aggregate inputs (Scherer, 1980). Thus, our model includes company size, in addition to asset specificity, uncertainty, and frequency.

3. Data from the electronic components industry

■ The above hypotheses were tested on survey data from the electronic components industry. We selected one industry, rather than several, to detect real differences in practice that might otherwise be confounded with industry-specific effects. This limits the generalizability of results, but does allow us to establish internal validity. The electronic components industry was chosen because its variety makes it a microcosm of American business, as can be seen in the following industry description (Electronic Industries Association, 1981).

Electronics concerns the conduction of electricity through a material such that the electrons' flow is influenced. The ability to influence electron flows (rather than simply to carry them) is what distinguishes electronic equipment from electrical equipment. In 1980, the electronic components industry posted factory sales in the United States of over 25 billion dollars. The many component producers (including some non-American companies) cover a broad spectrum. Generally, they sell to original equipment manufacturers (OEM's), though many OEM's (e.g., Texas Instruments) are themselves integrated backward into production of certain components.

Most components are categorized as "active" or "passive." Active components (such as semiconductors) contribute to signal energy in a circuit, whereas passive components do not. This distinction is important because the passive sector is more mature ("low tech"), with less product differentiation and more intense price competition. A capacitor (passive component) may sell for a few cents a pound and be treated as a commodity, whereas an integrated circuit (active component) may be engineering intensive, customized to the user's application, and treated as a highly differentiated product. Component producers vary not only in their products, but also in their strategies (e.g., low-cost producer vs. high-cost innovator), sizes, management styles, and distribution methods.

Component distribution proceeds through three different channels. The first two, company salespeople and manufacturers' representatives, involve no transfer of title to goods. Of these, reps are becoming increasingly popular. The third option is industrial distributors, independent wholesalers who purchase components for resale. Because distributors take title, they are less subject to the manufacturers' influence (particularly on pricing) than either direct salespeople or reps. Nonetheless, distributors are also becoming more popular. Many firms use all three, restricting each mode to certain product lines and customers. For example, a full line manufacturer may use distributors to sell passive components to small customers; reps to sell passive and active components to medium customers and active components to small customers; and direct salespeople to sell passive and active components to large customers. This study tests a transaction cost explanation for these assignments in cases where title stays with the manufacturer (i.e., reps vs. direct salespeople).

Sixteen recognized electronic component manufacturers participated in the study. Only recognized firms were included to permit a contrast between what might be presumed to be well-run direct sales forces and well-run reps.[5] The unit of analysis was the product line of a given company in a given territory or set of territories. A "territory" (defined by the firm) is a subset of customers covered by a sales force (rep or direct) reporting to a sales manager. Since most companies keep records and assign managers at the product-line-in-territory level, this unit of analysis facilitates data gathering.

[5] A list of recognized firms was generated from the *1980 Audit of Brand Recognition*, a survey in which purchasers of a given electronic component (e.g., switching diodes) listed the three manufacturers they would consider as suppliers. For all major categories of components, we selected every manufacturer mentioned by at least 10% of the purchasers. This procedure generated a very long list of recognized firms, many of which were on the West Coast. For convenience, non-West Coast firms were eliminated. With the endorsement of the EIA (Electronic Industries Association), the vice presidents of sales of 21 firms were contacted. Eleven have participated. In addition, nine recognized firms (none from the West Coast) suggested by EIA were contacted and five have participated. In total, 16 of 30 companies cooperated. To assess the seriousness of nonresponse bias, the 16 respondents and 14 nonrespondents were compared as to size, the sophistication of their product line, and whether they were rep or direct. The nonparticipants have little in common on these grounds. Since these three variables are important descriptors of electronic component manufacturers, the threat of nonresponse bias does not appear serious, although doubtless it is present.

The survey respondents were territory sales managers, who are in an excellent position to know both the selling environment and the firm's environment. Each manager is a boundary spanner, a person on both sides of the boundary between the firm and the customer in a particular territory. To be a sales manager, especially in this industry, one needs to have been a salesperson. Managers also know their territories, since the median length of time served in the territory is six years.[6]

Each sales manager was directed by top sales management to fill out a questionnaire and to return it directly to the research team. This questionnaire was extensively pretested and in total, 145 completely usable responses (of 172 questionnaires returned) are available.[7] The response rate per company is virtually 100% because company personnel followed up missing questionnaires.

4. The logistic response function

■ This section describes our specific model for the decision to use reps vs. a direct salesforce. Following the order in which the concepts described in Section 2 were introduced, the variables listed below are hypothesized to affect the likelihood of using a direct salesforce.

□ Measurement of variables.

Transaction specificity of assets (TSA). This is the average of six (standardized) variables representing managers' perceptions of:

(i) nature of the company: difficulty of a salesperson's learning the ins and outs of their company which are needed for success. Managers indicated their perception by circling a number from 1 to 7 on the following semantic differential scale:

1	2	3	4	5	6	7
Disagree						Agree

in response to the statement, "It's difficult to learn all the ins and outs of our company that a salesperson needs to know to be effective."

(ii) nature of the product: amount of extra training needed in this firm by a new salesperson who has experience in the product class (answer indicated in number of weeks of training).

(iii) confidential information: measured as a semantic differential in response to the statement, "An experienced salesperson's inside information could do us a lot of damage if it got out."

(iv) nature of the customer: measured as a semantic differential in response to the statement, "To be effective, the salesperson has to take a lot of time to get to know our accounts."

(v) importance of key accounts: percent of accounts given special attention.

(vi) customer loyalty: influence of personal relationships between salespeople and accounts on sales. Greater loyalty is measured as disagreement with the statement, "Personal relationships between our salespeople and accounts have little influence on sales of our product line."

---

[6] The median manager spends 35% of working time in the field, observing first-hand how the territory operates. Of the managers who supervise reps, one of every five has a representative's council, a forum for regular exchange between reps and managers. Such a forum increases the likelihood that managers know well the territories for which they report.

[7] The questionnaire itself was designed in accordance with the guidelines of the "key informant" literature (Campbell, 1955; Seidler, 1974). All questions that were not answered by at least 95% of the respondents were eliminated as having been overly difficult. The result, we believe, is a data set of high quality.

Uncertainty as environmental unpredictability (UEU). Expected deviation between forecast and actual sales in the next year, expressed as a percentage (plus or minus).

Uncertainty as difficulty of evaluating performance (UDEP). Perceived difficulty of measuring the results of individual salespeople equitably. Measured as semantic differential in response to "It is very difficult to measure equitably the results of individual salespeople."

Territory density (TD). Negative of the percentage of salespersons' time spent driving or flying, i.e., the less time spent traveling, the more dense the territory.

Company size (SIZE). 1980 company assets in dollars (Gupta, 1980).

On the basis of the motivation in Section 2, all of the variables above are hypothesized to have a positive effect on the likelihood of using a direct sales force. To account for differences in scale—semantic differential, percentages, dollars—each of these variables was standardized before estimating the response function. Specifically, each observation was transformed by subtracting the variable's mean and then by dividing by the standard deviation. Thus, standardized variables have a mean of zero and a standard deviation of one, and the magnitudes of response function coefficients may be directly compared.

In addition to these main effects, two interactions were also considered. As noted earlier, the effects of both types of uncertainty—environmental unpredictability and the difficulty of evaluating performance—are expected to be greater when transaction specificity of assets is high. This necessitates using multiplicative interaction terms.[8] The specificity/unpredictability interaction is denoted *ZUEUTSA*, and the specificity/difficulty of evaluating performance interaction is *ZUDEPTSA*.

Because of the binary dependent variable, the logistic response function is used to represent the impact of the five main effects and two interactions on the probability of going direct. Letting $X_{1j}, X_{2j}, \ldots, X_{7j} \equiv X_j$ stand for the seven factors described above for subject j, we have

$$P[D_j = 1|X_j] = \frac{e^{\beta_0 + \sum_{i=1}^{7} \beta_i X_{ij}}}{1 + e^{\beta_0 + \sum_{i=1}^{7} \beta_i X_{ij}}}, \tag{1}$$

where

$$D_j \equiv \begin{cases} 0 \text{ if manufacturers' reps are used, or} \\ 1 \text{ if a direct sales force is used,} \end{cases}$$

and $P[D_j = 1|X_j]$ is the probability that a firm with company and market characteristics X_j uses a direct sales force. Taking the natural logarithm of both sides in (1) yields the (linear) relation between the factors and the logit or log odds ratio:

$$\ln\left(\frac{P[D_j = 1|X_j]}{1 - P[D_j = 1|X_j]}\right) = \beta_0 + \sum_{i=1}^{7} \beta_i X_{ij}. \tag{2}$$

---

[8] Since all three of these variables are standardized, the interactions cannot logically be formed by simply multiplying two of them. Cooper and Nakanishi (1982) provide a solution to this problem using the zeta-squared transform:

$$\zeta^2(X) = \begin{cases} 1 + X^2 & \text{if} \quad X \geq 0 \\ (1 + X^2)^{-1} & \text{if} \quad X \leq 0. \end{cases}$$

Then the two desired interaction terms can be meaningfully constructed as

$$ZUEUTSA \equiv \zeta^2(UEU)\zeta^2(TSA)$$

and

$$ZUDEPTSA \equiv \zeta^2(UDEP)\zeta^2(TSA).$$

After being computed by these definitions, *ZUEUTSA* and *ZUDEPTSA* were also standardized before the response function was estimated.

The coefficients were estimated by maximizing the likelihood function:

$$L(D_j|X_j; \beta) = \prod_{j=1}^{N} P[D_j = 1|X_j]^{D_j}(1 - P[D_j = 1|X_j])^{1-D_j}, \quad (3)$$

where N is the number of subjects on which data have been collected. Maximization of (3) was accomplished with the Gauss-Newton nonlinear least squares method used by the BMD program BMDPLR (Dixon, 1981). The next section reports the results when this model (1) and measurement method were applied to the sales force integration data.

5. Empirical results

■ **Parameter estimates.** Case 1 of Table 1 gives the parameter estimates and their asymptotic standard errors for the seven hypothesized determinants of sales force integration. The most significant factors, based on the ratio of coefficient ÷ standard error, are difficulty of evaluating performance (*UDEP*), company size (*SIZE*), and transaction specificity of assets (*TSA*). All three have the hypothesized (positive) effect on the probability of using a direct sales force. With our sample of 145, the remaining four variables are not significant and have negative coefficients, which are inconsistent with the hypotheses.

The instantaneous rate of change of the probability of going direct with respect to a variable X_{ij} is

$$\frac{\partial P[D_j = 1|X_j]}{\partial X_{ij}} = \beta_i P[D_j = 1|X_j](1 - P[D_j = 1|X_j]) \quad (4)$$

(Domencich and McFadden, 1975, p. 84). Examining this derivative for the values of β_i in Table 1 leads to two conclusions. First, the variables that, at the mean (i.e., for $X_j = 0$) have the largest estimated effect on the probability of going direct, are *UDEP*, *TSA*, and *SIZE*. Second, in the neighborhood of the mean, each variable's impact on the probability of using a direct sales force is reasonably linear.

TABLE 1 **Parameter Estimates for Logistic Response Function**

Case 1: All Hypothesized Effects

Effect	Coefficient	Asymptotic Standard Error	Coefficient ÷ Standard Error
TSA	.616	.285	2.159
UEU	−.053	.276	−.193
UDEP	.782	.287	2.728
TD	−.172	.198	−.871
ZUEUTSA	−.027	.282	−.097
ZUDEPTSA	−.381	.295	−1.292
SIZE	.470	.204	2.307
Constant β_0	−.434	.188	−2.306

Case 2: Transaction Cost Effects Omitted

Effect	Coefficient	Asymptotic Standard Error	Coefficient ÷ Standard Error
SIZE	.547	.174	3.140
Constant β_0	−.405	.176	−2.302

l^* = logarithm of maximized likelihood.
Case 1: $l^* = -85.60$.
Case 2: $l^* = -92.87$.

□ **Importance of transaction-cost variables.** To evaluate the contribution of the set of transaction-cost variables over and above the results that could be obtained by using company size alone, we performed a logit analysis using only the latter factor. The estimated coefficients are listed as Case 2 in Table 1.[9]

The incremental benefit from including transaction costs in the analysis can be evaluated in two ways: statistical significance and predictive effectiveness. The logarithm of the maximized likelihood function is reported in Table 1 for the two models—the one including transaction cost effects and the one excluding them. The likelihood ratio test statistic is $c = 2(-85.60 + 92.87) = 14.54$. Under the null hypothesis that $\beta_i = 0$ for all of the transaction-cost variables, c has the χ^2 distribution with 6 degrees of freedom. Since the critical value for χ^2 at the .05 level is

$$\chi^2_{(6)} = 12.6,$$

the null hypothesis is rejected.

Alternately, the contribution of the transaction-cost variables can be examined in terms of predictive effectiveness. One index of effectiveness for comparing models estimated by maximum likelihood is Akaike's Information Criterion (Akaike, 1974):

$$AIC = -2(l^* - n), \tag{5}$$

where l^* is the logarithm of the maximized likelihood and n is the number of estimated parameters. This approach penalizes models having a large number of parameters, since the model with the smallest value of AIC is preferred.[10] In our application, the values of AIC for the two and eight parameter models are 189.74 and 187.20, respectively. Hence, the more complex model is again preferred. This result shows that the set of transaction-cost variables are not just statistically significant; one would also expect them to aid in predicting the degree of sales force integration for firms which are not included in the estimation sample.

6. Conclusion

■ Our estimated logistic function, with three significant parameters, provides support for our model of the appearance of integrated and nonintegrated sales forces. The significant predictor variables have the expected sign, which indicates support for the theoretical rationales underlying them. Although several expected effects were not observed, those transaction-cost effects that do appear improve upon a simple company-size model of integration.

Williamson (1979) argues that transaction-specific assets are the single most important determinant of vertical integration, followed by uncertainty. In our results, however, the order is reversed. Internal uncertainty, i.e., how difficult it is to evaluate individual performance, is strongly associated with the use of a direct sales force. Specificity, although strongly associated, has somewhat less of an effect. A likely explanation is that in this setting, the provision of a marketing service, the specificity of three of the four categories of assets—physical, site, and dedicated—is either minor or implausible. Where human

[9] Since the β-values have the same sign here as they did in Case 1, there is some evidence that multicollinearity between the set of transaction-cost variables and company size is not overly high.

[10] The statistic has been used for measuring predictive ability in a wide variety of settings including regression, time series analysis, multidimensional scaling, and cluster analysis (Rust and Schmittlein, 1982). Stone (1977) showed that using AIC to compare models is asymptotically equivalent to using the cross-validated likelihood function. For the logistic response function, Rust and Schmittlein (1982) also found AIC and cross validation to be very close in small samples (i.e., 10–12 observations per estimated parameter).

assets assume a prominent role, internal uncertainty is likely to assume considerable importance (Ouchi, 1979).

Contrary to the implications of Williamson's framework, the expected specificity/uncertainty interactions were not found; in this setting it appears that specificity and uncertainty have no incremental effect when they appear in combination. Further, frequency (density) appears to have no impact. Considerable difficulties are associated with measuring variables related to territorial density, e.g., workload, concentration of accounts, geographical dispersion, potential (Ryans and Weinberg, 1979). We suggest that measurement error might account for the weakness of our density measure. Recall that our measure of travel time is intended as a proxy for the ratio of potential to geographical dispersion. Had we been able to measure both potential and dispersion directly, the likelihood of error would have been much smaller.

Size of firm, the only nonterritory level variable, proves to be a powerful covariate. As expected, the larger the firm, the more likely it is to fill a territory with direct personnel.

These findings are for one type of integration (a marketing service) and one industry; hence, their generality remains to be established. Nonetheless, the results are encouraging, particularly to those who view the firm as an intendedly but imperfectly rational governance structure. Traditionally, economists have focused on production costs to the exclusion of transaction costs. Consequently, technological costs are viewed as the principal determinant of integration. The dominance of this paradigm led Coase (1972) to lament the state of affairs in industrial organization research at that date and to call for a more direct approach focusing on governance features. Our model is such an approach, and our results suggest that transaction-costs considerations are important determinants of integration.

References

AKAIKE, H. "A New Look at the Statistical Model Identification." *IEEE Transactions on Automatic Control*, Vol. 19 (1974), pp. 716–723.

ALCHIAN, A. AND DEMSETZ, H. "Production, Information Costs, and Economic Organization." *American Economic Review*, Vol. 62 (December 1972), pp. 777–795.

CAMPBELL, D.T. "The Informant in Quantitative Research." *American Journal of Sociology*, Vol. 60 (1955), pp. 339–342.

COASE, R.H. "Industrial Organization: A Proposal for Research" in U.R. Fuchs, ed., *Policy Issues and Research Opportunities in Industrial Organization, Economic Research, Retrospect and Prospect*. New York: Columbia University Press, 1972.

COOPER, L.G. AND NAKANISHI, M. "Standardizing Variables in Multiplicative Choice Models." *Journal of Consumer Research*, Vol. 10 (June 1983), pp. 96–108.

DIXON, W.J., ED. *BMDP Statistical Software*. Berkeley: University of California Press, 1981.

DOMENCICH, T.A. AND MCFADDEN, D. *Urban Travel Demand: A Behavioral Analysis*. Amsterdam: North-Holland, 1975.

Electronic Design, Audit of Brand Recognition by the Electronic Original Equipment Market. Rochelle Park, N.J.: Hayden Publishing Company, 1980.

ELECTRONIC INDUSTRIES ASSOCIATION. *Electronic Market Data Book*. Washington, D.C.: Electronic Industries Association, 1981.

GUPTA, N. "Some Alternative Definitions of Size." *Academy of Management Journal*, Vol. 23 (1980), pp. 759–766.

HOLMSTROM, B. "Moral Hazard and Observability." *Bell Journal of Economics*, Vol. 10 (Spring 1979), pp. 74–91.

KLEIN, B., CRAWFORD, R.A., AND ALCHIAN, A.A. "Vertical Integration, Appropriable Rents, and the Competitive Contracting Process." *Journal of Law and Economics*, Vol. 21 (October 1978), pp. 297–326.

MILES, R.H. *Macro Organizational Behavior*. Santa Monica: Goodyear Publishing Co., 1980.

MONTEVERDE, K. AND TEECE, D.J. "Supplier Switching Costs and Vertical Integration in the Automobile Industry." *Bell Journal of Economics*, Vol. 13 (Spring 1982), pp. 206–213.

OUCHI, W.G. "A Conceptual Framework for the Design of Organizational Control Mechanisms." *Management Science*, Vol. 25 (1979), pp. 833–848.

RESEARCH INSTITUTE OF AMERICA. "When, Where, and How to Use Manufacturers' Representatives." Staff Report, 1975.

RUST, R.T. AND SCHMITTLEIN, D.C. "A Bayesian Cross-Validated Likelihood Method for Comparing Alternative Specifications of Quantitative Models." *Marketing Science*, forthcoming.

RYANS, A.B. AND WEINBERG, C.B. "Territory Sales Response." *Journal of Marketing Research*, Vol. 16 (November 1979), pp. 453–465.

SCHERER, F.M. *Industrial Structure and Economic Performance*. Chicago: Rand-McNally, 1980.

SEIDLER, J. "On Using Informants: A Technique for Collecting Quantitative Data and Controlling Measurement Error in Organization Analysis." *American Sociological Review*, Vol. 39 (December 1974), pp. 816–831.

STONE, M. "An Asymptotic Equivalence of Choice of Model by Cross Validation and Akaike's Criterion." *Journal of the Royal Statistical Society*, Vol. 39 (1977), pp. 44–47.

TAYLOR, T.C. "A Raging 'Rep' idemic." *Sales and Marketing Management*, Vol. 127 (June 8, 1981), pp. 33–35.

TEECE, D.J. "Economics of Scope and the Scope of the Enterprise." *Journal of Economic Behavior and Organization*, Vol. 1 (1980), pp. 223–247.

WILLIAMSON, O.E. "The Economics of Organization: The Transaction-Cost Approach." *American Journal of Sociology*, Vol. 87 (1981a), pp. 548–577.

———. "The Modern Corporation: Origin, Evolution, Attributes." *Journal of Economic Literature*, Vol. 19 (December 1981b), pp. 1537–1568.

———. "Transaction-Cost Economics: The Governance of Contractual Relations." *Journal of Law and Economics*, Vol. 22 (October 1979), pp. 233–262.

———. *Markets and Hierarchies: Analysis and Antitrust Implications*. New York: Free Press, 1975.

[6]

Forward Integration into Distribution: An Empirical Test of Transaction Cost Analysis

GEORGE JOHN
University of Minnesota

BARTON A. WEITZ
University of Florida

1. INTRODUCTION

The issue of forward vertical integration has attracted a good deal of attention from researchers in several disciplines, including economics, marketing, and law. Many explanations have been offered for this phenomenon, including technological interrelationships involving economies of scale and scope (Chandler), uncertainty and risk considerations (Arrow, 1969), information externalities (Green), and strategic purposes. Blair and Kaserman (1983) offer an extensive survey of the extant literature in this area.

Of particular note, however, is the recent rise in prominence of the transaction costs analysis (TCA) of vertical integration. This approach consists of a blend of institutional economics, organizational theory, and contract law, and has been developed primarily by Oliver Williamson (1979, 1985). He views vertical integration as a response to the inability of arms-length market relationships to govern exchange efficiently under particular circumstances. The level of specialized assets[1] required to support the exchange, the uncertainty[2] surrounding the exchange, and the frequency[3] of exchange are

The authors are in alphabetical order. The financial support provided to the first author by the Graduate School Research Committee, University of Wisconsin is gratefully acknowledged. The comments of the *JLEO* reviewer are greatly appreciated.

1. Specialized assets are those investments in physical and/or human assets that have very limited salvage value outside the focal exchange.

2. Uncertainty refers to the condition of being unable to predict relevant contingencies.

3. Frequency refers to the distinction between one-shot exchange and recurrent exchange. We shall not deal with this variable here since we are interested only in recurrent exchange.

Journal of Law, Economics, and Organization vol. 4, no. 2 Fall 1988
 ISSN 8756–6222

identified as the principal factors that make market-mediated exchange inefficient.

Despite the increasing use of the transaction cost approach to explain forward integration, empirical tests of this line of reasoning are few. Some of the more prominent include make versus buy decisions in component sourcing (Monteverde and Teece), integration of the selling function (Anderson and Schmittlein), shipper-carrier relations (Palay), integration in the aluminum industry (Stuckey), and aerospace contracting relations (Masten). For a summary of these and other empirical TCA studies of long-term contracting, see Joskow. Clearly, there is a need to assess the validity of the particular propositions offered by TCA concerning vertical integration. Such evidence would advance our conceptual models by pinpointing areas of needed refinement, as well as begin to shed light on the diverse choices made by firms regarding forward integration.[4]

In this paper we present an empirical test of TCA propositions concerning forward integration by surveying a sample of industrial goods manufacturers. The variables implicated by the theory are measured via a questionnaire directed at a key informant within each firm. The resulting data are subjected to multiple regression and multinomial logit analysis to assess the degree of support for the predictions.

The remainder of the paper is divided into five sections. In section 2 we describe some of the institutional detail regarding industrial marketing channels and distinguish the principal alternative configurations. In section 3 we develop the link between forward integration and each of the key variables in transaction cost analysis. In section 4 the measures and data collection procedures are described. In section 5 we report the results of the analysis, and section 6 closes the paper with a discussion of the implications of the study.

2. DISTRIBUTION CHANNELS FOR INDUSTRIAL GOODS

One of the principal requirements for conducting an empirical investigation of TCA predictions is a high level of microanalytic detail concerning the alternative institutional arrangements. We begin by describing the organizational forms of distribution channels found in industrial goods markets.

The classification of channel structures in industrial markets is made difficult by the overlapping structures and inconsistent terminology found in the literature; see Stern and El-Ansary for a general discussion of distribution channels. Nevertheless, following Haas, Diamond, and Sutton, we can isolate

4. With respect to this diversity of choices, the available data (U.S. Bureau of the Census) show that industries vary considerably in their degree of forward integration. Further, casual observation reveals that such diversity extends to firms within industries as well.

two categories of channel organizations that differ with respect to the degree of forward integration. These researchers generally classify the various alternatives into direct and indirect channels. In the direct channel, the firm does not employ an independent reseller. Rather, it retains ownership of the product until it passes to the end-user. All of the downstream tasks are undertaken directly by company employees or else by such commission agents as manufacturers' representatives. The key attribute is that only the firm has any claim to residual profits.

The indirect channel classification comprises a bewildering array of institutional structures. The firm sells to independent resellers (such as distributors, wholesalers, retailers), who in turn resell the product to end-users or other resellers. These indirect channels vary by the type of intermediaries involved and the number of levels present within a particular system. Indirect channels are often "referred to collectively as distributors" (Sutton). Stern and El-Ansary provide a detailed description of several different types of distributors within the channel. All these indirect channels involve downstream firms that actually purchase the product and resell it. Since they take title to the product, residual profits are not claimed exclusively by the manufacturer.

From the standpoint of TCA, it is evident that direct channels represent relatively more forward integration than indirect channels. Thus, TCA predictions about vertical integration essentially speak to the choices made by manufacturers regarding direct versus indirect channels. As a recent survey of industry practice (Sutton) found, most firms can and indeed do use both direct and indirect channels simultaneously. A good illustration of multiple channels is IBM's using Computerland (a reseller) as a channel intermediary while making direct sales to end-users. Marketing specialists consider the multiplicity of channels and the management of these systems to be a critical managerial task (Stern and El-Ansary).

Multiple channel usage makes it infeasible to adopt the basic research design used in previous TCA studies. These studies typically have focused on only two disjunct categories representing the integrated and nonintegrated options. For instance, Anderson studied the internalization of the selling function in electronics firms by comparing sales territories serviced by sales branches with those serviced by commission agents. Overlapping territories where employee sales forces and commissioned agents operate concurrently were consciously excluded from the estimation sample. Likewise, when Monteverde and Teece and Walker and Weber compared the make versus buy decision for components, they excluded components that are both purchased and manufactured at the same time from their data. By contrast, we will examine indirect and direct channels used by industrial manufacturers, allowing for the possibility that these channels may be used simultaneously by some firms.

3. TRANSACTION COST ANALYSIS OF RESELLERS IN DISTRIBUTION CHANNELS

According to TCA, the firm's decision to use resellers is made on the basis of comparative institutional efficiency, In particular, it ascertains which of the alternatives constitutes the transaction-cost-minimizing condition. Such costs are distinct from production costs and are the "costs of running the system" (Arrow, 1969). Searching for information, bargaining, monitoring, and contract enforcing are all instances of these costs.

To some degree, transaction costs have earned the reputation of being capable of explaining anything in a post-hoc fashion because they have not been defined in an operational fashion. This state of affairs has been alleviated, however, by Williamson's (1979, 1985) elaboration of this approach. He provides testable implications of transaction-cost-minimizing analysis by elaborating the links between key attributes of transactions and institutional structures. Based on transaction costs logic, one can then match attributes of transactions with institutional structures that minimize these costs. Each of these attributes of transactions is discussed in turn below.

3.1. Asset Specificity

This significant attribute of transactions refers to the extent to which specialized or nonredeployable investments are needed to support an exchange. Example of such investments include railcars specialized to haul one brand of automobile (Palay), refrigerated trucks needed to ship unpasteurized beer, specialized software that communicates only with one firm's computers (Jackson), and dedicated production equipment (Monteverde and Teece).

Specialized human assets are also present to varying degrees in distribution channels. The time and effort employed to acquire firm-specific knowledge needed for downstream activities is perhaps the most common form of these investments found in distribution channels (Heide and John). Notice that such knowledge becomes largely useless if the relationship terminated.

A high level of specific assets has profound implications for forward vertical integration. The primary consequence is to expose the transaction in question to opportunistic behavior. Because nonredeployable specific assets make it costly to switch to a new relationship, the market safeguard against opportunism is no longer effective. The other party can expropriate the value of quasi-rents associated with these assets. Presumably, rational firms would not invest in them unless they could be safeguarded.

According to TCA, the ultimate safeguard for specific assets is to internalize the transaction in question. Vertical integration provides a safeguard because of (a) the better monitoring and surveillance properties of organizations relative to markets, and (b) the reduction of profits from opportunistic behavior since employees do not ordinarily have claims to profit streams. In the context of forward integration into wholesaling and/or retailing, the safeguarding of specific assets will involve internalizing the functions of independent resellers. We can summarize this as the following testable proposition:

Proposition 1. As the levels of specific assets needed to support distribution activities are increased, industrial firms will rely more heavily on direct channels.

3.2. Uncertainty

Williamson (1985) implicates uncertainty as the other principal factor involved in forward vertical integration decisions. Fundamentally, an inability to predict contingencies creates problems in writing contracts because these agreements are incomplete in some important respects. When unforeseen contingencies arise, market contracts experience strain in adapting to the changed circumstances because opportunistically inclined parties can try to interpret unspecified clauses to their own advantage. (It is important to note that contractual incompleteness is attributable to the limited cognitive capabilities of human actors.)

In a distribution channel it is evident that *environmental uncertainty* can exist with respect to many marketing activities, such as sales targets and promotional activities to support the introduction of new products. Clearly, institutional structures that permit sequential, adaptive decision making are needed when such uncertainty increases. Marketing specialists (Shapiro, Anderson and Weitz) have argued that one of the principal drawbacks of dealing with independent intermediaries is the difficulty of renegotiating agreements in light of changed circumstances. Similarly, organizational researchers (Stinchcombe) have shown that relationships incorporate more elements of hierarchy in response to increrases in uncertainty.

Transaction cost analysis posits that an appropriate response to increased environmental uncertainty is to internalize the transaction. First, vertically integrated structures permit sequential, adaptive decision making to proceed more smoothly because of administrative mechanisms. Authority structures permit quicker resolution of conflicts arising from differing interpretations of evolving circumstances. They enhance the information flow between the parties, thus enabling them to react better to the uncertainties. To summarize this as a testable proposition, we have:

Proposition 2. As downstream environmental uncertainties increase in industrial goods markets, manufacturers will rely more heavily on direct channels.

In addition to environmental uncertainty, Williamson (1985) introduces the notion of *behavioral uncertainty.* Unlike environmental uncertainty, which is exogenously imposed on the exchange, behavioral uncertainty arises within the context of the exchange itself due to the opportunistic inclinations of the transacting parties. Behavioral uncertainty refers to the difficulty of ascertaining the actual performance or adherence to contractual agreements. Stinchcombe has discussed in some detail the impact of such performance assessment difficulties on the structure of commercial relationships.

Behavioral uncertainty can take the form of false claims by downstream resellers that they have executed faithfully some agreed-upon channel activity (such as shelf stocking or cooperative advertising) while they simply pocket the remuneration for the activity or else save the costs of undertaking it. In such circumstances, greater control over reseller activities is desirable. While (costly) supervision can effectively reduce such blatant opportunism, a subtler problem arises when there are long lags between actions and market responses. Such lags in the downstream selling environment make it difficult to infer which actions were responsible for the observed outcomes. Related as such behavioral uncertainty is to performance issues, we advance the following proposition:

Proposition 3. As performance assessment difficulties in downstream activities increase, manufacturers will rely more heavily on direct channels.

3.3 Production Costs

Although TCA tends to downplay the significance of production costs and related technological effects on forward integration, the object, nonetheless, is to minimize the sum of transaction and production costs in making forward integration decisions. Following Williamson's (1985) treatment of these effects, we argue that larger firms will tend to integrate their channels more readily than smaller firms when economies of scale or scope are substantial. Summarizing, we have the following testable proposition:

Proposition 4. Industrial manufacturers who can exhaust economies of scale will rely more heavily on direct channels.

It should be noted that the above prediction is identical to that proposed by marketing specialists (Haas; Stern and El-Ansary). Their reasoning is quite different, however. Rather than relying on the assumption that firms strive to minimize transaction and production costs, they argue that firms will generally prefer to internalize activities wherever possible. Since larger firms are better able to afford the set-up costs involved, they will use direct channels more often. As the leading marketing channels textbook notes, independent resellers "exist only by virtue of the fact that suppliers and/or customers . . . cannot afford to integrate, and therefore must rely on such intermediaries. . . ." (Stern and El-Ansary: 129). TCA maintains that what matters is not whether the firm can afford to integrate but whether there is an incentive to integrate. In contrasting the two explanations, we would argue that the TCA reasoning is more appealing since it does not assume that firms are motivated to internalize activities as a general tendency. The justification for such an assumption derives from the power-oriented perspective on firm behavior developed by organization theorists. Since we are concerned with firm behavior in competitive markets, it seems more reasonable to invoke an efficiency perspective. Nevertheless, it should be stressed that the present study cannot rule out either explanation, should a firm size effect be found in the data.

4. EMPIRICAL STUDY

4.1. Research Design

A principal consideration in testing the TCA predictions advanced in the previous sections involves the operationalization of the dependent variable, vertical integration. Since the theory predicts that increasing levels of asset specificity and uncertainty result in greater forward integration, it becomes important to isolate a set of structures that can be unambiguously ordered with respect to the presence of forward integration. We accomplish this by examining industrial manufacturers and classifying their downstream channels into direct and indirect systems. The direct channel represents forward vertical integration. Since firms often utilize both kinds of channels, a quantified measure of the extent of forward integration is provided by assessing the fraction of that firm's sales going through the direct channel.

It should be stressed that this test involves a semi-microanalytic level of detail. We have ignored the institutional variation that exists within the indirect channel itself. Resellers can vary greatly in the degree to which vertical control is imposed on them by the upstream firm. For instance, an authorized dealer of a firm is likely to have far less discretion than a merchant wholesaler. Nevertheless, since they are both resellers who take title to the product and claim residual downstream profits, they are considered equivalent in our classification scheme.

To summarize, we intend to test the TCA predictions involving forward integration by examining industrial marketing channels. We focus on the use of direct versus indirect channels and classify those firms that use both types simultaneously as using "mixed" channels. The fraction of sales going through the direct channel is a quantified measure of the firm's position on the continuum of internalizing downstream activities.

4.2 Sample

The data reported here are obtained from a sample of industrial firms with sales over $50 million. The sample was drawn from a list of firms maintained by a commercial vendor. The responses of eighty-seven industrial goods firms constitute the data for estimating our models. An examination of the sample characteristics (table 1) reveals that there is substantial variation in the type(s) of channels used, ranging from exclusively direct to exclusively indirect, with the majority of firms drawing to some extent on both direct and indirect channels. The variety of products sold is very broad, including equipment, components, and operating supplies. This sample appears quite comparable to recently published marketing studies of channel types (Lilien, Coughlan). Despite the diversity of this sample, it should be emphasized that it is a nonrandom sample. The commercially available list used as our sampling frame may contain biases of unknown magnitude. We stress the need to cumulate evidence from multiple studies.

4. 3. Method

As the study concerns organizational-level decisions, a key informant survey was used to gather data. In this approach, the researcher uses one individual in each organization who is knowledgeable about the issues at hand and reports on behalf of the organization. These individuals are not selected at random from each organization. Rather, they are deliberately selected to be key informants by virtue of their position within the firm; see John and Reve for a detailed discussion of this approach.

The informants in this survey were sales managers. We can justify their choice on the following grounds. Decisions about channels typically reside at a reasonably high level within the sales function of a firm since the sales staff is the locus of contact between the focal firm and the downstream intermediaries. Further, channels decisions are not made for individual prod-

Table 1. Sample Characteristics

Measure	Average
Percentage of sales through direct channel	61%
Specific assets (Time required for new hire with prior experience to become familiar)	8.4 months
Environmental uncertainty (Average across 5 items on a 5-point scale response format)	3.0
Behavioral uncertainty (Typical time from initial contact to order placement)	4.6 months
Territory sparseness (Percentage of salesperson's time spent on travel)	23.0%
Annual sales	$133.4 million

ucts; rather, they are made for a line of related products. With these considerations in mind, it was felt that an appropriate key informant would be the sales manager in charge of a product line. Individuals in these positions are likely to be extremely knowledgeable about the downstream distribution function.

As described earlier, a commercial list of sales managers in firms with annual sales over $50 million was purchased and was used as the mailing list for the study.[5] A postcard was mailed to each of the individuals on the mailing list asking the firm to participate in the study. As an incentive to participate, the sales managers were told that a summary of the results would be provided to them. The survey instrument was developed with the assistance of on-site interviews with sales managers in about a dozen firms, who responded to an initial version of the questionnaire and gave us feedback that enabled us to identify potential problems with the questionnaire. After making the necessary changes, the final questionnaire was mailed to all the individuals in the sample who agreed to participate.

4.4. Measures

Each sales manager was asked to complete the questionnaire for a distinct self-selected product line; all the questions were answered at the level of this product line. The specific questions used to measure each of the variables involved in the propositions are described below.

4.5. Channel

The use of resellers was captured by responses to the following question:

What percentages of sales are made to the following types of customers?
________ end users
________ channel members (wholesalers, distributors, retailers)
100% total

The percentage sold to end-users (% DIRECT) constitutes the amount going through a direct channel. Sales to channel members represent the use of resellers.

4.6. Specific Assets

In order to measure this variable, we capitalize on the notion that products requiring a good deal of training and experience specific to the line represent situations where specific assets are present. This was measured with the following item:

5. The list included both industrial and consumer goods firms. Only the responses of the industrial goods manufacturers are analyzed here.

How much time is required for a newly hired salesperson with *experience in the industry* to become adequately familiar with your products and customers?
______months.

This measure (SPSKILLS) does not measure the overall level of skill needed; rather, only the nontransferable component is measured. It specifies a person with prior experience in the industry. To the extent that the skills are transferable, such an individual would not need much time to adapt to this situation. This measure is similar to one used by Anderson.

4.7. Environmental Uncertainty

The inability to predict relevant contingencies is measured with the rating scale items described below. These items capture the extent to which the downstream marketing environment is volatile and turbulent.

How would you describe these products compared to other products in general?

Stable market shares	1	2	3	4	5	Volatile market shares
Easy to monitor trends	1	2	3	4	5	Difficult to monitor trends
Stable industry volume	1	2	3	4	5	Volatile industry volume
Sales forecasts are quite accurate	1	2	3	4	5	Sales forecasts are quite inaccurate
Predictable	1	2	3	4	5	Unpredictable

The measure (ENVUNCT) was formed by computing the average response to these five items. Social science researchers use this summated scale strategy to enhance the reliability of measures. Such a summation is reasonable only if the items are unidimensional in a factor-analytic sense and are internally consistent. Evidence of unidimensionality is provided by extracting all the principal components in these data. The results showed that only the first principal component had an eigenvalue greater than one, which indicates that one factor adequately describes the variance in the items. Evidence of internal consistency was provided by computing Cronbach's alpha, and this estimate (0.73) is well above the suggested 0.6 cutoff for basic research.[6]

4.8. Behavioral Uncertainty

The second aspect of uncertainty addressed here is the difficulty of assessing performance. We measure this variable by capitalizing on the notion that it is more difficult to ascertain adherence to contractual agreements by downstream actors when critical points in the selling cycle are separated by relatively longer periods of time. When transactions are performed instantaneously, the performance of each party is more readily observable. If the

6. See Churchill for a discussion of these issues related to summated scales. The appendix describes an alternative measurement model for this scale. The substantive results were robust across these procedures.

market reacts with a lag to actions taken, however, it becomes more difficult to attribute output to efforts. Each survey respondent answered the following question:

What is the typical time between an initial contact concerning the product and the ultimate placement of an order? ________months.

This measure (BEHUNCT) measures the length of the selling cycle and indexes the difficulty of assessing downstream performance.

4.9 Scale Variables

There are two scale variables included in the study. In the first of these, we asked the informant to report the sales volume of the product line in question (SALES).

What is the annual sales volume of this product line? $________

The second scale variable described the density of sales territories. The density of a sales territory refers to the geographic concentration of customers. Denser territories make it possible to assign a company employee to that territory and to use that person's time efficiently. In relatively sparser territories, it may not be possible to exhaust the available time of company personnel assigned to that area. By contrast, independent resellers are better able to exhaust scale economies by aggregating the products of different firms. We measure territory sparseness as follows:

What percent of the typical field salesperson's time is spent on the following activities?

________ face-to-face selling
________ service, after sales support
________ paper work
________ travel time
________ other
100%

Our measure of (lack of) density (SPARSE) is the fraction of time reported for travel. Obviously, more time is spent on the road when the density of the territory is lower. This is the same indicator of density used by Anderson.

5. RESULTS

The first model estimated from the data is a multiple regression model with the fraction of sales made through the direct channel (% DIRECT) as the dependent variable. The results are displayed in table 2. Since all the propositions specify the expected sign of the coefficient,[7] their significance is tested via 1-tail tests at the usual 0.05 level.

7. The dependent variable was first transformed using a logistic function, $ln\left[\frac{p}{1-p}\right]$, in order to constrain the range of predictions to lie between 0 and 100 on the original scale.

Table 2. Regression Model of Channel Configuration

Dependent variable: $LN \frac{\% \text{ DIRECT}}{(1 - \% \text{ DIRECT})}$

Independent Variable	Coefficient	T-value
Constant	−1.061	0.203
SPSKILLS	0.147	2.608*
ENVUNCT	0.773	1.806*
BEHUNCT	0.218	3.001*
LNSALES	−0.057	−0.204
SPARSE	−0.059	−1.988*

R^2adj = 0.281.

*sig. at $p \leq .05$ (1-tail).

The model explains about 28 percent of the variation in sales volume through the direct channel. As the F-ratio indicates, this is a significant amount of explained variance. Turning to the individual coefficients, we see that specific assets (SPSKILLS) increase significantly the fraction of sales made directly to end-users (b = 0.147, t = 2.608). This result lends support for Proposition 1.

Regarding the uncertainty variables involved in Propositions 2 and 3, we see that the environmental uncertainty coefficient (ENVUNCT) is significant in the direction posited in Proposition 2 (b = 0.773, t =1.806). The behavioral uncertainty coefficient (BEHUNCT) exhibits a similar result (b = 0.218, t = 3.001), which supports Proposition 3.

The final set of independent variables are the scale effects variables. Sales volume (LNSALES) has no significant effect on the dependent variable (b = −0.057, t = −0.204). The other scale variable (SPARSE) indicates that sparser territories are related to significantly lower levels of direct channel sales (b = −0.059, t = −1.988). Thus, only mixed support is found for Proposition 4.

Sales volume excepted, the above results appear to provide considerable support for the TCA predictions. It is quite possible, however, that the linear model does not describe the organizational decision very well. Suppose these channel decisions were made in a relatively "lumpy" fashion where the firm chooses a direct, indirect, or mixed channel. The continuous dependent variable would not capture such a decision very well. Since the theoretical model is not sufficiently refined as to permit us to exclude either possibility, it would seem necessary to verify the robustness of the results. To achieve this, we estimated another model with these data. This consisted of a maximum-likelihood estimation of a multinomial logit model. The independent variables remain the same, while the dependent variable is respecified as a qualitative measure to represent the (possibly) discrete decision.

We placed the firms in the sample into three classifications; direct, mixed, and indirect channels based on a 90 percent rule. If a firm sold more than

90 percent of its volume through either a direct or an indirect channel, we classified that firm into the direct and indirect channel categories respectively. The remaining firms were classified into the mixed channel category. The 90 percent cutoff was established by inspecting the distribution of the dependent variable for natural breaks. This is the same classification rule used by Lilien.

This classification yielded 15 firms in the indirect channel category (17 percent), 39 firms in the mixed channel category (44 percent), and 33 firms in the direct channel category (38 percent). The following multinomial logit model describing the probability that a firm will fall into the ith category was estimated:

$$Prob\ (i/\bar{x}) = \frac{e^{\bar{x}\phi_i}}{\sum_{j=1}^{3} e^{\bar{x}\phi_j}}$$

where $\bar{x}$ is the vector of independent variables describing each firm and ϕ_i is the vector of coefficients associated with the i_{th} category.

Note that there is a set of ϕ_i coefficients associated with each category. Since these coefficients are determined only up to an arbitrary normalization, we have chosen the normalization $\phi_3 = 0$, where $i = 3$ describes the indirect channel. Each set of coefficients can now be interpreted as the effect of the independent variables on the probability of choice of that channel category relative to our chosen reference option (that is, the indirect category).

Table 3 displays the results of a maximum-likelihood estimation of this model. The Chi-square statistic displayed tests the hypothesis that the estimated coefficients (except the constant) are all zero. This is rejected at the 0.05 level.

Examining the significance of the ϕ_1 coefficients, we can see that SPSKILLS is significantly positive ($\phi = 0.187$, $t = 1.56$). Thus, as specific asset levels increase, the probability of using the direct channel increases relative to the probability of using the indirect channel. The environmental uncertainty measure displays a similar effect ($\phi = 1.66$, $t = 2.39$). The behavioral uncertainty measure is also significant in the expected directioin ($\phi = 0.553$, $t = 1.92$).

Turning to the scale-related variables, we see that sales (LNSALES) has no significant effect ($\phi = -0.011$, $t = -0.029$). Territory sparseness displays the anticipated significant negative coefficient, though ($\phi = -0.082$, $t = -1.78$).

As for the ϕ_2 coefficients, which assess the probability of the mixed channel category versus the indirect category, the specific assets coefficient is insignificant ($\phi = 0.097$, $t = 0.82$). The environmental uncertainty measure displays an expected positive coefficient, which is also significant ($\phi = 1.17$, $t = 1.80$). Similarly, the behavioral uncertainty measure displays a signifi-

Table 3. Multinomial Logit Model of Channel Configuration

Dependent variable: Direct, mixed, indirect channels
Reference category: indirect channel

Parameter ($\phi_{i=1}$)	Estimate	T-value
Constant	−4.446	−0.620
SPSKILLS	0.187	1.562*
ENVUNCT	1.660	2.394*
BEHUNCT	0.553	1.922*
LNSALES	−0.011	−0.029
SPARSE	−0.082	−1.781*
Parameter ($\phi_{i=2}$)		
Constant	−6.904	−1.062
SPSKILLS	−0.097	0.820
ENVUNCT	1.167	1.799*
BEHUNCT	0.480	1.686*
LNSALES	0.274	0.809
SPARSE	−0.075	−1.771*

Chi-Square (10 d.f.) = 31.64.
*sig. at $p \leq .05$ (1-tail).

Table 4. Independent Variable Derivatives

Variable	Direct	Mixed	Indirect
Constant	0.506	−0.688	0.182
SPSKILLS	0.023	−0.019	−0.004
ENVUNCT	0.137	−0.093	−0.043
BEHUNCT	0.024	−0.008	−0.016
LNSALES	−0.066	0.071	−0.005
SPARSE	−0.003	0.0003	0.002

cant, positive coefficient ($\phi = 0.48$, $t = 1.69$). The scale variable describing sales volume is insignificant ($\phi = 0.274$, $t = 0.81$), but the territory sparseness measure displays the expected significant negative effect ($\phi = -0.075$, $t = -1.77$).

The substantive results implied by these coefficients are more readily interpreted by examining the estimates in table 4. These estimates are derivatives that show how a change in any of the independent variables would affect the distribution of channel choices. Looking at the results of SPSKILLS, we see that as specific assets increase, the probability of the direct channel increases ($d_1 = 0.023$), while the probability of the mixed channel option decreases ($d_2 = -0.019$) as does the probability of the indirect channel ($d_3 = -0.043$). With respect to environmental uncertainty, increases in this variable result in more direct channels ($d_1 = 0.136$), fewer mixed channels ($d_2 = -0.093$), and fewer indirect channels ($d_3 = -0.043$). Behavioral uncertainty displays a similar pattern of results ($d_1 = 0.024$, $d_2 = -0.008$, $d_3 = -0.016$).

Turning to the scale variable, we find that larger volumes decrease direct channels (d_1 = −0.066), increase mixed channels (d_2 = 0.071), and decrease indirect channels (d_3 = −0.004). These effects are not statistically significant, though. With respect to territory density, we see that increased sparseness decreases direct channels (d_1 = −0.0028) but increases mixed channels (d_2 = 0.003) and indirect channels (d_3 = −0.002).

Taken together, the results of the two models are remarkably consistent. They increase our confidence in the robustness of the effects found in the data. Specific assets and uncertainty consistently increased the use of direct channels. As for the scale variables, territory sparseness consistently decreased direct channel use, while the sales volume measure had no effect in either model.

6. DISCUSSION

To the best of our knowledge, this is the first empirical test of TCA predictions involving forward integration into distribution. Aside from Anderson's study of manufacturers' agents versus employee sales forces, no other empirical results concerning downstream integration have been reported. The results obtained here are supportive of the basic refutable predictions made form the TCA perspective. We saw that firms were less likely to use reseller channels when specific assets levels were higher. Similar shifts were observed for higher levels of environmental uncertainty and behavioral uncertainty.

Our study has several methodological and theoretical implications. From a methodological standpoint, it is the first study that has accounted for the possibility that firms do not use a single means of reaching the end-user. Integration is a matter of degree rather than a binary choice. Along these lines, Stinchcombe has argued persuasively that the continuous nature of these shifts should not be underestimated. In fact, his analysis would suggest an even more microanalytic approach with explicit measures of the actual hierarchical mechanisms involved.

The design of an empirical test of TCA predictions rests on developing sufficient information about the institutional forms present in the context of interest. It would appear that empirical studies of TCA propositions are best conducted at a semi-microanalytic level of detail. Accounting data are probably unlikely to suit the needs of such research. Rather, researchers will have to rely on the organizational and sociological tradition of using questionnaires and rating scale data. Large sample sizes and "representative" selection have to be sacrificed in order to obtain the requisite detailed information. Consequently, it becomes important to cumulate results across a series of smaller studies.

From the standpoint of theory development, we have already noted that the basic refutable propositions of the TCA approach are supported in this study. Nevertheless, the causal mechanisms underlying these results still await direct testing. For instance, it is presumed that the firm's response to environmental uncertainty is prompted by the desire to make decision adaptively and sequentially. No direct evidence of this mechanism is currently available in the literature. Similarly, the effects of specific assets on the integration decision is presumed to be a reaction to the firm's vulnerability to opportunism. If, however, an exchange were governed by a norm of non-opportunism, then the model would become much more complex. Integration would presumably be a response only if the normative restraint were inadequate. Such an extension of the basic model rests on uncovering the conditions governing the appearance and maintenance of such normative restraints on opportunism.

Finally, with respect to the variables relating to the production cost, the present results contrast with the only other previous study that included production costs (Walker and Weber). They concluded that "comparative production costs" were responsible for most of the explanatory power of their model. Further, transaction costs variables received only "mixed" support in their study.

By contrast, the transaction cost variables were responsible for most of the explanatory power of the current models. Only one of the two production cost variables proved significant. One reason for insignificant results involving the sales volume measure of scale may be due to variance in the minimum efficient scale (MES) of distribution-related activities across the industries represented in our sample. Since we do not have a measure of minimum efficient scale to adjust the sales variable, our measure must be viewed with some skepticism. This possibility appears even more likely when one considers the significant supportive results obtained with the other scale variable. Unlike sales volume, the territory sparseness measure is not affected by interindustry differences in efficient scale. Time spent traveling is always an unproductive use of resources. On balance, it appears that both production and transaction costs are implicated in firms' decisions to integrate into the downstream channel. Nevertheless, the differences in results between the two studies suggest that further attention needs to be directed to the role of production costs in TCA models.

APPENDIX

Computing an average rating for five items described in section 4.7 to form the ENVUNCT measure assumes that these data are scaled intervally. Although this assumption has been used in the previous empirical studies of TCA propositions involving questionnaire data (Anderson and Schmittlien; Walker and Weber) and is standard practice in many disciplines, it is sometimes argued that rating scales provide only rank-order data. In order to assess the robustness of our results with respect to this assumption, an alternative measurement model was fitted and the vertical integration models were reestimated. This alternative was the Rasch latent trait model described by Wright and Stone.

Rather than assuming that the observed responses are intervally scaled, the Rasch model assumes that the probability of a response to a rating scale item i is a function of the amount of the trait β_j presents in the subject j and a parameter δ_i that indexes the amount of the trait reflected in the item.

Specifically,

$$Prob[x_{ji} = 1 \mid \beta_j, \delta_i] = exp(\beta_j - \delta_i)/[1 + exp(\beta_j - \delta_i)]$$

where $x_{ji} = 1$ when subject j responds favorably, and
0 when subject j responds unfavorably to item i.

Using a maximum-likelihood estimator (Wilkinson), one can obtain estimates of the amount of the trait present in each subject from the observed responses of all the subjects to all the items. These estimates of the trait are scaled intervally although the observed data are only categorical.

To apply this model to our data, we first dichotomize the responses to each of the five items. Responses above the midpoint on the scale were given the value 1 while responses below the midpoint were coded as 0. These represent the high and low uncertainty categories of responses. Then maximum likelihood estimates of the latent trait being measured were obtained for each subject. The resulting intervally scaled estimate of the trait for each subject β_j was used in place of the previously used measure (ENVUNCT) in the regression and multinomial logit models.

These reestimated models show no substantive differences compared to the originally estimated models shown in tables 2 and 3. All previously significant variables remain significant and retain their sign. Likewise, all previously insignificant variables remain insignificant. Thus, it appears that our assumption of interval data arising from the rating scale items does not affect the conclusions drawn from the study.

REFERENCES

Anderson, Erin. 1985. "The Salesperson as Outside Agent or Employee: A Transaction Cost Analysis," 4 *Marketing Science* 234–54.

Anderson, Erin, and David Schmittlein. 1984. "Integration of the Sales Force: An Empirical Investigation," 15 *Rand Journal of Economics* 385–95.

Anderson, Erin, and Benton Weitz. 1986. "Make or Buy Decisions: Vertical Integration and Marketing Productivity," 27 *Sloan Management Review* 3–20.

Arrow, Kenneth. 1969. "The Organization of Economic Activity: Issues Pertinent to the Choice of Market Versus Nonmarket Allocation," in *The Analysis and Evaluation of Public Expenditure: The PPB System*. Vol. 1. U.S. Joint Economic

Committee, 91st Cong., 1st Sess., Washington, D.C.: U.S. Government Printing Office 59–73.

———. 1971. *Essays in the Theory of Risk-Bearing*. Chicago: Markham.

Blair, Richard, and David Kaserman. 1983. *Law and Economics of Vertical Integration and Control*. New York: Academic Press.

Chandler, Alfred. 1977. *The Visible Hand: The Managerial Revolution in American Business*. Cambridge: Harvard University Press.

Churchill, Gilbert. 1979. "A Paradigm for Developing Better Measures of Marketing Constructs," 16 *Journal of Marketing Research* 64–73.

Coughlan, Anne. 1985. "Competition and Cooperation in Marketing Channel Choice: Theory and Application," 4 *Marketing Science* 110–29.

Diamond, William. 1963. *Distribution Channels for Industrial Goods*. Columbus: Ohio State University.

Green, Jerry. 1984. "Information in Economics," in K. Arrow and S. Honkapohja, eds., *Frontiers of Economics*. London: Basil Blackwell.

Haas, Robert. 1976. *Industrial Marketing Management*. New York: Petrocelli / Charter.

Heide, Jan, and George John. 1988. "The Role of Dependence Balancing in Safeguarding Transaction-Specific Assets in Conventional Channels," 52 *Journal of Marketing* 20–35.

Jackson, Barbara Bund. 1985. *Winning and Keeping Industrial Customers: The Dynamics of Customer Relationships*. Lexington, Mass.: Lexington Books.

John, George, and Torger Reve. 1982. "The Reliability and Validity of Key Informant Data from Dyadic Relationships in Marketing Channels," 19 *Journal of Marketing Research* 517–24.

Joskow, Paul. 1988. "Asset Specificity and the Structure of Vertical Relationships: Empirical Evidence," 4 *Journal of Law, Economics, and Organization* 95–117.

Lilien, Gary. 1979. "ADVISOR 2: Modeling the Marketing Mix Decision for Industrial Products," 25 *Management Science* 191–204.

Masten, Scott. 1984. "The Organization of Production: Evidence from the Aerospace Industry," 27 *Journal of Law and Economics* 403–18.

Monteverde, Kirk, and D. Teece. 1982. "Supplier Switching Costs and Vertical Integration in the Automobile Industry," 13 *Bell Journal of Economics* 206–13.

Palay, Thomas. 1984. "Comparative Institutional Economics: The Governance of Rail Freight Contracting," 13 *Journal of Legal Studies* 265–88.

Shapiro, Benson. 1977. *Sales Program Management: Formulation and Implementation*. New York: McGraw-Hill.

Stern, Louis, and Adel El-Ansary. 1982. *Marketing Channels*. Second Edition. Englewood Cliffs, N.J.: Prentice-Hall.

Stinchcombe, Arthur. 1985. "Contracts as Hierarchical Documents," in *Organization Theory and Project Management*, A. L. Stinchcombe and C. A. Heimer. Oslo: Norwegian University Press.

Stuckey, John. 1983. *Vertical Integration and Joint Ventures in the Aluminum Industry*. Cambridge: Harvard University Press.

Sutton, Harold. 1986. *Rethinking the Company's Selling and Distribution Channels*. Report No. 885. Conference Board.

U.S. Bureau of the Census 1980. *1977 Census of Wholesale Trade*. Geographic Area Services, Report No. WC77–A–52.

Walker, Gordon, and David Weber. 1984. "A Transaction Cost Approach in Make-or-Buy Decisions," 29 *Administrative Science Quarterly* 373–91.

Wilkinson, Leland. 1986. *SYSTAT: The System for Statistics*. Evanston, Ill.: SYSTAT.

Williamson, Oliver. 1979. "Transaction Cost Economics: The Governance of Contractual Relations," 22 *Journal of Law and Economics* 233–62.

———. 1985. *The Economic Institutions of Capitalism: Firms, Markets, Relational Contracting*. New York: Free Press.

Wright, Benjamin, and Michael Stone. 1979. *Best Test Design: Rasch Measurement*. Chicago: MESA Press.

[7]

The Costs of Organization

Scott E. Masten
University of Michigan

James W. Meehan, Jr.
Colby College

Edward A. Snyder
University of Michigan

1. Introduction

The tenet to which all transaction-cost economists subscribe is that the choice among alternative organizational arrangements turns on a comparison of the costs of transacting under each. To impart empirical content to this fundamental insight, theorists began to relate the incidence of transaction costs to observable attributes of transactions (Williamson, 1975, 1979; Klein et al.). These efforts, however, concentrated on factors aggravating the hazards of market exchange. By contrast, the limitations of internal organization have been treated primarily as a barrier to be overcome before integration would occur.

Although the empirical research to date has been generally supportive of the central transaction-cost propositions,[1] recognition that variations in internal organization costs may also play a role in the decision to integrate exposes an inherent weakness in the nature of these tests. Because of difficulties in observing and measuring transaction costs, analysts have had to rely on es-

We would like to extend our thanks for helpful comments to Keith Crocker, Alvin Klevorick, Ingo Vogelsang, Oliver Williamson, Bernard Yeung, and participants at seminars at Berkeley, UCLA, the University of Michigan, and the Antitrust Division of the U.S. Department of Justice, and at an NBER conference on Topics in Industrial Organization. We gratefully acknowledge the cooperation of Bath Iron Works and thank Mark McAliffe, Phil Nein, Don Spann, and Junius Brown for their cooperation in providing data. Jim Bohn provided excellent research assistance. The University of Michigan School of Business Administration and Colby College provided partial financial support.

1. See Williamson (1985) and Joskow for overviews of this literature.

 ISSN 8756-6222

timations of reduced-form relationships between observed characteristics and organizational forms. As we explain below, such indirect tests are unable to distinguish whether observed patterns of organization resulted from hypothesized changes in market transaction costs or from systematic, but as yet unexplored, variations in the costs incurred organizing production internally.

In this article, we give explicit attention to the role of internal organization costs in integration decisions and identify ways of overcoming the difficulties inhibiting direct tests of transaction-cost arguments. In particular, we show how econometric methods developed elsewhere can be used to reduce the information problems associated with estimating models of economic organization. We then apply these methods to analyze the organization of a sample of components from a large naval construction project. The nature of our data and the application of censored regression techniques permit us, unlike earlier empirical studies of integration decisions, to isolate the effects of attributes of transactions on the costs of organizing within and between firms and to provide dollar estimates of those costs.

Our results indicate that overall organization costs represent about 14 percent of total costs for the components and activities in our sample. Moreover, we find that these costs vary systematically with the nature of the transaction and that the savings from choosing organizational arrangements selectively can be substantial. Mistaken integration of the typical subcontracted component in our sample, for instance, would increase organization costs by approximately 70 percent, while subcontracting work currently performed inside the firm would, on average, generate market organization costs almost three times those incurred managing that work internally.

But the broader implications of the study lie in our findings regarding the relative contribution of variations in internal and market organization costs to the integration decision. Specifically, we find that the costs of dealing across a market interface, and hence the incentive to integrate, rise the greater the potential for holdups in a given transaction, as recent theorists have argued. In addition, however, the evidence indicates that variations in the level of internal organization costs also play an important role in integration decisions. Indeed, the importance of internal organization costs in our results leads us to reassess some of the earlier empirical literature on the determinants of vertical integration.

2. Conceptual Issues

2.1 The Form and Estimation of Transaction-Cost Arguments

2.1.1 A Tautological Formulation. The maintained hypothesis underlying transaction-cost analyses of organization form is that transactors choose organizational arrangements to minimize the expected costs of governing the transaction over the life of the relationship.[2] If we let I^* signify the institution

2. Governance or organization costs should be broadly construed to include both direct costs of conducting exchange and any corresponding inefficiencies in production or allocation as a result of these costs.

chosen, a representative model of the choice between two institutions—typically internal organization (I^o) and market exchange (I^m)—would be

$$I^* = \begin{cases} I^o, & \text{if } G^o < G^m, \\ I^m, & \text{if } G^o \geq G^m, \end{cases} \tag{1}$$

where G^o and G^m represent the costs of organizing under the corresponding alternative.

Analyses of organizational form requiring direct comparisons of the costs of transacting have been subject to criticism, however, on the grounds that such costs are difficult to observe and measure. Many hazards of exchange, such as inflexibility in response to changing circumstances or the need to litigate performance, are either implicit or latent to the transaction. And others, such as the increased demands placed on a manager's, regulator's, or judge's attention by bringing an additional transaction under his purview, or the losses due to withholding of information by either employees or subcontractors, while manifest, are often difficult to quantify.

In addition, attempts to compare the costs of organization must confront a basic selection problem: organization costs cannot be directly observed for organizational forms not chosen. Thus, even if the costs associated with internal administration could be adequately measured for supplies procured internally, the costs that would have occurred had the same supplies been acquired externally under, say, a long-term contract would not, by virtue of the integration decision itself, be observable. At best, one observes costs for the institution chosen so that direct comparisons with costs of alternative institutions are impossible. As a consequence, early claims that observed institutions minimize transaction costs were easy to make and impossible to refute.

2.1.2 Reduced-Form Analysis. To address this criticism, transaction-cost theorists began to relate the incidence of transaction costs to observable characteristics of the transaction and then base predictions of organizational form on those observed features.[3] Thus, suppose the true costs of organization are

$$G^o = \alpha X + e, \tag{2}$$

$$G^m = \beta Z + u, \tag{3}$$

where X and Z are vectors of attributes thought to influence the respective organization costs, α and β are coefficient vectors, and e and u are normally distributed random variables. After substituting into Equation (1), the probability of observing institution I^o becomes $\Pr(G^o < G^m) = \Pr(e-u < \beta Z-\alpha X)$.

3. An explicit statement of the need for matching institutions with attributes of the transaction can be found in Williamson (1979). Other contributions include Williamson (1975, 1985) and Klein et al.

Hypotheses regarding organization form can then be based on the signs and relative magnitudes of the coefficients α and β, rather than on the costs G^o and G^m.

The resulting model is amenable to qualitative choice estimation techniques such as probit and logit. Examples are previous empirical research on the economics of integration decisions by Monteverde and Teece (1982a), Masten (1984), and Anderson and Schmittlein. Again, the common strategy in each of these studies is to estimate organizational form as a function of observable characteristics such as the degree of asset specificity and the level of uncertainty or complexity associated with the transaction.

Since the coefficients in Equations (2) and (3) relate the exogenous variables to the costs of organization, these parameters have an appealing interpretation as the structure of organization costs underlying the choice among the observed institutions. Resulting estimates from qualitative choice models, however, provide at best only ordinal measures of those costs. The coefficients from a probit estimation, for instance, are the normalized difference between the coefficients of the underlying structural equations, or $(\beta-\alpha)/\sigma$, where σ is the standard deviation of $e - u$. Without independent information about the variance of $e - u$, the structural coefficients of the organization-cost equations can be identified only up to a proportionality factor.

Furthermore, if X and Z share common elements, only the difference between α and β can be identified.[4] Consider, for example, the hypotheses that the costs of market exchange, but not those of internal organization, rise as assets become more specific to a particular transaction. If we let β_k and α_k represent the corresponding coefficients, then it is possible to test the derived hypothesis that $\beta_k - \alpha_k > 0$. However, it is not possible to refute the underlying hypotheses that β_k and α_k are nonnegative. Thus, a finding that higher asset specificity leads to a larger probability of integration could, in principle, obtain even if the hypothesis that asset specificity raises contracting costs were invalid. As a result, existing tests of transaction-cost theories, while generally supportive, have in this sense been relatively weak.

2.1.3 Direct Tests. Stronger tests of the theory, and estimation of the actual costs of organization, are possible only if the measurement problems discussed at the beginning of this section can be resolved. Some now fairly standard econometric techniques can be helpful in this regard. For example, even though the costs associated with institutions not chosen cannot be observed for a particular transaction, the full structure of organization costs can be estimated if we know the selection process and if we can obtain data or proxies for the costs of organizational forms that *are* chosen. Thus, in integration decisions, if firms chose the lower-cost organizational alternative, and we

4. If a characteristic is thought to influence only one cost, then the corresponding coefficient in the other equation is implicitly zero and the numerator of $(\beta-\alpha)/\sigma$ contains only the remaining coefficient.

could observe the transaction costs incurred under the institution adopted, then application of switching regression techniques could provide consistent estimates of the costs of both market and internal organization.[5] The data burden could be further reduced by estimating the structural equations as a censored regression model analogously to the way actual and reservation wages are estimated in labor supply applications.[6] In that case, only cost data for one of the institutions is required. Thus, were G^o but not G^m available, the model would become

$$G = \begin{cases} G^o = \alpha X + e\,, & \text{if } G^o < G^m, \quad (4) \\ G^m = \text{n.a.}, & \text{if } G^o \geq G^m. \quad (5) \end{cases}$$

Consistent estimates of the coefficients of Equations (2) and (3) could then be obtained using either maximum likelihood or two-stage methods as long as either (i) an independent variable in X is not in Z or (ii) the covariance between e and u is 0.[7] In effect, the full set of coefficients is estimated by asking what structure of procurement costs most likely generated the observed pattern of procurement decisions given the observations of G^o and the characteristics of the transactions X and Z.

Generally, the ability to estimate the structural equations of the preceding model would offer two advantages over the reduced-form estimations used in prior research. First, unlike qualitative choice methods, censored regression techniques yield dollar estimates of the costs of organization. Second, while reduced-form models provide evidence about how characteristics of a transaction influence the relative costs of organizing under alternative arrangements, censored regression estimation can identify the magnitude of individual coefficients in the cost equations and therefore permits tests of hypotheses regarding the costs of organizing under each institution.

2.2 Transaction-Cost Differentials

By introducing the prospect of estimating the structural relationships underlying organization decisions, application of censored regression techniques stands to shed light on the issue raised at the outset of this article, namely, whether and to what extent variations in internal rather than market organization costs are responsible for observed variations in organizational form.[8] A

5. See the discussion and references in Maddala (223–8).

6. See Heckman (1980) and Hanoch. In the labor applications, wages are observed only for those who actually work. Nevertheless, one can infer from the decision to work and characteristics of workers the reservation wage schedule that most likely generated the pattern of observed employment given observed wages.

7. See Lee, Nelson, and the discussion in Maddala (228–9).

8. In terms of the model of the preceding section, recent transaction-cost theories have assumed a positive intercept but zero or small coefficients on the explanatory variables in the G^o equation.

prerequisite to conducting such tests, however, is the need to distinguish between the costs of internal and market exchange and then relate the incidence of each to the attributes of transactions in a discriminating way.[9]

As noted previously, recent transaction-cost arguments have tended to emphasize factors exacerbating the hazards of bargaining and incomplete contracting, activities identified most intensively with market organization. According to these arguments, the resources expended attempting to negotiate a favorable distribution of the gains from trade tend to be larger where relationship-specific investments have engendered appropriable quasi-rents (Williamson, 1975, 1979; Klein et al.). Efforts to suppress opportunism contractually, meanwhile, are limited by the costs of writing and enforcing contractual agreements, which rise, in turn, with the complexity and uncertainty associated with the transaction.

Organization within the firm mitigates these problems[10] but, by attenuating the residual claimant status of upstream transactors, sacrifices the high-powered incentive advantages of market exchange and, consequently, demands greater investments in monitoring and administration (Williamson, 1985:70,131–62; 1990). Although the costs associated with these activities present a clear deterrent to integration, theorists have paid scant attention to the factors that influence the level of these costs.

A prominent exception to this generalization is Ronald Coase, who has repeatedly asserted that understanding "the effect of activities in which a firm is already engaged on the cost of undertaking additional activities" is essential to explaining why particular operations are organized within specific firms (1988:40).[11] His own early speculation as to the incidence of those costs was

9. Meeting even the first part of this requirement is not straightforward. The sharp distinction often drawn between internal and market organization costs, while expedient, is artificial. In reality, organization entails a multiplicity of activities independent of the governing institution. Planning, bargaining, contracting, monitoring, enforcing, and so on are common to both internal and market exchange. What the choice of organization form does is influence the allocation of effort across the elements of this list. Hence, perceived differences in the incidence of organization costs within and between firms turn ultimately on one's conception of the nature of the firm—itself a matter of considerable dispute among economists. (For a sampling of opinions on the nature of the firm, see the Spring 1988 issue of this journal celebrating the 50th anniversary of Coase's treatise on the subject.) Inasmuch as our primary purpose in this article is to test received hypotheses, we will not explore these issues in depth. Arguments in support of the distinctions referred to below can be found in Williamson (1985:Chapter 6, 1990), Klein, and Masten (1988).

10. See the references in the note 9.

11. According to Coase,

> The way in which industry is organized is . . . dependent on the relation between the costs of carrying out transactions on the market and the costs of organizing the same operations within that firm which can perform this task at lowest costs. Furthermore, the costs of organizing an activity within any given firm depends on what other activities it is engaged in. A given set of activities will facilitate the carrying out of some activities, but hinder the performance of others. It is these relationships which determine the actual organization of industry. (1972:64)

Others who have argued the importance of internal organization costs are Demsetz, and Alston and Gillespie.

that "[t]he costs of organizing and the losses through mistakes will increase with an increase in the spatial distribution of the transactions organized, in the dissimilarity of the transactions, and in the probability of changes in the relevant prices" (1952:342–3). In other words, internal organization costs are likely to be higher for transactions that are differentiated—by either their location or characteristics—from other activities in which the firm is engaged, and for which there is a greater degree of uncertainty. Supervision and management of employees will be more difficult where managers are unfamiliar with the production process, while more complex or uncertain transactions demand a greater share of management's limited attention and would also tend, therefore, to be more expensive to administer.

Although Coase's predictions regarding the effects of similarity and uncertainty on internal organization costs seem reasonable, predictions about the choice among organizational arrangements require a comparative assessment. Thus, as already noted, complexity and uncertainty aggravate the costs of market exchange, as well as those of internal organization. Indeed, the differential effect of uncertainty and complexity is likely to favor integration over subcontracting: Whereas contracting demands prior anticipation of potential problems, internal organization permits adaptation to changing circumstances as they unfold (Williamson, 1975:25). Hence, higher levels of uncertainty and complexity should lead, on net, to a larger probability of integration.

The similarity of transactions, on the other hand, is unlikely to generate counteracting effects on the costs of market exchange for two reasons. First, parties engaged in bargaining across a market interface care primarily about final outcomes and not the manner in which goods or services are produced. Provided that the attributes of items exchanged can be adequately verified, high-powered incentives relieve the parties of the need for detailed knowledge about the production operations of their trading partners.[12] Second, to the extent that market exchange relies more heavily than internal organization on third-party dispute resolution, the knowledge and experience of judges and juries rather than of the transactors themselves will have a greater impact on the course and cost of litigation. Even if familiarity of the transactors with each others' techniques increases the probability of detecting opportunistic efforts to evade contractual obligations, it may do nothing to improve the prospects of successful enforcement.[13] Consequently, the effect of similarity on the costs of market exchange is likely to be insubstantial.

In Table 1, we summarize the relations between attributes and organization

12. Moreover, independent contractors have formal legal rights only over the results and not over the means by which the work of subcontractors is performed. See, for instance, Masten (1988:186). Notice that acquisition of expertise through hiring of a manager familiar with the relevant processes does not eliminate the added administrative burden incurred when unrelated activities are integrated within the firm; top management's ability to assess the performance of that manager—hence, the quality of the low-powered incentives they can bring to bear on him—will depend on their comprehension of the operations he oversees.

13. In other words, familiarity may help to make performance "observable" to the contracting parties but is unlikely to affect whether or not it is "verifiable" to a third party such as a court.

Table 1. Summary of General Hypotheses

	G^m	G^o	$G^m - G^o$
Transaction specificities	+	(+)	+
Uncertainty/complexity	+	+	+
Similarity of transactions		−	+

costs identified in the preceding discussion. (Parentheses indicate a potential but uncertain influence.) Transaction specificities and uncertainty and complexity tend to aggravate organization problems both between and within firms, but the differential effects consistently favor integration. Familiarity with an operation facilitates monitoring and supervision—activities engaged in most heavily within the firm. Hence, those transactions that are similar to ones in which the firm is already engaged are more likely to be integrated.

3. Naval Shipbuilding: Assets, Attributes, and Operations

In the remainder of this article, we apply the methodology described in Section 2.1 to estimate the structure of organization costs in a specific application, namely, the procurement of components and services by a large naval shipbuilder. Whereas previous empirical research on the determinants of vertical integration has dealt with manufacturing applications, the process of building a ship more closely resembles a construction project. Differences in the nature of construction and manufacturing operations, in turn, influence the circumstances that give rise to opportunism and that determine the level of organization costs more generally. Hence, before turning to the empirical results, we provide some background, first, on distinctive aspects of construction processes in general, and, then, on the nature and costs of naval construction in particular.

3.1 Distinctive Features of Construction Operations

The most salient feature distinguishing construction projects from manufacturing operations is the large, discrete, and immobile nature of the final product.[14] Whereas most manufacturing entails continuous processing of large quantities of products as they move from station to station, construction typically involves erection on site of a single or small number of finished units. This basic distinction underlies a number of differences in the nature of the production processes and assets employed in manufacturing and construction. In manufacturing operations, for instance, the portability of goods in-process means assets can be fixed, while high-volume production often makes specially designed and tooled assets economical. The capital and equipment used in construction, in contrast, are less likely to be specific to a particular transaction. To the extent that each construction project takes place on a

14. The role of mobility in distinguishing goods covered by the Uniform Commercial Code from construction, which is not covered, parallels the distinction made in the text. See Goetz.

unique site, the assets themselves are more likely to be mobile. And because the final product is often unique or produced in limited quantities, construction assets need to be adaptable for use in varying applications. As a result, physical asset specificities are less likely to be important determinants of organizational form in construction than in manufacturing.

The high-volume and continuous nature of most manufacturing operations also makes it possible to hold buffer inventories that absorb fluctuations and permit work to continue at one stage of production when problems arise elsewhere. The unique design and location aspects of construction projects, on the other hand, often limit the ability to hold inventories of work in progress. In such settings, timing and coordination become critical. As Robert Eccles notes, "Coordinating the work of [a large number of] labor specialties over the course of a project is a complex task. At any point in time a number of these specialties will be simultaneously involved on the project and often the work of one cannot proceed until a phase of work has been completed by several others" (337). At these stages, tasks must be strictly ordered for work to proceed. As a result, delays in a key task can have system-wide effects, hindering progress on a group of operations and forcing managers either to wait until the antecedent task has been completed or to uncover an alternative sequence of operations.

Where timely performance is critical, delay becomes a potentially effective strategy for exacting price concessions. Knowing that interruptions at one stage can reverberate throughout the rest of the project, an opportunistic supplier may be tempted to seek a larger share of the gains from trade by threatening to suspend performance at the last minute. Even though the skills and assets necessary to perform the task may be fairly common, the difficulty of identifying and arranging to have an alternative supplier in place on short notice introduces the prospect of strategic holdups. Expanding Williamson's original four-way classification, we refer to this latter source of holdups as *temporal specificity*.[15]

In principle, incentives for prompt performance could be created by specifying appropriate damages. And in fact, performance and installment contracts are common in construction settings (see, for instance, Lee and Png). But, in construction as in other settings, contracting offers only an imperfect solution to the problem of opportunism and is likely to become less attractive as the degree of complexity or uncertainty associated with the transaction increases.[16]

3.2 Determinants of Organization Costs in Naval Shipbuilding

In most critical dimensions, shipbuilding fits the construction model. Although the final product is obviously mobile, the bulk of the vessel is immov-

15. The original four are physical asset specificity, site specificity, human asset specificity, and dedicated assets (Williamson, 1985:55).

16. See, generally, Williamson (1979). Clarkson et al. provide an extended discussion of the limitations of stipulated damages using a construction contract as their principle illustration; see, especially, pp. 368–72.

able during most of its fabrication, requiring that much of the work going into a ship be performed on site. Furthermore, assembly of major subunits and of the ship itself must proceed in a precise order to avoid costly delays.[17] Meanwhile, holding buffer inventories as a safeguard against holdups is made impractical by uncertain demand and the low-volume, nonstandardized nature of many components. As a rule, a naval shipbuilder will have in process no more than a handful of ships and often only one or two ships of a particular class at a point in time. Orders for additional ships depend on the shipyard's performance history, its ability to make competitive bids, and congressional budgeting and allocation. Even for ships under contract, component specifications are often changed during the course of the contract to accommodate technological and military developments.

Moreover, modern naval vessels are complex entities. A navy cruiser, for instance, includes over 1,000,000 feet of cable, some 10,000 valves, and 150,000 feet of pipe. In addition to its basic structure, a ship must contain living quarters for its crew, propulsion and navigation equipment, and sophisticated communications, weapons, and guidance systems. Its military applications make the reliability of these complex systems critically important. Writing contracts with enough precision to assure desired performance but enough flexibility to permit adjustment in component and task specifications as circumstances require can be a formidable challenge.

In contrast to other construction applications, the specialized design of military vessels contributes to fairly high degrees of human asset specificity. Given the complexity of the tasks and the small number of producers of such ships, the skills, knowledge, and experience required of workers often demand extended apprenticeships to develop and may have limited value outside of a specific shipyard. Physical assets used in ship construction, on the other hand, tend to be much less relationship specific. Although some equipment such as cranes and ways—the platforms upon which ships are constructed—are location specific, most of the physical assets used in the construction process tend to be mobile to permit employment at various locations around the ship. And many basic assets, like welding and pipe-fitting equipment, also tend to be of a relatively standardized nature.

Finally, shipbuilding, like other construction operations, mainly involves organizing and coordinating a variety of relatively low-technology, labor-intensive activities associated with the physical fabrication and assembly of the final product. Highly technical, engineering-intensive activities, in contrast, tend to lie outside of a shipbuilder's main area of expertise.

3.3 Hypotheses

In Table 2, we relate the general hypotheses summarized in Table 1 to the particulars of shipbuilding. Again, the traditional transaction-cost arguments

17. An example is the installation of "interbottom piping" that carries fuel and ballast for the ship. These pipes run through the bottom or "tank" of the ship and must be fitted and covered by a layer of plating before successive tasks can be performed. If the work is not complete, subsequent stages of construction are, in the words of the firm's managers, "closed out." Delays at this stage of construction would ripple throughout the entire schedule.

Table 2. Summary of Specific Hypotheses

	G^m	G^o	$G^m - G^o$
Transaction specificities			
Physical asset	(+)		(+)
Human asset	+	(+)	+
Temporal	+	(+)	+
Uncertainty/complexity			
Complexity	+	+	+
Similarity of transactions			
Labor/capital intensity		−	+
Engineering intensity		+	−

regarding the role of relationship-specific investments suggest that both human and physical capital specificities should raise the costs of market organization, although the nature of construction may make physical asset specificities less important in shipbuilding than in other applications. The effects, if any, of these two variables on internal organization costs are expected to be smaller than on the costs of market exchange. There is no a priori reason why relationship-specific physical capital should be harder to manage than standardized assets. And, although integration may only imperfectly limit opportunism associated with relation-specific skills and knowledge embodied in workers, the net effect of human asset specificity on the difference between market and internal organization costs is generally argued to be positive (Williamson, 1975:29–30; Klein).

Of more consequence in this setting is the need for precise scheduling (temporal specificity) that raises the potential for strategic delays and thus the prospective cost of dealing with subcontractors. Scheduling concerns, by further taxing scarce managerial resources, may also raise internal organization costs. But the greater potential for strategic holdups in market transactions should increase the costs of contracting relative to internal organization and thus also increase the probability of integration. Similarly, complexity should also raise the cost both of contracting for required inputs and services and of administering production internally. But again, the differential effect should, for reasons outlined above, favor integration.

Finally, following Coase's argument, the similarity of a particular activity to the firm's primary operations should reduce the cost of managing that activity internally relative to subcontracting. Since shipbuilding primarily involves coordinating a large number of low-technology, labor-intensive tasks, we hypothesize that internal organization costs will be smaller, and thus the likelihood of integration greater, the more labor-intensive and the less engineering-intensive the production process.[18]

18. In other studies (Monteverde and Teece, 1982a; Masten et al.), engineering intensity has been used as a proxy for the amount of transaction-specific knowledge generated in developing a component, which would imply an opposite effect on the probability of integration. In this study, we include a separate measure for human asset specificity that we believe better captures the intended variable. See also the discussion in Section 5.

4. Evidence on the Structure and Costs of Organization in Shipbuilding

4.1 Data

To test the preceding hypotheses, we collected data using a survey design based on previous surveys by Monteverde and Teece (1982a), Masten (1984), and Anderson and Schmittlein. The survey covered a sample of tasks and components from the make-or-buy program of a large, naval shipbuilder and elicited information on each of the variables discussed in Section 3.3 as well as the mode of organization adopted for each component or activity.[19] A team of company officials consisting of the assistant to the vice president for production and the managers of the production planning and purchase specifications departments responded to each item on the survey based on their collective judgement.[20]

Definitions and descriptive details for the variables contained in the data are provided in Table 3. The independent variables corresponding to the hypotheses in Table 2 are based on ordinal rankings of each component relative to others in the production program using a 10-point scale and should be self-explanatory. Our examination of shipbuilding operations also revealed an auxiliary motive for integration not directly related to the transaction-cost hypotheses outlined previously. Given the lumpiness of orders for ships and of the construction process itself, shipbuilders may be unable to utilize skilled employees fully in their primary application for significant periods of time. To occupy these workers until their specialized skills are again needed, a company may integrate production of a variety of components that use related skills and that can be produced during slack periods and stored for later use. As a result, some components that would normally be procured by subcontract, like storage bins and spare parts boxes that require only ordinary sheet metal bending and welding skills, are produced inside the firm to balance the work loads of employees whose main duties are irregularly demanded. To control for this, a dummy variable (LOAD) was included as an indicator of whether a particular component or task had characteristics that would make it suitable for "load leveling."[21]

19. Random selection from a list of components and operations subject to procurement review on a regular basis generated 58 of the observations in the sample (32 make and 26 buy items). Because this list did not cover all aspects of ship production, the sample was supplemented with 16 additional items (11 make and 5 buy) drawn from the production program at large.

20. To gauge the reliability of the responses to the survey, we obtained a second set of responses for each transaction-cost variable from a naval architect who had been previously employed by the shipbuilder. The second respondent provided rankings for 72 of the 74 components in the original sample. The correlations between the two sets of responses for each variable were SCHEDULE, .73; HUMAN, .48; ASSET, .19; COMPLEX, .60; ENGINEER, .53; and LABOR, .45. Although the correlations are positive and significant for all six variables, the particularly low correlation between responses on the physical asset specificity measure suggests a high degree of measurement error for this variable. The advanced positions and greater collective experience of the primary respondents support use of the original data on a priori grounds.

21. Seven of the make and two of the buy items in our sample were identified as potential load levelers. Generally, the characteristics that make a component suitable for load leveling depend on the timing and skill requirements of the contractor and thus depend on the nature of the

In addition to these independent variables, we collected data on organization costs to permit estimation of the structural cost equations as discussed in Section 2.1. The difficulty of acquiring even the minimal information required to identify the censored regression model varies with the nature of the institutions and their costs. The problems of obtaining reasonable data on the costs associated with contracting, for instance, are likely to be severe. First, such costs will generally be incurred by each party to a transaction, so that information must be collected from two (or more) sources. Second, the most acute contractual failures occur only probabalistically over a period of time in the future, which requires that data be collected on the intangible expectations of the decision-makers.

In contrast, the costs of internal organization—expenses associated with activities like planning, directing, and oversight—besides accruing to a single organization, tend to occur in a more routine fashion.[22] Where costs have this nature, actual measurement or formulation of reasonable proxies may be possible. Accordingly, our efforts focused on obtaining data on the costs of internal organization *for those processes and components actually organized within the firm*. Specifically, our measure of the costs of internal organization was constructed as the number of hours devoted by management to planning, directing, and supervising a particular component or process times the average hourly management wage rate.

4.2 Empirical Results

Estimations of the censored structural model represented by Equations (4) and (5) were conducted using a two-stage procedure.[23] In the first stage, we estimated as a probit model the selection decision regarding whether to organize the process internally or to subcontract the work to an outside supplier. The reduced-form estimations at this stage are similar to estimations in earlier empirical studies of integration decisions except for the inclusion of proxies for temporal specificity and similarity.

In the second stage, we estimate the structural equations of the model. This is done, first, by estimating internal organization costs correcting for selectivity using an index constructed from the first-stage results. Estimates of the coefficients in the (unobserved) external organization-cost equation are then, in effect, inferred from the parameters of the probit and internal organization cost estimations. The following subsections report results from each stage of the estimation and present estimates of the dollar costs of organization. Dis-

---

particular project. Nevertheless, such components will tend to use relatively standardized skills and assets and permit flexibility in scheduling.

22. Not all internal organization costs fit this description. To the extent that a portion of the costs of internal organization result from things like labor strikes, which are probabilistic and for which some of the costs accrue to labor rather than the firm, the difficulties associated with measuring contracting costs apply as well to transactions within the firm. See Section 5.

23. See the references in note 7.

14 The Journal of Law, Economics, & Organization, V7 N1

Table 3. Variable Definitions and Descriptive Statistics

MAKE	= 1, if the production of the component or task was organized internally;	43 observations
	= 0, otherwise	31 observations
SCHEDULE	= a ranking of the importance of having the component or performing the task on schedule (median = 6)	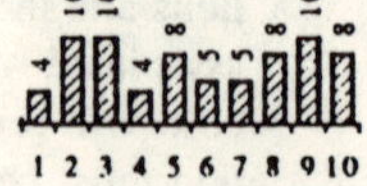
HUMAN	the degree to which skills, knowledge or experience of workers are specific to this application (median = 7)	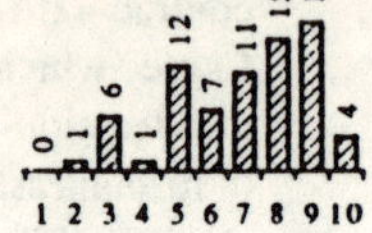
ASSET	= the degree to which facilities and equipment used in the production process are specific to this application (median = 3)	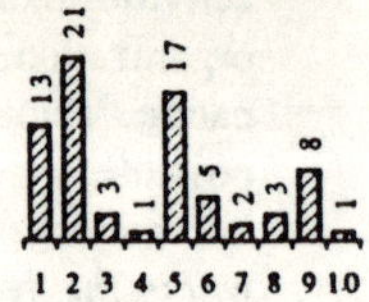
COMPLEX	= a ranking of the complexity of the component or task (median = 3)	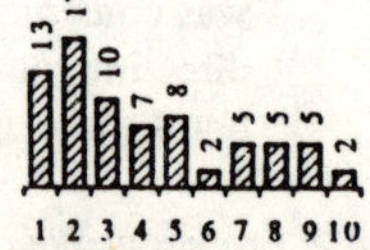
ENGINEER	= a ranking of the amount of engineering effort involved in developing the component (median = 3)	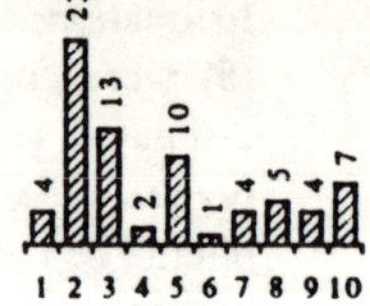
LABOR	= an index of the relative labor/capital intensity of the production process (median = 5)	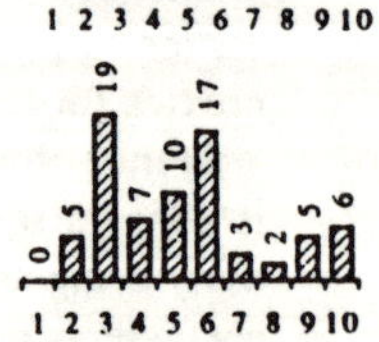
LOAD	= 1, if the component or task had characteristics making it a candidate for load leveling;	9 observations
	= 0, otherwise	65 observations
G^o	= costs of planning, directing, and oversight for integrated tasks or components ≡ (number of management hours × management wage rate)	Mean = \$38,690[a] Std. dev. = \$54,030

Number of observations = 74.

[a]For the 43 make observations.

cussion of the findings and their relationship to prior empirical research is deferred to Section 5.

4.2.1 Probit Estimations of the Make-or-Buy Decision. In Table 4, we present results from three alternative specifications of the selection equation. Column (1) shows results of a probit estimation of the decision to integrate production using only the proxies for specificity and complexity plus the variable LOAD to control for load-leveling concerns. This specification thus emphasizes the factors argued to aggravate market exchange hazards in the recent transaction-cost literature. Of the transaction-specificity variables, the coefficient on SCHEDULE is positive and significant as expected, indicating that production is more likely to be integrated the more critical scheduling of a task is to the project. Contrary to predictions, however, ASSET is significantly negative, while HUMAN is only marginally positive (the coefficient is significant at the .10 level in a one-tail test). Initial estimations indicated an insignificant or

Table 4. Probit Make-or-Buy Estimations

	(1)	(2)	(3)
CONSTANT	0.40531 (0.672)	−3.1229 (−2.720)	−2.5112 (−2.247)
SCHEDULE	0.29222 (3.027)	0.43285 (3.380)	0.37010 (3.031)
HUMAN	0.13899 (1.541)	0.22327 (2.154)	0.19888 (1.998)
ASSET	−0.15051 (−1.981)	−0.08512 (−0.971)	−0.10024 (−1.164)
COMPLEX	−0.75654 (−2.500)	−0.88865 (−2.656)	−0.85055 (−2.613)
$COMPLEX^2$	0.04744 (1.781)	0.06690 (2.218)	0.06291 (2.166)
ENGINEER		−0.18139 (−1.768)	−0.13805 (−1.429)
LABOR		0.42928 (3.754)	0.39893 (3.575)
LOAD	0.85908 (1.451)	1.3955 (1.895)	
χ^2	20.046 (6 d.f.)	37.529 (8 d.f.)	33.296 (7 d.f.)

t-statistics in parentheses $n = 74$.

slightly negative effect of complexity on the integration decision. Specification tests, however, revealed a nonmonotonic effect of complexity on observed organizational arrangements in this setting. Specifically, for relatively simple components, increases in complexity make it less likely that production would be internalized. Beyond some threshold, however, the probability of integration begins to increase as complexity rises. The results suggest that the deficiencies of contracting begin to overcome the administrative burden of internal organization in this industry only for the most complex tasks and components.[24] The effect of LOAD is also positive but only marginally significant.

The specification reported in column (2) incorporates measures reflecting the prediction that similarity favors integration as well as the variables embodying conventional transaction-cost concerns. The coefficients on both LABOR and ENGINEER are significant and support the hypothesis that integration is, in this application, more likely for more labor-intensive and less engineering-intensive activities. With respect to the other transaction-cost variables, the results for both SCHEDULE and COMPLEX are similar to those in column (1). The inclusion of ENGINEER and LABOR, however, alters the estimated effects of human and physical asset specificity. In particular, the coefficient on ASSET becomes insignificantly different from zero and the significance of the coefficient on HUMAN improves substantially.[25] The results also indicate that the firm is more likely to integrate activities that are suitable for use as "load levelers." Overall, the comprehensive model represented by the specification in column (2) predicts the organization form adopted correctly for 64 of the 74 observations in the sample.

Finally, column (3) shows for comparison results of the full model omitting LOAD. Although the results are similar to those in column (2), the exclusion of LOAD weakens the estimated correlations between integration and HUMAN, ENGINEER, and SCHEDULE. Since potential load levelers tend to use relatively standard skills and assets, involve little engineering, and

24. Because of the small sample size and large number of "steps" in the scale used to evaluate the independent variables, the resulting cells have too few observations to permit meaningful estimation using dummy variables for each step. We chose, therefore, to test for nonlinearities by adding quadratic terms for each of the variables both simultaneously and sequentially. We found no evidence that variables other than COMPLEX entered nonlinearly. The quadratic terms for complexity yield a minimum of 8.0 for the specification reported in column (1) and of 6.6 and 6.8 for columns (2) and (3). In the only other study that attempted to measure complexity, Masten (1984) found a lower probability of integration for relatively simple items but no significant difference between highly and moderately complex items. Further investigation of the effects of complexity in the present study revealed that the strength of the observed nonlinearity rests heavily on the 13 observations for which COMPLEX = 1.

25. The predicted effect of omitting ENGINEER and LABOR is consistent with the observed bias in the coefficients on HUMAN and ASSET: Since engineering intensity reduces the probability of integration, omission of ENGINEER, which is positively correlated with both HUMAN and ASSET, would bias the coefficients on HUMAN and ASSET downward. On the other hand, LABOR, which is negatively correlated with HUMAN and ASSET, is expected to increase integration. Hence, its exclusion reinforces this downward bias.

require flexibility in scheduling, the observed changes in the estimated parameters are consistent with the bias that we would expect from omitting this variable.

Overall, this stage of the analysis, which estimates a reduced-form model analogous to those employed in previous transaction-cost studies of integration, supports the proposition that variations in *both* market and internal organization costs influence the organization of economic activity. In particular, the results are consistent with hypotheses regarding (i) the potential for holdups in market transactions fostered, in this setting, by temporal and human asset specificities, and (ii) the costs of managing dissimilar, and, hence, unfamiliar activities within the firm.[26] But, as previously noted, the inability to identify the underlying cost structures using a reduced-form model tempers the strength of these conclusions.

4.2.2 Organization-Cost Estimates. In contrast to earlier studies, our data on internal organization costs permit us to estimate both the structural organization-cost equations and dollar costs of organization. Using the sample of integrated components, we estimated the coefficients for the internal organization-cost equation by regressing our measure of internal organization costs against each of the independent variables (with the exception of LOAD[27]) and a selection correction factor constructed from the probit results reported in column (3) of Table 4. Specifically, the organization-cost equations include the inverse Mills ratio $\lambda = f(z)/F(z)$, where z is the estimated value from the probit equation and f and F are the standard normal density and distribution functions, respectively.

Columns (1) and (2) of Table 5 report estimates of the coefficients for both linear and log specifications of the internal organization-cost equations.[28] The log specification has the advantage of constraining organization costs to be positive and provides a substantially better fit to the data. Despite the small sample size (only 43 "make" observations), both equations provide remarkably good estimates. As in the probit equations, complexity appears to have a nonmonotonic affect in the internal organization-cost equations, peaking at a value of approximately 5.3 in both specifications. The coefficient on SCHEDULE is not significant, indicating that the principal effect of SCHEDULE on

26. Davidson and McFetridge (1984, 1985) also employ a measure of similarity in their studies of technology transfer modes. Although their measure is different from ours, they find similar results with respect to the effects of similarity on the incentive to integrate.

27. The hypothesis that load-leveling activities are not more or less costly to manage than other activities is supported by the data. Inclusion of all eight independent variables in the organization-cost equation causes the estimated correlation coefficient between the errors in the selection and structural equations to exceed its logical upper bound, which causes problems in the correction of the standard errors for the endogeneity of the selection criterion. This is a fairly common problem with small samples such as the present one.

28. The internal organization-cost equations were estimated using LIMDEP version 5.1. The standard errors for these equations are corrected for both heteroskedasticity and the endogeneity of the selection correction index.

Table 5. Costs of Organization

	(1)	(2)	(3)	(4)
			$\ln(G^m)$	
	G^o	$\ln(G^o)$	$\beta_6, \beta_7 = 0$	$\sigma_{ou} = 0$
CONSTANT	61,458.1	10.3623	7.4009	6.4492
	(0.856)	(7.080)	(3.656)	(5.704)
SCHEDULE	−286.998	0.12453	0.59400	0.68817
	(−0.049)	(1.058)	(4.216)	(4.010)
HUMAN	−10,933.9	−0.18772	0.04874	0.10301
	(−2.443)	(−2.104)	(0.484)	(0.715)
ASSET	1494.09	−0.01961	−0.12173	−0.13045
	(0.404)	(−0.256)	(−1.421)	(−1.777)
COMPLEX	32,029.2	0.91355	−0.01618	−0.24362
	(1.853)	(2.615)	(−0.043)	(−0.563)
$COMPLEX^2$	−2995.95	−0.08630	−0.01374	0.00081
	(−2.027)	(−2.874)	(−0.420)	(0.023)
ENGINEER	13,491.4	0.25686		0.02066
	(3.765)	(3.592)		(0.192)
LABOR	−10,161.4	−0.40561		0.15339
	(−1.375)	(−2.652)		(0.809)
LAMBDA	−45,229.2	−0.63044		
	(−1.550)	(−1.068)		
$F(8, 34)$	5.2208	10.7124		
R^2	0.55125	0.71596		

t-statistics in parentheses.

the integration decision derives from the hazards of market exchange (see next paragraph). The degree of physical asset specificity also has no effect on the costs of internal organization, as expected. Contrary to expectations, however, HUMAN has a negative coefficient in these equations, suggesting that workers with more specific skills are less costly to manage. Finally, organization costs for this firm appear to be lower the more labor-intensive the process and the less engineering effort associated with the component, as the "Coase hypothesis" predicts.

The coefficients for the contracting cost equation corresponding to the log organization-cost estimates in column (2) are derived under two alternative assumptions: first, that the variables ENGINEER and LABOR affect only the costs of internal organization [column (3)]; and, second, that the errors in the internal organization cost and contracting cost equations are independent [column (4)].[29] The results under both assumptions are similar. Specifically, the coefficient on SCHEDULE is highly significant in both equations, indicating that scheduling concerns substantially increase the costs of contractual exchange in this application. Of the other traditional transaction-cost variables, only the physical asset specificity measure has a statistically significant influence on contracting costs, exhibiting a moderately significant, negative coefficient, contrary to hypothesis. The effect of ASSET on market organization costs, however, is not significantly different from its effect on those of internal organization, as indicated by the probit results. Finally, as predicted, the similarity measures ENGINEER and LABOR have no significant effect on contracting costs.

The second-stage results confirm the predictions of the theory and the findings of the first-stage selection estimation with regard to the effects of temporal specificity and the similarity of transactions. In particular, scheduling concerns raise the probability of integration by increasing the hazards of market exchange, while similarity fosters integration through its effects on internal organization costs. Complexity also exhibits a nonmonotonic effect on administrative costs that, although unanticipated, is consistent with the influence of this variable on the selection decision found in the first-stage estimates.[30] Finally, the second-stage estimates indicate that the correlation between human asset specificity and the likelihood of integration found in the first stage is a consequence of a decrease in internal organization costs rather than the increase in the costs of market exchange that the theory predicts. Hence, this result illustrates the hazards of relying on estimates from reduced-form models of economic organization.[31]

29. Intuitively, the coefficients for the market organization-cost equation, β, are found by substituting estimates of the coefficients from the internal organization-cost estimation, α, and of the covariance of e and u, σ, into the expression for the probit equation coefficients, $(\beta-\alpha)/\sigma$. See Hanoch, and Maddala (228–9, 252–5) for descriptions of the procedures used to calculate the coefficients and standard errors for these equations.

30. The second-stage findings with regard to complexity are in fact more troubling than those of the first stage. Although the nonmonotonic effect of complexity on the probability of integration would be consistent with a strictly positive, concave internal organization-cost equation and a strictly positive, convex market organization-cost equation, the nonmonotonicity in the internal organization-cost equation suggests a measurement or specification problem. The data, for instance, do not distinguish between product and process complexity, even though some of the items in the sample are more aptly classified as tasks than components. Other results, however, are robust to both omission and changes in specification of the complexity measure.

31. A possible explanation for the negative coefficient on HUMAN in the internal organization-cost equation is that relationship-specific human assets create a hostage that fosters cooperation by employees. Alternatively, skilled workers, whether their skills are general or specific, may require less oversight and supervision. If true, the latter would argue for including measures of both general and specific skill requirements in future empirical work. Neither of these explanations, however, can explain the differential effect of HUMAN on internal and market organization costs revealed in the probit selection estimation.

4.2.3 Estimated Organization Costs. Since the independent variables employed in this study are all ordinal in value, there is no natural interpretation of the coefficients in the second-stage equations. However, the structural equations can be used to estimate the costs of organization for each component given its attributes. In Table 6, we present estimated costs of organization for the 74 components in the sample. The first row shows the total estimated organization costs for these components given the organization form actually adopted. The estimated organization costs for the entire sample are \$3.6 million, which represents approximately 14 percent of the total value (\$25.8 million) of these components. This figure is 13 percent for the make items and 17 percent for those bought from outside suppliers. Note also that the estimated organization costs would rise substantially if all items were required to be either made internally or subcontracted, as indicated by the second and thirds rows of Table 6. The costs of organization for the 43 make items would rise from \$1.86 million to \$5.43 million, or from an average of \$43 thousand to \$126 thousand, were production of these components subcontracted. Integrating the "buy" items, on the other hand, increases estimated organization costs for the typical component by about 70 percent.[32] By this measure, the savings from selective organization appear to be substantial.

5. Discussion

In the preceding, we have applied fairly common econometric techniques and a new data set to advance the study of the determinants of organizational form and to estimate dollar costs of organization. The results support some but not all of the standard transaction-cost arguments. One of the principal findings is that temporal specificity can be a major determinant of organization form in some settings. The results consistently indicate that the prospect of holdups where the timing of performance is critical represents a significant hazard of contractual exchange in construction projects and increases the likelihood of integrating the corresponding activities.

Although generalization of this finding to other industries is hazardous, the literature suggests at least two other settings in which timing issues are important. Klein et al., in explaining why newspaper publishers tend to own their own presses while book publishers do not, observe that relative to newspapers, books are "planned further ahead in time and can be economically released with less haste. . . . No press is specialized to one publisher, in part because speed in publication and distribution to readers are generally far less important for books than newspapers, and therefore appropriable quasi rents are not created" (301, n. 6). Expropriation hazards associated with the need for prompt performance are also important in Edward Gallick's discussion of

32. No particular significance should be attributed to the asymmetries between the figures for organization costs as a percent of production costs or for the costs of mistaken integration, which would obviously be sensitive to the distribution of transactions in the sample.

Table 6. Estimated Organization Costs

	Make Items (n = 43)	Buy Items (n = 31)	Total (n = 74)
Estimated costs	$1,863,620	$1,717,710	$3,581,330
Costs if all components made internally	1,863,620	2,945,930	4,809,260
Costs if all components subcontracted	5,435,200	1,717,710	7,155,060

the organization of tuna fishing and processing where perishability issues are prominent.

Our results also provide evidence that integration becomes more likely in the presence of relationship-specific human capital and for at least very complex components. However, the organization-cost estimations indicate that this incentive to integrate arises primarily from the effects of these two variables on the costs of *internal* organization rather than on the costs of market exchange as the theory suggests. Furthermore, complexity has an unexpected nonmonotonic affect on both internal organization costs and the probability of integration, initially increasing and then decreasing the costs of organizing within the firm, with opposite effects on the likelihood that a transaction will be integrated. Fully satisfactory explanations for these findings are elusive.

The effects of physical asset specificity on both organization costs and integration vary across specifications of the equations. If anything, there is a weak indication that the need to employ relationship-specific physical assets reduces the costs of governing exchange through contracts in this setting. This finding may be somewhat less surprising in light of recent theory and evidence suggesting that problems associated with relationship-specific physical investments can be adequately dealt with via "quasi-integration," that is, the retention of title to specialized equipment by the prime contractor.[33] In fact, taking title to specialized tooling is a common practice in defense procurement (Masten, 1984).

Finally, the results of the probit estimations indicate that the particular firm we studied is less likely to integrate engineering-intensive activities and more likely to internalize labor-intensive ones. Our interpretation of these results is that the costs of internal organization are likely to be greater (both absolutely and relative to market organization costs) for activities outside of the firm's main area of expertise. Since management in construction settings largely specializes in administering the activities of diverse labor specialties focused on fabrication and assembly of a basic structure (in this case a ship), a

33. See Monteverde and Teece (1982b), and Masten et al. and cites therein.

construction firm is likely to find it easier to manage relatively low-technology, labor-intensive activities similar to its main line of business. The results of the structural equation estimations further support this interpretation. Specifically, ENGINEER and LABOR affect the costs of monitoring and supervising operations internally but not the hazards of market exchange.

Taken at face value, these results have a number of interesting implications.[34] First, while transaction-cost theory has emphasized the ways in which attributes of the transaction influence costs of market or contractual exchange (for which the probit results are supportive), the independent variables in our estimations, with the exception of SCHEDULE, have their principal influence on the costs of *internal* organization. This both illustrates the hazards of testing transaction-cost hypotheses using reduced-form equations and argues that greater attention should be paid to the determinants of internal organization costs as Ronald Coase has long contended.

Second, the findings regarding the effects of engineering effort on the integration decision raise questions about the interpretation of this variable in previous studies. Both Monteverde and Teece (1982a) and Masten et al. regard the positive effect of engineering effort on the decision to integrate production in the U.S. automobile industry as evidence that transaction-specific know-how generated in the process of developing new products creates quasi-rents that favor integration. Not only do the data in this study reveal no evident concern about appropriability problems associated with contracting for products embodying heavy doses of engineering know-how, but contracting actually becomes more likely as a component's engineering content increases. Given these results, the possibility must be considered that U.S. auto firms have developed over the years an expertise in managing engineering-intensive activities that reduce the costs of organizing the production of associated components internally and that the decision to integrate those components reflects more this proficiency in management than changes in the potential for holdups.

The importance of scheduling and load-leveling concerns and the effects of the engineering- and labor-intensity variables also underscore the need to know the industry being studied. Although the conditions of bounded rationality and opportunism may be universal, the factors that influence their incidence are likely to vary from one industry to another. As a result, it is almost imperative that case study techniques be combined with more formal-empirical analysis.

On a policy level, the cost estimates suggest that changes in regulations or legal rules that alter the nature of institutional arrangements can have significant efficiency implications. A change in legal rules that makes employees more like independent contractors, for instance, could, according to our results, more than double the cost of organizing those agents. The results also

34. Important qualifications regarding the robustness and generality of these conclusions follow.

provide a basis to assess the potential cost of antitrust prohibitions of meritorious vertical mergers.

However, in weighing these results, several caveats are in order. The present study was conducted with a small number of observations from a single firm in a fairly idiosyncratic industry. The complexity of the production process and scheduling issues may imply a disproportionate and atypical role for internal organization-cost considerations in construction settings. In addition to the construction aspects of shipbuilding, the organization of production in this application may also be influenced by government defense acquisition regulations (see Masten, 1984). Furthermore, since only data on internal organization costs were available, the burden of estimating both the internal and market organization-cost equations rests heavily on the 43 observations for the integrated components.

The cost equation estimates also depend critically on our internal organization-cost measure. To the extent that we miss important costs that are systematically related to one or more of the independent variables, our results will be biased. Thus, the negative correlation between organization costs and the amount of human asset specificity might result, for example, if union organization of skilled workers substituted in part for management organization or if costs associated with collective bargaining were split between employees and management. These costs (which might emerge as higher employee wages) and others of a similar nature would not be measured as part of organization costs in our data.

More generally, allowances must be made for the quality of the data used in both this and earlier studies of integration decisions. The independent variables employed in these studies have almost all been qualitative and are typically imprecise proxies for the variables of true interest. Results both supporting and opposing received theory may say more about the quality of the data than the validity of the theory. There is obviously a need both for refinement of these proxies and for new quantitative measures that permit cross-firm and cross-industry comparisons.

Given the idiosyncracies of shipbuilding and the limitations of the data, a recommendation that we redirect our research efforts toward improving our understanding of the nature and sources of internal organization costs would be premature. Nevertheless, the surprising importance of internal organization costs in this first attempt to distinguish their influence from that of market transaction costs suggests that analyses of integration decisions be broadened to encompass variations in costs of organizing within, as well as between, firms. Unfortunately, checking hypotheses against actual behavior poses a serious challenge, given the obstacles to obtaining even the limited quantity and types of data employed here.

References

Alston, Lee, and William Gillespie. 1989. "Resource Coordination and Transaction Costs: A Framework for Analyzing the Firm/Market Boundary," 11 *Journal of Economic Behavior and Organization* 191–212.

Anderson, Erin, and David Schmittlein. 1984. "Integration of the Sales Force: An Empirical Examination," 15 *Rand Journal of Economics* 385–95.

Clarkson, Kenneth, Roger Miller, and Timothy Muris. 1978. "Liquidated Damages v. Penalties: Sense or Nonsense?" 1978 *Wisconsin Law Review* 351–90.

Coase, Ronald. 1937 (1952). "The Nature of the Firm," 4 *Economica N.S.* 386–405 (reprinted in G. J. Stigler and K. E. Boulding, eds., *Readings in Price Theory*. Homewood, Ill.: Richard D. Irwin).

———. 1972. "Industrial Organization: A Proposal for Research," in V. R. Fuchs, ed., *Policy Issues and Research Opportunities in Industrial Organization*. New York: National Bureau of Economic Research.

———. 1988. "The Nature of the Firm: Origin, Meaning, Influence," 4 *Journal of Law, Economics, and Organization* 3–47.

Davidson, W. H., and Donald McFetridge. 1984. "International Technology Transactions and the Theory of the Firm," 32 *Journal of Industrial Economics* 253–64.

———, and ———. 1985. "Key Characteristics in the Choice of International Technology Transfer Mode," *Journal of International Business Studies* 5–21.

Demsetz, Harold. 1988. "The Theory of the Firm Revisited," 4 *Journal of Law, Economics, and Organization* 141–61.

Eccles, Robert. 1981. "The Quasifirm in the Construction Industry," 2 *Journal of Economic Behavior and Organization* 335–57.

Gallick, Edward. 1984. *Exclusive Dealing and Vertical Integration: The Efficiency of Contracts in the Tuna Industry*. Bureau of Economics Staff Report to the Federal Trade Commission.

Goetz, Charles. 1990. "Contagion and Quarantine among Contractual Regimes: A Code in the Node," working paper, University of Virginia Law School.

Hanoch, Giora. 1980. "A Multivariate Model of Labor Supply: Methodology and Estimation," in James P. Smith, ed., *Female Labor Supply: Theory and Estimation*. Princeton, N.J.: Princeton University Press.

Heckman, James. 1979. "Sample Selection Bias as a Specification Error," 47 *Econometrica* 153–61.

———. 1980. "Sample Selection Bias as a Specification Error with an Application to the Estimation of Labor Supply Functions," in James P. Smith, ed., *Female Labor Supply: Theory and Estimation*. Princeton, N.J.: Princeton University Press.

Joskow, Paul. 1988. "Asset Specificity and the Structure of Vertical Relationships: Empirical Evidence," 4 *Journal of Law, Economics, and Organization* 95–117.

Klein, Benjamin. 1988. "Vertical Integration as Organizational Ownership: The Fisher Body-General Motors Relationship Revisited," 4 *Journal of Law, Economics, and Organization* 199–213.

———, R. A. Crawford, and Armen Alchian. 1978. "Vertical Integration, Appropriable Rents and the Competitive Contracting Process," 21 *Journal of Law and Economics* 297–326.

Lee, L. F. 1976. "Estimation of Limited Dependent Variable Models by Two-Stage Methods." Ph.D. dissertation. University of Rochester.

Lee, Tom, and I. P. L. Png. 1990. "The Role of Installment Payments in Contracts for Services," 21 *Rand Journal of Economics* 83–99.

Maddala, G. S. 1983. *Limited-Dependent and Qualitative Variables in Econometrics*. Cambridge: Cambridge University Press.

Masten, Scott. 1984. "The Organization of Production: Evidence from the Aerospace Industry," 27 *Journal of Law and Economics* 403–17.

———. 1988. "A Legal Basis for the Firm," 4 *Journal of Law, Economics, and Organization* 181–98.

———, James Meehan, and Edward Snyder. 1989. "Vertical Integration in the U.S. Auto Industry: A Note on the Influence of Transaction-Specific Assets," 12 *Journal of Economic Behavior and Organization* 265–73.

Monteverde, Kirk, and David Teece. 1982a. "Supplier Switching Costs and Vertical Integration in the Automobile Industry," 13 *Bell Journal of Economics* 206–13.

———, and ———. 1982b. "Appropriable Rents and Quasi-Vertical Integration," 25 *Journal of Law and Economics* 321–8.

Nelson, Forest. 1977. "Censored Regression Models with Unobserved, Stochastic Censoring Thresholds," 6 *Journal of Econometrics* 309–27.

Williamson, Oliver. 1975. *Markets and Hierarchies: Analysis and Antitrust Implications*. New York: Free Press.

———. 1979. "Transaction-Cost Economics: The Governance of Contractual Relations," 22 *Journal of Law and Economics* 233–62.

———. 1985. *The Economic Institutions of Capitalism*. New York: Free Press.

———. 1988. "The Logic of Economic Organization," 4 *Journal of Law, Economics, and Organization* 65–91.

———. 1990. "Comparative Economic Organization: The Analysis of Discrete Structural Alternatives," mimeo, University of California, Berkeley, School of Business.

Part II
Contracting

[8]

COMPARATIVE INSTITUTIONAL ECONOMICS: THE GOVERNANCE OF RAIL FREIGHT CONTRACTING

*THOMAS M. PALAY**

I. Introduction

In recent years both economists[1] and lawyers[2] have studied the factors that lead private parties to adopt a particular institutional framework for their voluntary transactions. Their inquiry has been into the question of "governance choice." The term governance is a shorthand expression for the institutional framework in which contracts are initiated, negotiated, monitored, adapted, enforced, and terminated.[3] To date, however, the literature on the subject has been largely conceptual. One of its central theoretical propositions, attributable to both Williamson and Klein, Crawford, and Alchian, is that the most significant factor affecting the governance choice is the extent to which the parties have made idiosyn-

* Professor of Law, University of Wisconsin—Madison. This paper has benefited from the helpful criticisms and suggestions of Oliver Williamson, Yoram Ben-Porath, Peter Carstensen, Bill Clune, Victor Goldberg, Henry Hansmann, Neil Komesar, Rick Lempert, Ted Schneyer, Bill Whitford, and Richard Zerbe. An earlier draft was presented at the 1983 meeting of the Law and Society Association in Denver, Colorado. I have had almost as many financial backers as readers and I want to thank the Brookings Institution, the School of Public and Urban Policy of the University of Pennsylvania, and the Law School of the University of Wisconsin for their support.

[1] See, for example, Oliver E. Williamson, Transaction Cost Economics: The Governance of Contractual Relations, 22 J. Law & Econ. 233 (1979); Benjamin Klein, Robert G. Crawford, & Armen A. Alchian, Vertical Integration, Appropriable Rents, and the Competitive Contracting Process, 21 J. Law & Econ. 297 (1978); Victor P. Goldberg, Regulation and Administered Contracts, 7 Bell J. Econ. 426 (1976); and Kirk Monteverde & David J. Teece, Appropriable Rents and Quasi-Vertical Integration, 25 J. Law & Econ. 321 (1982).

[2] See, for example, Neil Komesar, In Search of a General Approach to Legal Analysis: A Comparative Institutional Alternative, 79 Mich. L. Rev. 1350 (1981); and Stewart Macaulay, Non-Contractual Relations in Business: A Preliminary Study, 28 Am. Soc. Rev. 55 (1963).

[3] As far as I can discern, the term governance was first used in this context by Williamson, *supra* note 1.

[*Journal of Legal Studies*, vol. XIII (June 1984)]

cratic investments in support of their transaction. Their reasoning is straightforward and familiar.[4] The more specialized the investment, the lower its value in its next best use. This heightens the risk of opportunistic behavior during both the performance and renegotiation of the contract.[5] Both sides, therefore, are willing to make increased expenditures to protect themselves against the possibility that the other party will act to obtain potentially appropriable quasi rents.[6]

This paper empirically tests the theory of governance choice within the context of real-world contracting between rail freight carriers and their shippers. These transactions are particularly interesting, as the contracts in question are often used to avoid regulatory constraints and are thereby made unenforceable in a court of law.[7] The study examines the effect of variation in the character of investment on the adaptation, monitoring, and informal enforcement of contracts. In broad outline it supports the basic proposition that as investment characteristics become more transaction specific, the associated institutional structure becomes increasingly unique to the parties and transactions it supports.

Section II briefly describes the data set and how the transactions were classified. Section III provides a short sketch of the contracts that were used. Section IV details the governance structure that supported the various types of transactions. The final section makes some concluding remarks.

II. The Data

The data are of two types: case studies and tabulations. The former involve a detailed description of particular transactions and their associ-

[4] As Williamson argues: "The crucial investment distinction is this: to what degree are transaction-specific (nonmarketable) expenses incurred. Items that are unspecialized among users pose few hazards, since buyers in these circumstances can easily turn to alternative sources, and suppliers can sell output intended for one order to other buyers without difficulty." Williamson, *supra* note 1, at 239.

[5] Opportunistic behavior refers to the proclivity of individuals to exploit the advantages to be attained from (1) the making of false or empty—that is, self-disbelieved—threats and promises concerning future conduct, or (2) the selective or distorted disclosure of information. Thus, related to the so-called moral hazard problem, it goes beyond, expanding the rational egoist characterization of economic actors to encompass varying degrees of strategic, myopic, and guileful behavior. Oliver E. Williamson, Markets and Hierarchies: Analysis and Antitrust Implications (1975).

[6] Klein, Crawford, and Alchian define the quasi-rent value of an asset as "the excess of its value over its salvage value, that is, its value in its next best *use* to another renter. The potentially appropriable specialized portion of the quasi rent is that portion, if any, in excess of its value to the second highest-valuing *user*." Klein, Crawford, & Alchian, *supra* note 1 at 298.

[7] Thomas Palay, The Avoidance of Regulatory Constraints through Informal Contracting (December 1983) (unpublished manuscript, University of Wisconsin Law School).

ated governance structures. The latter contain the summarization and cross-classification of the interview responses.

The data base was developed from a series of thirty-five field interviews held between October and December 1979 with rail carriers and their shippers.[8] The carrier interviews were held with the marketing and sales departments of three railroads, all of which were chosen for their willingness to be interviewed and their geographic proximity to Washington, D.C.[9] The shippers were, in general, matched to the carriers.[10] Though they were chosen because they moved a significant volume of their product on one of the three designated carriers, it proved infeasible in all cases to restrict their discussions to those railroads. Most of the shippers market nationwide and thus problems existed about the interviewees' personal familiarity with the details of the specific transaction I had discussed with the rail carrier. In addition, in order to maintain my promise to keep interviews confidential, it was impossible to tell shippers that I had talked with a particular carrier about a given transaction. Nevertheless, by choosing the interviews carefully I was fortunate enough to have many interviewees discuss transactions with the appropriate carriers and, in some instances, relate their answers to precisely the same transaction the carrier had described.

The interviews generated detailed discussions of fifty-one transactions, which may be broken into the following commodity groups:[11] finished automobiles (two shipper, six carrier); automobile parts (two shipper, seven carrier); aluminum (five shipper, three carrier); paper (two shipper, five carrier); steel (four shipper, six carrier); scrap (three shipper, two

[8] Unfortunately, seven of these had to be discarded because they were incomplete, the parties proved to be less than cooperative, or only one side of the transaction could be investigated.

[9] It is important to note that while only three railroads were used, each of the carriers consciously divided their sales and marketing functions into semi-autonomous commodity or car groups. That is, aluminum, steel, scrap, paper products, automobiles, and chemicals were generally handled by separate market managers located within semi-independent profit centers. Shippers who dealt with more than one marketing department of a given railroad often complained of the lack of coordination this system seemed to foster.

[10] That is, the rail users were chosen because their shipping needs required that they use one of the interviewed railroads. Although geographic proximity was not as important a consideration, limited interviewing resources precluded my seeing shippers located west of the Mississippi River and most were situated in the northeastern United States. The willingness of the companies to provide access to highly confidential material and to their corporate traffic department, without my having to use the public affairs office, played an important role in the selection process.

[11] The numbers in parentheses represent the number of transactions described from the perspective of the shipper and the carrier, respectively.

carrier); and chemicals (one shipper, three carrier). By concentrating on a small number of commodity groups I was able both to control somewhat for the type of investment that was undertaken and to develop some limited expertise in the transportation of these particular goods. This facilitated comparisons across transactions.

Conceptually, testing the hypothesis that governance structures vary systematically with the characteristics of the capital supporting the transaction is straightforward: identify the relevant classifications of investment characteristics and cross-classify these with the apparent form of the supporting governance structure. Three classifications of investment are used: nonspecific, moderately idiosyncratic, and highly idiosyncratic. While investment characteristics really form a more or less continuous spectrum running from perfectly fungible to perfectly idiosyncratic, little is lost by reducing the spectrum to these three discrete bands.[12]

Nonspecific investment involves capital that is easily transferable between users and uses. Alternative sources of supply, or alternative uses, for physical and human capital are readily available to the parties. Thus the identity of the party currently providing or receiving the benefit from the capital is irrelevant, for substitutes can be obtained at little (if any) additional cost. In the rail freight industry the movement of pulpboard, pulpwood, scrap, alumina, finished steel, iron ore, and sanitary tissue paper were each supported by nonspecialized capital. Standard boxcars, covered hoppers, or gondolas were used in each instance. Little was done in the way of transaction-specific planning or coordination.

The other two categories of investment both involve capital for which ex post alternative sources of purchase or supply are limited by the specialized requirements of the transaction. At the moderately idiosyncratic end of the interval are those transactions for which substitution, though not impossible, certainly is more difficult and involves more costly adaptations than does nonspecialized investment. The movements of semifinished aluminum, semifinished steel, and automobile parts fall in this category. For example, both semifinished metals are transferred in covered coil cars or specially designed and fitted boxcars. These cars can be shifted between shippers of semifinished metals, but their value is significantly reduced outside the movement of coils and sheet.

Transactions at the highly idiosyncratic end of the spectrum entail capital for which alternative sources of supply and use are even more restricted. Included here are the movements of chemicals and finished auto-

[12] These correspond to Williamson's categories: nonspecific, mixed, and idiosyncratic. Williamson, *supra* note 1, at 238–45.

TABLE 1
TYPE OF CAPITAL

Type of Capital	Number
Nonspecific:	
Pulpboard and sanitary paper	5
Pulpwood	2
Scrap metal	6
Alumina	4
Finished steel	3
Iron ore	2
Moderately idiosyncratic:	
Automobile parts	9
Semifinished steel	5
Semifinished aluminum	4
Highly idiosyncratic:	
Finished automobiles	8
Chemicals	4

mobiles. The latter, for instance, are moved in auto racks, which have but one use—the movement of finished automobiles. Once built, their worth in their next best use is roughly equivalent to their scrap value. What is more, the configuration of the decks and tie-downs makes it virtually impossible to transfer the railcars either between manufacturers or across models without substantial modification.

The fifty-one transactions examined, therefore, fall into the categories presented in Table 1.

III. THE CONTRACTS

The contracts discussed here generally involved a mixture of formally and informally derived terms. The formal elements, particularly the price term, were found in the published rate tariffs. Under the antidiscrimination provisions of the Interstate Commerce Act as it existed at the time of this study, the filed tariff constituted the entire agreement between the parties.[13] Thus the form of the agreement was supposed to be that of a long-term, incomplete contract completed on a spot or a short-term, nonrecurrent basis. In addition, substantive restrictions were placed on both price and service terms.

The informal elements of the agreement were used to supplement and complete the rate tariffs. In the cases that I studied they generally were negotiated and renegotiated on a short-term recurrent, or a long-term

[13] 49 U.S.C. § 11903 and 49 U.S.C. § 10761–62 (Supp. V, 1982). See also John Guandolo, Transportation Law (1979) 689–721 (3d ed. 1979) for a discussion of the Elkins Act.

incomplete basis, though occasionally spot contracts were used. The informal terms tended to involve (1) the number of cars the carrier would procure for, and dedicate to, the move; (2) the round-trip transit time between origin and destination; (3) specific service standards; and (4) the volume that shipper would guarantee carrier. These aspects of the agreement were not included in the tariff. To the extent that the resulting contracts violated the constraints imposed by the regulatory scheme they were unenforceable before either the Interstate Commerce Commission or a court of law.[14]

IV. The Governance Structures

The investment characteristics discussed in Section II can be cross-classified by governance structures. I identify five elements of governance structures that I expect to vary as investment characteristics vary: (1) the expected method of enforcement, (2) adaptations to changed circumstances, (3) the types of adjustments effectuated, (4) whether information for long-term planning was exchanged, and (5) whether structural planning was attempted. These were derived from a synthesis of the somewhat longer lists of Macneil and Wachter and Williamson.[15] Each aspect is discussed in turn.

A. *Enforcement*

The issue uppermost in the minds of the parties was how they were to obtain the performance promised when the contract in question was not enforceable in a court of law. Specifically, I was interested in how parties believed they ultimately would be protected from opportunistic behavior. The emphasis is not so much on how parties force their contracting opposites to provide specific performance, but on how they ensure that they receive what they are entitled to under the agreement. After all, the issue is not really *who* provides the service, but *whether* the precise service bargained for is ultimately delivered.

To compile a set of data on this issue I asked the interviewees to respond to four questions:

1. What, if anything, keeps [the other party] from backing out of his commitments to you?

[14] For more details of these contracts see Palay, *supra* note 7.

[15] Ian R. Macneil, The Many Futures of Contracts, 47 S. Cal. L. Rev. 691 (1974); Michael L. Wachter & Oliver E. Williamson, Obligational Markets and the Mechanics of Inflation, 9 Bell J. Econ. 549 (1978).

2. What ultimately protects you from his not keeping his promises and his side of the understanding?
3. What permits you to rely on his promises and representations? That is, how can you afford to make commitments or do things in reliance upon the agreement that you have with ———?
4. If he does fail to live up to his side of the understanding, do you have viable alternatives?

The technique required sacrificing the precision that might be obtained with a formal questionnaire, but two offsetting advantages made the course of action desirable. First, the informal conversational tone encouraged the interviewees, who were suspicious of academic interviews and concerned with the confidentiality of proprietary information, to be more open about important matters of institutional detail. Second, the absence of a formal questionnaire made it possible to proceed with the interviews without having to clear them through the firm's public affairs department.

The responses on enforcement were grouped by common features. Five subgroups were distinguished. They are cross-classified with investment characteristics in Table 2. There is an obvious pattern to this table. Where the investment is standardized, the enforcement mechanism tends to be market oriented. However, as the investment becomes more idiosyncratic, the means of ensuring enforcement tends, as predicted, to be transaction specific.

The first grouping described governance structures premised on the existence of potential or readily available substitutes (e_1). In particular, fourteen interviewees (nine railroad and five shipper) felt that their ultimate protection derived from their ability to exit from existing relations and easily procure alternative uses or sources of service for their equipment. The emphasis was on fulfilling the terms of the agreement by turning to substitutes rather than on enforcing the existing agreement. Cross-classifying the responses with investment characteristics yields the first column in Table 2.

For example, carrier R moved sanitary tissue paper for shipper K. To do so, the railroad invested heavily in both physical and human capital. But the investment involved little specialized equipment. The rolling stock tended to be free-running general service rail cars that were easily transferable among shippers, carriers, and uses. Either the fifty-foot/seventy-ton or the sixty-foot/one-hundred-ton boxcar was used. At the time of the interview each cost between $35,000 and $55,000. Neither the character of the product nor the nature of the transaction dictated any need for specialized handling or coordination. Carrier was particularly

TABLE 2
ENFORCEMENT AND INVESTMENT CHARACTERISTICS

Investment Characteristics	Type of Enforcement					Row Total
	e_1	e_2	e_3	e_4	e_5	
Nonspecific investment	14	4	2	1	0	21
Moderately idiosyncratic investment	0	0	7	11	0	18
Highly idiosyncratic investment	0	0	1	7	4	12
Column total	14	4	10	19	4	51

concerned that shipper K might use the cars on another railroad's routes. Rates were calculated on a ton per mile basis and shipper believed that the equipment per diem neither covered the cost of the cars nor contributed anything to fixed overhead. The railroad indicated that its primary protection from shipper's ability to take advantage of him at the renegotiation or recontracting phase was market related. If shipper failed to live up to the agreement, carrier could transfer its cars to some other user. When it came right down to it, R's willingness to bind its future to K was premised on its knowledge that it did not have to trust shipper to fulfill its end of the bargain. If K failed to deliver on its promise, R would suffer only momentary losses and could stop delivering equipment. As R's market manager stated:

> I don't have to trust what he tells me. We've got plenty of uses for fifty-foot boxes. If we provide [shipper] with cars and they use them to move paper over someone else's routes, it'll be a long time before I provide them with anything other than the bare minimum that I can get away with. The next time I'll be plenty wary about committing cars to them on a long-term basis. They'll sweat for them, and they're not going to be the best we've got.

Similarly, it was clear that carrier appreciated the constraints imposed on it because shipper had alternative means of transporting its sanitary paper to final customers. As carrier stated, "[c]ompetition from trucks is what keeps us from raising our prices too high. Our costs, and competition from other railroads, keeps us from setting them too low." The last sentence refers to the possibility that other railroads (competing either in carrier's market or in some other market of shipper) might protest a rate that is set below either fully allocated costs or variable cost.

Four of the fourteen e_1 transactions believed that it was the fear of exit that ultimately forced the parties to live up to their agreements. Interests were secured because of the existence of potential alternatives and not necessarily because of actual recourse to those substitutes. Shipper K, involved with R in the movement of sanitary tissue paper, described its primary protection from opportunistic conduct in these terms. Shipper K believed that its interests were ultimately secured by carrier R's reluctance to act in ways that would tempt K to "take its business elsewhere." It emphasized the *potential* for exiting rather than the act of doing so. In a sense, K's interests were secured by its ability to project a credible threat. With respect to the agreement on volume and equipment, K stated:

> When I or any one of our people promise some guy ten or fifteen carloads per day, we expect them to deliver the cars. If they won't, they know I'll use someone else. I've done it before.
>
> All bets are off when [carrier] stops sending me the cars. If he can't provide the equipment, then he knows I'm only going to dilly dally around so long. I can get service from [other carrier] or from trucks if I have to. I prefer to use rail and [carrier] has been good to us, but I work for [shipper], and my job is to deliver to our customers.

K argued that the rates were similarly constrained. It agreed that it was carrier's perception of the competition from trucks that guaranteed bargaining parity at the recontracting or renegotiating stage. The characteristics of the capital involved did not lock in either party once the initial contract was set. But shipper believed that its protection from opportunistic price increases did not come from actively seeking other suppliers of rail services. Rather, it was carrier's *concern* that shipper might do so that shipper relied upon for its protection.[16]

Common to the four transactions of the second group (e_2) (one railroad and three shipper) was the belief that opportunistic tendencies were controlled by a combination of actual alternatives and the implicit threat to withdraw any future service or volume. The premise was that parties would act to ensure the continuance not only of present contracts, but of future, expected ones as well.

The line between this category and the first is somewhat more pronounced than may be apparent at first glance.[17] Concern over future withdrawal of business will induce someone to refrain from opportunistic behavior today only if that party has, a priori, a nontrivial expectation that the future service or volume will materialize. In the instant cases, that expectation was created by one party's promise to the other. A, for instance, might say to B, "If you provide me with ten cars per day to

[16] Shipper indicated with respect to price that there is always the possibility of "going to the Commission," but while that alternative is available, recourse to it is relatively rare. Moreover, the commission only rarely "sets" prices. In general it simply approves or disapproves a protested rate.

[17] I am indebted to Stewart Macaulay for helping to make this point clear to me.

carry widgets today. I promise to provide you with at least 50 percent of the whatsits produced at our new plant next year."

The parties were doing something in exchange for future consideration. They would not know whether the other party would fulfill the promise until much later. To premise enforcement upon concern over the continuance of future contracts requires a degree of trust in one's trading partners that goes beyond the mere existence of actual and potential substitutes. Thus, the governance structure described by the respondents in group 2 combined both existence of alternatives (present and future) and, subtly, the presence of some degree of trust. The data are cross-classified with investment characteristics in Table 2, column 2.

A good example of this type of enforcement involves shipper H, a major user of iron ore. H produced finished steel and required rail transportation at three stages of its production process. By far its heaviest use of rail capacity was in the movement of raw materials—coal, coke, lime, and iron ore—which amounted to somewhere between forty and fifty million tons per year. The iron ore was mined in the northern Midwest where it was generally transformed into pellets, sinter, or reduced ore. It was then transported by ship to one of two ports. From the port it had to be moved by rail car two hundred miles to the mill site at destination.

The plant at destination was equipped solely for rail delivery. It was serviced directly by two railroads and had access to a third through reciprocal switching agreements. Rates from the ports were virtually identical and the question usually was which carrier could provide H the best service to the mills. The heavy density of iron ore pellets required that they be transported in either open-top hoppers or gondolas. Neither the hopper nor the gondola car was outfitted with equipment specific to the iron ore traffic. Hoppers are heavily used in the coal, grain, and alumina markets. Gondolas are also employed to transport machinery, lumber, clay, gravel, and metal scrap. Both cars, then, have significant alternative uses.

Though the transaction was relatively standardized, potential difficulties arose when H delivered the ore to port. Once there the ore was virtually assured to carrier X. Any other option involved nontrivial storage and inventory costs or additional transportation expenses.[18] The railroad could breach with current impunity the promise to provide the cars necessary for timely service. The existence of possible future business, though, kept the potential current problems—while significant—short-

[18] Thomas Palay, The Governance of Rail-Freight Contracts: A Comparative Institutional Approach (unpublished Ph. D. dissertation, University of Pennsylvania 1981).

term. Shipper H believed that its protection came ultimately from its ability to threaten to withhold future business from an offending railroad. It was also confident that carrier knew that it could count on H's future business if it acted in good faith. As H stated: "It's nothing that has to be said. I don't call up [X] and say 'if you don't do this you'll never see another pellet of ore again.' I don't have to. They know that if they produce the cars we'll keep giving them our business. Screw around with me, and that's the last trainload of ore they'll get—until we get desperate."

The third group (e_3) comprises ten respondents (six railroad and four shipper) who described the basis for protection as some combination of the elements cited by groups e_1 and e_4 or e_5. These answers are cross-classified with investment in column 3 of Table 2. In each case the parties talked of the existence of alternatives and said that the parties with whom they dealt had a reputation for fair dealing. Neither party was able, or willing, to say which of the two elements figured more prominently.

For instance, carrier T moved large quantities of aluminum sheet and plate to fabricating facilities located at various destinations throughout the United States. The transaction involved moderately idiosyncratic investment and the contract entailed trading volume for specified service standards and a guarantee of railcars. When asked to describe what it was that held the informal contractual relations together, T equivocated. In one breath it clearly mentioned and talked about trust and realized mutuality of interest. "We've been dealing with [shipper D] from the beginning. When they located and designed their plant they knew we'd be one of their primary carriers. I believe what they tell us. They know how we operate; that we're an honest bunch of people. Neither one of us plays games. I like dealing with them." Nevertheless, in the next breath carrier T was careful to point out its potential market alternatives: "We work very hard to maintain our image of integrity and fair play. We're very business-like. But I guarantee you that [shipper D] knows that if he pushes me once too often he'll find himself sitting around with a lot of aluminum sheet and no cars. Alternatively, we could stop investing money in new equipment for him."

In the fourth subgrouping (e_4) of nineteen transactions (thirteen railroad and six shipper),[19] opportunistic conduct was attenuated by a realized mutuality of interest, manifested in the parties' apparent reluctance to

[19] The ratio of railroads to shippers found in this category is virtually identical to the ratio of railroads (twenty-one) to shippers (nine) contained in the sample of idiosyncratic transactions.

exploit short-term advantages to the detriment of long-run relations. These responses are cross-classified in column 4 of Table 2.

Before investors make expenditures on idiosyncratic capital, their expectations must be reasonably secure. To facilitate the process both shippers and carriers felt it crucial to maintain reputations for honesty, integrity, and trustworthiness. Opportunistic conduct could destroy any established reputation effects. Concern over appearing honest, therefore, seems to have forced the parties to be so. In order to maintain reputations, shippers and carriers simply did not take advantage of the ex post small-numbers bargaining conditions. Instead, trust relations developed.

For instance, carrier X and shipper A were involved in the movement of finished automobiles which involved highly idiosyncratic investment. Each was asked to describe what, if anything, kept the other party from backing out of its commitments. Both parties indicated that "we need them as much as they need us," and the "business-like" behavior of the other. The parties had developed a relationship that, as carrier admitted, was both envied and suspected by the other divisions of railroad X. Shipper, though, was careful to describe the situation as being "strictly a good faith" relation, "honest and business-like, but not social."

Both shipper and carrier apparently were reluctant to exploit short-term advantages if it would lead to harm in the long-run relation. For example, amortization agreements were used to offset the risk that slumping auto sales, an auto industry strike, or a major design change might render the existing auto racks useless. Neither party, though, believed that the rack-car amortization agreements were legally enforceable. The understandings primarily were used to reduce ambiguity, to reinforce shipper's "moral commitment" to share the risk of idiosyncratic investment, and to reduce the unease of some of carrier's operations (as opposed to marketing) people.

Despite the legal unenforceability of these agreements, shipper had several times paid off the unamortized portion of cars when it discontinued use. Both parties pointed to the example of the "Epsilon" railcar, produced exclusively to move shipper's Epsilon model automobile. Shipper was initially quite taken with the concept and encouraged carrier to purchase a specified number of the railcars. Unfortunately, some time after the railcars went into service, shipper drastically altered the design of the Epsilon automobile, rendering carrier's equipment obsolete. The automobile manufacturer subsequently reimbursed carrier slightly more than \$1 million for the unamortized portion of the investment. Shipper felt that it was "in our best interest" to honor the agreement. As the director of transportation put it: "We've got to keep them healthy, viable and happy to guarantee that we'll get the equipment we need, when we need it."

The realized mutuality of interest also was manifested in an apparent willingness to undertake nonmandatory tasks that helped to facilitate and improve the working relationship itself. These investments in "transactional capital" often did not have an immediate or obvious return. Take, for instance, carrier X's willingness to accommodate shipper A by fully absorbing the cost of "switching" shipper's cars. The issue was not really the money, but rather the fact that this practice caused accounting and bureaucratic headaches for shipper. Upon learning of the problem, carrier unilaterally changed its policy on the issue to shipper's advantage. Carrier thought that the incident probably cost it about $50,000, but that the "investment" would pay for itself over time by strengthening the relationship with shipper. Carrier felt confident that the effort would be more than reciprocated.

The development of these relations takes both real resources and time. However, once the relations are successfully developed, both parties have the ability to make credible requests, reject inadequate offers, and make long-term commitments. Two years prior to the interview, for instance, "Richard Roe" at shipper A requested that railroad Y purchase thirty-five enclosed multilevel racks for a movement of finished automobiles from origin to destination. After confirming that thirty-five cars were in fact needed for the move and that a proper return would be realized if the promised volume materialized, the investment was made. Not so much as a letter promising the given volume of traffic was exchanged.[20] Y's explanation for going ahead with an investment valued between $1.5 and $2 million was the trust relations developed at both the individual and firm level. "As long as I have been here [shipper A] has never backed out of a commitment. They have a policy that when they promise something they follow through. [Richard Roe] is a real gentleman. I believe that he would never purposely hurt me."

Two different trust relations are critical in this last class of cases. The first is between individuals or departments, the second between firms. Where only the former exists the other parties can never be certain that a decision by an individual or a department will be backed up throughout the organization. Where both exist the parties have the further advantage

[20] Concededly there was an amortization agreement. However, as indicated, such understandings were little more than a written record of the particular agreement. They were, according to all the parties, unenforceable.

of being able to believe that actions will not be overruled, which helps both in making and in justifying decisions.

There appears to be no special formula for developing the necessary trust relations. "John Smith" at carrier X insisted that reputations of this nature simply develop from a policy of always being "straight with the customer." Each of the division heads under Smith used similar phrases to describe how they developed the reputations of their sections. Both indicated that in their section it was Smith's policy that "you tell the customer no tales."

Carrier X also gave shipper A a good deal of credit for having developed excellent relations at both the individual and firm level. Of the four major automobile producers, shipper A was the only one that carrier felt would deliver most of what it promised. Carrier said, for example, that the actual commitment of finished vehicles to the railroad was roughly 90 percent of the volume shipper promised.

The fifth category of enforcement (e_5) reduced opportunistic tendencies by combining the realized mutuality of interest described above with vertical integration. Involved here were four transactions (three railroad and one shipper), all of which entailed the movement of chemicals. In each instance, shipper owned its own rolling stock and rented track access and locomotive power from the carrier. The responses are cross-classified with investment characteristics in column 5 of Table 2.

A good example of this type of enforcement involves shipper E, a major producer of chemical products. Of those chemicals that were moved by rail, most traveled in tank cars or in covered hoppers. The former were among the most specialized cars in general use. They usually were constructed to be substance-specific. Glass or rubber linings, specialized pressure valves, and damage control equipment are but a few examples of the unique equipment employed. Quality control and safety concerns prevented the transfer of cars across products or manufacturers. Utilization patterns simply made it too costly to attempt to modify a car to handle a new product after each trip, and cleaning involved expensive facilities and technologies. In addition, shipper used carrier in a pipeline capacity. Thus specialized coordination and handling were required to maintain a constant flow.

To guarantee safety and quality control, shipper employed a governance structure premised on vertical integration. It owned in excess of ten thousand rail cars. To enforce the other aspects of any agreement realized mutuality of interest was employed. The chemical industry is, in the words of one market manager, a "handshake industry, where your word is your bond." Shipper E, for instance, wanted to move a million tons of a substance from origin to destination. Carrier X offered to transport the substance at a price of 69 cents per hundredweight. Carrier Y, however, offered to publish a rate of 65 cents per hundredweight. E readily accepted X's offer because (1) it felt it to be more realistic, but, more important, (2) it knew that when X's representative promised a particular rate that price would be in force for a significant period. Even after Y changed its filed rate to 75 cents per hundredweight, carrier X did not raise its price. As carrier X's chemical manager stated: "It's far more important that they believe I'm reliable than that we jack the price up on them. Maybe I could have gotten more out of them, but now I have them on the hook. Besides, they believe me when I come calling." E could have accepted Y's initial offer and then switched to X if the former raised its price. However, it was unable to accept the performance losses associated with any switch over. In addition, shipper was concerned that switching to railroad Y would create the impression that it was willing to deal "fast and loose" with the railroads.

B. Adjustments

The manner in which parties attempt to adjust contracts to changed circumstances is also a key element of a governance structure. The interviews were organized first to elicit the response of the parties to hypothetical changes in circumstances that might call for contractual modification. These preliminary responses set the stage for the more specific inquiries that follow. I therefore have data on two issues: the general reaction of parties to requests for adjustments and the nature of any adjustments that were made.

1. *Attitude toward Adjustments.* The parties responded to requests for adjustments in one of two ways: holding to original terms (a_1) or flexibility (a_2). The responses tended to correspond to the type of investment used to support the transaction. They are cross-classified with investment characteristics in Table 3.

The responses of eighteen nonspecific and two idiosyncratic transactions indicated an interest in holding the other party to the original negotiated terms. Two types of responses were classified in this manner. The first were those who denied the request as long as possible and who tried to enforce the initial contract term as originally negotiated. Thirteen of the transactions supported by nonspecific capital responded in this way. These parties assumed that the other side was, or should have been, able to project enough of the relevant future into the present to make appropriate risk-bearing or sharing decisions from the outset.

Shipper G's reaction to carrier's request for an increase in price is not atypical of this approach. G is a major producer of finished steel. It

TABLE 3
ATTITUDE TOWARD ADJUSTMENTS AND INVESTMENT CHARACTERISTICS

Investment Characteristics	Attitude Toward Adjustments: a_1	a_2	Row Total
Nonspecific investment	18	3	21
Moderately idiosyncratic investment	2	16	18
Highly idiosyncratic investment	0	12	12
Column total	20	31	51

employed rail transportation at all three stages of its production process. At the finished steel to consignee stage it moved approximately 45 percent of its total tonnage by rail. The finished steel was usually shipped in standard fifty- and sixty-foot boxcars, though some was moved in regular and covered gondolas. Most of this equipment was nonspecialized. All of it had a significant number of alternative uses. With the exception of covered gondolas, readily accessible substitutes were available.

The finished steel was sold on a price-absorbed basis. That is, it was purchased FOB nearest mill to customer. Therefore, the buyer (consignee) paid the freight bill from the mill nearest destination and the shipper paid the remainder. Technically the steel customer had the right to choose the route and negotiations should have taken place between the carrier and the consignee. The sheer number of customers, though, made it difficult for the railroad to deal separately with each steel consignee. In addition, the relative lack of bargaining power of the users of finished steel (vis-à-vis the railroads) had made it desirable for them to use shipper as their agent. Typically, therefore, the railroad's first approach on the price increase—before going to the consignee—was to the steel producer's traffic department. The theory was that if carrier could not get shipper's support for the price adjustment, the railroad was likely to be unsuccessful with the consignee.

In this instance, the proposed rate increase came on top of a recent general price increase. Shipper G's first formal notice was a letter indicating carrier's intention to raise the rate and requesting shipper's support. Though no specific mention was made of any preliminary informal discussions of the proposed increase, shipper indicated that it was not surprised at the request. This probably indicated either that it had received prior notice of the request or that it anticipated carrier's revenue problem at the time of the initial rate negotiation. Whatever the reason, shipper's initial formal response was negative. Carrier's representative requested a meeting between shipper's traffic department and carrier's marketing, pricing, and sales offices. After the conference shipper decided to reject carrier's request for support. They indicated that while there might be some merit to the request, carrier would have to live with the terms it had negotiated. As shipper's traffic manager asserted, the railroad, "like anyone else," had obligated itself for the long term to do something—in this case, to ship finished steel to destination—at "the negotiated rate," and any attempt to renegotiate the price because of a failure to anticipate future circumstances properly would meet stiff resistance.

The chances of the parties resolving those issues between themselves, shipper believed, were relatively slim. Carrier was not sure that it was prepared to take the matter all the way to the Interstate Commerce Commission. It believed that if the consignees ultimately lost before the ICC, they might switch to truck. G predicted that the most likely scenario would see the railroad pushing the issue to the point where the consignees began negotiating seriously with some trucking firms. If at that point shipper was still unwilling to back carrier's position, it would withdraw the proposal. If shipper were to back the proposal carrier would have to submit its figures to independent (from the railroad) verification. It would also have to be prepared to prove that the original price proposal was in fact "a mistake" rather than a calculated strategic move to attempt to lock the traffic in to carrier.

A second set of responses was also classified as indicating an interest in holding the other party to the original contract. The three nonspecific and two moderately idiosyncratic transactions of this group tended to characterize their reaction to requests for adjustments in terms of hesitancy rather than absolute resistance. They were willing to adjust initial understandings only if doing so would place their firm in a clearly superior position to that originally negotiated. There was more discussion of flexibility here than with the first group. However, when questioned further, they indicated only a theoretic flexibility. Only when more favorable terms could be worked out was there a true willingness to make adjustments. Initial terms were preferred unless concessions could be obtained that left the parties better off than they had been under the original contract.

The governance structure supporting the movement of sanitary paper exhibited this type of adjustment. Carrier described how shipper K had sought an adjustment in the number of boxcars assigned to movements originating at K's plant. Originally the agreement specified that carrier would provide shipper with a certain number of cars as long as shipper met specified volume commitments. Carrier anticipated that the agreement would run for "years." During my interview, carrier had first argued that its ultimate decision to permit the change was proof of its flexible attitude. But further questioning revealed that carrier's initial response to shipper K—in fact, its first several responses—had been to deny the request. At that time, shipper had proposed that carrier increase the number of cars assigned to the origin plant in exchange for a proportionate increase in the amount of pulpboard shipped with R. Carrier's reaction was to reject the proposal. As R explained: "The numbers just weren't there. The [initial understanding] was nothing special and their [new] offer didn't advance it any."

Several more attempts were made by shipper to increase its pool of available cars. Each was resisted by carrier in favor of the original terms of agreement. Finally, carrier offered to provide shipper with a number of boxcars above and beyond the present pool. K, in turn would have to agree not to contest a rate increase on the traffic. When asked to describe why it now was willing to make the adjustment, carrier responded: "It makes sense dollar-wise. The return's there. Our revenue on that movement is drastically increased."

Twenty-eight of the responses indicated an attitude toward adjustments that was a good deal more flexible. Sixteen of the moderately idiosyncratic and twelve of the highly idiosyncratic transactions were predisposed toward acting favorably upon the requests of their contracting partners. The possibility that they were being taken advantage of apparently did not worry them. On the contrary, the ability to change agreements in the face of problems or altered circumstances was perceived as essential to the preservation of their investments. For instance, both shipper A and carrier X, involved in the movement of finished autos, indicated that the parties were favorably predisposed toward making (or potentially having to make) adjustments in initial contract terms. Shipper in particular reiterated its basic policy of keeping carrier, and for that matter all railroads, "viable."

2. *Types of Adjustments.* The third facet of governance concerned the form of the contractual adjustments if and when they were made. Two types of adjustments were identified: unilateral (n_1) and negotiated (n_2). The data are summarized in Table 4 and indicate a tendency toward negotiated adjustments as the degree of idiosyncracy increased. In addition, as investment became more transaction specific, there was a greater willingness to trade present adjustments for future consideration. Slightly more than half of the transactions did not involve a major adjustment, so that a third category—no adjustments attempted (n_3)—appears to, but does not, vary systematically with investment characteristics.

Unilateral adjustments involved one party's announcement of a change without consulting the other. Negotiations were not seriously pursued.

TABLE 4
TYPES OF ADJUSTMENTS AND INVESTMENT CHARACTERISTICS

Investment Characteristics	Types of Adjustments				
		n_2			
	n_1	Present Tit-for-Tat	Future Consideration	n_3	Row Total
Nonspecific investment	4	7	0	10	21
Moderately idiosyncratic investment	0	4	4	10	18
Highly idiosyncratic investment	0	1	4	7	12
Column total	4	12	8	27	51

The initiating party cared little whether the relation itself was impaired. Five transactions involved adjustments of this nature. Four involved nonspecific investment, while one was supported by idiosyncratic capital. Railroad X, for instance, decided that the movement of pulpboard, which is transported in standardized equipment, was no longer compensatory. To rectify the situation, X announced a surcharge of *S* dollars per car, effective shortly after the announcement was made. No attempt was made to notify customers or encourage negotiations. In fact, on the day of the announcement executives from one of the large paper concerns were in the office of railroad X's market manager for forest products to discuss matters related to the price of pulpboard movements. No mention of the impending surcharge announcement was made. As X explained, "If you get people involved in a negotiation process, the whole thing can drag on for months." This is in marked contrast to the types of adjustments discussed below that were made by the same railroad (though a different marketing section) with respect to the movement of finished automobiles.

The alternative method of making adjustments was through negotiation. Two types of negotiated changes were evident. The first found the parties agreeing to change terms in exchange for fully compensatory, *present* consideration. Seven of the eleven nonspecific and five of the thirteen idiosyncratic transactions where adjustments were witnessed involved negotiations of this nature. Shipper A and carrier X, involved in the movement of finished automobiles, negotiated adjustments in this manner. Unilateral action was not seriously considered and the renegotiations generally involved an immediate quid pro quo.

One example illustrates the pattern. Despite their size and weight, finished automobiles are highly susceptible to damage from the environment, vandalism, and theft while in transit to final destinations. To reduce these losses, auto shipper A in the mid-1970s encouraged carrier to switch from open to enclosed auto racks. The change necessitated two types of investment in physical capital. First, there was the considerable cost either of enclosing the open equipment or of purchasing new, fully enclosed cars. Second, the fully enclosed auto rack is roughly nineteen feet high, while the standard clearance (bridge and tunnel heights) on carrier's route is much lower, requiring investments in higher clearances to complete the conversion. Many railroads, feeling that it was essential to accommodate the auto shipper, immediately began to increase their clearances, procure the necessary equipment, and renegotiate the rates. Carrier X, for a variety of strategic and financial reasons, refused to do so and continued to use the old cars.

During this same period, X renewed an old complaint. For many years it had been troubled by what it felt were noncompensatory movements of finished vehicles, especially the carloads of automobiles interchanged with railroads located in a particular region of the country. For reasons that had to do with the formula for splitting revenue on "foreign" (interchanged) movements, carrier believed that the routes were losing money. Carrier insisted that to make the routes compensatory it needed an increase of roughly *S* dollars per carload. The usual practice called for X to split its rate increase with all foreign lines. Carrier wanted to prevent payments to third parties whose share was already compensatory. Carrier X, therefore, proposed to shipper that in exchange for partially enclosing the auto racks, a fixed surcharge payable only to carrier be placed on each carload of automobiles. While this represented a radical departure from existing pricing practices, shipper eventually agreed despite the problems this might cause in its relations with other carriers.

Shipper attributed at least part of its willingness to accept the surcharge to carrier's careful preparation of its case. Unlike other divisions at carrier that faced similar problems, the automobile transportation section was very careful not to surprise or antagonize shipper. The groundwork for the surcharges had been laid months in advance, and A was carefully kept apprised of the situation. In the end, A even supported X's proposal before the ICC. Both shipper and carrier felt that a large part of the credit for the maintenance of cordial relations, even in the face of the price increases, could be given to "John Smith" at carrier who handled the situation in a "very business-like" manner.

The second type of negotiated adjustments were made in return for some implicit or explicit future consideration. Eight of the thirteen idiosyncratic transactions where adjustments were witnessed involved negotiations of this nature. For instance, railroad D indicated that it might provide additional cars to a steel mill for movements of semifinished steel, to increase its chances of receiving a lucrative movement at some point in the future. Alternatively, the carrier might provide needed equipment to

TABLE 5
LONG-TERM PLANNING AND INVESTMENT CHARACTERISTICS

	Information for Long-Term Planning		
Investment Characteristics	h_1 (No)	h_2 (Yes)	Row Total
Nonspecific investment	13	8	21
Moderately idiosyncratic investment	5	13	18
Highly idiosyncratic investment	1	11	12
Column total	19	32	51

preserve or enhance its reputation or to develop goodwill. On the shipper side, auto company G almost always approved a proposed rate increase. Its argument was, in effect, that by providing needed revenues to the railroads today it would help to guarantee that specialized investment would be undertaken in the future.

C. *Information for Long-Term Planning*

To be effective, any governance structure must entail exchanges of information for short-term, specific planning.[21] But the exchange of information for long-term forecasting as well as the sharing of proprietary and impacted data evidences a different attitude toward governing the transaction.[22] Thus, the fourth facet of governance explored with the parties was whether they exchanged long-term forecasting, proprietary, or impacted information with their contracting partners (h_1 = no, h_2 = yes). There is some indication from the data that parties to idiosyncratic transactions were more likely to be involved in exchanges of information for long-term forecasting than were the parties to nonspecific transactions. The data are summarized in Table 5.

D. *Information for Structural Planning*

Even more interesting in terms of the type of information exchanged is the fifth element of governance. The parties were asked whether the information necessary for structural planning was shared (s_1 = no, s_2 = yes). Structural planning involves the development of rules or procedures

[21] Macneil, *supra* note 15.

[22] Williamson defines impacted data as "mainly attributable to the pairing of uncertainty with opportunism. It exists in circumstances in which one of the parties to an exchange is much better informed than is the other regarding underlying conditions germane to the trade, and the second party cannot achieve information parity except at great cost—because he cannot rely on the first party to disclose the information in a fully candid manner." Williamson, *supra* note 5, at 14.

for dealing with long-term problems or unforeseen contingencies. Where markets were relied upon as the primary governance mechanism, little joint structural planning was evident. Nonspecific investments, therefore, tended to generate only infrequent exchanges of information for the purpose of structural planning.

With idiosyncratic transactions, in contrast, the data indicate that the parties were more likely to engage in exchanges of information for structural planning. Both formal and informal procedures for dealing with problems were established, and conversations were held to discuss the future course of the transaction. Many of the automobile transactions in particular involved regular conversations of this nature. For instance, automobile shipper B moved automobile parts with carrier Z. Because B maintained short inventories at its various assembly plants, it was crucial that Z provide consistent, on-time service. Shipper's procedures for dealing with carrier over these issues were relatively formalized. Each month shipper requested that a representative from each of the railroads with the most troublesome routes come to Detroit. At these discussions, B's traffic people would provide the railroads with a detailed analysis of the problems. They also made requests for improvements. If after thirty days carrier still was meeting its schedule less than 70 percent of the time, shipper would begin testing new routes. This might, as B put it, "mean spending a few more dollars," but it conveyed additional information to the railroad. If after sixty days carrier was still performing below standard, shipper might switch some traffic to another railroad. At all stages of the process the matter was handled in a reasonably formal manner, but with "plenty of give and take." As shipper put it: "We will make every effort to help them correct their problems. Usually the problem is legitimate and usually they fix it. If they can't, I want them to know that I don't like having to switch on them, but that I have to. We can't afford to have a plant close down. But I want the whole thing handled very business-like, with the minimum of bruised egos."

The data for idiosyncratic and nonspecific transactions are summarized in Table 6. It indicates that as investment becomes more idiosyncratic there is a greater likelihood that the exchanges of information necessary for structural planning will be made.

V. Conclusion

A consistent pattern emerges from this study. In this paper I have examined data on contractual enforcement, adaptations, and long-term planning. In each instance the predictions made by the general theory have been borne out by the data. Indeed, the combined force of the data is, if anything, more powerful than its component parts. Some rough

TABLE 6

STRUCTURAL PLANNING AND INVESTMENT CHARACTERISTICS

Investment Characteristics	Information for Structural Planning		
	s_1 (No)	s_2 (Yes)	Row Total
Nonspecific invesment	19	2	21
Moderately idiosyncratic investment	8	8	16
Highly idiosyncratic investment	1	10	11
Column total	28	20	48*

* Three interviewees provided insufficient data to permit an unambiguous classification.

TABLE 7

GOVERNANCE STRUCTURE AND INVESTMENT CHARACTERISTICS

Investment Characteristics	Governance Structure			
	Market (g_1)	Mixed (g_2)	Relational (g_3)	Row Total
Nonspecific investment	13	7	1	21
Moderately idiosyncratic investment	0	10	8	18
Highly idiosyncratic investment	0	2	10	12
Column total	13	19	19	51

measure of that force is suggested by showing the correlation between the increased use of long-term relational contracting devices and the existence of highly idiosyncratic investments by the parties, as is done in Table 7.[23] The qualitative data make it difficult to test these conclusions with precise statistical techniques. Inspection of the data, though, suggests that they tend to confirm the theoretical hypothesis advanced by institutional economists; namely, that the form of the institutional structure used to support contractual relations depends upon the character of the transaction being effected. Where the transaction involves idiosyncratic investment the governance mechanism is apt to be bilateral and unique to the parties. Conversely, as the investments become more standardized a concomitant reduction in governance specialization results.

[23] Table 7 is derived by aggregating the data presented in Tables 2–6. Category g_1 is made up of those parties classified as e_1, a_1, n_1, h_1, and s_1. Category g_3 is made up of those classified as e_4 or e_5, a_2, n_2, h_2, and s_2. Category g_2 is defined as any combination of the five elements described above, other than those defined as g_1 or g_3. Included among the governance mechanisms classified as "mixed" are the three ambiguous responses concerning the use of structural planning. In each instance, the governance structure would have been classified as mixed even if the responses had been unambiguous.

[9]

QUANTITY AND PRICE ADJUSTMENT IN LONG-TERM CONTRACTS: A CASE STUDY OF PETROLEUM COKE*

VICTOR P. GOLDBERG and *JOHN R. ERICKSON*
Northwestern University *California State University, Fullerton*

I. Introduction

MUCH economic activity takes place within a framework of complex, long-term contracts. While economists have shown increased interest in these contracts, surprisingly little is known about them, or, indeed, about how to analyze the contracting activity of private economic actors. A case study of the actual contracts used in one industry could provide sorely needed data about the way in which reasonably clever businessmen and lawyers cope with problems scholars might consider intractable. In this article, we provide such an analysis of contracts concerning a particular product—petroleum coke. We focus on the problems of quantity and price adjustment. We do not deal, except in passing, with the question of why the parties chose long-term contracts rather than short-term agreements or vertical integration by contract rather than by ownership.

In 1964, the Federal Trade Commission (FTC) launched an investigation into the possible anticompetitive effect of the long-term contracts under which eight oil refineries sold petroleum coke to the Great Lakes Carbon Corporation (GLC). The investigation culminated in a 1973 decision that these contracts violated the antitrust statutes.[1] The contracts

* Part of Goldberg's research was funded by a grant from Northwestern University School of Law. Part of Erickson's research was funded by a grant from the Great Lakes Carbon Company. The paper benefited from comments at seminars at UCLA (Economics), Toronto (Law), Stanford (Law), Virginia (Law), and Northwestern (Law).

[1] In the Matter of Great Lakes Carbon Corporation, et al., 82 F.T.C. 1529 (1973). The record of this case and the FTC's file serve as our primary source of information. The commission's internal classification of the case is 8805, and this number is used in referencing the location of documents. Complainants' exhibits are designated by CX. Exhibits by the defendants are designated by GLCX (Great Lakes Carbon), TX (Texaco), and MOX (Mobil). Proposed Findings of Fact and Conclusions of Law are found at 8805-1-3-2; these are

[*Journal of Law & Economics*, vol. XXX (October 1987)]

collected by the commission in its investigation are our primary source of data. The *Great Lakes Carbon* record and the FTC's nonpublic files included about ninety contracts, which account for about 80 percent of all the domestic petroleum coke contracts written between 1946 and 1973.[2] In addition, the FTC's Compliance Files provided us with a number of post-1973 contracts, while industry sources supplied us with a few more.

Long-term contracts enable economic actors to coordinate behavior, while stopping short of full, formal vertical integration. These contracts reflect the problems posed by the human characteristics of the transactors (their limited ability to process information, their propensity for strategic or opportunistic behavior); by the physical characteristics of the subject matter of the transaction (that is, problems with defining and monitoring quality, the production technology, the ease of access to alternative buyers or sellers, the relation-specific nature of the physical plant, and so forth), and by the reliability of external enforcement (legal enforcement or good will). These contracts embody the particular solutions developed by the contracting parties. Our working assumption here is that the solutions are correct—that is, that the contracts are "efficient" adaptations.[3] On the basis of this assumption, we can then work backward and ask why particular contract terms (or patterns of terms) might be efficient.[4]

Two caveats are in order. First, a written contract is at best an imperfect representation of the underlying economic relation. A written document is typically an incomplete specification of the terms and conditions. Moreover, even the terms and conditions explicitly included in the contract can be changed or suspended; indeed, adjustments to changed con-

denoted by the party's abbreviation followed by an F (for example, Complaint Counsel's Findings are CF). Documents introduced as evidence are designated by their FTC file number. Files were usually not paginated.

[2] The contracts were written by thirty different sellers of petroleum coke at forty-four different refineries. (In 1970, there were thirty-five refiners operating fifty-three coke-producing refineries.) The nature of the contracts varies considerably. Some are formal documents over twenty pages long, while others are two-paragraph letters saying that the parties renew their previous agreement with no changes. In a number of contracts, some confidential information (often concerning price) was deleted by the FTC.

[3] We have in mind a very narrow meaning of efficiency. The adaptations are efficient for the parties, not necessarily for any larger group (such as society as a whole).

[4] The theoretical framework for analyzing complex institutional arrangements in general, and long-term contracts in particular, has been developing over the last decade or so. See Victor P. Goldberg, Relational Exchange: Economics and Complex Contracts, 23 Am. Behavioral Scientist 337 (1980); Benjamin Klein, Robert G. Crawford, & Armen A. Alchian, Vertical Integration, Appropriable Rents, and the Competitive Contracting Process, 21 J. Law & Econ. 297 (1978); Oliver E. Williamson, The Economic Institutions of Capitalism: Firms, Markets, Relational Contracting, 1985; and The Economic Nature of the Firm: A Reader (Louis Putterman ed.), 1986.

ditions are frequently made without consulting the written contracts.[5] The documents will reflect the concerns of the parties as filtered through their lawyers and conditioned by their expectations regarding the reasonableness of the opposite party in adjusting to unspecified contingencies. Second, our working assumption is only a research strategy, not an article of faith. People do stupid things, and, in some instances, the best explanation of why a particular term was adopted is that the parties made a mistake. There are two countervailing forces influencing the likelihood that petroleum coke contracts would embody mistakes. On the one hand, considerable time and effort went into designing the contracts; contract terms were not simply lifted off the shelf. On the other hand, the long terms and the infrequent participation in the market by most of the buyers and sellers[6] meant that contract terms were not necessarily "equilibrium" terms—that is, the results of market forces rewarding winners and penalizing losers. The contract terms meet only the weak test of birth, not the stronger test of survival.

We have chosen not to rely on three common explanations: (*a*) the contract terms are imposed by the big and powerful on the small and weak; (*b*) the terms facilitate anticompetitive behavior;[7] and (*c*) the contracts reflect the risk preferences of the parties. We are not asserting that any of these propositions is false; we are simply trying to see how far we can go in explaining contract structure without invoking these three arguments. This research strategy was not, of course, adopted on a whim. It reflects our view that these propositions will not be of much help in explaining the structure of these, or most other, long-term economic relations. Indeed, we can go a step further and suggest that these propositions can impede (and have impeded) research on complex exchange by providing superficially appealing answers that have discouraged search along more fruitful lines.

In the next section, we provide some background on the petroleum coke industry. Section III analyzes the structure of coke contracts, emphasizing the duration, ease of termination, locus of decisions as to quantity, and the use of commission pricing. Section IV focuses on the price-adjustment mechanisms used in the coke contracts.

[5] See Stewart Macaulay, Non-Contractual Relations in Business: A Preliminary Study, 28 Am. Soc. Rev. 55 (1963).

[6] Some of the aluminum company buyers, for example, entered into a contract with only one coke supplier.

[7] This was, of course, the FTC's presumption in *Great Lakes*. For a complete analysis of the antitrust case, it would obviously be necessary to consider whether the contracts had a possible anticompetitive purpose or effect; that is the subject of a separate paper.

II. Petroleum Coke: Its Production, Processing, and Use

Petroleum coking is a process that takes the heavy residual oils left over from the initial distillation of crude oil and, through the application of high temperatures, produces gas oil and petroleum coke (often referred to as "green coke"). The former can be further processed into lighter distillate fuels, such as gasoline, turbine and diesel fuels, and light fuel oil. Coke accounts for less than 3 percent of the value of a barrel of oil. If not coked, the residual oil would be processed into heavy fuel oil or turned into asphalt. Thus, coking permits a low-value residual to be upgraded to more valuable light and middle distillate fuels. In 1970, fifty-three cokers were in operation in the United States. About 15 percent of the crude oil refined in the United States was coked.[8]

The principal constituent of green coke is carbon, which makes up from 82 percent to 92 percent of the total weight.[9] It also contains volatile matter, ash, sulphur, and trace metals. The amounts of sulphur and metals in coke depend directly on the origin of the crude oil from which it comes, and the amounts present determine the use to which it is put. High-sulphur coke, which is less valuable, is used primarily for fuel in utility boilers and cement kilns.

Most low-sulphur coke—about 40 percent of all green coke—is calcined. Calcining converts the coke from a hydrocarbon to a pure carbon. This eliminates the volatile elements, increases its hardness, and makes it an excellent conductor of electricity. At the same time, calcining reduces coke's suitability for use as fuel.[10] Most calcined coke is used for the production of anodes for the electrolytic cell reduction of alumina to aluminum.[11] Calcining reduces the weight of coke by 15–30 percent and raises its value substantially. In 1970, a ton of low-sulphur green coke sold for around $10, while a ton of calcined coke sold for around $30.[12] Production of one pound of aluminum requires approximately 0.5 pounds of green coke (or about 0.4 pounds of calcined coke).[13] About 3 percent of the cost of aluminum can be attributed to calcined coke.[14]

[8] Victor P. Goldberg & John R. Erickson, Long-Term Contracts for Petroleum Coke, 2-3 (Working Paper No. 206, Univ. California, Davis, Dep't Economics 1982).

[9] 82 F.T.C. 1529, 1532.

[10] 82 F.T.C. 1529, 1542–43.

[11] In the 1970s about 75–80 percent of the calcined coke produced in the United States was used for aluminum anodes, about half being sold to foreign users.

[12] CF, at 34.

[13] 8805-4-99-3.

[14] Aluminum prices in the late 1960s were about 25 cents per pound. Green coke sold for about $10 per ton and calcined coke for about $30. At the conversion rates noted in the text, the shares of the aluminum price attributable to green and calcined coke were 1 percent and 2.4 percent, respectively.

TABLE 1

Calcining Plants Owned by Great Lakes Carbon, 1964

Location	Capacity (tons/month)
Port Arthur, Texas:	
Started calcining operations 1935	3,000
Added second calciner 1938	9,000
Added third calciner 1952	18,000
Total	30,000
Calumet plant, Chicago, Illinois:	
Started calcining operations 1942	18,000
Added second and third units 1948	10,000
Added fourth unit 1959	8,000
Total	36,000
Wilmington plant, Wilmington, California:	
Started calcining operations 1940	12,000
Added second unit 1952	18,000
Total	30,000
Enid plant, Enid, Oklahoma: started November 1964	15,000
Casper plant, Casper, Wyoming	
Started processing 1956	2,500
Added second unit 1964	2,500
Total	5,000
Lockport, Lockport, Illinois: started 1937; abandoned 1958	7,500

Source.—F.T.C. 8805-4-2-1-1.

The GLC is the largest producer of calcined coke. Great Lakes' calciners, their initial dates of operation, and their capacity as of 1964, are shown in Table 1.[15] Twelve other firms operate twenty-one additional calciners, with a total capacity about twice that of Great Lakes.

Great Lakes served as a middleman, selling both green and calcined coke to end users. Other calcining firms also served as middlemen. In 1959, Kaiser Aluminum and Chemical Company became the first end user to build a calciner. In subsequent years, Kaiser added five additional calciners, and three other aluminum companies also built calciners. Although the major part of their calciner output was for their own anode production, the aluminum companies did sell some calcined coke to other

[15] According to industry sources, since 1964 capacity at the Port Arthur and Wilmington plants has roughly doubled, and at the Enid plant it has tripled. At the Chicago plant, it has been halved.

final users. While there has been a substantial amount of backward integration into calcining by aluminum companies, there has been very little forward integration by refiners. Continental Oil installed a calciner in 1956, but, by 1970, only four of the thirty-five coking refiners had installed calciners.[16]

Because coke is a low-value, bulky product, transportation costs play a significant role in the economics of coking. Unless a coker has access to ocean ports, or to a calciner within a radius of fifty miles, shipping by rail is the cheapest alternative. As an indication of the magnitude of these costs, we regressed 1968 rail freight rates against distance:[17]

$$F = 5.41 + \underset{(7.6)}{0.0038D}, \quad R^2 = .77, N = .85,$$

where F is freight rate per ton, and D is distance in miles. That is, shipping costs independent of distance were about $5 per ton, and shipping coke 1,000 miles costs about $4 more. At the time, high-quality coke sold for about $10 per ton freight on board (f.o.b.), while low-quality coke sold for about half that. Because calcined coke had a considerably higher value per pound, producers had an incentive to locate calciners near the source of supply and to transport calcined coke to the location of the end user. If a coker was located near a calciner, trucking was a reasonably inexpensive method of transport. In eleven instances, cokers and calciners were physically adjacent, so that no transportation (other than to or from the inventory pile) was necessary. Proximate location drastically reduced transportation costs, but other costs were likely to be higher. For example, it might require sacrificing economies of scale in the coking or calcining process. In addition, it could increase the contracting parties' vulnerability to opportunistic behavior by their counterparts.

The bulkiness of coke makes it expensive to store. Coke is also a fire hazard and a source of pollution unless it is put in covered storage.[18] The costs of storing coke include both the direct costs of preparing land and of providing railroad spurs, water sprays, bulldozers, and loading equipment and the opportunity cost of the land employed for storage. It also must include the possible costs arising from an accumulation of inventory, an accumulation that may cause a disruption in the refinery's operations.[19] Some of these costs arise regardless of whether the coke is stored at the

[16] More recently Arco and Gulf have built large calciners.

[17] The data are from 8805-4-2-2, pp. 276–78. The t-statistic is in parentheses.

[18] MOF, at 31–32.

[19] The production of coke has a "vast potential to disrupt the entire operation of the refinery due to its rapid accumulation" (MOF at p. 22).

refinery or elsewhere. But others, notably the opportunity cost of land, depend crucially on where the coke is stored. Economizing on inventory costs requires rapid processing to keep the total inventory low and rapid removal of inventory to lower-value storage areas. As we shall see in the next section, the latter is of particular importance in explaining the variation in the structure of coke contracts.

III. Structure of the Contracts

The parties to a long-term contract have a mutual interest in designing a contract that maximizes its value to both parties. They also, however, have a selfish interest in achieving a large individual share, even if doing so results in a reduced overall value. If the parties could costlessly constrain their noncooperative, opportunistic behavior, contracting would not be very difficult—or interesting. Much of the structure of contracts reflects the attempts of parties to constrain their noncooperative behavior in order to increase the total pie. In our discussion, we will emphasize the pie-increasing motives; but it should be understood that the opportunism problem is omnipresent.

In the long run, the parties involved want to assure the continuation of their relation while still maintaining enough flexibility to adapt the relation to changed circumstances. The more vulnerable a party is to termination, ceteris paribus, the greater the protection it would want. Thus, a coker with ample storage space and easy access to the sea would have little reason to rely on a particular customer, and it would not insist on a very long contract term with large penalties for early termination. On the other hand, a calciner built adjacent to a coker and with poor access to alternative coke suppliers would opt for greater protection.

The parties also face a short-run coordination problem. The coker's costs depend on the rate at which coke is removed from the refinery. If coke is removed too slowly, the coker is faced with a number of costly options. It could accelerate the search for new customers, reduce the selling price, add to inventory if storage space is available, reduce the production rate, or, in the limit, shut down its coking operation. The opportunity cost of refinery products not produced is a significant element of the cost of untimely removal. Because oil companies can substitute output from noncoking operations, the cost is related to the difference between the net returns from coking and the refiner's next best alternative. The buyer also faces costs if the rate of delivery deviates from the optimal rate. If too much coke arrives, the firm would have to store it or otherwise dispose of it. If too little, then the calciner must draw down inventory, acquire coke from an alternative supplier, produce at an inefficiently low rate, or, in the limit, shut down.

An integrated firm would face the same problem of balancing these various costs. The problems are compounded, however, when the decisions are to be made by independent firms. To facilitate coordinated, adaptive, sequential decision-making the parties could establish channels for conveying exchange-related information or set up procedures to deal with disputes, for example, arbitration. They could also build into the contract incentives for controlling the costs arising from miscoordination. Our primary focus will be on the locus of responsibility and on the incentive structures. In the remainder of this section we will focus on the means by which the contracts dealt with the long- and short-run coordination problems.

To facilitate exposition, we have divided the contracts into four groups: (1) sales of coke to Great Lakes Carbon for calcining (this covers most of the GLC contracts in the sample), (2) sales to aluminum companies, (3) commission contracts, and (4) the remainder. In an earlier draft, we included a large number of specific contract terms in the text. Most readers found that this impeded the flow of the argument. We, have, therefore, decided to omit the specific contract language and instead to paraphrase. For readers interested in the precise language, the contract terms are available separately as an Appendix.[20]

Great Lakes' Calcining Contracts.—A number of features common to most of the GLC contracts influenced their basic structure. The coker's capacity was usually considerably less than GLC's calciner capacity; for example, in 1963 GLC's Port Arthur calciner purchased at least 15,000 tons of coke from eight refiners and its Calumet calciner purchased a similar amount from six.[21] Moreover, GLC maintained more than 250 acres for coke storage at ten different locations. The storage capacity was about 3 million tons; in 1963 and 1964, its average inventory was about 2 million tons, which was equal to about one year's purchases.[22] Consequently, GLC was not particularly vulnerable to variations in the flow of coke from any single source. Sellers, on the other hand, generally had little storage capacity. If inventory was allowed to accumulate on the premises, the coker would have to shut down the coking operations. The cokers could have bought additional land—at a price—for storing coke inventory at the refinery and could have controlled—also at a price—the nuisance damages arising from storing coke at the refinery. We infer that

[20] Citations to this will be of the form: "Appendix, Term ——." A copy of the Appendix is on file at the editorial offices of the journal.

[21] 8805-4-2-1-1.

[22] 8805-4-2-1-1-. GLC's inventory was unusually high in those years.

the price for doing so was too high; on net, it was more profitable for most of these refiners to have the inventory moved away from the refinery.[23]

Almost all the GLC contracts were full output/immediate removal contracts with GLC bearing all the risks of changes in the rate of coke output. The coker was obligated to sell only if it produced.[24] The decision to produce was entirely in the hands of the coker. The coker could terminate without legal obligation if it ceased production of coke at the refinery. Termination for the purpose of selling to another buyer would, however, constitute a breach of contract. The contract was asymmetrical in that GLC did not have the option of ceasing performance without being liable for damages. Indeed, GLC typically agreed to provide immediate removal of the coke, so that a failure to remove coke rapidly enough would constitute a breach of its obligations.[25] GLC's nonperformance would be excused legally only for specified conditions having to do with changes in the coke's quality or for circumstances beyond the parties' control.[26]

The GLC contracts were generally of long duration, especially when a new coker was involved. Nine of the ten contracts written between 1946 and 1961 involving new cokers were for a period of at least ten years.[27] Contract length is, to be sure, a slippery concept. A contract might permit termination without penalty at a certain date prior to the stated termination date. For example, GLC's twenty-year agreement with American Oil gave each party the privilege of terminating with six months' notice at the end of the tenth and fifteenth years.[28] The stated twenty-year term does, nonetheless, convey some information. There would be a greater presumption of renewal at the tenth anniversary than for a straight ten-year agreement; a party terminating at the reopening date would have to meet a

[23] Conceivably, the refiner could have shipped the coke itself, rather than relying on GLC. It could have maintained the distant stockpiles or shipped the coke to stockpiles owned by others (including GLC). Thus, GLC's 1974 contract with Mobil's Beaumont, Texas refinery gave Mobil, in the event the contract were terminated, the right to store up to 400,000 tons of coke at GLC's Port Arthur facility; the agreement was for one year, with the option on a second year as well; prices for handling Mobil's inventory were specified in the contract. This was the only instance of such a term in the contracts. It seems quite certain that forward integration into inventory removal and storage by refiners was more costly than backward integration into removal and storage by calciners.

[24] Appendix, Term 1.

[25] Appendix, Term 2.

[26] Suspension or termination of the contract for failure to meet quality standards is discussed in Goldberg & Erickson, *supra* note 8, at 30–39. For a typical "force majeure" clause, see Appendix, Term 3.

[27] The one exception was a five-year contract with Skelly Oil in 1958 (8805-4-2-1-1, p. 30). Skelly had considerable space available for inventory storage.

[28] Appendix, Term 4.

higher standard of reasonableness to maintain its reputation with the trade.[29]

The primary determinant of contract length was the coker's need to protect its reliance interest. The small number of feasible alternative outlets for the coker meant that the value of the coker's investment would fall substantially if the relation were terminated. GLC's ample storage capacity and its multiple sources made it relatively less vulnerable.[30]

The Aluminum Contracts.—Ten contracts between coking refiners and aluminum producers were included in the record. Some significant features of these agreements are summarized in Table 2. Only the LaGloria-Alcoa contracts did not involve construction of either a new coker or a calciner. These agreements, not surprisingly, were for a much shorter period than the others. At three locations, the contracting parties were engaged in the simultaneous construction of an adjacent new coker and calciner.

The aluminum contracts differed considerably from the GLC agreements. Whereas, in the Great Lakes Carbon contracts, the refiner was responsible for determining whether, and how much, coke should be produced, in the aluminum contracts, the decision was in the hands of the buyer. All the contracts specified a minimum level of output. In no case did the buyer agree to take all the coker's output, even though in all but three instances the contract quantity was close to the coker's capacity. Moreover, in nine of the agreements, the coking refiner could not refuse to produce coke without being liable for damages.[31]

Six of the contracts allowed the buyer to reduce its purchases below the contract quantity under certain conditions. However, to provide some protection for the coker, the contracts included nonlinear pricing rules to discourage such reductions. The form these pricing rules took differed considerably. The differences are of less importance than the fact that

[29] A variant was a contract for three successive three-year terms. The contract stated that the parties could not terminate solely because the price was unsatisfactory without first engaging in good faith negotiation on the price (Appendix, Term 7).

[30] Two of GLC's calciners were built in close proximity to a single coker that supplied all its needs. The small calciner (50,000 tons per year) at Casper, Wyoming, had facilities to store one year's coke. The Wilmington, California, calciner was built near Mobil's large Torrance coker (coke output of about 500,000 tons per year). The calciner had storage capacity of about eight months (8805-4-2-1-1). Moreover, Mobile had additional storage capacity for coke in the event GLC's facilities were full (CX 5). In addition, GLC had access to the ocean and shipped most of the coke to Japan; in 1964, it sold 378,000 tons to Japan, about one-third of which was calcined (CX 1305).

[31] The one exception was the Humble-Kaiser agreement (CX 68). Because Humble had already accumulated a coke stockpile of 200,000 tons that could supply Kaiser's needs for four years, the cost to Kaiser of granting Humble discretion on production of coke was obviously not great. See Appendix, Term 8.

TABLE 2

ALUMINUM CONTRACTS

Refinery	Buyer	Exhibit Number	Contract Date	New Coker	New Calciner	Quantity Close to Coker Capacity	Contract Length (in years)	Calciner Adjacent
Gulf	Alcoa	CX 30	May 13, 1960	✓	‖	✓	10	...
Champlin	Swiss Aluminum	CX 20	June 2, 1960	✓	...	✓	11.5	...
Humble	Reynolds	CX 31	September 7, 1961	✓	✓	✓	10	✓
LaGloria	Alcoa	CX 34	January 23, 1962	...	‖	...	3	...
Humble	Kaiser	CX 68	April 1, 1963	...	✓	✓	8	§
LaGloria	Alcoa	CX 35	January 11, 1964	...	‖	...	3†	...
Cities Service	Swiss Aluminum	CX 25	February 1, 1964	✓	✓	...	8	...
Shell	Kaiser	CX 38	June 11, 1964	✓	✓	✓	8	✓
Atlantic-Richfield	Harvey	CX 17	December 22, 1965	✓	✓	...	15	✓
Humble	Reynolds	CX 418	March 1, 1967	✓*	✓*	✓	10‡	✓

* Expansion of coker and calciner roughly doubled capacity.
† Renewal of CX 34.
‡ Revision of CX 31.
§ Kaiser's calciner at Mead, Washington, was built specifically to process the high-sulphur coke produced by Humble's Billings, Montana, coker.
‖ The coke in these contracts is calcined for the aluminum company by Great Lakes Carbon.

nonlinear pricing rules were common. Nonlinear pricing was only used in contracts in which the buyer had some discretion as to how much of the output it required.

Alcoa's contract involving Gulf's new coker gave Gulf the right to shut down the coker if inventory at the refinery reached 10,000 tons (twenty days' output). Alcoa would have to pay a "standby" charge during the shutdown period of $75,000 per month.[32] With the contract price at $12 (before escalation) and the contract quantity 500 tons per day, Alcoa in effect paid for about 40 percent of the coke, whether or not it took any. Moreover, if Alcoa did not take most of the contracted amount, inventory would accumulate and the inventory constraint would quickly become binding. Alcoa could take coke at below the contract rate only if Gulf chose to produce at a reduced rate. Thus, Gulf was assured that Alcoa would have to take its interests into account when determining how much coke to take. Alcoa's contracts with LaGloria gave the coker less protection, although they still included nonlinear pricing. The price for the first 10,000 tons (35 percent of the contract quantity) was $14 per ton, while the price for the remainder was only $11.25.[33]

Two large cokers were constructed in conjunction with new calciners by Humble (with Reynolds) and Richfield (with Harvey). The Humble-Reynolds contract was entered into in September 1961, and the coker and calciner were in operation by spring 1963.[34] Reynolds agreed to take a minimum of 330,000 tons of coke per year, a quantity that it would either use itself or resell. Reynolds had the right to reduce its obligation if its estimated domestic aluminum primary ingot production were to fall below 420,000 tons per year. Since this output level would require only about 210,000 tons of petroleum coke, Reynolds in effect agreed that, in the event of a decline in demand for its aluminum, it would be fully responsible for disposing of the 120,000 tons of coke not needed for its own operations. For each ton by which Reynolds' projected aluminum production fell below 420,000, Reynolds was relieved of taking 0.78 tons.[35] Since its own coke usage would decrease by 0.5 tons, Reynolds' obligation to sell coke on the open market was reduced by 0.28 tons. Reynolds was obliged to pay 50 percent of the contract price whether or not the coke was produced.[36]

[32] Appendix, Term 11.

[33] Appendix, Term 12.

[34] See CX 31. The contract was for ten years from the date of first delivery with two five-year renewal periods.

[35] The minimum obligation was (330,000/420,000) times the projected aluminum output.

[36] Appendix, Term 13.

In 1967, the contract was revised since "Reynolds, because of the projected need for additional green . . . coke, has requested Humble to increase the quantity of green . . . coke supplied by it to Reynolds."[37] The new agreement was for 600,000 tons. The arrangement for dealing with a reduced demand for Reynold's aluminum was carried over to the new contract with only minor changes in the numbers. This contract added a new wrinkle by reducing the marginal price; the first 430,000 tons each year cost $12.50 while the price for the remainder was $10.50.

Since Reynolds' projected coke requirements for the early 1970s were only about 500,000 tons per year, the contract committed Reynolds to becoming a serious marketer of calcined coke.[38] Vertical integration into marketing enabled Reynolds to provide additional assurance to Humble that it stood ready to remove Humble's coke. This arrangement enabled Humble to achieve greater economies of scale than would have been possible if Reynolds were the only buyer and if it had agreed to take a smaller amount that was closer to its actual needs, or if it had agreed to a requirements contract.[39]

Alternatively, the parties could have set the quantity at the calciner's capacity and relied on other middlemen to remove the remaining coke. This is, in effect, what Richfield and Harvey did. Harvey agreed to construct, on land leased from Richfield and adjacent to Richfield's Watson, California, refinery, a calciner capable of handling about one-fourth the refinery's coke output. Richfield agreed to maintain a sufficient inventory of coke to assure a constant monthly flow of coke to keep Harvey's calciner operating at full capacity.[40]

The Richfield-Harvey contract period was fifteen years; however, under certain circumstances the contract could be terminated after only eight years (with two years' notice). The lease established a schedule of payments that was unrelated to the quantity of coke. Thus, by charging one price for the land and a second price per ton of coke, the parties established a two-part pricing system. The contract price of $3.10 per ton was only about one-quarter the current market price of equivalent quality coke, while the rental fee was above the fair market rate.

Richfield had two other buyers of coke from the Watson refinery. Mitsui had a one-year, renewable, fixed-price contract for 50,000–70,000 metric tons per year for sale to Japan; Mitsui had the exclusive right to

[37] CX 418. The contract was to run until the end of December 1978; it also had two five-year renewal periods.

[38] 8805-4-99-3.

[39] A requirements contract would have imposed all the risks of demand fluctuations on Humble and would have drastically reduced the protection of its reliance interest.

[40] Appendix, Term 14.

sell Richfield's coke in Japan and agreed not to sell coke outside Japan without Richfield's consent.[41] Wilson Carbon had an exclusive right under a six-year commission contract to sell Richfield's coke anywhere in the world other than to Harvey or in Japan. Wilson agreed to take a minimum of 200,000 short tons.[42] Thus, in the three contracts combined, Richfield had firm commitments to remove about two-thirds the coker's capacity. For the remaining one-third, Wilson had the first option, but Richfield reserved the right to determine whether the additional coke should be produced.[43] Mitsui and Harvey had lesser claims on coke beyond their contract maximum. Mitsui would be able to buy coke that Richfield had available at the contract price.[44] Harvey's contract terms did not carry forward to any additional sales.[45]

Commission Pricing.—Only two GLC contracts and none of the aluminum contracts utilized commission pricing. In contrast, nearly half the contracts involving other middlemen set the contract price as a fraction of the buyer's resale price. Other things being equal, commission pricing is more attractive the less the buyer does to the coke before reselling it. That is, commission pricing is easier to arrange and police if the reseller simply takes the order and arranges to ship the coke out of stockpiles maintained by the refinery than if he stores the coke, combining it with coke from other producers, or processes the coke (for example, calcining it).

Commission pricing was the standard for low-quality (high-sulphur) coke. The price to the middleman was usually 95 percent of the price at which the coke was resold. The contracts often covered the entire coker output, but they differed from GLC's contracts by allowing for intermediate storage.[46] Cokers promised to provide in advance an approximate schedule of coke production to facilitate the buyer's planning, but they refused to be bound by that schedule.[47] The contracts were for a much shorter duration than those involving calcinable coke. Contracts were typically for less than five years and termination was on relatively short notice.[48]

[41] CX 18.

[42] CX 19; Appendix, Term 17.

[43] Appendix, Term 18.

[44] Appendix, Term 19.

[45] Appendix, Term 20; Cities Service's coker at Lake Charles, Louisiana, also allowed for achieving scale economies in coking by having the coker contract with additional marketers. For Cities Service's method for allocating the uncommitted coke to the primary buyer, see Appendix, Term 21.

[46] Appendix, Term 22.

[47] Appendix, Term 23.

[48] Appendix, Term 24.

Commission pricing has a number of desirable properties. It provides, as a side effect, an automatic mechanism for adjusting prices over the life of the agreement. (The advantage of price adjustment will be discussed in the following section.) It also reduces the refiner's incentive to "cheat" in the quality dimension; the parties could therefore devote fewer resources to specifying quality and monitoring performance. Indeed, most of these contracts did not specify quality.[49]

Contracting parties can avoid some of the ex ante costs of gathering information by using commission pricing. With a fixed-price contract, the middleman has an incentive to line up resale contracts before negotiating the initial price. The coker also has an incentive to acquire information on the resale market lest the middleman use the additional information to extract the lion's share of the rewards. Commission pricing reduces the value of special price information and, therefore, permits the parties to develop the information in a more timely, less costly manner.[50]

One problem with commission pricing is that it impairs the middleman's incentive to search for customers willing to pay a high price. The reseller would be indifferent between price/effort combinations that yielded the same expected profit. The refiner, however, would not be indifferent since its compensation would depend on the resale price. It would prefer the high-price/high-effort combination. To guard against the reseller's choosing the "quiet life," the commission contracts typically included a ceiling on inventory accumulation and a minimum average price.[51] The minimum price was renegotiated frequently (often quarterly), and, if the parties could not agree on a minimum price, the contract would be terminable on short notice (often thirty days). However, the seller agreed not to offer to sell coke at or below the price offered by the reseller—the reseller could, in effect, match any outside offer.[52]

Great Lakes Carbon's two commission contracts nicely illustrate the complications that arise when the reseller does more than simply take orders for shipment from a stockpile maintained by the coker. Both in-

[49] Most contracts not using commission pricing did specify quality standards. They also spelled out the procedures for measurement and dispute settlement and established rules for dealing with coke that did not meet the quality standards. See Goldberg & Erickson, *supra* note 8, at 30–38.

[50] For similar arguments on the benefits of constraining "oversearching," see Roy W. Kenney & Benjamin Klein, The Economics of Block Booking, 26 J. Law & Econ. 497 (1983); Yoram Barzel, Some Fallacies in the Interpretation of Information Costs, 20 J. Law & Econ. 291 (1977); and Yoram Barzel, Measurement Costs and the Organization of Markets, 25 J. Law & Econ. 27 (1982). The same basic argument is used in the following section to explain why parties might find price-adjustment mechanisms to be mutually beneficial.

[51] For inventory ceilings, see Terms 22 and 24; for minimum price, see Terms 25 and 26.

[52] Appendix, Term 28.

volved new cokers being constructed in the Los Angeles area in the late 1960s. Each coker could hold up to two months of inventory, so that timely removal, while desirable, was not as critical as it was for other cokers dealing with GLC. The coke had a low-sulphur content, but there was not sufficient calcining capacity in the Los Angeles region to process it. This coke was destined for shipment outside the region; primarily to Japan.

The term of these contracts was substantially shorter than the other contracts involving new cokers—(three and five years, respectively). This shorter term reflects the coker's lesser reliance on a single purchaser. GLC had an advantage over other middlemen when the initial contracts were signed, since it already had extensive customer contacts in Japan, as well as ample storage capacity on the West Coast.[53] However, performance of the contract tended to erode its advantages vis-à-vis potential competitors. Because information developed by GLC regarding the existence of customers was revealed to the coker, GLC's market development effort was made available to potential competitors.[54] Indeed, both contracts were subsequently lost to competitors.

The inventory constraint meant that coke had to be removed even if it had not yet been sold. Therefore, the price to GLC was not set as a percentage of the f.o.b. price; it was set at 90 percent of the net resale price—resale price minus the costs incurred by GLC in reselling the coke if these costs had not been reimbursed by the customer.[55] This is similar to f.o.b. pricing, except that the costs of reselling are paid in what amounts to a cost-plus arrangement.[56] The contracts included complex variants on the minimum average price arrangement of other commission contracts. If the costs of resale exceeded the price, the coker would refund the excess to GLC. In that event, however, the coker would have the option of suspending deliveries to GLC.[57] The importance to the coker of removing inventory meant that it would be willing to accept a minimum average price of zero.

[53] In 1965, GLC exported 192,000 tons of noncalcined, high-quality (low-sulphur) coke to Japan; this was about 80 percent of the coke in this category exported by American firms. It accounted for about 90 percent of the calcined coke exported to Japan. See CX 1307.

[54] Because the price paid by GLC depended on GLC's selling price and its selling costs, the contract required that GLC make all materials related to costs available to the coker. See Appendix, Term 30.

[55] The costs included (*a*) all freight and other transportation charges, (*b*) all handling and storage charges, (*c*) the cost of any sizing of coke which in GLC's opinion increased the total market value of the coke more than the cost of processing, (*d*) bona fide selling commissions paid to third parties, and (*e*) taxes (CX 14).

[56] Appendix, Term 31.

[57] The two contracts treated this slightly differently; see Terms 32 and 33.

The coke covered by these agreements was either shipped directly to Japan or moved to GLC's storage facilities, where it was commingled with coke from other sources for subsequent shipment to Japan. If commission rates differed, or if some of the coke in GLC's inventory were purchased at a fixed price, then GLC would have an incentive to act opportunistically in designating the source of a particular shipment. The contracts provided a mechanism for constraining such behavior. If the average net price for a calendar year exceeded the average net price of all "Western Coke"[58] sold by GLC in that year, then GLC would have to repay the excess multiplied by the number of tons delivered under the contract during the year, GLC was responsible for determining the average selling price, but the seller had the right to require an audit, the cost of the audit being borne equally by the two firms.[59]

Other Contracts.—Union Oil and Collier entered into two contracts involving construction of an adjacent calciner and coker at two California locations—Oleum and Santa Maria. The agreements (CX 43, CX 66) illustrate nicely some of the points made above. The contracts were similar in a number of respects. Both were for full output of the coker and gave Union Oil the option of suspending, reducing, or discontinuing production of coke. Both were for long periods—the Oleum contract was for ten years[60] and the Santa Maria contract for twelve. However, there were significant differences, which stemmed largely from the availability of inventory storage capacity at the two sites. The Oleum site could store less than six months of coke output, while the Santa Maria site had a two-year capacity.

At Santa Maria, the stockpile was Collier's only protection from supply disruptions.[61] At Oleum, the contract included a very elaborate package that provided Collier with considerably more assurance of a continued supply. It also provided less assurance of removal than did the Santa Maria or GLC contracts.[62] The contract called for a minimum quantity of 1 million tons over ten years—approximately 40 percent of the coker's capacity. In the event that Union's production at the Oleum plant was reduced or discontinued (so that the minimum would not otherwise be

[58] For a precise definition, see Appendix, Term 34.

[59] In both contracts, an independent third party would determine the average selling price if the parties disagreed; see Appendix, Term 30.

[60] The contract was amended after two years and extended for an additional one-and-a-half years (CX 44).

[61] Appendix, Term 35.

[62] Collier received less assurance of a continued supply than did the aluminum companies. It also undertook a greater commitment to remove coke than did the aluminum companies.

obtained), it agreed to make up the deficiency with coke of similar quality from other sources at the contract price.

If inventory at the Oleum coker reached 50,000 tons (three months' output), Union could either offer it for sale (giving Collier the option to take the coke at a price 10 percent below the outside offer) or require Collier to remove the coke. In the latter event, Collier would pay only 50 percent of the contract price.[63] Thus, when there was external evidence of slack demand (inventory accumulation) and Union had confirmed this evidence through its inability to find buyers at prices below the contract price, Union would then share the cost of the demand reduction.

Carbon product producers were typically content to purchase their coke from middlemen. However, in some instances such producers chose to contract directly with a coker. The coker generally had more than one customer for its coke and was capable of carrying a reasonable amount of inventory; it was not purchasing removal services. As a result, the contracts typically gave very little protection to the reliance interest of either the buyer or the seller.

The carbon product contracts were either requirements contracts or for a fixed quantity.[64] The seller was obligated to deliver coke only if it produced. It had the right to determine whether, or how much, to produce.[65] If the seller did not produce sufficient coke, the buyer would be free to meet its needs elsewhere and would have the option of terminating the contract on short notice.[66] The term of the contracts was short—from one to five years. Moreover, in some of the agreements, the buyer had the right to shop for a better price. If the seller did not elect to meet the lower price, the contract could be terminated on short notice.[67]

IV. Price Adjustment

The parties did not enter into multiyear contracts in order to make bets on the future course of prices. Rather, they entered into these agreements

[63] Appendix, Terms 36 and 37.

[64] Air Reduction accounted for all three of the requirements contracts (CX 23, CX 39, CX 420).

[65] Appendix, Term 42 and 43.

[66] Appendix, Term 44.

[67] The three Air Reduction contracts fixed price for a period after which the buyer could search for a lower price. In the 1962 agreement, the initial price was firm for eighteen months, but this dropped to nine months in 1964 and zero months in 1967. See Appendix, Term 45. In a letter to the commission, a Union Carbide executive noted regarding one of its agreements with Cities Service: "Carbide ascertained it could procure comparable coke at a lower price. As the Carbide contract with Cities Service included a price protection clause, and Cities Service indicated it was unwilling to meet the lower offer made to Carbide, the contract was terminated according to its terms" (8805-4-2-1-4).

for the reasons developed in Section III. Having done so, they had to make some decisions regarding the price during the life of the agreement.[68] While they could simply establish a single price or a schedule of future prices that would be in force for the entire period, they also had the option of providing some mechanism for adjusting prices in light of changed circumstances. Nearly 90 percent of the pre-1973 contracts and all of the post-1973 contracts did provide some price flexibility.

Indexing is the most obvious price-adjustment mechanism, but there are others as well. The parties could simply agree to renegotiate price either at fixed dates (for example, quarterly or annually) or at one side's request. A hybrid mechanism involving indexing and negotiation utilizes an index with a maximum-minimum limitation. If the indexed price falls outside the predetermined range, the parties can either continue at the ceiling (or floor) price or renegotiate the agreement. Another way of adjusting to changing market conditions is to allow the parties to solicit outside offers and then permit the other party to match the offer. Commission pricing, by its very nature, automatically links the contract price to external market conditions.

Indexing has the obvious advantage of being easy to implement and beyond the control (usually) of the parties involved. It also has the obvious disadvantage of not tracking changing conditions perfectly. Ceteris paribus, the lower the correlation between an index and the "correct" current price, the less attractive will indexing be. Renegotiation has the advantage of allowing the parties to use accurate, current information in revising the contract. It also, of course, suffers from the fact that reopening the contract can result in strategic behavior, especially if one of the parties is vulnerable to a threat of nonrenewal. Other things being equal, the greater this vulnerability, the less attractive would be the prospect of renegotiating.

Given that price adjustment can be difficult and costly, why bother? What are the benefits to risk-neutral firms? We will suggest three reasons for incorporating a price-adjustment mechanism into a contract; only the last two, we believe, are apposite in the case of coke contracts.

First, adjusting the price to keep it in line with current market prices gives the parties the proper short-run price signals. If the parties have much discretion regarding the short-run quantity of coke, this could be important. However, for most coke, this is not the case. Coke is a by-product for the coking refiner; the buyer—especially Great Lakes Car-

[68] This does not mean that price problems have no effect on the structure of the contracts. As we show below, the increased rate of price change post-1973 did influence contract structure.

bon—often bought the coker's entire output. Quantity was determined by the demand for the refiner's lighter distillates, not for coke. Indexing a coke price to the market for this reason would be similar to indexing a home mortgage to the current rental rate so that homeowners could better take into account the opportunity cost of being their own tenants.

Two alternative reasons appear to be more plausible for explaining the usage of price adjustment mechanisms in petroleum coke contracts: reduction of precontract search and postagreement incentives to breach or behave opportunistically.[69] In both these explanations, the success of price adjustment depends on its ability to reduce the variance of outcomes. The reduced variance is not, however, valued for itself. Rather, it enables the parties to curtail behavior that is mutually harmful, thereby increasing the value of the agreement to both parties.

A party contemplating entering into a contract has an incentive to increase its expected share of the gains from trade by expending resources to improve its information on the future course of costs and prices. The more each spends to achieve an informational advantage, the smaller the pie. Ceteris paribus, the larger the variance of the outcomes, the more resources would be devoted to this effort. The parties have an incentive to incorporate into the initial agreement a device that would discourage this wasteful searching. By reducing the value of special information, price-adjustment mechanisms can do precisely that.

If, after the firms enter into a long-term agreement, the contract price differs substantially from the market price, then the loser could be reluctant to continue the agreement. In this event, the loser could breach and suffer the legal and reputational consequences. There are, however, a number of less severe alternatives to willing compliance. A buyer could, for example, insist on strict compliance with the quality standards; he could remove coke from inventory at a slower pace than otherwise; or he could read the contract literally—"working to the rules" as often happens in labor disputes or in centrally planned economies. If the probability of such wasteful behavior increases as the divergence between contract and market price widens, rules that narrow the gap—price-adjustment rules—become increasingly attractive.

The Pre-1973 Contracts.—None of the pre-1973 contracts was indexed specifically to changes in the aggregate price level.[70] Only five used a

[69] This argument is developed in Victor P. Goldberg, Price Adjustment in Long-Term Contracts, 1985 Wisconsin L. Rev. 532.

[70] Since changes in costs or in the market price concern changes in nominal values, adjustments for them implicitly involve some adjustment to changes in the overall price level. In this sense, all of the coke contracts that provided some price flexibility contain some mechanism for adjusting, albeit imperfectly, to changes in the overall price level.

TABLE 3

MAXIMUM-MINIMUM PRICE LIMITATIONS FOR GREAT LAKES CARBON CONTRACTS, PRE-1973

Seller	Exhibit Number	Contract Date	Base ($)	Maximum ($)	Minimum ($)
Sunray DX	CX 9	March 1, 1957	...	15	8
CRA	CX 408	January 18, 1957	...	15	8
CRA	CX 409	March 7, 1963	...	15	8
NCRA	CX 410	March 19, 1957	...	10	4
NCRA	CX 411	January 29, 1963	...	10	4
NCRA	CX 412	July 22, 1963	...	10	4
Ucan	8805-4-2-1-6	March 1, 1957	10	15	8
Derby	8805-4-99-1	April 30, 1968	10.50	15	7
La Gloria	CX 34*	January 23, 1962	12.00†	18.50	7.50
La Gloria	CX 35*	February 11, 1964	11.25‡	18.50	7.50

* La Gloria sold to Alcoa. Most of the coke was shipped directly to Great Lakes' calciner at Post Arthur for calcining on Alcoa's account.

† The base price of coke shipped directly to Alcoa was $14.75.

‡ The base price of coke shipped directly to Alcoa was $14.00.

broad-based measure of inflation—one utilizing the Wholesale Price Index (WPI) and the other four the WPI for other than farm products and food (and three of these four adjusted prices only on an annual basis)[71]

Over half the pre-1973 GLC contracts utilized a price index, and all except two of these had a maximum-minimum limitation. In all but one, the index was based on the price of the crude oil supplied to the refinery, with the price being adjusted either whenever the posted crude price changed or at monthly or quarterly intervals. Four of these contracts supplemented the crude oil index with an index of wages of oil refinery workers and one also included an adjustment for the WPI nonfarm component.[72] The actual maximum-minimum limitations were deleted by the FTC in most instances,[73] and all that remains is shown in Table 3. This skimpy evidence suggests that the price could diverge from the base by around 20–50 percent before reaching the ceiling (or floor).

GLC renegotiated rather than indexed at only three cokers prior to 1966. However, from 1966 through 1973, only three of the fourteen contracts included a price index. Of the remainder, two contracts utilized commission pricing (which implicitly indexes to the market price), and

[71] 8805-3-3-2, p. 5; CX 3, CX 24, CX 25, and CX 31.

[72] The three contracts that adjusted for crude oil and wages weighted the two equally (CX 1, CX 2, CX 6); the contract which indexed for crude, wages, and the WPI component weighted the three .75, .15, and .10, respectively.

[73] CX 1, CX 2, CX 4, CX 6, CX 8, CX 10, CX 12, and CX 416.

two were for one year or less. In the other seven contracts, price adjustment was accomplished by negotiation.

These contracts typically invoked the intentions of the parties to continue the agreement; negotiations were to be undertaken in "good faith," and in the event that negotiations failed, the current price would continue for a period of time—usually six to eighteen months—after which the agreement would terminate.[74]

Prices could be revised even if the contract did not explicitly provide for changes. The record contains numerous examples of price reductions to Great Lakes Carbon (and to others) during the slump in 1962–65.[75] Letters from two of GLC's suppliers give an indication of the nature of the revisions:

> As we explained to you this price increase to the March 19, 1957, contract level was requested and made only after the most careful consideration of all factors involved. As you know, we have now been on the reduced price basis for two years. We have been happy to work with Great Lakes throughout the years even to the extent of granting price relief when requested by your people. (CX 413)

> This is to confirm our discussion of June 17 at which time we agreed to abrogate the terms of our contract covering petroleum coke produced at our El Dorado Refinery for six months starting July 1, 1965. This is a contract dated June 27, 1956 as amended January 31, 1957 and October 2, 1959. In order to give you some assistance in your marketing program, we will invoice all shipments of El Dorado coke production between July 1, 1965 and December 31, 1965 at ——— per ton, F.O.B. El Dorado. It is understood that this revised price will apply only to the production during the indicated six months and that the other terms and conditions of the basic contract are unchanged. In the absence of any subsequent agreements, the price will revert to the contract schedule of ——— per ton, effective January 1, 1966. (CX 53)

These nonmandated price reductions were undoubtedly a factor in the increased reliance on renegotiation in the 1966–73 contracts. The favorable experience with voluntary renegotiation indicated that the costs associated with opportunistic behavior when the contract price is renegotiated need not be prohibitively high.[76] Moreover, the voluntary reductions reflected the failure of the price index to track market conditions accurately. That is, the expected costs of renegotiation fell at the same time that the expected benefits of indexing declined.

Most of the non-GLC middleman contracts either were commission contracts or utilized a simple price index. In only three instances did the

[74] Appendix, Term 60.

[75] CX 50, CX 51, CX 52, CX 53, CX 409, CX 411, CX 412, CX 413, CX 1323, and MOX 41. Revisions of prices in non-GLC contracts are illustrated in GLC 7, CX 405, and CX 406.

[76] Contrast this to the aluminum contracts discussed below.

parties explicitly state that price adjustment would be accomplished by negotiation, and one of these was not quite an arm's length agreement.[77]

Where aluminum companies constructed new calciners in reliance on supply by a particular coker, the contract price was typically fixed for a substantial period (see Table 4).[78] The only instance in which this was not so was the first Humble-Reynolds agreement. When that was revised, however, the parties eliminated the elaborate indexing formula (which covered over two pages in the 1961 agreement) and instead fixed the price for ten years. A similar adjustment was made in the arrangement between Mobil and Union Carbide (rows 6 and 7 of Table 4). The parties abandoned monthly indexing and instead agreed on a fixed price for the duration of the contract.

The substantial length of the period over which prices remain fixed in these contracts stands in sharp contrast to what existed in other petroleum coke contracts. The fixed price agreements all date to the period in which GLC was making the transition from indexing to negotiated price adjustment and most likely are a response to the same underlying factors—namely the poor correlation between available indexes and market conditions. Why was there a more exteme response in the aluminum contracts?

The aluminum contracts generally entailed greater insulation from current market conditions. Reopening a contract would mean that the parties would haggle over how to share the pie. The more the parties are isolated from alternative trading partners, the larger the size of the pie to be shared. The larger the pie, the more resources the parties would devote to pursuing it. That is, the higher reliance interest in the aluminum contracts would result in higher renegotiation costs, making frequent renegotiation relatively less attractive.

Moreover, the "good will" sanction would be a less effective constraint on negotiations for aluminum producers than for GLC. The past track record of GLC enhanced the coker's confidence that it would negotiate price adjustment in good faith, and its continued dealings with a large number of suppliers made maintenance of this good reputation worthwhile. The aluminum companies had neither the track record nor a large incentive to maintain their reputation for fair dealing in this market. Reynolds and Harvey, for example, had no other contracts.

The Post-1973 Contracts.—The petroleum coke industry was subjected to two major shocks in 1973. On June 5, the FTC handed down its deci-

[77] 8805-4-99-2, 8805-3-4, and CX 41. The last contract was between a coker and a joint venture of which the coker owned 50 percent

[78] Appendix, Term 66.

TABLE 4

PRICE ADJUSTMENT IN CONTRACTS INVOLVING END-USER'S NEW CALCINERS

Coker	Calciner	Contract	Date	Term of Contract (in years)	Period until First Revision (in years)	Index Period	Indexed to
Humble	Reynolds*	CX 31	1961	10	1	Annual	Wages in petroleum refining, WPI, all commodities except farm and food, Bunker C fuel oil price
Humble	Reynolds*	CX 418	1967	10	10	...	...
Humble	Kaiser*	CX 68	1963	8	8	...	...
Shell	Kaiser*	CX 38	1964	8	8	...	...
Richfield	Harvey*	CX 17	1965	15	5	Every three years	Bunker C fuel oil
Mobil	Union Carbide†	CX 404	1960	5	2	Monthly	Calcined coke sold to aluminum industry
Mobil	Union Carbide†	CX 405	1963	3¾	3¾	...	...

* Aluminum company.

† Mobil's contract was with General Carbon, but Union Carbide guaranteed payment (CX 406); Union Carbide also contracted with Marathon (CX 36), but that price clause was deleted from the record.

sion finding Great Lakes Carbon's long-term contracts in violation of the antitrust laws. The remedy required that GLC amend all its existing contracts so that they would extend for a period no longer than three years and all new GLC contracts be for a maximum of three years.[79] The remedy also restricted the length of the contracting period for the eight oil company respondents. The restrictions on contract length did not apply to other buyers or sellers of coke. The other shock was a tremendous increase in volatility in both the crude oil and the aluminum markets. Between 1973 and 1979, green coke prices rose from about $13 to $60, while calcined coke prices rose from about $30 to $120.[80]

Our ability to trace the effect of the post-1973 changes in the structure of petroleum coke contracts is limited by the availability of data. We have twenty-nine Great Lakes contracts,[81] but we have had access to only a handful of contracts involving other buyers. After analyzing the GLC contracts, we will discuss briefly the changes in the contracts involving aluminum companies.

Most of the GLC contracts contained a clause that reflected the restrictions imposed by the Commission's decision. The term was three years, and the parties could not extend the term of the contract prior to six months before the date at which the contract would expire.[82] The only contracts that were not for three years were a series of one-year contracts with Continental and a one-year contract with Midland in 1974 (which was succeeded by a three-year agreement). In both cases, GLC's last contract with the refinery prior to the FTC's decision was for only nine months,[83] so the short term of the postdecision contracts at these refineries was not related to the changed circumstances in the petroleum coke market. It is

[79] There were three exceptions: (*a*) if a new coker or calciner were involved, the maximum contract length was five years; (*b*) the limitation only applied if GLC took more than 50 percent of the coker's output (which had always been the case for its long-term contracts); (*c*) it could offer a longer term if it were meeting a competitive offer in good faith (so long as the offer was not from a new entrant).

[80] See Goldberg & Erickson, *supra* note 8, at Tables 9 and 10.

[81] Twelve of the contracts were from the Compliance File, 8805-3-3-2; the remainder were made available to one of the authors by Great Lakes' counsel. Some of the contracts were amended to increase prices. The commission's restrictions on renewal prevented the parties from extending the term of the agreement. If these amendments are not counted as "contracts" then the number of contracts falls to 25.

[82] Appendix, Term 67. The six-month renewal period was also mandated by the Commission: "It is further ordered, that respondent Great Lakes Carbon Corporation, its successors and assigns, shall not renew or extend any existing contract for the purchase or marketing of an amount in excess of fifty percent (50%) of the estimated annual production of petroleum coke at any refinery more than six (6) months prior to termination of the contract being renewed or extended" (82 F.T.C. 1529, 1672-73).

[83] 8805-3-3-2, pp. 43, 151.

clear, then, that the three-year restriction imposed by the commission was binding.

The three-year duration is misleading, however, since almost all the contracts could be terminated on fairly short notice. About two-thirds of the contracts could be terminated on three to six months' notice if the parties failed to agree on a new price. Only two contracts—both with Mobil—allowed for termination without cause by either party (three months' notice was required).[84]

The salient feature of the post-1973 contracts is, not surprisingly, the focus on the problem of price adjustment. The response to the increased variability of prices was a substantial decrease in the period between price changes. The contracts split approximately evenly between those relying on indexing and those relying on renegotiation. Through the beginning of 1976 the price of crude oil was the basis for indexing.[85] From July 1976 onward, however, if the contract provided for indexing, the only external price utilized was that of calcined coke.

The purpose of indexing in this period of high volatility was very different from its purpose in the previous period. There was no intention to ensure automatic price adjustment for the life of the contract. Rather it functioned as part of the renegotiation process. The index was only expected to be in force for short periods. Thus, half the contracts with prices indexed to crude oil called for renegotiation at a fixed interval of three to six months. The other half did not set a fixed date for renegotiation. Instead, they established a maximum and minimum (about 15 percent above and below the base price.) If the calculated price fell outside this range, one party could request price renegotiation. If the parties failed to agree on a new price, the contract would terminate in three months. Thus, indexing only provided a point of reference for renegotiation. That is, if one party did not accept the calculated price, it could request renegotiation, and, if the other party refused, it could terminate the agreement.[86] If the indexed price is expected to be closer to the market price than is the base price, then indexing would have reduced the rewards of opportunism associated with renegotiating the price.

Nine of the post-1973 GLC contracts were with Texaco—three contracts at three different sites. All nine contracts gave Texaco the right to

[84] A 1976 contract with Atlantic Richfield could be terminated after one year with 120 days notice.

[85] Eight contracts utilized indexes; all included the cost of crude oil; one added wages, and another added wages and refinery fuel costs and electricity (crude oil had a weight of 93 percent in this agreement).

[86] Appendix, Term 68.

terminate the agreement if it received a bona fide offer above the contract price; however, GLC could continue the agreement by matching the higher price.[87] This arrangement was adopted to adjust the contract price to rapidly changing market conditions, not to facilitate termination. Rapid adjustment to objectively determined information meant that that the parties were less likely to engage in bickering and similar behavior that would reduce the probability of their renewing the contract. The Texaco contracts also utilized one other form of price adjustment that relied on the continuation of the long-term relationship between the two firms—ex post pricing. In 1974 and 1975, when Texaco and GLC could not reach an agreement on price by the contractually determined deadline, they agreed to extend the negotiating period for a stated period. In the interim, they continued to perform with GLC paying at the preexisting price. When agreement was finally reached, the new price was applied retroactively. Thus, two 1974 contracts were effective as of January 1 even though they were not signed until August 26.[88]

In 1973, aluminum producers were performing under minimum quantity, fixed-price contracts. The fixed-price contracts provided the aluminum companies with an unanticipated windfall. Rather than simply accepting the windfall until the contract expired, the aluminum companies had the option of trading off part of the windfall to enhance their future access. Access could, of course, be achieved in other ways. The aluminum company could acquire nearby land for storing inventory, or it could find alternative suppliers. A new coker could be constructed at a convenient location before the existing contract expired. Our discussions with industry sources suggest that, with one notable exception (discussed below), contract prices were renegotiated upward.

The new prices were not, however, necessarily tied to a formal extension of the contract. Kaiser, which had the most coke contracts, did not extend its agreements; rather, it shifted to three-year contracts. Moreover, the new Kaiser contracts included price-adjustment mechanisms similar to those of GLC. Contract price was typically indexed, but prices could be renegotiated if the indexed contract price was out of line. In the GLC agreements, renegotiation was triggered by mechanical rules. The price could be renegotiated if the indexed price hit the ceiling or floor, or if sufficient time had passed. Kaiser's trigger was an announcement by either party that the current price was unacceptable. In that event, the parties would have a short period (about three months) to renegotiate a

[87] Appendix, Term 69.

[88] Appendix, Term 70.

price; if they failed, the contract would terminate after another three months.

Kaiser's willingness to accept such a renegotiation arrangement appears surprising given its vulnerability to opportunistic behavior by its suppliers. The increased volatility made tracking of current price more valuable than in the pre-1973 period, but we would have expected the parties to choose a less manipulable rule; for example, price could have been indexed to external prices (such as crude oil or calcined coke) and the parties could have been given the right to solicit outside offers, with their counterpart having the right of first refusal. Kaiser's willingness to go further than this might be explained by two factors. First, Kaiser had become increasingly less vulnerable to the loss of a single coke supplier; it operated six calciners, with the largest accounting for approximately one-fourth its capacity. Moreover, its calcined coke output had grown so that it now substantially exceeded Kaiser's internal needs. Kaiser looked more like a middleman than an aluminum company end user. Second, Kaiser's renegotiation of the fixed price, pre-1973 contracts might be viewed as an indication of its good faith; ceteris paribus, the more trust, the more viable the price renegotiation.

Kaiser's earlier contracts were indexed to crude oil, but most of the more recent ones were based on calcined coke prices. GLC's posted price of calcined coke was first used, but this proved unsatisfactory when GLC maintained the posted price in the early 1980s in the face of a price decline of about 30–40 percent.[89] Kaiser shifted to a measure based on actual Kaiser transaction prices that, although more subject to manipulation, better tracked the price of green coke.

The one exception regarding renegotiation was Richfield's contract with Harvey (subsequently Martin Marietta). The failure to renegotiate price led to considerable ill will, and the contract was allowed to expire in its fifteenth year. Richfield exercised its option to have the land returned and the calciner removed,[90] although it did permit Marietta to operate the calciner after the agreement expired (until Marietta's new calciner came on line). Marietta was supplied by a new coker built by Champlin Oil; the new calciner, a joint venture with Champlin, was located adjacent to the coker. It is generally believed in the industry that the demolition of the calciner was an unnecessary and costly result of the decision not to renegotiate prices.

[89] Peter Fasullo, Tim Tarrillion, & John Matson, Price of Dwindling Supply of Better-Quality Coke, Oil & Gas J. 198 (November 8, 1982).

[90] See Appendix, Term 15.

V. Concluding Remarks

The substantial amount of contractual detail we have provided indicates some of the ingenious solutions parties have devised for resolving some apparently intractable problems of coordination across organizational boundaries. We will not provide a full summary of all the features of the contracts. Instead, we will confine attention to a few points deserving special emphasis.

A refiner has to determine how much freedom it is willing to sacrifice in setting its rate of coke output, while a buyer must determine how much responsibility for accepting a given amount of coke it will bear. Since coke is a low value by-product accounting for less than 3 percent of the value of refined oil, the coker would prefer to decide how much coke it should produce on the basis of conditions in the oil market. Moreover, the less storage capacity available at the refinery, the more the refiner would value a buyer's promise to promptly remove whatever coke the refinery happens to produce. The full-output, immediate removal contracts that Great Lakes Carbon usually entered into provided the coker with this assurance. Nevertheless, when a coker entered into a contract in which it was to be the sole supplier of a calciner, it would almost invariably give up most of its freedom to determine its output rate in order to provide the buyer with sufficient assurance.

One of the most surprising findings was the frequent use of multipart, or nonlinear, prices to protect the seller's reliance. We must emphasize that considerable effort was necessary to reinterpret the contract language in a manner that would reveal the nonlinear pricing—this was not an easily observable fact that cried out for an explanation. We suspect that our efforts here will put subsequent researchers on guard and will result in the discovery of numerous other nonlinear pricing arrangements that had hitherto gone unnoticed.

Virtually all the GLC contracts that indexed to crude oil prices imposed maximum-minimum limits. However, while the maximum (minimum) was about 40–50 percent above (below) the base price in the low-inflation 1960s, it was only about 15 percent above (below) the base in the high-inflation 1970s. It would seem contrary to intuition that the limits would shrink as the rate of inflation rises. The apparent paradox is resolved by recognizing that the limitations served a completely different function in the two periods. In the former, the index was in force for the life of the contract. The limits came into play only if some major unanticipated change occurred, at which time the parties would then be forced to renegotiate in order to take the new circumstances into account. The limits would be reached only under rather extraordinary circumstances. In the latter case, indexing provided a point of reference for renegotiation. Frequent renegotiation, which kept the contract price in line with current market conditions, could be triggered either by setting fixed dates to renegotiate (for example, at quarterly intervals) or by setting narrow boundaries on an indexed price—boundaries that the parties expected would routinely be reached.

Increased price volatility resulted in contracts that were of shorter duration and easier to terminate. This is, of course, inconsistent with the notion that the parties would enter into long-term contracts to protect themselves from price fluctuations. It appears that the increased price volatility raises the costs of long-term contracts relative to both short-term contracts and integration by ownership.

We have had reasonable success explaining the structure of the petroleum coke contracts without invoking power, anticompetitive behavior, or risk preferences. Instead, we have focused on long-term reliance, short-term coordination, the costs of acquiring information, and other "relational" concepts. While a single case study may not prove anything, it can suggest which research strategies are more likely to prove fruitful. Furthermore, since the economic theory of contracts has heretofore largely ignored the empirical data, case studies of this sort should lead to a reshaping of the theorists' research agenda—a reshaping that would give more weight to the sorts of issues that prove to be important in this market.

[10]

Contract Duration and Relationship-Specific Investments: Empirical Evidence from Coal Markets

By PAUL L. JOSKOW*

This paper examines the importance of specific relationship investments in determining the duration of coal contracts negotiated between coal suppliers and electric utilities. Data for 277 coal contracts are used to perform the analysis. The results provide strong support for the view that buyers and sellers make longer commitments to the terms of future trade at the contract execution stage, and rely less on repeated bargaining, when relationship-specific investments are more important.

This paper seeks to test empirically the importance of relationship-specific investments in determining the duration of coal contracts negotiated between coal suppliers and electric utilities.[1] The analysis makes use of information for a large sample of coal contracts that were in force in 1979. It takes as a starting point Oliver Williamson's 1983 definitions and categorization of relationship-specific investments and applies them to the characteristics of coal market transactions. It also follows Williamson and Benjamin Klein, Robert Crawford, and Armen Alchian (1978) and assumes that risk aversion is not an important factor determining the structure of vertical relationships between coal suppliers and electric utilities.[2]

Coal market transactions are interesting to focus on because there is considerable variation in the duration and structure of vertical relationships between buyers and sellers. I observe spot market transactions, vertical integration, and a wide variety of longer-term contractual relationships with durations ranging from one year to fifty years.[3] My related work (1985) suggests that asset-specificity considerations may be an important factor affecting the structure of vertical relationships in coal markets. The empirical results reported below provide strong support for the hypothesis that buyers and sellers make longer *ex ante* commitments to the terms of future trade, and rely less on repeated negotiations over time, when relationship-specific investments are more important.

I. Contract Duration and Transaction-Specific Investments

The reliance on relationship-specific investments to support cost-minimizing ex-

*Department of Economics, Massachusetts Institute of Technology, Cambridge, MA 02139. The preliminary version of this paper was written when I was a Fellow at the Center for Advanced Study in the Behavioral Sciences. Leslie Sundt and Rafe Leeman provided valuable research assistance. Keith Crocker, Henry Farber, Oliver Hart, Scott Masten, Jean Tirole, and Oliver Williamson read preliminary versions and made useful suggestions. Three anonymous referees provided helpful suggestions. I benefited from seminar presentations at UCLA, Stanford, and MIT. Support from MIT and the Center for Advanced Study in the Behavioral Sciences is gratefully acknowledged. The views expressed here and any remaining errors are my sole responsibility.

[1]Electric utilities account for over 80 percent of domestic coal consumption.

[2]Other empirical work in this tradition includes Kirk Monteverde and David Teece (1982) and Scott Masten (1984), which focus on vertical integration; Keith Crocker and Scott Masten (1986), J. Harold Mulhern (1986), and Victor Goldberg and John Erickson (1982) which focus on long-term contracts; my paper (1985) which examines both vertical integration and long-term contracts.

[3]About 15 percent of electric utility coal consumption is accounted for by transactions with integrated suppliers, 15 percent is accounted for by spot market purchases, and about 70 percent is accounted for by contracts with durations of one to fifty years. See my paper (1985, pp. 50–54).

change is frequently advanced as an important factor explaining why we observe the use of long-term contracts that establish the terms and conditions of repeated transactions between two parties *ex ante*.[4] According to transactions cost theory,[5] when exchange involves significant investments in relationship-specific capital, an exchange relationship that relies on repeated bargaining is unattractive. Once the investments are sunk in anticipation of performance, "hold-up" or "opportunism" incentives are created *ex post* which, if mechanisms cannot be designed to mitigate the parties' ability to act on these incentives, could make a socially cost-minimizing transaction privately unattractive at the contract execution stage.[6,7] A long-term contract that specifies the terms and conditions for some set of future transactions *ex ante*, provides a vehicle for guarding against *ex post* performance problems.[8]

A coal contract generally specifies in advance a method for determining the price that the buyer is obligated to pay for each delivery (generally a formula for determining prices for deliveries at each point in time),[9] quantities that the seller is obligated to deliver and the buyer is obligated to purchase at each point in time (usually monthly),[10] the quality of the coal (Btu, sulfur, ash, and chemical composition), the source of the coal, and the period of time over which the contractual provisions are to govern the terms and conditions of trade.[11] The primary readily quantifiable characteristics of coal contracts that appear to vary widely from contract to contract are the quantity and characteristics of the coal contracted for and the length of time that the parties agree *ex ante* to commit themselves to the terms and conditions specified in the contract. It is this length of time to which the parties agree *ex ante* to abide by the terms of a contract that I refer to as the "duration" of the contract.[12]

My hypothesis is that the more important are relationship-specific investments, the longer will be the period of time (or number of discrete transactions) over which the parties will establish the terms of trade *ex ante* by contract. I therefore expect to observe that the variation in the agreed upon duration of contractual commitments is directly related to variations in the importance of relationship-specific investments.[13]

[4]Williamson (1979, 1983), Klein et al., Oliver Hart and Bengt Holmstrom (1986, pp. 1–2; 86–101). Other reasons for the use of long-term contracts have also been suggested. These include information lags, income effects and risk aversion, and improved monitoring of performance.

[5]I use the term "transactions cost theory" to refer generally to the work of Williamson (1979, 1983, 1985) and Klein et al.

[6]As Klein et al. discuss, the sunk investments create a stream of quasi rents that gives one party or the other (or both) some *ex post* bargaining power.

[7]The presence of these contracting hazards and imperfections in the ability of the transacting parties to protect against them does not mean that a deal will not be made. It simply means that the costs of making the transactions—the cost of the coal in this paper—will be higher than it would be if these hazards could be fully mitigated. Both parties have an interest in trying to structure the relationship so that a cost-minimizing deal can be struck.

[8]As discussed in my earlier paper (1985), reputational considerations may provide a natural market constraint on "bad behavior" *ex post*. Reputational constraints reduce the need to write inflexible long-term contracts to support cost-minimizing exchange in the presence of asset specificity. Reputational constraints are likely to be imperfect in coal markets, however. At the other extreme, vertical integration may be chosen to deal with *ex post* performance problems if satisfactory contractual solutions cannot be found.

[9]See my earlier paper (1986).

[10]The typical contract specifies a monthly and annual delivery schedule subject to minimum and maximum production and take obligations. The allowed variations from the contracted quantities in actual contracts that I have reviewed is fairly small.

[11]There are many other provisions as well, including arbitration provisions, force majeur provisions, resale provisions, etc. These provisions are fairly standard in long-term coal contracts, however.

[12]The actual duration of a contract could be longer or shorter than this. Buyers and sellers frequently voluntarily negotiate an extension of an existing contract. Contracts may also be broken through breach or mutual agreement. As far as I can tell from the data that I have reviewed, however, coal contracts are rarely terminated prematurely See my paper (1986, p. 2).

[13]To the extent that there are tradeoffs between contract duration and the incidence and structure of other contractual "protective" provisions, such as the method for determining price adjustment and quantities, these other provisions should be included in the analysis as well. As indicated above, however, there

II. Asset Specificity and the Contractual Duration of Coal Supply Relationships

Williamson (1983, p. 526) identifies four distinct types of transaction-specific investments, three of which appear to be relevant to different types of coal supply relationships. The three types of relevance to coal market transactions are:[14]

(a) Site Specificity: The buyer and seller are in a "cheek-by-jowl" relationship with one another, reflecting *ex ante* decisions to minimize inventory and transportation expenses. Once sited the assets in question are highly immobile.

(b) Physical Asset Specificity: When one or both parties to the transaction make investments in equipment and machinery that involves design characteristics specific to the transaction and which have lower values in alternative uses.

(c) Dedicated Assets: General investment by a supplier that would not otherwise be made but for the prospect of selling a significant amount of product to a particular customer. If the contract is terminated prematurely, it would leave the supplier with significant excess capacity. Although Williamson does not discuss it, I think that there is probably a "buyer" side analogy to the dedicated asset story as well. A buyer that relies on a single supplier for a large volume of an input *may* find it difficult and costly to quickly replace these supplies if they are terminated suddenly and effectively withdrawn from the market and, as a result, a large unanticipated demand is suddenly thrown on the market.

As discussed in more detail in the Appendix, I have put together a data base that includes information for nearly 300 contracts between electric utilities and coal suppliers that were in force in 1979. The data base includes information of various kinds regarding the characteristics of the individual coal contracts, the suppliers, the buyers, and the quality and quantity of the coal contracted for. The strategy was to use the information about the individual contracts in the data base and to attempt to measure, at least ordinally, differences in the importance of transaction-specific investments of one or more of the types identified by Williamson for each contract.

Williamson's notion of "site specificity" is the easiest to capture explicitly for coal supply relationships. For most electric generating plants, coal is purchased in one of three major coal-producing regions and then transported by rail, barge, and/or truck (often at least two of these transport modes are involved) to the power plant where it is burned. However, there are a relatively small number of plants that have been sited next to specific mines in anticipation of taking all or most of their requirements from that mine. These "mine-mouth" plants are generally developed simultaneously with the mines themselves. This appears to be a classic case of the cheek-by-jowl relationship that Williamson has in mind when he discusses site specificity.[15] The potential for *ex post* opportunism problems arising if the parties were to rely on repeated bargaining appears to be especially great in this case.[16] I there-

appears to be relatively little variation in these provisions in my data base, especially relative to the very large variation in contract duration. I therefore feel that it is safe to assume for purposes of this analysis that we have a sample of contracts that essentially holds these other provisions constant. In any event, we can measure the utilization of these other provisions only for a small fraction of the contracts in the data base and therefore cannot examine such tradeoffs directly. Note that the coal market is not subject to the kinds of price regulation discussed in Masten-Crocker and Crocker-Masten regarding natural gas contracts.

[14] The fourth is what Williamson calls "human asset specificity" (1983, p. 526). Jean Tirole has suggested to me that Williamson's four types of relationship-(or transaction) specific investment are simply different instances of the same phenomenon. I believe that this is correct. However, I find the distinctions to be quite useful for empirical applications.

[15] This is discussed in much more detail in my 1985 paper.

[16] Williamson (1983) states that common ownership is the predominant response to site specificity. My work with coal supply arrangements indicates that common ownership (vertical integration) is much more likely to emerge for mine-mouth plants than other types of plants, but that contracts are also used to govern exchange for about half of the mine-mouth plants constructed since 1960. We would probably see more vertical integration

fore expect that contracts for supplies for mine-mouth plants will be much longer than the average contract involving supplies to other types of plants, other things equal.[17]

Let us turn next to physical asset specificity. When coal-burning plants are built, they are designed to burn a specific type of coal (see my 1985 paper; Richard Schmalensee and myself, 1986; my paper with Schmalensee, 1985). By "type" of coal, I mean coal with a specific Btu, sulfur, moisture, and chemical content. The type of coal that a generating unit is designed to burn affects its construction cost and its design thermal efficiency. Deviations from expected coal quality can lead to a deterioration in performance or require costly retrofit investments. Thus when a plant is designed, the operator becomes "locked in" to a particular type of coal.[18]

The fact that a plant is locked in to a particular type of coal does not necessarily imply that the buyer is locked in to a specific supplier, however. Whether or not the plant design/coal characteristic lock in also leads to a lock in with the current supplier depends on other characteristics of the transaction. In particular, it is likely that the relationship between this type of asset-specificity and *ex post* hold up or opportunism problems is related to inter- and intraregional variations in coal quality, least cost supply technology, and transportation alternatives.[19]

The characteristics of coal produced in the United States vary systematically among the three major coal-producing regions. The eastern coal-producing districts produce high Btu coal of reasonably uniform quality. The midwestern coal-producing districts produce lower Btu coal that generally has a very high sulfur content. Coal quality is also more variable than that in the East. Finally, the western coal-producing districts generally produce coal with a much lower Btu content and a very low sulfur content. The quality of the coal varies quite widely throughout the western region.[20]

In addition to variations in coal quality among the regions, there are also systematic variations in the least-cost technology for producing coal and in the transportation alternative available. In the East, relatively small underground mines are economical and the supply of eastern coal can be expanded fairly quickly. Relatively abundant transportation alternatives, combined with relatively short average transport distances, mean that transportation is not likely to be a significant barrier to a buyer's obtaining alternative supplies. In the West, large surface mines that can be most economically expanded in large "lumps," are the least-cost production technology. Transportation alternatives are poor, the average transport distance quite long, large unit train shipments are the most economical transport method,[21] and utilities often must rely on one or two railroads to move the coal. The situation in the Midwest lies somewhere between these two extremes.[22]

for mine-mouth plants if state and federal regulation of electric utilities did not discourage it. I have argued elsewhere (1985) that to the extent that electric utility regulation biases coal supply arrangements at all, it is probably to make short-term purchases more desirable than they might otherwise be. While utilities might also like to integrate backwards into coal production to shift profits from a regulated to an unregulated activity, the regulatory process has discouraged this.

[17]I have included two plants in this category that are not technically mine-mouth plants but have economic characteristics that are identical to those of mine-mouth plants. For example, if a mine and a plant are connected by a transportation facility (a slurry pipeline or a rail line) built and owned by the supplier or buyer specifically to transport coal from a specific mine to a specific plant, the associated coal contract was grouped with the mine-mouth plants.

[18]Exactly how locked in, is a variable of choice, however.

[19]Transportation costs are on average a large fraction of delivered costs and lining up efficient transportation arrangements for large quantities of coal can be a time-consuming process.

[20]The midwestern region is sometimes broken up into two subregions (eastern and western interior) in discussions of coal supply. The western region is sometimes broken up into three or more subregions. Texas, where lignite coal is produced, is often considered a separate producing region. My data base has no contracts for Texas coal and I do not discuss that area here.

[21]Unit train cars are often owned or leased by the utility rather than by the railroad.

[22]See Martin Zimmerman (1981, pp. 17–36).

There are also systematic differences in the relative and absolute importance of spot markets in the three supply regions.[23] On average, from 1974 through 1982 spot market transactions accounted for roughly 15 percent of total domestic coal purchases by electric utilities. In 1982, spot market sales accounted for about 10 percent of coal supplies or about 60 million tons. However, in the western region, less than 2 percent of the coal delivered to electric utilities was purchased on the spot market or less than 5 million tons.[24] The spot market is more active in the Midwest, accounting for about 8 percent of deliveries in 1982 or about 10 million tons per year. The spot market is most active in the East where about 18 percent of deliveries went through the spot market in 1982 or about 45 million tons.[25]

These considerations imply the following: Coal suppliers are likely to be less able to exploit the lock-in effect associated with boilers designed to burn coal with specific characteristics in the East than in the West.[26] Thus the protection of a long-term contract is likely to be more desirable from the buyers' (and the sellers'—see below) perspective, for transactions involving western coal relative to transactions involving eastern coal, with midwestern coal falling somewhere in between.

Finally, let us turn to "dedicated asset" considerations. The available information in the data base does not make it possible for us to know specifically whether the supplier made general investments that would not have been made but for the prospect of selling a *significant amount of product* to a particular customer and if the contract is terminated prematurely it would leave the supplier with excess capacity (see Williamson, 1983, p. 526).[27] Williamson's conceptualization of dedicated assets implies that the importance of this factor in structuring coal supply relationships should vary with the quantity of coal that is initially contracted for, other things equal. The larger the annual quantity of coal that is contracted for, the more difficult it is likely to be for the seller to quickly dispose of unanticipated supplies (if the buyer breaches) at a compensatory price, and the more difficult will it be for a buyer to replace supplies at a comparable price if the seller withdraws them from the market. Thus, I expect that the greater the annual quantity of coal contracted for the longer will be the specified duration of the contract.

Because of systematic variations in the optimal scale and capital intensity of coal production across regions, dedicated asset considerations are also likely to be more important for western coal than for eastern coal. The greater heterogeneity in coal supplies and the difficulties of obtaining suitable transportation for it in the West, suggest that dedicated asset problems are likely to be more severe in the western than the eastern region. The very thin spot market in the

[23]Spot market sales also vary from year to year. Spot market transactions tend to be higher when coal miner strikes are anticipated as utilities seek to build up stockpiles or after coal mining strikes are over and stockpiles are replenished. The volume of spot market transactions also varies in response to unanticipated changes in coal supply and demand.

[24]The aggregate volume of spot market transactions for western coal is quite small compared to the annual quantity of western coal contracted for in a typical contract. The contracts for western coal in my data base have a mean quantity of about 1.8 million tons per and a maximum quantity of over 8 million tons per year.

[25]I believe that the wide variation in the importance of the spot market in different regions is largely related to the same economic considerations that lead me to conclude that the importance of asset specificity also varies from region to region.

[26]Generating plants located along the eastern seaboard that use coal essentially always use eastern coal. These plants are also more likely to have units that have multifuel capabilities than plants located elsewhere and can switch back and forth between coal and oil or gas (often with some performance penalty). See my paper with Frederick Mishkin (1977). Purchasers of eastern coal with multifuel capabilities will be less susceptible to opportunism problems when coal and oil prices are close together.

[27]Indeed, as a practical matter, it is unclear to me how one could ever go about determining this directly given the data that are likely to be available for analysis. The coal contracts that I have reviewed do sometimes have language that appears to recognize the dedicated asset notion directly, but the absence of an explicit statement cannot be assumed to imply that dedicated asset considerations are not important.

western region should be especially problematical for both sellers and buyers when large contractual commitments are breached because of the heterogeneity of the coal, the characteristics of least-cost production and the limited transportation alternatives. This all implies again that contracts for western coal should have longer contractual durations than contracts for eastern coal.

To summarize, if variations in the importance of relationship-specific investments do in fact lead to variations in the extent to which the parties precommit to the terms of future trade *ex ante*, I expect to find that the duration of contractual relationships specified at the contract execution stage will vary systematically with three primary observable characteristics of coal supply transactions. First, whether the plant taking the coal is a mine-mouth plant or not. I expect to observe longer-term contracts negotiated for mine-mouth plants. Second, with the region of the country in which the coal is produced. I expect the western region to have the longest contracts and the eastern region the shortest with the midwestern region having contracts with prespecified durations that lie in between. Third, with the annual quantity of coal contracted for. I expect that coal supply arrangements involving large annual quantity commitments will be supported by longer contracts than supply arrangements involving smaller quantities of coal.

III. Model Specification and Estimation

I am primarily interested in estimating a set of simple relationships between the duration of contractual commitments (*DURATION*) specified by the parties at the contract execution stage and, (a) the *annual* quantity (*QUANTITY*)[28] of coal contracted for, (b) a dummy variable (*MINE-MOUTH*) that takes on a value of 1 for a mine-mouth plant and zero otherwise, and (c) dummy variables that indicate the coal supply region in which the supplier is located (*MIDWEST* and *WEST*, so that regional effects are measured relative to contracts for eastern coal). Additional variables are considered in the next section.

The data base that I use includes information for approximately 300 coal supply contracts between domestic coal suppliers and investor-owned electric utilities. The contracts included in the data base were negotiated in various years up through 1979 and were in force at least for part of 1979. The data are discussed in more detail in the Appendix. Information on all variables of primary interest for this study is available for 277 of the contracts in the data base. I present estimates using both the full 277 observation sample as well as a subsample consisting of 169 contracts that involve deliveries dedicated to a single power plant.[29] Table 1 provides the mean, standard deviation, minimum and maximum values, and a brief description for all of the variables used in this section and subsequent sections for both the primary sample and the single-plant subsample. Table 2 is a correlation matrix for all of the variables in the two samples with the correlations for the 277 observation sample below the diagonal and those for the 169 observation subsample above the diagonal.

I work first with three simple specifications of the contract duration equation:

$$(1)\quad DURATION_i = a_0 + b_1 QUANTITY_i + b_2 QUANTITY_i^2 + b_3 MINE\text{-}MOUTH_i + b_4 MIDWEST_i + b_5 WEST_i + u_i$$

[28]Quantities are expressed in terms of the thermal (Btu) content of the coal. The basic results are not affected when quantities are expressed in tons. For the extensions reported in the next section, normalizing quantities for Btu content makes it possible to more accurately examine the effects, if any, of contract quantities relative to total plant and utility utilization of coal.

[29]Several people suggested to me that relationship-specific investment effects are most likely to be revealed for contracts that dedicate all supplies to a single plant. I also focus on this subsample to obtain the data necessary to explore issues discussed in the next section.

TABLE 1—SAMPLE STATISTICS

Variable	Observations	Description	Mean	Minimum	Maximum	Standard Deviation
DURATION	277	Contract Duration	12.75	1.00	50	10.43
	169	(years)	14.18	1.00	43	10.77
QUANTITY	277	Annual Contract	20.45	0.3696	183.00	24.62
	169	Quantity (trillion Btu's)	22.83	0.3696	183.00	27.05
PLANT PROPORTION	169	Fraction of Total Plant Use from Contract	0.44	0.03	1.00	0.35
UTILITY PROPORTION	169	Fraction of Total Utility Coal Use from Contract	0.19	0.003	1.00	0.23
PLANT QUANTITY	169	Plant Utilization of Coal (trillion Btu's)	51.47	2.95	172.42	41.69
UTILITY QUANTITY	169	Utility Utilization of Coal (trillion Btu's)	221.54	2.95	919.80	270.56
PLANT/UTILITY	169	Plant Use as Fraction of Total Utility Use	0.455	0.007	1.00	0.323
MINE-MOUTH	277	Mine-Mouth Plant	(*D* = 1; 14 Observations)			
	169	Dummy Variable	(*D* = 1; 14 Observations)			
WEST	277	Western Region	(*D* = 1; 54 Observations)			
	169	Supply Dummy	(*D* = 1; 44 Observations)			
MIDWEST	277	Midwestern Region	(*D* = 1; 68 Observations)			
	169	Supply Dummy	(*D* = 1; 47 Observations)			
DATE-71	277	Contracts Signed	(*D* = 1; 43 Observations)			
	169	1971–73: Dummy	(*D* = 1; 29 Observations)			
DATE-74	277	Contracts Signed	(*D* = 1; 116 Observations)			
	169	1974–77: Dummy	(*D* = 1; 71 Observations			
DATE-78	277	Contracts Signed	(*D* = 1; 72 Observations)			
	169	1978–79: Dummy	(*D* = 1; 38 Observations)			
YEAR	277	Year Contract Executed	1974	1955	1979	4.49
	169		1974	1955	1979	4.64

[a] Data sources and variable definitions can be found in the Appendix.
[b] The 169 observation subsample includes contracts dedicated to a single plant.

TABLE 2—CORRELATION MATRIX

277 Observation Sample	169 Observation Sample: *DURATION*	*QUANTITY*	*LOG-QUANTITY*	*MINE-MOUTH*	*MIDWEST*	*WEST*	*YEAR*	*PLANT PROP.*	*UTILITY PROP.*	*PLANT/UTILITY*	*PLANT QUANTITY*	*UTILITY QUANTITY*
DURATION	–	0.60	0.68	0.64	0.004	0.51	−0.57	0.58	0.43	0.05	0.29	0.02
QUANTITY	0.60	–	0.78	0.42	−0.04	0.28	−0.35	0.48	0.43	0.05	0.41	0.11
LOG-QUANTITY	0.64	0.80	–	0.30	0.02	0.32	−0.44	0.57	0.42	0.02	0.45	0.17
MINE-MOUTH	0.54	0.38	0.27	–	−0.09	0.41	−0.37	0.46	0.41	0.05	0.10	−0.05
MIDWEST	0.14	0.08	0.11	−0.06	–	−0.37	−0.20	0.04	−0.04	−0.06	−0.03	−0.15
WEST	0.41	0.25	0.26	0.39	−0.28	–	−0.10	0.46	0.40	0.16	−0.06	0.16
YEAR	−0.63	−0.39	−0.44	−0.31	−0.27	−0.08	–	−0.28	−0.11	0.13	−0.16	−0.11
PLANT PROP.	–	–	–	–	–	–	–	–	0.61	−0.11	−0.24	−0.14
UTILITY PROP.	–	–	–	–	–	–	–	–	–	0.66	−0.08	−0.36
PLANT/UTILITY	–	–	–	–	–	–	–	–	–	–	0.15	−0.57
PLANT QUANTITY	–	–	–	–	–	–	–	–	–	–	–	0.34
UTILITY QUANTITY	–	–	–	–								–

Note: Figures below the diagonal are for the 277 observation sample, those above the diagonal are for the 169 observation subsample.

$$(2)\quad DURATION_i = a_0 + b_1 LOG\text{-}QUANTITY_i + b_3 MINE\text{-}MOUTH_i + b_4 MIDWEST_i + b_5 WEST_i + u_i$$

$$(3)\quad \log(DURATION_i) = a_0 + b_1 LOG\text{-}QUANTITY_i + b_3 MINE\text{-}MOUTH_i + b_4 MIDWEST_i + b_5 WEST_i + \log(u_i)$$

where i indexes contracts and u_i is an error term whose characteristics will be discussed further below.

I have allowed (*QUANTITY*) to enter these relationships nonlinearly by introducing a quadratic in quantity (*QUANTITY-SQUARED*) in (1) and using the natural logarithm of quantity (*LOG-QUANTITY*) in equations (2) and (3). Since powerplants have useful lives of roughly forty years and the costs of breach are likely to decline over time as plants and mines age, I expect that the impact of quantity on contractual duration will diminish as quantity increases. The following pattern of coefficient estimates for the three equations is implied by the hypothesized relationship between asset specificity and contract duration:

(*i*) All of the b_i's should be positive, except for b_2, which could be positive, negative, or zero (no nonlinearity), although I expect that it will be negative.

(*ii*) b_4 should be smaller than b_5.

Equations (1), (2), and (3) are estimated in three different ways. First, I present ordinary least squares (OLS) estimates of each equation for both samples. Next, I present OLS estimates that introduce dummy variables which indicate the date that the contracts were executed. Finally, I present maximum likelihood estimates based on the assumption that we have a truncated sample drawn from a population with either a normal or a log-normal density function. I discuss the rationale and results for each estimation approach and also present OLS results for contracts with suppliers in each of the three regions.

A. *OLS Estimates*

If we assume that the u_i in (1), (2), and (3) are independently distributed and drawn from a normal distribution with mean zero, then OLS will yield an unbiased estimator of the coefficients of interest. I proceed first with this assumption and provide estimates for alternative assumptions about the error structure below. The OLS results are presented in Table 3. The first three columns are estimates for the three equations using the 277 observation sample. Columns 4, 5, and 6 contain estimates for the 169 observation subsample.

The OLS estimates are, in all cases, consistent with the hypothesized relationship between asset specificity and contract duration. The effects of annual contract quantity, region, and mine-mouth plants have the predicted signs and are estimated quite precisely. A mine-mouth plant is predicted to have a contract that is about 16 years longer than those of other plants. Contracts with eastern producers are 3 to 5 years shorter than those for western and midwestern producers. Contracts with western producers are 2 to 3 years longer than those with midwestern producers. The difference in duration between the *WEST* and the *MIDWEST* is generally not significant at the 5 percent level for the 277 observation sample, but is significant for the single-plant subsample. An increase in annual contract quantity of 22 trillion Btu's (roughly 1 million tons) yields about a 13-year increase in contract duration. As a general matter, the estimates are more precise for the sample of contracts dedicated to a single plant.

B. *OLS Estimates with Contract Date Dummies*

The desirable properties of the OLS estimates depend on the strong assumptions made about the error structure. Since the contracts in the data base were signed at many different times, it is natural to consider the possibility that contracting practices

TABLE 3—CONTRACT DURATION[a]

Independent Variables	277 Sample			169 Sample					2SLS Estimate
	DURATION (1)	*DURATION* (2)	*LOG-DURATION* (3)	*DURATION* (4)	*DURATION* (5)	*LOG-DURATION* (6)	*DURATION* (7)	*DURATION* (8)	Duration (9)
QUANTITY	0.4289 (0.0373)	–	–	0.4091 (0.0040)	–	–	–	–	–
QUANTITY-SQUARED	−0.0024 (0.00030)	–	–	−0.0020 (0.00003)	–	–	–	–	–
LOG-QUANTITY	–	4.4206 (0.3742)	0.5057 (0.0425)	–	4.2080 (0.4069)	0.4942 (0.0453)	4.2022 (0.4617)	4.2057 (0.4084)	5.1066 (0.812)
MINE-MOUTH	16.3300 (2.0496)	16.4317 (2.0045)	0.5104 (0.2279)	15.9583 (1.9106)	16.2300 (1.8421)	0.4616 (0.2050)	16.3432 (1.9426)	16.2284 (1.8477)	15.4391 (1.968)
MIDWEST	3.4267 (0.9682)	3.8795 (0.9821)	0.5154 (0.1116)	2.7832 (1.0928)	2.7843 (1.1032)	0.5785 (0.1228)	2.7317 (1.1295)	2.7848 (1.1065)	2.4268 (1.153)
WEST	5.3550 (1.357)	5.2033 (1.1641)	0.6142 (0.1323)	5.9856 (1.2346)	5.6108 (1.2586)	0.6844 (0.1401)	5.6456 (1.3406)	5.6391 (1.2751)	4.8916 (1.394)
PLANT PROPORTION	–	–	–	–	–	–	0.9729 (1.9806)	–	–
UTILITY PROPORTION	–	–	–	–	–	–	−2.0570 (2.5832)	–	–
PLANT/UTILITY	–	–	–	–	–	–	–	−0.2246 (1.4265)	–
Constant	3.6770 (0.6586)	−0.7902 (0.9579)	0.6014 (0.1089)	3.9334 (0.8109)	0.0155 (1.0917)	0.6242 (0.1215)	−0.0146 (1.0978)	0.1157 (1.2665)	−1.8922 (1.852)
Corrected *R*-squared	0.61	0.60	0.51	0.71	0.70	0.61	0.70	0.70	–
Observations	277	277	277	169	169	169	169	169	169

[a] OLS estimates. Standard errors of coefficient estimates are shown in parentheses.

changed over time. Not only might the duration of a typical contract have changed over time, but such changes may have been correlated with changes in contract quantities, supply location, and the development of mine-mouth plants over time. Failing to include variables indicated contract dates could then lead to a correlation between the independent variables and the error term. The OLS estimates would then be biased. To check to see if the estimates are sensitive to the presence of a left-out variable reflecting the contracting date, in Table 4, I report estimates of equations (1), (2), and (3) that have contract date dummies included. These contract date dummy variables are *DATE-71*, which is equal to one for all contracts signed between 1971 and 1973 inclusive, *DATE-74*, which equals one for contracts signed between 1974 and 1977, and *DATE-78* which equals one for contracts signed in 1978 and 1979. Since a separate variable for contracts signed prior to 1971 is not included, the coefficient estimates are all relative to pre-1971 contracts (i.e. the constant term). This aggregation of signing dates was made to reflect major shocks to coal supply and/or demand.[30]

[30] The 1971–73 period is just after the Clean Air Act Amendments of 1970 were passed, the 1974–77 period is the period after the Arab oil embargo and includes the subsequent increases in fossil fuel prices. The 1978–79 period coincides with the beginning of a slowdown in utility capacity additions. These periods are discussed in more detail in my paper (1986). The aggregation chosen is the same used to analyze pricing behavior in that paper. The results reported here are not sensitive to this aggregation, however. The same qualitative results are obtained if separate dummy variables are used for each year during the 1970's plus a separate dummy variable for pre-1965 and 1966–70 contracts.

TABLE 4—CONTRACT DURATION[a]

Independent Variables	DURATION (1)	DURATION (2)	LOG-DURATION (3)	DURATION (4)	DURATION (5)	LOG-DURATION (6)	DURATION (7)	DURATION (8)
QUANTITY	0.3120	–	–	0.3355	–	–	–	–
	(0.03547)			(0.0406)				
QUANTITY-SQUARED	−0.0018	–	–	−0.0018	–	–	–	–
	(0.00027)			(0.00029)				
LOG-QUANTITY	–	3.0482	0.3245	–	3.3485	0.3631	3.2847	3.3461
		(0.3655)	(0.0380)		(0.4330)	(0.0446)	(0.4923)	(0.4344)
MINE-MOUTH	13.9437	13.6701	0.3140	14.6494	14.6907	0.3792	14.5742	14.6800
	(1.8482)	(1.8260)	(0.1899)	(1.8495)	(1.8347)	(0.1891)	(1.9423)	(1.8403)
MIDWEST	1.6814	1.9761	0.3029	1.4906	1.6405	0.4083	1.5543	1.6323
	(0.8785)	(0.8952)	(0.0931)	(1.0544)	(1.0786)	(0.1112)	(1.1083)	(1.0821)
WEST	4.8429	4.8662	0.4831	5.1054	5.1731	0.5137	5.0697	5.1258
	(1.0301)	(1.0549)	(0.1097)	(1.2183)	(1.2524)	(0.1291)	(1.3338)	(1.2676)
PLANT PROPORTION	–	–	–	–	–	–	0.9930	–
							(1.8907)	
UTILITY PROPORTION	–	–	–	–	–	–	−0.9138	–
							(2.4975)	
PLANT/UTILITY	–	–	–	–	–	–	–	0.3785
								(1.3660)
CONSTANT	12.0145	9.4184	1.7205	9.2341	6.1982	1.4220	6.1583	6.0806
	(1.2526)	(1.5307)	(0.1592)	(1.5185)	(1.8612)	(0.1918)	(1.8853)	(1.9142)
DATE-71	−2.3734	−2.4564	−0.0988	−0.7282	−0.9103	−0.0311	−0.9389	−0.9455
	(1.2715)	(1.2876)	(0.1339)	(1.4890)	(1.5057)	(0.1552)	(1.5290)	(1.5154)
DATE-74	−6.6815	−7.3044	−0.5098	−3.9714	−4.3786	−0.3149	−4.3848	−4.4134
	(1.2647)	(1.1446)	(0.1190)	(1.3483)	(1.3685)	(0.1410)	(1.3789)	(1.3781)
DATE-78	−10.5052	−10.6151	−1.3926	−7.0789	−6.5193	−1.0317	−6.4995	−6.5749
	(1.2647)	(1.2976)	(0.1349)	(1.5540)	(1.6324)	(0.1682)	(1.6702)	(1.6493)
Corrected *R*-squared	0.70	0.69	0.67	0.74	0.73	0.69	0.73	0.73
Observations	277	277	277	169	169	169	169	169

[a] OLS/Contract date dummies. Standard errors of coefficient estimates are shown in parentheses.

While the introduction of these contract date dummy variables may help to control for contract date related correlations between the error term and the independent variables, the estimated coefficients of these variables themselves have no obvious economic meaning. This is because of the nature of the sample. Recall that I observe contracts *in force* in 1979. If we think of the population as consisting of contracts written for particular plants (i) in a particular year (t), we can observe a contract only if

$$(4)\quad DURATION_{it} \geq (1979 - \text{Contract } YEAR)$$

This means that of those contracts signed in 1970, I can observe, in 1979, only those that had durations of at least 9 years, while I will observe shorter contracts that were signed in later years. Even if there were no changes in contracting behavior over time, we would inevitably find that the coefficients of the contract date dummies indicate that the average length of a contract in the sample is negatively correlated with the date of the contract.[31] The coefficients of the contract date variables can therefore tell us nothing directly about the changes in contracting behavior over time.

With these considerations in mind, we can turn to the results reported in Table 4, columns 1 through 6. The results obtained are again consistent with the hypothesized relationship between asset specificity and contract duration. The coefficients of the quantity, mine-mouth, and regional variables

[31] In the sample, the simple correlation between contract date (*YEAR*) and *DURATION* is about −0.60. See Table 2.

continue to be of the predicted signs and relative magnitudes. The only interesting difference between these results and those reported in Table 3 is that the difference between the durations of contracts signed with western and midwestern producers is now generally statistically significant at the 5 percent level for both samples.

C. *Maximum Likelihood Estimates*

A third alternative for estimating these equations is to follow Keith Crocker and Scott Masten (1986), who work with a sample of natural gas contracts with similar sampling properties, and assume that the sampling procedure which chooses contracts in force in a single year (1981 in their paper) represents a classical sample truncation problem as discussed by G. S. Maddala (1983, pp. 165–170). The population of contracts then implicitly consists of all contracts written since the earliest contract in the data base. We obtain a truncated sample because we observe contracts only if the duration of the contract is greater than or equal to L_i, where L_i is equal to 1979 minus the contract date. In this case, OLS estimates of (1), (2), and (3) would be biased, because the sampling process is likely to induce a correlation between the independent variables and the error term.

We can obtain estimates with desirable asymptotic properties by specifying the likelihood function of the sample, given the nature of the sampling truncation, and then solve for the maximum likelihood estimates (MLE) of the coefficients of interest. Following Maddala (p. 166), I assume that the population relationship between contract duration and the independent variables has a normally distributed error and that each observation is truncated at L_i. This leads to a standard maximum likelihood estimator.

The maximum likelihood estimates are reported in Table 5, columns 1 through 6.[32] The results are again quite consistent with the hypothesized relationship between asset specificity and contract duration. The signs and magnitudes of the coefficients of *QUANTITY*, *MINE-MOUTH*, *WEST*, and *MIDWEST* are again as predicted. With the exception of the mine-mouth dummy in equation (3), the coefficients are estimated quite precisely. The magnitudes of the estimated coefficients in this table are difficult to compare directly with those in Tables 3 and 4 because of the need to incorporate the truncation effects into estimates of contract duration.[33] Correcting for the sample truncation, the estimates reported in Table 5, column 5, for example, yield the following expected durations: The expected duration evaluated at the means of the independent variables is 10.5 years (compared to a mean of 14.2 years for the truncated 169 observation sample). Mine-mouth plants have contracts with an expected duration that is about 12 years longer than the average non-mine-mouth plant. Midwestern contracts are about 3.5 years longer than eastern contracts. Western contracts are about 11 years longer than eastern contracts and 6 years longer than midwestern contracts. The difference between western and midwestern contracts is generally significant at the 5 percent level.[34]

D. *Estimates for Individual Coal Supply Regions*

Finally, in Table 6, I report estimates of the relationship between *DURATION*, *LOG-QUANTITY*, and *MINE-MOUTH* for

[32] The estimates were obtained using the MLE routine in the *Statistical Software Tools* package (Version 1.0 as of October 1986) developed by Jeffrey Dubin and R. Douglas Rivers running on an IBM XT. The estimates in cols. 3 and 6 assume that the density function is log-normal. Contracts executed in 1979 have been dropped since the likelihood function includes terms that require taking the logarithm of $L_i = (1979 - YEAR)$ which is zero for contracts written in 1979. Since the shortest contract in the data base has a duration of one year, we can impose a lower bound between zero and 1 on L_i to include all observations. Estimates obtained using different lower bounds does not change the results, so I simply report results for the sample excluding the small number of contracts in the data base executed in 1979.

[33] See Maddala (p. 167).

[34] I have also produced maximum likelihood estimates of equation (2) for subsamples consisting of pre-1974 contracts and those signed between 1974 and 1979. The hypothesized relationship between contract duration and the variables representing variations in asset specificity persists for both subsamples.

TABLE 5—CONTRACT DURATION[a]

Independent Variables	DURATION (1)	DURATION (2)	LOG-DURATION (3)	DURATION (4)	DURATION (5)	LOG-DURATION (6)	DURATION (7)	DURATION (8)	2SLS ESTIMATE DURATION (9)
QUANTITY	0.7948	–	–	0.5807	–	–	–	–	–
	(0.1046)			(0.0717)					
QUANTITY-SQUARED	−0.0043	–	–	−0.0030	–	–	–	–	–
	(0.00061)			(0.0004)					
LOG-QUANTITY	–	11.8527	0.6733	–	8.4367	0.6340	8.2709	8.4505	8.5737
		(1.5663)	(0.0897)		(1.0816)	(0.0816)	(1.0854)	(1.0815)	(3.5777)
MINE-MOUTH	16.5557	13.8763	0.2407	15.5484	14.4004	0.2736	14.1237	14.3841	15.4508
	(4.2407)	(3.8955)	(0.5714)	(2.9435)	(2.7764)	(0.4614)	(3.0120)	(2.7650)	(2.1083)
MIDWEST	8.3650	8.1377	0.4493	5.0050	4.7042	0.5376	4.4397	4.7468	2.4404
	(2.8188)	(2.5461)	(0.2281)	(2.5018)	(2.4511)	(0.2763)	(2.5221)	(2.4820)	(2.1797)
WEST	15.4864	13.8045	1.0500	11.7771	10.5506	1.0522	10.1238	10.4730	6.9477
	(4.1940)	(3.4244)	(0.0500)	(3.0124)	(2.4220)	(0.2416)	(2.6136)	(2.4095)	(1.8329)
PLANT PROPORTION	–	–	–	–	–	–	2.4401	–	–
							(3.7927)		
UTILITY PROPORTION	–	–	–	–	–	–	−2.0043	–	–
							(3.1937)		
PLANT/UTILITY	–	–	–	–	–	–	–	1.4626	–
								(2.1945)	
Constant	−18.4532	−35.6427	−0.4699	−6.9510	−19.0118	−0.2789	−19.0377	−19.7755	−36.1521
	(5.7203)	(7.2690)	(0.26709)	(3.4094)	(4.6758)	(0.2448)	(4.8545)	(4.8645)	(6.9717)
Log-Likelihood	−781.08	−769.29	−174.29	−475.17	−466.99	−101.60	−466.68	−466.83	−451.38
Observations	277	277	255	169	169	160	169	169	169

[a]Maximum likelihood estimates. Standard errors of coefficient estimates are shown in parentheses.

TABLE 6—CONTRACT DURATION[a]

Independent Variables	Dependent Variable: *DURATION* WEST (1)	MIDWEST (2)	EAST (3)	EAST (4)	WEST (5)	MIDWEST (6)	EAST (7)	EAST (8)
LOG-QUANTITY	3.4825	5.1249	4.2362	4.2968	3.5878	4.0269	4.408	4.4992
	(1.0714)	(0.7646)	(0.4668)	(0.4661)	(1.0992)	(0.6538)	(0.5798)	(0.5786)
MINE-MOUTH	18.4179	11.8107	–	17.6804	17.616	12.8372	–	17.0887
	(2.5064)	(5.1695)		(3.7348)	(2.3183)	(3.6363)		(3.8111)
Constant	6.819	1.365	−0.3975	−0.5265	7.2101	3.4075	0.4106	−0.6028
	(3.1610)	(5.1695)	(1.1159)	(1.1151)	(3.3441)	(1.8264)	(1.4256)	(1.4246)
Corrected R-squared	0.68	0.42	0.35	0.43	0.73	0.52	0.42	0.54
Observations	54	68	155	158	44	47	78	81

[a]OLS by region. Standard errors of coefficient estimates are shown in parentheses.

each coal supply region.[35] The samples do not include any mine-mouth plants using eastern coal, so columns 3 and 7 simply report the estimated relationship between *DURATION* and *LOG-QUANTITY*. There are in fact a few mine-mouth plants in the East and I have some information for three of them. These were not included in the sample because the data base did not have information on annual contract quantities for them. However, I was able to obtain information for delivered quantities for three eastern mine-mouth plants and have aug-

[35]I report only this variant of equation (2) to conserve space. It should be clear by now that the alternative specifications of (1), (2), and (3) do not yield any important differences in results.

mented the sample to include these plants, using delivered quantities rather than contract quantities as the values for the *QUANTITY* variable. These results are reported in columns 4 and 8 of Table 6.[36]

The effects of contract quantity and the mine-mouth dummy on contract duration are clearly not simply associated with the contracting behavior for coal from a particular region. The expected effects are found in each of the three regions. The coefficients of *QUANTITY* and *MINE-MOUTH* are of the expected signs and are estimated precisely in all cases. While there are differences in the magnitudes of the coefficients of these variables between the three regions, they are not very large numerically and equality of the coefficients of *QUANTITY* and *MINE-MOUTH* across regions cannot be rejected at standard significance levels. Contracts basically simply get longer as we move from East to West, other things equal.

IV. Alternative Measure of Asset Specificity

Clearly, the hypothesized relationship between contract duration and the variables that I have chosen to capture variations in asset specificity is quite robust to alternative specifications, samples, and estimating technique. Nevertheless, it is natural to ask whether there are alternative or additional factors that might explain the observed variations in contract duration. One argument that has been suggested to me is that it is not only the size of the contractual commitment that is likely to be important, but also the fraction of a plant's, and perhaps the utility's, requirements obtained from a specific contract. The argument is that as a larger fraction of a plant's requirements is associated with a specific supplier, "physical asset specificity" attributes are likely to be more important and lead to longer contracts. It has also been suggested to me that opportunism problems are likely to be less severe if the utility as a whole is not heavily dependent on supplies provided pursuant to a specific contract. These arguments imply that variables measuring plant and/or utility "dependence" on a specific contract should be introduced into the contract duration relationship.

To examine this possibility, I have included variables in (2)[37] that measure the fraction of a plant's requirements (*PLANT PROPORTION*) and the fraction of the total coal requirements of the utility (*UTILITY PROPORTION*) that operates the plant which are accounted for by a particular contract. As an alternative, I also estimate (2) introducing a variable that is equal to total plant utilization of coal divided by total utility utilization of coal (*PLANT/UTILITY*). I can estimate these relationships only for the contracts that are for delivery to a single plant because it is only for these contracts that I can construct a meaningful measure of plant specific dependence (i.e., the 169 observation subsample must be used).

The results are reported in columns 7 and 8 of Tables 3, 4, and 5. The coefficient estimates for *PLANT PROPORTION* and *UTILITY PROPORTION* are very imprecise. They are of opposite signs and are neither individually nor jointly significant at conventional significance levels. The coefficient of *PLANT/UTILITY* is also very imprecise and varies in sign depending on estimating technique. Introducing these variables has no effect on the estimates for the primary variables of interest. These results imply that a plant or utility that relies on a single supplier for a large fraction of its requirements, or that depends heavily on a specific plant, does not encounter significant hold-up problems per se. The lock-in effect associated with designing plants to burn a particular type of coal becomes a potential contractual problem only to the extent that the other asset specificity characteristics are active.

[36] The inclusion of these three additional observations does not change the aggregate results.

[37] Including these variables in (1) and (3) does not change the results and I report the results for (2) in order to conserve space.

V. Contract Quantity

Before concluding, it is useful to explore the role of asset specificity in determining annual contract quantities since this variable plays such an important role in the contract duration equation. A relationship between contract quantity and asset specificity potentially emerges because of the presence of all three types of asset specificity. First, other things equal, physical asset specificity considerations suggest that a plant operator would like to rely on a specific supplier producing a particular type of coal at a particular location to the greatest extent possible.[38] This implies that contract quantity should vary directly with the coal requirements of the individual plant (*PLANT QUANTITY*).[39] On the other hand, the more a utility comes to rely on a single supplier the more costly a breach of contract may be. This suggests that a utility may be willing to rely more on a single supplier for an individual plant the larger is total utility utilization of coal (*UTILITY QUANTITY*) given the utilization of a specific plant.

Second, in the case of mine-mouth plants, the nature of the *ex ante* location/investment decision involves the mutual expectation that all or most of a plant's requirements will be taken from the proximate supplier. This implies that the quantity per contract will be larger for mine-mouth plants, other things equal.

Finally, as discussed above, when utilities design plants to closely match specific coal quality attributes they will have an interest in relying more heavily on a specific supplier who contracts to supply coal from a seam with these characteristics. This is likely to be an especially important consideration for coal supplies from the western region.

I estimate the following relationship using the single-plant (169 observation) subsample to determine empirically whether and how these considerations affect annual contract quantities.

$$(5)\quad QUANTITY_i = c_0 + d_1 PLANT\text{-}QUANTITY_i + d_2 PLANT\text{-}QUANTITY_i^2 + d_3 UTILITY\text{-}QUANTITY_i + d_4 UTILITY\text{-}QUANTITY_i^2 + d_5 MINE\text{-}MOUTH_i + d_6 MIDWEST_i + d_7 WEST_i + v_i.$$

I expect d_1, d_3, d_5, d_6, and d_7 to be greater than zero, and d_7 should be larger than d_6.

Equation (5) is estimated in two different ways. First, OLS estimates are presented. Second, OLS estimates with a correction to reflect the possibility that I have a censored sample are also presented. The OLS estimates of the coefficients of (5) may be biased as a result of the sampling procedure discussed earlier. We observe contract quantity only if contract duration is greater than or equal to (1979 – contract *YEAR*), so we have a censored sample. This implies that the random error (v) in the contract quantity equation (5) may be correlated with the random error (u) in the contract duration equation. If this is the case, the random error (v) in the contract quantity equation will be a function of the independent variables in the contract duration equation. The OLS estimates of the coefficients of the independent variables in the quantity equation (5) would then be biased if they are correlated with the independent variables in the duration equation. In particular, independent variables that appear in the contract duration equation may appear to be significant when introduced as independent variables in equation (8) when in fact they are not.[40] Since three

[38] One might also argue that, other things equal, a buyer would rather rely on a single supplier to conserve on more traditional types of transactions cost associated with negotiating, monitoring, and enforcing contracts with multiple supplies.

[39] Ideally, we would like to look at specific generating *units* rather than specific generating *plants* where plants have multiple units with different design characteristics. Unfortunately, coal supply information is not available at the generating unit level.

[40] See George Judge et al. (1985, pp. 610–13) and James Heckman (1976, 1979).

TABLE 7—CONTRACT QUANTITY[a]

	Dependent Variable: *QUANTITY*			
	OLS		OLS/*H*	
Independent Variables	(1)	(2)	(3)	(4)
PLANT QUANTITY	0.2501	0.3133	0.2128	0.2827
	(0.0441)	(0.1573)	0.0489	(0.1578)
PLANT QUANTITY-SQUARED	–	−0.00066	–	−0.00067
		(0.0010)		(0.00099)
UTILITY QUANTITY	0.00349	0.0672	0.00393	0.06376
	(0.00689)	(0.0311)	(0.00685)	(0.03104)
UTILITY QUANTITY-SQUARED	–	−0.00007	–	−0.000063
		(0.00003)		(0.000032)
MINE-MOUTH	29.7932	27.1594	30.3261	27.775
	(6.8591)	(6.8997)	(6.8251)	(6.879)
WEST	13.5416	13.5865	8.4955	8.9738
	(4.6437)	(4.6259)	(5.4680)	(5.4597)
MIDWEST	5.2469	4.856	2.5832	2.4749
	(4.1841)	(4.1708)	(4.4371)	(4.4193)
H	–	–	−66.7618	−60.6647
			(38.7474)	(38.5749)
Constant	1.7329	−4.2283	10.6708	4.0997
	(3.5879)	(5.0515)	(6.2951)	(7.3027)
Corrected *R*-Squared	0.33	0.34	0.34	0.35
Observations	169	169	169	169

[a]Standard errors of coefficient estimates are shown in parentheses.

variables that appear in the quantity equation (5) also appear in the duration equation, this is a potential problem here.

We can obtain consistent estimates of the coefficients of (5) by obtaining maximum likelihood estimates of a reduced-form contract duration equation[41] to generate a sample selection correction H for each observation, adding the estimated values of H to (5) and then estimating the augmented equation (5) using OLS. The coefficient of H is then a consistent estimate of the covariance of u and v.

The results are reported in Table 7.[42] The OLS results appear in columns 1 and 2 and the OLS results with H introduced appear in columns 3 and 4. In both cases, estimates with and without quadratic terms in plant and utility quantities are reported. The results are generally consistent with my expectations. Larger plants tend to place larger orders and utilities with larger aggregate requirements do so as well, although the utility effect is generally small. The quadratic in plant quantity is not significantly different from zero. The coefficients of the mine-mouth dummy has the predicted sign and is estimated fairly precisely. Mine-mouth plants have contracts that are nearly 1.5 million tons larger (30 trillion Btu's) than other plants *ceteris paribus*. Regional differences in supply characteristics lead to larger contracts with western suppliers than with suppliers elsewhere. The coefficient of the correction variable H is negative, although not quite significant at the 5 percent level (two-tailed test), implying that the errors in the duration and quantity equation are negatively correlated. Including this correction does not have dramatic effects on the results for the coefficients of interest, however. The primary effect is to reduce the magnitude and significance of the coefficient of *WEST*.

[41]*QUANTITY* and *LOG-QUANTITY* are treated as being endogenous.

[42]The mean value for *H* is 0.076.

Finally, for the record, I report two-stage least square (*2SLS*) estimates of equation (2) in Table 3, column 9, and the equivalent of two-stage least squares for the maximum likelihood estimates of equation (2) in Table 5, column 9.[43] The estimates do not change in any important way from those obtained using the other estimating techniques in either case.

VI. Conclusions

The purpose of this paper has been to examine empirically hypotheses about the relationship between the duration of coal contracts and the presence of the three types of relationship specific investments discussed by Williamson (1983).[44] I argue that as relationship-specific investments become more important, the parties will find it advantageous to rely on longer-term contracts that specify the terms and conditions of repeated transactions *ex ante*, rather than relying on repeated bargaining. I make use of a large sample of coal contracts to examine this hypothesis. The empirical results obtained provide fairly strong support for this hypothesis. They are quite robust to alternative model specifications, samples, and estimating techniques. The results therefore provide additional empirical support for the view that the structure of vertical relationships between buyers and sellers is strongly affected by variations in the importance of relationship-specific investments.

[43]I assumed that *LOG-QUANTITY* is endogenous, and use the right-hand side variables in (5) as instruments for the *2SLS* results reported in Table 3, col. 9. Obtaining the equivalent of *2SLS* estimates for the case in which I treat the sample as being truncated and use maximum likelihood techniques, is more complicated. Following Maddala (pp. 234–40) and L. S. Lee et al. (1979), I proceeded in the following way. First, I estimate a reduced-form duration equation using maximum likelihood techniques. This allows me to obtain consistent estimates of H_i which can in turn be used to obtain consistent estimates of a contract quantity equation as discussed above. I use these estimates of the quantity equation to obtain predicted values of *QUANTITY* or *LOG-QUANTITY* which are then used in place of *QUANTITY* and *LOG-QUANTITY* to estimate equations (1) and (2) using maximum likelihood techniques. The results reported in Table 5, col. 9, assume that log(*PLANT QUANTITY*), log(*UTILITY QUANTITY*), *MIDWEST*, *WEST*, and *MINE-MOUTH* are exogenous variables. These variables are used to estimate a reduced-form duration equation using the maximum likelihood technique described earlier. An equation for log(*QUANTITY*) is then estimated using log(*PLANT QUANTITY*), log(*UTILITY QUANTITY*), *MIDWEST*, *WEST*, *MINE-MOUTH*, and *H* (generated from the reduced-form duration estimates) using OLS. The predicted values from this equation are then used instead of *LOG-QUANTITY* in (2) to obtain the maximum likelihood estimates reported. Specification (1) has also been estimated using this approach. The results appear to be robust.

[44]As well as similar considerations of transaction-specific investments identified by Klein et al.

APPENDIX

Here I discuss the sources of the data and the construction of the variables. The data base that I rely on was constructed from a variety of sources for use in a research project focusing on vertical relationships between electric utilities and coal suppliers. This is one of three papers that has been produced so far from this project.

The construction of the data base began with the choice of contracts to use in the analysis. Contracts were chosen if they appeared in *both* the 1981 and 1983 editions of *The Guide to Coal Contracts* (Pasha Publications) and for which information necessary for the project was reported. Contracts had to appear in both publications because some information that was desired appeared in one or the other publication, but not both. This also made it possible to check for errors and inconsistencies in the contract characteristics reported. To appear in both publications, contracts had to be in force in 1979. In five cases, actual contracts were used to supplement the data available from the primary sources.

This collection procedure resulted in a sample of 296 contracts (of which 277 had enough information to be used here) which generally had the following information, some of which is used in this paper and some of which I am using in related work:

1. Information required to calculate the agreed upon duration of the contract (see discussion below).
2. Contract quantities for 1979, 1980, and/or 1981 in tons.
3. The contract specifications for the Btu content and the sulfur content of the coal.
4. The identity of the seller and the location of the mine.
5. The identity of the buyer and the destination of the coal.
6. The base price for the coal at the time the contract was signed.
7. The actual price for the coal in 1979, 1980, and/or 1981.
8. Delivered quantities in 1979, 1980, and/or 1981.
9. Actual Btu and sulfur content of the coal.

Once the contract sample was selected, individual contracts were matched with specific utilities and power plants (where possible). Two publications were utilized to obtain coal quantity and quality (Btu content) information by plant and utility: *Cost and Quality of Fuels for the Electric Utility Industry* (U.S. Department of Energy, various years) and *Steam Electric Plant Factors* (National Coal Association, various years). For public utility holding companies, coal utilization for subsidiaries was aggregated. Jointly owned plants were assigned to the operating company.

The three coal supply regions represent aggregations of smaller U.S. Bureau of Mines (BOM) districts. The West was defined as including BOM districts 16 through 23. The Midwest included BOM districts 5, 9, 10, 11, 12, 14, and 15. BOM district 15 includes Texas, but we have no contracts for coal produced in Texas. The East includes coal from the remaining BOM districts, primarily in Appalachia. The differences between regions is discussed in more detail in my 1985 paper. The *Keystone Coal Industry Manual* (Mining Information Services) and an atlas were used to help locate mines in specific BOM districts.

The variable definitions and construction are as follows:

DURATION: Contract Duration: The contract data base generally provides information for the date the contract was executed, the termination date and (less frequently) the date of first delivery of coal. A specific month and year is often provided, but sometimes the source specifies only years. Because the contract execution date was available more often than the date of first delivery and because the two are generally quite close together, contract duration was measured as contract termination year minus execution year. Initial experimentation with duration measured using the date of first delivery or using month and year indicated that the results were unaffected, so the definition that preserved the largest number of contracts was used.

QUANTITY: Annual contract quantity in trillion Btu's. The contracted tonnage reported for 1980 (if that was not available, or obviously not representative, 1979 or, alternatively, 1981 were used instead) was multiplied by the contracted Btu content of the coal to arrive at the contract quantity variable.

MINE-MOUTH: Mine-mouth dummy variable that is equal to one if the plant is a mine-mouth plant and zero otherwise. The information in my 1985 paper combined with the coal destination information in the *Guide To Coal Contracts* was used to construct this variable. The Navajo and Mohave plants were included in this category as well since they have economic characteristics very much like a mine-mouth plant.

MIDWEST: A regional dummy variable that equals one if the coal is from a midwestern mine (as defined above) and zero otherwise. The contract data base provides information on mine location.

WEST: A regional dummy variable that equals one if coal is from a western mine (as defined above) and zero otherwise.

PLANT QUANTITY: Annual plant utilization of coal. Coal utilization by a plant to which a specific contract is dedicated (at least 90 percent of the coal delivered to a single plant) for 1980 (1979 or 1981 if necessary to match *QUANTITY*) in trillion Btu's. Obtained from the Department of Energy and National Coal Association publications identified above.

UTILITY QUANTITY: Annual utility utilization of coal. Coal utilization in 1980 (or 1979 or 1981 if necessary to match other data) by the utility operating a plant to which a contract is dedicated. Obtained from the Department of Energy and National Coal Association publications identified above.

PLANT PROPORTION: Delivered contract quantity in Btu's divided by plant utilization in Btu's. Delivered contract quantity in tons was pulled from the contract information for 1980 (or 1979 if 1980 was not available), and multiplied by the delivered Btu content of the coal to obtain quantities delivered to a specific plant under a contract dedicated to that plant. This figure was then divided by *PLANT QUANTITY*.

UTILITY PROPORTION: Delivered contract quantity in Btu's (as defined above in definition of *PLANT PROPORTION*) divided by utility utilization of coal in Btu's for 1980 (1979 or 1981 otherwise).

PLANT/UTILITY: *PLANT QUANTITY* divided by *UTILITY QUANTITY*.

YEAR: The year specified as the execution date of the contract.

DATE-71: A dummy variable that equals one for contracts signed in 1971, 1972, and 1973.

DATE-74: A dummy variable that equals one for contracts signed in 1974, 1975, 1976, and 1977.

DATE-78: A dummy variable that equals one for contracts signed in 1978 and 1979.

The mean, standard deviation, minimum, and maximum values of these variables for the 277 observation sample and the 169 observation (single delivery point) subsample are contained in Tables 1 and 2. The data for the variables used in this paper are available upon request.

REFERENCES

Crocker, Keith J. and Masten, Scott E., "Mitigating Contractual Hazards: Unilateral Options and Contract Length," Working Paper No. 449, Graduate School of Business Administration, University of Michigan, March 1986.

Dubin, Jeffrey and Rivers, R. Douglas, *Statistical Software Tools*, Version 1.0, Pasadena, March 1986.

Goldberg, Victor and Erickson, John, "Long Term Contracts for Petroleum Coke," Working Paper No. 206, Department of Economics, University of California-Davis, 1982.

Hart, Oliver and Holmstrom, Bengt, "The Theory of Contracts," Department of Economics Working Paper No. 418, MIT, March 1986.

Heckman, James, "The Common Structure of

Statistical Models of Truncation, Sample Selection and Limited Dependent Variables and a Simple Estimator For Such Models," *Annals of Economic and Social Measurement*, 1976, Vol. 5, 475–92.

______ "Sample Selection Bias as a Specification Error," *Econometrica*, January 1979, *47*, 153–61.

Joskow, Paul L., "Vertical Integration and Long Term Contracts: The Case of Coal-burning Electric Generating Plants," *Journal of Law, Economics and Organization*, Spring 1985, *1*, 33–80.

______ "Price Adjustment in Longer Term Contracts: The Case of Coal," mimeo., May 1986.

______ **and Mishkin, Frederick**, "Electric Utility Fuel Choice Behavior in the United States," *International Economic Review*, October 1977, *18*, 719–36.

______ **and Schmalensee, Richard**, "The Performance of Steam Electric Generating Plants in the United States: 1960–1989," Department of Economics Working Paper No. 379, MIT, July 1985.

Judge, George G. et al., *The Theory and Practice of Econometrics*, New York: Wiley & Sons, 1985.

Klein, Benjamin, Crawford, Robert and Alchian, Armen, "Vertical Integration, Appropriable Rents and the Competitive Contracting Process," *Journal of Law and Economics*, October 1978, *21*, 297–326.

Lee, L. S., Maddala, G. S. and Trost, R. P., "Testing for Structural Change By D-Methods in Switching Simultaneous Equations Models," *Proceedings of the American Statistical Association*, Business and Economics Section, 1979, 461–66.

Maddala, G. S., *Limited-Dependent and Qualitative Variables in Econometrics*, Cambridge: Cambridge University Press, 1983.

Masten, Scott E., "The Organization of Production: Evidence from the Aerospace Industry," *Journal of Law and Economics*, October 1984, *27*, 403–18.

______ **and Crocker, Keith, J.**, "Efficient Adaptation in Long-Term Contracts: Take-or-Pay Provisions for Natural Gas," *American Economic Review*, December 1985, *75*, 1083–93.

Monteverde, Kirk and Teece, David, "Supplier Switching Costs and Vertical Integration in the Automobile Industry," *Bell Journal of Economics*, Spring 1982, *13*, 206–13.

Mulhern, J. Harold, "Complexity in Long-term Contracts: An Analysis of Natural Gas Contract Provisions," *Journal of Law, Economics and Organization*, Spring 1986, *2*, 105–117.

Schmalensee, Richard and Joskow, Paul L., "Estimated Parameters as Independent Variables: An Application to the Costs of Steam Electric Generating Units," *Journal of Econometrics*, April 1986, *31*, 275–305.

Williamson, Oliver E., "Transaction-Cost Economics: The Governance of Contractual Relations," *Journal of Law and Economics*, October 1979, *22*, 233–61.

______, "Credible Commitments: Using Hostages to Support Exchange," *American Economic Review*, September 1983, *73*, 519–40.

______, *The Economic Institutions of Capitalism*, New York: Free Press, 1985.

Zimmerman, Martin, *The U.S. Coal Industry: Economics of Policy Choice*, Cambridge: MIT Press, 1981.

Mining Information Services, *Keystone Coal Industry Manual*, New York, 1981.

National Coal Association, *Steam Electric Plant Factors*, Washington, various years.

Pasha Publications, *Guide To Coal Contracts*, Washington, 1981; 1983.

U.S. Department of Energy, Energy Information Administration, *Cost and Quality of Fuels for Electric Utility Plants*, DOE/IEA-0191, Washington, various years.

[11]

Complexity in Long-term Contracts: An Analysis of Natural Gas Contractual Provisions

J. HAROLD MULHERIN
Clemson University

Long-term contracts in the coal, geothermal, uranium, and natural gas industries, among others, often include complex quantity and price provisions. Several explanations for contractual complexities of these kinds have been advanced. The earliest is that such complex provisions are a manifestation of market power. A second possibility is that the quantity and price provisions of long-term contracts are methods of allocating risk. A third explanation stems from the transaction cost framework of Coase, Klein et al., and Williamson (1979, 1985).

The transaction cost hypothesis maintains that economic organization varies systematically with the condition of asset specificity. This is amenable to empirical testing. Indeed, there is a growing empirical literature testing this hypothesis (Joskow, Masten, Monteverde and Teece, and Palay (1984, 1985)).

In this paper I analyze and empirically test a number of hypotheses on the role of the contractual provisions in the natural gas industry.[1] I compare the

This paper is derived from my doctoral dissertation at UCLA. Thanks are expressed to my committee (Benjamin Klein, Chair). Appreciation for comments on this paper is extended to Gabrielle Brenner, Keith Crocker, Scott Masten, Pablo Spiller, Michael Waldman, Oliver Williamson, and two referees. Earlier versions of this paper were presented at the meetings of the Law and Society Association, San Diego, California, June 1985, and the meetings of the European Association for Research in Industrial Economics, Cambridge, England, September 1985.

1. Simultaneous empirical research on the natural gas industry has been performed by Masten and Crocker. They examined the role of one of the contractual clauses, the take-or-pay provision, also studied in this paper. Their data set comes from a period of price controls, while that of the present study comes from a period prior to price controls. A comparison of the results of Masten and Crocker and those of the present paper will be made below.

Journal of Law, Economics, and Organization vol. 2., no. 1 Spring 1986
 ISSN 8756-6222

transaction cost premise with hypotheses based on market power, risk allocation, and non-price competition. The primary result is that the transaction cost hypothesis is most consistent with the observed provisions of natural gas contracts.

The first section of the paper discusses the structure of the natural gas industry, emphasizing the contracts that existed during the 1940s and 1950s. In section 2 I state and empirically test predictions of the transaction cost hypothesis as to the role of the provisions of these contracts. Alternative hypotheses are reviewed in section 3. The final section provides a summary and conclusion.

1. THE NATURAL GAS INDUSTRY

The natural gas industry is composed of the production, pipeline, and distribution sectors. In the industry's early growth period between 1920 and 1940, the three sectors were vertically integrated. However, federal legislation passed in the 1930s led to vertical divestiture in the industry. The Public Utility Holding Company Act of 1935 explicitly severed the pipeline and distribution sectors. The original cost regulation of pipeline rates by the Federal Power Commission (FPC) subsequent to the Natural Gas Act of 1938 provided a disincentive for pipelines to produce their own gas. This led to a substantial decrease in integration between the pipeline and production levels.[2]

Since 1940, production, transmission, and distribution have been conducted primarily between unaffiliated entities bound together by long-term written agreements. From 1940 to 1954, the contractual exchange of gas between producers and pipelines was conducted in an unregulated setting. But the 1954 *Phillips* decision placed natural gas producers under FPC jurisdiction, including control of wellhead prices (*Phillips Petroleum* v. *Wisconsin*, 347 U.S. 672 [1954]).

The focus of this study is on the producer-pipeline contracts of the 1940–54 period. Information on the contracts comes from data collected by the FPC. The data set is described in the appendix.

Some background on natural gas contracts is useful. A producer-pipeline contract exclusively dedicated the gas of a particular well to one pipeline. The contract prescribed whether the delivery point of the gas was to be at the wellhead or at the pipeline. This effectively determined whether the producer or the pipeline owned the gathering line connecting the well and the pipeline.

The contracts in the 1940–54 period had an average length of twenty years. To facilitate the flow of the contracted reserves over such a long time, the

2. For an elaboration of the effects of this regulation, see Mulherin (1985).

contract set a daily contract quantity which determined the average daily amount of natural gas that the pipeline would take annually. This quantity was expressed as a fraction of reserves to deplete a well in a given period of time. For example, a daily contract quantity of 1/10,000 would deplete a well in roughly twenty-seven years; 1/7,300 would do so in twenty years.

The pipeline paid for the gas as it was taken. But if the daily contract quantity multiplied by 365 days exceeded the actual amount of gas that the pipeline had taken in a particular year, the pipeline was required to make up the monetary difference between the minimum quantity and the amount taken. Thus the specification of the daily contract quantity denoted how much gas the pipeline had to take or pay for in a given year. A daily contract quantity which implied the depletion of a well in a shorter period indicated that the take-or-pay provision was of a greater magnitude.[3]

Complementing the quantity provisions of natural gas contracts were clauses providing for the adjustment of price. One prevalent price adjustment provision was the most-favored-nation clause. If a contract contained such a clause, then the pipeline was obligated to increase the price paid in that existing contract to the level paid by the same pipeline to other producers in a defined geographic region.

Some natural gas contracts contained a different adjustment provision called the price renegotiation clause. Under this provision, the producer and the pipeline merely agreed to renegotiate the price at prespecified dates. Arbitration might be prescribed in the event that the producer-pipeline negotiations broke down.

2. THE TRANSACTION COST HYPOTHESIS

Regulation encouraged separate ownership of natural gas wells and pipelines. Assume that such a condition obtains. The question, then, is how will the interface between wells and pipelines be accomplished?

This is a complicated issue. I focus attention on three features: (1) the gathering lines; (2) contractual safeguards concerned with procurement; and (3) price adjustment features. The transaction cost hypothesis predicts that the ownership of the gathering lines will vary with the organization of the gas field. It also predicts that procurement safeguards will appear in response to differential procurement hazards. And it further predicts that special price adjustment mechanics will be introduced as price indeterminacies become more severe. Consider each of these features.

3. In more recent contracts, the take-or-pay provision is based on "deliverability" rather than reserves (Masten and Crocker).

108 / JOURNAL OF LAW, ECONOMICS, AND ORGANIZATION II:1, 1986

2.1. The Ownership of Gathering Lines

Gathering lines are durable, site-specific assets. Well owners will be more prepared to make such investments if they can easily sell gas to a variety of pipelines. Pipelines will be more prepared to make such investments if they are dealing with many rather than only a few producers. The point at which "delivery" is made—at the wellhead, in which case the gathering lines are owned by the pipelines, or at the pipeline, in which case the gathering lines are owned by the producer—thus becomes the variable of interest.

A crude test of the transaction cost hypothesis can thus be made using the data described in the appendix. The variables used in the test are:

DELIVERY POINT:	0 if at the wellhead; 1 if at the pipeline[4]
NOSELLRS:	Number of producers in a natual gas field
NOPURCHS:	Number of pipelines in a natural gas field

With these variables, the hypothesis is that the delivery point will be positively related to NOPURCHS and negatively related to NOSELLRS. Since this test entails a qualitative choice model, a logistic specification was employed.[5] The number of observations was 3,818. The results are:

$$\text{DELIVERY POINT} = \underset{(.047)}{.119} + \underset{(.015)}{.061}\ \text{NOPURCHS} - \underset{(.003)}{.042}\ \text{NOSELLRS}$$

Standard errors are in parentheses. All coefficients are significant at the 95 percent level. The model chi-square is 541, $d.f. = 2$, which is also significant at the 95 percent level. The results are consistent with transaction cost reasoning.

2.2. The Take-or-Pay Provision

The take-or-pay provision specifies the minimum amount of natural gas for which the pipeline must pay the producer on an annual basis, even if that amount is not taken. The fact that the provision is take-*or*-pay rather than take-*and*-pay allows the pipeline to vary the daily, monthly, and annual quantities taken in response to the fluctuating demand for natural gas. Instead of having to maintain large inventories to meet demand changes, the pipeline is able to use the natural storage of the original well. While economizing on storage costs, the take-or-pay provision reduces the likelihood that the pipe-

4. In the data, 65 percent of the contracts specified a delivery point at the well and 35 percent specified delivery at the pipeline.

5. For a discussion of qualitative choice models, see Pindyck and Rubinfeld (273).

line would make use of *ex post* bargaining opportunities created by the features of natural gas.

The fugacity and common pool existence of natural gas imply that production delays are quite costly to the producer. After a producer's well is constructed, the pipeline to which the well is connected might threaten to delay taking gas from the producer as a means of appropriating rents. The producer might invoke a court injunction against such delays, but in the time taken to secure court enforcement the producer would lose a substantial amount of reserves to neighboring producers. Due to the costs of defining the property rights of underground reserves, it would be difficult for a court to discern the quantity drained from the producer and to determine the proper penalty for the pipeline.

The commitment to take or pay for a minimum daily contract quantity of natural gas clearly delineates the obligation of the pipeline, reducing the pipeline's incentive to use drainage as a strategic bargaining tool. If the pipeline delays taking a producer's gas, the pipeline must still pay the producer the amount specified by the take-or-pay provision. Hence, the costs borne by the producer are significantly reduced, mitigating the source of the pipeline's strategic behavior.[6]

Drainage can be assumed to increase with the number of producers in a field. Hence, the transaction cost hypothesis would predict a positive relation between the magnitude of the take-or-pay provision and the number of producers in a field.

The threat of drainage due to production delays is stronger as the number of contractual alternatives falls. The transaction cost hypothesis would predict a negative relation between the number of pipelines in a field and the magnitude of the take-or-pay provision.

The take-or-pay provision would also be expected to vary with the legal regime controlling drainage within a particular state. Where the control of drainage was stronger, the magnitude of the take-or-pay provision would be expected to be smaller. Congressional testimony has stated that Texas was more successful in controlling the drainage of natural gas compared to other major natural gas producing states such as Louisiana and Oklahoma. Such success was attributed to the active oversight of natural gas production by the Texas Railroad Commission. Through the commission's imposition of production quotas for each field, the protection of correlative rights, and other conservation measures, the ability of a producer to drain a common natural gas pool was lower in Texas.[7] Of course, even within Texas, as the number of

6. The possible correlation between drainage and the take-or-pay provision has also been noted in Broadman and Montgomery, Canes and Norman, and Masten and Crocker.

7. For a historical reference to the role of the Texas Railroad Commission in controlling the drainage of natural gas, see *Amendments to the Natural Gas Act: Hearings before a Subcommittee*

producers in a field increased, the legal regime would be less successful in controlling drainage (Libecap and Wiggins, 1984).

The transaction cost hypothesis on the role of the take-or-pay provision can be tested with the following variables.

TOP:	Daily take/estimated reserves[8]
BUYSTAR:	Number of pipelines in a field/contract price
SELLSTAR:	Number of producers in a field/contract price[9]
DUM:	Dummy variable equal to 1 for contracts in Texas

The transaction cost hypothesis would predict that TOP is negatively related to BUYSTAR and DUM and positively related to SELLSTAR. A test was performed by running OLS on the contracts from the data that contained information on the take-or-pay provision (N = 632). The results are:

$$\underset{}{TOP} = \underset{(.08)}{2.31} - \underset{(.34)}{.71}\ BUYSTAR + \underset{(.06)}{.11}\ SELLSTAR - \underset{(.09)}{.92}\ DUM$$

The R-square of the equation was .163. Standard errors are in parentheses. All coefficients are significant at the 95 percent level. The signs of the coefficients support the transaction cost hypothesis.[10]

The results resemble those of Masten and Crocker, who implemented a similar model in an environment of price controls. Their model regressed the magnitude of the take-or-pay provision on the number of producers and pipelines in the field, the Herfindahl index for pipeline concentration in a

---

of the Senate Committee on Interstate and Foreign Commerce on S. 1498, 81st Cong., 1st Sess. 31–65 (1949). For a more recent discussion of the same point, see *Natural Gas Issues: Hearings before the Subcommittee on Fossil Fuels of the House Committee on Energy and Commerce*, 97th Cong., 2nd Sess. 1358–59 (1982).

8. In the data, the observations for the ratio of the daily take to reserves were as follows:

Ratio	No. Observations
1/10,000	457
1/9,000	3
1/8,000	95
1/7,000	77
	632

9. The specification of BUYSTAR as the number of pipelines divided by the contract price and SELLSTAR as the number of producers divided by the contract price is formally derived in Masten and Crocker.

10. The sign of DUM implies that Texas was more successful than states such as Louisiana and Oklahoma in controlling the drainage of natural gas. In contrast, Libecap and Wiggins (1985) found that, compared to Wyoming and Oklahoma, Texas was less successful in unitizing oil leases. The results of Libecap and Wiggins and those of this paper are not in direct conflict due to the differences in the form of energy and the states under comparison. Yet the difference in results and the detail to which Libecap and Wiggins have analyzed oil production suggests that further study of natural gas conservation is warranted.

region, and a term denoting the binding nature of federal price controls. They found that the magnitude of the take-or-pay provision was negatively related to the number of pipelines and the pipeline Herfindahl index and was positively related to the number of producers and the price control variable. All coefficients were significant at the 90 percent level.

2.3. Price Adjustment Provisions

Complementing the quantity specifications of natural gas contracts were price provisions such as the most-favored-nation and price renegotiation clauses. These adjustment provisions have been structured to allow a price response to new information within an otherwise long-term agreement. These clauses have thereby reduced the cost of natural gas contracts by lowering the number of contingencies that had to be explicitly stated in the contracts.

A notable feature of the natural gas contracts written during the 1940s and 1950s is that the price adjustment provisions were not tied to general price indexes. In the data, only 2 percent of the contracts had price escalators based on a general index. A general index was not used because the price in the natural gas industry might have no defined correlation with the overall economy. The price provisions were also not based on a national natural gas price index, because across geographic regions the cost and demand conditions in the industry varied substantially.[11]

Price escalation either was left up to the specific trading partners (through the price renegotiation provision) or was based on the price in a defined geographic region (through the most-favored-nation clause). Within a region, the cost conditions of wells were similar (MacAvoy: 24). This ability to structure homogeneous cost conditions in natural gas contracts contributed to the origination and survival of the most-favored-nation clause in that industry and is contrasted with the absence of such a clause in the automobile industry (Klein: 335) and the coal industry (Carney: 217) due to heterogeneity across contracts.

While the most-favored-nation clause and the price renegotiation provision both facilitate price adjustments, the two provisions imply different incentives for the pipeline. The lack of a defined criterion with which to obtain a new price under a price renegotiation clause introduces the possibility of opportunistic behavior by the pipeline at the renegotiation date. If the producer had few contractual alternatives, the pipeline might attempt to hold down the new price or to induce side payments. A court or an arbitrator might be unable to determine if this delay was an expression of normal bargaining methods or was instead a product of opportunistic behavior.

11. For a discussion of the heterogeneous demand and cost conditions in the natural gas industry, see *Amendments to the Natural Gas Act: Hearings before a Subcommittee of the Senate Committee on Interstate and Foreign Commerce on H.R. 4051*, 80th Cong., 2nd Sess. 527 (1948).

112 / JOURNAL OF LAW, ECONOMICS, AND ORGANIZATION II:1, 1986

The most-favored-nation clause offers stricter control of pipeline incentives by specifying an automatic trigger for price increases.[12] The fact that the trigger would be activated by new purchases in an area provides an expectation that producers in existing contracts will always receive a price that covers the investment in production facilities. This lessens the likelihood of opportunistic behavior by the pipeline and would be more valuable in areas with fewer pipelines.[13]

While reducing the likelihood of opportunistic behavior by the pipeline, the most-favored-nation clause enables a timely adjustment to changing market conditions over the life of the agreement. The usefulness of this adjustment feature would increase with the length of the contract.[14]

This discussion suggests that the use of the most-favored-nation clause is negatively related to the number of pipelines and positively related to the length of the contract. This hypothesis can be tested with the following variables:

MOSTFN:	0 if the most-favored-nation clause is absent;[15]
	1 if the most-favored-nation clause is present[16]
NOPURCHS:	Number of pipelines in a field
TERM:	Length (in years) of a contract

The variable MOSTFN is assumed to be negatively related to NOPURCHS and positively related to TERM. The hypothesis was tested by using a logistic specification on the data reporting information on price adjustment provisions (N = 2234). The results are:

$$\underset{(.188)}{\text{MOSTFN} = .41} - \underset{(.011)}{.023}\ \text{NOPURCHS} + \underset{(.009)}{.052}\ \text{TERM}$$

Standard errors are in parentheses. All coefficients are significant at the 95 percent level. The model chi-square is 61.4, $d.f. = 2$, which is also significant

12. The adjustment features of the most-favored-nation clause applied to any higher prices involving the pipeline over an area such as a Texas Railroad Commission district, several counties or parishes in a state, or within a hundred-mile radius of the well. The most-favored-nation clause would be activated as the pipeline purchased new gas in the area to meet the increased demand of existing customers or to make extensions to meet the demand of new customers. The clause would also be activated by the higher prices that resulted from the pipeline's compliance with contracts in the area that had price renegotiation provisions.

13. A similar point is made by Norman.

14. The decision to use a most-favored-nation clause and the choice of contractual length are made at the same time. Hence, care must be taken in posing the length of the contract as a variable affecting the likelihood of the use of the most-favored-nation clause. My interpretation is that the use of a lengthier contract is a reaction to the perception of a greater possibility of opportunism. Given this greater possibility, there is an increased role for the most-favored-nation clause, both to mitigate opportunism and to ensure a response to changes in market conditions over the life of the contract.

15. The absence of the most-favored-nation clause implies the use of a price renegotiation clause, a general price index, or no index at all.

16. The proportional of contracts having a most-favored-nation clause was 78 percent.

at the 95 percent level. The qualitative direction of the coefficients of NOPURCHS and TERM are consistent with the transaction cost hypothesis.

3. SOME RIVAL HYPOTHESES

In the literature that comments on the provisions of natural gas contracts, hypotheses based on market power, risk allocation, and non-price competition have been proposed. This section reviews these rival hypotheses and offers empirical analysis of their applicability to natural gas contracts.

3.1. Market Power

One view of the role of the contracts in the natural gas industry is that such arrangements were used to extend the market power of the producer.[17] This view would posit that where competition from other producers was absent, the producer might structure the contract so as to impose costs on the pipeline. This imposition of costs would lower the return to the pipeline and increase the return to the producer.

One implication of the market power hypothesis is that a producer with market power would require the pipeline to bear the costs of constructing the gathering line. As the number of producers in a field fell, the producer would be less likely to own the gathering line. Hence, the hypothesis would predict a positive relation between DELIVERY POINT and NOSELLRS in the regression in section 2.1. Yet the results indicated a significant, negative relation which does not support the market power hypothesis.

Market power might also enable the producer to "force" the pipeline to commit to a larger amount of gas by means of a take-or-pay provision of greater magnitude. As the number of producers in a field was lower, the market power hypothesis would predict a larger take-or-pay amount. In the regression in section 2.2, one would expect a negative relation between TOP and SELLSTAR. Yet the regression indicates a significant, positive relation which does not support the market power premise.[18]

Another possible market power hypothesis is that the most-favored-nation clause was used to support a pipeline monopsony cartel.[19] The viability of

17. This view often turns up in congressional testimony. See, for example, Temporary National Economic Committee, *Report on Natural Gas and Natural Gas Pipelines in the U.S.A.*, monograph no. 36, part 1, 76th Cong., 3rd Sess. 4 (1940).

18. Since SELLSTAR is the ratio of the number of producers in a field divided by the price in the transaction, a qualification must be placed on this interpretation of the regression. Price is an endogenous variable that is affected by the number of producers and pipelines in a field. Hence, the sign of the coefficient of SELLSTAR in the regression in section 2.2 is not as clear a refutation of the market power hypothesis as the sign of the coefficient of NOSELLRS in the regression in section 2.1.

19. A similar argument which states that a most-favored-nation clause might facilitate a seller cartel can be found in the opinion of the Federal Trade Commission, *In the Matter of Ethyl Corporation et al.*, Docket no. 9128, 68–76 (1983).

such a cartel could be undermined if the cartel members could cheat by paying prices in individual contracts that were above the chosen cartel price. The presence of the most-favored-nation clause might lessen the incentives for such cheating since the offer of a higher price to one producer would activate higher prices in the pipeline's other contracts in the same area.

The likelihood of cheating on a cartel can be assumed to increase with the number of pipelines in the cartel. If the most-favored-nation clause is used to reduce cheating, then the occurrence of the provision would be expected to rise with the number of pipelines in an area. The empirical results in section 2.3 show otherwise. The occurrence of the most-favored-nation clause is negatively related to the number of pipelines in a field.

3.2. Risk Allocation

Several authors have argued that the provisions of natural gas contracts serve a competitive function by allocating risk between pipelines and producers. For example, MacAvoy (66) and Norman (11) have stated that the price adjustment provisions of natural gas contracts distribute the risk of price fluctuations. In the absence of a price escalator, the producer would not be able to reap any gains from future price increases and would thereby bear the risk of such increases. When the adjustment provisions were present, the pipeline would have to pass on any price increases in the industry and would thereby bear the price risk.

The party bearing the risk would be expected to be compensated through an alteration in the initial price. The price risk hypothesis predicts a negative relation between the price in a contract and the presence of a price adjustment provision.[20]

To test this hypothesis, MacAvoy constructed a model which regressed the initial price of a producer-pipeline contract on terms including dummy variables for the presence of the most-favored-nation and price renegotiation clauses. Using subsets of the data described in the appendix of this paper, MacAvoy (264) found that the coefficients of the price adjustment dummies often had significant, positive signs. This result does not support the price risk hypothesis.

Recent papers have also conjectured that the take-or-pay provision allocates risk (Broadman and Montgomery, Canes and Norman). The view is that the take-or-pay provision guarantees more stabilized cash flows for the pro-

20. If the price in a producer-pipeline contract could go down as well as up, the price risk hypothesis would be different. Risk-averse producers would prefer a fixed price and would have to be paid a premium to bear a variable return. A positive relation between the price and the presence of an adjustment provision would be predicted. But because producer-pipeline contracts offered no downside price exposure, a producer would prefer the presence of an escalator and would have to be paid up front to forsake future possible price increases. Hence, the price risk hypothesis formulates a negative relation.

ducer and enables the sharing of risk between the producer and the pipeline. The reason that stabilized cash flows are desired by the producer is not stated. Sizeable bankruptcy costs in the production sector may have been the implicit assumption (Warner).

By reducing the variability of a producer's cash flow, the take-or-pay provision may lessen the probability of bankruptcy and thereby increase the producer's expected value. Such a role would be more useful the smaller the producer, because as firm size falls the proportionate effect of bankruptcy costs is greater (Warner: 345). The risk allocation/bankruptcy cost hypothesis would postulate that small producers would use the take-or-pay provision relatively more than major energy companies.

To test the bankruptcy cost hypothesis, the contracts from the data that contained information on the take-or-pay provision (N = 632) were segregated according to whether they involved small producers or major energy companies. The amount of the two groups was fairly equal—48 percent were small producers and 52 percent were major companies. But the use of the take-or-pay provision was swayed toward the major companies—68 percent of the contracts containing the provision involved major companies while 32 percent involved small producers. Using a chi-square test the difference in use is statistically significant in the opposite direction of the bankruptcy cost hypothesis (chi-square = 22.15, *d.f.* = 1). The take-or-pay provision does not appear to be used to allocate risk so as to lessen bankruptcy.

3.3 Non-Price Competition

A third competing hypothesis is that the take-or-pay provision is a means of avoiding federal price controls. In a setting of binding price controls, a pipeline might offer to make faster payments by increasing the magnitude of the take-or-pay provision. Yet the data for this study come from contracts written prior to the imposition of controls on wellhead prices. The existence of the take-or-pay provision in the pre-1954 period indicates that the provision has a function independent of price controls. The recent research by Masten and Crocker, however, suggests that price controls do affect the magnitude of the take-or-pay provision.

4. SUMMARY AND CONCLUSION

In this study I have reviewed several hypotheses as to the role of the contractual provisions in the natural gas industry. The transaction cost hypothesis was shown to be more consistent with the data than the competing hypotheses. The assertion that the contractual provisions existed only to facilitate non-price competition could be immediately disproven by the occurrence of the provisions in an environment free of price controls. Past research has empirically rejected the risk allocation hypothesis and the present study

116 / JOURNAL OF LAW, ECONOMICS, AND ORGANIZATION II:1, 1986

rejected a corollary which relied on bankruptcy costs. Empirical tests also did not support the market power hypothesis.

By contrast, the contracting nexus between natural gas producers and pipelines is consonant with transaction cost economizing. The tests were applied to the ownership of gathering lines, the magnitude of the take-or-pay provision, and the use of the most-favored-nation clause. The results of the tests were that, indeed, the contractual provisions used in particular producer-pipeline agreements were systematically affected by the the nature of the bilateral contracting hazards.

The results lend additional support to the transaction cost framework. Specific to the natural gas industry, the finding of an inherent competitive source of the arrangements in the natural gas industry contradicts the historical association of the arrangements with market power. In a more general context, the results suggest that one must penetrate the operations of an industry before placing a "noncompetitive" label on "unusual" methods of organization.

APPENDIX

Exhibit 2-LC of Federal Commission Docket G-9277 forms the data base for the empirical tests of this paper. Subsequent to the 1954 *Phillips* decision, the FPC requested that natural gas producers submit information on all existing contracts for the sale of natural gas. The information was compiled for the FPC by Foster Associates, Washington, D.C. The contracts in Exhibit 2-LC span the period 1938–54.

Table 1 of Exhibit 2-LC contains information from natural gas contracts including the following: seller and purchaser; county and state in which gas is produced; type of gas and type of contract; delivery point; and contract length and price. There are 6,397 observations in table 1. Of these, 2,579 refer to gas transportation, direct sales, processing, or casinghead gas agreements, or they had missing data. To allow the concentration on producer sales to pipelines, these 2,579 observations were deleted from the data used in this paper. The remaining 3,818 observations in table 1 were used to test the gathering line hypothesis in section 2.1.

Table 3 of Exhibit 2-LC contains information from individual contracts including the seller and purchaser and the presence or absence of a most-favored-nation clause. There are a total of 4,266 observations in table 3. Due to missing data, not all of the observations in table 3 could be matched with those in table 1. The merging process produced 2,234 observations that could be used to perform the regression in section 2.3.

Table 3 also contains 632 observations providing information on the ratio of the daily take to reserves. All of these observations could be used to enable the testing of the transaction cost hypothesis in section 2.2 and the bankruptcy cost hypothesis in section 3.2.

REFERENCES

Broadman, Harry G., and W. David Montgomery. 1983. *Natural Gas Markets after Decontrol*. Washington, D.C.: Resources for the Future.

Canes, Michael A., and Donald A. Norman. 1983 "Analytics of the Take-or-Pay Provision in Natural Gas Contracts." American Petroleum Institute discussion paper no. 029.

Carney, Edmund M. 1978. "Pricing Provisions in Coal Contracts." Rocky Mountain Mineral Law Institute, *Proceedings of the Twenty-Fifth Annual Institute*.

Coase, R. H. 1937. "The Nature of the Firm," 4 *Economica* 386.

Joskow, Paul L. 1985. "Vertical Integration and Long-term Contracts: The Case of Coal-burning Electric Generating Plants," 1 *Journal of Law, Economics, and Organization* 33.

Klein, Benjamin. 1984. "Contract Costs and Administered Prices: An Economic Theory of Rigid Wages," 74 *American Economic Review* 332.

———, Robert G. Crawford, and Armen A. Alchian. 1978. "Vertical Integration, Appropriable Rents, and the Competitive Contracting Process," 21 *Journal of Law and Economics* 297.

Libecap, Gary D., and Steven N. Wiggins. 1984. "Contractual Responses to the Common Pool: Prorationing of Crude Oil Production," 74 *American Economic Review* 87.

———. 1985. "The Influence of Private Contractual Failure on Regulation: The Case of Oil Field Unitization," 93 *Journal of Political Economy* 690.

MacAvoy, Paul. 1962. *Price Formation in Natural Gas Fields*. New Haven: Yale University Press.

Masten, Scott E. 1984. "The Organization of Production: Evidence from the Aerospace Industry," 27 *Journal of Law and Economics* 403.

———, and Keith J. Crocker. 1985. "Efficient Adaptation in Long Term Contracts: Take-or-Pay Provisions for Natural Gas." 75 *American Economic Review*.

Monteverde, Kirk, and David J. Teece. 1982. "Appropriable Rents and Quasi-Vertical Integration," 25 *Journal of Law and Economics* 321.

Mulherin, J. Harold. 1984. "Vertical Integration and Long Term Contracts in the Natural Gas Industry." Ph.D. dissertation, University of California, Los Angeles.

———. 1985. "Specialized Assets, Governmental Regulation, and Organizational Structure in the Natural Gas Industry." Mimeo.

Norman, Donald A. 1984. "Indefinite Pricing Provisions in Natural Gas Contracts." American Petroleum Institute, draft working paper.

Palay, Thomas. 1984. "Comparative Institutional Economics: The Governance of Rail-Freight Contracting," 13 *Journal of Legal Studies* 265.

———. 1985. "Avoiding Regulatory Constraints: Contracting Safeguards and the Role of Informal Agreements," 1 *Journal of Law, Economics, and Organization* 155.

Pindyck, Robert S., and Daniel L. Rubinfeld. 1981. *Econometric Methods and Economic Forecasts*. New York: McGraw Hill.

Warner, Jerold B. 1977. "Bankruptcy Costs: Some Evidence," 32 *Journal of Finance* 337.

Williamson, Oliver E. 1979. "Transaction Cost Economics: The Governance of Contractual Relations," 22 *Journal of Law and Economics* 233.

———. 1985. "Assessing Contract," 1 *Journal of Law, Economics, and Organization* 177.

[12]

Efficient Adaptation in Long-Term Contracts: Take-or-Pay Provisions for Natural Gas

By SCOTT E. MASTEN AND KEITH J. CROCKER*

To avoid repeated bargaining in transactions supported by durable, transaction-specific investments, parties may decide to specify the terms of future trade in a long-term contract at the outset of the relationship (see, for example, Benjamin Klein, Robert Crawford, and Armen Alchian, 1978; and Oliver Williamson, 1979). A principal limitation of long-term contracting, however, is its inflexibility in the face of fluctuations in supply and demand: although contingent claims contracts permit adaptation to changing circumstances, contingent performance is costly to stipulate and even more difficult for courts to administer. To mitigate these hazards, parties will therefore wish to choose contract terms that minimize the need for costly adjudication while maintaining incentives for appropriate adaptation.

This paper examines the incidence of "take-or-pay" provisions in contracts between natural gas producers and pipelines from this perspective. Take-or-pay clauses require purchasers to pay for a contractually specified minimum quantity of output, even if delivery is not taken. The existence of such provisions and efforts by pipelines to have them abrogated in the face of declining demand during the most recent recession have generated a debate regarding the role such terms play in allocating gas resources. A common perception has been that take-or-pay provisions are an artifact of wellhead price regulation: by assuring a minimum payment, take obligations raise the expected value of a contract to a producer and thereby circumvent the effect of the price ceiling. To the extent that producers of high-cost gas were able to command higher obligations, some pipelines have been induced to purchase and sell more expensive gas to end users while leaving lower-cost supplies with smaller take requirements in the ground. The implication of this view is that take provisions are anomalies that distort market incentives and should therefore be nullified, permitting pipelines to adjust purchases in a more appropriate manner.

The problem with this explanation is that the incidence of take provisions is not limited to regulated gas supplies, but is also a feature of contracts covering unregulated pre-1954 interstate and pre-1978 intrastate gas, as well as of recently deregulated categories of new "high-cost" gas.[1] Moreover, take-or-pay clauses are also encountered in contracts for

*Graduate School of Business Administration, University of Michigan, Ann Arbor, MI 48109, and Department of Economics, University of Virginia, Charlottesville, VA 22901, respectively. This paper was presented at the Third Annual Conference of the Rutgers University Advanced Workshop in Public Utility Economics and Regulation, May 1984. We thank Michael Canes, Maxim Engers, Matt Gelfand, Richard Higgins, Douglas Kinney, Jonathan Skinner, the University of Virginia Microeconomics Workshop, and an anonymous referee for helpful suggestions. Financial support was provided by the Federal Trade Commission. The views presented are our own, not those of the Commission, individual commissioners, or staff.

[1]See H. G. Broadman and M. A. Toman (1983); and M. E. Canes and D. A. Norman (1983). Take provisions were also an integral part of producer-pipeline contracts throughout the essentially unregulated period before area pricing was adopted in 1960. The *Phillips* decision in 1954 gave the Federal Power Commission jurisdiction to regulate wellhead prices of gas sold in interstate commerce. The initial regulatory efforts, however, sought to institute cost-based rates on a well-by-well basis. Using this approach, the Commission never progressed beyond regulating the parties to the original decision. The result was a prodigious case backlog. According to Paul MacAvoy and Robert Pindyck, "...The Commission itself forecast that it would not finish its 1960 case load until the year 2043" (1975, p. 13). Area rates, that effectively froze prices at the market levels of 1958–59, were an attempt to lend tractability to the regulatory process.

coal and other unregulated commodities.[2] In view of this, both H. G. Broadman and M. A. Toman, and M. E. Canes and D. A. Norman have suggested that take obligations might be a means of allocating risk between producers and pipelines. High take provisions reduce risk for producers by guaranteeing a minimum return on investments in well capacity. Unfortunately, such arguments do not provide a practical basis upon which to evaluate observed contractual arrangements without knowledge of the relative risk preferences of the parties involved.

This paper offers an interpretation of take-or-pay provisions that relies on neither risk aversion nor the existence of regulatory price ceilings. Instead, we argue that take obligations can be viewed as a mechanism for effecting appropriate incentives for contractual performance, and show that efficient breach considerations define an optimal take percentage as a function of characteristics of the transaction. These incentives are distorted, however, by the existence of regulated price ceilings, causing the adoption of take obligations *in excess* of optimal levels.[3] Whether a policy to reduce "excessive" take provisions to *ex post* optimal levels can be justified on the basis of regulatory interference depends on the regulatory environment expected to govern the development of future gas reserves.

Section I develops these arguments and applies them to contracting in the natural gas industry. Section II presents an empirical test of the model employing actual data on producer-pipeline contracts and well characteristics.

I. Performance Incentives in Long-Term Contracts

Once a transaction-specific investment has been made, only imperfect market alternatives exist and both the buyer and seller are locked into a bilateral monopoly relationship. To prevent contention over the resulting quasi rents from dissipating too large a portion of the gains from trade, the parties may try to secure a mutually advantageous distribution through a contract, the duration of which will depend in part on the durability of the associated investments. In industries with particularly durable capital, it is not uncommon to observe contractual agreements that extend for ten years or more.[4]

Over such long horizons, the need for adaptation to changing circumstances, and hence the desire for flexible arrangements, may be substantial. But a tradeoff generally exists between the flexibility provided for in a contract and the ease with which it can be implemented: a single contractual stipulation is relatively straightforward for courts to enforce in comparison to multiple contingent claims which require that both the parties and the courts establish the state that has actually transpired. The more provisions stipulated, the greater the scope for both honest misinterpretation and intentional deception, and thus the greater the likelihood of a dispute requiring costly adjudication.

To minimize these costs, the parties will wish to stipulate terms that do not require court verification of exogenous events. Accordingly, contracts usually employ unilateral options rather than contingent clauses to accommodate adaptation.[5] The goal is to

[2] As Canes and Norman note, E. M. Carney (1978) discusses the use of take-or-pay provisions in coal contracts. Similar arrangements also appear in other contracts as minimum bill provisions.

[3] Except where explicitly noted, we will be referring throughout the paper to private optimality in exchange between a buyer and a seller. The social efficiency of any contractual provision depends upon whether private valuations are distorted from social valuations by the existence of externalities or other factors. We show here that the presence of price regulation does not in and of itself justify the abrogation of take-or-pay obligations.

[4] Victor Goldberg and John Erickson, for instance, note that in their sample, "Nine of ten contracts...involving new [petroleum] cokers were for a period of at least ten years" (1982, p. 10). Coal contracts are of similar duration (Carney, p. 197). Also see below.

[5] The notion of a unilateral option is analogous to the self-selection behavior often observed in theoretical models of bargaining in an environment of asymmetric information (see, for example, Milton Harris and Robert Townsend, 1981).

design contracts in ways that reconcile the exercise of such options with joint profit-maximizing behavior.[6]

The adoption of take-or-pay provisions in long-term contracts can be usefully interpreted in this light. Fluctuations in demand or costs may make it unprofitable or even inefficient to carry out the original objectives of a contract. By altering incentives to accept or reject delivery, take provisions can induce buyers to release investments to their alternative uses only when it is efficient to do so.

A. *Natural Gas Production and Contracting*

These considerations bear directly on the organization of production and exchange in the natural gas industry. Most natural gas is purchased by pipelines from independent producers for distribution to customers in regional markets. Like oil production, the extraction of gas requires large, durable, location-specific investments in facilities and equipment. However, unlike the field market for oil which is characterized by a functioning spot market, gas sales tend to be governed by extended contracts averaging fifteen to twenty years in length. This disparity in contractual structures governing commodities that are so closely related in production technologies may be traced to differences in transmission alternatives. Whereas pipelines represent virtually the only economically feasible form of transportation for gas, oil may be transported by truck or barge as well as by pipeline, thereby reducing the extent to which oil producers are locked into a bilateral relationship.[7]

Uncertainty regarding future market conditions can make it hazardous to commit resources contractually to a particular application, however. For example, in the face of a decline in gas demand, it may become more economic to sell gas to an alternative pipeline (if the decline is regional) or to store it for future use (if the decline is economy-wide). Since uncertainty increases with the distance of the relevant horizon, the need to provide for adaptation is most acute in longer term agreements. The prevalence of take-or-pay clauses in both long-term coal and gas contracts is consistent with this reasoning. Take obligations encourage efficient adaptation by relating the payment schedule in a contract to the alternative values of the resources either in sale to alternative customers or in storage for future use.

Alternative sale values of a product in transaction-specific relationships are limited by the design and location of specialized investments. For natural gas, the most important determinant of that value is the number and proximity of alternative pipelines. The fewer the connections to pipelines, the less likely that a producer will be able to dispose of gas at a price comparable to that in the original contract. In the extreme, the sale of gas to an alternative customer may require the construction of costly new transmission facilities.[8]

[6]That joint profit-maximizing behavior does not always coincide with the private incentives of the parties to an exchange is a familiar proposition:

> ...joined as they are in an idiosyncratic condition of bilateral monopoly, both the buyer and seller are strategically situated to bargain over the disposition of any incremental gain whenever a proposal to adapt is made by the other party. Although both have a long-term interest in effecting adaptations of a joint profit-maximizing kind, each also has an interest in appropriating as much of the gain as he can on each occasion to adapt. Efficient adaptations which would otherwise be made thus result in costly haggling or even go unmentioned, lest the gains be dissipated in costly subgoal pursuit. [Williamson, p. 242]

[7]A more complete discussion of oil field markets and how they differ from those of gas is given in S. L. McDonald (1971).

[8]Alternative sale possibilities are sometimes governed by the particulars of the supply contract between a producer and a pipeline. Often, the contract governs only a portion of the well's output, which is sold to the contracting pipeline on a first refusal basis. In other cases, particularly, when the field is served by a single pipeline, the entire output of a well is "dedicated" to a particular pipeline for the life of the contract. When gas demand is low, however, pipelines have little incentive to enforce these dedication clauses. Indeed, given the present surplus, many pipelines are attempting to renegotiate their purchase obligations downward and would welcome sale to alternative buyers (see D. Norman, 1984).

Because of this, and the fact that the demand for energy resources often fluctuate on a nationwide basis, the best alternative employment for both coal and gas is often to store it for future use. Since the product can usually be left in the field, storage is generally less costly for the producer than the customer. The resource value of stored gas may be diminished, however, by the proximity of other wells: gas not extracted may be drained away by other producers operating in the same field. To attenuate the problem of competitive extraction and protect landowners from drainage, the primary gas-producing states have instituted well-spacing rules and prorationing of output among the wells in a field.[9] The prorationing formulae generally used assign each producer an interest in the field based on surface ownership and well deliverability. Gas demand is divided among the various producers by the assignment of production allowables based on each producer's interest in the field.

But such intervention, while mitigating the drainage problem, does not eliminate it. The formulae are, at best, imprecise rule-of-thumb estimates of gas location relative to surface ownership. Moreover, a production allowable conveys only the *opportunity*, not the guarantee, to produce a given amount of gas in a specified period of time. An operator who is unwilling or unable to produce his allowable faces the prospect of drainage to those who do.[10] Consequently, most gas production remains governed by the *Rule of Capture*: "Possession of the land...is not necessarily possession of the gas. If an adjoining, or even distant, owner drills on his own land, and taps your gas, so that it comes into his well and under his control, it is no longer yours, but his."[11]

In general, the desirability of reallocating resources away from their intended use depends critically on their value in alternative applications. In the case of gas, the appropriate take obligation in each instance will depend on the nature of the well and its relation to other wells, piplines, and markets.

B. *Take-or-Pay and Breach of Contract*

To illustrate these concerns, consider the relationship between a pipeline (or buyer) and producer (or seller) of natural gas, both of whom are assumed to be risk neutral. After gas has been discovered but prior to investing in production and transmission facilities, the parties write a contract specifying a capacity level and the terms under which the product is to be exchanged in subsequent periods. The value of this capacity to the pipeline depends upon such things as weather patterns, economic fluctuations, and the prices of alternate fuels, all of which are uncertain at the time the contract is written and the well drilled. If we let θ represent this uncertainty, and define

$v(\theta)=$ the value of the well to the pipeline, net of transmission costs and gross of payments to the producer; and

$y=$ the payment made by the pipeline to the producer for a contractually specified quantity of gas;

then, once θ is revealed, the pipeline and the producer would receive $v(\theta)-y$ and y, respectively—*if* the exchange takes place: for low values of θ, and hence of v, the pipeline would wish to breach the contract with the producer. Specifically, the pipeline would wish to discontinue deliveries whenever $v(\theta) < y$.[12] Were this to occur, the pipeline would

[9] Gas and oil prorationing differ in several significant respects, reflecting the greater importance of extraction rates on the amount of oil that is ultimately recoverable. For a more complete discussion, see R. E. Sullivan (1955).

[10] Both Texas and Oklahoma have attempted to ensure that producers are equally able to sell their allowables by requiring pipelines to purchase ratably (according to each producer's interest) from their suppliers in a field. However, other states do not require ratable take (Sullivan, p. 348), nor does this approach preclude disproportionate purchases by different pipelines.

[11] *Westmoreland and Cambria Natural Gas Company v. Dewitt, 130 Pa. St. 235, 18A. 724, 725* (1889).

[12] For analytical tractability, we consider a model in which gas deliveries are discontinued in a discrete fashion; i.e., the purchaser either "takes" the gas at the contract price, or else "pays" the contractually specified percentage of the full obligation and releases all of the gas contracted for to its alternative use. With a few exceptions, the continuous analog to this model in which

then earn no net return,[13] and the producer would seek the next highest value of his capacity, $s(\alpha)$, which is a function of well attributes, α.

Since efficiency requires that gas be used in its highest value, breach would in fact be efficient if $s(\alpha) > v(\theta)$. But for $s(\alpha) < v(\theta) < y$, the pipeline would wish to breach even though it would be inefficient to do so. Figure 1 depicts the ranges of $v(\theta)$ for which the buyer would wish to breach and for which breach would be efficient. In general, there is a tendency, as illustrated in the diagram, for breach to occur too frequently in unsecured agreements.

The pipeline could, however, be induced to reject delivery efficiently by imposing a penalty for nonperformance, $\delta = y - s(\alpha)$. This penalty, known as "expectation damages," is commonly employed by the courts and would normally apply to gas contracts in the absence of a stipulated take obligation.[14] If the courts always and unerringly chose this award, there would be little need to stipulate damages in the contract. But the uncertainty associated with judicial rulings encourages costly litigation. By stipulating damages, the parties avoid the costly process of determining the appropriate penalty in the courts, and rejection of deliveries becomes an option that may be unilaterally invoked by the purchaser.

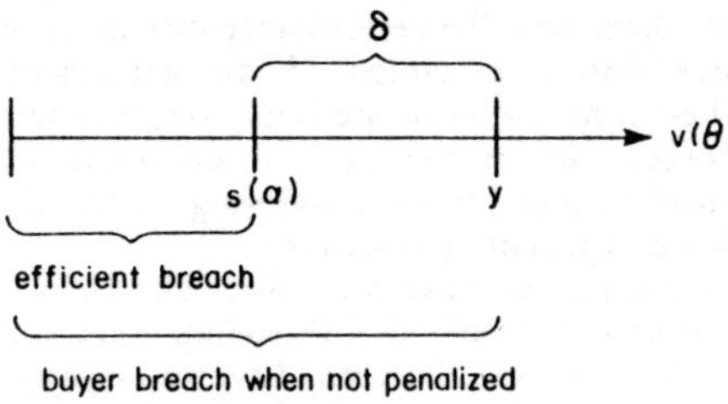

FIGURE 1

Since the optimal penalty for breach declines as a well is depleted, gas contracts usually express the penalty for refusing delivery as a fraction of reserves or deliverable capacity. In that way, the penalty obtaining in each successive period covered by the contract adjusts automatically to the declining level of remaining reserves. Written as a percentage, γ, of the contractually specified payment, the penalty described above becomes

$$\gamma = 1 - s(\alpha)/y. \tag{1}$$

Since y must be at least as great as $s(\alpha)$ to cover the fixed costs of production and induce the producer to enter the contract with the pipeline, the optimal take percentage will be nonnegative. As a rule, $s(\alpha)$ will equal y only when the producer can sell his output to another pipeline that comparably values the gas, which is unlikely unless the producer is already connected to several pipelines. At the other extreme where gas has no alternative value to the producer, the optimal take percentage is 100 percent, which would be the case, for example, were all of the gas drained away by nearby wells if not extracted by the producer himself.

C. *The Effects of Regulation*

In general, contract terms perform two functions. First, they permit parties to establish a division of the gains from trade that allows both to cover fixed costs; and second,

---

the buyer may gradually decrease the quantity of gas taken from the producer yields the same qualitative results.

[13] By no net return, we mean zero revenues. Note that a pipeline's willingness to fulfill the terms of a contract may also depend on the opportunity to purchase alternative low-cost gas supplies. In that case, his return in the event of breach would be $\max\{0, \bar{v}\}$ where $\bar{v}$ is his net revenue from the alternative purchases. This possibility does not affect the optimal breach penalty discussed below.

[14] The efficiency of the expectation damage has been demonstrated elsewhere; see, in particular, J. H. Barton (1972), and Steven Shavell (1980). Richard Pierce (1983) has noted that under the Uniform Commercial Code, a pipeline would be liable to a producer for "the difference between the market price and the contract price of the gas available but not taken" (p. 79), precisely the penalty described above. Note that take provisions only address the problem of buyer breach, and as such are only adopted where the principal source of uncertainty is on the demand side of the transaction, a condition true of both coal and gas production. In practice, parties must base their choice of δ on the conditional expectation of $s(\alpha)$ in the event of breach.

they determine the performance incentives in force during execution of the agreement. When contract terms are freely set, transfers between the parties prevent distributional considerations from interfering with the choice of incentive structures.

Thus far we have seen that take obligations serve the second of these functions, and that buyers and sellers may have an incentive to specify such terms even in the absence of regulation and risk aversion. The presence of price controls, however, may distort those incentives. In the case of natural gas, wellhead price restrictions prohibit certain divisions of gains and create an excess demand for gas production capacity. As a result, producers may engage in nonprice competition for capacity through the choice of contract terms. In that regard, raising take obligations will, *ceteris paribus*, increase the amount the seller receives when the buyer rejects delivery, thereby raising the expected value of the contract to the seller.[15] By setting a take percentage greater than the optimal level, the parties in effect sacrifice some efficiency in performance incentives in order to achieve a higher level of investment. The take percentage that would be chosen in a regulated transaction becomes

$$(2) \qquad \gamma = 1 - s(\alpha)/y + D,$$

where $D > 0$ reflects the excess demand induced by the presence of binding price constraints.[16]

[15]Because an increase in γ both raises the amount paid in the event of breach and reduces the number of states in which breach occurs, it is possible that beyond some point an increase in γ could, depending on the distribution of θ, reduce the expected value of the contract to the seller. In equilibrium, however, more restrictive price ceilings lead unequivocally to higher take percentages on the margin (see our 1984 working paper).

[16]The additive form of equation (2) follows directly from the model in our earlier paper where we characterize efficient contracts between a producer and a pipeline. The choice of γ in an efficient contract is shown to be a second-best response to the existence of a regulatory price ceiling.

II. Empirical Results

Here we employ data on natural gas producer-pipeline contracts and associated well attributes to test the relationship characterized by equation (2), which we rewrite for estimation purposes as

$$(3) \qquad \gamma_i = 1 - s(\alpha_i)/y_i + \xi D_i,$$

where ξ is a coefficient measuring the effects of excess demand, D_i, on take percentages. Prior to estimating this relationship, we describe the data used in the estimation and construct a proxy for D_i.

A. *Gas Contracts and Well Characteristics*

The data used for this study were obtained from several sources. Information regarding price and take obligations was obtained from a survey (EIA-758) conducted by the Energy Information Administration (EIA) in 1982. Through this survey, the EIA obtained detailed data on 659 contracts governing the interstate sale of natural gas from 615 wells located in the lower 48 states. The contracts included in the survey were randomly selected from post-1978 wells which qualified for incentive pricing under Sections 102, 103, 107, and 108 of the Natural Gas Policy Act (NGPA, 1978).[17] Since the data were obtained in disaggregated form, we were able to examine the relationship between take obligations and well characteristics on a well-by-well basis.

Information on the characteristics of the wells governed by these contracts was obtained independently from records at the EIA. Data availability reduced the sample to approximately 300 contracts governing onshore gas priced under NGPA sections 102 ("new" natural gas), 103 ("new" onshore production wells), and 107 ("high cost" gas from deep wells, tight sands, Devonian shales or geopressurized brine).

[17]For a more complete explanation of the survey methodology, see EIA, "Natural Gas Producer/Purchaser Contracts..." (1982).

The variables employed in the estimations are:

γ_i = the contractually specified take percentage for a contract covering gas produced from well i;

$\bar{p}_i$ = the applicable price ceiling (if any) for this gas in October 1981;

p_i^0 = the actual contract price for the gas in October 1981;

D_i = a measure of excess demand for gas from well i;

$DEPTH_i$ = the depth in feet of well i;

$BUYERS_i$ = the number of independent pipelines serving the gas field tapped by well i;

$SELLERS_i$ = the number of independent producers operating in the corresponding field;

$HERF_i$ = the Herfindahl numbers equivalent for the concentration of pipelines in the FERC gas region corresponding to well i,

$$= [\Sigma_t (R_{it}/T_i)^2]^{-1};$$

where R_{it} is the dedicated reserves of interstate pipeline t in FERC gas area i, T_i is the total amount of reserves dedicated to interstate pipelines in the gas area, and the summation is taken over all of the interstate pipelines with reserves in the gas area.[18]

B. *Excess Demand*

As a proxy for the effect of a price ceiling on the demand for gas, let

$$D_i = p_i^* - \bar{p}_i \quad \text{if} \quad p_i^0 = \bar{p}_i;$$
$$= 0 \quad \text{if} \quad p_i^0 < \bar{p}_i$$

where p_i^* is the price that would have obtained for well i in the absence of price constraints, and $\bar{p}_i$ is the applicable price ceiling. Thus, if the constraint on price is not binding, $D_i = 0$, and γ is affected only by $s(\alpha)$. If the ceiling is binding, however, D measures the difference between the unconstrained and ceiling prices.

Since p_i^* cannot be observed for $p_i^* \geq \bar{p}_i$, we employ maximum likelihood techniques to construct an estimate for this variable. Where the observations of the dependent variable are truncated, as is the case here, Tobit is an appropriate estimation procedure.[19] In particular, suppose that $p_i^* = aW_i + e_i$, where W_i is a vector of well characteristics affecting p_i^*, and e_i is normally distributed with zero mean and variance σ^2. Then the observed price in a contract covering well i would be

$$p_i^0 = p_i^*, \quad \text{if} \quad p_i^* < \bar{p}_i,$$
$$= \bar{p}_i, \quad \text{if} \quad p_i^* \geq \bar{p}_i.$$

The likelihood function of the ith observation is

$$L_i = f(aW_i) \quad \text{if} \quad p_i^0 < \bar{p}_i,$$
$$= 1 - F(aW_i) \quad \text{if} \quad p_i^0 = \bar{p}_i.$$

Estimates for p_i^* are derived by maximizing the likelihood function,

$$\Lambda_i = \prod_1^N L_i,$$

with respect to a and σ^2.

Results of the estimation of p_i^* are reported in Table 1. The price at which gas is exchanged in an unregulated transaction depends upon the costs of drilling and connecting the well to a pipeline, as well as on the relative bargaining positions of the transactors. In general, one would expect drilling costs, and hence price, to be positively related to the depth of the well. Also, a large

[18] In order to construct a pipeline, the Natural Gas Act (1938) requires that the transmission company obtain a certificate of public convenience and necessity from FERC. One requirement is that the transmission company demonstrate "adequacy of reserves"; i.e., a sufficient supply of gas to keep the pipeline in operation. As a result, gas reserves are often contractually "dedicated" to individual pipelines. Thus one indicator of the proximity and capacity of pipelines in a geographical region is the number of pipelines that have dedicated reserves in the area and the relative size of those reserves. The information used to compute this measure was obtained from EIA, "Gas Supplies of Interstate Natural Gas Pipeline Companies–1980," (1980).

[19] See, for example, G.S. Maddala (1983).

TABLE 1—ESTIMATION OF p^*

Variable	Coefficient	*T*-Ratio	Mean
CONSTANT	1.0623	10.890	1.000
DEPTH	$.27465 \times 10^{-3}$	4.4689[a]	10368.
HERF	.35661	2.7472[a]	4.8687
BUYERS	.34237	2.6665[a]	4.5709
SELLERS	−.06202	−2.4156[b]	9.3041

Chi-square: 403.333 with 4 degrees of freedom[c]
Number of observations: 296
Proportion of observations for which $p^0 < \bar{p}$: .1757

[a] Indicates significance beyond the .01 level.
[b] Indicates significance beyond the .05 level.
[c] Indicates significance beyond the .001 level.

number of buyers and sellers in a particular gas field would tend to undermine the respective group's bargaining position, with corresponding effects on price. In addition, to the extent that connection costs are reduced by the proximity of transmission lines, increases in the concentration of pipelines serving an area should also raise the value of the transaction. The availability of alternative pipelines depends both on their number and transmission capabilities. The Herfindahl measure defined above provides a proxy for the proximity of pipeline capacity to a particular well.

As can be seen from Table 1, the coefficient on each of the variables has the expected sign and is significant beyond the .05 level.

C. *Take-or-Pay Percentages*

We may now turn to estimating the effects of alternative values and excess demand on take percentages. To derive an estimate of $s(\alpha)$, the alternative value of a well, recall that this value will be the maximum of two alternatives: the resource value, which is the discounted value of the gas if left in the ground to be sold at a later date less losses due to drainage by other wells; and the sale value, which is the net value of the gas from sale to another pipeline.

Letting X_i be a vector of attributes affecting the resource value and Z_i a vector affecting the sale value, the expected value of the gas in an alternative use may be represented as

$$s(\alpha_i) = (\beta_1 X_i + \beta_2 Z_i) q_i,$$

where q_i is the capacity of well i, and β_1 and β_2 are coefficient vectors.[20]

Substituting into equation (3) and adding an error term, ε_i, yields

$$(3') \quad \gamma_i = 1 - \beta_1 \frac{X_i}{p_i^0} - \beta_2 \frac{Z_i}{p_i^0} + \xi D_i + \varepsilon_i.$$

The theory of the preceding section predicts that well characteristics, X and Z, which raise (lower) the alternative value of developed capacity should lead to a decrease (increase) in the size of take obligations, and thus implies negative (positive) values of the corresponding coefficients in β_1 and β_2. Meanwhile, we would expect that the more constraining the price ceiling, that is, the greater $p_i^* - \bar{p}_i$, the larger should be γ_i, implying $\xi > 0$.

In determining the resource value of the gas, the larger the number of sellers in a field, the greater the drainage that would occur if a producer were forced to "shut in" his supplies, and hence, the lower this alternative value. The alternative sale value in turn would be expected to increase with the availability of alternative purchasers as measured by the number of buyers in the field and the number of pipelines in the region. Hence, *BUYERS* and *HERF* should both raise the expected alternative value of a well, implying a lower take percentage, and *SELLERS* should reduce $s(\alpha)$ and raise γ.

The ordinary least square (*OLS*) estimates of (3′) are presented in Table 2. (The prefix *S* on a variable indicates that it has been divided by price, see equation (3′). Also note that γ is expressed in percentage terms rather than as a fraction.) Each of the coefficients in this regression has the predicted sign and is

[20] It would be possible to estimate $s(\alpha)$ as the maximum of its resource and sale values using switching regression techniques (see Maddala). We have chosen instead to let well characteristics affect the *expected* value of $s(\alpha)$ additively for its relative computational ease.

TABLE 2—ESTIMATION OF TAKE OBLIGATIONS

Variable	Coefficient	*T*-Ratio	Mean
CONSTANT	82.0822	43.6650	1.000
SSELLERS	.4833	2.0927[a]	3.9819
SBUYERS	−1.3136	−1.7589[b]	2.1080
SHERF	−.8646	−1.7929[b]	2.3270
REGCONST (D)	1.85132	3.9956[c]	2.8897

F: 13.24079 with 4 and 294 degrees of freedom[c]
Number of observations: 299
$R^2 = .1526$

[a]Indicates significance beyond the .05 level.
[b]Indicates significance beyond the .1 level.
[c]Indicates significance beyond the .001 level.

statistically significant beyond the 10 percent level. The evidence is thus consistent with the hypothesis that take percentages are designed to influence adaptation in long-term contracts and, in particular, are negatively related to the alternative value of gas reserves. Moreover, price ceilings seem to have the predicted effect on take provisions, raising the percentage paid for nondelivery. The findings indicate that, at the mean, a 1 percent decrease in the price ceiling will lead to a 6 percent increase in the take obligation. For the mean values of the independent variables, the regulatory price ceiling increases the predicted take obligations from 79 to 85 percent.

III. Conclusions

The results of this paper suggest that the incentive to provide flexibility in long-term contracts is an important consideration in the design of contract terms, and that the nature of those terms can be predicted on the basis of characteristics of the transaction. In particular, we have identified an efficiency motivation for the inclusion of take-or-pay provisions in long-term agreements: take obligations induce purchasers to release output to alternative uses only when it is efficient to do so. These incentives may be distorted, however, by the existence of regulated price ceilings. In the case of natural gas, government regulation of wellhead prices appears to have caused nonprice competition in take obligations leading to higher percentages than would prevail in the absence of such regulation.

Empirical tests presented in the paper support the hypotheses of the model. Take percentages are significantly lower for wells associated with small numbers of sellers and large numbers of buyers, each of which raise the alternative value of the gas, a result which seems to apply more generally: E. M. Carney, for example, has noted that, in coal contracts, "If... the coal mine has no access to other markets, the seller obviously has more need for a take or pay clause than he would otherwise"; while, on the other hand, "If the seller can get his product to other markets, the take or pay provision is often tempered to reflect that fact" (p. 226).

The evidence presented here refutes the common perception that take-or-pay provisions are soley an artifact of wellhead price regulation and hence serve no useful purpose in the absence of regulation. Providing that externalities do not result in a divergence of private and social valuations,[21] take obligations contained in contracts written in unregulated environments provide for efficient adaptation to changing circumstances in long-term contractual relationships. Whether a policy to reduce excessive take provisions to *ex post* optimal levels should be advocated on the basis of regulatory interference depends upon both the current regulatory status of the gas covered by the contract and the regulatory environment expected to govern the sale of gas discovered in the future. For example, if the gas under consideration has

[21]Where a field is exploited by a single producer, the gas production process involves no obvious externalities. With more than one operator, however, gas not sold by one producer may be captured and profitably marketed by other producers in the same field. In that event, the social value of "shut in" gas is apt to exceed the value of that gas to the original producer, leading to the adoption of take provisions in excess of socially optimal levels. To the extent that the drainage problem is exacerbated by the number of sellers in the field, the results in Table 2 suggest that take percentages are raised by less than one-half of 1 percent above the socially optimal level for each additional producer in a given field. This implies that, on average, take percentages exceed their socially optimal levels by less than two percentage points due to the externalities associated with competitive extraction from a common pool.

been deregulated and deregulation is expected to continue in the future, the possibility of private bilateral renegotiation obviates the need for intervention. With the removal of the price ceiling, the efficiency gains arising from the reduction of take obligations can be distributed between the buyer and seller through price adjustments, effecting a true Pareto improvement.[22]

Contract terms should also be upheld for categories of gas that currently remain regulated if price regulation is expected to be extended into the future: the precedent established by a reduction of take percentages from the second-best levels stipulated in the contracts could seriously distort capacity investment decisions for future wells. On the other hand, if future discoveries are expected to be sold in an unregulated environment, the efficiency gain from a one-time reduction in take obligations is not offset by adverse precedential effects on future investment. In this event, a prima facie case can be made for intervention to reduce take obligations to levels consistent with efficiency absent regulation. However, these potential benefits must be weighed against the ability of the government to intervene advantageously. Inasmuch as optimal take percentages depend upon characteristics of individual wells, effective intervention would require well by well adjustments. Given the government's previous record on well-specific regulation (see fn. 1), the practicality of this solution is in doubt.

[22] While such renegotiation is certainly not costless, it is likely to be less expensive and more precise than either judicial or legislative intervention.

REFERENCES

Barton, J. H., "The Economic Basis of Damages for Breach of Contract," *Journal of Legal Studies*, June 1972, *1*, 277–304.

Broadman, H. G. and Toman, M. A., "Non-Price Provisions in Long-Term Natural Gas Contracts," Resources for the Future, Washington, 1983.

Canes, M. E. and Norman, D. A. "Analytics of Take-or-Pay Provisions in Natural Gas Contracts," Discussion Paper No. 029, American Petroleum Institute, Washington, 1983.

Carney, E. M., "Pricing Provisions in Coal Contracts," in *Rocky Mountain Mineral Law Institute*, New York: Matthew Bender, 1978, 197–230.

Goldberg, Victor and Erickson, John, "Long Term Contracts for Petroleum Coke," Department of Economics Working Paper No. 206, University of California-Davis, September 1982.

Harris, Milton and Townsend, Robert, "Resource Allocation Under Asymmetric Information," *Econometrica*, January 1981, *49*, 33–64.

Hawkins, C. A., *The Field Price Regulation of Natural Gas*, Tallahassee: Florida State University Press, 1969.

Klein, Benjamin, Crawford, R. G. and Alchian, Armen A., "Vertical Integration, Appropriable Rents and the Competitive Contracting Process," *Journal of Law and Economics*, October 1978, *21*, 297–326.

Libecap, G. D. and Wiggins, S. N., "Contractual Responses to the Common Pool: Prorationing of Crude Oil Production," *American Economic Review*, March 1984, *74*, 87–98.

MacAvoy, Paul W. and Pindyck, Robert S., *The Economics of the Natural Gas Shortage (1960–1980)*, New York: Elsevier, 1975.

McDonald, S. L., *Petroleum Conservation in the United States: An Economic Analysis*, Baltimore: Johns Hopkins University Press, 1971.

Maddala, G. S., *Limited-Dependent and Qualitative Variables in Econometrics*, Cambridge: Cambridge University Press, 1983.

Masten, S. E. and Crocker, K. J., "Regulation and Nonprice Competition in Long Term Contracts for Natural Gas," Working Paper, University of Virginia, December 1984.

Norman, D., "Indefinite Pricing Provisions in Natural Gas Contracts," Discussion Paper No. 034, American Petroleum Institute, Washington, 1984.

Pierce, Richard J., "Natural Gas Regulation, Deregulation, and Contracts," *Virginia Law Review*, 1983, *68*, 63–115.

Shavell, Steven, "Damage Measures for Breach of Contract," *Bell Journal of Economics*, Autumn 1980, *11*, 466–90.

Sullivan, R. E., *Handbook of Oil and Gas Law*, New York: Prentice-Hall, 1955.

Williamson, Oliver E., "Transaction-Cost Economics: The Governance of Contractual Relations," *Journal of Law and Economics*, October 1979, *22*, 233–62.

Energy Information Administration (EIA), "Natural Gas Producer/Purchaser Contracts and Their Potential Impacts on the Natural Gas Market," DOE/EIA-0330, Washington: USGPO, 1982.

______, "Gas Supplies of Interstate Natural Gas Pipeline Companies—1980," DOE/EIA-0167 (80), Washington: USGPO, 1982.

[13]

Transactions Costs and the Efficient Organization of Production: A Study of Timber-Harvesting Contracts

Keith B. Leffler
University of Washington

Randal R. Rucker
Montana State University

A transaction costs framework is developed to explain the choice between lump-sum and per unit payment provisions in private timber-harvesting contracts. Predictions about which contract type minimizes the transaction costs of presale measurement and contract enforcement and monitoring are derived and tested using private timber sales contracts from North Carolina. The empirical results provide strong support for the transaction costs approach and also reject several predictions from a risk-based model. The transaction costs framework also provides insights into the choice between negotiated and competitive sales procedures.

The work on this paper was completed while Rucker was in the Department of Economics and Business at North Carolina State University. For comments on earlier drafts, we thank Doug Allen, Lee Alston, Yoram Barzel, Gardner Brown, Carlyle Franklin, Bob Higgs, R. Glenn Hubbard, Ron Johnson, Chuck Knoeber, Jeff LaFrance, Dean Lueck, Nancy Margolis, Steve Margolis, Scott Masten, Ian Munn, Peter Nickerson, Peter Pashigian, Eric Rasmusen, V. Kerry Smith, Vince Smith, George Stigler, Wally Thurman, Doug Young, and an anonymous referee as well as participants in seminars at the University of Chicago, Clemson, North Carolina State, Montana State, Seattle, Arizona, and Simon Fraser and in the Summer 1989 National Bureau Conference on Topics in Industrial Organization. We also thank the Political Economy Research Center for financial support and Karen Carlton for secretarial support. Wade Dorsey, Myra McCrickard, Jeff Ward, and Barry Weinmann provided valuable research assistance.

[*Journal of Political Economy*, 1991, vol. 99, no. 5]

Individuals and firms have incentives to develop institutions and adopt contractual arrangements that minimize the dissipation resulting from transaction costs.[1] In any particular instance, the precise nature and relative magnitude of transaction costs will be determined by the physical properties of the goods being exchanged and the characteristics of the buyers and sellers involved. As a result, institutions and contract provisions will differ across goods and with the characteristics of buyers and sellers. Detailed analyses of particular production processes, like the analysis presented in this paper, can therefore improve our understanding of the relationship between transaction costs and observed institutions and contracts. Such studies are few, presumably because of the difficulty in identifying and quantifying the relevant transaction costs of policing and enforcing input exchange agreements.

The specific production activity we study is timber harvesting. We focus on this activity because the most valued input, standing timber, is produced (in large part) naturally. This limits substantially the dimensions of the transaction costs associated with production.

In Section I we describe the nature of timber harvesting, focusing on the sources of transaction costs in that production process and on alternative means of assembling productive inputs. We conclude that transaction costs will be minimized if the timber owner transfers standing timber (rather than logs) to downstream resource owners.

In Section II we analyze the transaction costs associated with alternative contractual arrangements through which timber is purchased: lump-sum versus per unit harvested contracts. In that section we develop a transaction costs–based model that yields a variety of implications concerning the determinants of the choice of payment provisions in timber-harvesting contracts. We also compare the predictions of our transaction costs approach with those of a risk-based model. In addition, our approach provides insights into the choice between negotiated and competitive sales procedures.

In Section III we test the implications of our analysis using primary data on individual private timber-harvesting contracts in North Carolina.[2] We find broad support for the transaction costs approach. In addition, for those cases in which the risk and transaction costs ap-

[1] Cheung (1969*b*), Williamson (1971, 1979), Alchian (1977), Barzel (1987), and Allen (1991) discuss the nature of transaction costs and the distinction between costs of exchange (such as transportation) and transaction costs arising from devoting resources to exploiting (or preventing exploitation of) incomplete information about goods' attributes.

[2] Published transaction cost studies using private contract data include Cheung (1973), Umbeck (1977), Hallagan (1978), Alston and Higgs (1982), Alston, Datta, and Nugent (1984), Libecap and Wiggins (1984), Masten and Crocker (1985), Mulherin (1986), and Joskow (1987, 1988).

proaches yield different predictions, the transaction costs effects are found to dominate. In Section IV we provide concluding comments.

I. Transaction Costs in Timber Harvesting and the Efficient Organization of Inputs

Consider an individual who owns the property rights to a tract of timber and who has made the decision to sell the entire tract. To produce logs, the owner must apply to the trees labor and capital currently owned by others. Two contrasting methods of organizing these required inputs are that (1) the timber owner can hire logging resources to cut his timber and then sell logs to the mill or (2) he can sell to the mill or the logger the right to remove standing timber.[3] Because the levels of the potential transaction costs associated with these alternatives may differ greatly, the timber owner's choice of production method can have a substantial impact on the costs of producing logs. For example, if he retains the rights to the trees and hires loggers by the hour, they will have little incentive to exercise care in topping the trees or in minimizing stump heights. If, on the other hand, he sells the standing trees, the owners of the logging resources may create erosion problems and will be more reluctant to clean up messy slash. In either case, the incomplete specification and measurement of the attributes being transferred motivate each resource owner to incur (transaction) costs to measure and monitor what he buys and to exploit the incompletely measured attributes being sold. Thus the choice of who buys what from whom will significantly affect the level of transaction costs accompanying production and thus the level of output.

Although tracts of standing timber vary widely in species composition, tree quality, and density, in the short run the timber owner cannot significantly alter the value of a particular tract. In contrast, the owner of the logging resources has numerous opportunities to exploit the costliness of monitoring his behavior. For example, the value of the harvested timber is influenced by the care in felling (neighboring trees should be protected) and bucking (the log lengths should be proper) and the diligence exercised in separating logs from

[3] We are interested in the initial stage of production. Thus we abstract from the contractual arrangements among the various downstream resources and focus on differences in the relationship between the timber owner and the logging resources, whether the latter are owned by the logger, the mill, or further downstream resource owners. This issue of the degree of vertical integration in an industry (which we ignore) is one frequently analyzed in a transaction costs context (see, e.g., Coase 1937; Williamson 1971; Klein, Crawford, and Alchian 1978; Cheung 1983).

slash and in minimizing stump heights. In addition, the net value of the output to the buyer is affected by his success in limiting shirking by his employees and in enforcing the appropriate use of other logging resources.

A contract in which a timber owner transfers standing timber to the owner of logging resources ensures that the owner of the logging resources will bear the costs of differences in output value resulting from his economic actions. Such an organization of production provides an incentive for the owner of the logging resources to eliminate shirking and inefficient logging practices, thus minimizing transaction costs.[4] We expect, therefore, that transferring logging rights to standing timber will be the best way to minimize the cost of producing logs.

This expectation is supported by the empirical evidence. We collected some 200 timber contracts (see Sec. III) and interviewed over 20 forestry consultants, buyers, and sellers. In this process, we did not learn of a single tract in which the timber owner hired logging resources and sold logs to the mill.[5]

II. Costly Information and Opportunism in Timber Markets: Minimization of Transaction Costs through the Choice of Payment Method

When a timber owner sells standing timber to a mill or to an owner of logging resources, payment for these rights can be made in a variety of ways. Two payment arrangements are used typically in the timber industry: (1) a lump-sum payment in which the total payment amount is determined at the time the contract is signed or (2) a payment schedule per unit of output in which payments depend on the amount of timber harvested.[6] Previous analyses and discussions of contract choice for natural resources have emphasized the risk-sharing characteristics of lump-sum versus per unit sale contracts.[7] We, however, emphasize the difference in transaction costs.

[4] See Barzel (1987) for a discussion of these issues in a more general context.

[5] This excludes, of course, the case (which we do not consider) of vertically integrated wood-products companies, which typically mill logs from their own land and often hire logging resources to harvest their standing timber. In addition, we focus on "natural" tracts. Tree farms, in which the timber owner might be able to exercise substantial control over the characteristics of the trees, are not included in our data set.

[6] With respect to the incentives of buyers and sellers, the per unit and lump-sum payments in timber sales contracts are analogous to the royalty and bonus payments in mineral and petroleum contracts and to share and fixed-rent payments in agricultural labor contracts.

[7] See, e.g., Leland (1978) and Mead et al. (1985). For similar discussions of labor contracts, see Cheung (1969*a*), Higgs (1973), and Stiglitz (1974).

A Model of Lump-Sum Contracts[8]

Consider a lump-sum contract in which a tract of standing timber is sold to the high bidder.[9] We assume that bidders are homogeneous: if all the attributes of the tract are known, all bidders will place the same value (v) on the tract. Also, they all employ the same bidding strategy and have the same "uninformed" prior distribution function, $G(v)$, with expected value μ_0 and variance σ^2. All bidders are risk neutral and are profit maximizers. They also correctly estimate how many offers, N, will be made for the resource.

The risk-neutral seller (or his agent) provides public information about the sale, and this information is used by bidders in formulating $G(v)$. Each bidder then is able to collect further private information through presale measurement at a cost of M. This presale measurement occurs through a timber cruise in which a sample is taken of species and product composition, count, size, and condition of the trees on the tract.

Individual private information results in a sample value estimate for bidder j of i_j. Each individual's measurement sample is drawn independently from the same distribution $F(i|v)$. Bidder j combines the prior, $G(v)$, with his sample information, i_j, to form a modified estimate of the expected value of the resource, μ_{1j}, based on the presumption that i_j is the highest-valued information sample.[10] The bid then made by bidder j, B_j, is less than μ_{1j} (by an amount ΔX_j) because competitors by assumption are expected to have lower (modified) estimates of the tract value.[11]

A zero-profit equilibrium is obtained by allowing the number of bidders in the auction to be endogenous. The expected payoff to a prospective bidder from bidding is

$$\frac{\Delta X}{N} = \frac{E[\mu_1 - B(N)]}{N} = \frac{v - E[B(N)]}{N}, \qquad (1)$$

where ΔX is the expected return to the winning bidder over a large number of (identical) tracts, E is the expectation operator, and $E[B(N)]$ is the expected winning bid in a sale with N bidders. On average (over a large number of tracts), the modified estimate (after

[8] The auction framework developed below for lump-sum sales is a "common-values," sealed-bid auction model adapted from French and McCormick (1984). Their model is, in turn, an adaptation of models by Wilson (1977), Johnson (1979), and Ramsey (1985).

[9] Because private timber sale contracts are usually fairly short-term (24 months or less), we abstract from any temporal aspects of these contracts.

[10] That is, the winner's curse is taken into account (see Wilson 1977; French and McCormick 1984). Note that for all but the winning bidder, μ_{1j} is a biased estimate of the true value of the tract (v).

[11] See French and McCormick for elaboration of this point.

private measurement) of the expected value of the resource held by the high bidder (μ_1) will equal the true value of the tract; that is, $E(\mu_1) = v$. New bidders will enter until the expected payoff from bidding ($\Delta X/N$) is equal to the expected cost of presale measurement, M, that is, until each bidder's expected profits are zero, or $E(\pi_b) = (\{v - E[B(N)]\}/N) - M = (\Delta X/N) - M = 0$.[12] This equilibrium condition can be written as

$$E[B(N^*)] \equiv B^* \equiv v - M \cdot N^*, \tag{1'}$$

where N^* and B^* are the number of bidders and the bid (the seller's revenue) in equilibrium.

In the equilibrium described by equation (1′), it is apparent that the resource owner "pays" all measurement costs, in the sense that increases in $M \cdot N^*$ reduce B^* on a dollar-for-dollar basis. This result is reasonable in our context of landowners that hold relatively small tracts and have very inelastic supplies of standing timber. Even in a broader context, where economywide changes in M would induce changes in v (through changes in log prices) and thereby in B^*, equation (1′) captures the incentives of the individual timber owner. Any innovative activity in contracting by the individual timber owner that reduces M will yield a corresponding increase in the equilibrium bid for the tract.

As suggested by Barzel (1982) in a more general context, the individual seller therefore has an incentive to influence buyers' measurement activity. The seller would prohibit presale measurement completely if he could do so without incurring any costs, that is, if this prohibition did not reduce the number of bidders or alter the bidders' beliefs concerning the tract's value. More realistically, the seller will have incentives to reduce M, thereby lowering total presale measurement costs ($M \cdot N^*$) and increasing his revenues (B^*).[13] He might accomplish this by, for example, cutting roads into the stand, providing aerial photos, supplying detailed area-specific cruises, hiring reputable third parties to provide tract information, and so forth.

There are also contractual means of reducing buyers' presale measurement incentives. If purchaser payment is made contingent on the volume and quality of logs removed from the tract, the purchaser

[12] The number of bidders will be finite given that the expected payoff, $\Delta X/N$, decreases as the number of bidders increases. This occurs for two reasons: first, the probability that a particular bidder will win the auction decreases as the number of bidders increases, and second, bidders will decrease the adjustment to their postmeasurement estimate of value, ΔX, as the number of bidders increases (see French and McCormick [1984, p. 423] for elaboration).

[13] A decrease in M induces a less than proportional increase in N^*. The reason is that ΔX (which in equilibrium equals $M \cdot N^*$) decreases as N increases. Total measurement costs therefore decrease and seller's revenue increases.

will have less incentive to measure the timber before the sale. A landowner may therefore be able to limit dissipation due to presale measurement and increase his net returns by using a contingent-payment contract. We now turn to a discussion of such contracts as a means of reducing presale measurement.

A Model of Per Unit Contracts

Under a per unit harvested contract, the total payment made by the buyer is determined by the actual volume and composition of timber harvested. This type of contract greatly reduces a prospective buyer's incentives for presale measurement because such measurement gives him no useful information to exploit. In fact, buyers and timber consultants have told us that buyers frequently do not bother to conduct presale cruises of per unit sales. For simplicity, we therefore assume that no presale measurement takes place for per unit sales. Thus if presale measurement were the only source of transaction costs, we would expect all resource sales to be conducted on a per unit basis. But other transaction costs must also be considered. In particular, payment method will influence the buyer's incentive to harvest the tract efficiently.

In figure 1, let P be the per unit value of the logs obtained from a particular tract of standing timber.[14] The line MC_H, the expected marginal cost of harvest (or of transforming standing timber into logs), slopes upward because, for example, some of the standing timber is further from the logging road or is on terrain that is more difficult to log.[15] The right to harvest the timber is granted to the bidder offering the highest per unit payment, R.[16] Because the net

[14] The per unit contracts we model are "ideal" in the sense that we assume that they specify a per unit payment for each grade and species of timber on the tract. For simplicity, the discussion presumes a tract with one species and one grade of timber.

[15] We assume that harvest by a single buyer is efficient. This will be the case if marginal costs of harvest increase because of tract characteristics or there are significant fixed costs of harvesting a timber tract.

[16] We constrain the per unit bid not to vary with harvested quantity (this constraint conforms with our observation that harvest-dependent per unit payments are not used in practice). We can identify two reasons for not specifying reduced per unit payments with increased harvest as a means of increasing a buyer's preferred level of harvest. First, in per unit contracts, different payments are typically offered for different grades and species of timber. If each per unit payment varied with measured harvest, the cost of formulating and assessing bids likely would increase substantially. Second, buyers would have greater incentives to cheat on reported species type and grade. For example, if the high-volume payment for a more expensive species falls below the low-volume payment for a less expensive species (given the large number of potential species-grade combinations, this is likely), a buyer with a tract that turns out to have an unexpectedly low volume of low-value timber might attempt to reduce his payments by reporting the low-value grades as high-value grades. Obviously, sellers' costs of monitoring harvest levels could increase significantly.

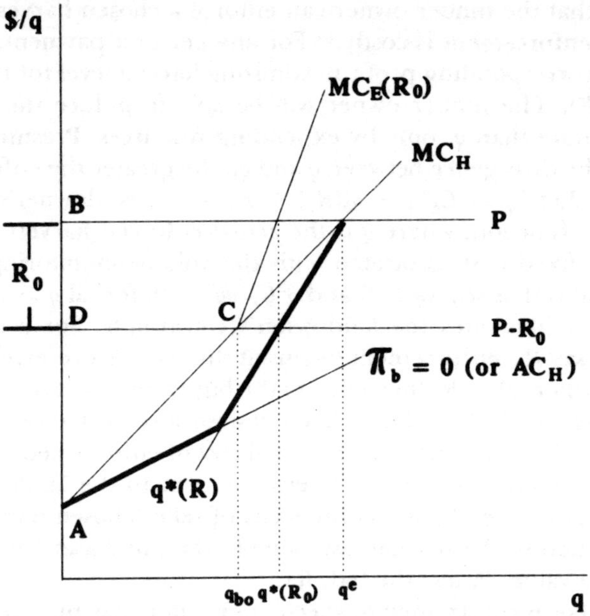

FIG. 1.—Per unit payment contracts: buyer's and seller's profit-maximizing harvest levels for given per unit bids.

value of additional harvest to the buyer is now $P - R$, the per unit contract affects the harvesting incentives of the buyer. For example, the buyer's profit-maximizing harvest with an initial per unit payment of R_0 in figure 1 is q_{b0}, which is less than the harvest level that would maximize the joint profits of the buyer and the timber owner, q^e.[17] This contrasts with a lump-sum sale, in which the buyer harvests q^e, where MC_H equals P.[18]

The seller can control the harvest incentive problem created with a per unit payment by specifying and enforcing the level of harvest.[19]

[17] Note that with a per unit bid of R_0 and a harvest level of q_{b0}, the buyer's quasi rent is area *ADC*. In fact, for all bids less than $R = AB$ (the difference between P and the marginal cost intercept), a buyer choosing the level of harvest makes positive rent. Hence, without minimum harvest levels, competition implies a bid of *AB* and the incentive not to harvest. This adds to the speculative incentives to default on timber contracts discussed at length by Rucker and Leffler (1988).

[18] Some monitoring of the buyer's activities on a lump-sum contract may nonetheless be required. The reason is that the landowner wants to prevent the buyer from engaging in activities that reduce the value of his resource in other current uses (e.g., farming on land bordering roads used to access the timber tract) or in future uses (either timber or nontimber). These monitoring costs are present under both payment schemes.

[19] The specification of "harvest levels" is common in contracts for natural resources. For example, oil leases often specify minimum flow requirements, and timber contracts require that all timber larger than a specified diameter be harvested. In agricultural labor contracts the labor input of share tenants may be specified (Cheung 1969*a*).

Assume that the timber owner can enforce a chosen harvest level, q, but that enforcement is costly.[20] For any per unit payment, R, there will be a corresponding profit-maximizing harvest level for the buyer, $q_b = q_b(R)$. The timber owner will be able to induce the buyer to harvest more than q_b only by expending resources. Presumably, the greater the divergence between q and q_b, the greater the enforcement costs, C_E. Let $C_E = C_E[q - q_b(R)] + F_E$ be the landowner's enforcement cost function, where q is the actual enforced harvest level and F_E is the fixed cost associated with the volume-monitoring system. Assume also that $\partial C_E/\partial q > 0$ and $\partial^2 C_E/\partial q^2 > 0$, for all $q > q_b(R)$.

Figure 1 illustrates the landowner's constraints. For a given per unit bid, say R_0, enforcement begins at the buyer's preferred harvest level q_{b0}, where $P - R_0$ (net value to the buyer) intersects the marginal harvesting cost (MC_H). The seller's desired level of harvest is $q^*(R_0)$, the harvest level at which the marginal cost of enforcement, $MC_E(R_0)$, equals the marginal benefits of enforcement to the landowner, R_0. The line labeled $q^*(R)$ shows the locus of seller-chosen harvest levels as a function of the net harvest value to the purchaser (the per unit stumpage value, P, less the bid, R).

The seller is constrained to specify per unit payment–harvest combinations that result in nonnegative buyer profits. This constraint is shown in figure 1 by the average cost of harvest, which we label $\pi_b = 0$; areas above $\pi_b = 0$ are regions of positive profit for the bidders.[21] The seller is therefore limited in his choice of combinations of R and q to points on or above $\pi_b = 0$, implying that the profit-maximizing combinations are restricted to points on the heavily shaded line segments in figure 1.

As indicated by the preceding discussion, the landowner's problem is to choose a per unit payment R and a harvest level q to

$$\max_{q,R} \pi_L = R \cdot q - C_E[q - q_b(R)] - F_E \qquad (2)$$
$$\text{subject to } \pi_b = (P - R)q - C_H(q) \geq 0,$$

where π_L is the landowner's profit, π_b is the buyer's profit, and $C_H(q)$ is the total harvest cost.

[20] The ensuing discussion is a description of the ex ante equilibrium harvest level. Our characterization of ex post behavior is that the harvest level actually enforced will vary with the revealed volume of logs on the tract. If the actual volume is small (large), the marginal cost of harvest will be high (low) and the enforced harvest level will be low (high). This characterization is consistent with actual contracts that normally specify harvest levels in terms of "merchantable" timber or minimum diameters rather than in absolute levels of harvest.

[21] Figure 1 illustrates a case with zero fixed costs of harvest. No substantive changes result from incorporating positive fixed costs and the resulting U-shaped average cost.

The Kuhn-Tucker conditions for a maximum in (2) are

$$\frac{\partial \mathcal{L}}{\partial q} = R - MC_E + \lambda[MC_H - (P - R)] = 0, \tag{3}$$

$$\frac{\partial \mathcal{L}}{\partial R} = q - \frac{\partial C_E}{\partial q_b} \cdot \frac{\partial q_b}{\partial R} + \lambda \cdot q = 0, \tag{4}$$

$$\frac{\partial \mathcal{L}}{\partial \lambda} = (P - R)q - C_H(q) \geq 0; \quad \text{if} > 0, \text{then } \lambda = 0. \tag{5}$$

To interpret these conditions, suppose initially that the bidder's zero-profit constraint is not binding, that is, that $\lambda = 0$ and $\pi_b > 0$. In this case, expression (4) indicates that the landowner will increase the per unit payment (R) until marginal benefits and marginal costs are equal. For a given harvest level, the marginal benefit from a $1.00 increase in R is the level of harvest (q). The marginal cost is the increased enforcement cost resulting because an increase in the per unit bid reduces the buyer's preferred harvest level. If the bidder's zero-profit constraint is binding, then $\pi_b = 0$, $\lambda < 0$, and expressions (3) and (4) each have an additional negative term, $\lambda[MC_H - (P - R)]$ and $\lambda \cdot q$. These terms represent the profit the seller must give up to the buyer if the seller increases harvest or per unit payments when the buyer's zero-profit constraint is binding.[22]

A striking result of this analysis is the possibility that the landowner's profits may be maximized at a bid-harvest combination in which the buyer's zero-profit constraint is not binding; that is, the seller's maximum profits may occur at bid-harvest levels implying positive buyer profits.[23] In such a situation, the benefits to the landowner of a higher per unit payment will be outweighed by the higher costs of enforcing any given level of harvest that result because the higher payment reduces the buyer's desired harvest. Models that assume that the constraint on buyer profits is binding (such as those developed in other contexts by Cheung [1968], Stiglitz [1974], and

[22] The per unit payment-harvest combination that maximizes the seller's profit is not seen trivially in fig. 1. In an unpublished appendix (available from the authors), we describe both graphically and algebraically the solution to the seller's problem for linear marginal harvest and enforcement costs. We also derive and discuss the conditions under which the buyer's profit constraint is binding. The result is that the buyer's zero-profit constraint is not binding if the costs of enforcement are high relative to the costs of harvest. Intuitively, when enforcement is cheap, it pays the landowner to enforce a harvest level that extracts all the buyer's profits.

[23] Of course, we expect buyers' profits to be competed away as they expend resources to become preferred negotiating buyers. Thus we might predict relatively larger "entertainment" expenses by private timber buyers, efforts to be the first buyer to knock on a prospective seller's door, or agreement by buyers to incur "extra" expenses building roads or cleaning up slash.

Leland [1978]) preclude this outcome. The possibility that it may be in the interest of both risk-neutral resource owners and prospective buyers to agree on lower per unit payments than would be offered under unrestricted competition simply is not allowed.

Landowners can restrict competition by negotiating the sale of their timber with a single (or limited number of) buyer(s) or by considering only invited bids. Restrictions on competition have no similar benefits in our model of a lump-sum contract, where limiting the number of bidders simply reduces the seller's revenues. We therefore predict greater reliance on negotiated sales for per unit contracts than for lump-sum contracts.

Figure 2 shows an enforcement cost equilibrium for a nonbinding buyer zero-profit constraint. The profit-maximizing bid-harvest combination is R^*, q^*, with the seller's total revenue equal to $R^* \cdot q^*$. Part of this revenue is dissipated in enforcing the contracted quantity, as shown by the vertically shaded enforcement costs, E^*. Of the potential value of the timber (*ABC*), a portion also is dissipated by a buyer's shirking in harvesting (shown by the diagonally shaded area, S^*).[24] The seller also bears the fixed costs associated with monitoring harvest levels, F_E. The seller's profit, π_L^*, is thus the potential value of the timber as logs minus the total transaction costs, $E^* + S^* + F_E$, minus the buyer's profit ($\pi_b^* = \pi_b^+ - \pi_b^-$).[25]

The Choice between Lump-Sum and Per Unit Contracts

For either a lump-sum or a per unit contract, the net value to the landowner of a tract of timber is the potential value of the tract minus the costs associated with presale measurement and enforcement. The resource owner will choose the payment provision that maximizes his expected net return. Of course, it would be possible for the seller to use a mixed contract that combines a lump-sum payment with contingent per unit payments. In our investigation of timber-harvesting contracts, however, we have not learned of a single instance of such a mixed contract. Significant fixed costs for each of the relevant transaction costs—presale measurement and enforcement—can explain the dominance of the pure contract types.

Given a choice between a pure lump-sum or a pure per unit contract, the seller's profit-maximizing decision is determined by whether the transaction costs from a lump-sum contract ($M \cdot N^*$) are less than or greater than those from a per unit contract ($E^* + S^* + F_E$) plus

[24] Of course, enforcement costs are incurred because of shirking. Although one might label $E^* + S^*$ shirking costs, we find it useful to distinguish the direct cost expended, E^*, from the value never produced, S^*.

[25] Figure 2 is drawn for the case in which F_E is zero.

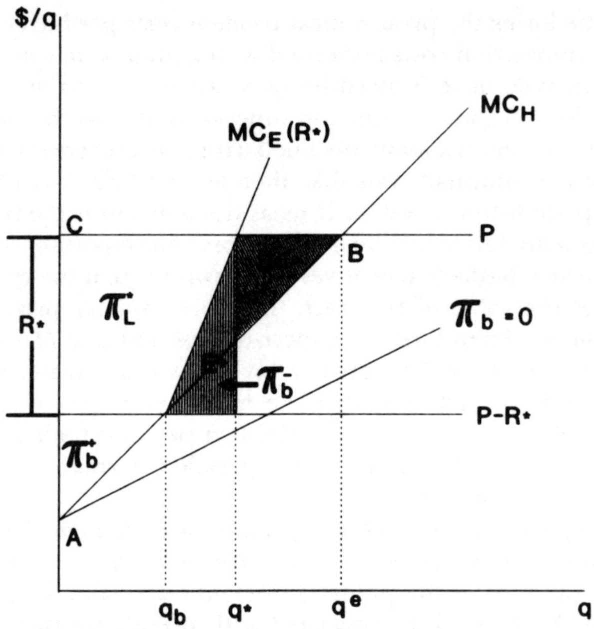

FIG. 2.—Equilibrium per unit contracts with nonbinding buyer zero-profit constraint. Seller's profits = π_L^*, buyer's profits = $\pi_b^* = \pi_b^+ - \pi_b^-$, enforcement costs = E^*, and shirking costs = S^*.

any buyer's profit. Although we cannot specify a priori when $M \cdot N^*$ will be greater or less than $E^* + S^* + F_E + \pi_b^*$, we can identify observable variables that have independent effects on the transaction costs of lump-sum sales ($M \cdot N^*$) or per unit sales ($E^* + S^* + F_E$) and also on the buyer's profit from per unit sales. Thus we can predict the conditions under which contracts with per unit payment provisions are more or less likely to be chosen than lump-sum contracts. These predictions result from identifying factors that change (1) the costs to prospective buyers of presale measurement and (2) the costs to landowners of enforcing specified harvest levels on per unit contracts. Factors affecting these costs include the physical characteristics of the tract and characteristics of both buyers and sellers.

Predictions Concerning the Choice of Payment Provisions

Consider first the factors affecting presale measurement costs. Presale measurement provides a sample of information concerning the actual value (quantity and quality) of timber on the tract. This information is obtained at a cost. Our discussion above suggests that, ceteris paribus, the lower the presale measurement costs per buyer (M), the lower the transaction costs associated with a lump-sum contract.

The individual buyer's incentive to measure is based on the likelihood that he will gain information superior to that of the competing bidders. If the information obtained from measurement indicates that the tract is unusually valuable, then he may be able to obtain the tract at a price below its value. If measurement shows the tract to be of unexpectedly low value, he avoids a loss. An important feature of the prospective bidders' incentives to measure is that the greater the variance of the value of the tract, the more valuable private information will be. Therefore, we expect that M and also $M \cdot N^*$ (total measurement costs) will be greater for tracts with greater variance. Thus our first prediction is that the more heterogeneous (i.e., the more variable) the tract, the more likely a per unit timber contract. Similarly, the less reliable the seller's presale information, the more likely a per unit contract.

The dissipation due to excessive presale measurement ($N^* \cdot M$) will increase not only when buyers' incentives to measure increase (because the variance of the premeasurement tract value is larger) but also when the fixed costs associated with presale measurement increase.[26] Thus we predict that when buyer measurement is more expensive, per unit contracts are more likely.[27] In addition, when the cost of measurement is prohibitive (because of high fixed costs of presale measurement), buyers will be unwilling to purchase timber on a lump-sum basis and per unit contracts will prevail.[28]

An additional prediction results from differences in enforcement costs on lump-sum and per unit contracts. Where the seller's cost of monitoring buyer-harvesting activity is low, the transaction costs of per unit contracts (and the buyer's profit, if any) are low and per unit contracts are more likely.

The reigning alternative to the transaction costs explanation for

[26] We limit this statement (and the associated predictions) to changes in the fixed costs associated with presale measurement. The direction of the effect on M of a change in the marginal costs of presale measurement is determined by the elasticity of the marginal benefit curve for presale measurement, a value on which we have no information.

[27] In our model, presale buyer measurement does not alter the value of the tract; hence it is never efficient. If, however, buyers use timber for very different purposes and if the specific characteristics valued by buyers are "taste attributes," presale buyer measurement is nonduplicative and likely efficient. Hence for very unusual tracts with rare species, we expect efficient buyer presale measurement and an increased likelihood of lump-sum contracts.

[28] If buyers do not undertake presale measurement on a lump-sum contract, a "lemons" phenomenon (Akerlof 1970) is likely to result. A solution to such a problem in the present context is to use per unit payment contracts.

contract choice is risk aversion. The presale measurement associated with a lump-sum contract acts to reduce the total risk shared by the buyer and seller as compared to the total risk shared under a per unit contract.[29] Given risk aversion, the greater the riskiness (variability or heterogeneity) of a tract, the more valuable the risk reduction of the presale measurement. Thus the more heterogeneous a tract, the less likely a per unit contract.[30] This prediction contradicts that of the transaction costs model, implying that we may be able to determine empirically whether transaction costs or risk is the more important factor in this aspect of contract choice.

III. Empirical Tests of the Transaction Cost Theory of Contract Choice

The analysis of Section II yields predictions that per unit contracts are more likely when (*A*) presale measurement costs are higher as a result of (1) more heterogeneous tracts, (2) less reliable seller-provided presale information, and (3) more expensive buyers' presale measurement and (*B*) monitoring of harvesting activities is relatively cheap. To test these hypotheses, we collected data on private timber-harvesting contracts by interviewing timber buyers, sellers, and forestry consultants throughout North Carolina.[31] We obtained information on empirical proxies for the variables suggested by the theory of Section II for 188 usable timber-harvesting contracts from recent years.[32] Sample sizes from individual interviewees ranged from three to 27 sales, depending on the patience of the source. A description of these empirical proxies and of their predicted effects follows. Table 1 displays the variable names, variable definitions, predicted effects, and sample statistics for these proxies. Table 2 presents a correlation matrix.

[29] Under a lump-sum contract, the seller still bears some risk because prior to the sale, there is uncertainty concerning the level of the high bid.

[30] Leland (1978) formally derives an analogous prediction in a model with a risk-averse resource owner selling to competing risk-averse buyers, but with no explicit treatment of presale measurement.

[31] North Carolina is a major timber-growing state, with over 90 percent of both the inventory of standing timber and timberland area being privately owned. In 1984, more than 400 million cubic feet of timber with a value of $241 million was harvested from private land in North Carolina, with timber ranking second in value only to tobacco among the state's agricultural crops (U.S. Department of Agriculture 1988). Only 23 percent of the timberland in the South is owned by the forest industry. Ten percent is publicly owned. The remaining 67 percent is owned by individuals and companies not in the business of growing trees. We focus on this latter group of owners.

[32] As we indicate below, the size of the sample of usable contracts depends on the empirical specification chosen for testing the model.

TABLE 1

Variable Definitions, Predicted Effects, and Sample Statistics (153 Observations)

Variable	Definition	Effect: Presale Measurement	Effect: Enforcement	Predicted Sign	Mean	Minimum	Maximum	Standard Deviation
PERUNIT	Payment provision (0 = lump-sum, 1 = per unit)				PERUNIT = 1; 31 observations			
%PINE*	Percentage pine sawtimber (omitted from regressions)				43.59	0	100	26.33
%HARDWOOD	Percentage hardwood sawtimber	+		+	18.64	0	98.3	23.37
%PULP	Percentage pulpwood	−	+	?	33.52	0	100	26.87
%C&SAW	Percentage pine chip-and-saw	−	+	?	4.25	0	56.4	8.34
VOLUME	Volume of timber on the tract	+	−	?	581.3	1.43	4,111.1	649

LOWVAR	Low-variance timber tract (1 = low-variance, 0 = not low-variance)	+		+	LOWVAR = 1; 15 observations			
NSPECIES	Number of species (1–18 integer valued)	–		–	6.84	1	18	3.34
CONSULT	Consultant involved in sale (0 = no consultant, 1 = consultant)	–	+	?	CONSULT = 1; 139 observations			
NIPF	Nonindustrial private forest owner (0 = large owner, 1 = small [NIPF] owner)	+	–	?	NIPF = 1; 141 observations			
ACCESS	Access conditions (0–4 integer variable, 0 = poor)	–		–	2.29	0	4	1.44
BUYSIZE	Buyer size (0 = small, 1 = medium, 2 = large)	–		–	1.16	0	2	.82
THIN	Thinning sale (0 = harvest, 1 = thinning)		+	+	THIN = 1; 24 observations			
VALUE	Tract value ($1,000's)		–	–	54.14	0	393	67.60

* This variable is the tract composition variable that is omitted from the regressions.

TABLE 2

Correlation Matrix (153 Observations)

	PERUNIT	%HARDWOOD	%PULP	%C&SAW	VOLUME	LOWVAR	NSPECIES	CONSULT	NIPF	ACCESS	BUYSIZE	THIN	VALUE
PERUNIT	1.000												
%HARDWOOD	−.167	1.000											
%PULP	.433	−.404	1.000										
%C&SAW	.064	−.295	−.049	1.000									
VOLUME	−.122	−.043	−.054	.087	1.000								
LOWVAR	.490	−.210	.654	−.007	−.234	1.000							
NSPECIES	−.303	.580	−.205	−.196	.261	.281	1.000						
CONSULT	−.122	.182	−.293	.005	−.087	−.124	.189	1.000					
NIPF	−.034	−.113	−.025	.121	−.251	−.067	−.058	−.008	1.000				
ACCESS	.058	−.099	.032	−.054	−.084	.072	−.116	.048	−.060	1.000			
BUYSIZE	−.276	−.128	−.027	.028	.268	−.198	.029	−.133	−.063	.006	1.000		
THIN	.498	.025	.178	−.053	−.137	.341	−.103	.012	−.008	.189	−.259	1.000	
VALUE	−.204	−.113	−.164	.125	.901	−.235	.141	−.054	−.157	−.061	.293	−.200	1.000

Variable Descriptions

A. Presale Measurement Cost Variables

1. *Tract heterogeneity variables.*—Tract heterogeneity is determined by such factors as the composition and volume of the timber on the tract. North Carolina forests contain hardwood sawtimber, which is quite variable in value; pine sawtimber, which is more uniform in value; and pine chip-and-saw and pulpwood timber, which is homogeneous in value. The tract composition variables used in our empirical analysis are the following:

%HARDWOOD$_i$: The percentage of hardwood sawtimber on tract *i*. An increase in %HARDWOOD (offset by an equal reduction in the tract composition variable omitted from the regressions, the percentage of pine sawtimber, %PINE) is predicted to increase the likelihood of per unit contracts.

%PULP$_i$ and %C&SAW$_i$: The percentage of pulpwood and pine chip-and-saw on tract *i*. This heterogeneity effect predicts that an increase in either %PULP or %C&SAW (again offset by a reduction in %PINE) will reduce the likelihood of per unit contracts.

Two other variables also measure differences in tract heterogeneity:

VOLUME$_i$: The volume of timber on tract *i*. With composition held constant, an increase in volume increases the variance of a tract's value,[33] thereby increasing presale measurement expenditures. This heterogeneity effect therefore predicts that an increase in VOLUME will increase the likelihood of per unit contracts.

LOWVAR$_i$: A dummy variable assigned a value of one on the 10 percent of the sales in our sample with the lowest variance.[34] The

[33] To see that an increase in volume increases variance, consider a tract with one tree that, because of its perceived size and quality (according to the seller-provided information), has an expected value of $110, and prospective buyers' perceptions are that the actual value of the tract is either $100 or $120, both with a probability of .5. Now suppose that the number of trees on the tract doubles to two. If the expectations concerning the second tree are identical to those of the first (i.e., with composition held constant), the tract now has an expected value of $220 with potential realized values of $200 with probability .25, $220 with probability .50, and $240 with probability .25. The variance of the tract thus increases from 100 to 200 with the increase in volume.

[34] In our data set, we identify low-variance tracts as those with a low proportion of sawtimber and a low volume. Because there is no way to know precisely how changes in these two factors affect tract variance, we test for sensitivity of our empirical results to different definitions of the low-variance tracts in our sample. The estimated coefficients on the other variables in our model are not sensitive to these modifications, and, in general, the estimated coefficient on LOWVAR is not affected either. The exception to this is that (as would be expected) the significance of the estimated coefficient on LOWVAR diminishes as its definition is changed to include higher-variance tracts.

ex ante variance in the value of a tract will determine whether presale measurement is worthwhile. For low-variance tracts, the fixed costs of cruising (transporting material and personnel to the tract) will likely outweigh the benefits, implying that buyers will choose to undertake no presale measurement (cruise). Assuming that buyers will not enter into a lump-sum contract without cruising the tract,[35] we predict a higher likelihood of per unit contracts on low-variance tracts.

2. *Seller-provided presale information variables.*— Factors such as the detail and specificity of seller-provided presale information will also determine the presale variance of a tract's value. Variables included to measure this effect are the following:

$NSPECIES_i$: An integer variable for the number of species identified in the seller's presale cruise information. The more species identified, the more detailed (and therefore more reliable) the seller's cruise.[36] As NSPECIES increases, we predict per unit contracts to be less likely.

$CONSULT_i$: A dummy variable assigned a value of one if the seller hired an independent forestry consultant to provide presale information and to conduct the sale. This effect predicts that the use of a consultant (with his experience and reputational capital behind his cruise) will increase the reliability of a seller's presale information, thus decreasing the likelihood of per unit contracts.

$NIPF_i$: A dummy variable assigned a value of one if the timber seller is a nonindustrial private forest (small) landowner. Small landowners with little experience in the timber market will likely provide poorer-quality presale information. This effect therefore predicts a higher likelihood of per unit contracts on NIPF tracts.

3. *Buyer presale measurement variables.*—We have also argued that higher buyer presale measurement costs will encourage use of per unit contracts. Possible empirical proxies for buyers' measurement costs include weather conditions, tract locations, tract access, and the buyer's size and experience. Of these, we were able to construct the following two variables:

$ACCESS_i$: An integer variable measuring the access conditions to a tract. Interviewees rated the accessibility of each tract on a scale of

[35] This assumption is consistent with comments made by a number of the individuals we interviewed that they would not purchase certain tracts on a lump-sum basis because the tracts were not worth the time and effort required to cruise them.

[36] The types of trees on the various tracts in our sample are generally the same. The tracts have loblolly pine, Virginia pine, white pine, and a variety of hardwood species: white oak, poplar, maple, walnut, sweet gum, red oak, and ash. Some seller cruises distinguish, e.g., the different types of pine; others do not. Some cruises count only the major species on the tract; others count them all.

zero to four, with zero indicating poor and four indicating excellent access. As access to the tract improves (ACCESS increases), buyers' presale measurement costs fall and per unit sales become less likely.

$BUYSIZE_i$: An integer variable measuring the buyer's size and experience. Each buyer is included in one of three size categories (small = 0, medium = 1, or large = 2). Larger buyers will be more experienced at presale measurement and will cruise more tracts at a lower average cost. Thus we predict that the larger the buyer, the lower the likelihood of per unit sales.

B. Enforcement/Monitoring Cost Variables

Per unit contracts will be relatively cheaper and will be chosen more often when the seller has substantial incentives to monitor the harvest regardless of the contract used. The variable we use to measure this effect follows:

$THIN_i$: A dummy variable assigned a value of one for thinning sales and zero for harvest (clear-cut) sales. Because the postharvest timber value on a thinning sale can be substantially affected if the wrong trees are harvested, contract-independent monitoring incentives will exist for thinning sales. We therefore predict a greater likelihood of per unit contracts on thinning sales.

Other enforcement cost predictions are related to the seller's costs under a per unit contract of monitoring the quantity of timber removed from a tract. The cost of such monitoring depends on the composition of the tract. Pulpwood is simply weighed, while sawtimber (both hardwood and pine) is typically stick-scaled, a procedure that involves measuring the length and the diameter of the small end of each log and converting these measurements to the specified payment units (thousands of board feet). To monitor harvest levels on a per unit contract, the landowner must therefore understand the appropriate scaling procedure (or procedures) and also monitor the volume of logs harvested.[37] We include three variables to measure these effects:

$\%PULP_i$ and $\%C\&SAW_i$: Defined above. The costs of monitoring harvest will fall as the proportion of sawtimber falls (%PULP or %C&SAW increases).[38] This effect predicts, therefore, that an in-

[37] The costs incurred by the landowner to understand the appropriate scaling procedure (which do not vary with the level of enforcement effort) are the empirical counterpart of the fixed costs of enforcement (F_E) mentioned in Sec. II.

[38] The reason is that landowners will have an incentive to observe the sizes and count the number of logs on trucks with sawlogs rather than simply count the number of trucks with pulpwood.

crease in either %PULP or %C&SAW on a tract will increase the likelihood of a per unit contract.

$VOLUME_i$: Defined above. With tract composition held constant, an increase in volume increases the truckloads of logs the timber owner observes and counts, thereby increasing harvest-monitoring costs and reducing the likelihood of per unit contracts.

Because the predicted effects for these three variables are opposite of the heterogeneity-related predictions discussed earlier, we have no predictions for them. A change in tract composition between pine and hardwood sawtimber, however, does not entail any change in harvest-monitoring costs, so that our analysis does provide a prediction for %HARDWOOD.

Three other variables also measure the seller's monitoring costs:

$VALUE_i$: The market value of the timber on tract *i*. With volume and tract composition held constant, an increase in a tract's value resulting from an increase in the per unit log value (*P*) leads to an increase in the optimal per unit payment (R^*); this increases the dissipation associated with a per unit contract, thereby decreasing the likelihood of a per unit contract.[39]

$CONSULT_i$: Defined above. Consultants will have more experience monitoring harvesting behavior, thus reducing the cost of enforcement. This effect therefore predicts a greater likelihood of per unit contracts on sales involving a consultant.

$NIPF_i$: Defined above. Small (NIPF) landowners will be less proficient at monitoring harvesting behavior than larger (more experienced) landowners. This effect therefore predicts a lower likelihood of per unit contracts on NIPF sales.

Because the enforcement cost effects for CONSULT and NIPF act in the opposite direction of the presale measurement cost effects discussed earlier, our analysis provides no prediction for their empirical effects.

Empirical Results

Our data set includes information on 188 tracts for most of the variables discussed above. We could not, however, obtain value estimates for 35 of these tracts. Table 3 presents coefficient estimates from

[39] This result can be seen as follows. In expression (1), an increase in the per unit value of the timber (with volume and composition held constant) will increase v and $E[B(N)]$ by equal amounts; it will have no effect on the costs associated with a lump-sum contract. In our unpublished appendix, we show that an increase in the per unit price (*P*) increases the optimal per unit payment (R^*). Thus, in fig. 2, an increase in *P* increases the per unit payment and therefore the size of the triangles representing dissipation on the per unit contract.

three logit regressions explaining the choice of payment provision. The likelihood ratio tests in all cases reject the null hypothesis that the variable coefficients are jointly equal to zero. Regression 1 includes all the variables discussed for the 153 observations with complete data. The regression results support every prediction of the transaction costs model. In all cases the estimated coefficient has the predicted sign and is significant at the 11 percent level or less.[40]

Regressions 2 and 3 allow evaluation of the full data set. In regression 2, we exclude the value variable and estimate the model using all 188 contracts. Regression 3 has the same specification as regression 2 but uses only the 153 contracts used in regression 1. Generally, the results for the variables with a priori predictions are unchanged.

The regression results reported in table 3 demonstrate the robustness of our empirical results and provide strong support for our transaction costs theory of contract choice. We now compare the predictions from our model with those from a risk-based model.

A Comparison of Transaction Costs and Risk-based Predictions

As discussed above, a lump-sum contract leads to presale measurement, which reduces the total risk shared by the buyer and seller. A risk-based model therefore predicts that the more heterogeneous a tract, the less likely a per unit contract.[41] Thus risk-based predictions on the tract composition variables are that an increase in %PULP or %C&SAW will increase the likelihood of per unit contracts and that an increase in %HARDWOOD will decrease the use of per unit contracts. Similarly, a risk-based analysis predicts that an increase in NSPECIES (which indicates an increase in the quality of seller-provided information) will increase the likelihood of per unit contracts and that an increase in VOLUME (which increases tract variance) will reduce the likelihood of a per unit contract.

From the estimated coefficients in regression 1 of table 3, the positive estimated coefficients on %PULP and %C&SAW support a risk-based model (though they are not inconsistent with the transaction costs model). The positive coefficient on %HARDWOOD and the negative coefficient on NSPECIES are, however, contrary to the pre-

[40] There are considerable differences in the geographical characteristics and market conditions in different regions of North Carolina. To correct for potential bias from the omission of such factors, we included dummy variables for five different regions in North Carolina. These variables were not significant, and their inclusion had little effect on the other estimated coefficients. Also, omitting the insignificant variables CONSULT and NIPF did not affect either the estimated coefficients on the other variables or the fit of the model.

[41] The risk-based predictions discussed are consistent with the predictions from the model developed by Leland (1978).

TABLE 3

REGRESSIONS EXPLAINING THE CHOICE BETWEEN LUMP-SUM AND PER UNIT TIMBER-HARVESTING CONTRACTS

	PREDICTIONS		REGRESSIONS		
EXPLANATORY VARIABLE	Transaction Costs Model	Risk Model	1 (N = 153)	2 (N = 188)	3 (N = 153)
Constant			.11 (.06)	−.39 (−.27)	−.77 (−.40)
%HARDWOOD	+	−	.04 (1.59) [.06][1]	.04 (2.53) [.01][1]	.04 (1.99) [.02][1]
%PULP	?	+	.04 (2.05) [.04][2]	.06 (3.55) [.00][2]	.06 (2.91) [.00][2]
%C&SAW	?	+	.08 (1.77) [.08][2]	.06 (1.61) [.11][2]	.07 (1.68) [.09][2]
VOLUME	?	−	.003 (2.00) [.05][2]	.001 (1.68) [.09][2]	.001 (1.29) [.20][2]
LOWVAR	+		1.97 (1.50) [.07][1]	1.29 (1.01) [.16][1]	1.59 (1.22) [.11][1]

NSPECIES	−	+	−.52 (−2.99) $[.00]^1$	−.54 (−3.59) $[.00]^1$	−.55 (−3.10) $[.00]^1$
CONSULT	?		−.37 (−.38) $[.70]^2$	−.31 (−.41) $[.68]^2$	−.13 (−.14) $[.89]^2$
NIPF	?	−	−.21 (−.19) $[.85]^2$	−.63 (−.86) $[.39]^2$	−.11 (−.01) $[.92]^2$
ACCESS	−		−.30 (−1.21) $[.11]^1$	−.17 (−.89) $[.19]^1$	−.27 (−1.16) $[.12]^1$
BUYSIZE	−	−	−.87 (−2.19) $[.01]^1$	−.79 (−2.25) $[.01]^1$	−.95 (−2.40) $[.01]^1$
THIN	+		3.61 (3.57) $[.00]^1$	3.68 (4.28) $[.00]^1$	4.04 (3.98) $[.00]^1$
VALUE	−	+	−.03 (−1.46) $[.07]^1$	...	...
Likelihood ratio test			78.5	99.4	75.6
Correct predictions (%)			86.9	86.7	86.9

NOTE.—The dependent variable is PERUNIT: lump-sum = 0, per unit = 1. Numbers in parentheses are asymptotic t-values. Numbers in brackets are p-values, which indicate the minimum level of test significance for which the hypothesis that the coefficient is zero is rejected. Superscripts on p-values indicate whether they are for one-tailed or two-tailed tests.

dictions of the risk-based model but are as predicted by the transaction costs model. The positive coefficient on VOLUME also fails to support the prediction of the risk-based model, and it is not inconsistent with our transaction costs approach.

Additional predictions from the risk-based model are based on the observation that the seller bears more revenue risk on a per unit contract than on a lump-sum contract. By hypothesizing plausible differences in risk aversion (or the ability to diversify the riskiness of selling a timber tract) within the set of buyers and the set of sellers in our sample, we obtain further contrasts in the predictions of the transaction costs approach and a risk approach. The sellers in our sample are relatively small landowners (as compared to large industrial landowners such as Georgia Pacific). Most of them (see table 1) are classified as NIPF landowners: those who typically sell their timber themselves (or with the assistance of a consultant) once every 20 or 30 years. The non-NIPF sales in our sample are typically corporate sales. The NIPF sellers are presumably more risk averse than these other sellers, who can diversify tract-specific risk through more frequent timber sales. Thus a risk-based model would predict a lower likelihood of per unit contracts on NIPF sales. If large buyers (because they purchase more tracts) are assumed to be better able to diversify the risk associated with a particular tract of timber than small buyers, then per unit sales are less likely on sales involving large buyers. Thus the risk-based predictions are that the coefficients on NIPF and BUYSIZE will both be negative. The negative estimated coefficient on BUYSIZE therefore supports the predictions of both the risk model and our transaction costs model. The lack of significance of the coefficient on NIPF fails to support this prediction of the risk model.

Finally, if we add a further standard assumption of the risk aversion literature—decreasing absolute risk aversion—we obtain an additional risk-based prediction opposite to that of the transaction costs model. An increase in the value of the tract should, on average, be associated with greater seller wealth. Given decreasing absolute risk aversion, this increased seller wealth will lead to an increased willingness of the seller to bear the risk of the timber sale. Hence, a risk-based approach predicts an increased likelihood of per unit sales as tract value increases. The negative and significant coefficient on VALUE in table 3 therefore supports the transaction costs model but not the risk model.

Negotiated Sales: Per Unit versus Lump-Sum

Our transaction costs model of the choice between lump-sum and per unit contracts suggests that per unit payments for the quantity of the resource actually harvested are an effective method of reducing presale measurement costs. The discussion also demonstrates that under certain circumstances, landowners will maximize their profits by restricting competition for their timber. The intuition for this, again, is that for any given harvest level, the increase in enforcement costs associated with a higher per unit bid may more than offset the additional revenues associated with a higher bid. There are no similar enforcement cost–based incentives to restrict competition in the analysis of lump-sum sales. We therefore predict a greater reliance on negotiated sales for per unit than for lump-sum contracts.

In our sample of private timber-harvesting contracts, 94 percent of the per unit sales and 20 percent of the lump-sum sales were negotiated. This is a statistically significant difference, which again supports the transaction costs model of contract choice.[42]

IV. Concluding Comments

Empirical studies of the effects of transaction costs on the organization of production are few in number. This paper contributes to that literature by applying a transaction costs–based analysis to the choice of payment provisions in private timber-harvesting contracts. Our empirical results provide strong support for the predictions from such a transaction costs–based analysis, at the same time rejecting several contrasting predictions from a risk-based model. Our analysis also provides a transaction costs explanation for why negotiated sales instead of competitive sales may yield maximum net benefits to the resource owner under some circumstances. Again, our empirical results support this explanation.

Our investigation of the choice between payment provisions for timber focuses on two types of transaction costs: the costs of enforcing desired harvest levels and presale measurement costs. Analyses of contracts for the sale and lease of other natural resources often acknowledge the costs associated with enforcing desired harvest or use levels when per unit or royalty payments are specified. Presale measurement costs, however, typically are ignored. For example, a survey of the literature on public oil-leasing policies indicates that differences in incentives for presale measurement under different payment provisions (a critical component of our model and a potentially important source of dissipation) have been completely overlooked (see, e.g., Leland 1978; Robinson 1984; Mead et al. 1985).

The two types of timber-harvesting contracts that we analyze are extremes on a continuum with "pure" lump-sum sales at one end and

[42] The t-statistic from the test for the equality of the proportion of negotiated per unit and lump-sum sales is 9.56.

"pure" per unit sales at the other. We found no instances of "mixed" timber-harvesting contracts that specified both a lump-sum payment and a per unit payment. By contrast, private and public oil leases include both a lump-sum component (the bonus payment) and a per unit component (the royalty payment). We hypothesize (in Sec. II) that mixed contracts for timber may be absent because of large fixed costs associated with the lump-sum and the per unit components of timber-harvesting contracts. Investigation of this and alternative hypotheses concerning the use of mixed contracts can be accomplished only through detailed interresource comparisons of transaction costs.

References

Akerlof, George. "The Market for 'Lemons': Quality Uncertainty and the Market Mechanism." *Q.J.E.* 84 (August 1970): 488–500.

Alchian, Armen A. "Some Economics of Property Rights." In *Economic Forces at Work*. Indianapolis: Liberty Press, 1977.

Allen, Douglas. "What Are Transaction Costs?" In *Research in Law and Economics,* edited by Richard Zerbe and Victor Goldberg. Greenwich, Conn.: JAI, 1991.

Alston, Lee; Datta, Samar K.; and Nugent, Jeffrey B. "Tenancy Choice in a Competitive Framework with Transactions Costs." *J.P.E.* 92 (December 1984): 1121–33.

Alston, Lee J., and Higgs, Robert. "Contractual Mix in Southern Agriculture since the Civil War: Facts, Hypotheses, and Tests." *J. Econ. Hist.* 42 (June 1982): 327–53.

Barzel, Yoram. "Measurement Cost and the Organization of Markets." *J. Law and Econ.* 25 (April 1982): 27–48.

———. "The Entrepreneur's Reward for Self-Policing." *Econ. Inquiry* 25 (January 1987): 103–16.

Cheung, Steven N. S. "Private Property Rights and Sharecropping." *J.P.E.* 76 (November/December 1968): 1107–22.

———. *The Theory of Share Tenancy*. Chicago: Univ. Chicago Press, 1969. (*a*)

———. "Transaction Costs, Risk Aversion, and the Choice of Contractual Arrangements." *J. Law and Econ.* 12 (April 1969): 23–42. (*b*)

———. "The Fable of the Bees: An Economic Investigation." *J. Law and Econ.* 16 (April 1973): 11–33.

———. "The Contractual Nature of the Firm." *J. Law and Econ.* 26 (April 1983): 1–21.

Coase, Ronald H. "The Nature of the Firm." *Economica* 4 (November 1937): 386–405.

French, Kenneth R., and McCormick, Robert E. "Sealed Bids, Sunk Costs, and the Process of Competition." *J. Bus.* 57 (October 1984): 417–41.

Hallagan, William S. "Share Contracting for California Gold." *Explorations Econ. Hist.* 15 (April 1978): 196–210.

Higgs, Robert. "Race, Tenure, and Resource Allocation in Southern Agriculture, 1910." *J. Econ. Hist.* 33 (March 1973): 149–69.

Johnson, Ronald N. "Auction Markets, Bid Preparation Costs and Entrance Fees." *Land Econ.* 55 (August 1979): 313–18.

Joskow, Paul L. "Contract Duration and Relationship-specific Investments: Empirical Evidence from Coal Markets." *A.E.R.* 77 (March 1987): 168–85.

———. "Price Adjustments in Long-Term Contracts: The Case of Coal." *J. Law and Econ.* 31 (April 1988): 47–83.

Klein, Benjamin; Crawford, Robert G.; and Alchian, Armen A. "Vertical Integration, Appropriable Rents, and the Competitive Contracting Process." *J. Law and Econ.* 21 (October 1978): 297–326.

Leland, Hayne E. "Optimal Risk Sharing and the Leasing of Natural Resources, with Application to Oil and Gas Leasing on the OCS." *Q.J.E.* 92 (August 1978): 413–37.

Libecap, Gary D., and Wiggins, Steven N. "Contractual Responses to the Common Pool: Prorationing of Crude Oil Production." *A.E.R.* 74 (March 1984): 87–98.

Masten, Scott E., and Crocker, Keith J. "Efficient Adaptation in Long-Term Contracts: Take-or-Pay Provisions for Natural Gas." *A.E.R.* 75 (December 1985): 1083–93.

Mead, Walter J.; Moseidjord, A.; Muraoka, D.; and Sorensen, P. *Offshore Lands: Oil and Gas Leasing and Conservation on the Outer Continental Shelf.* San Francisco: Pacific Inst. Public Policy Res., 1985.

Mulherin, J. Harold. "Complexity in Long-Term Contracts: An Analysis of Natural Gas Contractual Provisions." *J. Law, Econ. and Organization* 2 (Spring 1986): 105–17.

Ramsey, J. B. *Bidding and Oil Leases.* Greenwich, Conn.: JAI, 1985.

Robinson, Marc S. "Oil Lease Auctions: Reconciling Economic Theory with Practice." Discussion Paper no. 292. Los Angeles: Univ. California, 1984.

Rucker, Randal R., and Leffler, Keith B. "To Harvest or Not to Harvest? An Analysis of Cutting Behavior on Federal Timber Sales Contracts." *Rev. Econ. and Statis.* 70 (May 1988): 207–13.

Stiglitz, Joseph E. "Incentives and Risk Sharing in Sharecropping." *Rev. Econ. Studies* 41 (April 1974): 219–55.

Umbeck, John. "The California Gold Rush: A Study of Emerging Property Rights." *Explorations Econ. Hist.* 14 (July 1977): 197–226.

U.S. Department of Agriculture. Forest Service. *The South's Fourth Forest: Alternatives for the Future.* Forest Resource Report no. 24. Washington: Government Printing Office, 1988.

Williamson, Oliver E. "The Vertical Integration of Production: Market Failure Considerations." *A.E.R. Papers and Proc.* 61 (May 1971): 112–23.

———. "Transaction-Cost Economics: The Governance of Contractual Relations." *J. Law and Econ.* 22 (October 1979): 233–61.

Wilson, Robert. "A Bidding Model of Perfect Competition." *Rev. Econ. Studies* 44 (October 1977): 511–18.

[14]

PRETIA EX MACHINA? PRICES AND PROCESS IN LONG-TERM CONTRACTS*

KEITH J. CROCKER *and* *SCOTT E. MASTEN*
Pennsylvania State University
University of Michigan

I. Introduction

AMONG the primary motives for writing contracts identified in both the law and economics literatures is the desire to protect against the hazards inherent to exchange where one or both parties have invested in reliance, or relationship-specific assets, in support of the transaction.[1] Because such investments have a higher value in their intended than in their next best use, parties have an incentive to engage in haggling or other forms of opportunism in hopes of influencing the distribution of the resulting quasi rents. Contracts promote efficiency by securing the distribution of those rents ex ante, thereby avoiding costly repetitive bargaining over the terms of trade and reducing the risk for each party of relying on the performance of the other.

In reality, this description of the role and functioning of contracting is oversimplified. As a number of legal and economic scholars have emphasized, contracts are not the precise, mechanically enforced documents often encountered in economic theory.[2] Indeed, contracts are extremely

* We would like to thank Russell Pittman and participants at seminars at Columbia University, the University of Chicago, the University of Illinois, the University of Michigan, and Pennsylvania State University for helpful comments. Research support from Pennsylvania State University and the University of Michigan School of Business Administration is gratefully acknowledged.

[1] See, for example, Benjamin Klein, Robert G. Crawford, & Armen A. Alchian, Appropriable Rents and the Competitive Contracting Process, 21 J. Law & Econ. 297 (1978); Oliver E. Williamson, Transaction-Cost Economics: The Governance of Contractual Relations, 22 J. Law & Econ. 233 (1979); and Steven Shavell, Damage Measures for Breach of Contract, 11 Bell J. Econ. 466 (1980).

[2] See, for example, Ian R. Macneil, Contracts: Adjustment of Long-Term Economic Relations under Classical, Neoclassical, and Relational Contract Law, 72 Nw. U. L. Rev. 854 (1978); Kenneth W. Clarkson, Roger Leroy Miller, & Timothy J. Muris, Liquidated Damages v. Penalties: Sense or Nonsense? Wis. L. Rev., 1978, at 351; Charles J. Goetz &

[*Journal of Law & Economics*, vol. XXXIV (April 1991)]
 0022-2186/91/3401-0003$01.50

imperfect tools for controlling opportunism. Parties may resort to all sorts of tactics to evade or chisel on performance. In that regard, contracts do not so much define the terms of trade as establish the procedures and alter the threat points from which parties compete over the division of transactional surpluses. An important element in designing contracts then becomes economizing on the costs associated with resolving disputes and governing exchange.

In this article, we examine the processes by which parties adjust prices in long-term contracts from this more relational view of contracting. That contracts often contain provisions for the periodic adjustment of prices is not all that surprising. Both relative prices and the general price level can change substantially over the extended time periods covered by many contracts, making original prices inappropriate to future conditions. What is possibly more surprising is the variety of processes that contracting parties have devised to effect such adjustments. Pricing provisions vary from definite escalators that establish a predefined schedule of prices over the life of the contract to vaguely worded renegotiation provisions. But while there have been a number of recent explanations for why parties might wish to provide for price flexibility[3] and some empirical work on how well contract prices track "market prices,"[4] there has been little systematic analysis of how parties choose among alternative pricing processes.[5] By focusing on the manner in which price adjustments are admin-

Robert E. Scott, Principles of Relational Contracts, 67 Va. L. Rev. 1089 (1981); Timothy J. Muris, Opportunistic Behavior and the Law of Contracts, 65 Minn. L. Rev. 521 (1981); Victor P. Goldberg, Toward an Expanded Theory of Contract, 10 J. Econ. Issues 45 (1976); Victor P. Goldberg, Price Adjustment in Long-Term Contracts, Wis. L. Rev., 1985, at 527; Williamson, *supra* note 1; Oliver E. Williamson, The Economic Institutions of Capitalism: Firms, Markets, Relational Contracting (1985); Oliver E. Williamson, The Logic of Economic Organization, 4 J. L. Econ. & Org. 65 (1988); and Benjamin Klein, Contract Costs and Administered Prices: An Economic Theory of Rigid Wages, 74 Am. Econ. Rev. 332 (1984).

[3] See A. Mitchell Polinsky, Fixed Price vs. Spot Price Contracts: A Study in Risk Allocation, 3 J. L. Econ. & Org. 27 (1987); Goldberg, Price Adjustment, *supra* note 2; and Victor P. Goldberg & John R. Erickson, Quantity and Price Adjustment in Long-Term Contracts: A Case Study of Petroleum Coke, 31 J. Law & Econ. 369 (1987).

[4] See Dennis W. Carlton, The Rigidity of Prices, 76 Am. Econ. Rev. 637 (1986); and Paul L. Joskow, Price Adjustment in Long-Term Contracts: The Case of Coal, 31 J. Law & Econ. 47 (1988).

[5] One exception is Harold Mulherin's 1986 article, in which he seeks to explain, among other things, the adoption of most-favored-nation clauses in natural gas contracts in existence during the period 1940–54; J. Harold Mulherin, Complexity in Long-Term Contracts: An Analysis of Natural Gas Provisions, 2 J. L. Econ. & Org. 105 (1986). Victor Goldberg and John Erickson's 1987 article (*supra* note 3) also looks at issues similar to those considered here as they apply to price adjustment in petroleum coke contracts. That article, however, relies on case study methods to explain observed contractual provisions, whereas this one employs more formal econometric techniques to evaluate contract design. Although

istered, we hope to provide additional insights into the role of various pricing provisions and the factors affecting contract design more generally.

We begin in the next section with a discussion of the trade-offs involved in designing contracts implied by relational contracting theory. We then discuss in Section III how these arguments relate to the design of processes for the adjustment of prices in long-term relationships. In Section IV, we apply those insights to explain the specific price adjustment processes adopted in a sample of long-term natural gas contracts. Section V contains our conclusions.

II. Relational Contracting

Most of the economic literature on contracting treats contracts in a mechanistic fashion. Once a contract is entered, the obligations of the parties for the duration of the agreement are fully prescribed. Contractors accommodate future uncertainty by stipulating contingent claims. Issues relating to enforcement are rarely afforded explicit discussion, but the presumption is clear that courts will either direct specific performance or apply appropriately measured damages to assure that the intentions of the parties are fulfilled. Overall, the incentives and the distribution of rents contained in the contract are definitive and immune to efforts to evade performance or to reopen the agreement to further negotiation.

Familiarity with actual contracting reveals that contracts rarely exhibit the precise, unequivocal character suggested by this traditional view. First of all, courts are not the reliable enforcers of contractors' intentions that are often envisioned. The legal system does not costlessly and unerringly assess remedies. On the contrary, there are reasons to believe that courts systematically deviate from efficient awards. Claims for damages, for example, are subject to a requirement of "proof with reasonable certainty." In cases where lost profits cannot be adequately established, recovery is likely to be limited to the cost of reliance, implying lower than optimal awards on average. And even if court-determined damages were not systematically biased, the cost of adjudicating damage awards would diminish the attractiveness of litigated enforcement.

Second, and largely as a result of these imperfections in enforcement, parties often engage in conduct designed to escape performance or force

our approach permits systematic tests on a larger set of contracts, we do miss much of the detail useful in evaluating contract terms that is available only through case studies. Paul Joskow's 1985 and 1988 articles also contain a considerable amount of useful case detail. See Paul L. Joskow, Vertical Integration and Long-Term Contracts: The Case of Coal Burning Electric Generating Plants, 1 J. L. Econ. & Org. 33 (1985); and Joskow, *supra* note 4.

renegotiation of contract terms. A short list of tactics contractors might exploit in attempting to effect a redistribution of the gains from trade includes capitalizing on ambiguous terms, suing for trivial deviations, making false claims of dissatisfaction, withholding relevant information, interfering with or failing to cooperate in the other party's performance, and failing to mitigate damages where a breach has occurred.[6] The success of any of these tactics depends on, among other things, how easily they can be detected and substantiated in court, but the uncertainty associated with litigated outcomes will generally leave some such tactics potentially profitable.

Finally, rather than defining the full set of obligations under the contract at the outset as implied by the standard economic treatment, contracts often leave terms and duties to future determination. Where uncertainty about what will constitute optimal behavior at the time of performance is great, it may be better to leave aspects of that performance open to negotiation rather than to constrain parties to specific but potentially inappropriate actions. Contracts in which parties intentionally defer decisions about price, quantity, or other aspects of the exchange until well into the term of the agreement are in fact quite common.[7]

These factors combine to suggest that contractual relationships, especially long-term ones, are rarely implemented in the mechanical way typically envisioned in economic theory but are characterized instead by an ongoing process of negotiations over the terms of trade. Contracts, from this perspective, become simply a means of structuring those negotiations, and litigation merely a negotiation tactic—a view supported by the small number of cases that go to trial relative to the number of actions filed. In this more relational view of contracting, "formal legal procedures are but a step in a longer process of negotiation. Filing a complaint and pre-trial procedure can be tactics in settlement bargaining."[8]

The problem is to devise a structure that encourages rent-increasing

[6] For more extensive lists and further discussion, see Goetz & Scott, *supra* note 2; Muris, *supra* note 2; Clarkson *et al.*, *supra* note 2; and Robert S. Summers, "Good Faith" in General Contract Law and the Sales Provision of the Uniform Commercial Code, 54 Va. L. Rev. 195 (1968). Such behavior "together with the other party's efforts to counteract them" create what Charles Goetz and Robert Scott refer to as "evasion costs." See Charles J. Goetz & Robert E. Scott, The Mitigation Principle: Toward a General Theory of Contractual Obligation, 69 Va. L. Rev. 967, 977 (1983). The important points are that, although the nature of strategic behavior within a contract will differ, opportunism occurs within as well as outside contractual agreements and that attempts to force a reallocation of contractual surpluses and efforts to counter them, whether through legal channels or less formal means, dissipate part of the rents accruing to exchange.

[7] For specific examples, see Goldberg & Erickson, *supra* note 3; and below.

[8] Stewart Macaulay, An Empirical View of Contract, 1985 Wis. L. Rev. 465, 468 (1985).

adjustments (flexibility) but discourages rent-dissipating efforts to redistribute existing surpluses (opportunism). Although more detailed and precise agreements make evasion more difficult, contingent claims contracting becomes costly very quickly in complex or uncertain environments. Failure to account adequately for uncertainty, however, may leave gains from adaptation unrealized or, if one party is greatly disadvantaged by ensuing developments, induce the types of costly efforts to evade performance or force a renegotiation described above.

The advantage of less precise, "relational" contracts that leave terms to future negotiation is that, because they do not attempt to explore and stipulate responses to every possible event, such agreements are considerably simpler to draft than contingent claims contracts yet at the same time remain flexible in the face of changing circumstances. As Victor Goldberg has argued, in designing relational contracts, emphasis shifts from devising "a detailed specification of the terms of the agreement to a more general statement of the process of adjusting the terms of the agreement over time—the establishment, in effect, of a 'constitution' governing the ongoing relationship."[9] The drawback is that such broad statements often afford the parties considerable latitude for dispute over what constitutes satisfactory performance and therefore introduce the prospect of having to engage in costly bargaining on a regular basis—the avoidance of which presumably motivated the use of long-term contracts in the first place.[10]

In practice, parties attempt to strike a balance between flexibility and opportunism in a variety of ways. To limit the nature and scope of renegotiations in relatively open-ended agreements, parties may restrict either the set of permissible adjustments or the process by which such changes are to be implemented. For example, the contract may permit negotiation over price or quantity requirements only at specified intervals or may designate which party has the right to initiate such renegotiations. Certain types of bargaining tactics may also be excluded, such as strikes or refusals to accept delivery. Delay as a tactic in negotiations is often made less attractive by stipulating that renegotiated terms apply retroactively to all deliveries after renegotiations were initiated. Alternatively, parties may attempt to expand the scope for negotiation and adjustment within rela-

[9] Goldberg, Toward an Expanded Theory, *supra* note 2, at 428.

[10] See Klein *et al.*, *supra* note 1; Williamson, *supra* note 1. For evidence that the size of quasi rents affects the length of contractual agreements, see Paul L. Joskow, Contract Duration and Relationship-specific Investments: Empirical Evidence from Coal Markets, 77 Am. Econ. Rev. 168 (1987); and Keith J. Crocker & Scott E. Masten, Mitigating Contractual Hazards: Unilateral Options and Contract Length, 19 Rand J. Econ. 327 (1988).

tively precise agreements by including provisions such as force majeure or gross inequity clauses.

Ultimately, the degree to which transactors leave the details of performance to future resolution will reflect the nature of the transaction. In the words of Oliver Williamson, "What is needed, evidently, is some way for declaring admissible dimensions for adjustment such that flexibility is provided under terms in which both parties have confidence. This can be accomplished partly by (1) recognizing that the hazards of opportunism vary with the type of adaptation proposed and (2) restricting adjustments to those where the hazards are least."[11]

III. Price Adjustment Processes in Long-Term Contracts

Here we apply the relational contracting perspective described above to analyze the nature of price adjustment processes. Unlike most earlier studies of price adjustment that emphasize either the reasons parties might want to allow for price flexibility[12] or the correlation between contract and market prices,[13] we focus on the question of *how* parties adjust prices. Thus, our concern is less with what prices actually result than with the processes by which they get determined.[14]

[11] Williamson, *supra* note 1, at 251.

[12] For discussions of alternative theories, see Goldberg, Price Adjustment, *supra* note 2; Goldberg & Erickson, *supra* note 3; Joskow, *supra* note 4; and note 14 *infra*.

[13] See, for example, Carlton, *supra* note 4; and Joskow, *supra* note 4. There are reasons to question whether market prices are the appropriate standard against which to evaluate contract prices. As Goldberg has argued, "[T]he relevant price to each party is its opportunity cost—the net price it could get from the next best trading partner. In a market for a standardized commodity, the list price and these two opportunity costs are roughly the same. However, in a long-term contract in which the parties deliberately isolate themselves from the external market, these three prices are more likely to diverge." See Goldberg, Price Adjustment, *supra* note 2, at 540.

[14] Focusing on process obviously begs the question of what parties are trying to accomplish in adjusting prices. Generally, economists have identified three motives for price adjustment: risk sharing, incentive alignment, and, most recently, transaction-cost based arguments. Risk-sharing arguments see the goal of price adjustment as stabilizing the surplus of the more risk-averse party (see, for example, Polinsky, *supra* note 3). In the incentive explanation, prices in variable quantity contracts are adjusted to provide appropriate price signals to the transactor having discretion over quantity.

The third rationale interprets price adjustment in a more relational manner. According to Goldberg, a goal of price adjustment is to reduce relational frictions or "postagreement jockeying." Changes in market conditions during execution of a fixed-price contract may leave one or the other party in an unfavorable position relative to his outside opportunities. That party then becomes more likely to engage in rent-seeking activities designed to evade performance or force a redistribution of contractual surpluses. "If the probability of wasteful behavior increases as the divergence between contract price and opportunity costs of the aggrieved party widens, price-adjustment rules which narrow the gap become increasingly attractive." See Goldberg, Price Adjustment, *supra* note 2, at 533. Also see Richard E.

A. *Methods of Price Adjustment*

Redetermination Provisions. Price adjustment processes can be divided into two basic categories, redetermination processes and renegotiation processes. Redetermination provisions establish prices by formula. The most extreme, rigid form is a definite escalator that adjusts prices according to an explicit, predefined schedule, increasing prices at a stipulated rate, for example. While the price that applies at a particular date is easily determined by reference to the contract, definite escalators have the obvious disadvantage of failing to make use of information arising over the course of the relationship and thus suffer many of the deficiencies of fixed-price contracts.

Indefinite escalators, in contrast, attempt to relate contract prices to market conditions as they unfold. The process of determination is still formulaic, but the equation now ties price to market data such as a general price index or the price of some important input or substitute product. Implementation thus remains straightforward, while prices become more flexible. But the same factors that prompt the use of long-term contracts limit the practicality of indexing. Specifically, the relationship-specific nature of many of the assets used in producing, transporting, or consuming a product isolates the parties from market alternatives. The more isolated the transaction in question, the more likely is it that indexed prices will fail to track the parties' respective opportunities.

To make use of information more closely related to the transaction at hand, parties have devised adjustment provisions such as most-favored-nation and right-of-first-refusal clauses that tie contract prices to prices obtained in similar transactions or to best alternative offers. Still, even these may miss cost or demand changes specific to a particular transaction and thus adjust prices imperfectly. In addition, the need to seek out and validate outside prices makes these provisions more costly to implement than index formulae and, being less definite, introduce a somewhat greater prospect of strategic behavior.

Renegotiation Provisions. Each of the indefinite pricing processes described above, while leaving price indeterminate at the time the contract

Speidel, Court Imposed Price Adjustments under Long-Term Supply Contracts, 76 Nw. U. L. Rev. 369, 373 (1981). An implication of this argument is that parties will wish to set prices so that ex post distributions of rents are divided equitably (see Scott E. Masten, Equity, Opportunism, and the Design of Contractual Relations, 144 J. Theoretical & Institutional Econ. 493 (1986)) to effect what Oliver Williamson has called "hazard equilibration" (for example, Williamson, *supra* note 2, at 34). We have implicitly adopted this relational explanation as our maintained hypothesis. Although we do not attempt to test the latter against alternative theories of price adjustment directly, evidence in support of one or the other is occasionally noted.

is written, is still definite in the sense that the price at which the parties will trade is determined definitively by the contract once the state of the world has been verified. Under renegotiation provisions, however, the distribution of rents under the contract is indeterminate up to the point at which the parties reach agreement on price. The ability to take into account the full range of relevant information before settling on price affords the transaction a considerable degree of flexibility.

This is not to say that such negotiations are totally unconstrained. Parties may structure the negotiation process by, for example, defining in the contract the sequence of offers and acceptances or specifying the defaults if agreement cannot be reached. Even contracts that place no express restrictions on the strategies of the parties provide more structure than no contract at all. As long as agreements are sufficiently definite to be considered valid contracts,[15] the law imposes a duty of good faith in execution of ambiguous terms.[16] Circumstances in which a duty to deal in good faith might come to bear include situations where a contract leaves the power to specify price or quantity to either or both parties. "Contract cases condemn the abuse of these powers as a form of bad faith in performance, even when the objectionable conduct is within the letter of the contract or when the contract says nothing at all about how the powers are to be exercised."[17] Thus, the law generally requires that quantity decisions in variable quantity contracts be made in good faith and seeks to deter variations whose purpose is to extort concessions from the other party.[18] More important for the issue at hand, "good faith prohibits a party from setting unreasonably high (or low) prices under an 'open price' provision."[19]

The advantage of renegotiation provisions is that they permit the parties to take full advantage of current information in adjusting prices.

[15] Although contracts that are too vague may be found void for want of definiteness, the Uniform Commercial Code states explicitly, "An agreement for sale which is otherwise sufficiently definite . . . to be a contract is not made invalid by the fact that it leaves particulars of performance to be specified by one of the parties. Any such specification must be made in good faith and within the limits set by commercial reasonableness" (U.C.C. § 2-311(1)).

[16] Generally, "[e]very contract [covered by the Uniform Commercial Code] imposes an obligation of good faith in its performance and enforcement" (U.C.C. § 1-203). The duty to deal in good faith, moreover, applies only to the *execution* and not the *negotiation and formation* of a contract. See Summers, *supra* note 6, at 220. Summers refers to good faith as "a phrase which has no general meaning or meanings of its own, but which serves to exclude many heterogeneous forms of bad faith" (*id.* at 201) and provides an extensive discussion of various practices constituting bad faith.

[17] Summers, *supra* note 6, at 239.

[18] See, generally, Muris, *supra* note 2, at 556–64, and cities therein.

[19] Summers, *supra* note 6, at 239–40.

Hence, they provide a high degree of flexibility. But they also expose the parties to the costs of having to negotiate mutually acceptable terms. Although the good faith requirement places restrictions on the use of the most flagrant negotiating tactics, considerable scope may remain for exercising more subtle, though still costly, bargaining strategies.

B. The Choice of Adjustment Process

The choice between redetermination and renegotiation provisions will reflect the relative costs of governing relationships under the respective arrangements. On the one hand, renegotiation provisions generally offer wider latitude to respond to changing conditions but subject the parties to the need to negotiate prices on a regular basis. Redetermination provisions, on the other hand, avoid the expense of negotiations but are less sensitive to relationship-specific events and are therefore more likely to generate acute hazards in extreme situations.[20] By relating the magnitude of these costs to characteristics of a transaction, it should be possible to predict the adjustment process most likely to be adopted to govern a particular relationship.

The literature on relational contracting suggests several factors that are likely to influence the degree to which contracts leave performance to future discretion. The most prominent consideration is the extent to which the environment associated with the transaction is complex or uncertain.[21] According to Charles Goetz and Robert Scott, for example, contracts will tend to be more relational in character where[22] "the parties are incapable of reducing important terms of the arrangement to well-defined obligations. Such definitive obligations may be impractical because of the inability to identify uncertain future conditions or because of inability to characterize complex adaptations adequately even when the contingencies themselves can be identified in advance."

Applied to pricing provisions, this suggests that the hazards of relying on relatively mechanical price adjustment processes will be smaller when the parties are fairly confident about future conditions or the variables of concern are easily quantifiable. Devising a satisfactory index may prove difficult, however, when the relevant information is costly to obtain or

[20] Witness, for example, *Aluminum Co. of America v. Essex Group, Inc.*, 499 F.Supp. 53 (W.D.Pa. 1980) (discussed in Goldberg, Price Adjustment, *supra* note 2) or the well-known experience of Westinghouse with its uranium supply contracts in the 1970s (see, for example, Paul L. Joskow, Commercial Impossibility, the Uranium Market, and the Westinghouse Case, 6 J. Legal Stud. 119 (1977)).

[21] See, for example, Macneil, *supra* note 2, at 901; and Williamson, *supra* note 1, at 238.

[22] Goetz & Scott, *supra* note 2, at 1091.

certify in court. The more uncertain the environment in these dimensions, the higher the likelihood that prices determined by formula will be severely disadvantageous to one of the parties. In such settings, renegotiation provisions, which institutionalize the ability to adapt to extreme conditions, reduce the incentive to employ the most costly evasion tactics. But they do so at a greater cost of arriving at prices on a day-to-day basis.

The greater uncertainty associated with distant horizons makes inflexible pricing particularly hazardous in longer-term agreements.[23] What were parameters in the short run become variables in the long run, increasing the dispersion of possible states of the world. The probability of being locked into an unprofitable undertaking and, hence, of efforts to subvert the agreement, will therefore be larger the more time separating acceptance and performance. We would thus expect renegotiation provisions to become more common as the duration of the contract increases.

The use of relational contracts is also often associated with the degree to which transactors need to invest in relationship-specific assets. Oliver Williamson, for example, generally posits a direct correlation between relational contracting and relationship-specific investments.[24] One reason for the latter is that the existence of appropriable quasi rents often motivates long-term affiliations, which, as just noted, favor the use of flexible arrangements. The effect of asset specificities on the incentive to write more relational contracts holding contract duration constant is less clear, however. On the one hand, increases in the size of appropriable quasi rents might be expected to increase the amount of resources transactors would be willing to expend attempting to negotiate a favorable distribution of those rents, making recurring negotiations unattractive.[25] On the other hand, investments in relationship-specific assets would inhibit the design and implementation of formulaic adjustment processes by insulating traders from similar transactions, thereby raising the costs associated

[23] See, for example, Williamson, *supra* note 1, at 238; Macneil, *supra* note 2, at 901; and Goetz & Scott, *supra* note 2, at 1091.

[24] Williamson, *supra* note 1.

[25] In explaining the relative infrequency of renegotiation provisions in contracts between petroleum coke refiners and aluminum producers, for instance, Goldberg and Erickson reason, "The aluminum contracts generally entailed greater insulation from current market conditions. Reopening a contract would mean that the parties would haggle over how to share the pie. The more parties are isolated from alternative trading partners, the larger the size of the pie. The larger the pie, the more resources the parties would devote to pursuing it. That is, the higher reliance interest in the aluminum contract would result in higher renegotiation costs, making frequent renegotiation relatively less attractive." See Goldberg & Erickson, *supra* note 3, at 391. The comparison is to upstream contracts between the coke refiners and suppliers of unrefined coke.

with redetermination as well.[26] Thus, although larger quasi rents are likely to lead to longer-term agreements, the differential effect of quasi rents on the costs of redetermination and renegotiation provisions, holding contract duration constant, appears to be ambiguous.

Finally, the choice of price adjustment processes is likely to interact with nonprice dimensions of the contract such as quantity, timing, and product specifications. At a superficial level, flexibility in price and in these other dimensions can be thought to act as substitutes: the more flexibility allowed in quantity, for instance, the less need there will be for flexibility in price. But the relational contracting approach also provides a more substantive rationale for expecting such a trade-off.

In fixed-quantity contracts, price adjustments are zero sum in nature.[27] As a result, reaching agreement on adjustments to a contractually established, but inequitable, price is likely to be difficult. However, unlike renegotiation provisions that provide expressly for such modifications and limit the tactics that can be employed in arriving at a settlement, redetermination provisions give much greater support to the status quo and actually provide an arsenal of legal tactics to protect the existing distribution of rents. The prospect of having to resort to litigation, delay, and similar tactics to affect adjustments makes inflexible pricing extremely hazardous where quantity variations are contractually restricted.

The relative disadvantage of redetermination provisions decreases, however, when quantity is variable. First, in response to an unfavorable price, the party with discretion over quantity may temper his losses by adjusting output or purchases, generally without exposing himself to the threat of costly litigation.[28] Second, and more important, where contracts permit variation in quantity, there is a greater chance of finding modifications to price *and* quantity that will be mutually beneficial. The result is that disputes are more likely to be settled with minimum disruption to

[26] Higher quasi rents might also increase the frequency and expense of evasion efforts. Moreover, the duty to deal in good faith that the law imposes on transactors during contract performance should constrain the most blatant manifestations of opportunism and thus temper the effect of quasi rents on the costs of renegotiation. Again, the fact that good faith requirements apply only to performance and not formation of a contract distinguishes negotiations during the term of the contract from those at contract renewal intervals. See text around notes 15–19 *supra*.

[27] Compare Williamson: "[P]rice adjustments have an unfortunate zero-sum quality, whereas proposals to increase, decrease, or delay delivery do not." See Williamson, *supra* note 1, at 251. See also, Michael L. Wachter & Oliver E. Williamson, Obligational Markets and the Mechanics of Inflation, 9 Bell J. Econ. 549 (1978).

[28] Quantity variations also may be held to good faith requirements. In particular, the courts seek to deter variations made for strategic purposes. See Muris, *supra* note 2, at 556–64, and cites therein.

the relationship where mechanically determined prices are accompanied by flexibility in other substantive dimensions of the agreement.

IV. Price Adjustment in Natural Gas Contracts

From the inception of the industry, sales of natural gas between producers and pipelines have been governed by contracts averaging ten to fifteen years in duration. The use of price-adjustment provisions in those contracts was common prior to the introduction of wellhead price regulation. The most frequently used provisions were two-party most-favored-nation (MFN) clauses that indexed contract price to the price paid by the purchaser to other suppliers in a stipulated area and renegotiation provisions, typically calling for open-ended price discussions every four or five years.[29]

Following the *Phillips* decision in 1954,[30] however, the Federal Power Commission began the process of regulating wellhead prices that culminated in 1960 in the introduction of area rate price ceilings for interstate gas sales. As part of that regulation, the commission also introduced restrictions on the types of price escalators parties could adopt and the frequency with which prices could be adjusted in contracts for gas sold below ceiling prices. The commission's objection to indefinite escalators was based on the belief that such provisions permitted price increases based on events having no relation to the economics of a particular sale.[31] Nevertheless, in a decision to ease those restrictions soon thereafter, the commission indicated a grudging appreciation of the role of price flexibility in facilitating long-term contractual relationships:[32]

> We reaffirm our earlier findings that the use of long-term contracts for the sale of natural gas by producers to pipelines or to others is desirable and appropriate in the public interest but that indefinite escalation provisions are, in general, contrary to the public interest. However, it also appears that elimination of all indefinite escalation provisions would be too restrictive to enable the industry adequately to cope with possible changing economic conditions over the span of long term contracts. Therefore, *to permit pricing flexibility and to provide an incentive for long term contracts,* we should permit future contracts to contain limited price-redetermination provisions.

[29] See Edward J. Neuner, The Natural Gas Industry (1960); Mulherin, *supra* note 5; and J. Harold Mulherin, Specialized Assets, Governmental Regulation, and Organizational Structure in the Natural Gas Industry, 142 J. Theoretical & Institutional Econ. 528 (1986).

[30] Phillips Petroleum Company v. Wisconsin, 347 U.S. 672 (1954).

[31] See U.S. General Accounting Office, Comptroller General, Information on Contracts between Natural Gas Producers and Pipeline Companies, 14 (February 22, 1983).

[32] *Id.* at 26, emphasis added.

Although the Federal Power Commission, and its successor, the Federal Energy Regulatory Commission (FERC), continued to limit the nature and frequency with which prices could be adjusted during the period of gas regulation, regulators did permit parties to adopt contract provisions that stipulated how gas prices were to be determined *in the event that gas sales were deregulated.*[33] As the prospect of deregulation increased prior to and following the passage of the Natural Gas Policy Act (NGPA) of 1978, the significance of such deregulation provisions increased. Below, we examine evidence regarding the relation between adjustment processes contained in these deregulation provisions and the characteristics of gas transactions in light of the discussion in the preceding section, using data collected when many categories of gas were either already deregulated or scheduled to be so in the near future.

A. *Deregulation Provisions*

Our information on contract terms was obtained from a 1982 survey (EIA-758) conducted by the Energy Information Administration (EIA) covering wells that qualified for incentive pricing under sections 102, 103, 107, and 108 of the Natural Gas Policy Act.[34] Through this survey, the EIA compiled detailed data on 659 contracts governing the sale of natural gas from 615 wells located in and off the coast of the lower forty-eight states. We then independently augmented this data with information on well characteristics from public records at the Department of Energy. Missing observations in the sample and limits on our ability to identify attributes of wells reduced the sample to 234 contracts governing onshore gas sales under NGPA sections 102 ("new" natural gas), 103 ("new" onshore production wells), and 107 ("high-cost" gas from deep wells, tight sands, Devonian shales, or geopressurized brine).[35]

[33] *Id.* at 28. Permissible pricing provisions were limited to (1) definite escalator clauses, (2) tax reimbursal provisions, and (3) limited indefinite escalators that adjusted price no more frequently than every five years. Later (1966), provisions that raised the price to the highest allowed regulatory rate were also permitted (18 C.F.R. 154.93).

[34] U.S. Department of Energy, Energy Information Administration, Natural Gas Producer/Purchaser Contracts and Their Impacts on the Natural Gas Market, Publication No. 0330 (1982). The NGPA established a time schedule for deregulation by gas category with high-cost section 107 gas deregulated as of November 1979, and sections 102 and 103 gas deregulated between January 1985 and July 1987, depending on the depth of the well.

[35] The EIA-758 survey data on contract terms was obtained under a confidentiality agreement with the Energy Information Administration. Over a third (233) of the contracts in the original data set covered offshore wells for which well characteristics data were unavailable. Correlation of the remaining observations with information obtained from FERC-121 filings (Application for Determination of the Maximum Lawful Price under the Natural Gas Policy Act) yielded basic well and field characteristics data on 392 contracts

TABLE 1

PRICE ADJUSTMENT PROVISIONS

	Adjustment Process			
	Redetermination			Renegotiation
	Equal to	Highest of	Selected by Seller	Based on
Total contracts	102	67	13	52
Adjustment factors:				
Definite escalator	10	37	5	2
Fuel index	. . .	31	6	1
Other price index	. . .	1	1	1
Two-party most-favored nations	4	12	. . .	. . .
Three-party most-favored nations	87	57	13	15
Market factors	. . .	13	1	39
Other	3	27	3	2
Other provisions:				
Market out	29	21	7	6
Maximum price	10	27	2	9
Minimum price	24	23	1	10
Right of first refusal	19	2	3	6
Price arbitration provision	40	40	7	34

Contract provisions relating to or affecting price can be remarkably complex.[36] Table 1 provides a sense of the diversity of natural gas pricing

representing 235 onshore gas fields. Missing values on one or more variables and exclusion of contracts written prior to the introduction of area rate regulation in 1960, and of section 108 contracts, which were not deregulated under the NGPA, left a sample of 234 contracts containing deregulation provisions. The majority of these (79 percent) were written during or after the year in which the NGPA was passed.

[36] We had access only to the Department of Energy's survey data and not to the original contracts. The following, however, is a sample deregulation clause provided by the Energy Information Administration:

Redetermination may be requested at time of deregulation and at each succeeding January 1 thereafter by seller who will select a redetermined price from one of the following:

(1) Initial price of $6.169 effective December 1, 1981, escalating monthly thereafter based on Section 102 escalation factors;

(2) The price in effect immediately prior to redetermination;

(3) Average of the two highest prices, selected by seller, being paid for substantially comparable gas produced in South Louisiana, onshore and offshore, escalated monthly by the Section 102 escalation factor, including taxes [a most-favored-nation clause]; or

(4) A price equivalent to 80 percent of the price of No. 2 fuel oil. defined as 100 percent of the average price per MMBtu for No. 2. fuel oil as published in *Platt's Oilgram* for "South and East Terminals, New York Harbor District." The average fuel oil price each month will be calculated from the arithmetic average of the daily arithmetic averages of the high and low quotations for each day of the month used. To convert price per gallon to

provisions. The column headings in the table—"equal to," "highest of," "select by seller," and "based on"—indicate the basic processes natural gas contracts employ to guide the establishment of prices, while the row headings list the most common reference prices or "adjustment factors," and the cells indicate the frequency with which each combination of processes and factors appears in the sample. Notice that more than one factor may be referenced in a given contract.

The adjustment processes are listed from least to most relational moving left to right across the table. The most precise process used in natural gas contracts set price either "equal to" or as the "highest of" some combination of the adjustment factors. Once the reference price or prices are established, the corresponding contract price is determined by the formula adopted in the agreement. An alternative that provides more flexibility is to permit one party, in this case, the seller, to select price from among a set of prices determined by the adjustment factors listed in the contract. Giving the seller some discretion over price allows greater opportunity to conform price to unusual circumstances (and to behave opportunistically) than would "equal to" or "highest of" contracts. Finally, renegotiation provisions indicate only that renegotiations should be "based on" or take into consideration specific factors such as prices paid by other pipelines or simply "market factors." Unlike "selected by seller" contracts in which the seller chooses price unilaterally, this adjustment process requires that the parties reach agreement before price is established.

The trade-off between precision and flexibility may be influenced not only by the adjustment process but also the adjustment factors selected. Definite escalators, for example, are extremely precise but inflexible. Fuel indices are also fairly precise but track only general market conditions, whereas most-favored-nation clauses use more well-specific information but must rely on the firm's ability to identify and document prices received by other producers.[37] Other provisions also influence the amount

price per MMBtu, each gallon will be deemed to contain 0.138691 MMBtu [a fuel-tied provision].

Redetermined prices, including tax reimbursement, shall not exceed 110 percent of the price of No. 2 fuel oil as determined above [a maximum price provision].

If buyer, at its sole discretion, determines that the total price being paid for all or a portion of the gas is not economical, buyer may elect not to pay the price and notify seller of the price it is willing to pay. If seller is unwilling to accept such price, it can cancel the contract [a market-out provision].

See U.S. Department of Energy, *supra* note 34, at 9.

[37] Most-favored nation clauses may be either two-party or three-party. Two-party clauses

of flexibility in the contract. Maximum and minimum prices may limit price increases or decreases or may trigger renegotiation, as may "market out" provisions that allow a purchaser to refuse deliveries if gas is "unremarketable" at the current contract price. The nature and scope of renegotiations may, in turn, be structured by arbitration provisions or buyer-right-of-first-refusal clauses that give the purchaser the option of either meeting third-party offers or releasing the seller from the contract. Finally, contracts may differ with regard to how often adjustments can or must take place and how and by whom adjustments are initiated.

Although the diversity of adjustment processes suggests a continuum of contract types, data and statistical limitations prevent estimation of the full variety of contract clauses.[38] Nevertheless, the hypotheses discussed in Section III can be tested by partitioning the data in a variety of ways. We begin by examining the adoption of redetermination versus renegotiation provisions.

B. *Pricing Processes and the Frequency of Adjustment*

The discussion in Section III*B* suggests that renegotiation provisions are more likely to be adopted the more uncertainty associated with the transaction, the longer the duration of the contract, and the more restrictive the nonprice aspects of the agreement. Information on contract duration and nonprice provisions were provided in the original data.[39] Given that natural gas is a fairly homogeneous product, the main dimension other than price over which the parties have control is quantity. The amount of quantity flexibility permitted in the contract is governed by take-or-pay provisions, which require purchasers to pay for a contractually specified minimum quantity of output even if delivery is not taken.[40]

tie price to the prices paid by the buyer to other sellers, while three-party MFNs tie price to prices paid by *any* buyer in a specified region. A number of papers have interpreted such MFNs as devices to facilitate collusion; see, for instance, Charles A. Holt & David T. Scheffman, Facilitating Practices: The Effects of Advance Notice and Best-Price Provisions, 18 Rand J. Econ. 187 (1987), and cites therein. For alternative explanations, see Mulherin, *supra* note 5; and David A. Butz, Durable Good Monopoly and Best-Price Provisions, 80 Am. Econ. Rev. 1062 (1990).

[38] There are 7,620 possible combinations of the processes, factors, and other provisions listed in Table 1 alone.

[39] In twenty-seven of the contracts in our sample, the deregulation provision was added after the original contract was signed. In those cases, DURATION is the number of years remaining on the contract beyond the signature date of the deregulation provision.

[40] The size of take-or-pay obligations range from 0 to 100 percent of the stipulated contract maximum. For more detailed discussions of these provisions, see Scott E. Masten & Keith J. Crocker, Efficient Adaptation in Long-Term Contracts: Take-or-Pay Provisions for Natural Gas, 75 Am. Econ. Rev. 1083 (1985); Mulherin, *supra* note 5; and Scott E. Masten, Minimum Bill Contracts: Theory and Policy, 37 J. Indus. Econ. 85 (1988).

The lower the required take percentage, the more discretion buyers have over the quantity of gas exchanged, and, hence, the less restrictive is the contract in this regard.

Constructing a meaningful proxy for the uncertainty associated with a given transaction is problematic. On the surface, a measure of energy market volatility, such as the variance in oil prices around the date the contract was signed, would seem suitable. However, uncertainty of a type that a researcher can easily capture in an index could also be accounted for and incorporated in a contract by the parties themselves.[41] The uncertainty that poses the biggest hazard to contracting is specific to a particular transaction and therefore hard to quantify adequately with a statistic. Even though we include a variable, OILVAR, in the estimations to represent disturbances in energy markets generally (see Table 2), a finding that this type of uncertainty does not influence the choice between renegotiation and redetermination provisions would be consistent with the theory.[42]

Although relational contracting arguments offer no firm prediction regarding the effects of asset specificities on the adoption of renegotiation provisions, the importance of this variable in general discussions of relational contracting motivates its inclusion here as well. In gas transactions, asset specificities are primarily locational. Once in place, the immobility of pipelines and wells limits the ability of both producers and purchasers to seek alternative trading partners if the original partner were to behave opportunistically. The smaller the number of buyers and sellers in the immediate vicinity, the greater the hazards of ex post negotiation. Accordingly, our proxy for appropriable quasi rents, QUASIR, is inversely related to the number of buyers and sellers serving the field in which

[41] The fuel index to which prices in natural gas contracts are most commonly tied (see Table 1) is the BTU (British thermal unit) equivalent price of no. 2 or no. 6 fuel oil. In fact, the use of fuel indices is highly correlated with the level of energy market volatility measured by OILVAR, suggesting that indexing to oil prices is a useful way of adjusting gas rates when energy market volatility is a major source of uncertainty.

[42] This measure of uncertainty did not perform well in our earlier estimations of the determinants of contract length. See Crocker & Masten, *supra* note 10. A dummy variable representing discrete changes in the nature of energy markets following the oil embargo in 1973 had a more profound influence on contract duration but, because gas pipelines and producers did not begin to insert deregulation provisions regularly in contracts until around 1978, could not be used to estimate the structural equations in the present study. In their study of jet engine procurement, Keith Crocker and Kenneth Reynolds were able to develop a measure of engine-specific technological uncertainty and found that such uncertainty did result in the adoption of more flexible procurement contracts. See Keith J. Crocker & Kenneth J. Reynolds, The Efficiency of Incomplete Contracts: An Empirical Analysis of Air Force Engine Procurement (Working Paper No. 9-90-1, Pennsylvania State Univ., Dep't Economics 1990).

TABLE 2

DATA DEFINITIONS AND DESCRIPTIVE STATISTICS

	Definition	Mean	Minimum	Maximum
RENEG	= 1 if renegotiation provision, = 0 if redetermination provision	.222	0	1
BASEDON	= 1 if the adjustment process in the contract is "based on," = 0 otherwise	.222	0	1
EQUALTO	= 1 if the adjustment process is "equal to," = 0 otherwise	.436	0	1
HIGHEST	= 1 if the adjustment process is "highest of," = 0 otherwise	.286	0	1
SELECBY	= 1 if the adjustment process is "select by seller," = 0 otherwise	.056	0	1
DURATION	= the duration of the contract (in years)	12.979	1	20
TAKEPCT	= the contractually specified take percentage	79.085	0	100
QUASIR	= 1/[(the number of independent purchasers serving the field in which the well is drilled) × (the number of independent producers operating in the field)]	.199	0	1
OILVAR	= the standard error of real oil prices over the eight quarters in and preceding the year in which the contract was written	.316	0	1.01
REGCONST	= $p^* - \bar{p}$, if the price constraint is binding, where p^* is the predicted unconstrained price and $\bar{p}$ the ceiling price; = 0 otherwise	2.6614	0	7.48

the well is located and is constructed to reflect the hypothesis that each additional buyer or seller has a diminishing effect on the size of quasi rents at stake.[43]

[43] Thus, introducing an additional buyer or seller to a location where there are already one hundred transactors has less of an effect on quasi rents than doing so where there is just a single buyer and seller operating in a particular gas field.

We have argued elsewhere that drainage problems may also increase the potential for holdups in natural gas transactions; where a producer is exposed to the threat of drainage

Finally, our earlier research indicated that nonprice competition in response to price ceilings in place at the time the contract was written may influence other contract terms.[44] Again, although we have no specific hypothesis regarding how nonprice competition should affect the choice among price-adjustment provisions scheduled to apply *after* deregulation, we include the variable REGCONST as a measure of the degree to which the price constraint was binding at the time the contract was written in order to control for this possibility.[45]

In addition to the basic estimation, we perform two sets of corrections. Because contract duration and take percentages are endogenous contract terms,[46] we correct for the possibility of simultaneity bias by substituting predicted values, DURATION* and TAKEPCT*, from reduced-form estimations of these variables.[47] In addition, there is a potential selection bias associated with truncation of the sample for contracts whose lengths

---

by other sellers operating in the same field, a purchaser might seek to force price concessions by delaying purchases from the producer. See Masten & Crocker, *supra* note 40; and Crocker & Masten, *supra* note 10. Additional variables included to reflect the extent of the drainage on the choice of adjustment process were, like QUASIR, insignificant and did not significantly influence other results.

[44] See Masten & Crocker, *supra* note 40; and Crocker & Masten, *supra* note 10.

[45] The extent to which price ceilings are binding depends on whether a particular transaction is subject to price constraints and the price that would obtain in the absence of a price ceiling. Since the latter is observable for those transactions where a price ceiling is not binding, it is possible to estimate unconstrained prices for all contracts as a function of characteristics of the transaction using Tobit estimation procedures. The estimated unconstrained price can then be compared to actual price ceilings to obtain a measure of the degree to which the ceilings are binding. See Masten & Crocker, *supra* note 40, for a formal description of the procedures used to estimate this variable. Because contract price is an endogenous variable, the price equation is estimated in reduced form. The independent variables employed in the estimations are listed in note 47 *infra*.

[46] More flexible contracts, for example, may induce the parties to adopt longer-term agreements.

[47] In addition to OILVAR and QUASIR, the regressors in these estimations included or were functions of the following variables: well depth; the number of purchasers serving the corresponding gas field; the number of producers operating in that field; a Herfindahl-numbers-equivalent measure of the concentration of pipelines serving each FERC gas region; gross national product in the year in which the contract was written; and dummy variables corresponding to gas regions, whether the purchaser was a gas pipeline company, and post–oil embargo and post-NGPA contracts. Because the reduced-form equations for these variables do not involve the adjustment process variables (which are endogenous to the system), we were able to estimate contract duration and take percentages using a larger sample than that used to estimate the structural equations in the text. In particular, because deregulation provisions appeared only in relatively recent vintage contracts, the expanded sample included many older vintage contracts, which permitted the use of the two era dummies described above in the reduced-form estimations. See note 42 *supra*. The exogenous variables listed above that do not appear in the process estimations, and that therefore identify the system, are significant beyond the $.1 \times 10^{-10}$ level in both the contract-duration and take-percent equations.

TABLE 3

PROBIT ESTIMATION OF ADJUSTMENT PROCESSES

Dependent Variable = 1 If Renegotiation Provision

	(1)	(2)	(3)	(4)
CONSTANT	−2.85160	−5.86105	−5.55308	−5.34007
	(−5.169)	(−4.993)	−(4.519)	(−4.444)
QUASIR	.116193	.0894184	.250413	.183061
	(.353)	(.269)	(.723)	(.540)
OILVAR	−.610790	−.220057	−.525018	−.456681
	(−1.632)	(−.574)	(−1.259)	(−1.108)
DURATION	.0670760	. . .	. . .	. . .
	(3.499)			
TAKEPCT	.0146802	. . .	. . .	. . .
	(3.073)			
DURATION*	. . .	.0955810	.0757232	.0780524
		(3.298)	(2.250)	(2.366)
TAKEPCT*	. . .	.0440879	.0476193	.0411660
		(3.575)	(3.695)	(3.498)
REGCONST	.0703153	−.0479919	−.113803	
	(.937)	(−.594)	(−1.313)	
H	. . .	. . .	−10.1294	−9.16021
			(−1.573)	(−1.376)
χ^2	32.887	35.813	43.156	41.416
df	5	5	6	5

NOTE.—*t*-ratios are in parentheses.

were less than the date of the survey minus the date the contract was written. Estimations were also conducted including a variable, *H*, that corrects for this bias along lines first suggested by Heckman.[48]

Probit results of estimations of the use of renegotiation provisions are reported in Table 3.[49] The coefficients in column 1 are uncorrected for simultancity and selection biases. Column 2 results have been corrected for simultaneity, and column 3 for both simultaneity and selectivity. Col-

[48] See James Heckman, Sample Selection Bias as a Specification Error, 47 Econometrica 153 (1979); and G. S. Maddala, Limited-Dependent and Qualitative Variables in Econometrics (1983), chs. 6 and 8. Specifically, $H = [(1/\sigma)g((L - \beta X)/\sigma)]/[1 - G((L - \beta X)/\sigma)]$, where L = 1981 minus the year in which the contract was written, and g and G are the standard normal density and distribution functions with variance σ^2. Joskow faces the same selection problem. See Joskow, *supra* note 4. Note that the density in the numerator of Joskow's definition of *H* should be $g(L - \beta X)$, as above.

[49] The estimations use RENEG as the dependent variable. The argument could be made that because "select by seller" provisions give some discretion to one of the parties to choose price, it is really more relational than the other redetermination processes. In addition to the probit estimations reported in Table 3 and the multinomial logit estimations described below, we also ran probit estimations combining "select by seller" and "based on" as the dependent variable. The results were not qualitatively affected by this change.

umn 4 reports the corrected results omitting REGCONST for comparison.

The results in all four equations are similar. The greater uncertainty associated with contracts of longer duration, for instance, appears to favor more flexible pricing. Specifically, the adoption of renegotiation provisions increases with the duration of natural gas contracts. Using column 3, the results indicate that, at the mean values of the right-hand-side variables, a one-year increase in contract length increases the probability of selecting renegotiation as the adjustment process by approximately three percentage points.

The results also support the predicted relationship between the use of renegotiation provisions and the size of take-or-pay percentages.[50] In all specifications of the equation, renegotiation provisions are significantly more likely to be adopted where quantity flexibility is limited. At the means, a percentage point decrease in take-or-pay obligations increases the probability of adopting redetermination provisions by about two points. Thus, the potential for mutually advantageous adjustments where quantity is variable appears to reduce the disadvantage of redetermination relative to renegotiation. Stated conversely, the flexibility of renegotiation provisions are more highly valued where quantity variation is limited. Notice that this contrasts with what would be expected if the role of prices in contracts were mainly to provide buyers with the incentive to choose quantity optimally.[51] In that case, price flexibility would be most important in variable-quantity contracts and would, in fact, serve no function at all in fixed-quantity agreements. The fact that price flexibility appears to be more important where take obligations are high thus supports the relational view of contracting in which process and evasion costs play a more central role.

Neither QUASIR nor OILVAR, however, has a significant effect on the choice of price-adjustment process.[52] Although previous research by Joskow and by ourselves indicates that the presence of asset specificities motivates the use of longer-term contracts, there is no indication here that the level of quasi rents influences the choice between redetermination and renegotiation provisions.[53] This result may reflect either: (1) the success of good faith requirements in attenuating opportunism or offsetting effects

[50] Both DURATION and TAKEPCT are obviously measured with greater precision than the characteristics proxied by QUASIR and OILVAR.

[51] See note 14 *supra*.

[52] There also appears to be no pronounced effect on the choice of adjustment mechanism to apply after deregulation resulting from the prior existence of price ceilings under regulation.

[53] Joskow, *supra* note 10, and Crocker & Masten, *supra* note 10.

of quasi rents on the costs of alternative adjustment processes as hypothesized earlier, or (2) simply the poor quality of the available proxies. And while the theory unambiguously predicts greater reliance on renegotiation provisions the greater the level of uncertainty associated with a transaction, the type of general market uncertainty measured by OILVAR would be easy to account for in a contract and thus should not greatly impair the efficiency of redetermination relative to renegotiation.

Such easily quantifiable uncertainty should, however, influence the frequency with which price adjustments occur. Although indexing can accommodate most measurable variations in the surrounding environment, all contracts are fixed-price contracts over the intervals between adjustments. Since fixed-price contracts do not account even for generic uncertainty, the hazards of lengthening the period between adjustments should rise with measurable changes in market volatility. More generally, we would expect contractors to choose the frequency with which they schedule adjustments to balance the expense of implementing each adjustment against the increasing likelihood that interim prices will become incompatible with the surrounding conditions as the period between adjustments lengthens. Because renegotiated adjustments are more expensive to execute than formulaic changes, we would expect renegotiations to be scheduled at greater intervals. More uncertainty, meanwhile, should raise the expected costs of delaying adaptations in either contract type and therefore lead to more frequent adjustments.

Information on the frequency of adjustments was available for 214 of the observations in the preceding sample, with scheduled frequencies distributed among five categories as follows: less than one year (33), annually (100), biennially (44), three to five years (20), and more than five years (17). The following results from an ordered probit estimation on these five categories reveal significant correlations between the frequency of adjustment and both the adjustment process and the level of general energy market volatility:[54]

$$\begin{aligned}\text{frequency of adjustment} = {} & \underset{(4.706)}{1.61170} + \underset{(.995)}{.283574}\text{*QUASIR} \\ & + \underset{(6.960)}{2.63896}\text{*OILVAR} - \underset{(-.793)}{.01184}\text{*DURATION} \\ & - \underset{(-.555)}{.00172}\text{*TAKEPCT} - \underset{(-4.347)}{1.11108}\text{*RENEG.}\end{aligned}$$

[54] For discussions of ordered response models like ordered probit, see Takeshi Amemiya, Advanced Econometrics (1985); or Maddala, *supra* note 48. The categories are ordered from lowest to highest frequency of adjustment; *t*-ratios are in parentheses. Results using predicted values of DURATION, TAKEPCT, and RENEG were consistent with those reported.

TABLE 4

ESTIMATED FREQUENCIES OF PRICE ADJUSTMENTS

	ADJUSTMENT FREQUENCIES (by Years)				
	>5	3–5	2	1	<1
OILVAR = .311:					
Redetermination	.01	.05	.19	.64	.11
Renegotiation	.14	.19	.34	.32	.01
OILVAR = .610:					
Redetermination	.00	.01	.06	.60	.33
Renegotiation	.03	.08	.26	.57	.06

Table 4 reports estimated probabilities of choosing each of the frequency categories for redetermination (RENEG = 0) and renegotiation (RENEG = 1) provisions using the preceding equation. In the top half of the table, the probabilities are evaluated at the mean values of each of the variables other than RENEG. In the bottom half, the probabilities were recalculated using a value of OILVAR one standard deviation above the mean. These OILVAR values correspond roughly to the values of this variable in 1975 and 1980, respectively. At the initial value of OILVAR, the distribution of redetermination frequencies is centered around annual adjustments, with three-quarters of the contracts predicted to adjust prices at intervals of one year or less. The distribution for renegotiation provisions, in contrast, centers around biennial revisions, with adjustments predicted to occur with a frequency of one year or less in only a third of the agreements. Both distributions shift toward more frequent modifications following periods of increased energy market volatility, however, with adjustments scheduled at intervals of one year or less rising to 94 percent of redetermination contracts and 63 percent of renegotiation contracts. Other variables, included as controls, show no significant affect.

Thus, overall, the process and frequency of price adjustment chosen by transactors in natural gas contracts are consistent with the magnitude and incidence of costs hypothesized earlier. In particular, the frequency-of-adjustment estimations provide evidence that renegotiation is a more costly way to effect price changes than is redetermination. This cost is overcome, however, as the relative inflexibility of redetermination provisions becomes more burdensome. The latter is likely to occur, in turn, where the duration of the contract is long (hence, uncertainty about the costs of future performance great) and quantity flexibility (and the corresponding prospect of reaching mutually advantageous modifications) limited, as the process choice estimations attest. Finally, general market uncertainty appears to affect the frequency but not the process by which prices get adjusted, a finding consistent with the proposition that only uncertainty that is relationship specific and noncontractible undermines the performance of redetermination processes.

C. *Multinomial Logit Estimations of Process Selection*

An alternative way of estimating the process selection decision that makes use of more information is to partition the sample by the four adjustment processes: "equal to," "highest of," "selected by seller," and "based on." Both "equal to" and "highest of" use relatively mechanical formulae for determining price and are in that regard the least relational of the processes, other things being the same. At the other extreme, "based on" merely sets a reference point—in the majority of cases, just market factors—for negotiations and is thus the most relational.

By conferring discretion over price to the seller, the final category, "select by seller," offers a greater degree of flexibility than either "equal to" or "highest of" provisions. But the seller's power to select price also affords him considerable control over the distribution of rents. As a result, "select by seller" contracts usually restrict the set of prices from which the seller may choose. Furthermore, whereas price changes in fixed-quantity contracts have a zero-sum nature, the buyer's ability to withhold purchases in variable quantity agreements would tend to constrain seller opportunism and introduce the prospect of mutually beneficial modifications. Hence, other things being the same, we would expect "select by seller" processes to be more common in long-term but *low*-take requirement contracts.

Results of multinomial logit estimations on these four processes are reported in Table 5.[55] Note that BASEDON is the omitted category so

[55] If we assume that transactors wish to maximize the net benefits from exchange, the choice among adjustment processes becomes a straightforward application of McFadden's random utility model, for which multinomial logit is a standard estimation procedure. See Daniel McFadden, Conditional Logit Analysis of Qualitative Choice Behavior, in Frontiers in Econometrics 105 (Paul Zarembka ed. 1974). Although the apparent ordering of adjustment processes in terms of their flexibility might suggest application of an ordered response model, such models require that the categories representing the dependent variable be logically and consistently ranked with respect to a single latent index. See Amemiya, *supra* note 54, at 292. The choice among adjustment processes, however, involves trade-offs in multiple dimensions; transactors, for example, care not only about the responsiveness of adjustment processes to changes in the surrounding environment but the degree to which contracts deter opportunism as well. Thus, higher take percentages raise the value of price flexibility, which should increase the use of more flexible processes like "select by seller" and "based on," but also increase the relative costs of implementing "select by seller" processes by expanding the scope for seller opportunism. Where there are reasons to suspect that the logical requirements are violated, "[w]e should be cautious in using an ordered

TABLE 5

MULTINOMIAL LOGIT ESTIMATION OF ADJUSTMENT PROCESSES

	Equal to	Highest of	Selected by Seller
CONSTANT	13.1560	15.1251	12.8149
	(3.747)	(4.221)	(3.222)
QUASIR	−.340730	−.304543	−.633058
	(−.524)	(−.429)	(−.545)
OILVAR	−.138487	.797736	1.05796
	(−.172)	(.952)	(.926)
DURATION*	−.118348	−.189396	−.124344
	(−1.963)	(−2.690)	(−1.231)
TAKEPCT*	−.130374	−.141549	−.15049
	(−3.605)	(−3.826)	(−3.736)
REGCONST	.352129	.0338269	.224031
	(2.128)	(.189)	(.857)
H	17.7407	16.0577	19.9631
	(1.484)	(1.331)	(1.608)
		χ^2 = 71.009	
		df = 18	

NOTE.—The omitted category is "based on"; *t*-ratios are in parentheses.

that the coefficients reflect the effect that each of the right-hand-side variables has on the probability that a particular adjustment process will be adopted relative to BASEDON.

The coefficients on DURATION and TAKEPCT are again all of the correct sign and, with the exception of the coefficient on DURATION for the category SELECBY, significant beyond the .05 level. However, none of the three included processes differ significantly *from each other* with respect to these two variables. In addition, as in the probit equations, neither QUASIR nor OILVAR contribute to our ability to distinguish among the categories, except for weak evidence that increasing

---

model because if the true model is unordered, an ordered model can lead to serious biases in the estimation of the probabilities. On the other hand, the cost of using an unordered model, when the true model is ordered, is a loss of efficiency rather than consistency" (*id.* at 293). Nevertheless, the following results from an ordered probit estimation of the categories ranked from least ("equal to") to most flexible ("based on") are presented by comparison and are consistent with the probit results reported in Table 3:

$$\begin{aligned}\text{adjustment process} = &-\underset{(-1.877)}{1.22480} - \underset{-(.053)}{.013548}\text{*QUASIR} + \underset{(.149)}{.045687}\text{*OILVAR}\\ &+ \underset{(1.793)}{.040834}\text{*DURATION*} + \underset{(2.037)}{.013676}\text{*TAKEPCT*}\\ &- \underset{(-1.616)}{.114668}\text{*REGCONST} - \underset{(-1.184)}{1.74285}\text{*}H.\end{aligned}$$

energy market volatility led to the adoption of more "highest of" processes relative to "equal to" processes (the hypothesis that the coefficients on OILVAR for "highest of" and "equal to" are the same can be rejected at the 10 percent level in a one-tail test).[56] Finally, the results indicate that "equal to" is more likely to be chosen than "highest of" or "based on" the larger REGCONST.

Table 6 presents estimated probabilities of adopting each of the adjustment processes for alternative take percentages and contract durations based on the estimates reported in Table 5. The first row reports the probabilities evaluated at the means of each of the independent variables. In the remaining rows, the probabilities associated with selected values of the indicated variables (and the mean values of the other independent variables) are presented. As indicated by the table, the relative probabilities vary in directions consistent with our hypotheses. Specifically, the probability of using "based on" increases for long-term and high-take percentage contracts. For twenty-year, 100 percent take-or-pay agreements, that probability becomes 66 percent. Transactors are more likely, however, to let the seller choose price in long-term but low-take percentage contracts. Although the estimated probabilities remain small, a twenty-year contract with zero-take percent has a 25 percent probability of using "select by seller" as the adjustment process. The probability of adopting "highest of," in comparison, declines as contract length and quantity restrictions rise, reaching its maximum of 68 percent for single-year, variable-quantity agreements. The estimated probabilities for "equal to" *relative* to "based on" also move in the predicted direction, rising for short-term and low-take percentage agreements.

Overall, the results do not suggest much of a basis for distinguishing between "equal to" and "highest of" provisions in process terms. Although the relative probabilities suggest that the implicit costs of "highest of" provisions rise more rapidly with contract length and quantity restrictions than do those of "equal to" provisions, the differences are not statistically significant. The results, however, support the claim that the hazards of both should rise more rapidly than those of renegotiation provisions. Permitting the seller to choose price, meanwhile, appears intermediate between these extremes in the sense that this process is neither significantly inferior to explicit renegotiation in dealing with the uncertainty associated with longer-term contracts nor substantially better in this regard than the more mechanical processes of "equal to" and "highest of." But the infrequency with which "select by seller" is chosen in

56 "Highest of" contracts are also more likely than "equal to" contracts to contain a fuel index provision. See Table 1.

TABLE 6

ESTIMATED PROBABILITIES FOR SELECTED VALUES OF DURATION AND TAKE PERCENTS

	Equal to	Highest of	Selected by Seller	Based on
At mean values of all variables	.514	.303	.060	.123
DURATION:				
= 20	.497	.181	.056	.266
= 1	.387	.542	.049	.022
TAKEPCT:				
= 100	.353	.181	.032	.434
= 0	.308	.483	.210	<.0001

practice suggests that the hazards of assigning price discretion to a single party are large in most settings. And although the likelihood of adopting "select by seller" increases the more power afforded the buyer to mitigate seller opportunism through quantity variations, the uniformly low estimated probabilities for this category indicate that other concerns not addressed in this article also play a role in the decision to adopt this process.

V. CONCLUSIONS

The terms on which parties actually trade in contractual relationships do not, like Athena, spring full-blown from the brow of Zeus. Ultimately, they are the outcome of a process of negotiations guided broadly by the rules set out in the contract and by the applicable law. Occasionally, the contract is so clear and the law so obvious that application of the contract is virtually automatic. But frequently the contract or the law is vague and the responsibilities of the parties ambiguous, leaving ample room for opportunistic behavior. Such imprecision, moreover, is often intentional. Transactors deliberately adopt terms like "good faith" and "best efforts" to describe their obligations under contractual agreements.

In light of these facts, it seems more appropriate to view contracts as means of establishing procedures for adapting exchange and resolving disputes rather than purely as incentive mechanisms. Whereas economic theory normally treats contract price as firm once chosen, the relational contracting approach regards contractually stipulated prices as little more than starting points for future negotiations. Thus, purchase decisions are made not just in response to price signals in the contract but also for any effect they might have in eliciting a more favorable price. The more precise the contract, the more secure the agreement. But some scope for opportunism inevitably remains, and the problem for transactors be-

comes devising agreements flexible enough to permit rent-increasing adaptations but rigid enough to deter rent-dissipating efforts to reallocate contractual surpluses.

In this article, we have applied relational contracting theory to analyze the processes by which parties adjust prices in long-term relationships and to conduct some preliminary tests of propositions derived from that literature. Generally, the theory predicts that transactors will value flexible arrangements most highly where uncertainty about circumstances at the time of performance is greatest. Conversely, environments where opportunism is expected to be rife or where economic conditions are relatively simple and static will tend to favor more precise but rigid agreements.

Our findings indicate that price adjustment processes tend to be more flexible the longer the duration of the contract, presumably reflecting the greater uncertainty associated with performance at more remote dates. Transactors, meanwhile, appear more willing to adopt mechanical pricing arrangements where contracts allow flexibility in other dimensions such as quantity, a finding consistent with the proposition that evasion costs will be lower where the possibility exists of realizing mutually advantageous modifications in price and other aspects of performance. We did not, however, find any evidence that a higher level of appropriable quasi rents favors redetermination over renegotiation independent of its effect on contract length—a result that may reflect the relative ease of formulating satisfactory adjustment formulae where there exists a significant number of similar transactions. The difficulty of constructing a satisfactory measure of quasi rents using our data, however, leaves this proposition open to future investigation.

Finally, as one might expect, market volatility that is easily quantified does not appear to undermine the efficiency of formulaic price-adjustment processes relative to renegotiation. Increases in generic uncertainty do, however, increase the frequency with which parties schedule price adjustments. Furthermore, the interval between adjustments tends to be greater in contracts containing renegotiation rather than redetermination provisions, which is consistent with the higher costs of implementing negotiated price changes.

The tendency for conventional economic theory to treat contract execution in a mechanical fashion stems in part from a failure to appreciate the richness of real-world contractual relationships and the laws that govern them. The evidence provided here suggests that an approach oriented more toward contracting as a process can be useful in explaining at least some of that diversity. At a minimum, it poses a challenge to economists to account for and explain a widely used class of contracts in which performance is often only vaguely circumscribed by the terms of the agreement.

Bibliography

Amemiya, Takeshi. *Advanced Econometrics*. Cambridge, Mass.: Harvard University Press, 1985.

Butz, David A., "Durable Good Monopoly and Best-Price Provisions." *American Economic Review* 80 (1990): 1062–76.

Carlton, Dennis W. "The Rigidity of Prices." *American Economic Review* 76 (1986): 637–58.

Clarkson, Kenneth W.; Miller, Roger Leroy; and Muris, Timothy J. "Liquidated Damages v. Penalties: Sense or Nonsense?" *Wisconsin Law Review*, 1978, pp. 351–90.

Crocker, Keith J., and Masten, Scott E. "Mitigating Contractual Hazards: Unilateral Options and Contract Length." *Rand Journal of Economics* 19 (1988): 327–43.

Crocker, Keith J., and Reynolds, Kenneth J. "The Efficiency of Incomplete Contracts: An Empirical Analysis of Air Force Engine Procurement." Working Paper No. 9-90-1. University Park: Pennsylvania State University, Department of Economics, 1990.

Goetz, Charles J., and Scott, Robert E. "Principles of Relational Contracts." *Virginia Law Review* 67 (1981): 1089–1150.

Goetz, Charles J., and Scott, Robert E. "The Mitigation Principle: Toward a General Theory of Contractual Obligation." *Virginia Law Review* 69 (1983): 967–1024.

Goldberg, Victor P. "Toward an Expanded Theory of Contract." *Journal of Economic Issues* 10 (1976): 45–61.

Goldberg, Victor P. "Regulation and Administered Contracts." *Bell Journal of Economics* 7 (1976): 426–48.

Goldberg, Victor P. "Price Adjustment in Long-Term Contracts." *Wisconsin Law Review*, 1985, pp. 527–43.

Goldberg, Victor P., and Erickson, John R. "Quantity and Price Adjustment in Long-Term Contracts: A Case Study of Petroleum Coke." *Journal of Law and Economics* 30 (1987): 369–98.

Heckman, James. "Sample Selection Bias as a Specification Error." *Econometrica* 47 (1979): 153–61.

Holt, Charles A., and Scheffman, David T. "Facilitating Practices: The Effects of Advance Notice and Best-Price Provisions." *Rand Journal of Economics* 18 (1987): 187–97.

Joskow, Paul L. "Commercial Impossibility, The Uranium Market, and the Westinghouse Case." *Journal of Legal Studies* 6 (1977): 119–76.

Joskow, Paul L. "Vertical Integration and Long-Term Contracts: The Case of Coal Burning Electric Generating Plants." *Journal of Law, Economics, and Organization* 1 (1985): 33–80.

Joskow, Paul L. "Contract Duration and Relationship-specific Investments: Empirical Evidence from Coal Markets." *American Economic Review* 77 (1987): 168–85.

Joskow, Paul L. "Price Adjustment in Long-Term Contracts: The Case of Coal." *Journal of Law and Economics* 31 (1988): 47–83.

Klein, Benjamin. "Contract Costs and Administered Prices: An Economic Theory of Rigid Wages." *American Economic Review* 74 (1984): 332–38.

Klein, Benjamin; Crawford, Robert G.; and Alchian, Armen A. "Vertical Integration, Appropriable Rents, and the Competitive Contracting Process." *Journal of Law and Economics* 21 (1978): 297–326.

Macaulay, Stewart. "An Empirical View of Contract." *Wisconsin Law Review*, 1985, pp. 465–82.

McFadden, Daniel. "Conditional Logit Analysis of Qualitative Choice Behavior." In *Frontiers in Econometrics*, edited by Paul Zarembka, pp. 105–42. New York: Academic Press.

Macneil, Ian R. "Contracts: Adjustment of Long-Term Economic Relations under Classical, Neoclassical, and Relational Contract Law." *Northwestern University Law Review* 72 (1978): 854–905.

Maddala, G. S. *Limited-Dependent and Qualitative Variables in Econometrics*. Cambridge: Cambridge University Press, 1983.

Masten, Scott E. "Equity, Opportunism and the Design of Contractual Relations." *Journal of Institutional and Theoretical Economics/Zeitschrift für die gesamte Staatswissenschaft* 144 (1986): 493–509.

Masten, Scott E. "Minimum Bill Contracts: Theory and Policy." *Journal of Industrial Economics* 37 (1988): 85–97.

Masten, Scott E., and Crocker Keith, J. "Efficient Adaptation in Long-Term Contracts: Take-or-Pay Provisions for Natural Gas." *American Economic Review* (1985): 1083–93.

Mulherin, J. Harold. "Complexity in Long-Term Contracts: An Analysis of Natural Gas Provisions." *Journal of Law, Economics, and Organization* 2 (1986): 105–18.

Mulherin, J. Harold. "Specialized Assets, Governmental Regulation, and Organizational Structure in the Natural Gas Industry," *Journal of Institutional and Theoretical Economics/Zeitschrift für die gesamte Staatswissenschaft* 142 (1986): 528–41.

Muris, Timothy J. "Opportunistic Behavior and the Law of Contracts." *Minnesota Law Review* 65 (1981): 521–90.

Neuner, Edward J. *The Natural Gas Industry*. Norman: University of Oklahoma Press, 1960.

Polinsky, A. Mitchell. "Fixed Price versus Spot Price Contracts: A Study in Risk Allocation." *Journal of Law, Economics, and Organization* 3 (1987): 27–46.

Shavell, Steven. "Damage Measures for Breach of Contract." *Bell Journal of Economics* 11 (1980): 466–90.

Speidel, Richard E. "Court Imposed Price Adjustments under Long-Term Supply Contracts." *Northwestern University Law Review* 76 (1981): 369–422.

Summers, Robert S. " 'Good Faith' in General Contract Law and the Sales

Provisions of the Uniform Commercial Code." *Virginia Law Review* 54 (1968): 195–267.

U.S. Department of Energy. Energy Information Administration. "Natural Gas Producer/Purchaser Contracts and Their Potential Impacts on the Natural Gas Market." Publication No. DOE/EIA-0330. Washington, D.C.: U.S. Government Printing Office, 1983.

U.S. General Accounting Office, Comptroller General. "Information on Contracts between Natural Gas Producers and Pipeline Companies." RCED-83-5. Washington, D.C.: U.S. Government Printing Office, 1983.

Wachter, Michael L., and Williamson, Oliver E. "Obligational Markets and the Mechanics of Inflation." *Bell Journal of Economics* 9 (1978): 549–71.

Williamson, Oliver E. "Transaction-Cost Economics: The Governance of Contractual Relations." *Journal of Law and Economics* 22 (1979): 233–62.

Williamson, Oliver E. "Credible Commitments: Using Hostages to Support Exchange." *American Economic Review* 83 (1983): 519–40.

Williamson, Oliver E. *The Economic Institutions of Capitalism: Firms, Markets, Relational Contracting*. New York: Free Press, 1985.

Williamson, Oliver E. "The Logic of Economic Organization." *Journal of Law, Economics, and Organization* 4 (1988): 65–93.

Part III
Regulation and Positive Political Economy

[15]

Franchise bidding for natural monopolies—in general and with respect to CATV

Oliver E. Williamson

Professor of Economics, Law, and Public Policy
University of Pennsylvania

The orthodox attitude among economists toward regulation is one of "disdain and contempt." The general reputation is not undeserved, but it fails to discriminate among different economic activities and different types of regulation. An effort to distinguish between those circumstances in which regulation, in some form, is immanent from those in which market modes can be made to work relatively well is needed.

Discriminating assessments of regulated industries (extant and proposed) will be facilitated by examining transactions in much greater microanalytic detail than has been characteristic of prior studies of regulation and proposed alternatives thereto. My examination of franchise bidding for natural monopoly discloses that this mode suffers from much more severe contractual disabilities than have hitherto been acknowledged. Faced with both technological and market uncertainties, CATV, circa 1970, does not appear to be among the circumstances for which unassisted franchise bidding can be expected to work well.

1. Introduction

■ The limits of regulation are manifold and, in a general way at least, have been examined elsewhere by others. Merely to show that regulation is flawed, however, does not establish that regulation is an inferior mode of organizing economic activity. For one thing, the disabilities of regulation are apt to vary with both the type of activity regulated and the form of regulation attempted. Secondly, before regulation is supplanted, there is an obligation to assess the properties of the proposed alternative—not only in general, but also specifically with respect to the activity in question. If the proposed mode is flawed in similar or different respects, the purported advantages of shifting out of regulation may be illusory.

The present paper is primarily concerned with the efficacy of

---

Oliver E. Williamson received the S. B. from M. I. T. in 1955, the M. B. A. from Stanford University in 1960, and the Ph. D. from Carnegie-Mellon in 1963. When he is not working on his sequel to *Markets and Hierarchies* or his time is not preempted by this journal, he can sometimes be found bounding irrationally at a squash court.

Research on this paper has been supported by a grant from the National Science Foundation (NSF SOC 72-05550 A02). The author acknowledges, without implicating, the helpful comments on an earlier version of the paper of Susan Ackerman, William Baxter, Victor Goldberg, Paul Joskow, Alvin Klevorick, Arthur Leff, Paul MacAvoy, and Richard Nelson.

franchise bidding schemes as an alternative to regulation in the provision of public utility services in circumstances in which there are nontrivial economies associated with monopoly supply. Granting that regulation is highly imperfect, assessed in terms of an abstract ideal, what are the conditions under which franchise bidding is a vastly superior solution to the supply of "traditional" public utility services?[1] In particular, should public utility regulation be extended to cover community antenna television systems or should franchise bidding be used instead (Posner, 1969, pp. 642–643)?

My assessment of franchise bidding for the supply of CATV services, *circa* 1970, is that it differs mainly in degree, rather than in kind, from the regulation that such bidding is intended to supplant—though this does not deny that franchise auctions may sometimes have attractive properties for the supply of natural monopoly services (see Section 5). In circumstances, however, where franchise bidding predictably and actually converges toward regulation, the purported advantages of franchise bidding as compared with regulation are problematical.

I attempt here to examine franchise bidding issues in somewhat finer microanalytic detail than has been done previously. My emphasis on contractual detail is to be contrasted with that of Richard Posner, who argues that "[t]o expound the details of particular regulations and proposals . . . would serve only to obscure the basic issues" (1972, p. 98). I submit, however, that the strategy employed elsewhere to study the employment relation (Williamson, Wachter, and Harris, 1975) and vertical integration (Williamson, 1971) has general application. In both instances, it was necessary to examine the contracting process in greater detail than had been done previously to discern the types of difficulties which market mediated exchange encounters and, relatedly, to establish in what respects and why internal (collective or hierarchical) organization offers an advantage.

It is of interest in this connection to observe that what Posner has referred to as the "economic approach to law" (1975) is characteristically deficient in microanalytic respects. The economic approach which Posner favors traces its intellectual origins, in antitrust respects at least, to Aaron Director and his students (Posner, 1975, p. 758, n. 6). As I have observed elsewhere, this tradition relies heavily on the fiction of frictionlessness and/or invokes transaction cost considerations selectively (Williamson, 1974a; 1974b). However powerful and useful it is for classroom purposes and as a check against loose public policy prescriptions, it easily leads to extreme and untenable "solutions."[2] What Arthur Leff has referred to as a "legal approach to economics" (1975), in which transaction costs are more prominently

[1] By traditional natural monopoly services I mean electricity, gas, water, and telephone. See Joskow (1975, p. 18) and Jorden (1972, p. 154).

[2] Posner regards Ronald Coase's classic paper "The Problem of Social Cost" (1960) as the entering wedge to the "new law and economics field" (1975, p. 760). It is noteworthy that this important and influential paper is in two parts: the first part features frictionlessness; the second qualifies the earlier discussion to make allowance for frictions. Much of the follow-on literature, including franchise bidding, is largely or wholly preoccupied with frictionlessness or deals with frictions in a limited or sanguine way.

and systematically featured, is, I think, a necessary supplement to (and sometimes substitute for) the Director-Posner tradition.[3]

My assessment of the problems of supplying natural monopoly services suggests that there are no friction-free alternatives. Choice among alternative modes nevertheless has to be made. Among the relevant factors to be considered in evaluating alternative modes of organizing natural monopoly are the following: (1) the costs of ascertaining and aggregating consumer preferences through direct solicitation; (2) the efficacy of scalar bidding; (3) the degree to which technology is well developed; (4) demand uncertainty; (5) the degree to which incumbent suppliers acquire idiosyncratic skills; (6) the extent to which specialized, long-lived equipment is involved; and (7) the susceptibility of the political process to opportunistic representations and the differential proclivity, among modes, to make them. (Of special relevance in this last connection is the tendency for regulation, once put in place, to assert ancillary powers, thereby to expand its jurisdiction, often with dysfunctional consequences. Although it is beyond the scope of the paper to assess this issue here, creeping "ancillariness" is one of the more severe disabilities to which regulation is subject.) The more confidence one has in contracting and in the efficacy of competition—both at the outset and at contract renewal intervals—the more one tends to favor market modes. Conformably, regulation, in some form, is relatively favored when one is dubious that incomplete contracting will yield desired results and when competitive processes are prone to breakdown.

It should be noted in this connection that variants within both market and regulatory modes exist. Discriminating assessments within as well as between modes are accordingly indicated. Also, a once-for-all verdict with respect to the supply of a particular natural monopoly service is unwarranted. The better mode at an early stage of an industry's development may no longer be better later on when a lesser degree of uncertainty prevails. To the extent that difficult transition problems are apt to be posed in shifting from one mode to the other, this should be acknowledged and taken expressly into account at the outset.

More intensive study of the abstract properties of alternative modes at successive stages will be needed before a more confident matching of modes with activities can be accomplished. Considering the primitive state of comparative institutional analysis, however, more than abstract study is needed. Microanalytic examination of a number of *individual cases* will also be instructive. Among the cases that might be selected for examination, the "study of extreme instances often provides important leads to the essentials of the situation" (Behavioral Sciences Subpanel, 1962, p. 5). Subject to the conditions that only gross inferences are to be attempted and that the system is observed to respond to disturbances in a coherent way, such observations offer a relatively economical way by which to secure insights into the properties of a complex organization. The case study reported here is used only for gross inference purposes,

[3] For an important contribution to the contracting literature, of which I became aware only recently, see Macneil (1974). The "relational" contracts described by Macneil are examined in a regulatory context by Goldberg (1976), whose treatment of the issues is independent of, but in a spirit that is consonant with, that developed here.

appears to satisfy coherence requirements, and introduces a hitherto missing element of reality testing into the evaluation of franchise bidding for natural monopolies.

Franchise bidding under steady state conditions is treated in Section 2. The more interesting issues relating to the efficacy of franchise bidding do not appear, however, until uncertainty is introduced. These are developed in Section 3. The Oakland, California, experience with franchise bidding for CATV is then described and evaluated in Section 4. Concluding remarks follow in Section 5.

2. The simple franchise bidding scheme

■ Partly out of a sense that the defects of regulation are so serious that patching it up is not worth the effort and partly out of a conviction that market solutions have not been given a fair chance to deal with the problems for which regulation has been devised, numerous proposals have appeared recently suggesting that market modes be used more imaginatively. Many of these suggestions are traceable, directly or indirectly, to what has come to be known as the economics of property rights literature.[4] Ronald Coase's study of the Federal Communications Commission (1959) is an early and classic example. A more recent issue to come up for consideration is the organization of community antenna television (CATV) systems, of which Posner's study (1972) is an illustration.

Posner's evaluation of CATV franchising relies in part on Harold Demsetz' earlier treatment of the question, "Why regulate utilities?" (1968). Demsetz contends that even though efficiency considerations may dictate that there be only one supplier in a natural monopoly industry, the unregulated market price need display no elements of monopoly.

□ **The basic argument.** Conventional analysis is flawed by a failure to distinguish between the number of *ex ante* bidders and the condition of *ex post* supply. Even though scale economies may dictate that there be a single *ex post* supplier, large numbers competition may nevertheless be feasible at the initial bidding stage. Where large numbers of qualified parties enter noncollusive bids to become the supplier of the decreasing cost activity, the resulting price need not reflect monopoly power. The defect with conventional analysis is that it ignores this initial franchise bidding stage.

Franchise bids which involve lump-sum payments should be distinguished from those where the franchise is awarded to the bidder who offers to supply at the lowest per unit price. Awarding an exclusive franchise to the noncollusive bidder who will pay the largest lump-sum fee to secure the business effectively capitalizes the monopoly profits which thereafter accrue. But the product or service for which such a franchise is granted will be priced on monopolistic terms. To avoid this outcome, the franchise award criterion of lowest per unit price is favored. George Stigler, among others, evidently finds the argument persuasive (1968, pp. 18–19; 1974, p. 360).

Demsetz illustrates the argument by examining a hypothetical example in which the state requires automobile owners to purchase

[4] For a survey of this literature, see Furubotn and Pejovich (1972); for a selection of readings, see Furubotn and Pejovich (1974).

automobile license plates annually, where the plates in question are produced under decreasing cost conditions. To simplify the argument he strips away "*irrelevant complications*, such as durability of distribution systems, uncertainty, and irrational behavior, all of which may or may not justify the use of regulatory commissions but none of which is relevant to the theory of natural monopoly; for this theory depends on one belief only—price and output will be at monopoly levels if, due to scale economies, only one firm succeeds in producing the product" (1968, p. 57; emphasis added).[5] Provided that there are many qualified and noncollusive bidders for the annual contract and that the contract is awarded to the party that offers to supply at the lowest per-unit price, "the winning price will differ insignificantly from the per-unit cost of producing license plates" (Demsetz, 1968, p. 61).

Demsetz and others evidently believe, moreover, that the argument is not vitiated when the simple case is extended to include such complications as equipment durability and uncertainty. Equipment durability need not lead to wasteful duplication of facilities since, should a potential supplier offer superior terms, trunk line distributional facilities can be transferred from the original supplier to the successor firm (Demsetz, 1968, p. 62). Whether regulation is warranted as a means by which to cope more effectively with uncertainty is met with the observation that "[l]ong-term contracts for the supply of [nonutility services] are concluded satisfactorily in the market place without the aid of regulation" (1968, p. 64).

The dominant theme that emerges, occasional disclaimers to the contrary notwithstanding,[6] is that franchise bidding for natural monopolies has attractive properties. It is a market solution that avoids many of the disabilities of regulation. Demsetz' concluding remarks, in which he registers his "belief that rivalry of the open market place disciplines more effectively than do the regulatory processes of the commission" (1968, p. 65), are plainly in this spirit.

□ **Some objections.** *Marginal cost pricing.* Lester Telser takes issue with Demsetz' treatment of natural monopoly on the grounds that franchise bidding gives no assurance that output will be priced efficiently on marginal cost terms (Telser, 1969, pp. 938–939):

> [Demsetz] leaves readers with the impression that he is content with a situation in which the firm is prevented from obtaining a monopoly return and he does not raise the question of efficiency. Hence he implies that direct regulation of an industry subject to decreasing average cost is unnecessary if it is prevented from obtaining a monopoly return. . . . This misses the point. The controversy concerns regulation to secure efficiency and to promote public welfare. It does not concern the rate of return.

Another way of putting it is that Demsetz does not identify the relevant social welfare function or evaluate his results in welfare terms. Failure to do so, coupled with the prospect that franchise

[5] To the extent that Demsetz' treatment of natural monopoly is limited to a critique of elementary textbook discussions, the argument goes through. Plainly, however, Demsetz and others also contend that it has real world relevance. The "irrelevant complications" referred to in the text are conspicuously present when this latter application is attempted. As will be apparent, the purported superiority of franchise bidding is a good deal more difficult to establish when these conditions are present.

[6] Demsetz is somewhat more cautious about the merits of franchise bidding and highlights the qualifications to his argument in his reply to Telser's critique (Demsetz, 1971).

bidding will not lead to efficient marginal cost pricing, is, in Telser's view, a critical shortcoming of Demsetz' approach.

Demsetz has responded to these criticisms by observing that marginal cost pricing was of secondary importance to his paper (1971, p. 356). Although a complete treatment of the natural monopoly problem would require that efficient pricing be addressed, his original article did not pretend to be complete (1971, p. 356). He furthermore considers it doubtful that regulation leads to more efficient pricing than an appropriately elaborated bidding scheme (1971, pp. 360–361).

I suggest, for the purposes of this paper, that the marginal cost pricing issue be set aside and that the frictions associated with franchise bidding, which are glossed over in previous treatments, be examined instead. To the extent that filling the *lacunae* in Demsetz' "vaguely described bidding process"—which Telser mentions (1971, p. 364) but does not investigate—involves the progressive elaboration of an administrative machinery, the advantages of franchise bidding over regulation are uncertain. If, despite such machinery, the price-to-cost tracking properties of regulation are arguably superior to those of franchise bidding, the purported advantages of franchise bidding are further suspect.

Irrelevant complications. The irrelevant complications to which Demsetz refers—equipment durability and uncertainty—and dismisses in the context of his automobile license plate example are really the core issues. To be sure, steady state analysis of the type he employs sometimes yields fruitful insights that have wide reaching applications. I submit, however, that the interesting problems of *comparative institutional choice* are largely finessed when the issues are posed in steady state terms. Frank Knight's admonitions to this effect, although expressed in a different institutional context (1965, pp. 267–268), have general application. The basic argument, which applies both to Knight's interest in whether internal organization matters and to Demsetz' concern with market modes of contracting, is this: Rates of convergence aside, any of a large variety of organizing modes will achieve equally efficient results if steady state conditions obtain.[7] In circumstances, however, in which the operating environment is characterized by a nontrivial degree of uncertainty, self-conscious attention to both the *initial* and *adaptability* attributes of alternative modes is warranted.

Demsetz' treatment of franchise bidding emphasizes the initial supply price aspect and, as developed below, treats the matter of adaptability in a rather limited and sanguine way. As will be apparent, franchise bidding for public utility services under uncertainty encounters many of the same problems that the critics of regulation associate with regulation; as Victor Goldberg (1976) argues, the problems inhere in the circumstances.

[7] Consider in this connection whether, from an allocative efficiency point of view, it really matters if franchises are awarded on the basis of a lump-sum fee rather than a lowest supply price criterion. I submit that the monopoly distortions commonly associated with the former mode of contracting will tend to vanish if steady state conditions obtain. The reasoning here is that steady state conditions facilitate low cost price discrimination, in which event the marginal customer is supplied on marginal cost terms, and/or that customers can more effectively organize their side of the market and bargain to an efficient result.

3. Franchise bidding under uncertainty

■ It will be useful to examine franchise contracts of three types: once-for-all contracts, which appear to be the type of contract envisaged by Stigler; incomplete, long-term contracts, which are favored by Demsetz; and recurrent short-term contracts, which Posner endorses.

□ **Once-for-all contracts.** Stigler's views on franchise bidding are limited mainly to an endorsement of Demsetz' prior treatment of these matters. He observes simply that "[n]atural monopolies are often regulated by the state. We note that customers can auction off the right to sell electricity, using the state as the instrument to conduct the auction, and thus economize on transaction costs. The auction . . . consists of a promise to sell cheaply" (1968, p. 19). Since he gives no indication to the contrary, Stigler apparently intends that such bidding be regarded as a serious alternative to regulation under actual market circumstances—which is to say under conditions of market and technological uncertainty. Failure to refer to recurrent bidding also suggests that the bidding scheme proposed is of the once-for-all variety.[8]

Once-for-all contracts of two types can be distinguished: complete contingent claims contracts and incomplete contracts. The former require that each prospective franchisee specify the terms (prices) at which he is prepared to supply service now and, if price changes are to be made in response to uncertain future events, the conditional terms under which he will supply service in the future. It is generally appreciated that complete contracts of this kind are impossibly complex to write, negotiate, and enforce (Radner, 1968). The underlying transactional disabilities have been set out elsewhere (Williamson, 1975, Chap. 2; Williamson, Wachter, and Harris, 1975).

Given the infeasibility of complete contingent claims contracts, incomplete once-for-all contracts might be considered. Contractual incompleteness, however, is not without cost. Although incomplete once-for-all contracts are feasible in the sense that bounded rationality constraints are satisfied, such contracts pose hazards by increasing the risk of opportunism. The problems here are substantially those discussed below in conjunction with incomplete long-term contracts.

□ **Incomplete long-term contracts.** Demsetz evidently has in mind that franchise awards be of a long-term kind in which adaptations to unanticipated developments are accomplished by permitting renegotiation of terms subject to penalty clauses (1968, pp. 64–65). Such renegotiation would be unnecessary, of course, if the parties to the contract could agree, at the outset, to deal with unanticipated events and to resolve conflicts by employing a joint profit maximizing decision rule, thereafter to share the gains of the resulting adaptation. General agreements to this effect are not self-enforcing, however, unless the profit consequences are fully known to both of the parties and can be displayed, at low cost, to an impartial arbitrator. Absent this, each party will be inclined, when the unanticipated events occur, to manipulate the data in a way that favors its interests (Williamson, 1975, pp. 31–33, 91–93).

---

[8] Possibly, however, Stigler intends that Demsetz' discussion of renegotiation and/or rebidding should apply. Demsetz' treatment of these matters appears below.

To be sure, aggressive self-interest seeking of a myopic kind is attenuated both by the existence of informal sanctions and by an appreciation between the parties that accommodation yields long-run benefits (Macaulay, 1963). But the hazards of opportunism scarcely vanish of these accounts. Among the problems to be anticipated when incomplete long-term contracts are negotiated under conditions of uncertainty are the following: (1) the initial award criterion is apt to be artificial or obscure; (2) execution problems in price-cost, in other performance, and in political respects are apt to develop; and (3) bidding parity between the incumbent and prospective rivals at the contract renewal interval is unlikely to be realized. Consider these several conditions *seriatim*.

(1) *Artificial or obscure initial award criterion*. The promise to "supply cheaply" is scarcely a well-defined commitment unless the quality of service is well specified and scalar valued bids possess economic merit. Posner recognizes the former and proposes that subscriber preferences regarding quality be ascertained by a preaward solicitation. The mechanics involve (1972, p. 115):

> . . . an "open season" in which all franchise applicants were free to solicit the area's residents for a set period of time. This would not be a poll; the applicants would seek to obtain actual commitments from potential subscribers. At the end of the solicitation period, the commitments received by the various applicants would be compared and the franchise awarded to the applicant whose guaranteed receipts, on the basis of subscriber commitments, were largest. In this fashion the vote of each subscriber would be weighted by his willingness to pay, and the winning applicant would be the one who, in free competition with the other applicants, was preferred by subscribers in the aggregate. To keep the solicitation process honest, each applicant would be required to contract in advance that, in the event he won, he would provide the level of service, and at the rate represented, in his solicitation drive.

The comparability problems that would otherwise be posed if both price and quality were permitted to vary at the final competition stage are thus avoided. The preaward solicitation not only prevents the quality level from being set by a political body, but also relieves the need to choose among disparate price-quality mixes, on grounds that are uncertain, at the final competition.

However imaginative this preaward solicitation process of Posner, it is not obviously practicable. For one thing, it assumes that subscribers are able to assess quality-price packages abstractly and have the time and inclination to do so—which poses a bounded rationality issue.[9] For another, it aggregates preferences in a rather arbitrary way.[10] Finally, it assumes that subscribers will demand that winners

[9] To observe that "customers face and overcome [such problems] daily in choosing among products that differ in quality as well as price" (Posner, 1972, p. 115) is scarcely dispositive. Issues peculiar to the supply of natural monopoly services are not even raised. For example, quality variability of electricity supply is apt to entail voltage variations or prospective supply interruptions, the implications of which are apt to be difficult to assess. Secondly, variable load pricing issues, with which most consumers have little familiarity, may be posed. Third, collective choice issues which do not appear for most consumer goods must be faced in deciding on electricity supply. Fourth, long-term interaction effects between electricity price and substitutes and complements are rather strong, albeit difficult to sort out in the context of hypothetical solicitations.

[10] Thus, if price-quality package A wins the competition, on Posner's criterion, over price-quality mixes B, C, D, and E, where A is a high price, high quality mode and B through E are all variants on a low price-quality mix, does it follow that package A is socially preferred?

provide the level of service at the rate represented or can otherwise obtain satisfaction for failure to perform. This poses execution issues and is discussed in (2) below.[11]

If, additionally, the prices at which service is supplied are to vary with periodic demands—a measure which often has efficient capacity rationing properties for public utility services—a complex variable load pricing schedule, rather than a single lowest bid price, must be solicited. Vector valued bids clearly pose award difficulties.

The upshot is that, although franchise awards can be reduced to a lowest bid price criterion, this is apt to be artificial if the future is uncertain and the service in question is at all complex. Such awards are apt to be arbitrary and/or pose the hazard that "adventurous" bids will be tendered by those who are best suited or most inclined to assume political risks. Again, this gives rise to execution issues, to which we now turn.

(2) *Execution problems.* Even if contract award issues of the kinds described above either were absent or could be dismissed as *de minimis*, we would still have to face problems of contract execution. It is at the execution stage and in conjunction with contract renewal that the convergence of franchise bidding to public utility regulation is especially evident.

I assume, for the purposes of this subsection, that there is a strong presumption that the winner of the bidding competition will be the supplier of the public utility service over the entire contract period. Only in the event of egregious and persistent malperformance would an effort be made to replace the winning franchisee.

The assumption is supported by the following considerations. First, the award of a long-term contract plainly contemplates that the winner will be the supplier over a considerable period. A leading reason to make the contract long term is to provide the supplier with requisite incentives to install long-lived assets.[12] If any slight failure to perform in accordance with the franchisor's expectations would occasion rescission of the franchise, the long-term contract would be a fiction and its investment purposes vitiated.

The prospect of litigation delays and expenses also discourages an effort to displace a franchisee. Moreover, even if such an effort were successful, nontrivial transition costs would be incurred. (These are discussed further in (3) below.) Finally, franchise award agencies, like other bureaucracies, are loath to concede or be accused of error. As Eckstein puts it, publicly accountable decision makers "acquire political and psychological stakes in their own decisions and develop a justificatory rather than a critical attitude towards them" (1956, p. 223). Since displacement may be interpreted as a public admission of

[11] Similar problems arise with respect to the matter of who in the community is to be supplied service and at what connection costs: Connect everybody who requests it at a flat charge? Only those who live in areas where connected service exceeds some threshold? Anyone who bears his own incremental costs? Although a single standard can be stipulated by the contracting agency, is this optimal and ought such a connection standard to remain fixed for the duration of the contract?

[12] The short-term contracting procedure favored by Posner contemplates the transfer of long-lived assets from the winning franchisee to a successor firm. Appropriate investment incentives would thereby be realized. For the reasons developed in (3) below, I am skeptical of the properties of the asset transfer procedure described by Posner.

error, franchise award agencies predictably prefer, when faced with malperformance, to negotiate a "compromise" solution instead.

Price-cost relations. In circumstances in which long-term contracts are executed under conditions of uncertainty, fixed price bids are apt to be rather unsatisfactory. If the environment is characterized by uncertainty with respect to technology, demand, local factor supply conditions, inflation, and the like, price-cost divergences and/or indeterminacies will develop.

To be sure, some of these divergences can be reduced by introducing price flexibility by formula (Fuller and Braucher, 1964, pp. 77–78; Goldberg, 1975, p. 19). Adjustment for changes in the price in response to some index of prices is one possibility. This, however, is a relatively crude correction and unlikely to be satisfactory where there is rapid technical change or where local conditions deviate significantly from the index population. More precise tracking of prices to costs will be realized if, instead of fixed price contracts, cost plus (or cost sharing) contracts are negotiated. All of the difficulties associated with the execution of defense contracts of the cost sharing kind then appear, however (Scherer, 1964; Williamson, 1967). Problems of auditing and of defective incentives are especially severe. (These, it will be noted, are disabilities associated with regulation. Franchise bidding is designed to overcome them.)

Other performance attributes. A lack of specificity in the contract with respect to the quality of service and a failure to stipulate monitoring and accounting procedures accords latitude to franchisees during contract execution. Despite *ex ante* assurances to the contrary, franchisees can rarely be made to fulfill the spirit of an agreement if net revenues are enhanced by adhering to the letter of the contract only (CTIC, 1972a, p. 11). Moreover, technical standards, by themselves, are not self-enforcing; enforcement requires that a policing apparatus be devised (CTIC, 1973, p. 7). Since individual consumers are unlikely to have the data or competence to evaluate the quality of service in a discriminating way (Goldberg, 1976) and since both setup cost and specialization of labor economies will be realized by assigning the quality evaluation function to a specialized agency, centralization is indicated. But again, the convergence toward regulation should be noted.[13]

It may not be sufficient, moreover, merely to specify a common quality standard for all bidders. Thus, suppose that one bidder proposes to achieve the specified quality target by installing high performance, long-lived equipment, that a second proposes to have backup equipment ready in the event of breakdown, and that the third claims that he will invest heavily in maintenance personnel. Although only one of these may fully satisfy the requirements, both subscribers and the franchising agency may lack the *ex ante* capacity to discern which. Granting the franchise to the low bidder only to discover that

[13] The Cable Television Information Center expresses the issue as follows (1973, p. 7):

[T]echnical standards do not enforce themselves. Enforcement requires testing the system, evaluation of the tests, and deciding upon corrective actions required. These activities add to the administrative burden of regulation. A franchising authority should not adopt standards unless it is willing to shoulder the burden of enforcement.

he is unable to perform as described is plainly unsatisfactory. Although penalty clauses in contracts can help forestall such outcomes, it is often the case—as the history of defense contracting suggests—that successful bidders are able to have terms renegotiated to their advantage.

Accounting ambiguities coupled with the disinclination of franchising agencies to allow winning bidders to fail permit franchisees to use accounting data in a strategic way—to include the threat of bankruptcy—during renegotiations. The introduction of monitoring and accounting control techniques can prevent such outcomes, but this measure then joins the winning bidder and the franchising agency in a quasi-regulatory relationship.

Politics. In circumstances in which renegotiation is common and perhaps vital to the profitable operation of a franchise, political skills assume special importance. Prospective suppliers who possess superior skills in least cost supply respects but who are relatively inept in dealing with the franchising bureaucracy and in influencing the political process are unlikely to submit winning bids.[14] To the extent that political skills override objective economic skills, the advantages of franchising over regulation are placed in question.

Indeed, if franchisees are subject to less stringent profit controls than regulated firms (where the latter are subject to rate of return constraints), it may well be that franchising encourages greater political participation. The argument here is that the incentive to invest private resources to influence political decisions varies directly with the degree to which the resulting advantages can be privately appropriated—and that franchised firms have an appropriability advantage in this respect.[15]

(3) *Lack of bidding parity during contract renewal.* Lest meaningful competition at the contract renewal interval be upset, participation in contract execution should not place winners of the original competition at a substantial advantage over nonwinners. As discussed generally elsewhere (Peacock and Rowley, 1972, p. 242; Williamson, 1975, pp. 26–35), however, and as expressly developed in the context of CATV in the following subsection, there are reasons to believe that bidding parity at contract renewal intervals will not obtain.

□ **Recurrent short-term contracts.** A leading advantage of recurrent short-term contracting over long-term contracting is that short-term contracts facilitate adaptive, sequential decisionmaking. The requirements that contingencies be comprehensively described and appropriate adaptations to each worked out in advance are thereby avoided. Rather, the future is permitted to unfold and adaptations are introduced, at contract renewal intervals, only to those events which actually materialize. Put differently, bridges are crossed one (or a few) at a time, as specific events occur. As compared with the

[14] Note that a merger between parties who possess economic qualifications and those with political skills yields private and probably social gains in these circumstances. Such a merger actually occurred in the case study reported in Section 4.

[15] This assumes that regulation is not a farce and that management engrossing is strictly limited under regulation. Note also that the argument assumes that the *marginal* net gains of influencing the political process are greater under the franchise mode. For a discussion of politics and regulation, see Alfred Kahn (1971, pp. 326–327).

contingent claims contracting requirement that the complete decision tree be generated, so that all possible bridges are crossed in advance, the adaptive, sequential decisionmaking procedure economizes greatly on bounded rationality.

Additionally, under the assumption that competition at the contract renewal interval is efficacious, the hazards of contractual incompleteness which beset incomplete long-term contracts are avoided. Failure to define contractual terms appropriately gives rise, at most, to malperformance during the duration of the current short-term contract. Indeed, recognizing that a bidding competition will be held in the near future, winning bidders may be more inclined to cooperate with the franchising authority, if specific contractual deficiencies are noted, rather than use such occasions to realize temporary bargaining advantages.[16] Opportunism is thereby curbed as well.[17]

The efficacy of recurrent short-term contracting depends crucially, however, on the assumption that *parity among bidders at the contract renewal interval is realized.*[18] Posner faces and disposes of this issue (1972, p. 116):

> [T]he fact that the cable company's plant normally will outlast the period of its franchise raises a question: Will not the cable company be able to outbid any new applicant, who would have to build a plant from scratch? And will not the bargaining method therefore be ineffective after the first round? Not necessarily: in bidding for the franchise on the basis of new equipment costs, new applicants need not be at a significant disadvantage in relation to the incumbent franchisee. For example, once a new applicant is franchised he could negotiate to purchase the system of the existing franchisee, who is faced with the loss of the unamortized portion of his investment if his successor builds a new system. Insofar as the economic life of a cable plant is considered a problem when the franchise term is short, it can be solved by including in the franchise a provision requiring the franchisee, at the successor's option, to sell his plant (including improvements) to the latter at its original cost, as depreciated.

I find these views overly sanguine. For one thing, equipment valuation problems are apt to be rather more complex than Posner's remarks suggest. Secondly, Posner focuses entirely on nonhuman capital; the possibility that human capital problems also exist is nowhere acknowledged. To be sure, human asset benefits which accrue during contract execution and which give incumbents an advantage over outsiders will, if anticipated, be reflected in the original

[16] This assumes that winning bidders are not fly-by-night operators, but instead are interested in remaining in the business on a continuing basis. Other things being equal, the franchising authority can be expected to continue with the current supplier or shift to a new supplier at the contract renewal interval depending on its experience with the current winner during the contract period.

[17] Similar considerations have a bearing on the performance of the franchising agency. Posner puts the argument as follows (1972, pp. 115–116):

> [If] the duration of the franchise . . . is long, the parties may not have foreseen all of the circumstances that might require modification of its terms. Although this is a problem common to all contracts, the peculiarity here is that one of the contracting parties is not a true party in interest but a public body charged with overseeing the interest of the other parties (subscribers). Experience with regulatory agencies suggests that one cannot assume such a body will represent the consumer interest faithfully. When the cable company asks for a modification of the contract by virtue of an unforeseen change in circumstances, the public body may react ineffectually or perversely.

With short duration contracts, "no modification of . . . terms need be entertained" (Posner, 1972, p. 116), in which event the distortions referred to are avoided.

[18] For prior discussions of bidding parity and its absence at contract renewal intervals, see Peacock and Rowley (1972, p. 242) and Williamson (1975, pp. 26–35).

bidding competition. But "buying in" can be risky and the price tracking properties of such strategies are easily inferior to average cost pricing in resource allocation respects. The upshot is that recurrent bidding (at, say, four-year intervals) is riddled with contractual indeterminacies.

Concern over plant and equipment valuation is, of course, mitigated if the investments in question are relatively unspecialized. I conjecture that this is the case for Demsetz' automobile license plate example. If, with only minor modifications, general purpose equipment (for the cutting, stamping, painting, etc.) can produce license plates efficiently, then a franchisee who fails to win the renewal contract can productively employ most of this same equipment for other purposes, while the new winner can, at slight cost, modify his own plant and equipment to produce the annual requirement efficiently.

Alternatively, concern over plant and equipment poses no problem if its useful life is exhausted during the contract execution interval. As Posner's remarks suggest, however, and as is generally conceded, it is inefficient to install utility plant and equipment of such short duration.

Unlike Demsetz' license plate manufacturers, moreover, most utility services (gas, water, electricity, telephone) require that *specialized* plant and equipment be put in place. The same is true of CATV. Since the construction of parallel systems is wasteful and since to require this to be done would place outside bidders at a disadvantage at the contract renewal interval, some method of transferring assets from existing franchisees to successor firms plainly needs to be worked out.

Posner contends that this can be handled by stipulating that plant and equipment be sold to the successor firm, at its option, at the original cost less depreciation of the predecessor franchisee. Consistent with his emphasis on fundamental policy choices, Posner declines to supply the details. Unfortunately, however, the details are troublesome.

For one thing, original cost can be manipulated by the predecessor firm. For another, even if depreciation accounting procedures are specified under the original franchise terms, implementation may still be contested. Third, original cost less depreciation at best sets an upper bound—and perhaps not even this, since inflation issues are not faced—on the valuation of plant and equipment. The successor franchisee may well offer less, in which case costly haggling ensues. Finally, even if no disputes eventuate, Posner's procedures merely provide a legal rule for transferring assets. He does not address the economic properties of the procedures in investment incentive and utilization respects.

Whether the accounting records of original costs can be accepted as recorded depends in part on whether the equipment was bought on competitive terms. The original franchisee who is integrated backwards into equipment supply or who arranges a kickback from an equipment supplier can plainly rig the prices to the disadvantage of rival bidders at the contract renewal interval. Furthermore, and related, the original cost should also include the labor expense of installing plant and equipment. To the extent, however, that the allocation of labor expense between operating and capital categories is not unambiguous, the original winner can capitalize certain labor expenses to the disadvantage of would-be successors. Auditing can be employed to limit these distortions, but this has the appearance of regulation. Even if carefully done, moreover, the results are apt to be disputed. Inasmuch as information on true valuation is asymmetrically distributed to the disadvantage of outside parties, the burden of showing excess capitalization falls heavily on the would-be new supplier.

Reaching agreement on depreciation charges, which are notoriously difficult to define (especially if obsolescence is a problem and maintenance expenditures can be manipulated in a strategic manner), poses similar problems. Therefore, costly arbitration, for both original equipment valuation and depreciation reasons, is apt to ensue.[19] Rate base valuations of a regulatory kind thereby obtain.

---

[19] The City of Los Angeles anticipated such difficulties in its ordinance on franchise award and execution (Ordinance No. 58,200). The ordinance stipulates that the City has a right to purchase the property of a franchise or find a purchaser therefore and further provides that

. . . in the event said franchise shall expire by operation of law, said city shall have the right, at its option, declared not more than one (1) year before the expiration of the franchise term as herein fixed, which right an option is hereby reserved to said city, to purchase and take over the property of such utility, and in the event that said city shall so exercise its right under such option the said city shall pay to the said grantee the fair value of the property of such utility as herein provided.

(d) The term "fair value" as used herein shall be construed to mean the reasonable value of the property of such utility having regard to its condition of repair and its adaptability and capacity for the use for which it shall have been originally intended. The price to be paid by the City for any utility shall be on the basis of actual cost to the utility for the property taken, less depreciation accrued, as of the date of purchase, with due allowance for obsolescense, if any, and the efficiency of its units to perform the duties imposed on them; no allowance shall be made for franchise value, good will, going concern, earning power, increased cost of reproduction or increased value of right of way or allowance for damages by reasons of severance.

(e) That the valuation of the property of such utility proposed to be purchased upon the termination of said franchise as herein provided, or otherwise, shall be determined by a board of three arbitrators of whom one shall be appointed by the city, one by the grantee, and the third by the two arbitrators so appointed. Said arbitrators shall be appointed within thirty days after the declaration by the city of its option to purchase said property of such utility, or to find a purchaser therefor. In case said arbitrators fail to make and file an award within the time hereinafter limited, a new board of three arbitrators shall be appointed as hereinbefore prescribed. The board of arbitrators shall immediately upon the appointment of its members enter upon the discharge of its duties. Any vacancy in the board of arbitrators shall be filled by the party who made the original appointment to the vacant place.

(f) In the event the grantee shall fail to appoint an arbitrator within thirty days after the declaration by the city of its option to purchase the property of such utility or to find a purchase therefor, or in the event of the death or resignation of such arbitrator so appointed and such grantee, its successors or assigns, shall fail to appoint an arbitrator to fill such vacancy within ten (10) days thereafter, or in the event the two arbitrators appointed by the city and grantee, as hereinbefore provided, shall fail to appoint a third arbitrator within sixty (60) days after the declaration of the city of its option to purchase the property of such utility, or to find a purchase therefor, then upon application made either by the city, or by said grantee after (5) days' notice in writing to the other party, such arbitrator shall be appointed by the presiding Judge of the Superior Court of the State of California, in and for the County of Los Angeles, and the arbitrators so appointed shall have the same powers and duties as though he had been appointed in the manner hereinabove prescribed.

(g) The award of the arbitrators must be made and filed with the City Clerk of said city within three (3) months after their appointment, and a majority of the arbitrators who agree thereto may make such award.

Indeed, the valuation of physical assets is predictably more severe under franchise bidding than under regulation. For one thing, earnings in the regulated firm are a product of the rate base and the realized rate of return. Clearly, the regulated firm can be conciliatory about the rate base if in exchange it receives allowable rate of return concessions. Additionally, the regulatory agency and regulated firm are prospectively joined in a long series of negotiations. Errors made by either party on one round are less critical if these can be remedied at the next rate review interval (or if, in a crisis, interim relief can be anticipated). More is at stake with asset valuation under franchise bidding, since degrees of freedom of both rate of return and intertemporal kinds are missing. Accordingly, more contentious bargaining leading to litigation is to be expected.

A related difficulty with Pósner's physical asset valuation scheme is that it merely sets an upper bound. Inasmuch, however, as procurement on these terms is left to the successor firm's option, there is little reason to expect this figure to prevail. Without stipulating more, the successor firm would presumably offer to buy the specialized plant and equipment at its value in its best alternative (nonfranchised) use. This will normally be a small fraction of the depreciated original cost. Predecessor and successor firms thus find themselves confronted with a wide bargaining range within which to reach an exchange agreement. Since competitive forces sufficient to drive the parties to a unique agreement are lacking, additional haggling (which is a social cost) can be anticipated. Albeit vexing, the details, which are neglected by Posner, nevertheless matter; the frictionless transfer on which he appears to rely is simply not to be had on the terms described.

Conceivably superior asset valuation and franchise bidding schemes can be devised which mitigate these problems.[20] It is patently incumbent, however, on those who believe that large numbers competition can be made effective at the contract renewal interval to come forward with the requisite operational details. Without such specificity, one must consider dubious the contention that low cost reassignment of physical assets can be effected at the contract renewal interval for franchised services which require specialized and long-lived plant and equipment to be installed. Rather, nontrivial haggling and litigation expenses appear to infect Posner's proposal.

Moreover, human asset problems, which Posner and Demsetz fail even to mention, also need to be faced. Again, the matter of fungibility arises. To the extent that the skills of operating the franchise are widely available or, alternatively, that employees of the incumbent firm deal with rival bidders and the incumbent's owners on identical terms, no problems of this kind appear. If, however, nontrivial spec-

For a discussion of franchise valuations of a similar kind in connection with New York City's award of CATV franchises, see CTIC (1972a, pp. 16–17).

[20] One possibility is for each willing bidder, at the contract renewal interval, to indicate his asset valuation at the time he enters his bid on the quality and price of service. The problem here is that asset valuations and service bids are not independent. Franchisees will be prepared to pay dearly for assets if in the process they can charge a high price.

Other schemes might be explored (see note 19, *supra*) and possibly some can be shown to have attractive properties. It is plainly the case, however, that a good deal of hard thinking about the mechanics of the asset valuation process is needed before the rebidding scheme can be considered complete.

ialized skills and knowledge accrue to individuals and small groups as a result of on-the-job training and experience, the first of these conditions is violated. If, additionally, employees resist transfer of ownership in the bidding competition, rivals are put to a disadvantage.

The matter of nonfungibility of labor has been discussed elsewhere by Friedrich Hayek (1945, pp. 521–522) and Jacob Marschak (1968, p. 14) and has been addressed in the context of task idiosyncracy by Peter Doeringer and Michael Piore (1971, pp. 15–16) and by Williamson, Wachter, and Harris (1975). The thrust of this literature is that significant differences sometimes develop between experienced and inexperienced workers in the following respects: (1) equipment idiosyncracies, due to highly specialized or incompletely standardized, albeit common, equipment, are "revealed" only to experienced workers; (2) processing economies of an idiosyncratic kind are fashioned or "adopted" by managers and workers in specific operating contexts; (3) informal team accommodations, attributable to mutual adaptation among parties engaged in recurrent contact, develop and are upset, to the possible detriment of group performance, when the membership is altered; and (4) communication idiosyncracies evolve (with respect, for example, to information channels and codes), but are of value only in an operating context where the parties are familiar with each other and share a common language.

As a consequence, it is often inefficient fully or extensively to displace the experienced labor and management group that is employed by the winner of the initial franchise award. Familiarizing another group with the idiosyncracies of the operation and developing the requisite team production and communication skills are costly. Accordingly, incumbent employees, who alone possess the idiosyncratic knowledge needed to realize least-cost supply, are powerfully situated to block a franchise reassignment effort.

The cost disadvantage referred to will obtain, however, only insofar as incumbent employees deal with the current ownership and outside bidders differently. The strategic advantage which they enjoy in relation to inexperienced but otherwise qualified employees is one which can be exercised against both the current owner and his bidding rivals alike. The issue thus comes down to whether current and prospective owners are treated differently at the contract renewal interval.[21] I conjecture that they will be. The main reason is that *informal* understandings (with respect to job security, promotional expectations, and other aspects of internal due process) are much

[21] Relevant in this connection is the following issue: Why have incumbent employees failed to exploit fully their idiosyncratic advantage over inexperienced employees during the contract execution period—in which event there is no unliquidated idiosyncratic gain to be differentially awarded at the contract renewal interval? A distinction between moving equilibrium and discrete bargaining behavior is relevant in this connection. For one thing, there may be adjustment lags in the system which are tolerated during the operating period but for which correction is possible at the contract renewal interval. For another, collective action is necessary to appropriate the idiosyncratic gains. Enterprise owners may work out a *modus vivendi* with managers and labor representatives in which management and labor, in exchange for ownership support (including job security, emoluments, etc.), consciously decline to absorb the full idiosyncratic gain. Out of recognition that the "leadership" is in this together, a reserve of unliquidated idiosyncratic gain has strategic advantages.

easier to reach and enforce in familiar circumstances than in unfamiliar ones.[22]

This is not to say that employees cannot or will not strike bargains with outsiders, but rather that such bargains will be more costly to reach, because much more attention to explicit detail will be required, or that there is greater risk associated with an informal (incompletely specified) agreement with outsiders. Where additional detail is sought, outsiders will be at a disadvantage in relation to insiders, because the costs of reaching agreement are increased. If, instead, employees are asked to trust the outsider to behave "responsibly" or, alternatively, the outsider agrees to accept the interpretation placed on incomplete agreements by the employees when unanticipated events not expressly covered by the employment contract develop, the implied risks are great and corresponding premia will find their way, directly or indirectly, into the bid price. As a consequence, idiosyncratic employment attributes coupled with the inability of outsiders to reach equivalent agreements at equal expense place original franchisees at an advantage at the contract renewal interval. Thus, human capital considerations compound the bidding difficulties which physical asset valuation problems pose. To contend that bidding parity can be expected at the contract renewal interval is accordingly suspect for this reason as well. Put differently, if original winners of the bidding competition realize nontrivial advantages in informational and informal organizational respects during contract execution, bidding parity at the contract renewal interval can no longer be presumed. Rather, what was once a large numbers bidding situation, at the time the original franchise was awarded, *is converted into what is tantamount to a small numbers bargaining situation* when the franchise comes up for renewal.

Contracting schemes which avoid these risks, which have superior price tracking properties, and which do not experience offsetting disabilities are plainly to be preferred. Since both the risk bearing and price tracking properties of regulation are arguably superior to those of franchise bidding, and if franchise bidding in practice is, in most other respects, difficult to distinguish from regulation, the net gain of franchise bidding over regulation is not transparent.[23]

It might be argued, of course, that the incumbency advantage will be anticipated at the outset, in which event discounted certainty equivalent profits will be bid down to zero by large numbers competition for the original award. This is not, however, an entirely satisfactory answer. For one thing, to come in at a price below cost for the initial award (perhaps even a negative price) and to set price at the level of alternative cost at contract renewal intervals easily result in resource utilization of an inferior kind. Additionally, buying-in

[22] For a sociological discussion of some of the problems of succession, see Gouldner (1954). Macneil observes that "the elements of trust demanded by participant views of relations make identity important, and simple transfer therefore unlikely" (1974, p. 791).

[23] A distinctive limitation of regulation, to which franchise bidding is presumably less subject, is the proclivity of regulators progressively to expand the reach of regulation to include "ancillary" activities. More generally, the greater autonomy and degree of specialization associated with regulation, as compared with franchise bidding agencies, may have unfavorable long-run rigidity consequences. In particular, regulatory authorities are apt to resist vigorously anything which threatens their demise.

strategies are risky. The alternative supply price can be influenced by the terms the franchisor sets on subsequent rounds, including terms that may obsolete the learning by doing advantages of incumbents.

□ **A summing up.** Once-for-all bidding schemes of the contingent claims contracting kind are infeasible and/or pose execution hazards. Incomplete long-term contracts of the type envisaged by Demsetz alleviate the first of these problems but aggravate the second. A whole series of difficulties long familiar to students of defense contracting and regulation appears. The upshot is that franchise bidding for incomplete long-term contracts is a much more dubious undertaking than Demsetz' discussion suggests.

Posner's proposal that franchise terms be kept short is designed to overcome the adaptability problems associated with incomplete long-term contracts, but his discussion is insufficiently microanalytic and/or critical of the disabilities of short-term contracts to expose their shortcomings. The fundamental limitation of the argument is that, despite Posner's procedural stipulations (1972, p. 116), bidding parity at the contract renewal interval between the original winner and rival successor firms cannot safely be presumed. To the contrary, there are reasons to doubt such parity, in which case the adaptability and price to cost properties that Posner associates with recurrent contracting[24] are not to be had on the frictionless (or low cost) terms he describes.

To be sure, some of the difficulties which infect the Posner proposal can be mitigated by introducing an extensive regulatory/arbitration apparatus. Assessing plant and equipment installations, auditing related accounting records, and arbitrating disputes between incumbent and rival firms over physical asset valuations are illustrative. But then franchise bidding and regulation differ only in degree.

It is perhaps unsurprising, in view of the foregoing, that Posner's recurrent bidding proposal has not been widely adopted. Rather, most CATV franchise awards are for ten to fifteen years, and contractual incompleteness has been handled by progressively elaborating a regulatory structure (CTIC, 1972c, pp. 9–12)—a result which conceivably reflects a desire by CATV operators to insulate themselves from the rigors of competition. I submit, however, that the drift toward regulation is also explained by performance defects associated with CATV franchise awards which are caused in part by contractual incompleteness (CTIC, 1972c, p. 9).

Still, the contractual incompleteness defects described above might conceivably be remedied by progressively refining CATV awards in the future. Stipulating appropriate penalties for unsatisfactory performance and setting out complex conditional responses to contingent events may serve to promote efficient adaptation and mitigate haggling expenses. Elaborating the contract in these respects is not costless, however, and franchising agencies often lack the resolve to exact penalties as prescribed.[25] Although times have surely

[24] The basic argument is that "[e]ach bidder would submit a plan of service and schedule of rates. As long as there was more than one bidder and collusion among the bidders was prevented—conditions that ought not to be insuperably difficult to secure—the process of bidding subscriber rates down and quality of service up would eliminate monopoly pricing and profits" (Posner, 1972, p. 115).

[25] Note, moreover, that not only are contract remedies "among the weakest of

changed for the better, it is sobering to note that the limits of franchise contracts were described some 70 years ago as follows (Fisher, 1907, pp. 39–40):

> Regulation does not end with the formulation and adoption of a satisfactory contract, in itself a considerable task. If this were all, a few wise and honest men might, once in a generation supervise the framing of a franchise in proper form, and nothing further would be necessary. It is a current fallacy and the common practice in American public life to assume that a constitution or a statute or a charter, once properly drawn up by intelligent citizens and adopted by an awakened public, is self-executing and that the duty of good citizens ends with the successful enactment of some such well matured plan. But repeated experience has demonstrated—what should have been always apparent—the absolute futility of such a course, and the disastrous consequences of reliance upon a written document for the purposes of living administration. As with a constitution, a statute, or a charter, so with a franchise. It has been found that such an agreement is not self-enforcing. . . . [Moreover, the] administration may ignore or fail to enforce compliance with those essential parts of a contract entrusted to its executive authority; and legal proceedings . . . are frequently unavoidable long before the time of the franchise has expired.

At the risk of oversimplification, regulation may be described contractually as a highly incomplete form of long-term contracting in which (1) the regulatee is assured an overall fair rate of return, in exchange for which (2) adaptations to changing circumstances are successively introduced without the costly haggling that attends such changes when parties to the contract enjoy greater autonomy. Whether net gains are thereby realized turns on the extent to which the disincentive effects of the former (which may be checked in some degree by performance audits and by mobilizing competition in the capital market forces (Williamson, 1972)) are more than offset by the gains from the latter. This is apt to vary with the degree to which the industry is subject to uncertainties of market and technological kinds.

4. A case study

■ Although the case study reported below cannot claim to be representative, it does reveal that many of the franchise concerns discussed in the previous section are not purely imaginary.[26] The study both

---

those the legal system can deliver, [b]ut a host of doctrines and techniques lies in the way even of those remedies" (Macneil, 1974, p. 730). Until franchisers and the legal system can be persuaded to behave otherwise, it is fatuous to contend that franchisees can be induced to behave in ideal ways by the introduction of a complex set of penalty clauses.

[26] It is also noteworthy that many of the franchising concerns reported by the Cable Television Information Center are consonant with those set out in Section 3. Among the concerns and recommendations of the CTIC are the following (CTIC, 1972a):

> (1) The renewal period has proven to be a period of great pressure on the city, with the cable operator often threatening to discontinue service immediately unless renewal is promised (p. 16).
> (2) The franchising authority will . . . want to include buyback provisions as part of its effort to insure continuity of service. The provision should include . . . a method of evaluation or termination (S. 4, p. 6).
> (3) [The] right of transfer should be limited at the initial stages of the systems' development, and perhaps flatly forbidden before construction, to avoid trafficking in franchise awards (p. 17).
> (4) Results of system performance and tests should be submitted periodically to ensure the system's quality (p. 24).
> (5) [Day to day regulation involves] considering consumer complaints and passing on requests for rate increases (p. 25).
> (6) Once a procedure has been developed for considering rate changes, the proposed

indicates the importance of evaluating proposals to scrap regulation in favor of market alternatives in more microanalytic terms and discloses that, in practice, franchise bidding for CATV (and presumably other public utility services) has many of the qualities of regulation.

□ **The Oakland CATV experience.** On June 19, 1969, the Council of the City of Oakland, California, passed a city ordinance which provided for the granting of community antenna television franchises. The main features of the ordinance, for the purposes of this paper, were:[27]

(1) the franchise award was to be nonexclusive;
(2) the franchise duration was not to exceed twenty years;
(3) the City was authorized to terminate a franchisee for noncompliance after thirty days' notice and a public hearing;
(4) the franchisee was directed to supply a complete financial statement to the City annually and the City was given the right to inspect the franchisee's records;
(5) the City had the right to acquire the CATV system at the cost of reproduction;
(6) the City Manager was authorized to adjust, settle, or compromise any controversy that might arise among the City, the franchisee, or subscribers, although aggrieved parties could appeal to the City Council;
(7) failure to comply with time requirements of the franchise were grounds for termination;
(8) inasmuch as failure to comply with time requirements would result in damages that would be costly to assess, an automatic fine of seven hundred and fifty dollars per day would be imposed for each day beyond the three-year target completion date that the franchisee took to install the system;
(9) any property of the franchisee that was abandoned in place would become the property of the City;
(10) a surety bond of one hundred thousand dollars was to be obtained by the franchisee and renewed annually;
(11) property of the franchisee was to be subject to inspection by the City;
(12) the CATV system was to be installed and maintained in accordance with the "highest and best accepted standards" of the industry.

Operationalizing the bidding process. The above constituted the basic legislative authority and ground rules. Rather, however, than solicit bids immediately, the Department of General Services engaged instead in a set of preliminary discussions with prospective franchisees.[28] Simultaneously, community groups were requested to advise the City on the types of services to be offered. The resulting

changes are to be measured against the standard of what is fair to the system and to the subscribing public (p. 30).

(7) One of the most neglected areas in ordinances has been enforcement. Mechanisms such as arbitration, provision for leaseback, and the ability to seek court action will aid in achieving the type of Cable system the community wants (p. 45).

[27] City of Oakland, Ordinance No. 7989 C.M.S., June 19, 1969.

[28] The dialogue period was described to me by Mark Leh, Assistant Manager of Electrical Services of the Department of General Services, Oakland.

dialogue was intended to elicit information regarding cost, demand characteristics, technical capabilities, etc., and would help define the "basic service," which would then be stipulated in the contract. Comparability among bids for a standardized service would thereby be facilitated.

Ten months later, on April 30, 1970, the City of Oakland apprised five applicants that the City would receive their amended applications to construct, operate, and maintain a nonexclusive CATV system franchise within the City. The main features, for the purposes of this paper, of the invitation to bid were:[29]

(1) Two systems were to be provided:
 (a) System A, which is the basic system, would permit the subscriber to receive the entire FM radio band plus twelve TV channels distributed as follows: nine local off-the-air channels; one or more newly created local origination channels; and one channel assigned to the City and School District. Payment of a monthly charge of "*X*" plus connection charges (see items (5) and (6), below) would permit the subscriber to receive System A.
 (b) System B would provide special programming and other services. The mix of programming and other services were left unspecified, however. The charges for System B were to be determined later by the franchisee with the approval of the City Council.

(2) All areas within the city limits of the City of Oakland were to be served.

(3) Franchise duration was set at fifteen years.

(4) The franchisee was to make annual payments to the City of 8 percent of gross receipts or $125,000, whichever was greater.[30]

(5) Connection charges for each of four customer classes[31] were stipulated, and thus common for all bidders. It was further stipulated that no additional fee be charged to the subscriber for switches or converters needed to receive System A.

(6) The basic bid consisted of designating the monthly fee "*X*" which would be charged to each subscriber for the first TV and FM outlet connected in his living unit, with an additional monthly charge of $0.2X$ to be paid for each additional outlet in his living unit. This would entitle the subscriber to receive System A.

(7) The franchisee was to provide the City and School District with certain free connections and services, including studio facilities for originating programming for up to twenty hours per week.

(8) The system to be installed was to be a dual cable system, and

---

[29] City of Oakland, "Invitation to Submit Amended Applications for a Community Antenna Television System Franchise," April 30, 1970.

[30] The $125,000 figure was built up in successive $25,000 annual increments, starting with zero in 1970 and reaching $125,000 in 1975, thereafter to continue at this level.

[31] The four customer classes were: noncommercial housed in buildings with less than four living units; noncommercial housed in multiple unit apartments, motels, hotels; commercial; and special, including low density users. The installation charge was $10 for noncommercial subscribers housed in buildings with less than four living units.

each of the cables was to be capable of carrying the equivalent of thirty-two video channels. A series of minimum technical specifications concerning signal quality, cable characteristics, installation methods, automatic controls, etc., were stipulated.

(9) Service requirements were described in general terms. The details were to be defined by the franchisee subject to Council approval.

(10) The system was to be 25 percent complete within eighteen months of franchise acceptance, with an additional 25 percent being completed in each succeeding six month period, so that the system would be fully completed in three years.

(11) Proposals to raise rates to subscribers could be submitted annually. (No indexing or other criteria were offered in this connection.)

Bid acceptance. Bids were made on July 1, 1970, the lowest being the bid of Focus Cable of Oakland, Inc., which stipulated an "*X*" (see items (1) and (6), above) of $1.70 per month.[32] The next lowest bid was by Cablecom-General of Northern California, which set a rate of $3.48.[33] The TelePrompTer Corporation bid was $5.95 (Libman, 1974, p. 34).

Focus Cable apprised the City at the time of its bid that Tele-Communications, Inc. of Denver, Colorado, whose participation had been vital to the qualification of Focus as an applicant, had elected to withdraw from the Focus Cable proposal.[34] Focus Cable reorganized the corporation under the laws of California and included a copy of the Articles of Incorporation, dated July 1, 1970, with its bid. Inasmuch as Focus had entered the lowest bid (by a factor of two), was the only local bidder, and represented an ethnic minority,[35] the City was reluctant to reject their bid for lack of financial capability and technical qualifications. However, awarding the franchise to Focus plainly posed hazards.

It appeared that these were greatly mitigated when TelePrompTer Corporation proposed on July 16, 1970, to enter into a joint venture with Focus Cable to construct and develop the Oakland franchise. As a part of the joint venture, TelePrompTer agreed to provide all needed financing for the project.[36] Why TelePrompTer was prepared to do this at a monthly charge less than 30 percent of its own bid was not disclosed. Presumably, however, the prospect of earning substantial returns on System B was a contributing factor.[37] Focus Cable

[32] Amended Application for a Franchise to Construct, Operate and Maintain a Community Antenna Television System within the City of Oakland submitted by Focus Cable of Oakland, Inc., July 1, 1970.

[33] Memorandum from the City Manger to the City Council, dated September 28, 1970, p. 3.

[34] See note 32, *supra*.

[35] Minority group involvement in cable—in ownership, employment, and programming respects—is prominently featured in the CATV literature (CTIC, 1972c, p. 13). The FCC requires cable operators to establish affirmative action plans (CTIC, 1972a, p. 34).

[36] Letter from Leonard Tow, Vice President of TelePrompTer, Inc., to Harold Farrow of Focus Cable, dated July 16, 1970.

[37] The rate on System B was not included in the original bid but was to be negotiated later. As things worked out, and probably ought to have been anticipated, most subscribers elected to receive System B—at a considerably higher rate than System A.

advised the City of Oakland, in a letter dated July 21, 1970, that "the proposed financing of Focus by TelePrompTer can and will provide the ideal marriage of local investors, CATV expertise, and over-all financial strength to best develop the CATV franchise in Oakland."[38] The Focus contribution to this ideal marriage was its local investor attributes.

The agreement between Focus and TelePrompTer provided that each should have equal ownership at the outset but that TelePrompTer would convert this to a majority interest immediately and could exercise options after the first year which gave it ownership of 80 percent of the capital stock outstanding.[39] The joining of TelePrompTer with Focus was thought to warrant completing the negotiations. A report to the City Council from the City Manager and the City Attorney, dated September 28, 1970, concluded as follows:[40]

> Part of the concept of Systems A and B in the specifications was, by competitive applications, to obtain a rate sufficiently low on System A which would encourage the early development of System B. It is staff opinion that the low rate submitted by Focus would motivate such a development. Also, the low rate will assure the widest utilization of System A by families of all economic means.
>
> Focus is the applicant which has submitted the lowest basic monthly subscriber rate. The question has been raised as to whether Focus meets the specifications due to changes in its organization. From a legal standpoint, the organizational change does not disqualify Focus from further Council consideration. It is staff opinion that the proposed agreements between Focus and TelePrompTer, with the additional guarantees by TelePrompTer, will result in a useful combination of initial local representation with one of the largest and best qualified CATV firms in the United States.

Focus Cable and TelePrompTer Corporation entered into a Subscription Agreement on September 21, 1970, in anticipation of being awarded the franchise. Two hundred shares at ten dollars per share were to be paid for by the organizers of Focus.[41] Additionally, the Agreement provided:[42]

> The Corporation shall purchase equipment and products from TPT [TelePrompTer] for use in its business in preference to other sources to the extent that the quality and workmanship of such equipment and products are comparable to such other sources. If TPT shall sell any such equipment or products to the Corporation, the price to be charged shall not exceed an amount which would be reasonably comparable to the charge for like equipment and products if obtained from an independent supplier dealing on an arm's length basis.

The Subscription Agreement also set out the TelePrompTer option to acquire an 80-percent ownership position at an option price per share of $10.[43] The purchase of eight hundred shares at ten dollars per share would thus give TelePrompTer an 80-percent ownership position for an outlay of eight thousand dollars.

The Council of the City of Oakland awarded the CATV franchise to Focus Cable on November 10, 1970.[44] Focus Cable accepted the franchise on December 23, 1970.[45]

---

[38] Letter from Focus Cable to the City Manager of Oakland, dated July 21, 1970.

[39] Stock Transfer Restriction and Purchase Agreement, dated September 21, 1970, Appendix A to Focus Cable of Oakland, Inc., Subscription Agreement.

[40] See note 33, *supra*.

[41] See Subscription Agreement, note 39, *supra*, p. 2.

[42] *Ibid.*, p. 12.

[43] See note 39, *supra*, p. 6.

[44] City of Oakland Ordinance No. 8246 C.M.S., November 10, 1970.

[45] Statement from Leonard Tow, Treasurer, Focus Cable of Oakland, to City of Oakland, dated December 23, 1970.

Execution of the franchise. A rate for System B of $4.45 per month was requested by Focus Cable on March 10, 1971, and was approved on March 11, 1971.[46] The combined rate for System A and System B thus came to $6.15 per month.

Construction, which was due to be completed on December 28, 1973, did not go so quickly as the franchise specifications called for, fewer households subscribed to the service than anticipated, and costs escalated. Focus Cable appealed to the City to renegotiate the terms of the franchise. A reduction in the penalty period and the penalty fee was sought; a stretch-out of the construction period was requested; and a downgrading of the cable requirement was proposed. The Staff of the Office of General Services summarized the requested changes as follows:[47]

> Focus is requesting that: further construction be limited to a dual trunk/single feeder cable configuration; a two-year construction extension be granted; only 90% of the households be served at the end of the two years with the remaining 10% to be served only under specified conditions; activation of the dual cable system be deferred until adequate demand develops; damage payments for construction delays be waived; rates of $1.70 for basic services and $6.15 for extended services continue but that additional set rates be increased; extended service subscribers be reduced from 38 to 30 channels; and that reductions be made in the city and school spectrum allocations.

The Staff then considered four alternatives: (1) insist that the terms of the original franchise be met; (2) negotiate a revised agreement with Focus; and terminate the franchise, in which event (3) proposals from other commercial cable operators would be invited, or (4) shift the franchise to public ownership. The first was rejected because it would require great effort by the City "to obtain a satisfactory result from a recalcitrant operator. Citizen complaints about service will proliferate and require enormous effort to resolve. Litigation may result."[48] The third was rejected because other operators were thought unlikely to provide any more than the "minimum requirements of the 1972 Cable Television Report and Order"—"28-Channel capacity, some two-way capacity, three channels for local use, and 'significant' local programming"—offerings which were characterized as "significantly less than would be provided by Focus' recommended plant revisions."[49] Furthermore, public ownership was rejected for philosophical and financial reasons.[50] The second alternative, which the Staff characterized as the compromise solution, was accordingly proposed.[51]

In the course of reviewing Focus Cable's problems, the Staff reported that Focus claimed to have invested $12,600,000 to date and that Focus estimated that this would increase to $21,400,000 if the dual system were to be completed. The Staff disputed these figures and offered its own estimate of $18,684,000 as the completed capital cost of the dual system. The original Focus estimate, by contrast, was $11,753,000. The Staff attributed the increase over the initial estimate to "possible mismanagement of construction activities; inflation,

---

[46] Oakland City Council Resolution No. 51477 C.M.S., dated March 11, 1971.

[47] Inter-Office Letter from Office of General Services to Office of the City Manger, dated April 5, 1974, p. 1.

[48] *Ibid.*, attachment, p. 4.

[49] *Ibid.*, attachment, p. 5.

[50] *Ibid.*, attachment, p. 5.

[51] *Ibid.*, attachment, p. 8.

which was compounded by Focus' not meeting the original construction schedule; and an underestimate by Focus of the mileage and unit costs necessary to build the Oakland system."[52]

Since 437 miles, or 55 percent of the system, were already completed and furnished with dual cable, the Staff recommended that the system be completed as a dual cable system. The second cable, however, would not be energized until a later date. Since only the one cable was to be energized, a reduction of channel capacity on System B resulted, and a reduction of city and school spectrum allocations was proposed. The subscriber to the extended service (now designated A/B) would receive 12 channels on System A and 18 channels on System B.[53] Also, the Staff was agreeable to the proposal that a construction extension of two years be granted and that only 90 percent rather than 100 percent coverage be attempted.[54] Additionally, the Staff recommended that Focus pay the City $240,000 for lost revenues, due to the delay, during the period 1973 to 1976 and that any delays beyond December, 1976, be assessed at the rate of $250 rather than $750 per day.[55] Finally, the Staff recommended that the monthly rate for the initial System A connection remain at $1.70 and that the initial System B connection remain at $4.45 (so that System A/B remained at $6.15), but that the monthly rate on additional outlets for System A be increased from $.34 to $1.70 and that the rate for additional System B outlets be set at $3.00.[56]

The "compromise" that finally emerged and was approved by City Council had the following provisions:[57] (1) A shift from the dual to a single cable system was permitted with the understanding that additional transmission capacity would be put in place within one year after it was ascertained that the "additional transmission capacity will attract sufficient revenues to provide a per annum rate-of-return on the gross investment required, over a 10-year period, equivalent to ten percent."[58] (2) The minimum franchise fee was increased by $25,000 in 1974 and each year thereafter. (3) Damages were assessed at the rate of $250 per day from December 18, 1973, until the first reading of the amended franchise—which resulted in a penalty of $36,000—rather than $750 per day for the entire period from December 18, 1973, until system completion—a penalty which would have been greater by a factor of 20 or more and which might have precipitated bankruptcy. (4) A deferred construction schedule was approved. Finally, (5) the monthly rate on additional connections was increased from $.34 to $1.70 per month on System A and was set at $3.00 per month on System B.

The City passed an ordinance on May 30, 1974, to reflect most of these changes.[59] Attorneys for Focus forwarded Letters of Accep-

[52] *Ibid.*, attachment, p. 8.

[53] *Ibid.*, attachment, pp. 10–11.

[54] *Ibid.*, attachment, pp. 8–9.

[55] *Ibid.*, attachment, pp. 11–12.

[56] *Ibid.*, attachment, pp. 12–13.

[57] Memorandum from Office of General Services to Office of City Manager summarizing actions taken by the City Council at work sessions concerning Focus Cable, dated April 22, 1974.

[58] *Ibid.*, attachment I.

[59] City of Oakland, Ordinance No. 9018 C.M.S., Amending Ordinance No. 8246 C.M.S., and Ordinance No. 7989 C.M.S., Relating to the Community Antenna Television System Franchise, dated May 30, 1974. The only significant exceptions from the

tance by Focus and TelePrompTer on June 14, 1974, and sent a check from TelePrompTer Corporation made payable to the City of Oakland in the amount of $36,000.

Focus Cable filed a progress report on November 15, 1974, which showed that 11,131 subscribers were connected. Of these, 770 took the basic service at $1.70 per month (of which 206 had additional outlets), and 10,361 had the extended service at $6.15 per month (of which 974 had additional outlets). This represented an overall penetration rate of 36 percent.[60] The Office of General Services recommended that Cable Dynamics, Inc. of Burlingame, California, be retained as consultants to "devise and perform tests to establish the degree of compliance" with technical requirements of the franchise.[61] Cable Dynamics estimated that the costs from Autumn 1974 to June 1976 would be approximately $10,750.[62] Focus agreed to reimburse the City for these costs up to an amount not to exceed $10,750.[63]

□ **An evaluation.** The franchising procedures employed by the City of Oakland, especially at the initial reward stage, are not without merit. As compared, for example, with those in New York City, which awarded noncompetitive, 20-year contracts to Manhattan Cable TV and to TelePrompTer to supply CATV in Manhattan,[64] the Oakland exercise had the appearance of a genuine bidding competition. Franchise specifications were standardized and, with respect to System A at least, carefully described. Bidding competition in terms of a simple promise to sell cheaply (by designating the value "*X*" at which System A services would be supplied) was thereby facilitated. However, numerous problems, many of which were anticipated in the discussion of incomplete long-term contracts, developed. Thus, consider each of the previously described disabilities which sometimes infect franchise awards: (1) the artificiality or obscurity of the initial award criterion, (2) the development of execution problems in price-cost, other performance, and political respects, and (3) the absence of bidding parity at the contract renewal interval.

(1) *Initial award.* Awarding the franchise on the basis of the lowest bid of "*X*" to supply System A service simplified the award criterion, but the promise to supply cheaply proved to be specious. The lack of attention to System B (which was treated as a futuristic service and, except for capacity requirements, was left relatively undefined) in both quality and price respects may well have contributed to "adventurous" bidding on the part of Focus. Trafficking in the franchise award quickly ensued.

To have regarded System A, which essentially supplies improved off-the-air signals, as the "basic system" was misguided. Over 90 percent of the subscribers took the combined A/B service, although the additional service thereby obtained was relatively mundane

---

compromise described in the text are the following: the additional connection rate for System B was set at $1.30 per month and it was stipulated that System B should provide not less than 18 video channels.

[60] Attachment to City of Oakland Inter-Office Letter from Office of General Services to City Manager, dated November 20, 1974.

[61] Letter, *ibid.*, p. 2.

[62] Attachment to letter, *ibid.*

[63] Letter, see note 60, *supra*, p. 2.

[64] *New York Times*, July 29, 1970, p. 1.

(mainly the import of distant signals). The rate on the combined service, however, was three-and-a-half times as great as the basic System A service. Surely a more careful effort to assess subscriber preferences at the outset would have revealed that System A lacked appeal. Indeed, inasmuch as most of the prospective franchisees were experienced in supplying CATV services in other areas, it is difficult to understand the preoccupation with System A services during the extended precontract discussion between the franchisor and the prospective franchisees. The possibility that the Staff was gullible and deliberately misled during these precontract discussions cannot be dismissed.[65]

Whatever the case—given the demand and technological uncertainties associated with CATV (CTIC, 1972c, pp. 5, 12) and the complexity of the service, in quality and product mix respects—reducing the award criterion to the lowest bid price for System A resulted in a strained and perhaps bogus competition.

(2) *Execution difficulties. Price-cost relations.* Whether the Focus bid of $1.70 per month for System A can be regarded as close to "per unit production cost" is doubtful in view of the following factors: (1) the disparity among bid prices raises a question as to whether an economically meaningful competition was conducted; (2) System B prices, which appear to be the more relevant dimension, were negotiated subsequent to the bidding competition; and (3) true cost levels are difficult to ascertain—partly because the vertically integrated supply relation obscures these, partly because inflation rates during the construction period have been abnormally high, and partly because the Staff lacks an auditing capability. What is evident is that Focus and the Staff of the Office of General Services are, together with the City Council, involved in a long-term bargaining relationship over prices and costs in which political interests, bureaucratic interests, and franchise viability all play a role.

Other performance attributes. The stipulation that the CATV system be installed and maintained in accordance with the "highest and best accepted standards" of the industry coupled with technical specifications did not yield a well-defined quality outcome.[66] Sufficient customer complaints over quality have been registered with the Staff of the Office of General Services[67] that the Staff, unable itself to assess the quality of service, has arranged for a consultant to test the degree of compliance of service with technical requirements.

Politics. Whether the winning bid by Focus involved "buying in" is uncertain. An inference that buying in did occur is supported by the following considerations. (1) The next lowest bid was double the Focus bid while the TelePrompTer bid was more than triple the Focus bid. (2) The timing and nature of the Focus reorganization

[65] As Posner surmised, it is hazardous to permit a public agency by itself to declare subscriber preferences for service.

[66] Partly this may be because "[a]n initial high signal quality may, over time, slowly degrade to the point where the signal quality is not acceptable" (CTIC, 1973, p. 9); partly it is that signal quality is multidimensional and varies with the capability of the system to receive off-air and microwave signal as well as headend and cable attributes (CTIC, 1973, pp. 19-24).

[67] The existence of customer complaints regarding quality of service was disclosed in an interview with Mark Leh (see note 28, *supra*).

suggest a foot in the door strategy—the object being that, once in, the franchising authority would be inclined to work with Focus and its affiliates in an accommodating manner. (3) Focus' local bidder status was affirmatively regarded by the franchising authority and evidently supported politicking.[68] Finally, (4) the extensive renegotiations undertaken by Focus, with evident success—the Staff acceded to most of Focus' requests and the City Council approved a "compromise" in which energizing of the second cable was deferred (with a cutback in System B services to 18 channels); the annual franchising fee was increased slightly; damages were reduced drastically; construction deadlines were extended; and rates on additional System A and B connections were increased—reinforce this judgment.

(3) *Frictionless takeover or transfer.* Although the enabling ordinance provided for buying up of the plant and equipment of the franchisee, the City was plainly not prepared to upset the original award. The reasons appear to be that incumbents are strategically positioned to bargain—both in terms of service interruptions and the litigating and other expenses which franchise termination would entail—and, relatedly, because franchising agencies lack resolve. This lack of resolution appears to be attributable to the reward structure in bureaus. Unable to appropriate the gains that reassignment of the franchise would prospectively yield and unwilling to concede error, the bureaus favor "accommodation" whenever contract execution difficulties appear.

The interruptions and expenses which franchise termination would experience are presumably explained, in part at least, by physical and human asset problems of the kinds discussed in Section 3. Absent rules for valuing the CATV plant and equipment that are at once rational, unambiguous, and inexpensive to employ, physical asset valuation problems predictably arise.[69] Inasmuch as such rules had not been devised (and, realistically, perhaps could not have been devised) for the Oakland franchise, litigation expenses and delays would attend any effort to take over the physical plant in question.

The risk of service interruptions and related malfunctions would

[68] Libman (1974) reports that the award of the Oakland CATV franchise to the Focus group, despite its lack of expertise and adequate financing, and the subsequent implementation of the franchise appear to have been influenced by political considerations. A more spectacular and unambiguous case is afforded by the CATV competition in Johnstown, Pennsylvania, where Irving Kahn, the former chief executive and chairman of TelePrompTer, the nation's largest operator of cable TV, was tried and convicted of bribery and perjury. Kahn has also admitted bribing public officials in Trenton, New Jersey, to secure their votes. Politics appears also to have been a decisive factor in the award of CATV franchises in New York City. (See note 64, *supra.*) Whether this holds for CATV awards in large cities more generally is uncertain. The incidence of corruption with respect to franchise awards for other types of services is also an open question.

[69] Indeed they did arise. Witness that the completed system estimate by Focus exceeded the Staff's estimate by almost three million dollars. Note also that it is ill-advised to permit the franchisee to become affiliated with a firm that supplies equipment and products for the construction of the plant. The risk here is that the procurement costs of these items will be overstated, thereby to build up the rate base of the franchisee and improve its bargaining position during rate negotiations. Despite claims that equipment will be procured on competitive terms, this is costly to check and violations are difficult to prove conclusively. The Oakland Staff suspects unwarranted equipment cost escalation in the estimates by Focus of plant valuation, but admits that it has no definitive proof.

be compounded if the human assets associated with the franchise had acquired, in a learning by doing process, nontrivial task idiosyncracies. Given that the Staff lacked qualifications in the CATV area and was evidently unwilling to solicit bids from other experienced CATV operators (possibly because the Staff was unwilling to accept the risk of embarrassment should the new operator also prove to be deficient), the transfer of human assets would need to be worked out if City ownership were to be attempted. The incentive to displace the original franchisee would be attenuated to the extent that a frictionless transfer of such human assets could not be anticipated.

The upshot is that, good intentions to the contrary notwithstanding, *unassisted* franchise bidding for CATV conducted and executed under conditions of uncertainty has dubious properties. The franchising authority that assumes an accommodating posture is merely legitimating monopoly, while a concerted effort to exercise control requires the agency to adopt a regulatory posture. The purported dichotomy between "regulatory controls" on the one hand and "natural economic forces" on the other is accordingly strained. It confuses the issues to characterize market solutions as "natural" where these are actually supported by an administrative apparatus of considerable complexity.[70]

5. Concluding remarks

■ That franchise bidding for CATV, *circa* 1970, has superior properties to regulation is not transparent. Microanalytic assessments of franchise bidding, both as an abstract exercise and in the context of a specific case study, suggest a mixed verdict. Not only is simple franchise bidding for CATV beset with numerous transactional difficulties, but the institutional infrastructure that predictably develops to check dysfunctional or monopoloid outcomes has many of the earmarks of regulation.

Surely no one would dispute that "[t]he correct way to view the problem is one of selecting the best type of contract" (Demsetz, 1968, p. 68). But one also needs to be instructed on how to proceed. Although it may be possible to disallow some contracting modes on static allocative efficiency grounds,[71] the more interesting cases, I submit, involve an examination of the efficiency properties of alternative contracts executed under conditions of uncertainty. Contrary to normal practice, attention to transactional detail is needed if the real issues are to be exposed. Additionally, a check on the operational properties of abstract contracting modes is usefully made *by examining one or more actual cases* in which different modes are being employed.[72] As P.T. Bauer and A.A. Walters observe, "the com-

[70] Posner employs this dichotomy in his 1969 discussion of natural monopoly, in which he urges that "even in markets where efficiency dictates monopoly we might do better to allow natural economic forces to determine business conduct and performance subject only to the constraints of antitrust policy" (1969, p. 549). He declines, however, to handle the CATV issue in this way but instead favors the market assisted bidding scheme described in Section 3, the administrative problems associated with which are formidable.

[71] For example, awarding a franchise to the bidder who will pay the largest lump-sum amount will serve to capitalize the monopoly profits but, at least transitionally, will lead to a higher price and lower output than will an award of the franchise to the bidder who offers to supply at the lowest price.

[72] To be sure, one swallow does not make a spring, and a single case study does not settle the franchise bidding for CATV issue. It is thus to be hoped that more such

plexity, instability, and local variation of many economic phenomena imply that the establishment or understanding of relationships requires that analysis be supplemented by extensive observation, and also that the inquiry must often extend beyond statistical information to direct observation and use of primary sources" (1975, p. 12). The case study of CATV franchising in Oakland, California, as reported in Section 4, is in this spirit. The complexity of this contracting problem exceeds that of Demsetz' automobile license plate example by several orders of magnitude. That a different understanding of franchise bidding obtains is not, perhaps, unsurprising.

The "appropriate" level of transactional detail is not well defined and may vary with the circumstances. The following proposal is advanced as a means by which to get at the transaction cost issues: Progressively refine the degree of detail until contractual problems are plainly exposed. Then ask the question, "Do these issues have comparative institutional significance in the context of the specific problems at hand?"

The level of detail that I have found useful in studying related transactional phenomena is what might be called a semimicroanalytic level of detail. Given the infeasibility of complex contingent claims contracting for the services in question, the properties of incomplete long-term and sequential spot contracts need to be assessed. When unassisted market processes prospectively or actually founder—because the hazards of incomplete long-term contracts are severe and sequential spot contracting is beset with indeterminacies and/or distortions—alternatives to autonomous contracting, of which regulation is one, plainly warrant consideration.

It is relevant in this connection to note that there are striking regularities among the incentives to organize internal labor markets (Williamson, Wachter, and Harris, 1975), the incentives for vertical integration (Williamson, 1971), and the incentives to regulate (or otherwise substitute an administrative apparatus for unassisted market exchange). The particulars differ, but the disabilities of recurrent market contracting which give rise to each of these nonmarket or market assisted modes are substantially the same. To the extent that the organizational failures framework set out elsewhere has generality (Williamson, 1975), such commonalities are to be expected.

Lest the argument appear unsympathetic to the franchise bidding approach, I should point out that there are circumstances where I suspect that regulation or public ownership can be supplanted by franchise bidding with net gains. Local service airlines and, possibly, postal delivery are examples.[73] The technology for both is well developed, demand is likewise well defined, and idiosyncratic skills appear to be negligible. Furthermore, displacement can be made without posing serious asset valuation problems—since the base plant (terminals, post offices, warehouses, etc.) can be owned by the government and other assets (planes, trucks, etc.) will have an active second-hand market. It is not, therefore, that franchise bidding is

studies will be performed. In the meantime, I submit, the Oakland experience gives occasion for pause.

[73] A careful microanalytic assessment of both is needed, however, before the franchise bidding mode is introduced. Disabilities that are not apparent on the surface may be disclosed.

totally lacking in merit,[74] but that those who have favored this mode have been insufficiently discriminating in their endorsement of it.

An unbiased assessment of the abstract properties of alternative modes will be facilitated by examining the transactional attributes of each in microanalytic detail.[75] It will be useful for this purpose to regard rate of return regulation as a highly incomplete form of contracting in which the prospects for windfall gains and losses are strictly limited and, in principle and sometimes in fact, adaptations to changing circumstances are introduced in a low cost, nonacrimonious way. The frequency and extent to which such adaptations are required and the differential ease with which these are effectuated by alternative modes are important in making an informed comparative institutional choice.

References

BAUER, P. T. AND WALTERS, A. A. "The State of Economics." *Journal of Law and Economics*, Vol. 18 (April 1975), pp. 1–24.

BEHAVIORAL SCIENCES SUBPANEL, PRESIDENT'S SCIENCE ADVISORY COMMITTEE. *Strengthening the Behavioral Sciences*. Washington, D. C.: U.S. Government Printing Office, 1962.

COASE, R. H. "The Federal Communications Commission," *Journal of Law and Economics*, October 1959, 2, 1–40.

———. "The Problem of Social Cost." *Journal of Law and Economics*, Vol. 3 (October 1960), pp. 1–44.

CTIC. *How to Plan an Ordinance*. Washington, D.C.: 1972(a).

———. *A Suggested Procedure*. Washington, D.C.: 1972(b).

———. *Cable: An Overview*. Washington, D.C.: 1972(c).

———. *Technical Standards and Specifications*. Washington, D.C.: 1973.

DEMSETZ, H. "Why Regulate Utilities?" *Journal of Law and Economics*, Vol. 11 (April 1968), pp. 55–66.

———."On the Regulation of Industry: A Reply." *Journal of Political Economy*, Vol. 79 (March/April 1971), pp. 356–363.

DEWEY, D. J. "An Introduction to the Issues," in H. J. Goldschmid, H. M. Mann, and J. F. Weston, eds., *Industrial Concentration: The New Learning*, Boston: 1974, pp. 1–14.

DOERINGER, P. AND PIORE, M. *Internal Labor Markets and Manpower Analysis*. Lexington, Mass.: D. C. Heath, 1971.

ECKSTEIN, H. "Planning: The National Health Service," in R. Rose, ed., *Policy-Making in Britain*, London: 1969, pp. 221–237.

FISHER, W. L. "The American Municipality," in Commission on Public Ownership and Operation, *Municipal and Private Operation of Public Utilities*, Part I, Vol. I, New York, 1907, pp. 36–48.

FULLER, L. AND BRAUCHER, R. *Basic Contract Law*. St. Paul: West Publishing Co., 1964.

FURUBOTN, E. AND PEJOVICH, S. "Property Rights and Economic Theory: A Survey of Recent Literature." *Journal of Economic Literature*, Vol. 10 (December 1972), pp. 1137–1162.

———. *The Economics of Property Rights*. Cambridge, Mass.: Ballinger, 1974.

[74] Not only might franchise bidding be usefully introduced in some cases where regulation is now employed, but it should continue in circumstances in which it is plainly efficacious. The award of gas station franchises on turnpikes is an example of the latter.

[75] As Donald Dewey has observed, "[T]he disdain and contempt for regulation [by economists] is nearly universal" (1974, p. 10). Although much of regulation is indeed contemptible, I submit that *some* of the problems for which regulation has been devised are really intractable—in the sense that *all* of the feasible modes of organization are beset with difficulties. Arguments favoring market modes in which these difficulties are not squarely faced should accordingly be regarded with skepticism.

GOLDBERG, V. P. "Regulation and Administered Contracts." *The Bell Journal of Economics*, Vol. 7, No. 2 (Autumn 1976).

GOULDNER, A. W. *Industrial Bureaucracy*. Glencoe, Ill.: 1954.

HAYEK, F. "The Use of Knowledge in Society." *The American Economic Review*, Vol. 35, No. 4 (September 1945), pp. 519–530.

JORDAN, W. A. "Producer Protection, Prior Market Structure, and the Effects of Government Regulation." *Journal of Law and Economics*, Vol. 15 (April 1972), pp. 151–176.

JOSKOW, P. L. "Regulatory Activities by Government Agencies." Working Paper No. 171, Department of Economics, M.I.T., December 1975.

KAHN, A. E. *The Economics of Regulation: Vol. 2, Institutional Issues*. New York: Wiley, 1971.

KNIGHT, F. H. *Risk, Uncertainty, and Profit*. New York: 1965.

LEFF, A. A. "Teams, Firms, and the Aesthetics of Antitrust." Draft manuscript, February, 1975.

LIBMAN, J. "In Oakland, a Cable-TV System Fails to Live Up to Promises." *Wall Street Journal* (September 25, 1974), p. 34.

MACAULAY, S. "Non-Contractual Relations in Business." *American Sociological Review*, Vol. 28 (1963), pp. 55–70.

MACNEIL, I. R. "The Many Futures of Contracts." *Southern California Law Review*, Vol. 47 (May 1974), pp. 691–816.

MARSCHAK, J. "Economics of Inquiring, Communicating, Deciding." *The American Economic Review*, Vol. 58, No. 2 (May 1968), pp. 1–18.

PEACOCK, A. T. AND ROWLEY, C. K. "Welfare Economics and the Public Regulation of Natural Monopolies." *Journal of Public Economics*, Vol. 1 (1972), pp. 227–244.

POSNER, R. A. "Natural Monopoly and Its Regulation." *Stanford Law Review*, Vol. 21 (February 1969), pp. 548–643.

———. "Cable Television: The Problem of Local Monopoly." RAND Memorandum RM-6309-FF, May 1970, p. 35.

———. "The Appropriate Scope of Regulation in the Cable Television Industry." *The Bell Journal of Economics and Management Science*, Vol. 3, No. 1 (Spring 1972), pp. 98–129.

———. "Theories of Economic Regulation." *The Bell Journal of Economics and Management Science*, Vol. 5, No. 2 (Autumn 1974), pp. 335–358.

———. "The Economic Approach to Law." *Texas Law Review*, Vol. 53, No. 4 (May 1975), pp. 757–782.

SCHERER, F. M. *The Weapons Acquisition Process: Economic Incentives*. Boston: 1964.

STIGLER, G. J. *The Organization of Industry*. Chicago: Univ. of Chicago Press, 1968.

———. "Free Riders and Collective Action: An Appendix to Theories of Economic Regulation." *The Bell Journal of Economics and Mangement Science*, Vol. 5, No. 2 (Autumn 1974), pp. 359–365.

TELSER, L. G. "On the Regulation of Industry: A Note." *Journal of Political Economy*, Vol. 77 (November/December 1969), pp. 937–952.

———. "On the Regulation of Industry: Rejoinder." *Journal of Political Economy*, Vol. 79 (March/April 1971), pp. 364–365.

WILLIAMSON, O. E. "The Economics of Defense Contracting: Incentives and Performance," in *Issues in Defense Economics*, New York: 1967, pp. 217–256.

———. "The Vertical Integration of Production: Market Failure Considerations." *The American Economic Review*, Vol. 61. No. 2 (May 1971); pp. 112–123.

———. "Administrative Controls and Regulatory Behavior," in H. M. Trebing, ed., *Essays on Public Utility Pricing and Regulation*, East Lansing, Mich.: 1971b, pp. 411–438.

———. "Patent and Antitrust Law: Book Review." *Yale Law Journal*, Vol. 83 (January 1974a), pp. 647–661.

———. "The Economics of Antitrust: Transaction Cost Considerations." *University of Pennsylvania Law Review*, Vol. 122 (June 1974b), pp. 1439–1496.

———. *Markets and Hierarchies: Analysis and Antitrust Implications*. New York: Free Press, 1975.

———, WACHTER, M. AND HARRIS, J. "Understanding the Employment Relation: The Analysis of Idiosyncratic Exchange." *The Bell Journal of Economics*, Vol. 6, No. 1 (Spring 1975), pp. 250–278.

[16]

Regulation and administered contracts

Victor P. Goldberg

Associate Professor of Economics
University of California, Davis

This paper explores the ramifications of introducing administered contracts—long-term, collective contractual relationships—into economic analysis with attention being focused on the implicit regulatory contract. The perspective afforded by the administered contracts framework suggests that the economist's case against regulation has been overstated. Many of the problems associated with regulation lie in what is being regulated, not in the act of regulation itself. Further, many of the perceived failures of regulation (for example, entry restrictions) can be seen to have a plausible efficiency rationale.

1. Introduction

■ The failure of regulation has been widely chronicled in recent years.[1] Extension of public utility regulation into new areas—e.g., cable television and hospitals—calls forth widespread opposition from economists (and others) and the momentum for deregulation of a number of activities has been building. However, regulation's low repute is in part based on misconceptions about the regulatory process and the private contract alternatives.

In this paper we present a conceptual framework offering a different perspective on regulation and institutional choice. The emphasis is on aspects of contractual complexity typically glossed over in economic analyses of regulation (and economic theory generally). The paradigmatic contract of economic theory (and of law)[2] is a discrete transaction conveying a well-defined object (the ever popular widget) in exchange for cash. This characterization is adequate for many purposes, but it diverts attention from some aspects of contract that will be of particular significance in a regulatory context. This discrete transactional mold is apt to be singularly inappropriate for representing relations which are to take place over a long period of time and in which the parties will have to deal with each other regularly over a

---

This research was partially supported by a post-doctoral fellowship from the Public Choice Center, Virginia Polytechnic Institute and State University. The author would like to thank the following for comments on earlier drafts: George Berger, Paul Joskow, Blair Lord, Ian Macneil, Alan Olmstead, John Roemer, Warren Samuels, Kathy Swartz, Gordon Tullock, David Warner, and Oliver Williamson. An earlier version of this paper was presented at the Seminar on Problems of Regulation and Public Utilities held at Dartmouth College, August 5, 1975.

[1] "Among economists the disdain and contempt for regulation is nearly universal; if effective, it is thought to be pernicious, and if ineffective, a waste of resources" (Dewey, 1974, p. 10). See also MacAvoy (1970, p. viii) and Green and Nader (1973, p. 881); for a detailed statement of the antiregulation case, see Posner (1969).

[2] For a detailed discussion of the role of the discrete transaction paradigm in the law of contracts, see Macneil (1974); for discussion of some of the economic implications, see Goldberg (1976a).

wide range of issues (many of them unknown in advance). A second suppressed problem concerns the reliance of individuals on agents (for gathering information, making decisions, negotiating contracts, adjusting the terms of ongoing relationships, and so on). It is convenient to distinguish the discrete transaction of traditional theory from contracts which exhibit prominently one or the other (or both) of these elements—an ongoing relationship and agency. Such contracts will be called "administered contracts."[3] Regulation can be viewed as an implicit administered contract in which both elements are significant.[4]

By attempting to analyze regulation within a discrete transaction framework, economists have suppressed the most significant aspects of the regulatory arrangement and this has led to an overstatement of the case against regulation. First, that framework generates the wrong criteria against which regulation is to be evaluated. Second, when viewed in an administered contracts perspective, regulatory policies that would appear indefensible in a discrete transactions world can be seen to have a (loose) efficiency rationale. And finally, a failure to appreciate the complexity of contractual arrangements in the private sector is apt to leave the analyst unduly sanguine as to the efficacy of private market solutions to problems in the regulatory sector.

The argument below should not be construed as a brief for wall-to-wall regulation. Nor should it be taken to mean that current regulatory policies are the best we can do. They are not. The point is simply that if one is interested in seriously analyzing regulation and other institutional alternatives, it is necessary to open up the "black box" of contract.

2. The administered contracts framework

■ Before analyzing the complexities that arise in a world of administered contracts, it is useful to elaborate upon some of the aspects of such a world. We begin this section by expanding upon the distinction between the discrete transaction and the ongoing contractual relationship. We then turn to a discussion of agency and the related issues of the nesting of contractual relationships and the blurred borderline between private contract and social contract. Next we introduce a convenient simplification—the notion that the agent is putting out a bid for a long-term contract for the right to serve his constituency. Finally, we will make some remarks concerning the difficulties entailed in developing satisfactory welfare or efficiency criteria in an administered contracts framework.

□ **Relational contracts.** The pure discrete transaction of economic theory involves the contemporaneous exchange of claims or rights

[3] Pure discrete transactions exist only as theoretical abstractions. All contracts will have at least some relational and agency aspects (as will be made clear in the following section) and it might therefore be better to eliminate the "administered contract" terminology. We prefer, however, to use it now to emphasize the distinction between contracts in which the relational and/or agency aspect is important and the narrower contracts implicit in most economic theorizing.

[4] In the next section we shall broaden the notion of the agency relationship so that it will be unnecessary to distinguish between actual contractual relationships (those explicitly recognized as creating contractual duties) and implicit contractual relationships.

between the contracting parties.[5] The identity of the parties and the social milieu within which the contract is consummated are irrelevant. The exchange is cloaked in anonymity with one party selling to the market and the other buying from the market. This is an extreme caricature of contract and in its purest form it has no real world counterpart. Contract typically involves the projection of exchange into the future, with contemporaneous exchange as a special case. Entering into a contract will generally entail placing restrictions on the contracting parties' future options. Freedom of contract is the freedom to impose restrictions on one's future behavior.[6]

For a wide range of activities, recognition of the duration of the contract and the extensiveness of the future restrictions would add complexity to the analysis but little insight. For many other activities, however, the length of the agreement, the nature of the restrictions, and the complexity of the issues arising between the formation stage[7] of the contract and its termination will be of crucial interest. Consider the difficulties in designing contracts to deal with long-term relationships such as development and procurement of complex defense hardware, construction of a chemical plant embodying substantial state of the art advances, joint ventures, franchise agreements, or marriage. While the parties might want to go into considerable detail at the formation stage concerning the rights and obligations of each party given various contingencies,[8] it will often prove too costly to specify the precise terms of the contract and it will be desirable instead to use rough formulae or mutual agreement to adjust the contract to current situations.[9] As the relational aspects of the contract become more significant, emphasis will shift from a detailed specification of the terms of the agreement to a more general statement of the process of adjusting the terms of the agreement over time—the establishment, in effect, of a "constitution" governing the ongoing relationship.[10]

☐ **Agency.** Frequently one party to a transaction—the firm—engages

[5] For a detailed discussion of the characteristics of discrete transactions and relational contracts, see Macneil (1974, pp. 735–805).

[6] See Clark (1939, p. 87) and Macneil (1974, p. 810).

[7] In contractual relations, rights and duties often arise before the formation stage of the contract. In civil code countries, the obligation to bargain in good faith has long been explicitly recognized. Kessler and Fine (1964) show that this continental law doctrine is not totally foreign to common law jurisdictions. See, for example, *Hoffman v. Red Owl Stores, Inc.*, 26 Wis. 2d 683, 133 N.W.2d 267 (1965).

[8] For examples of some attempts to specify at least some of the terms of the marriage contract, see Weitzman (1974, pp. 1278–1288).

[9] For a discussion of some of the factors making long-term, incomplete contracts desirable, see Williamson (1971, 1973, 1974), Macneil (1974), and Goldberg (1976a). Coordination by long-term contract blends into coordination by vertical integration. It is not hard to imagine *interfirm* coordination mechanisms that are stronger and more accepted by the relevant parties than some *intrafirm* mechanisms. The convenient fiction of economic theory that monolithic firms coordinate internal behavior perfectly and engage only in discrete, anonymous contracts with external parties leads us to ignore the great similarities between internal and external coordination. For an approach which stresses interorganization coordination, see Richardson (1972).

[10] The constitution can be in large part implicit, being defined largely by the social (and legal) context within which the agreement was made. The standard marriage contract provides a good example. The general question of the nesting of transactions in deeper relationships is discussed briefly in Section 2 and in more detail in Macneil (1974).

in similar transactions with a large number of other parties—the consumers—who each enter into very few such transactions. The consumers will, in many instances, find it desirable to act collectively through an agent both to negotiate the terms and to administer the contract over time. In an analogous situation, employees will find that a union can fill this role, negotiating multiyear contracts which determine both compensation and working conditions and also providing a method for seeing that the terms of the contract are adhered to (or a means for changing the working conditions without reopening the contract).

We can view individual transactions as being governed by contracts on (at least) two levels. The provider enters into contracts with individual customers with the content and interpretation of these contracts governed by another level of contract—the collective contract—between the provider and the agent. Regulation can also be viewed in this manner with the implicit contract between the regulated firm(s) and the regulatory agency serving as the collective contract.[11] Indeed, we can go much further than this. Conceptually, we can treat judges and legislators as agents enforcing and revising the rules under which individual transactions take place. Thus, the absence of a formal administered contract does not preclude us from analyzing a certain set of transactions as if it were governed by such a contract. For example, the law of product liability can be viewed as a collective contract governing the terms under which numerous individual contracts are consummated; further, changes over time in the content of product liability law can be viewed as efforts by the agents (courts and legislatures) to adjust the terms of the collective contract to changing circumstances.[12]

In this sense, all transactions, however well defined they might appear, are nested in a complex shifting pattern of contractual jurisdictions which, taken together, establish the rights and obligations of the respective parties and the roles of the agents. The structures of the set of contracts governing particular transactions can, of course, differ substantially. The responsiveness of the agents to their clientele, the division of authority between agents, and the freedom of individuals to shift between jurisdictions all will vary.[13] Nevertheless, this formulation does call attention to the fact that the problems of determining the appropriate common law rules for governing specific sets of transactions will in many ways be analogous to the problems

[11] There is no reason for the collective contract to be explicitly recognized as a valid contract. Indeed, even if it has no legal recognition it might still be of tremendous practical importance; see, for example, Friedmann's discussion of collective bargaining agreements in Great Britain (1951, pp. 26–27).

[12] Brown (1974, p. 149) notes that the common law can be treated as a standard form contract. We are suggesting a slightly different interpretation. The common law is embedded in a social contract which establishes a procedure for adjusting the specific terms of the contract over time.

[13] Agency relationships might be very short-lived and might involve small numbers. Single individuals or small groups might engage agents to customize services for them (e.g., stock brokers or trustees). One party might sometimes act both as a party to the transaction and an agent for the other party (e.g., a doctor or a department store certifying, in effect, the product's quality). Since in the context of regulation we shall generally be more interested in long-run collective agency relationships, these qualifications will generally not be of much importance in this paper. They can, however, be of much greater interest in a general theory of agency. For an exhaustive taxonomy of agency concepts, see Mitnick (1974).

faced by regulators and other administrators of collective contracts. It also emphasizes that private explicit contract inevitably blends into implicit social contract of which regulation is but a special subset. Finally, it provides us with an individual—the agent—on whom we can focus our attention. That the agent might be a fictitious character does not detract from his pedagogic value.

We shall assume throughout that the agent is a faithful representative of his principals' interests. While a wildly unrealistic assumption, the benevolent agent, like the benevolent dictator of traditional welfare economics, is a convenient analytical construct. This assumption does, however, preclude discussion of the politics of regulation—particularly the charge that regulators are susceptible to political influence by producer interests.[14] It is indeed true that the institutions of regulation are subject to political abuse. We must bear in mind, however, that all institutions, including those of private contract, are. It is by no means obvious that integrating political considerations into the analysis will make regulation a relatively less attractive alternative; detailed investigation of that point, however, is beyond the scope of this paper.[15]

How might we model economic processes in a world in which agency is important and restrictions on entry into (and exit from) jurisdictions are pervasive? One possibility would be to take a general equilibrium Walrasian approach. This, however, is apt to be uninteresting or impracticable.[16] Instead we shall focus on the decisions of an agent with a fixed constituency; this is roughly the counterpart to Marshallian partial analysis in an agency world. (As we shall see in the next section, however, the analysis has strong Schumpeterian overtones.)[17]

□ **A bidding for the market paradigm.** To facilitate analysis, we shall focus on an agent who must devise, put out to bid, and administer a collective contract for the provision of electricity, telephone service, or some other so-called natural monopoly industry. The assumption that there is a unique formation stage for the collective contract does some violence to reality, particularly for some of the more subtle relational contracts (e.g., the implicit contract of the common law). The assumption does, however, greatly simplify the discussion and usefully centers on the decision problem of the benevolent agent with a defined constituency (or jurisdiction).[18]

---

[14] See, for example, Bernstein (1955), Stigler (1971), and Posner (1974).

[15] For a more detailed discussion of the politics of regulation and private contract, see Goldberg (1974); see also Galanter (1974).

[16] It is doubtful that sufficient institutional content can be introduced into such models to make them very interesting. On a more heuristic level, however, the study of "appropriate jurisdiction" might yield useful insights. For example, if most health insurance is provided through group insurance, then we might ask whether the group administrator is the appropriate agent for all aspects of the contract or whether some decisions should be left to "lower" agents or reserved for "higher" agents. An example of the former would be giving the individual member a choice of insurers or insurance packages; an example of the latter would be a legislative or judicial rule that the insurance coverage does not lapse for one year after an individual has been laid off. For a discussion along these lines, see Lord (1975).

[17] A third approach, which is largely ignored here, would be to focus on the agent's problems of building and maintaining his constituency.

[18] Certainly the initial bidding abstraction would appear far less objectionable than the conventional Walrasian fiction of an auctioneer quoting prices.

Demsetz[19] relies on bidding for the whole market in his debunking of the standard natural monopoly justification for regulation—namely the allegation that there might be room for only one efficient producer. The fact that technology requires that only one producer exist does not preclude an initial bidding competition for the right to be the sole provider. If collusion among bidders can be avoided, competitive bidding "for the field" should eliminate monopoly profits, since any bidder who included monopoly profits in his bid would run the risk of being undercut. Expected profits would, therefore, be zero and, since Demsetz assumes away risk and uncertainty, there will be no risk premium. Thus, competitive bidding solves half the monopoly problem: excessive profits. However, if this solution entailed merely equating price and average cost, there would still be misallocation since, with decreasing costs, price would exceed marginal cost. This second problem can be solved, as Demsetz implies, by adopting a multipart tariff, charging the consumers marginal cost plus a lump sum just sufficient to yield the provider a normal profit. Thus, there is no reason in principle that a natural monopoly industry need be inefficient.

This argument assumes away problems due to risk or transactions costs to focus attention on the logical inconsistency of the narrow natural monopoly rationale. Of course, as Demsetz has shown elsewhere, if we can assume away risk and transactions costs, then, as long as there is freedom of contract (that is, the state does not artificially set some transactions costs greater than zero), the private market will always yield efficient outcomes. Monopoly, for example, would not be inefficient, since consumers could (costlessly) band together and bribe the monopolist to set price equal to marginal costs even if there were no potential competitors.[20]

The demolition of the natural monopoly rationale is not merely a testimonial to the power of the "zero transactions cost" assumption. The argument highlights the fundamental similarity between regulation and a private contract for the right to serve. It further suggests that in searching for a rationale for regulation we should look not at the shape of the long-run average cost curve, but instead at the complexities involved in devising and administering such a contract. Indeed, natural monopoly industries will be characterized in this paper not by their alleged decreasing average costs, but by the features which make long-term relationships between consumers and producers desirable and which further make it extremely difficult to determine at the outset the specific terms of that relationship.

□ **Desiderata.** Working within the discrete transaction paradigm, economists have developed an elaborate and elegant optimization framework which provides a rigorous definition of economic efficiency. In an administered contracts world we are not so fortunate. We must first concede that even if the agent were to perform perfectly, the outcomes need not be socially desirable—there is no reason to presume that decision-making has been decentralized along the proper lines. That is the price we must pay for confining ourselves to partial analysis.

[19] Demsetz (1968); for a critical discussion of Demsetz, see Williamson (1976).

[20] See Demsetz (1966, p. 64). For a discussion of some of the conceptual difficulties that arise in a zero transactions cost world, see Goldberg (1976a, pp. 46–48).

The agent must, explicitly or implicitly, give appropriate weights to the preferences of his clientele—that is, he must somehow construct a partial social welfare function. Further, he must ascertain those preferences and where preferences are ill-defined—as would be common in administered contracts—the agent will, in effect, be called upon to manufacture group preferences.[21] Hence, welfare criteria will be based on the agent's weighting and characterization of reasonable preferences.

In the discrete transaction paradigm, the parties are concerned with the price and quantity of clearly defined inputs or outputs and make their optimizing production or consumption decisions accordingly. The agent at the formation stage of an administered contract typically confronts a far more complex problem. The longer the anticipated relation and the more complexity and uncertainty entailed in that relation, the less significance will be placed on the price and quantity variables at the formation stage. The emphasis will instead be on establishing rules to govern the relationship: rules determining the appropriate length of the relationship; rules determining the process of adjustment to unexpected factors that arise in the course of the relationship; and rules concerning the termination of that relationship.

One can, with suitable caution and humility, apply the logic of optimization to aspects of the agent's choice problem. Indeed, one reason for formulating the problem as we have is to facilitate such analysis. Thus, by holding other aspects of the problem constant, it should be possible to determine the optimal length of a contract as a function of certain parameters (such as the exogenous rate of technological change). Nevertheless, in the discussion that follows we shall shy away from attempting to develop any rigorous criteria for efficiency and shall instead content ourselves with judging arrangements by some "reasonable" criteria. Such a nondefinition of efficiency will not sit well with most economists. Having scaled the dizzying heights of optimality, it is difficult and a bit anticlimactic to have to plumb the murky depths of reasonableness.

3. Protecting the producer's right to serve

■ Suppose that potential bidders for a contract realize that successful performance requires them to install long-lived, specialized capital equipment that has a very thin resale market. Their bid will depend in part on their expectations concerning the future availability of that market. These expectations will, in turn, be influenced by the existence of restrictions on the consumers' ability to exit. The investment might, however, prove to be a serious miscalculation and the winner might find that it cannot even cover variable costs. Then termination would be cheaper than continuation. In this event, making it easier for producers to terminate the contract will enhance the attractiveness of the arrangement (lower the supply price). Hence, the

[21] Alternatively we could say that the agent must determine the principal's true preferences and then, given the principal's ignorance of the relationship between his preference mapping and the choice set, the agent must attempt to construct that relationship. Thus, in a world in which a rational principal *must* delegate much of the task of evaluating alternatives to agents, we cannot judge the success of the agents against a standard based on the principal's perceptions of the relationship between the available alternatives and his utility to be derived therefrom.

producers will find that restrictions on either their behavior or the consumers' behavior will affect their supply price.

Consumers are in a similar position. To take advantage of a particular service might require the installation of long-lived complementary equipment. The consumer might be reluctant to purchase an all-electric house if he has no assurance that electricity will be available at "reasonable prices" over the life of the house. On the other hand, the consumer will want to avoid being locked into an inferior technology; for example, he might want the flexibility to transmit data by microwave rather than telephone lines if he were to see fit.

Increasing the protection of the producer's right to serve will make the contract more attractive to producers but, *ceteris paribus*, will make it less attractive to consumers. Likewise, increased protection of the consumers' right to be served will be valued by consumers and be treated as an additional cost by producers. Thus, at the formation stage the agent must determine the appropriate protection for both the right to serve and the right to be served.

Consider the following stylized example. The provider can name only one price that is fixed for the duration of the contract. Consumers have no interest in protecting their right to be served. (Therefore, the producer is free to terminate at will.)[22] Potential bidders know that as the durability of the plant increases, the marginal costs of production will fall; if the contract is terminated at any time, however, the scrap value of the plant will be zero. The consumers want to maintain their freedom to terminate the agreement so that they can take advantage of lower prices and/or superior technologies as they appear. The only variable under the agent's control is the level of protection of the right to serve.[23]

The optimal protection will be that at which the expected marginal benefits to the consumers of increased durability and decreased producer risk (lower prices) are just offset by the expected marginal costs of decreased flexibility. If the optimal protection is substantially greater than zero, this means that the agent finds it in the long-run interest of his principals to restrict their future options;[24] the effective achievement of their long-term interests requires that barriers be erected to their pursuit of short-run self-interest.[25]

Observation of private contracting parties suggests that they often will provide such protection in their contracts. Long-term commercial leases, requirements contracts, and exclusive dealing contracts are

[22] Price determination in long-term contracts will be discussed in more detail in Section 4. Protection of the consumers' right to be served will be discussed in Section 5; for a detailed analysis of the right to be served, see Goldberg (1976b)

[23] Protection depends on both the length of the contract and the penalties for breach at any time during the life of the contract. It is assumed for expositional convenience that these can be aggregated.

[24] It should be remembered that the very essence of contract is the restriction of future options. It is the economist's failure to take cognizance of that fact which leads to the treatment of long-term restrictions on behavior as aberrational.

[25] Formal models of the agent's choice problem can be extended to take into account such complications as (1) consumer reliance on the continuance of the relationship (protection of the right to be served), (2) more complex pricing formulae, and (3) interactions with insurance or alternative risk spreading devices. While insurance will often be a substitute for restrictions, it can also be a complement; it might, for example, be best to insure against some contingencies and to include restrictive contract clauses to control insurance premiums.

commonly observed.[26] Liquidated damages for premature termination or cancellation are also common.[27] For example, for sale of nuclear power plants General Electric's catalog listed termination charges in 1974 beginning at $72,000 per month.[28] The natural monopoly sector has characteristics which generally make protection of the producer's reliance especially attractive—very high capital-output ratios and capital which is both extremely long-lived and relatively immobile.[29] It is therefore reasonable to expect that the agent would design contracts with substantial protection of the producer's right to serve.

The fact that such protection would be desirable from the consumer's point of view has important implications for the analysis of regulation.[30] Two closely related criticisms of regulation are that it unduly restricts entry[31] and that it discourages technological change

[26] In practice, these often provide much less protection than they appear to provide on paper. See the comments of businessmen in *Columbia Nitrogen Co. v. Royster Guano Co.* 451 F.2d 3 (4th Cir. 1971). On the other hand, it is probable that meaningful long-term contracts would be more common were it not for their possible conflict with the antitrust laws. See *Standard Oil Co. of California v. United States*, 337 U.S. 293 (1949) and *FTC v. Motion Picture Advertising Co.*, 344 U.S. 392 (1953).

[27] Courts will refuse to enforce what they regard to be penalty clauses. The line between unenforceable penalty clauses and enforceable liquidated damage clauses is a fuzzy one. See Dawson and Harvey (1969, pp. 19–34) and Macneil (1975, pp. 699–702).

[28] Kwitny (1974, p. 39). In 1973 Combustion Engineering won a series of contracts in which it dramatically increased the customer's freedom to back out of deals. While the increased freedom (reduced protection of the right to serve) might ultimately prove desirable, it is clear that Combustion Engineering has exposed itself to substantially greater risks. The *Wall Street Journal* notes the company officers and directors were heavy sellers of the stock in 1973. It further states:

> Within Combustion, the debate over these risks has grown so hot that a contracting executive has come to this newspaper with documents describing the new contracts. He argues that the risks are unacceptable and could cost Combustion hundreds of millions of dollars within a decade. He shows evidence that others in the company are worried too (Kwitny 1974, p. 38).

[29] It could be argued that these characteristics are the *result* of protective regulation. Indeed the argument in the following footnote suggests that the protection of the right to serve will generally lead to more capital intensive production techniques. Thus we are implicitly assuming that if there were no protection for the right to serve, the efficient capital-output ratio would still be very high or if that is not the case, the optimal technique would be extremely expensive. For most of the industries generally classified as natural monopolies that would seem to be a reasonable assumption.

[30] The discussion in the text focuses on growth and innovation and ignores internal efficiency issues such as the influence of regulation on factor proportions. The analytical framework can be extended to encompass such issues. For example, it seems clear that the level of protection of the right to serve does influence the choice of production techniques. As protection is increased, producers will adopt technologies which take advantage of this increased protection and this will almost certainly lead to the adoption of more capital-intensive techniques. The choice of flexible pricing rules (to be discussed in the next section) can also influence factor proportions decisions. The Averch-Johnson (1962) model would be a special case in which the right to serve has absolute protection (entry is blockaded) and in which rate of return pricing (rather than some other flexible pricing mechanism) is used. In this broadened context the A-J overcapitalization result must be reinterpreted. The optimal factor proportions of the A-J model will not (except by accident) be optimal when we take into account the factors that make flexible pricing and protection of the right to serve (and the right to be served) attractive. (It should be noted that there are other reasons for not taking the A-J implications seriously; see Joskow (1974).)

[31] Posner (1969, p. 612) for example, states:

> But limitations on entry are worse than superfluous; they constitute a barrier to entry that may perpetuate monopoly long after a market has ceased to be naturally monopolistic.

by protecting existing producers from competing technologies.[32] To be sure, such limitations on entry must appear inefficient in a discrete transaction world. Entry barriers do enable the producer to charge a higher price in the short run than he could without the barriers; likewise, the regulator who, for example, protects UHF station owners from CATV competition is undoubtedly in error within this framework. But this short-run analysis ignores the importance of the protection of the right to serve. Would the firm have come into the market initially without some protection from competition? Would it have come in on terms as favorable as it did? What will be the rate of supply of innovations in the future if potential suppliers realize they will not be protected by the regulator? That is, if we view the protection afforded by the regulatory agent as *forward looking*, we can see it as a goad to innovation rather than a hindrance. Restrictions on entry by firms with identical or competing technologies provide a (possibly beneficial) haven from the Schumpeterian gale of creative destruction. Schumpeter[33] put the point eloquently:

> . . . restrictions . . . are, in the conditions of the perennial gale, incidents, often unavoidable incidents, of a long-run process of expansion which they protect rather than impede. There is no more of a paradox in this than there is in saying that motorcars are traveling faster than they otherwise would *because* they are provided with brakes.

Thus, a regulator acting as the consumers' agent would desire some shielding of existing producers from competing technologies. Regulation could, perhaps, be criticized for doing too much shielding or shielding the wrong producers, but to be valid such criticism first requires that we adopt a framework that enables us to determine the appropriate restrictions on producers and consumers.[34]

Even if it is true that regulation is too protective of existing technologies, there is no reason to presume that private contract would lead to the optimal amount of protection. The consumers' private agent will adopt some of the same practices as would the regulator (public agent). We can thus suggest four points. First, some technology suppression will likely be desirable from the consumers' viewpoint regardless of the institutionally determined identity of the agent. Second, institutional arrangements relying on private agents will frequently have restrictive mechanisms similar to those employed in regulated industries. Third, if they do not employ such mechanisms, they will often rely on a mixed bag of substitute rules to achieve roughly the same goal—patents,[35] trade secrets, and creation

The only justification for regulating entry that seems at all appealing . . . is that a true market test of a new entrant's efficiency may fail to materialize due to the regulatory agency's power to prescribe minimum rates.

[32] See, for example, Green and Nader (1973, p. 881), Kahn (1971, pp. 32–45), Posner (1971, pp. 29–30), and Noll (1971, p. 25).

[33] Schumpeter (1950, p. 88). The reader is strongly urged to read the two paragraphs preceding the quoted material.

[34] In terms of policy we should be concerned not only with the appropriate restrictions but with designing mechanisms that facilitate removing restrictions that no longer serve their purpose. For an analysis along these lines concerning protection of the right to be served, see Goldberg (1976b).

[35] A patent is another manisfestation of the right to serve. During the life of the patent, the patentee has the exclusive right to sell the product and can enjoin others from doing so or collect damages (if he can afford to protect his claim). In an institutional engineering context there are great difficulties determining the proper mix of legal devices for protecting the right to serve. It should be clear, however, that all such

of property rights in customers are examples.[36] Finally, sometimes private market mechanisms will simply not be adequate and the private market will fail to provide goods and services that would (and should) be made available under alternative institutional arrangements.[37]

4. Flexible pricing

■ Consider the options concerning pricing arrangements open to an administrator of a long-term contract. One option is simply to charge a lump-sum payment payable at the beginning of the period with goods and services then provided costlessly during the period the contract is in force. An almost equivalent alternative would be to provide for a fixed annual payment. If the buyer has access to capital at better terms than the potential sellers, it is to his advantage to acquire the financing and to pay the supplier up front. If the contract were terminated, then the buyer might find the task of attaining a refund more difficult (and expensive) than the task of ceasing payment and would therefore prefer annual payments. But aside from such relatively minor issues, these two options are rather similar. A third option would be to establish a price schedule fixed for the duration of the contract. The schedule can entail all sorts of complex arrangements—two-part tariffs, quantity discounts, cash discounts, and the like. But the significant factor is that the price schedule, no matter how complex, is agreed to when the contract is signed.

Another option would be for the agent to leave the price term open to varying degrees. Rather than specify future prices in advance, he could simply specify a process whereby such prices would be determined.[38] Such flexible pricing can take a number of different forms. The French administrative law doctrine of *imprévision*[39] and, to a lesser degree, the common law doctrines of frustration and quasi-contract are examples of such flexible pricing at the implicit social contract level. Alternatively, price could be adjusted according to some formula. A cost-of-living escalator is the simplest example of

devices (including patents) are quite imperfect, and, furthermore, that the array of institutional alternatives is much richer and more complex than standard economic analyses suggest.

[36] See *National Fire Insurance Co. v. Sullard*, 89 N.Y.S. 934: 97AD233 (1904) in which insurance agents were given property rights in customers. Joskow (1973, p. 404) complains that recognition of this right has severely slowed the adjustment of the liability insurance industry to superior distribution methods.

[37] It is quite possible that institutions of private contract can provide *less* flexibility than those of regulation and can in some instances lead to too much protection of an obsolete technology. Private property rights in insurance customers mentioned in the previous footnote, provide one likely example. In a somewhat different context, Dunham (1972, p. 14) notes that private restrictive covenants written at one point in time establish a set of transactions costs at a later date which can substantially slow adjustment to a changing world.

[38] Flexibility will be important for elements other than price as well. For a discussion of flexibility in long-term relationships from both a planning and legal viewpoint, see Macneil (1975).

[39] Friedman (1951, p. 34) notes: "It is in regard to administrative contracts that the famous doctrine of *imprévision* was first developed. Since 1905, French administrative tribunals have adjusted terms of administrative contracts in favour of the private contractor where a change of circumstances, such as a substantial rise in costs, would make it inequitable to hold him to the terms of the agreement. This has inspired most of the recent developments of the doctrine of frustration."

this approach. Prices could be set in relation to some presumably exogenous price, for example, the spot market price.[40] Or the price might be set as a function of gross revenues.[41] Fuller and Braucher summarize well the array of options:[42]

> Flexibility is sometimes sought . . . by leaving the price in a supply contract to be set by agreement from time to time. The agreement may contain a general arbitration clause . . . or it may contain a specific provision for arbitration in the event of a failure of the parties to agree on price. Frequently no standard is established for the arbitrator other than the implied one of general fairness and prevailing price levels. At other times the agreement will include a formula that interlocks the price to be paid by the buyer with the price of the same product, or a related product, on some designated market. At other times, particularly in agreements between corporations affiliated in ownership or management, price will be determined by actual cost to the seller plus a percentage for profit. In such "cost plus" contracts an elaborate definition of "cost" will usually be required, as well as considerable faith in the processes by which cost accountants purport to allocate costs where more than one product is being manufactured or sold.

Flexible pricing techniques are risk shifting devices,[43] but they are much more than that. Price flexibility preserves the decisionmaker's ability to adjust to changing conditions. It provides the opportunity to make better short-run allocation decisions under the umbrella of the long-term contract.[44] In a complex world, agents (or contracting parties generally) are unable to specify the characteristics of the product at the formation stage.[45] Thus, in designing a contract for an ad-

[40] In *Socony-Vacuum*, long-term contracts for gasoline fixed the price on the basis of the prevailing spot market price. Industry members agreed to a procedure of buying "excess" gasoline in the spot market in order to raise prices, demonstrating that such external prices need not be truly exogenous. *United States v. Socony-Vacuum Oil Co.*, 310 U.S. 150 (1940). Similarly, about half the wholesale meat sales are for future delivery with the price being the one reported in the "Yellow Sheet" on the date of delivery; for a discussion of alleged manipulation of Yellow Sheet prices by major meat packers, see Kwitny (1974). Fishlow (1974, p. 269) notes that in Brazil, where indexing has been built into many long-term contracts, the choice of an index has become a political issue.

[41] In American shopping centers tenants pay a fixed rent or five to six percent of the gross, whichever is larger; Fuller and Braucher (1964, p. 79) note that such arrangements have become very common in long-term leases for commercial real estate generally. Such pricing is also common for franchising arrangements and royalty payments.

[42] Fuller and Braucher (1964, pp. 77–78). For a detailed discussion of the variety of flexible pricing techniques, see "Business Practices and the Inflexibility of Long-Term Contracts" (1950).

[43] The defense contracting literature suggests that as the government bears a larger share of the risks of cost overruns—that is, as the contract type shifts from fixed price to cost plus fixed fee—bidders will decrease their bid price; see Moore (1967, p. 49), and Feeney, McGlothlin, and Wolfson (1964). While the federal government is probably better able to bear the risks than defense contractors, it is not obvious that a wise agent would shift the risk from, say, a cable television firm to a local community.

[44] The importance attached to flexibility is well illustrated by behavior in the paper industry. According to Macaulay (1963, p. 60):

> The standard contract used by manufacturers of paper to sell to magazine publishers has a pricing clause which is probably sufficiently vague to make the contract legally unenforceable. The house counsel of one of the largest paper producers said that everyone in the industry is aware of this because of a leading New York case concerning the contract, but that no one cares.

[45] While the argument in the text concerns the flexibility to adapt to changes in specifications, the inability to specify quality at the formation stage and subsequent difficulties in monitoring it will also increase the attractiveness of cost-based pricing in contracts for long-term provision of a bundle of services. Problems associated with determining and monitoring quality are discussed in Section 6.

vanced weapons system embodying a number of advances in the current state of the arts, construction of a complex new chemical plant,[46] or a telephone system to be operated over a long period of time, the agent will desire flexibility to adapt his plans to incorporate new knowledge developed during the performance of the contract (or developed exogenously) and to adapt also to possible changes in the principals' preferences. It would be extremely difficult to maintain such flexibility with a fixed price if the desired changes entailed increased costs for the providers.[47] If the change orders can be isolated, the contract at the formation stage might appropriately call for a fixed price plus a cost-based adjustment for changes in specifications;[48] if the changes are likely to be a significant aspect of the product being procured or if assigning costs to the changes in specifications is very difficult, then the agent might desire to extend cost-based pricing to the entire contract.

Many of the techniques used in other flexible pricing contracts are ill-adapted to problems in the regulatory sector. Cost-of-living escalators can adjust for the risks entailed in a changing price level but are of no help in adjusting to changes in relative factor scarcity, quality changes, or production techniques. Prices might be tied to spot market prices, but spot markets for most regulated industries seldom exist (nor would the likelihood of their existence be much enhanced under alternative nonregulatory regimes); even if they did exist, there would be great difficulties in determining the relevant spot price since costs often depend on customer characteristics (like location), the availability of fuel, and other localized factors. Comparability with benchmark producers (government or private firms) offers some guidance, but, as the long controversy over the comparability of TVA to private utilities showed, conclusive inexpensive answers are not likely to be found.

It seems reasonable to conclude that the agent would desire some flexible pricing mechanism in the long-term contract for provision of a natural monopoly service. While some of the techniques discussed in the previous paragraph might be utilized (e.g., fuel adjustment clauses), it is quite likely that there will be a large cost-based component. In particular, one form of cost-based pricing—rate of return regulation—appears to be at least a plausible choice. It is not obvious that any of the other imperfect flexible pricing mechanisms (including the special case of prices fixed at the formation stage) will be superior.[49]

---

[46] For constructing petrochemical plants, *Business Week* notes: "Most of the industry has switched to a negotiated, cost-plus-fixed-fee type of contract from the old fixed-price bid where the contractor with the lowest bid got the project." See "Fluor Gambles on a Flock of New Orders," *Business Week*, November 9, 1974, p. 129.

[47] If the changes led to lower costs, the fixed fee would deprive the customers of the savings; it would also greatly curtail the agent's incentives to lower quality standards since his principals would not be rewarded with lower prices to offset the quality reduction.

[48] We must stress that in actual commercial ongoing contractual relationships, adjustments often will be made regardless of the wording of the formal contract; see Macaulay (1963).

[49] The problems arising from cost-based pricing have been discussed extensively in the defense contracting literature; see Scherer (1964). See also the discussion in Section 6.

5. Protecting the consumers' right to be served

■ The discussion of pricing in the previous section assumed that only a single price was to be charged. Since most observed long-term contracts deal with a single customer, it is not necessary in those contexts to discuss rules for designing a price structure. However, in collective contracts this is no longer true and, consequently, the complexity of the agent's task is increased. He must now determine an initial rate structure and rules for adjusting the structure over time; this includes rules governing the conditions under which service to specific individuals or classes of customers can be terminated and rules governing the prices offered to new customers.

While for much economic activity customer protection against termination (or a sudden price increase) is not important, in some instances it would be very valuable. A franchise contract in which the very existence of one of the parties is threatened by termination provides one private sector example.[50] Protection of the right to be served is generally of greater import in the regulated sector.[51] The customer will find a great distinction between its *ex ante* and *ex post* demand. Before locating its plant at a particular site, a firm will have a number of options and, therefore, its demand for, say, rail services will be more elastic than after the plant has been built. *Business Week* provides a graphic example of the extent to which customers will rely on the continuance of the relationship and of the costs that will arise if that reliance is misplaced:[52]

> The magnitude of even a short hiatus in Penn Central service is so great that auto, steel and chemical industries, among other businesses located along the 19,000 mi. of line, say there is no way even to plan for alternative service. Victor Long, director of logistics for General Motors says, "You can't make contingency plans for something of this scope." Long says 42 GM plants are served exclusively by Penn Central, and some of them would be affected within 24 hours. Ford Motor Co., with 29 plants exclusively on the PC, says, "There is no way we could sustain our operation." Dupont adds: "A shutdown would mean insurmountable problems for every shipper."

There are three roots for the customers' demand for protection of the right to be served. First, once the relationship has begun, the supplier will be isolated to some degree from competition and will be in a position to "hold up" the consumer. A simple example would be the automobile mechanic who agrees to fix a car, takes it apart, and then says he will put it together again at three times the originally agreed upon price.[53] Generally, after the consumer has entered into the relationship with the producer, he will find himself vulnerable to price increases or the threat of termination; the producer will be in a position to price discriminate in an attempt to capture the "*ex post* consumer surplus."[54] In addition to protection from being held up,

---

[50] See Macaulay (1970) and Kessler (1957).

[51] The rights to serve and be served are not totally independent. The fact that the customer's options are generally restricted by the regulatory arrangement increases the importance of the right to be served. Protection of the right to be served in the form of the common carrier rule long precedes the appearance of the modern institutions of regulation.

[52] "Penn Central Puts Off Doomsday," *Business Week*, February 17, 1975, p. 30.

[53] The consumer would be protected under one or more common law doctrines (e.g., preexisting duty or unconscionability) or Section 2-209 of the Uniform Commercial Code. These represent a response by agents at a different level (judicial and legislative) to the hold up problem.

[54] Since the consumer's demand curve can look very different after he has made a commitment to the long-term contract, it is important when discussing price discrimina-

the customers will desire protection from arbitrary and capricious treatment. Finally, they will want to deal with the problem of "honest mistakes." The customers want to make investment decisions on the basis of reasonable price expectations but the producer finds that a particular service is no longer (or never was) profitable; the customer therefore would like some protection for his reasonable price expectations against the good faith decisions of the supplier to terminate or to increase prices.[55]

It should be clear that protection of the right to be served is not the only mechanism which consumers can use to achieve their goal. They could engage in stockpiling, maintain multiple suppliers, maintain standby capacity, insure, or perhaps even resort to vertical integration. Determination of the appropriate mix of these imperfect alternatives is obviously a complex problem. It is reasonable to suggest, however, that protection of the right to be served would frequently play a prominent role in the mixes chosen by agents for contracts to serve the natural monopoly industries.

Protection of the right to be served does not come costlessly. The agent must therefore balance the benefits of protecting the right against the costs such protection entails. The problem conceptually is similar to that of protecting the right to serve discussed in Section 3. Producers might be reluctant to initiate particular services if they do not have the freedom to adjust prices (or terminate) if future circumstances warrant. This problem is in part mitigated by regulatory policies which generally require the utility to extend services and by compensation schemes which base utility earnings on the overall operations of the firm, not on individual services—i.e., rate of return regulation. Given these institutional constraints on the supplier, the more likely effect will be that service will be overextended and that particular services will be kept alive too long.[56] If the firm is to make a reasonable profit, the cost of providing unprofitable services must be covered by some subset of the customers; in effect, customers will pay an insurance premium in the form of higher prices. In addition, if prices are prevented from adjusting to short-run changes in supply and demand conditions, there will be persistent short-term resource misallocation.[57]

---

tion to distinguish between *ex ante* and *ex post* demand curves. This distinction generally appears to be ignored in analyses stemming from a discrete transaction orientation.

The producer can increase his revenue by a more indirect means by using the threat of termination to discipline trouble makers—for example organizers of dealers, tenants, or customers. This is, of course, analogous to the firing of union organizers.

[55] What if consumers are uninformed and do not perceive the risks? Should we encourage them to expose themselves to such risks because their ignorance shields them from the undesirable results discussed in the text? We can still suggest an alternative efficiency-based argument for justifying protection. Failure to adopt protection today against the unperceived future risks can lead to significant losses in the future, and these future losses can cause social dislocations which would make society as a whole worse off for having failed to adopt protective measures today. This notion is analogous to Calabresi's "secondary costs" of accidents; see Calabresi (1970, pp. 39–67). Consumers, in effect, delegate to the agent the tasks of evaluating the risks and of determining the efficacy of alternative responses to the risks.

[56] It should be pointed out that the utility can to some extent offset these forces by degrading quality and by using selective marketing practices.

[57] The vulnerability of the individual customer to arbitrary treatment by the utility suggests that substantial procedural protection of the individual's right to be served would be desirable. However, if the firm must go through extensive and expensive

We do not intend to consider here how the agent should balance protection of consumer reliance against the costs of possible higher average prices and static misallocation. The point we do want to stress is that analyses in the discrete transaction tradition tend to focus only on these cost elements—primarily the static misallocation problems—and ignore the possibility that some of these costs might well be worth bearing. Modeling which derives efficiency conditions with the implicit assumption that there should be no protection of the right to be served will, except by accident, give wrong and misleading answers.

6. Administering the contract

■ If, as the above argument suggests, contracts for the provision of a natural monopoly service will be long-term agreements with cost based pricing, then the agent's task is not done once the contract has been let.[58] As Posner notes, a whole new set of issues arises:[59]

> What our discussion of the pernicious side effects of profit regulation crucially implies is that if an attempt is made to limit a company's profits the government must also concern itself with dimensions of firm behavior that could otherwise be left to the free market, such as the efficiency with which the firm employs capital and other resources, the rate and direction of its inventive activity, its expansion into other markets, and . . . the structure of its prices. These are areas in which a natural monopolist left to itself might be expected at least to approximate satisfactory performance. Once its profits are constrained—even partially—the monopolist's incentives to economically efficient and progressive performance are distorted, and much broader regulatory controls of company activity become necessary.

He is right in observing that once we begin to attempt to limit the firm's profits, we have taken the first step down the slippery slope and must then engage in a lot of other detailed oversight. He is wrong, however, in suggesting that the roots of our difficulties lie in the institutions of regulation. The problems are intrinsic to the service, not to the act of regulation itself.

That is, if the regulatory relationship were replaced by a private contract, the problems faced by the private agent would differ mainly in degree rather than in kind from those that plague regulators and provide a field day for their critics. Indeed, even in a rather simple private sector contract like a university food service contract[60] one can observe on a lesser scale the whole panoply of regulatory horrors.

---

proceedings to terminate customers it might find it cheaper to continue serving them, even if those customers are behaving in a manner detrimental to the group as a whole (for example, not paying their bills). It should not be difficult to work out examples in which the high price of due process will lead to substantial antigroup behavior. Starr (1971), for example, argues that increased due process protection of tenants in public housing has made it extremely difficult for the authorities to deal with "problem" tenants; this, he suggests, is a primary cause of the deterioration of public housing.

58 Since we are using the bidding for the market notion only metaphorically, there is no need to consider the problems that arise if such a contract were actually being put out to bid. If, however, we were considering the possibility of franchise bidding as a substitute for regulation, such a comparision would be appropriate. For an example of the difficulties that arise in this regard, see Williamson (1976) and Goldberg (1976c).

59 Posner (1969, pp. 605–606).

60 The university is in the not-for-profit sector and therefore the contract is not a purely private market affair, but this is not terribly important. The bulk of the contract food industry does deal with the private sector; see "America's Eating-Out Splurge," *Business Week*, October 27, 1975, p. 45. We focus on the university primarily because we have had first-hand experience in negotiating and administering such a contract.

Such contracts typically last for three years with the price for the last two years to be determined on the basis of expected costs plus a specified rate of return on sales. The university, like the regulator, must determine which costs are allowable; it must further decide on how detailed its monitoring of the firm should be, and on how much discretion the firm's management should have in making decisions that will affect costs.[61] The university must also determine what it will consider to be a "reasonable profit," and it must decide how much effort it should exert to ascertain the firm's true profits. In particular, it will have to monitor intra-firm transfers between the fiscal entity under its jurisdiction and the firm's central headquarters (for various managerial services) or supplier divisions. The problem is analogous to the difficulties encountered by a state regulatory agency analyzing the cost allocations made by AT & T for long distance calls, or the prices for equipment charged operating companies by Western Electric.[62]

Quality of service raises a number of problems. The agent must devise criteria and a process for changing the quality of service (and perhaps the price) if experience indicates that the initial quality level chosen was inadequate (or too high). The quality criteria must be flexible enough so that the management is not precluded from taking advantage of bargains. (That is, the contract should not require that only Brand X coffee be used or that pork chops be served on Monday nights.) Yet the standard must be objective enough so that the agent can convey the standards to the provider and monitor compliance.

The agent will find that there are substantial problems in monitoring compliance. To perform the task satisfactorily, he must immerse himself in trivia. Is there sufficient choice of breakfast cereals? Do they run out of the main entrees too often? Are they using "choice" meat in the stew? The agent will have to investigate consumer complaints regarding the general quality of service. He will find that it is too expensive to monitor everything effectively and, consequently, some noncompliance will get by, yet it is also likely that a not insignificant amount of resources will go toward monitoring. It is not too fanciful to suggest that the ratio of time spent quibbling over trifles to industry value added is higher in the contract food service industry than in the telephone industry or other regulated industries.[63]

The food service example might not adequately capture the complexity of the problem. Consider, therefore, a business firm purchasing private line services from a telephone company.[64] How is the buyer to monitor performance? The methods and criteria it adopts would probably not differ much from those developed by the reg-

[61] Of particular importance are decisions concerning the quality of service; these will be discussed below.

[62] One difference from the regulatory context is the relative ease the university has in terminating the contract. Termination and putting a contract to bid again are costly, but they are options which are available and, from time to time, are used. The university also has the option of vertically integrating and providing the service itself which many, in fact, do; it also has the option of more complete vertical disintegration—having no collective contract and relying on the market—an option which is also sometimes taken.

[63] For criticism of the emphasis regulatory agencies place on trivia, see MacAvoy (1971), Lewis (1967), and Posner (1969).

[64] See also Williamson (1976) for a discussion of some of the problems in the context of a cable television contract.

ulators. The one substantial difference between the two cases is the relative simplicity of this private agent's task. He can establish performance criteria in terms of the goals of members of the firm. While these goals are not necessarily so mutually consistent as traditional profit maximizing models assume, they are likely to be far more homogeneous and ascertainable than the goals of the community at large. Hence, the difficulties of determining consumer preferences (or what consumer preferences ought to be) are greatly diminished in the private line example. The more homogeneous preferences and clearer feedback signals of the private arrangement might lead to the choice of a different (and more effective) set of monitoring techniques, but at least in their broad outlines the tasks of the public and private agent are the same.[65]

Capital poses a number of problems for regulators, both in its measurement and in the monitoring of capital decisions (to control the tendency to expand the rate base). The same sort of issues arise, albeit in a somewhat different form, within long-term contracts for the provision of services in which fixed, specialized capital must be used (e.g., the food service contract, or a cable television agreement). If the life of the capital does not coincide with the life of the contract, then when the contract expires (or is prematurely terminated) it will be necessary to determine the capital consumption—if the capital is owned by the customers or their agent—or the "fair market value" of the surviving capital—if it is owned by the provider but must (or ought to)[66] be sold back to the other party or to the new provider. In either case the task can be a complex and expensive one to perform. If the rate of capital consumption is variable (depending on the level of output and maintenance effort) then the rules that the agent uses to determine capital consumption will, in effect, determine the relative price of capital; the rules could lead to factor proportion alterations not unlike the Averch-Johnson effect.[67]

---

[65] For a description of California's system for monitoring quality of telephone service, see Public Utilities Commission (1972). Performance standards include a number of technical criteria—for example, the call completion rate should be at least 98 percent (pp. 13–14)—and methods for measuring complicance. While there often are substantial economies of cost spreading which make the collective establishment and monitoring of quality standards desirable, this does not mean that the agency should (or does) centralize all quality decisions. Indeed, one criterion for satisfactory performance is a rate of fewer than 6.5 customer trouble reports per 100 stations per month (pp. 12–13). Quality variations clearly are discernible in many dimensions (for example, the choice between private and party lines) and it would generally be desirable to leave such decisions to the customer. The extent to which quality decisions should be delegated by the agent is an "appropriate jurisdiction" issue (see note 16) which, while fascinating, is beyond the scope of this paper.

[66] The contract could actually require such resale at "fair" prices or the fact that the capital is worth so little to the holder without the franchise could make resale extremely likely, although not inevitable. Williamson (1976) has a detailed discussion of the treatment of capital in the cable television contract which includes a description of the process for transferring equipment from the provider back to the city. See also Macaulay's (1966, pp. 90–91) description of termination compensation in automobile dealership franchise contracts.

[67] In the food service the capital is owned by the university and capital consumption is priced by paying a fee as a percentage of gross revenue to cover rent for land, buildings, tables, dishwashers, etc. Percentage of the gross compensation to an input of production (which is common in a number of other contexts such as shopping center leases) will typically lead to overuse of that input—at least according to traditional welfare criteria. When it is realized that using the price system is not costless and that

What should be the agent's role in capital expenditure decisions that arise during the life of the contract? To what extent should he "duplicate" the supplier's efforts in evaluating capital expenditures? Extensive supervision is costly both in terms of the out-of-pocket costs of monitoring and in terms of the sacrifice of the benefits of the provider's presumed expertise, a sacrifice which can be very great if the knowledge gained from operating programs is a useful input in capital decisions. On the other hand, giving the provider a relatively free rein will induce him to recommend (or undertake) capital expenditures which, if the capital "pricing" rules are improperly specified, can lead to an excess of capital. Perhaps a more serious problem is the producer's incentive to try to influence capital decisions so as to enhance his relative advantage in future bidding. This can take the form of recommending equipment which takes advantage of idiosyncracies of the providing firm. There is, indeed, an incentive to develop such idiosyncracies (similar to the incentive to differentiate one's product) so as to increase the relative disadvantage of new bidders.

The preceding discussion should not be taken to mean that the problems raised are insoluble. They are, indeed, resolved regularly in a manner apparently satisfactory to the contracting parties. Whether they are solved as well as they could be in terms of the contracting parties' interests and whether the solutions are also in the best interest of those not party to the contract are more difficult questions. The point is, however, that the solution ultimately agreed to will be imperfect by the criteria of traditional welfare economics and, further, that the imperfections will be similar to those that arise under regulation. Long-term, flexible pricing contracts with cost-based, profit-limitation features will discourage internal efficiency, discourage hard bargaining with labor and other suppliers, encourage gold plating, and encourage excessive capital formation. That is, the provider will have incentives to act very much like a regulated firm. Likewise, the agent will have incentives to act very much like a regulator, analyzing the cost figures of the provider, determining whether the measured profits meet the criteria laid out in the initial contract, monitoring quality and capital decisions, and so forth.

7. Concluding remarks

■ It is important to reiterate that we are not making a case for regulation. This essay might more appropriately be looked upon as "the case against the case against regulation." Many of the problems that arise in regulated industries would arise even if the industries were not under the jurisdiction of a regulatory agency (although the magnitude of the problems need not be the same).[68] Further, some of

there are other reasons for resorting to percentage of the gross pricing (see the discussion of flexible pricing in Section 4), then it is no longer clear that there really is "overuse." What we have is merely a factor proportion alteration, not necessarily a factor proportion bias.

[68] For a suggestive discussion of the difficulties involved in franchise contracts for provision of cable television, see Williamson (1976). Of course, the alternative to regulation need not be a publicly let franchise contract; it could simply be private individual contracts made under the jurisdiction of the public law of contract including, perhaps, the antitrust laws. While analysis of the impact of these bodies of law on an unregulated natural monopoly sector is well beyond the scope of this essay, there is reason for pessimism, or at least caution. The law of contracts has not in general been very successful in adapting to relational exchange patterns; it has maintained its

the regulatory problems perceived by economists are largely illusory; they are the result of stacking regulatory outcomes against irrelevant standards generated by models which suppress the contractual complexities inherent in the so-called natural monopoly sector.[69]

The administered contracts approach provides a very different perspective for examining regulatory institutions. The "justification" of regulation is seen to rest not on narrow natural monopoly (declining long-run average costs) grounds; rather it rests on the long-term relational matters stressed here. Thus, the observed emphasis by regulatory agencies on protection from competition, which appears quite anomalous within the standard framework, has a plausible explanation in this broader context.

Perhaps of greater importance, the administered contracts framework opens up new areas of search for innovations in regulatory institutions. Current research typically begins with an optimization model and seeks innovations which will satisfy static efficiency conditions within the framework of the model; peak load pricing and the optimal fair rate of return provide examples of this genre. Our approach places a relatively greater emphasis on mechanisms for maintaining, adjusting, and, perhaps, terminating long-term relationships. Further, it suggests sources for institutional innovation heretofore largely ignored by economists studying regulation. The emphasis on rights to serve and be served raises the natural question of how, if at all, those rights should be protected. Such a formulation suggests the relevance of analytical tools and institutional forms responsive to such questions as: how should *X*'s right to breathe clean air be protected from *Y*'s productive activity which pollutes that air? Thus, we are led to consider the efficacy of such legal instruments as injunctions, damage rules, and other forms of protecting rights.[70] A second source of innovation is observation of the behavior of privately contracting parties. How do businessmen design, police, and adjust their long-term relationships? Can any of the techniques that have evolved in the private sector be fruitfully transferred to the public sector?

The implications of this essay go beyond altering our perspective on regulation. Economic theory generally ignores the complexity of contractual arrangements by implicitly assuming that most exchange takes place in the discrete transaction form. Indeed, some of the theoretical breakthroughs of recent years (for example, time-dated commodities and contingent markets) have taken the form of forcing complex relationships over time into a discrete transaction mold. We

doctrinal integrity in large part by relinquishing jurisdiction (for example, to regulatory agencies) so that it has become a law of leftovers, "general rules adequate for regulating those transactions which are either not complicated enough or numerous enough to have stimulated the development of separate bodies of rules" (Summers, 1969, p. 567). See also Macneil (1974) and Friedman (1965). Antitrust law presents a veritable mare's nest for a deregulated natural monopoly sector: multiyear contracts, termination of customers, refusal to provide services to competitors (e.g., not permitting local telephone companies to tie in with a larger telephone network), and similar issues will bring the activities of the producers into constant conflict with the law (although many such activities would likely be desirable). Further, it is quite probable that the judicial remedy would take the form of a regulatory decree, in effect establishing a mini-regulatory agency; see Posner (1970, pp. 386, 388) and Timberg (1954).

[69] See the discussion of comparative institutional analysis in Demsetz (1969).

[70] See generally Coase (1960) and Calabresi and Melamed (1972); for an analysis of protection of the right to be served in this spirit, see Goldberg (1976b).

hope that this essay has been sufficiently suggestive to encourage theorists to explore seriously the implications of opening up the black box of contract.

References

AVERCH, H. AND JOHNSON, L. "Behavior of the Firm under Regulatory Constraint." *The American Economic Review*, Vol. 52, No. 5 (December 1962), pp. 1052–1069.

BERNSTEIN, M. H. *Regulating Business by Independent Commission*. Princeton: Princeton Univ. Press, 1955.

BROWN, J. P. "Product Liability: The Case of an Asset with a Random Life." *The American Economic Review*, Vol. 64, No. 1 (March 1974), pp. 149–161.

"Business Practices and the Inflexibility of Long-Term Contracts." *Virginia Law Review*, Vol. 36 (1950), pp. 627–647.

CALABRESI, G. *The Cost of Accidents*. New Haven: Yale Univ. Press, 1970.

——— AND MELAMED, A. D. "Property Rules, Liability Rules, and Inalienability: One View of the Cathedral." *Harvard Law Review*, Vol. 85 (April 1972), pp. 1089–1128.

CLARK, J. M. *Social Control of Business*, 2nd ed. New York: McGraw-Hill Book Company, 1939.

COASE, R. H. "The Problem of Social Cost." *Journal of Law and Economics*, Vol. 3 (October 1960), pp. 1–44.

DAWSON, J. P. AND HARVEY, W. B. *Cases on Contracts and Contract Remedies*, 2nd ed. Mineola, N.Y.: The Foundation Press, 1969.

DEMSETZ, H. "Some Aspects of Property Rights." *Journal of Law and Economics*, Vol. 9 (October 1966), pp. 61–70.

———. "Why Regulate Utilities?" *Journal of Law and Economics*, Vol. 11 (April 1968), pp. 55–66.

———. "Information and Efficiency: Another Viewpoint." *Journal of Law and Economics*, Vol. 12 (April 1969), pp. 1–22.

DEWEY, D. J. "The New Learning: One Man's View," in H. J. Goldschmid, H. M. Mann, and J. F. Weston, eds., *Industrial Concentration: The New Learning*, Boston: Little, Brown and Company, 1974, pp. 1–14.

DUNHAM, A. "Separation of Ownership from Decisions about Usefulness," in G. Wunderlich and W. L. Gibson, Jr., eds., *Perspectives on Property*, State College, Pa.: Institute for Research on Land and Water Resources, Pennsylvania State University, 1972.

FEENEY, G. J., MCGLOTHLIN, W. H., AND WOLFSON, R. J. *Risk Aversion in Incentive Contracting: An Experiment*. The Rand Corporation, RM-4231-PR, August 1964.

FISHLOW, A. "Indexing Brazilian Style: Inflation with Tears?" *Brookings Papers on Economic Activities*, No. 1. Washington D.C.: The Brookings Institution, 1974, pp. 261–280.

FRIEDMAN, L. M. *Contract Law in America*. Madison: University of Wisconsin Press, 1965.

FRIEDMANN, W. "Changing Functions of Contract in the Common Law." *University of Toronto Law Journal*, Vol. 9 (1951): pp. 15–41.

FULLER, L. AND BRAUCHER, R. *Basic Contract Law*, St. Paul: West Publishing Company, 1964.

GALANTER, M. "Why the 'Haves' Come Out Ahead: Speculations on the Limits of Legal Change." *Law and Society Review*, Vol. 9 (Fall 1974), pp. 95–160.

GOLDBERG, V. P. "Institutional Change and the Quasi-Invisible Hand." *Journal of Law and Economics*, Vol. 17 (October 1974), pp. 461–492.

———. "Toward an Expanded Economic Theory of Contract." *Journal of Economic Issues*, Vol. 10 (March 1976a), pp. 45–61.

———. "Protecting the Right to be Served by Rregulated Industries." Unpublished manuscript, 1976b.

———. "Competitive Bidding and the Production of Pre-Contract Information," Unpublished manuscript, 1976c.

GREEN, M. AND NADER, R. "Economic Regulation vs. Competition: Uncle Sam the Monopoly Man." *Yale Law Journal*, Vol. 82 (April 1973), pp. 871–889.

JOSKOW, P. L. "Cartels, Competition and Regulation in the Property-Liability Insurance Industry." *The Bell Journal of Economics and Management Science*, Vol. 4, No. 2 (Autumn 1973), pp. 375–427.

———. "Inflation and Environmental Concern: Structural Change in the Process of Public Utility Price Regulation." *Journal of Law and Economics*, Vol. 17 (October 1974), pp. 291–327.

KAHN, A. E. *The Economics of Regulation: Principles and Institutions, Volume II: Institutional Issues*. New York: John Wiley and Sons, 1971.

KESSLER, F. "Automobile Dealer Franchises: Vertical Integration by Contract." *Yale Law Journal*, Vol. 66 (1957).

——— AND FINE, E. " 'Culpa in Contrahendo,' Bargaining in Good Faith and Freedom of Contract: A Comparative Study." *Harvard Law Review*, Vol. 77 (January 1964), pp. 401–449.

KWITNY, J. "Combustion Engineering's Order Surge May Have Been Based on Risky Deals." *Wall Street Journal*, May 7, 1974, p. 38.

———. " 'Yellow Sheet' Guides Prices of Most Meat, But How Reliable Is It?" *Wall Street Journal*, December 6, 1974, p. 14.

LEWIS, B. W. "Emphasis and Misemphasis in Regulatory Policy," in G. Shepherd and T. G. Gies, eds., *Utility Regulation*, New York: Random House, 1967.

LORD, B. M. "An Analysis of the Market for Medical Expense Insurance: Some Implications of Contractual Relationships." Unpublished Ph.D. dissertation. University of California, Davis, 1975.

MACAULAY, S. "Non-Contractual Relations in Business: A Preliminary Study." *American Sociological Review*, Vol. 28 (February 1963), pp. 55–67.

———. *Law and the Balance of Power: The Automobile Manufacturers and Their Dealers*. New York: Russell Sage Foundation, 1966.

MACAVOY, P. W. *The Crisis of the Regulatory Commissions*. New York: W. W. Norton and Company, 1970.

———. "The Formal Work-Product of the Federal Power Commissioners." *The Bell Journal of Economics and Management Science*, Vol. 2, No. 1 (Spring 1971), pp. 379–395.

MACNEIL, I. R. "The Many Futures of Contract." *Southern California Law Review*, Vol. 47 (May 1974), pp. 691–816.

———. "A Primer of Contract Planning." *Southern California Law Review*, Vol. 48 (January 1975), pp. 627–704.

MITNICK, B. M. "The Theory of Agency: The Concept of Fiduciary Rationality and Some Consequences." Unpublished Ph.D. dissertation. University of Pennsylvania, 1974.

MOORE, F. T. "Incentive Contracts," in S. Enke, ed., *Defense Management*, Englewood Cliffs, N.J.: Prentice Hall, 1967.

NOLL, R. *Reforming Regulation*. Washington, D. C.: The Brookings Institution, 1971.

POSNER, R. A. "Natural Monopoly and Its Regulation." *Stanford Law Review*, Vol. 21 (February 1969), pp. 548–643.

———. "Taxation by Regulation." *The Bell Journal of Economics and Management Science*, Vol. 2, No. 1 (Spring 1971), pp. 22–50.

———. "A Statistical Study of Antitrust Enforcement." *Journal of Law and Economics*, Vol. 13 (October 1970), pp. 365–419.

———. "Theories of Economic Regulation." *The Bell Journal of Economics and Management Science*, Vol. 5, No. 2 (Autumn 1974), pp. 335–358.

PUBLIC UTILITIES COMMISSION OF THE STATE OF CALIFORNIA. "Investigation into the Need and Requirements for a General Order Governing Standards of Telephone Service to be Furnished by Telephone Utilities in the State of California." Decision No. 80082, Case No. 9353, March 21, 1972.

RICHARDSON, G. B. "The Organization of Industry." *Economic Journal*, Vol. 82 (September 1972), pp. 883–896.

SCHERER, F. M. *The Weapons Acquisition Process: Economic Incentives*. Boston: Graduate School of Business Administration, Harvard University, 1964.

SCHUMPETER, J. A. *Capitalism, Socialism and Democracy*, 3rd ed. New York: Harper and Row, 1950.

STARR, R. "Which of the Poor Shall Live in Public Housing?" *Public Interest*, Vol. 23 (Spring 1971), pp. 116–124.

STIGLER, G. "The Theory of Economic Regulation." *The Bell Journal of Economics and Management Science*, Vol. 2, No. 1 (Spring 1971), pp. 3–21.

SUMMERS, C. W. "Collective Agreements and the Law of Contracts." *Yale Law Journal*, Vol. 78 (March 1969), pp. 525–575.

TIMBERG, S. "The Antitrust Aspects of Merchandising Modern Music: The ASCAP Consent Judgment of 1950." *Law and Contemporary Problems*, Vol. 19 (Spring 1954), pp. 294–322.

WEITZMAN, L. J. "Legal Regulation of Marriage: Tradition and Change." *California Law Review*, Vol. 62 (September 1974), pp. 1169–1288.

WILLIAMSON, O. E. "The Vertical Integration of Production: Market Failure Considerations." *The American Economic Review*, Vol. 61 (May 1971): pp. 112–123.

———. "Markets and Hierarchies: Some Elementary Considerations." *The American Economic Review*, Vol. 63, No. 2 (May 1973), pp. 316–325.

———. "The Economics of Antitrust: Transaction Cost Considerations." *University of Pennsylvania Law Review*, Vol. 122 (June 1974), 1439–1496.

———. "Franchise Bidding for Natural Monopolies—In General and with Respect to CATV." *The Bell Journal of Economics*, Vol. 7, No. 1 (Spring 1976), pp. 73–104.

[17]

THE ORIGINS OF UTILITY REGULATION AND THE "THEORIES OF REGULATION" DEBATE*

GEORGE L. PRIEST
Yale Law School

I. Introduction: *The Journal of Law and Economics* and the Modern Understanding of the Motivations for Regulation

For at least the past twenty years, the academic literature has debated explanations of the origins and underlying motivations of the establishment and operation of commissions directly regulating industry in the United States. I will describe this literature as the "theories of regulation" debate. Although there were important precursors, the debate became prominent in 1971 with the publication of George J. Stigler's article, "The Theory of Economic Regulation,"[1] in which Stigler proposed the theory, quite contrary to then-conventional wisdom, that regulation by commission could be considered a commodity and analyzed like other commodities as subject to the forces of demand and supply: demand by affected interest groups and supply, in the first instance, by legislators and after by regulators. The debate was focused three years later by Richard A. Posner in his article, "Theories of Economic Regulation."[2] Posner contrasted Stigler's "economic" theory to two alternative approaches: the widely accepted "public interest" theory, according to which regulation is imposed by government to correct market failures in

* Presented at the John M. Olin Centennial Conference in Law and Economics at the University of Chicago Law School, April 7–9, 1992. The author is the John M. Olin Professor of Law and Economics, Yale Law School. I am very grateful to Jean Doerr, Susan J. Grelick, Eric Posner, and Brooks Fudenberg for excellent research assistance over many years on this article and to Fred McChesney, Kathleen Cleaver, and participants at the Faculty Colloquium, Emory Law School, for helpful comments.

[1] George J. Stigler, The Theory of Economic Regulation, 2 Bell J. Econ. & Mgmt. Sci. 3 (1971).

[2] Richard A. Posner, Theories of Economic Regulation, 5 Bell J. Econ. & Mgmt. Sci. 335 (1974).

[*Journal of Law & Economics*, vol. XXXVI (April 1993)]

order to benefit consumers and to enhance social welfare, and a theory related to, but somewhat cruder than, Stigler's economic theory: the "capture" theory, according to which a regulatory agency, though perhaps created to pursue public interest goals, later comes under the dominant influence of—is captured by—the industry subject to regulation. Posner concluded that none of the three theories was totally successful in explaining the incidence of commission regulation but that Stigler's economic theory was clearly the most promising avenue for future research.[3]

This debate over the motivations of regulation has continued since and has exerted an extraordinary influence on public policy. Reducing the public interest justification for regulation to merely one of several available theories and, beyond that, to an unconvincing member of the set seriously challenged the widely accepted basis for government control of so-called market failures. More specifically, it significantly contributed to the movement toward broad deregulation of industry which, along with the parallel adoption of the economic approach toward antitrust law, constitutes the greatest intellectual triumph in U.S. public policy of modern times. To fully appreciate the significance and the modern influence of the "theories of regulation" debate, however, it is important to understand the foundation on which it was built.

Stigler's 1971 article and the debate it engendered followed more than a decade of sustained criticism of the origins and effects of regulation and of antitrust enforcement, most of which appeared in studies published in the *Journal of Law and Economics*. From the very first issue of the *JLE*, its founding editor Aaron Director and his successor Ronald H. Coase solicited, encouraged, and, through their own work and ideas, stimulated studies of both direct industry regulation and regulation through antitrust enforcement whose common theme was the debunking of the then-widespread view that government interference in the economy, either through regulation or the antitrust laws, served broad public interest goals. The consistent themes of the *JLE* attacking regulation and extolling competition and economic freedom contributed importantly to the broader intellectual debate over socialism and planned economies.[4] A brief canvas of some early *JLE* issues will remind the reader of the extraordinary uniformity of the approach as well as of the continuing

[3] *Id.* at 356.

[4] For a flavor of the underlying social context of this debate during the late 1950s and early 1960s, see G. Warren Nutter, The Structure and Growth of Soviet Industry: A Comparison with the United States, 2 J. Law & Econ. 147 (1959) (warning of vastly more rapid future economic growth in the Soviet Union than in the United States).

impact of this work: volume 1 contained John McGee's debunking of the *Standard Oil* case[5] and Gale Johnson's critique of agricultural subsidies;[6] volume 2, Ronald Coase's expose of the origins and the regulatory rationale of the Federal Communications Commission (FCC)[7] and Jack Hirshleifer's articles on the ethics of capitalism;[8] volume 3, Coase's broader critique of the effects of liability rules on the control of externalities[9] and Lester Telser's critical analysis of the prohibition of resale price maintenance;[10] volume 4, Coase's undermining of the postal monopoly[11] and Thomas Moore's broad critique of occupational licensing.[12] As *JLE* issues progressed, the criticism of regulation and of the antitrust laws expanded in scope and effect: volume 5 contained the famous Stigler-Friedland study of the ineffectiveness of electricity regulation,[13] Coase's further study of communications regulation,[14] Yale Brozen's study of minimum wage laws,[15] and Rosemary Hale and J. E. Hale's critical review of antimerger enforcement.[16]

Many studies published in the *JLE* were directed at the operations of

[5] John S. McGee, Predatory Price Cutting: The Standard Oil (N.J.) Case, 1 J. Law & Econ. 137 (1958).

[6] D. Gale Johnson, Government and Agriculture: Is Agriculture a Special Case? 1 J. Law & Econ. 122 (1958). It also contained George Stigler's famous study of The Economies of Scale, 1 J. Law & Econ. 54 (1958), and Gary Becker's still insufficiently appreciated Competition and Democracy, 1 J. Law & Econ. 105 (1958). Though I do not emphasize work of this nature because of the more specific focus of this article, significant attention was given by articles in the *Journal* to the operation of competitive markets, such as Stigler's article on scale economies, as well as to the relationship between economic and political freedom. For example, see Becker, *id.;* Jacob Viner, The Intellectual History of Laissez Faire, 3 J. Law & Econ. 45 (1960); George J. Stigler, Private Vice and Public Virtue, 4 J. Law & Econ. 1 (1961).

[7] R. H. Coase, The Federal Communications Commission, 2 J. Law & Econ. 1 (1959).

[8] Jack Hirshleifer, Capitalist Ethics—Tough or Soft? 2 J. Law & Econ. 114 (1959); The Secretary [Jack Hirshleifer], The Sumptuary Manifesto, 2 J. Law & Econ. 120 (1959).

[9] R. H. Coase, The Problem of Social Cost, 3 J. Law & Econ. 1 (1960).

[10] Lester G. Telser, Why Should Manufacturers Want Fair Trade? 3 J. Law & Econ. 86 (1960).

[11] R. H. Coase, The British Post Office and the Messenger Companies, 4 J. Law & Econ. 12 (1961).

[12] Thomas G. Moore, The Purpose of Licensing, 4 J. Law & Econ. 93 (1961).

[13] George J. Stigler & Claire Friedland, What Can Regulators Regulate? The Case of Electricity, 5 J. Law & Econ. 1 (1962).

[14] R. H. Coase, The Interdepartment Radio Advisory Committee, 5 J. Law & Econ. 17 (1962).

[15] Yale Brozen, Minimum Wage Rates and Household Workers, 5 J. Law & Econ. 103 (1962).

[16] Rosemary D. Hale & J. E. Hale, More on Mergers, 5 J. Law & Econ. 119 (1962).

specific regulatory agencies such as the FCC[17] and later the Interstate Commerce Commission[18] and former Civil Aeronautics Board[19] and Federal Power Commission (FPC).[20] Each of these agencies regulated what most accepted to be a competitive industry. For these examples, as well as for the regulation of industries such as the merchant marine[21] and the service occupations,[22] the weaknesses in the justifications for regulation were readily apparent; the primary mission of the related *JLE* article was to fully air (and so expose) the nominal excuse for regulation and then to demonstrate regulation's adverse effects. Far more influential criticism of regulation, however, derived from studies debunking the regulation, not of competitive industries, but of industries seemingly characterized by natural monopoly. For natural monopoly industries, the critical task was more difficult because there existed a widely accepted justification for regulation in economics: to benefit consumers by reducing price closer toward marginal cost. For this reason, the case of natural monopolies provided the strongest battleground over government interference in markets. Even economists accepted that, in contexts of natural monopoly, price was likely to depart from marginal cost. But if it could be shown that, in contexts of natural monopoly, government interference could not enhance social welfare, how could government interference ever be justified in contexts where claims of "market failure" were far more controversial?

Of all the articles published during these years in the *JLE* (or elsewhere) criticizing the regulation of natural monopolies, surely the two most important were the Stigler-Friedland study showing that regulatory commissions had no apparent effect on electricity prices[23]—the seminal empirical attack on public utility regulation—and Harold Demsetz's 1968 essay, "Why Regulate Utilities?"[24] Demsetz's article raised the question

[17] See notes 7 and 14 *supra;* Harvey J. Levin, Federal Control of Entry in the Broadcast Industry, 5 J. Law & Econ. 49 (1962).

[18] George W. Hilton, The Consistency of the Interstate Commerce Act, 9 J. Law & Econ. 87 (1966).

[19] Michael E. Levine, Landing Fees and the Airport Congestion Problem, 12 J. Law & Econ. 79 (1969); Michael E. Levine, Regulating Airmail Transportation, 18 J. Law & Econ. 317 (1975); also see David G. Davies, The Efficiency of Public versus Private Firms: The Case of Australia's Two Airlines, 14 J. Law & Econ. 149 (1971).

[20] Edmund W. Kitch, Regulation of the Field Market for Natural Gas by the Federal Power Commission, 11 J. Law & Econ. 243 (1968).

[21] Clinton H. Whitehurst, Jr., The Merchant Marine Act of 1936: An Operational Subsidy in Retrospect, 8 J. Law & Econ. 223 (1965).

[22] See note 12 *supra*. Also see Charles R. Plott, Occupational Self-Regulation: A Case Study of Oklahoma Dry Cleaners, 8 J. Law & Econ. 195 (1965).

[23] See note 13 *supra*.

[24] Harold Demsetz, Why Regulate Utilities? 11 J. Law & Econ. 55 (1968).

to a new level by arguing powerfully that the conditions of natural monopoly of local utilities such as electricity, gas, or water were never sufficient to justify regulation by commission in any form. As I shall later show,[25] the concluding sentences of Demsetz's article suggested the idea that Stigler would later develop as his economic theory of regulation. Thus, Stigler's economic theory of regulation published in 1971 and Posner's 1974 comparative review were built on a decade and a half of sustained and unrelenting criticism in the *JLE* of the operation of industrial regulation, demonstrating uniformly adverse effects and a generalizable absence of coherent or defensible rationale.

The "theories of regulation" literature, in essence, continued to ask the question Posner put in 1974: can the existence and operation of regulatory commissions best be explained by some public interest theory or by some theory relating to the pursuit of private interests, typically at public expense?[26] In the succeeding years, there have been significant advances in the definition of the economic theory, the most important by Sam Peltzman (again, published in the *JLE*) focusing on the importance of the marginal voter in coalition building.[27] In addition, the approach has been substantially aided by the public choice school.[28] Not surprisingly, the literature has been dominated by demonstrations of the influence of private interests.[29] Indeed, it was claimed as early as 1984 that the "economic theory of regulation long ago put public interest theories of politics to rest."[30] Nevertheless, there remain important defenders of public interest explanations,[31] and even some supporters of the economic theory still seek to find a role for "ideology," unrelated to economic interests, in the design and implementation of regulatory policy.[32]

This article, however, is critical of this literature and of its basic conception that it is useful to attempt to discover and verify some single

[25] See Part II *infra*.

[26] For a recent review of this literature, see Michael E. Levine & Jennifer L. Forrence, Regulatory Capture, Public Interest, and the Public Agenda: Toward a Synthesis, 6 J. L. Econ. & Org. 167 (1990).

[27] Sam Peltzman, Toward a More General Theory of Regulation, 19 J. Law & Econ. 211 (1976).

[28] See the Levine & Forrence review, *supra* note 26.

[29] As I shall explain below, there are very grave deficiencies in the effort to define the contrasting "public interest" with any specificity.

[30] Joseph P. Kalt & Mark A. Zupan, Capture and Ideology in the Economic Theory of Politics, 74 Am. Econ. Rev. 279 (1984).

[31] Michael E. Levine, Revisionism Revised? Airline Deregulation and the Public Interest, 44 L. & Contemp. Probs. 179 (1981); Levine & Forrence, *supra* note 26.

[32] See Kalt & Zupan, *supra* note 30 (defining the range of regulatory "slack" as available for the pursuit of the public interest). See also Levine & Forrence, *supra* note 26, for the same point.

theory that explains the broad range of commission regulation. As I shall try to show, I believe that the effort to ascribe regulatory effects to a "theory" largely deflects attention from the dynamic relationship between the regulator and the regulated firm or industry played out most frequently within a long-term relationship closely resembling more familiar forms of long-term contracts. I believe that the focus on regulation by commission (indeed, the theory is a theory of commission regulation) is misguided and that the differences between regulation by commission and by other regulatory techniques are much less important than has generally been appreciated.

I will attempt to illustrate the point—and the futility of the "theories of regulation" approach—by examining in a preliminary way the history of public utility regulation, the subject of the Stigler-Friedland and Demsetz studies which initiated the debate. I will argue that a careful review of the early history of public utility regulation renders impossible any clear-cut distinction between competing public interest and private interest "theories." The history, moreover, shows that the "theories of regulation" approach ignores more important and more tractable issues regarding the interaction of regulators and the regulated firm that are likely to prove more fruitful for the understanding of regulation. For the public utilities and, I shall suggest, for other areas of regulation, the interaction between the regulator and the regulated firm or industry is difficult to distinguish from long-term contracting, dominated by predictable problems of unilateral or mutual adjustment over time in response to changing conditions. Several recent papers chiefly directed at the regulation of cable television have suggested the similarity between regulation and long-term contracting.[33] This article generalizes the point and illustrates its operation in the context of the transition during the early years of this century from municipal regulation by franchise to state regulation by commission. In the process, it challenges earlier studies explaining the origins of commission regulation[34] and suggests that the problem of regulatory design, importantly illuminated twenty-five years ago by Harold

[33] A. Prager, Firm Behavior in Franchise Monopoly Markets, 21 RAND J. Econ. 211 (1990); M. A. Zupan, Cable Franchise Renewals: Do Incumbent Firms Behave Opportunistically? 20 RAND J. Econ. 473 (1989). For an earlier discussion, see O. E. Williamson, Franchise Bidding for Natural Monopolies—in General and with Respect to CATV, 7 Bell J. Econ. 73 (1976), which, lightly rewritten, appears in Oliver E. Williamson, The Economic Institutions of Capitalism (1985), at ch. 13 (emphasizing problems with specifying and enforcing franchise contracts).

[34] In particular, see Stigler & Friedland, *supra* note 13; and Gregg A. Jarrell, The Demand for State Regulation of the Electric Utility Industry, 21 J. Law & Econ. 269 (1978).

Demsetz, is substantially more complicated than has earlier been appreciated.[35]

Part II of this article reviews the history of the "theories of regulation" literature, indicating why the institution of commission regulation has received such prominent attention and how the analysis of public utility regulation by Stigler-Friedland and Demsetz has contributed to the literature. Part III then discusses the history of public utility regulation more carefully, examining, though necessarily without comprehensiveness, several decades of municipal regulatory activity that preceded the adoption of the commission form criticized by Stigler and Friedland and Demsetz. Finally, Part IV explains the difficulties of focusing on the commission form and attempts to refocus our understanding of regulation and its effects from a long-term contracting viewpoint.

II. Commission Regulation of Public Utilities in the Theories of Regulation Debate

As described earlier, the evaluation of commission regulation of public utilities—in particular, services such as electricity, gas, and water—has been of central importance in the theories of regulation debate. There are three basic reasons that the search for a theory of regulation has focused on public utility commissions. First, regulation by commission represents the most sustained form of government interference in the otherwise competitive marketplace of the United States. A continuously sitting commission, with perpetual jurisdiction over all aspects of a firm's or an industry's operations including constraint of its rate of return, is the closest analogue to the government planning characteristic of socialist economies. Thus, though often below the surface, the debate over the welfare-enhancing or welfare-diminishing effects of commission regulation is a debate over socialism versus capitalism.

Second, the public utilities have long been operated as monopolies and have been believed to be natural monopolies: industries characterized by declining average costs over the relevant range of output, thus industries for which the introduction of competition would lead total production costs to increase. Industries meeting these conditions have traditionally provided the strongest public interest justification for regulation. In addi-

[35] For discussions emphasizing the problems of franchise contracting, see Williamson, Franchise Bidding for Natural Monopolies, *supra* note 33; Williamson, The Economic Institutions of Capitalism, *supra* note 33; Richard Schmalensee, The Control of Natural Monopolies 68–72 (1979).

tion to any noneconomic goals, regulation seemingly can achieve the powerful economic goal of constraining monopoly pricing toward marginal cost in order to enhance social welfare. Indeed, this social welfare justification is so widely accepted that the natural monopoly case is viewed as the prototypical context for government regulation. Virtually all public interest justifications for regulation in industries not characterized by natural monopoly consist of claims that the alleged market imperfection in the particular industry will generate an effect resembling natural monopoly.

Third, the history of commission regulation in the United States strongly points toward the centrality of the public utility context and is suggestive that some single economic theory may be more explanatory than the public interest theory deriving from the analysis of natural monopoly. Except for the handful of federal regulatory commissions, the principal example of commission regulation in the United States is regulation of public utilities. Almost all states have established continuously sitting public utility commissions. Moreover, these commissions were introduced relatively uniformly in the various states within a very short compass of time. Figure 1 displays the cumulative adoption by state of regulatory commissions with authority to regulate rates for electric utilities and, separately, for gas utilities within twenty large states. As is evident, state regulatory commissions were first created in the late 1880s (in Massachusetts) but then were inaugurated with sudden uniformity in the decade and a half following 1907. Figure 1 shows that, by 1922, electric regulatory commissions had been introduced in thirty-seven of the forty-eight states and gas commissions in eighteen of twenty large states.

This rough simultaneity in timing across states is not easily reconciled with the explanation that regulatory commissions derived solely from the existence of natural monopoly. That is, it is very hard to believe that the average cost curves of electric and gas utilities only began to slope downward after 1907, switching in direction at roughly the same time in each of these diverse states. This seeming coincidence of commission establishment might surely suggest that some deeper underlying source exists for the establishment of regulatory commissions.

For these various reasons, it is not surprising that, as part of the ambitious assault on the foundations of regulation waged in the pages of the *Journal of Law and Economics*, careful attention was given to the public utility–natural monopoly case. Two studies published just a few years apart severely challenged the conventional justification for public utility regulation and directly stimulated the theories of regulation debate. The first study, published in 1962 by George J. Stigler and Claire Friedland,

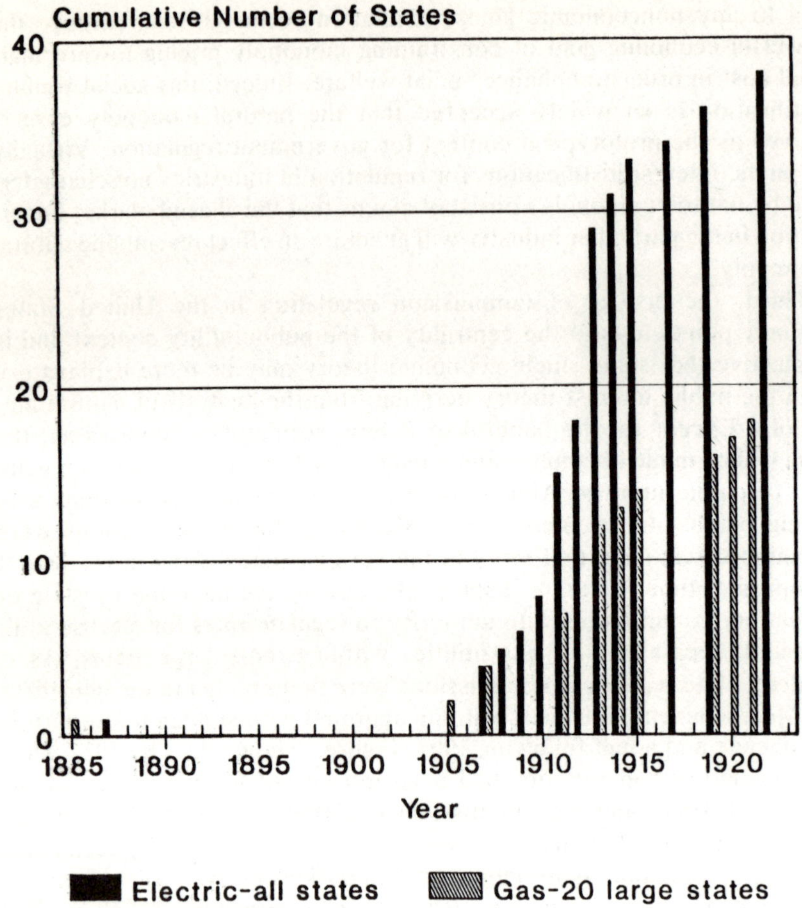

FIGURE 1.—Adoption of commission rate regulation electricity and gas. Sources.—George J. Stigler & Claire Friedland, What Can Regulators Regulate? The Case of Electricity, 5 J. Law & Econ. 1 (1961); William K. Jones, Regulated Industries 65 (1st ed. 1967).

provocatively entitled "What Can Regulators Regulate?"[36] sought to measure the impact of commission regulation on electric utility rates and profits. Stigler and Friedland treated the close timing of the establishment of state regulatory commissions as enabling a form of event study, segregating the data into preregulation and postregulation periods. They measured the effects of regulation by commission in three different ways:

[36] Stigler & Friedland, *supra* note 13.

they regressed utility revenue per kilowatt-hour against measures of costs, income, and urbanization; they investigated two different indices of price structure, looking for evidence of cross-subsidization in favor of consumers or other small-volume users; and they looked at the effect of the introduction of commission regulation on stock prices and, thus, on returns of the regulated firms. Uniformly, they found no differences in any dimension associated with commission regulation across states with or without rate-setting commissions or across periods before or after the creation of commissions.[37]

Stigler and Friedland concluded that regulatory commissions had no demonstrable effect because the electric utilities, though natural monopolies in city delivery, were subject to effective long-term competition with suppliers of other energy sources[38] such as oil, gas, and coal. Because they were subject to extensive competition in the long run, the utilities were unable to secure rents that were of sufficient magnitude for regulators to restrain, given the operational inadequacies of commission regulation. Stigler and Friedland were skeptical of the ability of regulatory commissions to overcome problems of their dependence on the regulated firm for information as well as of regulatory lag. They estimated that "pure monopoly profits in the absence of regulation would [have to] be 10 or 20 percent above the competitive rate of return [and] prices would [have to] be on the order of 40 or 80 percent above long run marginal cost" before ineffective regulators might have an impact. They concluded, however, that profit and rate levels of this dimension were impossible for the electric utilities given the extent of long-term competition.[39]

Stigler and Friedland did not raise the question, but publication of their findings must have alerted readers to the puzzle relating to the underlying motivation for regulation. That is, if the adoption of regulatory commissions with rate-setting authority could not be shown to have reduced electricity rates, what was its purpose?[40] To my knowledge, it was Harold Demsetz's 1968 article, equally provocatively entitled "Why Regulate Utilities?"[41] that provided the first published suggestion of a theory of

[37] *Id.* at 5–11.

[38] *Id.* at 11.

[39] *Id.* at 12.

[40] It is possible to read the Stigler-Friedland discussion as suggesting that commissions may have been created with the expectation that there were monopoly profits to constrain but that the expectation was erroneous.

[41] Demsetz, *supra* note 24. Of course, it is likely that the idea was widely discussed among the Chicago economics group at the time Demsetz was writing his article.

the motivation for commission regulation,[42] a suggestion similar to the theory that Stigler would later develop. Demsetz's point, however, was little more than an aside in a much broader and more general analysis of the regulation of natural monopolies. I do not know that Demsetz himself pursued the theory of regulation issue. But his criticism of the regulation of natural monopolies—again, the bedrock case for public interest justifications—was so devastating that it substantially fueled the subsequent "theories of regulation" inquiry.

Demsetz's article demonstrated that there were *no* conditions under which regulation by commission could be guaranteed to optimize social welfare. Demsetz argued that a governmental entity could constrain a monopolist utility to competitive levels of price and output, without need for commission regulation, by auctioning a franchise contract to manage the natural monopoly to a group of competing potential operators. According to Demsetz's analysis, the focus of the conventional analysis of regulation on natural monopoly in supply and distribution of a service was myopic. Notwithstanding technological monopoly in supply, a governmental entity could create competitive conditions by engendering competition for the field, that is, for the right to operate the natural monopoly itself. Thus, Demsetz proposed that the government auction off the right to provide, say, electricity or gas service to a set of competing firms. The auction would lead the prospective bidders to propose a combination of price and quality that would closely approach competitive levels.[43]

It followed from Demsetz's demonstration that regulation by commission could never be automatically defended. The central issue for regulatory policy, instead, was whether a continuously sitting regulatory commission, given its inherent limitations, could ever achieve results equal to an auction. Demsetz forcefully stated that it was his belief "that the rivalry of the open market place disciplines more effectively than do the regulatory processes of the commission."[44]

[42] Of course, there were many earlier cynical comments about regulators and regulatory corruption that implied benefit to regulated firms, for example, Horace Gray, The Passing of the Public Utility Concept (1942), cited in Jarrell, *supra* note 34, at 269, but this work had no demonstrable influence on the economics literature.

[43] Though irrelevant to Demsetz's larger point, Lester Telser contentiously argued that Demsetz's auction would result in Chamberlinian monopolistic competition, rather than price equal to marginal cost. See L. G. Telser, On the Regulation of Industry: A Note, 77 J. Pol. Econ. 937 (1969). Telser's point, however, was chiefly related to his broader advocacy for his analysis of the "core" and had no empirical or historical dimension. See Harold Demsetz, On the Regulation of Industry: A Reply, 79 J. Pol. Econ. 356 (1971).

[44] Demsetz, *supra* note 24, at 65. This judgment of Demsetz was supported by both the

In his conclusion, Demsetz put forward the idea that Stigler would later develop into his more complete economic theory of regulation. Having demonstrated that there is no necessary link between natural monopoly and commission regulation, Demsetz intimated that the natural monopoly defense for regulation may well be a pretext disguising a regulatory regime that benefited and, therefore, might be demanded by the regulated monopolists themselves. According to Demsetz, "[R]esort to the rivalry of the market place [through the adoption of Demsetz's competition for the franchise proposal] would relieve companies of the discomforts of commission regulation. But it would also relieve them of the comfort of legally protected market areas."[45] His final sentence dramatically challenged the defenders of regulation, especially those within the regulated industries themselves, to show that regulation did not exist to serve their economic interests: "If the managements of utility companies doubt this belief, I suggest that they reexamine the history of their industry to discover just who it was that provided most of the force behind the regulatory movement."[46] George Stigler's "Theory of Economic Regulation" paper formalizing Demsetz's speculation was published three years later, and Posner's review of the competing theories, three years after that. The "theories of regulation" debate had begun.

As described earlier, in succeeding years, a consensus developed in favor of Stigler's economic theory of regulation, built on the Stigler-Friedland and Demsetz foundation. Indeed, few scholars purport to defend public interest explanations of regulation. With respect to the public utilities, the most important subsequent work is a study by Gregg A. Jarrell reanalyzing the early history of electric utility regulation to identify with greater precision the determinants of the demand for commission regulation implied by Stigler's economic theory.[47] Jarrell examined the electric utility industry in the years prior to those studied by Stigler and Friedland to determine why some states created regulatory commissions earlier than others. According to Jarrell, prior to the creation of commissions, individual municipalities had attempted to control the exploitation of natural monopoly advantages by aggressively awarding new franchises

Stigler-Friedland finding of no-commission effect and the findings of an earlier *Journal* article that had found that the price of natural gas sold in interstate commerce subject to FPC regulation was 5–6 percent higher than gas sold in intrastate commerce exempt from regulation. See Robert W. Gerwig, Natural Gas Production: A Study of Costs of Regulation, 5 J. Law & Econ. 69 (1962), cited in Stigler, *supra* note 1.

[45] Demsetz, *supra* note 24, at 65.

[46] *Id.*

[47] Jarrell, *supra* note 34.

to competing electric companies.[48] Jarrell interpreted the economic theory of regulation to imply that the demand for regulation by commission would be greater in states in which municipal encouragement of competition of this nature had been the greatest.[49] Jarrell found that, in the preregulatory commission period, electricity prices and firm profits were lower in those states that had earliest adopted rate-setting commissions but that these differences declined after the creation of regulatory commissions.

Jarrell interpreted these findings as confirmatory of both the Stigler-Friedland and Demsetz studies. First, they showed that competition in the precommission period successfully reduced rates more effectively than regulation. Second, the findings that profits were higher under regulation suggested that regulatory commissions were created as a result of industry demand rather than to pursue the public interest.[50]

The next part reviews the early history of public utility regulation in additional detail. As we shall see, Harold Demsetz's analysis of natural monopoly regulation possessed not only an analytical brilliance but also a historical acuity. The history, however, suggests a different interpretation of the origins and significance of the introduction of regulatory commissions.

III. Public Utility Regulation in the Precommission Period

Study of the motivations for the introduction of commission regulation of public utilities in the early decades of the 1900s, regrettably, has neglected careful consideration of the extensive regulation of utilities by municipal governments that preceded the creation of state commissions. Beginning in the early decades of the nineteenth century, municipalities regulated the utilities that served them through a method of franchise contracting similar to that Harold Demsetz imaginatively described a century later. These franchise contracts were openly sensitive to the problems of utility monopolization, and they incorporated terms limiting price and mandating features of service quality attempting to control for these problems. In a period of increasing urbanization, conditions of supply and demand must have changed substantially over time, altering both the conditions of profit maximization to the utility and the benefits and costs to the citizenry of the service being provided. Not surprisingly, municipal

[48] *Id.* at 273–75.

[49] That is, Jarrell's hypothesis is that the utilities wanted to avoid competition and thus demanded the creation of a state regulatory commission that they could capture to enact restrictions preventing further competitive entry.

[50] *Id.* at 287.

franchise contracts were changed over time attempting to respond to changes in the underlying markets.

Regulation by franchise contract was introduced in New York City as early as the 1820s for gas and the 1830s for street railway transportation (powered by horse),[51] and it extended through the early decades of the 1900s until supplanted in many, though not all, states by the creation of permanently sitting regulatory commissions. Over these years, franchises were granted—and thus cities subjected to regulation—virtually all services benefited by the use of public rights-of-way: gas, electricity, water, sewer, street railways, telegraph, and, separately, telephone, subways, railroad terminals, ferries, private bridges, tunnels and toll roads, as well as service industries no longer marketable today: pneumatic tubes, electrical conduits, refrigeration, central heating, and electric signal services. Municipal regulation by franchise was quickly responsive to innovation: Alexander Graham Bell received his telephone patent in 1876; the first telephone exchange was regulated by municipal franchise in 1878 (New Haven).[52] Thomas Edison succeeded with the carbon filament in 1879; the first central electric station was installed, subject to franchise, during the same year (San Francisco).[53]

The system of municipal regulation by franchise, however, suffered many problems. As we shall see, there is substantial evidence of persistent difficulties relating to specifying the franchise contract, adapting it over time to new conditions, and monitoring compliance with the contract for the benefit of the citizenry. These various problems closely resemble now well appreciated problems in the execution of long-term contracts for the supply of a product or service,[54] except that, for municipal utilities, they appear more difficult since municipal franchise contracts incorporated more diverse sets of services and, for reasons to be explained, extended for longer terms than typical long-term contracts in modern commercial settings.

As we shall see, in response to these many problems, as city govern-

[51] Franchise, New York Gas & Light Co., May 12, 1823; Franchise, New York & Harlem Railroad Co., April 25, 1831. 1 Wilcox, at 545–46. All of the detailed information with respect to utility franchise terms is taken from Delos F. Wilcox, Municipal Franchises (2 vols. 1911); and Edward W. Bemis, Municipal Monopolies (1899). The Wilcox volumes constitute an attempt to compile a census of all franchise contracts entered by municipalities from, as the author puts it, "a large number of cities"; 1 Wilcox, at viii (incorporating contracts from cities as diverse as New York, LaCrosse, Wis., and Saginaw, Mich.).

[52] 1 Wilcox, *supra* note 51, at 217.

[53] *Id.* at 135.

[54] See, for example, P. L. Joskow, The Performance of Long-Term Contracts: Further Evidence from Coal Markets, 21 RAND J. Econ. 251 (1990).

ments gained experience in administering utility franchises, municipalities amended franchise contract design and administration in systematic ways. Although initial franchise agreements often defined performance requirements with broad and general standards, later contracts incorporated provisions that were increasingly detailed, seeking greater benefit to the citizenry through more complete specification of the price structure and of service requirements. More precise specification of terms, however, created a different set of difficulties. And over time, franchise contracts were amended further to be made more flexible, frequently defining requirements again in terms of general standards, but now to be administered in their details by council subcommittees or boards of arbitrators.

Though implemented by means of contract, this method of control begins to resemble the operation of a regulatory commission. Indeed, as I shall attempt to show, the adoption of regulation by commission cannot be claimed to differ qualitatively from the regulation by city council or, often, by specialized committee that preceded it in many jurisdictions. As a consequence, in contrast to the implication of the "theories of regulation" debate, the introduction of regulation by state commission may not represent obviously either the imposition of new and more burdensome controls on public utilities or their escape from excessive municipal competition or regulation. Though I believe that we know too little at this point to reach a confident conclusion as to the ultimate social welfare effects of the shift from regulation by franchise to regulation by commission, it is not clear that regulation by commission can be distinguished from an advanced stage in the evolution of municipal franchise contractual form.

A. *The Legal Basis of Municipal Franchise Regulation and Its Implications*

The underlying motivation for the regulation of public utilities in the United States is more mundane than either the idealistic basis of the public interest theory or the craven basis of the economic or capture theories: public utility companies voluntarily entered contracts subjecting themselves to regulation in order to gain authority to use public rights-of-way for laying gas and water pipes, stringing telephone and electric poles, burying electrical wires, and laying street railway tracks. Regulation of the utility's activities and terms of business resulted from a negotiation between the municipal government and the utility in a context that both parties recognized saved the utility the costs of negotiating with and securing rights from the individual property owners they intended to serve. Thus, the utility secured the valuable right to employ public rights-of-way in return for its acceptance of the terms and limitations imposed by the municipal government.

In order to critically evaluate the terms of specific franchise contracts themselves, it is useful at the outset to consider the available terms of trade between an aspiring franchisee and a municipal government possessing authority to grant public rights-of-way. Though this point has not been emphasized, Harold Demsetz's proposal for employing franchise contracts to create "competition for the field" derives from specific, but unstated, presumptions about the particular structure of property rights and the particular legal regime in effect at the time of contracting. For reasons explained below, the property rights structure and legal regime that Demsetz presumes do not closely resemble property rights ever in effect in any American city. As a consequence, the implementation in fact of utility franchise contracts departs systematically from Demsetz's theoretical construct.

Demsetz's basic intuition was to substitute market processes for the actions of a continuously sitting commission possessing authority to approve or deny specific utility decisions. Demsetz proposed that, in contrast to continuous regulation, a governmental entity should establish an auction at which prospective utility operators would bid for the right to manage the utility for a limited period of time.[55] To best benefit the citizenry, the governmental entity would offer the contract to that prospective operator who offered the optimum combination of price and quality.[56] The bidding competition stimulated by the auction would lead the operators to bid away monopoly profits, so that the winning bid would be an offer of a quality of service at a near-to-competitive price.[57]

Demsetz's proposal rests on two unstated presumptions: first, a legal regime in which the governmental entity possesses exclusive authority to grant or deny a utility the right to provide the service and, second, a property rights structure according to which the governmental entity owns the capital plant of the utility and conducts a bidding competition, in essence, for management services. First, in order to achieve the result of competitive levels of price and service, Demsetz presumes that the governmental entity possesses an enforceable legal monopoly over the provision of the service in question which it can delegate unilaterally on

[55] See, generally, Demsetz, *supra* note 24.

[56] Oliver Williamson has emphasized the difficulty of defining ex ante optimal price and quality (Williamson, Franshise Bidding for Natural Monopolies, *supra* note 33; Williamson, The Economic Institutions of Capitalism, *supra* note 33), but this concern is irrelevant to Demsetz's analytical point.

[57] But see Telser, *supra* note 43.

terms of its own choice. As we shall see, without legal monopoly, Demsetz's competitive solution cannot be guaranteed. Second, in Demsetz's auction, prospective franchisees bid over the price structure and quality of service only, with no reference to capital investments, whether initial or continuing. Demsetz, thus, is presuming that the capital investment in the plant is complete at the time of the auction and that the governmental entity will reclaim possession of the utility's plant at the end of the franchise term in order to conduct a new round of bidding. In subsequent bidding rounds, the previous operator may compete, but without any specific advantage over other bidders except, perhaps, reputational value gained from its previous term of administration. The previous operator surely possesses no inherent property interest that would affect the subsequent negotiation.

Given Demsetz's presumptions, his conclusion that monopolization can be controlled without continuous regulation follows directly. Given the legal regime and property rights structure in force in the nineteenth century, however, an entirely different set of problems of utility control arise that are ignored or would be difficult to manage through Demsetz's auction proposal. First, during the nineteenth century, there was no inherent legal municipal monopoly of utility services, nor did municipal or state governments generally possess the authority to limit entry. Demsetz's proposal seems to imagine a municipality with the authority to negotiate terms in return for the unilateral grant of something resembling the modern certificate of public convenience and necessity. But this legal construct postdates the regime of municipal franchises and appears to have been introduced only after the establishment of state regulatory commissions. During the nineteenth century, with the exception of services such as the federal post office and money supply, all other American enterprises were available for open entry by any aspiring entrepreneur. Most typically, state governments possessed authority to confer corporate charters, but the corporate charter chiefly provided only the benefit of limited corporate liability, not monopoly. Municipal government authority, in contrast, was limited to the regulation of those rights-of-way that had been dedicated to the public either through custom or expressly in return for development authorization. Thus, municipal regulatory authority derived solely from jurisdiction over public rights-of-way.

Second, for the provision of almost all public utility services, American cities relied exclusively on private capital for initial and subsequent investment.[58] The nineteenth century was a period of extremely low levels

[58] The principal exception, to be discussed further below, was water service, which was publicly supplied by roughly half of American cities.

of state and local government expenditure, financed chiefly by a property tax, of course, without an income tax. Government expenditures on public works were not unknown, but remained highly controversial throughout much of the century.[59]

As a consequence, the actual negotiation of utility franchise contracts during the nineteenth century was not conducted, as Demsetz images, between a monopolist government and a group of firms competing to provide management services. Rather, actual negotiations were conducted between a city government with authority limited to control of public rights-of-way and, in the first instance, an independent entrepreneur who bore all responsibilities and risks of capital investment and, at times of subsequent renewal, a firm that owned the capital plant then providing current service to city citizens.

There are various implications for the nature of franchise negotiation where the legal regime does not grant the governmental entity control over entry and where the property rights structure requires both management services and both initial and continuing capital investment to be provided privately, not publicly. First, without control over entry, a governmental entity can offer in return for the franchise contract only the value of using public rights-of-way. The use of public rather than private rights-of-way is beneficial chiefly because it enables the utility to avoid the costs of negotiating rights-of-way with the utility's customers themselves. There is no doubt that the transaction cost savings of negotiation with the city, rather than with individual landowners, were substantial. Nevertheless, there must surely have been limits to the value of these savings.

The level of transaction cost savings places an important constraint on the extent to which the governmental entity in negotiation can compel the utility to reduce price below the monopoly level. Demsetz's conclusion that the governmental entity can require price to be set at competitive levels can only be guaranteed where the magnitude of the transaction costs of individual negotiation would preclude provision of the service entirely, either because of the absolute magnitude of these costs in relation to the expected rate of return or because of hold-up problems. If these transaction costs were sufficiently large to otherwise preclude entry, then, whether there were one or many aspirants for the utility franchise, the governmental entity could extract all but a fraction of monopoly returns by specifying price and quality in return for access to public rights-of-way.

[59] See, for example, Theodore Pease, The Frontier State, 1818–1848, at 194–215 (1922) (discussing public improvement expenditures in Illinois).

On the other hand, where the transaction cost savings are relatively less substantial, the conditions of negotiation become more complicated. As we shall see, the lengthy terms of actual utility franchises suggest that there may have been substantial investment risks facing entrepreneurs, especially in the early years of utility operation. In addition, there are examples throughout the period of what appear to be duplicative construction—examples of multiple sets of water or gas pipes being built to serve individual customers—suggesting the existence, though hardly dominance, of potential competition for utility services.[60] Where there is no governmental power to limit entry and where the savings in transaction costs that the government can offer to a franchisee are relatively limited, it may not be possible for the governmental entity to extract full monopoly profits from the potential franchisee.

An outcome cannot be derived in theory without the introduction of restrictive (and, historically, totally hypothetical) assumptions regarding the various hold-up opportunities. But it is easily imaginable, for example, that a utility may choose to invest in the transaction costs of negotiation with individual landowners (a fixed cost) rather than to accept a city's zero profit constraint.[61] Alternatively, one might imagine a context in which one firm has obtained a municipal franchise agreeing to a price structure generating zero profits set by the governmental entity, while a competing firm enters the market without a franchise to cream-skim, taking advantage of familiar natural monopoly pricing problems. Of course, one can also imagine conditions that would generate Demsetz's competitive price and quality result—sharply declining costs and multiple, noncollusive bidders—but those conditions may be difficult to approximate in fact. Indeed, I have found no historical examples of Demsetz-like auctions in my research on municipal franchises.

Demsetz's second central presumption is that the governmental entity possesses the capital plant of the utility, auctioning off little more than a contract for management services. Demsetz must also be presuming, implicitly, that the governmental entity makes all continuing capital investments in plant. These conditions, too, were unknown to American cities in the nineteenth century.

The provisions of the utility franchise contract are likely to be different where the governmental entity chooses to rely solely on private invest-

[60] 1 Wilcox, *supra* note 51, at 441.

[61] The issue is complicated because it was probably necessary for a utility to enter some contract with a municipal government if only to extend its service across public streets to reach other citizen-customers. Whether the city government could exercise hold-up powers or would bow to demands of citizen-customers would affect this negotiation.

ment. The level of actual capital invested, of course, will be heavily affected by the expected rate of return. As a consequence, the outcome of the negotiation over the price structure and the minimum quality of service will affect the ultimate level of investment. Again, analytically, Demsetz's proposed auction could be amended to include a specification of minimum initial investment and some level of continuing investment, but obviously the difficulties of ex ante prediction and ex post monitoring multiply.

In addition, relying on private capital investment complicates the conditions of negotiation at the end of the term of a franchise. Again, Demsetz's competitive price and quality result derives from entirely unrestricted bidding for the new franchise. In the real world, however, after the utility has been placed in operation, the franchisee and governmental entity become locked in a position that perhaps more closely resembles bilateral monopoly. In principle, the governmental entity could deny further authorization to use public rights-of-way, even requiring the utility to tear up and dismantle its pipes or rails. Such a threat, however, may not be realistic since subsequent duplication of the fixed investment would raise average costs for any successor. Moreover, serious timing issues would arise: a citizenry which had come to rely on the provision of utility services would hardly benefit from retrogression to preservice days. While the governmental entity could seek to encourage the utility to convey the plant to a successor, it could not compel a transfer. And if the governmental entity were to seek to acquire the plant for itself, the Constitution would require compensation to the franchisee. Again, one can imagine conditions under which some transfer of utility management might be arranged in order to constrain monopolistic behavior, but again, the conditions may be difficult to approximate in the real world of franchise contracting.

As we shall see, the actual provisions of municipal utility franchises in the nineteenth century suggest the importance of these various contractual problems and illustrate the difficulties of regulation by contract. These provisions and the ways in which they were amended over time also indicate the complexity of the evaluation of the welfare effects of the shift from regulation by contract to regulation by commission. The next parts review various features of actual municipal utility franchises. Part *B* surveys the principal provisions of franchise contracts generally. Part *C* presents a history of electric utility franchises in two major cities over a twenty-five-year period. Part *D* discusses the seemingly aberrant case of waterwork utilities—the utility most prominently owned and managed by governmental entities in contrast to private firms.

B. Basic Provisions of Municipal Franchise Contracts

Municipal utility franchises shared in common many characteristic provisions unrelated to the specific service subject to regulation.

1. *Franchise Duration.* Although not necessary to his analytical point, Demsetz implies that optimal regulation by contract would set a relatively short duration for the franchise in order to allow responsive readjustment as underlying market conditions changed.[62] Quite in contrast, the durations of municipal franchises were quite long: twenty, thirty, sometimes fifty years.[63] A relatively long contractual duration is not surprising in the initial grant of a franchise given reliance on private investment in the context of a novel service. Lengthy franchise durations, however, prevail over the entire period, suggesting that concerns about returns on or the stimulus for continuing investment may have been substantial. A lengthy franchise duration, of course, also constrains the range of governmental opportunism.

Franchise durations of such length obviously complicate the specification of a price structure and minimum quality of service. Even if confident in estimating today's competitive price, who can predict the competitive price in thirty years? As we shall see, however, utility franchises also incorporated many provisions allowing readjustment of basic provisions which make difficult analysis of the implications of the thirty- or fifty-year basic term.

2. *Price.* All franchises specified a price structure. In the years of initial service within a given city, franchise provisions relating to price and quality of service tended to incorporate standards of great generality, such as the 1888 electricity franchise in Duluth, which required only that electricity was to be provided "at reasonable prices,"[64] or the 1890 Cedar Rapids electricity franchise, which forbade the utility to "charge unreasonable or exorbitant rates for light or power."[65] Again, in the early years, prior to municipal experience in regulation, several cities limited price by reference to external indices, such as the 1852 franchise of the

[62] For a discussion of this issue, see Williamson, Franchise Bidding for Natural Monopolies, *supra* note 33, at 83–90, criticizing the proposal for recurrent short-term contracts by Demsetz, *supra* note 24; and Richard A. Posner, The Appropriate Scope of Regulation in the Cable Television Industry, 3 Bell J. Econ. & Mgmt. Sci. 98 (1972).

[63] For example, Franchise, Detroit Gas Co., October 31, 1893 (30 years), 1 Wilcox, *supra* note 51, at 655; Franchise, City Railway Co, Wheeling, W. Va., March 1902 (fifty years), 2 *id.* at 427.

[64] 1 *id.* at 161.

[65] 1 *id.* at 175.

Erie (Pa.) Gas Light Co. which set price as "not exceeding the average rate charged by other cities . . . on the shore of Lake Erie,"[66] or the 1882 natural gas franchise in Toledo, which defined the maximum price as "on equal terms and at reasonable prices, reference being had to the cost of producing and delivering the same and the prices for like supplies in other cities."[67]

In later years and especially at franchise renewals, however, many franchises incorporated rate schedules that were minutely detailed. For example, the 1906 Denver electricity franchise defined a rate structure that included one set of rates for illumination, calculated by kilowatt-hour, by year and by sixteen-candle lamp, and a separate, equally detailed set of rates for power use, presumably chiefly for commercial users.[68] On establishing detailed rate schedules of this nature, many franchises attempted to anticipate future changes. The 1906 Kansas City gas franchise, for example, established a rate of twenty-five cents per 1,000 cubic feet for the first five-year period, twenty-seven cents for the second five-year period, and thirty cents thereafter.[69]

Increasingly over time, however, utility franchises appear to introduce techniques for allowing greater flexibility in rate determination. A gas franchise in Philadelphia in 1897, for example, set the price of gas at $1 per 1,000 cubic feet but provided that the rate could be changed by city ordinance. In order to protect the utility, the franchise prohibited the city council from reducing price below ninety cents prior to 1908; below eighty-five cents prior to 1913; below eighty cents prior to 1918; or below seventy-five cents during the remaining ten years of the franchise.[70] More generally in these years, however, franchises delegate authority for changes in price and in the price structure to arbitrators or committees of disinterested persons. A good example is the provision in a 1908 Saginaw, Michigan, gas franchise that gives both the franchisee and city the authority to request price changes, to be determined by a board of five arbitrators.[71] Similarly, a 1905 gas franchise in Cincinnati delegates price setting to the city's board of public service, subject to judicial review.[72]

[66] 1 *id.* at 647.

[67] 1 *id.*

[68] 1 *id.* at 186–87. This franchise was issued after a consolidation of competing utilities, described in more detail in Part C *infra.*

[69] 1 Wilcox, *supra* note 51, at 614.

[70] 1 *id.* at 567–71.

[71] 1 *id.* at 585.

[72] 1 *id.* at 596–97. To illustrate the difficulty of evaluating the welfare effects of the shift from regulation by franchise to regulation by commission, Ohio utilities are commonly

3. *Quality of Service.* Most franchises incorporated specifications of minimum service quality. Again, in the early years, these provisions may resemble aspirations more than hard-line requirements: for example, New York's 1823 and 1833 gas franchises required that the product be "of a quality, brilliancy or intensity equal to the gas in use for the public lamps in the City of London."[73] Changes over time in the methods adopted in utility franchises for the specification of minimum quality resemble changes in the specification of the price structure. Following the initial definition of broad and general standards, franchise provisions become increasingly detailed, incorporating service requirements specifying minimum candle-power, minimum gas capacity, defining details of underground burying,[74] or electric pole height and maintenance.[75] Still later, however, more mature franchises return to general quality standards, while delegating more precise monitoring of construction and service maintenance requirements to a city engineer, commissioner, or board of public works.[76]

4. *Adjustment over Time.* Though municipal utility franchises were contracts and strictly enforceable according to contract law, there appear to have been many techniques through which a city could secure renegotiation of franchise provisions. First, many franchises incorporate adjustment provisions explicitly, such as the provision in a Saginaw, Michigan, gas contract providing for the city council to review and reset prices every five years.[77] Second, many franchise authorization statutes subjected municipal franchises to city ordinances, although limits were often placed on the extent to which a city council could change basic terms.[78] Thus, the city council through subsequent ordinance could mandate a change in service or terms, if not directly, then at least to bring utility management back to the bargaining table. Third, franchises were renegotiated and reissued in many different contexts, for example, where the utility wanted authorization to extend service to new customers or where the utility itself wished to renegotiate some term. Franchise contracts

regarded as having been made subject to commission regulation in 1911. See the citations to Stigler and Friedland, *supra* note 13; and William K. Jones, Regulated Industries 65 (1st ed. 1967).

[73] 1 Wilcox, *supra* note 51, at 545.

[74] Franchise, Colorado Edison Electric Light Co, March 24, 1883, 1 *id.* at 184.

[75] Franchise, Jersey City Electric Light Co., October 11, 1887, 1 *id.* at 150.

[76] Franchise, Columbus Electric Light, March 28, 1887, 1 *id.* at 177; Franchise, East River Gas Co. of Long Island City, April 19, 1892, 1 *id.* at 543.

[77] Franchise, East Saginaw, Mich., January 26, 1886, 1 *id.* at 582.

[78] See, for example, the limits established by the 1897 Philadelphia gas franchise; text at note 70 *supra*.

were renegotiated on any consolidation with another utility or where a utility changed its operations (say, by some form of vertical integration) not clearly authorized in the initial contract. In addition, there are many examples of simple renegotiation of the franchise duration—for example, extending its duration by twenty or thirty years—substantially prior to the expiration of the original franchise.[79]

5. *Exclusivity and Competition.* Franchise contracts were seldom exclusive, conferring monopoly rights, although they were more likely to be exclusive in the early years of provision of the service. Indeed, at the time of the first development of a utility, the franchise less closely resembles a regulatory device than a patent: a governmental grant to an enterpriser to encourage an undeveloped and uncertain business. The 1823 gas franchise to the New York Gas Co. (south of Grand to Canal), for example, was exclusive while the 1833 gas franchise to the Manhattan Gas Light Co. (all other areas north) was expressly nonexclusive.[80]

The importance of the absence of exclusivity provisions cannot accurately be evaluated without particular information about the extent of potential competition. It is clear that city governments often threatened competition, but it is not clear how significant in fact the threats became. As Jarrell reported, municipalities frequently issued duplicative franchises, even for seemingly natural monopoly services such as gas or electric supply. Many of these efforts, however, appear to be little more than another negotiation tactic of a city levied against an incumbent utility. On some few occasions, there is evidence of later consolidation with a competing operator (again, to obtain authority to consolidate, the utility needed to renegotiate its franchise).[81] But subsequent consolidations of this nature are rare, in contrast to consolidations between utilities servicing different areas of the same city.

Finally, many franchises incorporated provisions empowering the municipality to buy out the utility on various terms, most commonly at historical cost of investment. Wilcox reports many threats of buy-outs by municipalities, chiefly as a tool of contract negotiation, but few that were ever exercised.[82]

6. *Cross Subsidization.* Stigler and Friedland could not find significant

[79] See, as an example, the serial renegotiation of the Salt Lake City electricity franchises; Part *C infra*.

[80] 1 Wilcox, *supra* note 51, at 545–46.

[81] For example, see the more detailed discussion *infra* of the franchise of the Reorganized Denver Consolidated Electric Co., May 15, 1906, 1 *id.* at 184.

[82] See, for example, the discussion of franchises involving the New Haven Water Company, Part *D infra*.

shifts as between the precommission and commission periods in subsidization of low-volume users or of consumer in contrast to commercial users. Their finding is consistent either with extensive cross subsidization of this nature under municipal franchise regulation or its absence. Without greater information about costs, it is difficult to judge whether the price structure specified for residential versus commercial users or among residential users constituted a subsidy or not. Nevertheless, occasionally various specific groups are singled out for undeniable preferences in municipal franchises, not a surprising form of regulatory behavior.[83] Virtually all municipalities negotiated for free service for city departments and other public institutions such as libraries or parks.[84] Other franchises, for example, required railways to give free transport to mailmen or individuals going to funerals[85] or to offer special rates for "workingmen."[86] Still others prohibited utilities from employing convict labor, mandating union labor.[87]

C. The History of Some Electricity Franchises More Carefully Described

A better view of the dynamics of the system of regulation by municipal franchise comes from a review of case histories in individual cities.

The Development of Electricity Franchises in Salt Lake City.[88] Salt Lake City entered its first electric franchise contract in 1881, shortly after the first reduction to operation of central electric systems in 1879. This early franchise was skeletal, resembling a patent, granted both "for the purpose of conveying electrical currents by means of wires to be used for lighting, and also conveying steam by means of pipes to be used for heating and propelling machinery, and for other purposes." There is no evidence that steam service by pipe was ever established. In 1893, the city entered a new and more detailed franchise for electrical service. The franchise had a term of twenty-five years and was expressly made subject to ordinances later to be adopted by the city council, including ordinances

[83] See Richard A. Posner, Taxation by Regulation, 2 Bell J. Econ. & Mgmt. Sci. 22 (1971).

[84] City street lighting was an exception, for obvious reasons, since the city was the only user of the service. The 1823 and 1833 New York franchises, for example, set a maximum price of $15 per lamp for the city. See 1 Wilcox, *supra* note 51, at 545.

[85] Franchise, Chicago West Division Railway, 1907, 2 *id.* at 148.

[86] City Ordinance amending Franchise, Detroit City Railway Co., January 3, 1889, 2 *id.* at 351–52.

[87] Franchise, Nashville Gas Co., February 20, 1900, 1 *id.* at 587.

[88] The Salt Lake history is taken from 1 *id.* at 153–61.

setting electric prices. Surely because of the concern over council price authority, the franchise guaranteed the utility a minimum price per customer of $1.50 per month. The contract also incorporated a detailed specification of maximum prices and provided a discount of 10 percent for the city, hospitals, and other charitable and religious institutions. The franchise provided that pipes, conduits, and poles were to be located "at such points and places as shall be designated by the city engineer . . . and under the supervision of said city engineer and the board of public works."

In succeeding months, the city granted two other competing franchises for electricity service. These franchises were much the same in content, though they added specific provisions dealing with street lamps: the franchisee was to furnish arc lamps to the city at a charge of $10 per month for each 2,000 candlepower lamp for all-night service. The contracts also provided that the franchisees were to provide free service for city offices and the library and "to construct the most practical device for consuming or arresting the smoke in all instances wherein coal is used for fuel." It is not clear that these competing franchises were ever exercised, and they were acquired by the dominant 1893 franchisee in subsequent years.

In 1903, following the buy-out, the city renegotiated the 1893 franchise, reissuing it for a new twenty-five-year term. Thus, ten years into the twenty-five-year term of the 1893 franchise, the city in effect extended the franchise for an additional ten years. The new franchise reincorporated many terms of the earlier contract but changed it to require the franchisee to provide additional arc lights to the city free of charge over specified periods and to set a deadline of 1914 for all electrical wires to be removed from poles and buried underground. Two years later, in 1905, the city renegotiated and reissued the franchise again, this time for a fifty-year term. The 1905 franchise was accompanied by a detailed council ordinance setting electrical prices at twelve cents per kilowatt-hour and $1.50 per month per arc light or eleven cents per kilowatt-hour and $1 per month for incandescent lights. The price ordinance provided that consumers paying their bills within seven days were to receive a 10 percent discount, though not below a minimum of $1 per month, fifty cents per month lower than the minimum in the 1893 franchise. The franchise required the utility to provide the city fifty-two incandescent lamps for the city square as well as service to all public buildings free of charge.

Most important, the franchise introduced new terms dealing with future prices. It specified that the city agreed "that it will not, by ordinance or resolution, make any rules or regulations in regard to the price of lighting" different from the prices set in the ordinance, except on a showing of a material change in operating costs. According to the agreement, if "there shall hereafter be any new inventions or improvements that will materially reduce the cost of producing or distributing either gas or electric energy for lighting or heating purposes," or "if there shall hereafter be any conditions which shall materially enhance the cost of producing or distributing either gas or electrical energy," then the parties agreed that there would be a "reasonable readjustment" of the rates. If new rates could not be agreed on, the parties agreed to refer the issue for decision by a panel of three arbitrators. A successor franchise was issued in 1906, and Utah adopted a utility regulatory commission in 1917.[89]

The Development of Electricity Franchises in Denver.[90] Denver's first electricity franchise was entered in 1883 with the Colorado Edison Electric Light Company providing for underground service. As with other early franchises, this grant exhibits less concern with monopolization than with encouragement of the enterprise and protection of the public. The franchise placed few restrictions on the utility's operations, but required the company to post a $25,000 bond to indemnify the city from any claims relating to the burial of underground lines. Four years later, in 1887, the city entered another franchise with a different company, Denver Light, Heat and Power, authorizing pole lines and conduits, in contrast to the earlier underground system. The 1887 franchise introduced a mandatory service provision according to which the city council retained authority to mandate the extension of service along any city block on which six customers requested the company's service. Where the 1883 franchise appears to represent the city's hope that service would be established, the 1887 franchise charged $5,000 as a franchise fee.

Shortly thereafter, the two companies merged to become the Denver Consolidated Electric Company, a merger ratified by the council without apparent change in franchise terms. The record is vague as to how the city sought to restrain the monopoly in succeeding years. In 1900, however, the city issued a new electric franchise to a businessman, Charles A. Lacombe, subsequently revised in 1901. The 1901 franchise included a ten-year city contract for the provision of street lighting at a specified rate ($7.50 per month per light), and it specified a schedule of maximum charges (ten cents per kilowatt-hour for lighting; four cents, for power). The franchisee was charged a fee of 3 percent of gross receipts and the city retained buy-out rights according to a schedule beginning at $230,000 at the end of the first year to $40,000 at the end of the tenth year. To protect the buy-out option, the contract compelled the franchisee to main-

[89] Stigler & Friedland, *supra* note 13, at 13.

[90] The Denver history is taken from 1 Wilcox, *supra* note 51, at 184–88.

tain the plant "in as good order and condition as the same was when erected and constructed." The franchise explicitly prohibited Lacombe from selling or conveying the plant to any current electric company, that is, the competing monopoly, Denver Consolidated.

According to reports, following the award of the second, competing franchise to Lacombe, a rate war developed between the two electricity suppliers. Denver Consolidated, the previous monopolist, is reported to have dropped its rates to as low as two and one-half cents per kilowatt-hour. After some period, the rate war forced Lacombe into receivership. The rate war had led both Lacombe and Denver Consolidated to enter many low-rate service contracts with consumers. Denver Consolidated arranged a plan according to which it, too, would enter receivership, shed itself of its low-rate contracts, buy up the Lacombe's assets (free of Lacombe's low-rate contracts), and reorganize, charging higher rates.

In 1906, the City Council entered a new franchise with Denver Consolidated for a twenty-year term. This franchise, however, was far more detailed than any that had been entered previously. The franchise set maximum rates at ten cents per kilowatt-hour (the rate to which it had agreed with Lacombe), with a discount for early payment, but a minimum guarantee of five cents per month per lamp or $1 per month per consumer. The franchise also incorporated a detailed price structure for nonresidential uses as well as specifications regarding quality of service. In addition to the price constraint, the franchise charged the utility two and one-half percent of gross receipts during the first year, escalating to 4 percent after the eighth year. The franchisee also agreed to pay the city a fee of $1 million apportioned over the twenty-year franchise term. Colorado supplanted the franchise with a state regulatory commission in 1917.[91]

D. *Municipal Ownership: The Curious Case of Waterworks*

As stated earlier, Demsetz's proposal for establishing competition for the field presumes that the governmental entity owns the capital plant of the utility and auctions a contract for management services, with bidders competing over price and quality. Again, despite the prevalence of the franchise contract mechanism throughout the nineteenth century, I have discovered no examples of such an auction process.[92] Indeed, during

[91] Stigler & Friedland, *supra* note 13, at 13.

[92] I have found only one example of municipal ownership of a utility with other than municipal employees providing the service. Wilcox reports that the city of Denver acquired a small water plant in South Denver that had been constructed privately prior to annexation of the area by the city. After the city gained possession of the company, it leased the plant to the private water company monopolist then providing service to the remainder of the city under franchise. 1 Wilcox, *supra* note 51, at 440.

the nineteenth century, municipal ownership of utilities was extremely limited. For example, it is estimated that, of electrical power plants in the United States, 8 percent were publicly owned;[93] of municipal street railways, less than 1 percent were publicly owned.[94]

The one central exception to the predominance of private ownership of utilities is waterworks. Table 1 below, indicates the relative number of publicly and privately owned waterworks in the United States from 1800 to 1896. Table 1 shows that, though the proportion of publicly owned waterworks remained low prior to the Civil War, the absolute difference was not substantial. The large growth of waterwork plants occurred after 1880, with an exceptional spurt after 1890. Publicly owned plants were slightly more common, such that, by the end of the century, publicly owned works had reached a proportion of 53 percent of all operating plants. The author of this statistic reports separately that, of the 3,179 public or private waterworks in existence in 1896, slightly less than half (1,505) had been originally constructed by public entities, but that over the century 205 privately constructed works had been acquired by public entities, and twenty publicly constructed works had been sold to private owners.[95]

There is no clear explanation for why, of the variety of public utilities, water supply was the most likely to be publicly owned and managed. The history of the provision of water in a particular city, however, is illustrative of various of the concerns affecting municipal ownership and suggests the close similarity between municipal ownership, regulation by franchise, and regulation by commission.[96] The city of New Haven, Connecticut, was founded in 1638, but it was not until 1849 that a private firm, the New Haven Water Company, was issued a charter by the state legislature to provide water supply. Despite the charter, the Water Company did not initiate service. In 1853, citizens voted to issue bonds for a municipal water supply, though opposition later developed and, the next year, when the citizenry was to vote on final ratification, the proposal was defeated.

The private Water Company began operations in 1859. A further amendment by the state legislature to its charter in 1860 authorized the company to employ public rights-of-way, but without a limit on price. The company, of course, was obligated to secure service contracts with individual consumers and with the city itself. In 1862, the city entered a

[93] This figure is for 1902. William K. Jones, Regulated Industries 14 (2d ed. 1976).

[94] Two out of 789. This figure is for 1890. See Edward W. Bemis, Street Railways, in Municipal Monopolies 505, 565 (Edward W. Bemis ed. 1899).

[95] M. N. Baker, Water-Works, in Bemis ed., *id.* at 26.

[96] This history is taken from 1 Wilcox, *supra* note 51, at 409–17.

TABLE 1

PUBLIC OWNERSHIP OF WATER WORKS IN THE UNITED STATES, 1800–1896

	Number of Operating Plants		
Year	Public	Private	Percent Public
1800	1	15	6.3
1805	2	21	8.7
1810	5	21	19.2
1815	5	21	19.2
1820	5	25	16.6
1825	5	27	15.6
1830	9	35	20.5
1835	15	39	27.8
1840	23	41	35.9
1845	27	43	38.6
1850	33	50	39.7
1855	48	58	45.3
1860	57	79	41.9
1865	68	94	42.0
1870	116	127	47.7
1875	227	195	53.8
1880	293	305	49.0
1885	447	566	44.1
1890	806	1,072	43.9
1896	1,690	1,489	53.2

SOURCE.—M. N. Baker, Water-Works, in Municipal Monopolies 16 (Edward W. Bemis ed. 1899).

twenty-year contract with the company for the provision of water for city purposes. The contract required that the company lay ten miles of pipe within six years and established a schedule of annual prices. The contract gave the city the right to renew the contract and provided that, if the city objected to the prices claimed by the company, the renewal price structure would be set by a commission to be appointed by a superior court. Under the contract, the city obtained the right to purchase the plant and franchises of the company after ten years at historical cost plus 10 percent.

In succeeding years, other companies sought charters in order to provide competing service, which the New Haven Water Company opposed vigorously. According to Wilcox, "[a]fter several years struggle," a competing company obtained a charter on the condition of ratification by New Haven citizens, who overwhelmingly endorsed competition by a vote of 2,978–116. Wilcox reports, however, that the new company was absorbed by New Haven Water in 1876.

According to Wilcox, as the end of the twenty-year contract approached, there were increasing demands for public ownership. An act of the legislature authorized the city to purchase the works, if approved by the citizenry. The act also established an investigating committee, chaired by a Yale professor, Simeon E. Baldwin, to estimate the appropriate price. The final determination of price, however, was to be made by the Superior Court. Wilcox reports that the investigating committee recommended a price of $1.4 million; appraisers appointed by the court, a price of $1.1 million, but that the company, "by active political methods . . . carried on a campaign before the election to make the people believe that the court would award over $1.8 million." The citizenry soundly defeated the public ownership proposal. Baldwin, however, was severely criticized for his role and was accused of corruption by a National Civic Federation official, who emphasized that Baldwin later became a shareholder of the company and its legal counsel.

Thereafter, the city renewed its contract with the company in 1881 for a ten-year period with an option to renew indefinitely on terms to be determined by three arbitrators. The contract was renewed again in 1891, again in the context of substantial agitation in favor of a municipal buy-out. After substantial political dispute, the company submitted three alternative proposals to the city. The first proposal was a ten-year contract, with an option to renew on the same terms, that fixed rates for private consumers at current levels but required the city to pay $20,000 for public water and gave the city the right to purchase the company for just compensation at any time. The second proposal was a thirty-year contract that, again, fixed rates for private consumers at current levels but now provided for free public water and limited the city's right to purchase the company prior to the end of the thirty-year term only on the demonstration of a breach of contract.

The third proposal, of greatest interest since it was the proposal accepted by the city, provided for a contract of perpetual length, free water for public purposes, but no longer with the promise to fix rates to private consumers at current levels. Instead, the contract provided that rates to private consumers were to be readjusted once every five years through arbitration. The contract provided that "the arbitrators should not fix the rates at a point too low to pay all operating costs, renewals, extensions, and every other kind of expense, including interest on funded and unfunded debt, and in addition thereto an 8 percent dividend on the company's existing capital stock, together with a reasonable return, not exceeding 8 percent, upon other capital that might be invested from time to time in additions or extensions of the plant."[97]

[97] 1 *id*. at 415.

This agreement was executed in 1891. Connecticut established a public utility regulatory commission in 1911.[98]

IV. Regulation by Franchise and Commission Compared

This brief review of the characteristics of municipal utility regulation by franchise suggests the need for a substantial reinterpretation of the establishment of utility regulatory commissions. First, it is clear that the debate engendered by Harold Demsetz over the ultimate necessity of continuous commission regulation must be informed by a discussion of the legal and property rights foundations from which regulatory power derives. Demsetz's endorsement of regulation by contract presumes government control over entry and government ownership of the capital plant of the utility. Where the governmental entity lacks the power to prohibit entry and where it relies on private resources for capital investment, the comparison of regulation by franchise and by commission is different. The auction that Demsetz proposes becomes far more complicated, and the ability of the auction process to generate the result of price equal to marginal cost becomes increasingly heroic.

As we know, historically, municipalities, with respect to almost all public utilities, chose not to develop or acquire the capital plant of their utilities but to enter long-term contracts incorporating provisions seeking to restrain monopoly behavior. One obvious advantage of this approach is the escape by the governmental entity from the need to accurately determine the level and scope of investment in the utility and from the need to provide by contract or by subsequent governmental action for continuing investment or from opportunistic dissipation by the franchisee. Without more, it is difficult to conclude that public ownership, with recurrent short-term franchises let out through auction, represents a more effective means of enhancing social welfare.

Yet, even without the complications added by municipal ownership of the plant, many problems attended the effort to regulate monopolies by franchise, as Oliver Williamson has emphasized in an early essay addressing cable television.[99] Given the reliance of the municipality on private investment of capital, it was necessary to enter franchise contracts of exceptionally long duration. Because of the natural monopoly characteristics of many utilities, long duration franchises gave rise to the substantial prospect of monopoly pricing. Price and quality of service could be controlled by contract, but the determination of the appropriate price

[98] Stigler & Friedland, *supra* note 13, at 13.

[99] Williamson, *supra* note 33.

and quality specifications over a long period is very difficult. As we have seen, municipal franchises incorporated provisions allowing for adjustment, and cities made use of various other techniques to secure adjustment. The power to adjust, however, simply shifts the potential source of opportunism, requiring further contractual protections, such as the introduction of limits on price reductions and of minimum prices. All of these contractual provisions are reflective of the difficulties of regulation by franchise.

Over time, there appears to have been a systematic transformation in the utility franchise form. Early franchises incorporated provisions of great generality. Later franchises attempted more detailed specifications of contractual requirements. Toward the end of the nineteenth century, however, franchises for many different public services—electricity, gas, water—began to incorporate provisions providing for the subsequent adjustment of terms by independent groups of arbitrators, committees, or boards, charged to provide for amendments fair to both city and utility. Again, without more, it is difficult to distinguish state regulatory commissions established between 1907 and 1922—for example, from the board of arbitrators established in the 1891 New Haven water franchise—from the panel of arbitrators to be appointed according to the 1903 Salt Lake electricity franchise, or from the groups of disinterested citizens to be similarly convened in other cities.[100]

As a consequence, analysis of the social welfare effects of the adoption of continuously sitting regulatory bodies requires reexamination. The history makes clear that the establishment of state utility commissions in the 1907–22 period is a historical event of much less moment than has been generally appreciated. Much of the passion that has been devoted to this subject derives from the apparent contrast between what has been thought to be a laissez-faire regime of competition or, perhaps, regulation by contract in contrast to a socialistic regime of continuous and pervasive commission regulation. This characterization, however, is suspect. Is it more or less socialistic for city governments to increase taxes in order to build or purchase utilities, subcontracting management by a Demsetz-style auction, or to rely almost entirely on private capital investment, but requiring periodic adjustment to limit monopoly pricing?

Moreover, the creation of regulatory commissions appears to represent neither a shift from a free to a regulated market, as suggested by Stigler and Friedland, nor a shift from a market controlled by competition to a market controlled by captured regulators as suggested by Jarrell. It would be foolish to conclude that there were no differences between regulation

[100] For example, see sources cited in notes 71, 72, and 76 *supra*.

by municipal franchise and by state commission, but it is a complicated issue to determine exactly what the changes were. It is not surprising that Stigler and Friedland found little effect on the price level, price structure, or returns on utility investments.

Similarly, without more detailed analysis city by city, it is very difficult to characterize the level of competition of the precommission period. Jarrell's empirical conclusions derive from his assumption that, prior to the introduction of regulation by commission, public utilities were constrained to charging competitive prices. But this assumption has little basis. There is substantial evidence of the desire to enter markets in competition with existing utilities. This evidence, however, suggests that regulation by franchise failed to fully extract all monopoly profits. That is, whether by contract or commission, if regulation is successful in reducing price to marginal cost, there will be no benefit to a competitor to enter the market. In the context of regulation, attempts at competitive entry demonstrate that the regulated firm is earning greater than competitive profits. Thus, the evidence of efforts to enter the market may as easily support the conclusion of monopolization prior to the commissions rather than—as Jarrell claims—the threat of potential competition constraining municipal utilities to zero profits. Jarrell did find that electricity prices were significantly lower prior to commission regulation in the states that introduced commissions relatively early than in states that introduced commission regulation later. But, given the difficulties in evaluating the difference between regulation by franchise and by commission, it is hazardous to infer too much from the result.[101]

Indeed, the history suggests that to evaluate either the municipal or commission experience in terms of "public interest" versus "economic" theories of regulation is not illuminating. Many commentators have noticed that the content of the "public interest" theory is often difficult to define.[102] It is particularly difficult with respect to the regulation of public utilities. Perhaps in the ideal world of welfare economics the public inter-

[101] There are many questions relating to Jarrell's distinction between states regulated by comission early and later. Following Stigler, Jarrell regards a state as subject to commission regulation three years after the establishment of a state commission. See Jarrell, *supra* note 34. According to this definition, he contrasts five states subjected to commission regulation prior to 1912, twenty-five states subjected to commission regulation between 1912 and 1917, and two states subjected to commission regulation between 1917 and 1922. *Id.* at 286. If Jarrell used the actual year of the establishment of the state commission, instead of his three-year assumption, the numbers would be eighteen states prior to 1912, thirty-three states between 1912 and 1917, and three states between 1917 and 1922. More seriously, of course, it is difficult to know the extent to which regulation by state commission differed from municipal regulation.

[102] For example, see Levine & Forrence, *supra* note 26.

est can be defined as equal to adopting marginal cost pricing or recouping the equivalent of average costs with the smallest effect on output. Yet, how is it possible to evaluate any city's price structure to ascertain how close it complies to this standard? In contrast, to claim that the public interest is vindicated by any constraint on the full monopoly price is a shallow achievement.

More important, the "theories of regulation" approach misconstrues the relationship underlying regulatory behavior. Municipal regulation by franchise resembles a peculiar form of long-term relational contracting. The city council or citizenry on the one hand and the utility on the other are at once buyers and sellers of the other's services or assets. The city council is buying services on particular terms at the same time that it is selling its control over the public rights-of-way. The provisions of the initial franchise and the adjustments introduced in subsequent years represent the mutual pushing and tugging of buyers and sellers linked over time in a complicated contractual relationship. To seek to define the relationship in terms of a single "public interest," "economic interest," or "capture" theory is as futile as asserting that one can characterize a long-term contract for, say, coal supply in terms of a "buyer" or "seller" theory. The search for a single theory of regulation of this nature does not illuminate regulatory behavior.

Regulation by commission is hardly different. Aside from cases of total corruption, the assertion that an agency has been "captured" by a utility or is serving that utility's economic interests necessarily is too crude a depiction of the regulatory relationship. The authority of the regulator is independent of the regulated firm and monitoring of the regulator is independent. The more important issue is to identify and evaluate the determinants of the relationship and of its changes over time. As we have seen in repeated examples, it appears to have been often helpful in the execution of an arms-length franchise contract for a municipality to rely on independent boards or panels of citizens or arbitrators for the resolution of difficult issues that might arise in the future.

Regrettably, we know too little today to evaluate the impact of the establishment of regulatory commissions. There has been little study of the detail of early commission activity: How often were rates or service evaluated? When did commissions effectively extend the rate-of-return approach, suggested in the New Haven Water Company franchise? How was a single state commission able to effectively supplant tens or hundreds of municipal city councils in performing regulatory review? It is necessary to understand the mechanics of a change in regulatory regime before deriving a theory of it.

[18]

The Institutional Foundations of Regulatory Commitment: A Comparative Analysis of Telecommunications Regulation

Brian Levy
and
*Pablo T. Spiller**

1. Introduction

This paper provides a comparative assessment of the impact of core political and social institutions on telecommunications regulatory structures and utility performance outcomes in five countries – Argentina, Chile, Jamaica, the Philippines and the United Kingdom.[1] Although in recent years institutional analyses have made major gains in accounting for the conduct of regulatory and other economic policies in the United States and elsewhere, the empirical assessment of some key hypotheses has been constrained by the fact that over long periods of time the US's core American political institutions (institutions identified as key explanators of policy outcomes) have changed only slowly.[2] Cross-country comparative analyses are one way to release this constraint.

Utilities privatization and regulatory reform are increasingly billed as the way to improve service quality and to lower prices. Here we argue that such expectations may not always be attainable. In particular, looking at the problem of utilities regulation through the lens of transaction cost economics – with its micro-analytical perspective, its emphasis on discriminating alignment and remediableness, and its view of regulation as a contracting problem – provides an understanding of the determinants of performance of privatized utilities in different political and social circumstances. Our objective is to highlight how political institutions interact with regulatory processes and economic conditions in exacerbating or ameliorating the potential for administrative expropriation or manipulation, and hence determining the economic performance of the sector.

We argue that the credibility and effectiveness of a regulatory framework – and hence its ability to facilitate private investment – varies with a country's political and social institutions. Further, we argue that performance can be satisfactory with a wide range of regulatory procedures, as long as three complementary mechanisms restraining arbitrary administrative action are all in place: (a) substantive restraints on the discretion of the regulator, (b) formal or informal constraints on changing the regulatory system, and (c) institutions that enforce the above formal – substantive or procedural – constraints. Our evidence suggests that regulatory commitment can indeed be developed in what appear to be problematic environments, that without such commitment long-term investment will not take place, that achieving such commitment may require inflexible regulatory regimes that go against prevailing academic views, that in some cases public ownership of utilities is the default mode of organization, and furthermore that such ownership may be the only feasible alternative.

Political and social institutions not only affect the ability to restrain administrative action, but they also have an independent impact on the type of regulation that can be implemented, and hence on the appropriate balance between commitment and flexibility. For example, relatively efficient regulatory rules (e.g., price caps, incentive schemes, use of competition) usually require substantial discretion granting to the regulators. Thus, unless the country's institutions allow for the separation of arbitrariness from useful regulatory discretion, systems that grant too much administrative discretion may not generate the high levels of investment and welfare expected from private-sector participation. Conversely, some countries have regulatory regimes that drastically limit the scope of regulatory flexibility. Although such regulatory regimes may look inefficient, they may in fact fit the institutional endowments of the countries in question, and may provide substantial incentives for investment.

Our analysis may be especially relevant for the design of regulatory policy in developing, newly industrializing and previously socialist countries, where lack of economic development may be related to a generalized lack of administrative restraints.[3] But the results are also relevant in understanding the historical evolution of utilities regulation and ownership in developed countries. Indeed, as the analysis of the UK case highlights, restraining regulatory discretion seems to be behind the development of regulatory institutions in developed countries as well.[4]

A word of caution is in order, though. Our effort at comparative analysis has some important limitations. The need for detailed analyses of the political, social and regulatory institutions of each country naturally limits the number of cases that we were able to analyse.[5] Consequently, we do not offer formal statistical tests of our central propositions (as such tests would require a methodology not feasible at this stage of our research) but instead provide an analytical framework and casual but systematically collected and researched evidence. While we believe that our results provide strong support to some core propositions aligned with the new institutionalism, the spirit of the paper is exploratory – as much an exercise in hypothesis formulation as in hypothesis testing.

2. The Analytical Framework

A. *The Problem of Utilities*

Three special features characterize utilities and provide the starting point for our analysis. First, most (but not all) utility services are characterized by important economies of scale and scope. Second, most utilities' assets are highly specific and non-redeployable (although the extent of sunk investments varies with the application and with technology). Third, these services typically have a broad range of domestic users, usually overlapping with the voting population of the country. Viewed through the lens of the new institutional economics, these characteristics create contracting problems that undercut the ability of ordinary market mechanisms to deliver first-best performance.[6]

Economies of scale and scope and highly specific assets imply that the number of providers of basic utility services is going to be relatively small. Because a large proportion of the utilities' assets are sunk, a utility will be willing to operate even if it cannot recover its sunk investments as long as it covers its operating costs.[7] Widespread domestic consumption implies that the pricing of utilities is always going to be political.[8] Furthermore, the whiff of monopoly (particularly when ownership is concentrated in foreign hands) increases the gains from political action.

The combination of significant investments in durable, specific assets with the high level of politicization of utilities has the following result: utilities are highly vulnerable to administrative expropriation of their vast quasi-rents. Administrative expropriation may take several forms. Although the easiest form of administrative expropriation is the setting of prices below long-run average costs, it may also take the form of specific requirements concerning investment, equipment purchases or labour contract conditions that extract the company's quasi-rents. Where the threat of administrative expropriation is great, private investors will limit their exposure.[9] Thus, countries where administrative discretion is the norm may find that public ownership of utilities arises because the hazards of direct private investment are so great.[10]

Politics and technology strongly interact in shaping the potential for administrative expropriation. Sectors with very small sunk investments or with rapid asset depreciation will not be prime candidates for administrative expropriation.[11] Similarly, administrative expropriation may not be expected in the short run in countries or jurisdictions experiencing rapid growth in the demand for utilities services, as the costs of investment delays may limit the political gains from opportunistic behaviour. In the longer run, however, the fight for control over the institutions of government, and the corresponding division of spoils, will continuously expose the utilities to potential administrative or outright expropriation, even in rapidly growing economies.

B. Resolution of the Regulatory Problem: A Framework for Empirical Analysis

This section lays out a general framework for empirical, country-specific analysis of the extent to which the regulatory problems outlined above have been resolved, explains why the resolution took the form it did, and discusses the relation between regulatory outcomes and the performance of private utilities. Subsequent sections fill in the details.

REGULATORY DESIGN: GOVERNANCE AND INCENTIVES

In trying to understand different countries' abilities to commit to particular processes and institutions, we find it useful to look at regulation as a design problem. Regulatory design has two components: *regulatory governance* and *regulatory incentives*. We define the governance structure of a regulatory system as the mechanisms that societies use to constrain regulatory discretion and to resolve conflicts that arise in relation to these constraints.[12] The regulatory incentive structure comprises the rules governing utility pricing, cross- or direct-subsidies, entry, interconnection, etc. In contrast to regulatory governance, the structure of regulatory incentives has been the central preoccupation of virtually all theoretical work on regulation. A main result of this study, though, is that such emphasis is inadequate. Although we find that regulatory incentives indeed affect performance, their impact (positive or negative) comes to the forefront only if regulatory governance has successfully been put into place.[13]

Both regulatory governance and incentives are choice variables in the hands of policy-makers. The choices, however, are constrained ones. Choices as to regulatory governance are constrained by the specific institutional endowment of the nation, which both determines the form and the severity of the regulatory problems and shapes the range of options available for resolving them. Choices as to regulatory incentives are also constrained by a nation's specific institutional endowment. Moreover, a nation's choice of the governance features of the regulatory system will have an independent effect on the type of regulatory incentives that are viable.

INSTITUTIONAL ENDOWMENT AND REGULATORY GOVERNANCE

Following North (1990) and others, we define the *institutional endowment* of a nation as comprising five elements. First there are a country's legislative and executive institutions. These are the formal mechanisms (a) for appointing legislators and decision-makers and for making laws and regulations, apart from judicial decision making; (b) for implementing these laws, and (c) that determine relations between the legislature and the executive. Second, the country's judicial institutions. These comprise its formal mechanisms (a) for appointing judges and determining the internal structure of the judiciary and (b) for impartially resolving disputes among private parties, or between private parties and the state. Third are customs and other informal but broadly accepted norms that are generally understood to constrain the actions of individuals or institutions. Fourth is the character of the contending social interests within a society and the balance between them, including the role of ideology. Finally, there are the administrative capabilities of the nations. Each of these elements is subject to change, and the determinants of each can also be the subject of study. In this paper, though, we treat each of these elements as exogenous – as the institutional endowment of a particular nation. Here we highlight the first two, and comment on the remaining three whenever appropriate.

The form of a country's legislative and executive institutions influences the nature of its regulatory problems. The crucial issue is to what extent the structure and organization of these institutions impose constraints upon governmental action. The range of formal institutional mechanisms for restraining governmental authority includes the following: explicit separation of powers between legislative, executive and judicial organs of government;[14] a written constitution that limits the legislative power of the executive and is enforced by the courts; two legislative houses elected under different voting rules;[15] an electoral system calibrated to produce either a proliferation of minority parties or a set of parties whose ability to impose discipline on their legislators is weak;[16] and a federal structure of power, with strong decentralization even to the local level.[17] Utility regulation is likely to be far more credible – and the regulatory problem less severe – in countries with political systems that constrain executive and legislative discretion. Note, however, that credibility is often achieved at the expense of flexibility. The same mechanisms that make it difficult to impose arbitrary changes in the rules may also make it difficult to enact sensible rules in the first place, or to efficiently adapt the rules in the face of changing circumstances. Thus, in countries with these types of political institutions, the introduction of reforms may have to await the occurrence of a drastic shock to the political system.

Legislative and executive institutions may also limit a country's regulatory governance options. In some parliamentary systems, for example, the executive has substantial control over both the legislative agenda and legislative outcomes.[18] In such countries, if legislative and executive powers alternate between political parties with substantially different interests, specific legislation need not constitute a viable safeguard against administrative discretion, as changes in the law would follow directly from a change in government.[19] Similarly, if the executive has strong legislative powers, administrative procedures and administrative law by themselves will not be able to constrain the executive, which will tend to predominate over the judiciary in the interpretation of laws. In this case, administrative procedures require some base other than administrative law.

A strong and independent judiciary could serve as the basis for limiting administrative discretion in several ways. For example, the prior development of a body of administrative law opens the governance option of constraining discretion through administrative procedures.[20] Also, a tradition of efficiently upholding contracts and property rights opens the governance option of constraining discretion though the use of formal regulatory contracts (licences). This option is particularly valuable for countries where the executive has a strong hold over the legislative process. Further, a tradition of judicial independence and efficiency opens the governance option of using administrative tribunals to resolve conflicts between the government and the utility within the contours of the existing regulatory system. Finally it provides assurances against governmental deviation from specific legislative or constitutional commitments that underpin the regulatory system. While there are no simple ways of measuring judicial strength, two features seem to us to be key determinants: the extent of perceived judicial corruption and whether the courts have a history of deciding against the government. A corrupt judiciary that attempts to be independent may easily find its corruption publicly disclosed, with a clamp down following.[21] Similarly, a judiciary that seldom decides against the government, even on contract disputes, cannot be interpreted to be strong.[22]

INSTITUTIONAL ENDOWMENTS AND REGULATORY INCENTIVES

If the regulatory incentive structure is to promote welfare, it should facilitate investment, allocatively efficient pricing, and the introduction of new services and technologies. Yet regulatory incentives cannot be implemented in an institutional vacuum. The country's institutional endowment, the character of distributive politics, and the nature of its regulatory governance structure all affect the potential for the successful design of regulatory incentives.

Consider first the constraints that the nation's institutional endowment imposes on the design of regulatory incentives. Administrative capabilities – the ability of the nation's professionals (e.g., academics, lawyers, bureaucrats) to handle complex regulatory concepts and processes in a relatively efficacious manner, without triggering excessive disputes and litigation – are of particular relevance. These capabilities will determine the potential for the successful implementation of complex regulatory designs. Thus, regulatory systems that call for complex implementation will be inadequate in nations with weak administrative capabilities.

As for the impact of distributive politics, it can constrain the extent of allocative efficiency that can be achieved by regulatory incentives. A major feature of telecommunications distributive politics is the demand for cross-subsidization from businesses to residential users, which has translated in many countries into very high prices for long-distance or international calls. Unless eliminated, such cross-subsidization limits the potential for exploiting the advantages of competition.

Finally, and perhaps more important, the institutional realities of some countries may be such that resolution of governance problems constrains the range of regulatory incentive options to third (or even fourth) best. In some countries, the only way to constrain administrative arbitrariness may be to almost totally withdraw administrative discretion. The resulting governance considerations would constrain the range of workable regulatory incentive designs to those that provide only limited flexibility. In telecommunications, where technological change is rapid, the cost of this reduction in regulatory flexibility is high – but so too is the cost of failing to adequately restrain discretion.

Yet, even given these constraints, the individual country studies suggest that in most cases there exists a broad range of discretion for policy-makers as to the design of regulatory governance and incentive structures. Indeed, utility performance appears to be best in countries that have achieved a good fit between their exogenous institutions and their regulatory governance and incentive designs, and worst in those instances where regulatory design proceeded without attention to the exogenous institutional realities. Furthermore, the quality of design of regulatory incentives emerges in the country studies as an independent influence on performance.[23]

C. A Decision Tree

The decision tree presented in Figure 1 summarizes the above discussion and sets the stage for analysis of the five countries in a way that highlights the impact of a country's exogenous institutional endowment on its regulatory design.[24] The heavier lines in the figure are branches represented by observations in our sample. Because our framework has implications for other institutional environments, we present the decision tree in its general formulation. We make four sets of distinctions.

The first distinction is between those countries that have domestic institutions capable of credibly refraining from arbitrary administrative action and those that do not. Our framework suggests that the existence of an independent judiciary with a reputation for impartiality, and whose decisions are enforced, is a necessary condition for making these credible commitments. As discussed further below, among the countries studied, Chile, Jamaica and the United Kingdom had in place a well-functioning judiciary, while Argentina and the Philippines did not. Countries lacking a well-functioning judiciary will face difficulties in the short term in developing a regulatory system capable of sustaining efficient levels of private participation and investment, and there is little reason for them to devote substantial scarce resources to such an effort. Instead alternative mechanisms of securing commitment (like international guarantees) will be necessary.

Among countries capable of using regulation to secure commitment, the second distinction is between those countries whose electoral, legislative and executive institutions are structured in a way that enables them to achieve credible regulatory commitments via legislation and those countries which can best achieve credible commitments by embedding their regulatory systems in the operating licences of private companies. As we discuss below, legislation may provide regulatory credibility in political systems that do not generate unified governments, like presidential systems with multi-chamber legislatures, fragmented parties and nonsimultaneous

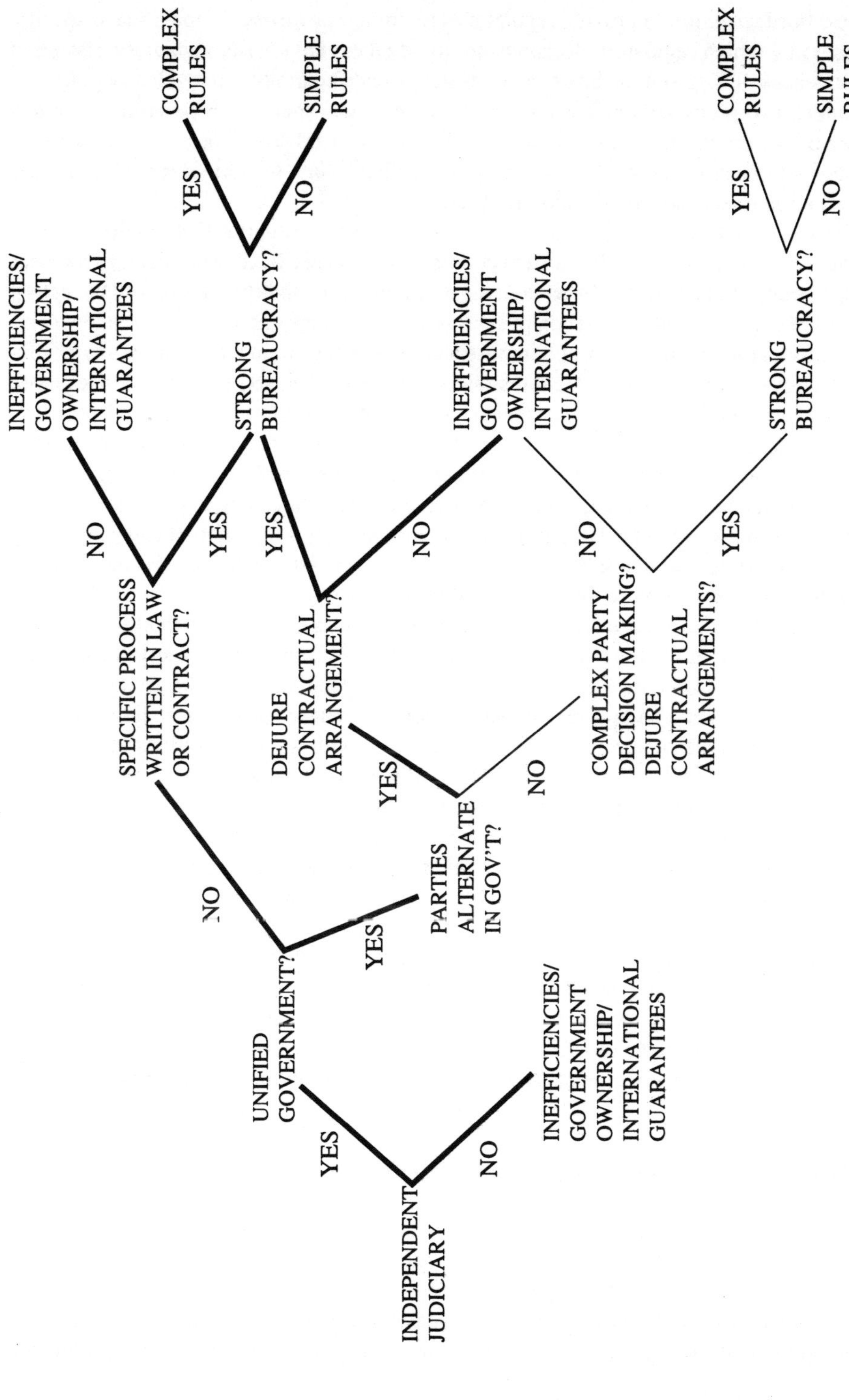

Figure 1 A Decision Tree

elections. For legislation to provide regulatory credibility, however, it should make specific the process by which regulatory decisions are to be taken. Otherwise, regulatory discretion will be unchecked. Legislation, however, does not provide credibility to regulatory policy in, for example, two-party parliamentary systems where parties alternate in government. In this case, regulatory credibility can be obtained by basing the regulatory process in contract law, rather than administrative law.[25] As will be seen, Chile falls into the former category (as does the US), and Jamaica and the UK into the latter.

The third distinction, not depicted in Figure 1, is between countries that require specific, substantive rules to achieve credibility and countries that can use flexible regulatory processes and still restrain arbitrary action. In general, the potential for flexibility in design will be highest in two sets of countries. The first set comprises those whose exogenous institutional endowments include informal norms or bodies of administrative law that restrain the arbitrary use of governmental power even if explicit legal restraints are absent. The second set comprises those where an institutionalized process of argumentation and consensus formation sets de facto limits on the extent to which a private utility can be subjected to administrative expropriation. Among the countries studied, although neither Jamaica nor the UK can provide credibility though legislation, Jamaica falls into the category of countries requiring specific, substantive rules to achieve regulatory credibility, while the UK can achieve such credibility with a more flexible regulatory process. Chile, while able to use legislation as its regulatory instrument, also has the ability to achieve credibility with a more flexible regulatory framework.

Among countries that require very specific, substantive rules to achieve credibility, the fourth and final distinction in Figure 1 is between those that have strong administrative capabilities and those that do not. Countries with strong administrative capabilities can put in place a regulatory system based on specific, substantive rules that can both attract investment by restraining arbitrary action and promote efficiency and flexibility. Countries with weak capabilities may have to settle for less efficient rules for their regulatory system to work. Among the countries studied, Chile falls into the former category and Jamaica the latter.

Viewed from a different perspective, the decision tree identifies three complementary sets of mechanisms to restrain arbitrary action. First are substantive restraints on regulatory discretion, which can take the form of either process regulation or of specific, substantive rules (i.e. distinctions 3 and 4). Second are restraints on changing the regulatory system, of either the legislative or licensing variety (i.e. distinction 2). Finally, there are institutions, notably a judiciary, for enforcing both the substantive restraints and restraints on system changes (i.e. distinction 1). A central hypothesis to be explored in the comparative country analysis is that for private performance to be satisfactory all three mechanisms must be in place and must be properly aligned with the specific character of a country's background institutions.

3. The Institutional Background of the Country Cases

This section describes the exogenous variables – the institutional background of each of the five countries[26]. Section 4 then provides the link between these and our endogenous variables – regulatory regimes and regulatory performance.

Table 1 provides a snapshot of the main institutional characteristics of Argentina, Chile, Jamaica, the Philippines and the United Kingdom, and relates them to the potential for opportunistic

Table 1 Institutional Features of Argentina, Chile, Jamaica, Philippines and United Kingdom

COUNTRY	LEGISLATIVE AND EXECUTIVE INSTITUTIONS	JUDICIAL INSTITUTIONS	SOCIAL CONFLICT	SOCIAL NORMS	ADMINISTRATIVE CAPABILITIES
ARGENTINA	Separation of powers with fragmented party structure	Weak and politically manipulable	Basic urban-rural conflict	Rent seeking. Lack of respect for constitutional order	Corrupt bureaucracy, but highly qualified professional class
CHILE	Separation of powers with fragmented party structure. Orderly alternation of power except during Gen. Pinochet's regime	Strong and professional; defended private property during socialist period	Regional balance	Respect for judiciary	Highly respected bureaucracy and qualified professional class
JAMAICA	Parliamentary system with two strong parties	Strong and professional; upheld utility contracts against government prior to 1966 and defended private property during the first Manley administration	Small middle class holds political balance. No major regional differences. Violent urban poor	Respect for judiciary and electoral outcomes	Small professional class. Politicized bureaucracy
PHILIPPINES	Separation of powers with weak parties and strong presidency. Until 1960s partial US supervision. Military regime during Marcos	Weak and corrupt	Regional competition among members of elite	Rent seeking. No outright expropriation of elite ownership	Weak and corrupt bureaucracy
UNITED KINGDOM	Sovereign parliament with strong two-party system	Very strong and professional; upholds contracts against the government. Weak administrative law	Large middle class holding political balance	Strong respect for bureaucratic process and for judiciary	Very strong bureaucracy

government behaviour. In exploratory research of the kind described here, there is an ever-present risk of expost rationalization in interpreting the role of exogenous variables. To obviate this risk, we have tried as much as possible to anchor our depictions of the exogenous institutions of the five countries in prior scholarly writings. Further, we alert the reader wherever we push our interpretation of the behaviour of a country's institutions beyond previous interpretations. We divide the countries into three groups: *traditional parliamentary systems* (Jamaica and the UK), *the archetypal presidential systems* (Chile), and *rent-seeking presidential systems* (Argentina and the Philippines). Each group has distinct implications for what type of regulatory regimes are workable.

A. *Traditional Parliamentary Systems: Jamaica and the United Kingdom*

Jamaica and the UK provide the observations for the Figure 1 branch that answers yes to the 'unified government' question. The political systems of Jamaica and the UK are parliamentary, characterized by a strong judiciary and electoral rules that tend to generate two strong parties.[27] As a consequence, the majority party invariably has an absolute majority in Parliament and controls both the government and the legislature.[28] The two countries' judicial institutions are also similar.[29] Britain has led the world in the development of a judiciary with an exceptional reputation for probity. Jamaica's judiciary is also well regarded and has ruled against the government on numerous occasions.[30] Note, though, the implications for the judiciary of a political system based upon a sovereign two-party parliament, with no written constitution: under such a system, the parliament is free to act as it pleases, so long as it follows generally accepted procedures (on which more later), but the courts have no formal restraining authority.[31] To a large extent because of this feature of parliamentary politics, in neither country has the judiciary developed a strong administrative law doctrine, although both have a long contract law tradition and have upheld contracts against the government.[32] In both countries, then, administrative decisions are essentially undertaken in the dark.[33] Agencies do not necessarily justify their decision (although the UK Office of Telecommunications Regulation does),[34] nor necessarily hold public hearings.[35,36] Judicial review of agency decisions is not customary in either country.[37] Furthermore, in the UK, regulatory review is not a strong weapon for the regulated firms and intervenors,[38] because regulators can make decisions that effectively prevent judicial review.[39]

Thus, the formal institutions of government in the UK and Jamaica allow for substantial governmental discretion. This governmental discretion can translate into important policy shifts, with the judiciary playing a minor role in restraining administrative discretion. Informal rules of legislative decision making, however, restrain both governments' ability to undertake policy shifts without consulting interest groups. For example, over the years the UK has developed decision-making processes that tend to limit the endemic secrecy of parliamentary system governments by allowing interest group consultations. Although both these countries have the potential to undertake large policy shifts, some amount of consensus in policy-making is required. The necessity for consensus-making procedures arises as much from the need to legitimize governmental decision-making as from the need to avoid cracks in the governing party with the consequent loss of legislative support. Ways to develop consensus and conduct interest-group consultations vary from country to country; they include the role and use of ad-hoc commissions and white and green papers,[40] the use of collective ministerial responsibility,[41] as well as the use of party organizations to settle disagreements prior to parliamentary action. Within-party consensus-building measures are useful for single-party governments not just because they grant stability and credibility to their actions, but also because they provide legitimacy to the party leadership. Legitimacy is important in safeguarding against other factions' attacks and in maintaining backbenchers' support.[42]

In the UK, furthermore, at the level of policy implementation, the Westminster model of government defines the prerogatives and responsibilities of politicians and bureaucrats,[43] with mutually recognized boundaries of authority, even where their power is not explicitly constrained. Jamaica and the UK differ, however, in the extent of professionalism of the bureaucracy. While the UK's bureaucracy is professional and largely apolitical, the politicization of the bureaucracy during the first administration of Jamaica's Prime Minister Manley seems to have had an irreversible effect in reducing the qualifications and role of its bureaucracy.[44]

Thus both the UK and Jamaica have electoral systems that provide for great legislative flexibility and judiciaries that do not strongly restrain administrative actions. As a consequence, neither can base its governance structure on legislative acts. They need further constraints. As we will see, both found them in contract law.

B. The Archetypal Presidential System: Chile

Chile, with its architypal presidential system,[45] is the country in our sample that provides the observations for Figure 1 branch that answers no to the 'unified government' question. Between 1973 and 1989, Chile went through a period of military rule under General Augusto Pinochet. This period, however, stands out as a 15-year exception to more than 100 years of rule by civilian government. For the rest of this 100-year period, the country was governed by a constitution that embodied the principles of separation of powers, orderly transfer of authority, and regular elections between competing parties. For an extended period, voters were divided among multiple parties, with none strong enough to legislate except by coalition. Legislators' independence from central party apparatus led to the development of a legislature with a strong sense of local representation.[46] A series of constitutional reforms between 1958 and 1973 shifted the balance of authority in favour of the presidency and elevated national (rather than regional) politics and parties to centre stage. These reforms granted more executive powers at the same time as they developed stronger checks and balances.[47] The reforms increased the potential for conflict between the legislative and executive branches, which became evident during the regime of President Salvador Allende. Thus, while not entirely resistant to extreme pressure, Chile's longstanding set of legislative and executive institutions and the nature of its checks and balances can be seen as potentially providing some credible safeguards against arbitrary changes in the regulatory regime governing utilities. This period of extended stability, broken only by the military takeover in 1973, developed in Chile a strong respect for institutions.[48]

Chile's strong, professional and independent judiciary provides a particularly effective check on the government, on issues of both constitutional and statutory interpretation. For example, Salvador Allende's 1970–73 government repeatedly clashed with the courts over issues of expropriation and compensation, with the courts refusing to back down. Its large pool of highly qualified professionals, has served Chile well in providing governments of the different parties with access to qualified political appointees.

Chile's diffuse political power, then, provides opportunities for designing regulatory governance structures along several alternative lines. Because specific legislation is more difficult to change in Chile than, say, in the UK, specific legislation may play a more important role in the regulatory governance structure of Chile than the UK. On the other hand, Chile's strong judiciary provides also for implementing regulatory governance based purely on procedures or contract law.[49]

C. Rent-Seeking Presidential Systems: Argentina and the Philippines

Argentina and the Philippines provide the observations for Figure 1 branch that answers no to the 'independent judiciary' question. These countries share some common political features. First, both have modelled their formal political institutions upon those of the US, creating a complex system of checks and balances.[50] Indeed, both countries experienced quite extended periods of constitutional rule during which executive authority was largely restrained. Yet structure is not determinative: the history of both countries has been punctuated by periods of extra-constitutional rule in which governmental authority was concentrated in the president (see Hill and Abdala 1993, and Esfahani 1993).[51] Second, in both countries, the endemic lack of respect for constitutional order has translated into a corrupt bureaucracy and judiciary, and into turns to the military as the panacea for interest group conflicts.[52,53]

Although the governments of both the Philippines and Argentina have traditionally followed 'beggar-thy-neighbour' policies towards political opponents, the governing Filipino elites have followed, even during the Marcos regime, a 'non-expropriation' norm whereby assets of political opponents are not expropriated outright (Esfahani, 1993). Instead, since control over the government rotates among elite groups, business owners not aligned with the elite in power tend to be subject to administrative expropriation (see Esfahani, 1993).

To summarize, both Argentina's and the Philippines' institutional frameworks seem to be sufficiently weak, and the scope for executive dominance sufficiently strong, that our framework suggests that regulatory governance has to go beyond the choices of legislation, procedures or contract law.[54] We discuss these issues in section 4B.

4. Exogenous Endowments and Regulatory Commitment Mechanisms

This section describes and interprets the regulatory experience of the five countries in question. The discussion of regulation is organized around the three mechanisms to restrain arbitrary administrative action that were identified earlier: (a) substantive restraints on the discretion of the regulator that are written into the design of a regulatory system; (b) restraints on changing the regulatory system; and (c) institutions for enforcing both the substantive restraints and restraints on system changes. Each subsection sets the stage for discussing regulation by briefly describing the evolution of telecommunications ownership in the relevant countries.

As the analysis reveals, across the five countries and different periods, regulatory systems worked and attracted private investment at reasonable rates of return only when all three mechanisms were in place. Moreover, the evidence suggests that the exogenous institutional endowments of individual countries have influenced both whether they were able to put in place workable governance designs for their regulatory systems and, if so, the specific forms of such

Table 2 Regulatory history and commitment mechanisms: Jamaica and the UK

				Restraining Mechanism		
COUNTRY/ PERIOD	OWNERSHIP	REGULATORY HISTORY	PRIVATE PERFORMANCE	SUBSTANTIVE RESTRAINTS	RESTRAINTS ON SYSTEM CHANGES	ENFORCEMENT OF RESTRAINTS
JAMAICA –1966	Privately owned with separate domestic and international companies.[1]	Rate of return (7–9%) on assets stipulated in the licence. Ad hoc rate boards responsible for rate reviews. Decisions challengeable in courts.	Sustained network expansion up to 1962 Steady, moderate rate of return.	Monopoly rights plus precise rate of return for long period, written in the licence.	Licence cannot be altered without consent of company.	Strong judiciary.
JAMAICA 1966–75	In 1962 government announced intention to change regulation system at licence renewal time. Sale of JTC to CTC[2] in 1966. In 1971 government takes majority stake in new international operations company, and in 1975 takes over JTC.	New licence issued in 1966 specifies JTC to be regulated by JPUC. Licence specifies rate of return to be fair and reasonable, although Telephone Act specifies 8% return. JPUC interprets legislative mandate to be not binding. JPUC institutes rate increases based on investment performance. Sustained regulatory conflict.	Initial network expansion, then slowdown. Low profitability.	'Fair' rate of return.	None, given generality of licence.	Strong judiciary.
JAMAICA 1987–	Creation of TOJ[3] to combine JTC and JAMINTEL. Privatization starts in 1988.	Licence stipulates rate of return (17.5–20%) on shareholders' revalued assets. Speedy arbitration. Government cannot challenge investments. Government to monitor quality, and may require quality improvements.	Major investment in domestic network. Reduction in real prices and sustained high profitability.	Monopoly rights plus precise rate of return for long period, written into licence.	Licence cannot be altered with consent of company.	Strong judiciary.
UNITED KINGDOM 1984+	Publicly owned from 1912 until privatization in 1984.	Licence specifies price cap and a complex mechanism to resolve regulatory conflicts.	Take-off of investment in 1982, with large gains in national welfare.	Main regulatory issues, including RPI–X, with a specific X, written into licence.	Licence can only be changed with consent of company or through a precise process requiring the approval of three separate bodies. Informal restraints on abuse of power by sovereign.	Strong judiciary, plus informal norms of governmental decision making.

Notes:

1. International Company: Cable and Wireless (West Indies). Domestic Company: Jamaica Telephone Company (JTC). Majority shareholder, the Telephone and General Trust of the UK.
2. CTC: Continental Telephone Company.
3. TOJ: Telecommunications of Jamaica, a joint venture between the government of Jamaica and Cable and Wireless.

workable governance designs for their regulatory systems and, if so, the specific forms of such designs. See Tables 2 to 4 for a summary of the information presented below.

A. *Traditional Parliamentary Systems: Jamaica and the United Kingdom*

Table 2 summarizes the chronology of telecommunications ownership, regulation and performance in Jamaica and the UK[55]. Three features of the chronology are especially noteworthy and are examined in some depth below. First, both the UK and Jamaica have had sustained periods of high levels of private investment in telecommunications: in Jamaica before 1962 and after 1987 in the UK since corporatization and privatization (1982 and 1984 respectively). Second, during the periods of high investment, regulation took different forms in the two countries. In Jamaica, rate-of-return regulation has been the standard regulatory method. although with important differences between the pre-1962 and post-1987 periods; in the UK, on the other hand, price-cap regulation was introduced for the first time in the regulation of British Telecommunications (BT). Finally, although both Jamaica and the UK had periods in which private ownership was associated with strong investment, Jamaica experienced a long decade (from the early 1960s to the mid-1970s) during which private investment lagged.

In this section we attempt to explain these three features in the light of the framework developed earlier. The thrust of this section is the following: First, despite seeming differences in their regulatory frameworks, the strong commonalities in the two countries' regulatory governance structures have roots in the similarities of their exogenous institutional endowments. Second, the differences in the substantive restraints developed in both countries can be traced to important variations in their respective exogenous endowments. Third, in all three high-investment periods, the regulatory systems were appropriately aligned with exogenous endowments in a way that created workable mechanisms to restrain arbitrary action. Finally, Jamaica's disastrous 1966–75 experience was the consequence of a misalignment between its exogenous institutions and the chosen regulatory governance structure.

THE HIGH INVESTMENT PERIODS

As Table 2 describes, Jamaica has had two high investment periods: the first continued until the government's decision (in 1962) to switch from licence-based, rate-of-return regulation to a US-style Public Utility Commission-based regulatory framework. The second period started with the creation and privatization of Telecommunications of Jamaica (TOJ) in 1987. The UK's high investment period began with BT's corporatization and its subsequent privatization in 1984. As we discuss below, these events provide the observations for the Figure 1 branch that answers yes to the 'dejure contractual arrangement' question.

Although the regulatory incentive schemes in the three periods are quite dissimilar (Jamaica having in both periods a rate-of-return regulation with specific profitability targets and strong limitations on regulatory discretion, while the UK has no formal profitability targets in its price-cap regime), the regulatory governance structures are quite similar. The licences served as contracts between the regulated companies and their respective governments, since attempts by the governments to deviate from the licence specifications could be, and were, challenged in court. For the judiciary to serve as a credible arbitrator, however, the licences must be specific enough that judicial outcomes are predictable. Licences, then, can serve as an effective restraint to administrative action. Indeed, in the three episodes, licences have been very specific about price-setting procedures. Both Jamaican licences require that prices provide the company with a specific rate of return (7–9% on real operating assets in the pre-1966 period, and 17.5–20% on revalued shareholder's net worth since 1987). The 1987 licence also limits the ability of the regulator to disqualify investments or to delay price increases through administrative silence. Furthermore, the 1987 licence provides for speedy arbitration to resolve price-setting conflicts. Both Jamaican licences specifically granted the company the ability to challenge government decisions in court. BT's 1984 licence (and all its amendments) is equally specific in its price-setting procedures. Price-setting powers are granted to BT, with only ex-post supervision by the regulator to see that regulated prices follow the price cap structure specified in the licence. In both countries, attempts by the regulator to alter the main features of the regulatory regime require a licence modification. In Jamaica, licence modifications require the agreement of the company. In the UK, licence modifications involve a well-specified process which, to be undertaken against BT's will, requires the agreement of the Monopolies and Mergers Commission (MMC) and of the Secretary of Trade and Industry (the Board of Trade). Furthermore, an attempt by the regulator to circumvent such a process can be challenged in court.

Thus, in both Jamaica and the UK the use of very specific licences provided the companies with substantial assurances about the expected profitability of their investments.[56] Furthermore, because these licences were specified for long periods of time, they were not easily modified and were enforceable in the courts, the companies were assured of substantial regulatory stability.[57]

The emphasis on contract rather than administrative law in providing regulatory credibility in both Jamaica and the UK is consistent with the nature of their political institutions. Their systems of parliamentary sovereignty imply that the mere existence of a law governing regulation, even if it is very precise and specific, provides very little assurance that the current regulations will not be subsequently modified. On the other hand, the courts in both Jamaica and the UK have a strong history of upholding contracts among private parties. Jamaican courts were called to resolve contract (regulatory) disputes between the government and the regulated company before 1962, while the UK courts dealt with electric power licence interpretation issues prior to World War II. While UK courts have yet to hear and decide a case against a regulator of the privatized utilities, it seems that the threat of legal action has in fact restrained the United Kingdom's regulators.[58,59] No disputes over the terms of the 1988 Jamaican licences have yet been brought to court.

To summarize, in the three periods with substantial private investment, the three regulatory regimes specified important substantive restrictions on the discretion of the regulator; furthermore, there were serious impediments to changing the regulatory regimes, and finally, in all three episodes, there was an institution that could credibly be called upon to enforce both the substantive restrictions on the regulator and the stability of the regulatory regime.

DIFFERENCES IN REGULATORY GOVERNANCE

Although both the UK and Jamaica have based their respective regulatory governance structures on licences, BT's licence has a measure of flexibility that Telecommunications of Jamaica's (TOJ) does not have: BT's licence can be amended against its will; TOJ's cannot. Amending BT's licence against its will, however, is no minor task. It requires agreement among the Director General of Telecommunications, the Monopolies and Mergers Commission and the Secretary of Trade and Industry. These three authorities can be expected to differ with one another in their regulatory views; indeed, two of them (the Director General and the Monopolies and Mergers Commission) enjoy more than a modicum of independence from the government of the day. As Spiller and Vogelsang (1993a) show, the traditional independence of the MMC and the inability of the Secretary of Trade and Industry to dictate decisions to the Director General of Telecommunications[60] imply that the multiplicity of veto points make a licence amendment against BT difficult, though not impossible.

Jamaica's licences have never had that measure of flexibility. Since the beginning of utility regulation,Jamaica's licences have required the agreement of the company for any amendment.[61] That requirement has given the regulated company substantial bargaining power. As a consequence, even dramatic technological or political changes may fail to bring about changes in the regulatory environment.[62] While such rigidity could be criticized from a purely normative perspective, Jamaica's institutional endowment provides the clue for the need to introduce institutional rigidities in the regulatory governance. In the UK, regulatory flexibility was built on a foundation of a long tradition of informal checks and balances and the use of independent, expert commissions. By contrast, Jamaica has never had a system of administrative checks and balances. The Jamaican Public Utilities Commission, created in 1966, was the first and only experiment with independent commissions and as the next section shows, the result was quite disastrous. Furthermore, the repercussions of the politicization of the bureaucracy during the first administration of Prime Minister Manley in the early 1970s eliminated the potential for using delegation of regulatory responsibilities as a source of commitment (Spiller and Sampson 1993).[63] This has not yet been tried. Our framework suggests, then, that attempting to design in Jamaica a regulatory governance system with as much flexibility as that in the UK will most probably undermine the credibility of Jamaica's regulatory process, and hence negatively impact on the sector's performance.

DIFFERENCES IN REGULATORY INCENTIVES

Jamaica and the UK differ not only in their regulatory governance structures, but also in the nature of their regulatory incentive structures. Jamaica pursued a straightforward rate of return regulatory system,[64] while the UK introduced price-cap regulation. Because the normative inefficiencies of rate-of-return regulation had been discussed at length in the economic literature by the early 1980s, and because price caps were already widely discussed as superior to rate of return, by the late 1980s,[65] it is proper to question whether Jamaica's regulatory system introduced in the late 1980s was the result of a mistake, capture, or of the constraints imposed by the institutional background of the country.

Although we cannot reconstruct the mental processes by which Jamaica's government privatized TOJ and compare it to that undertaken by the UK government, it is clear that in both instances substantial emphasis was given to how to design the regulatory system to be applied to the privatized company, in the case of the UK, through the commissioning of several white papers[66], and in the case of Jamaica, through numerous cabinet meetings.[67] While capture and mistakes are difficult to discard as reasons for any regulatory decision,[68] our framework sees the institutional background in Jamaica as limiting the potential implementation of a flexible price-cap regime.[69] In the UK, the regulator's revision of the price-cap rules is constrained by a very specific process built around the integrity and credible independence from government of the various layers of authority required to approve licence amendments, and around a range

Table 3 Regulatory history and commitment mechanisms: Chile

PERIOD	OWNERSHIP	REGULATORY HISTORY	PERFORMANCE	RESTRAINING MECHANISMS: SUBSTANTIVE RESTRAINTS	RESTRAINING MECHANISMS: RESTRAINTS ON CHANGES SYSTEM	RESTRAINING MECHANISMS: ENFORCEMENT OF CONSTRAINTS
1930–58	Controlled by ITT. (International Telephone and Telegraph)	Regulatory law open-ended; no independent regulatory body. Government had right to intervene in the company's operations. Disputes to be resolved by Supreme Court.	Initially, relative rapid expansion, then slow-down.	Vague. Based on legislation	Vagueness provided for administrative discretion in interpreting law.	Strong judiciary.
1958–1973	Partial takeover of CTC[d] by government in 1967, government intervention in 1971, and total takeover in 1974. ENTEL created to provide long-distance services in 1964.	Regulatory sub-agreements in 1958 and 1967 eliminated vaguess concerning rate of return (now at 10% instead of up to 10%) and imposed new investment obligations.	Network expansion accelerates prior to intervention and nationalization.	Strengthened with 1958 sub-agreements.	Separation of powers and divided legislature. Constitutional changes in 1958 and 1967 increased powers of national parties.	Strong judiciary.
1987+	Privatization in 1988.	Detailed benchmark regulation for non-competitive market segments. Price regulation based on performance of theoretically efficient firm, recalibrated every 5 years with interim indexation. Law stipulates process to be followed to compute rate of return to efficient firm. Explicit arbitration procedure for recalibration. Regulatory decisions appealable to Supreme Court.	Unprecedented high rates of network expansion and traffic growth subsequent to privatization.	Very explicit, precise price regulation based on rate of return of efficient firm, plus explicit process for defining non-competitive activities subject to price regulation. Both stipulated by law.	Separation of powers and divided legislature.	Explicit conflict resolution process, with strong judiciary as final arbiter.

Notes: d-CTC-Compañía de Teléfonos de Chile

of informal norms in the UK, which ensures that the process cannot easily be manipulated. Such a process, however, could not readily be transferred to Jamaica. Jamaica lacks the multiple layers of independent authority necessary to build in credible UK-style restraints.[70] Since price caps are by nature transitory,[71] it is reasonable to expect the X factor to be increased opportunistically at the next price-cap renewal. As a consequence, the regulated company will limit its exposure, unless the initial price-cap regime would provide it with substantial up-front rents.[72] In other words, UK-style RPI–X price-cap regulation is not readily transferable.

REGULATORY MISALIGNMENT: JAMAICA 1966–1975

In 1962 the Jamaican government decided to move, at licence renewal time, from a licence-based to a PUC-style regulatory structure. In 1966 the government issued new licences to the domestic company based on the Jamaican Public Utilities Act of 1966, which mandated 'fair' rates of return. It also established a permanent and independent regulatory commission, the Jamaican Public Utilities Commission (JPUC), to oversee regulation of domestic telephone and electricity services. The JPUC had substantial administrative discretion and promoted participation in the regulatory process by a wide range of interest groups. This episode provides the observation for the Figure 1 branch that answers no to the 'dejure contractual arrangement' question.

From its inception the relationship between the JPUC and the domestic company (the Jamaica Telephone Company – JTC) were acrimonious, and the conflict increased over time. Price increases fell substantially behind inflation, and the JPUC introduced a policy of promising price increases conditional on quality improvements and investment levels. The domestic operations company stopped all investment programmes in 1962 following the government's decision to change the regulatory regime. Except for a short period following the US-based Continental Telephone Co.'s takeover of domestic telephone operations, there was no network expansion until the 1980s.

The primary reason for this acrimony and the deteriorating performance of JTC was the absence of substantive restraints in the regulatory system. The JPUC was created to replicate the operations and freedoms of a US-style PUC. The JPUC invited participation from interest groups, undertook hearings and made determinations without strong constraints. The enabling legislation only required it to set 'fair and reasonable' rates. Although the JPUC Act of 1966 granted the Jamaican courts the right to review JPUC's decisions, during the 1966–75 period the judiciary did not provide any important restraint to the JPUC. Indeed, given the vagueness of the licence, the 'unreasonableness' criterion required to overturn a governmental decision became a very stringent standard to overcome.[73] The JPUC was, for all purposes, unchecked, except for the direct intervention of the government.[74] Thus, during this period, the judiciary could not be called to provide the regulatory credibility inherent in the pre-1966 and post-1987 regulatory regimes.

B. The Archetypal Presidential System: Chile

Table 3 provides a summary chronology of telecommunications ownership, regulation and performance in Chile.[75] As in Jamaica, Chile's regulatory history can be separated into high and low investment periods. During the high investment periods, regulation took very different forms rate of return – in 1958–71 and benchmark regulation from 1987 on. The low investment periods were a) from the end of World War II until the late 1950s and b) from the Allende government, through the intervention in 1971 and nationalization in 1974, until the regulatory reforms of the mid-1980s. Here we focus only on the period under private ownership (up to 1971 and following 1987). In this section we attempt to explain and interpret these patterns in the light of the framework developed earlier. The thrust of the section is as follows: first, during periods of high investment, the regulatory schemes were better aligned with Chile's exogenous endowments than during the low investment period; second, that such alignments restrained arbitrary action in the three dimensions noted above.

THE LOW INVESTMENT PERIOD

The Compañía de Teléfonos de Chile (CTC) was operating as early as 1880. In 1930 it entered into a contract with the government (later written as Law No. 4791/30) which remained in effect until the government intervention of 1971. The 1930 contract provided CTC with a 50-year concession, indexed its tariffs to 'peso-gold', stipulated a return on assets of up to 10%,[76] protected the company against termination of the concession,[77] and required from the company a particular investment programme over the next few years. The contract provided the government with the ability to take over the company's operations under vaguely defined terms (Galal 1993). While the 1930 law seems to have provided an impetus to telecommunications investments, investments started to lag and conflict with the government over tariffs and costs developed. The sub-agreements negotiated in 1958 and 1967 resolved these conflicts. The 1958 sub-agreement assured CTC of a 10% rate of return (rather than up to 10% as in the 1930 law), and CTC agreed to start an eight-year development plan. The 1967 sub-agreement maintained the rate of return and redefined costs and CTC agreed to an expansion plan up to 1971, committing itself to increase lines from 1971 at a rate of 6–7% per annum.

Although many other reasons may be behind the low investment levels prior to the sub-agreement of 1958,[78] the vagueness of Chile's telecommunications law did not provide strong safeguards against opportunistic behaviour by the government, particularly as the post-war period was one of rapid political change. The telecommunications statute specified a maximum, but not necessarily binding, rate of return of 10%. The vagueness of the law had two main implications: first, regulators had substantial discretion in its interpretation; second, because of its vagueness, government could modify the law through regulatory decrees, as it did in 1958 and 1967.[79] Thus, not only did the regulatory regime provide wide latitude to the regulator, but there were no important limitations to changing the regulatory system itself. The sub-agreements of 1958 and 1967 did not change the regulatory incentive structure, but rather improved upon regulatory governance. The change in performance that followed can be related directly to such an improvement. This period, then, provides an observation for the Figure 1 branch that answers no to the 'specific process written in law or contract' question. This period resembles Jamaica's JPUC period. In both instances, regulatory governance structures were not aligned with the countries' institutional endowments and neither restrained regulators' discretion nor limited the potential for changing the regulatory systems. In both cases, network expansion was limited.

THE HIGH INVESTMENT PERIODS

While the regulatory schemes of 1958–71 and 1987+ are quite different (see Table 3), both attempt to limit regulatory discretion. In both cases, limits to regulatory discretion are attained through specific legislation. As noted, the sub-agreements of 1958 and 1967 eliminated the vagueness of the previous law by assuring CTC a 10% rate of return (while at the same time imposing new investment obligations). The post 1987 regulatory regime is of a different nature. After experimenting with a variety of regulatory schemes as a prelude to privatization, Chile's military government introduced a new regulatory law that remains in force to this day. The new law provides precise details for the implementation of rate-of-return regulation of the 'non-competitive' market segments. Furthermore, the law specifies the process to be used in determining which segments are non-competitive and hence subject to regulation. The process involves a determination by the Antitrust Resolutive Commission, following a reference from the telecommunications regulator (the Sub-Secretary for Telecommunications).

Price regulation for the non-competitive services is designed to provide a rate of return to a theoretically best-practice efficient firm. The specificity of the telecommunications law is such that it specifies how to compute the cost of capital of the putatively efficient firm,[80] and how to compute given the cost of capital, the maximum prices (based on a long-run marginal cost model for each of the individual services at the point of departure) for the regulated services. Note, though, that Chile permits entry even into these regulated segments.[81] This benchmark is recalibrated every five years (with indexation in interim periods) by the regulator in consultation with the private companies. The law also specifies an explicit arbitration process in the event of disagreements – with the courts as final arbiter.[82]

Because the law is so specific, regulatory changes require new legislation, as the law's specificity provides very little latitude for alternative interpretations. New legislation would have to overcome institutional obstacles, like bicameralism and an divided legislature with a minority president. The post-1987 period, however, provides a particular source of flexibility that did not exist in 1958–74. Because regulation is to be undertaken only in 'non-competitive' segments, the boundaries of price competition are not fixed in the legislation, but rather are allowed to be changed by decisions of the antitrust commission. It was possible to initiate such specific legislation at that time because Chile's government was unified under the military, thus partially resolving any legislative obstacles to the creation of a complex regulatory system. This of course does not mean that only through military regimes can such specific legislation be achieved. In fact, other democratically elected governments have introduced similarly specific legislation in other regulatory areas.[83]

Thus, during the post-1987 period, and to some extent following the sub-agreements in 1958 and 1967, governance structures were designed to limit regulatory discretion. These structures were particularly aligned with Chile's institutional environment. Specific regulatory laws in Chile provide regulatory credibility, because specific legislative changes are not easy to implement. Finally, deviations from both specific regulatory instructions and attempts to change the system by governmental actions can be easily challenged in the courts. The Chilean judiciary has a record of hearing – and impartially resolving – regulatory disputes. Indeed, since privatization, it has become involved in a series of disputes surrounding the regulation of telecommunications concerning, in particular, the determination of competitive boundaries (see Galal 1993).

These two periods, however, provide very different limitations on regulatory discretion. While regulatory discretion during the 1958–71 period was more limited than during the period prior to the sub-agreements of 1958–67, it was still much higher than during the 1987+ period. Since 1987, short-run regulatory discretion in pricing has been almost completely eliminated, as the

1987 law specifies not only the procedures to be followed, but also the way information is to be processed. These episodes, then, provide observations for the Figure 1 branch that answers yes to the 'specific process written in law or contract' question.

We should note, however, that such legislative specificity would not have provided the same type of commitment in Jamaica or the UK, where laws can be amended much more easily than in a presidential system like Chile's. While specificity of the sort designed in Chile could be stipulated in a licence (à la UK or Jamaica), such high degree of specificity and complexity requires that those active in enforcing the licence (i.e., the company executives, the bureaucrats and the courts)[84] be able to effectively navigate its complexity. While the UK bureaucracy has traditionally attracted highly qualified professionals, it is questionable whether the Jamaica counterpart has the necessary depth and experience. As a consequence, it is reasonable to speculate that the introduction of Chilean-style regulatory incentives in Jamaica could have triggered continuous litigation, forcing the Jamaican courts to make highly technical interpretations, with an unstable outcome being highly probable. In terms of Figure 1, the UK and Chile provide observations for the branch that answers yes to the 'strong bureaucracy' question, while Jamaica provides observations for the branch that answers no to that question.

To summarize, the evidence presented here is consistent with our main hypothesis that performance is related first and foremost to the extent to which regulatory governance structures are aligned with the institutional endowments of the country. While the incentive structures of Chile's post-1987 period are particularly strong, they would not be credible in the absence of appropriate regulatory governance.

C. Rent-Seeking Presidential Systems: Argentina and the Philippines

Table 4 provides a summary chronology of telecommunications ownership, regulation and performance in Argentina and the Philippines.[85] Three features are particularly noteworthy and will be examined in some detail below: first, in neither country has a workable regulatory governance structure been successfully put in place; second, telecommunications development in the Philippines has been characterized by a 'political investment cycle'; third, investment levels have been reasonable in Argentina since privatization, but were accompanied by very high rates of return. In this section we attempt to explain and interpret these patterns in the light of the framework developed above. The main thrust of this section is as follows: the gaps in the exogenous institutional endowment of the two countries account for their chronic failure to establish workable regulatory governance structures; as a consequence, investment decisions have been made with very short horizons, with negative implications for long-term performance.

REGULATORY GOVERNANCE PROBLEMS

In 1990 Argentina's main state-owned telecommunications company, ENTel, was split and later sold to two separate private consortia (one headed by Telefónica of Spain, the second headed by France Cable and Radio and Stet of Italy).[86] The rules under which the private companies were to operate have repeatedly been changed, with pricing a vivid example: one set of pricing rules was announced when private investors were invited to bid for ENTel; these rules were changed during negotiations with the bidders; were changed twice more in 1991 when the initial agreements came into conflict with broader macroeconomic policies; and were renegotiated yet again in late 1992. Underlying the fluid state of the regulatory system around

Table 4 Regulatory history and commitment mechanisms: Argentina and the Philippines

				RESTRAINING MECHANISMS		
COUNTRY	OWNERSHIP	REGULATORY HISTORY	PERFORMANCE	SUBSTANTIVE RESTRAINTS	RESTRAINTS ON SYSTEM CHANGES	ENFORCEMENT OF RESTRAINTS
ARGENTINA	Main telephone companies nationalized in 1946, to form a national company (ENTEL). Divided into two regional companies and privatized in 1990.	Licence-based regulatory framework, specified initial two years based on rate of return, followed by 5 years with price cap with X=0. Exclusive licence to be extended to 10 years only if minimum investment targets are met. In fact, price freeze instituted four months after privatization. Companies negotiated indexation based on US CPI. Regulatory agency created under the Ministry of Economy, Appeals only to the Minister. Regulatory framework currently under review.	Highly profitable to initial investors. Investment levels match or exceed licence renewal requirements. Very high prices (in US$). and quality problems remain. Too soon to determine full impact on welfare.	Explicitly price adjustment formula.	Licence amendments require company's agreement.	Very little, as government seems to be able to deviate from licence specifications without triggering judicial review. Politicized and weak judiciary.
PHILIPPINES	Private since inception, with ownership shifting from GTE to private Filipino parties in 1967.	Longstanding regulation by commission with vague mandate, lack of political independence and modest power.	Alternation between stagnation and periods of moderate investment, following political cycle. Very high unmet demand. Profitability unknown.	None.	None.	None.

the time of the privatization, the initial price level for the basic telecommunication pulse[87] was negotiated *after* the companies submitted their bids and *after* the bids were adjudicated, but *before* the companies signed their licence agreements in 1991.[88] The two winning consortia negotiated hard to set the initial price level before taking control of, and paying for, the two operating companies, suggesting that they were not confident that the proposed regulatory scheme would actually be implemented. Indeed, although the regulatory systems specified in the operating licences granted at privatization incorporated substantive restraints of some type or another, what actually was implemented (i.e., a price freeze, followed by indexation to US CPI) bore no resemblance to what was specified in the original licences.[89] We have found no evidence that the affected companies tried to force implementation of their licence specifications through appeals to the courts. However, this is not surprising, given the politicization and corruption of the Argentine judiciary.

The Philippines also has not had a system that imposed any substantive restraints on regulatory discretion. Formally, the telecommunications sector has been under the control of a regulatory commission since colonial times: before 1972 the Public Service Commission (PSC) was responsible for all utilities; subsequently responsibilities passed to a specialized telecommunications regulatory agency. However, at no time have either the boundaries of authority of the regulatory agency or the substance of its regulatory mandate ever been clearly delineated. Other than the splitting of the PSC into its component parts, there have been no systematic efforts at telecommunications regulatory reform, at least since the Philippines obtained its independence in 1946. Given the fragmentation of the Philippines legislature and the potential for judicial corruption, the system limits the ability of the regulator to promote competition without legislative support. While Argentina and the Philippines' traditionally fragmented legislatures could provide a basis for stable regulatory regimes, in fact lack of informal restraints, weak judiciaries and disregard for the rule of law in both polities have meant that opportunities for enacting restraints on changing the regulatory system are very limited.[90] Furthermore, the existence of corrupt judiciaries in both countries seems to constitute a basic institutional flaw, as they cannot be trusted to restrain the regulators nor to resist changes in the regulatory systems.

INVESTING IN THE FACE OF ADVERSITY

It is reasonable to ask how investment takes place at all in countries with such weak governance structures. The answer resides in the extraction of short-term rents. Measuring profitability rates in the Philippines is an impossible task, given the extent of corruption in procurement (Esfahani 1993). But 'short-termism' can be seen in the rhythm of telecommunications investment in the Philippines, which is attuned to the ebb and flow of political actors 'friendly' to the telecommunications utility rather than to the business cycle. In particular, Esfahani (1993) shows a repeated three-pronged investment pattern: first, investment in telecommunications takes off immediately following the inauguration of governments aligned with the group controlling the main telecommunications utility (PLDT); second, investment tails off in the later years of the regime; and third, investment stagnates in periods when relations with the group in power are more distant. As a consequence, sector performance has been poor, especially in the provision of local service. Between 1950 and 1991, the number of telephones in service expanded at a modest average rate of 4% per annum, with bursts of moderate growth in fixed assets punctuated by periods of stagnation. As of 1991, record unmet demand for telephones amounted to almost 65% of the number in service.

In Argentina, 'short-termism' is apparent in the extremely high profitability of the licensees. For example for the eleven months ending on 30 September 1991, the rate of return to Telecom's operator was 26.9%, while that of Telefónica's was 203%. The returns to both consortia were also quite remarkable, 58% and 72% respectively (Hill and Abdala, 1993, Table 8). While 1991 investments were not higher than anticipated, during 1992 both companies increased their lines by twice the number required by their licences to maintain their ten-year exclusivity period.[91]

5. Final Comments and Open Questions

The evidence presented in the previous section can be interpreted as follows. First, private utilities were aggressive investors whenever the three restraining mechanisms identified in Tables 2 to 4 were in place (Chile 1958–70 and post-1987, Jamaica pre-1962 and post-1987, and the UK post-1984). By contrast, out of the remaining four cases where the three mechanisms were not in place, only Argentina has experienced any significant private investment by telecommunications utilities (although only two years have elapsed since privatization). And that experience has been accompanied by unusually high rates of return.

Second, there were substantial variations in the specific forms of the three mechanisms. These variations appear to derive from the nature of each country's exogenous institutions. Chile incorporated substantive restraints into its regulatory incentive structures by specifying precisely how regulated prices were to be determined. Jamaica and the UK limited administrative discretion by granting the regulated company freedom to set prices subject to some overall price constraints – rate-of-return in the case of Jamaica, price-cap in the case of the UK – and limiting the ability of the regulator to interfere with such decisions. Restraints on changing the regulatory system were also in place in those three countries during the periods when the regulatory incentive structures limited administrative discretion. The character of these restraints, however, varied across the three countries according to their exogenous institutional endowments: UK and Jamaica used licences, while Chile used specific regulatory legislation.

Third, all three countries whose regulatory systems successfully constrained the discretionary power of regulators have independent and well regarded judiciaries. And in all three countries, these judiciaries have a record of hearing regulatory disputes and resolving them impartially. Thus, while in seven of the nine regulatory episodes discussed here, countries were endowed with exogenous institutions capable of restraining arbitrary administrative action, only in five of these seven did governments actually use these exogenous endowments to put in place regulatory systems that restrained such action and, in turn, were successful in attracting private investment. The remaining two episodes (Jamaica between 1962 and 1975, and Chile before the sub-agreements of 1958 and 1967) appear to be cases of missed opportunities. In both episodes there was a basic flaw in the design of regulatory governance – a failure to build substantive regulatory restraints into the system itself. Chile's 1930 law imposed a ceiling (but no floor, until amended in 1958) on the rate of return, and also gave the government the right to intervene in the company's operations under vaguely defined circumstances. Jamaica's regulatory system between 1966 and 1975 was modelled on the US system and promoted participation in an open-ended regulatory process by a wide range of interest groups – but without the procedural and judicial safeguards that traditionally have protected utilities in the US. Consequently, in both episodes private utilities eventually failed to invest, and the resulting conflicts with government culminated in nationalization.

The two remaining cases, the Philippines and Argentina, are more of a mixed bag. In the Philippines the exogenous domestic institutions have historically provided an inadequate foundation upon which to erect a regulatory system capable of restraining administrative discretion. Private ownership seems to be based on rents extracted through the political process. For all their historical weaknesses, Argentina's political institutions may provide some basis for making credible commitments, providing the judiciary achieves a modicum of independent credibility and enforcement capability. If democracy becomes a permanent feature of Argentina, then power is likely to become more fragmented than at present, both between the executive and the legislature and within the legislature itself. Thus, regulatory reforms that limit administrative discretion either through licences (with specific and limiting provisions) or through very specific legislation, may prove difficult to change and may thereby provide investors with safeguards for future investments. The Philippines' stable political institutions, however, would seem to frustrate even such a mildly positive assessment (Esfahani 1993).

Our analysis suggests that the foundation of a successful regulatory policy consists of the development of a regulatory governance structure that, given the nature of the country's institutions, is adequate to constrain arbitrary administrative action and also encourages private investment. An exclusive focus on regulatory governance, however, is inadequate as it offers only limited guidance as to what should be the specific content of substantive regulatory rules. Thus, a unified approach to regulatory policy must incorporate regulatory incentives (that is, rules concerning pricing, entry and interconnection) into the analysis, and also consider the impact of the specific content of such rules on the efficiency with which private utilities perform. Exclusive emphasis on the latter, on the other hand, may result in a totally inadequate regulatory structure.

At this point it may be useful to speculate on what alternatives are available to countries that lack the crucial exogenous formal and informal institutions outlined here. Our discussion suggests that in those countries private investment will require the development of alternative safeguards. One example of a safeguarding mechanism is a privatization programme that distributes share ownership (and thus a stake in the performance of the privatized company) among a broad section of the population. Building a broad base of shareholders was important in the privatization of telecommunications in the UK, and played a modest role in the Chilean, Argentinean and Jamaican processes (but was a vital component of other Chilean utility privatizations; see Spiller 1993). Attempts at widespread ownership require the prior development of a stock market, with relatively sophisticated security regulations which may be lacking in some countries. Similarly, widespread ownership may require the existence of private institutional investors (e.g. pension funds, insurance companies) that provide a low-cost conduit for widespread and diversified stock ownership The UK, Chile and to some extent Jamaica have developed these types of institutions, thus facilitating the establishment of investment safeguards.[92] A second option is to privatize enterprises sequentially (and to have sequential sales of shares in individual enterprises). Since the success of the later steps of a sequenced programme depends upon whether the privatizing government abides by the agreements made in the earlier stages, the cost to government of reneging on its early agreements can be high. Argentina provides the clearest example from the case studies of this approach. Its privatization of telecommunications was the first dramatic step in a sweeping programme to privatize public enterprises. The potential impact on the remainder of the programme afforded the private buyers of the telecommunications utility some confidence that the Argentine government would refrain from ex post administrative expropriation (Hill and Abdala 1993). Unless the required institutions develop as the privatization process progresses, investors will be increasingly reluctant to invest since the end of the privatization period may witness an unravelling of the government's self-restraint.

As for international substitutes for missing national foundations, Jamaica and the Philippines in the 1950s came closest of all the countries studied to using this mechanism. Jamaica's judicial system continues to recognize the Privy Council in London as the final arbiter of Jamaican court decisions, a feature that may partially account for its continued credibility. Even though the Philippines was formally granted independence from the US in 1946, for the next fifteen years the continuity of pre-independence institutions, the strong US leverage and specific agreements that protect US investors all helped to provide a predictable and safe environment that facilitated investment by both Filipino and US investors.

The potential exists to go much further in using international institutions as substitutes for weaknesses in domestic commitment capability. One innovation that has begun to receive attention is for an international institution like the World Bank to provide private investors (and lenders) with guarantees against non-commercial risk, including the risk of administrative expropriation. These guarantees are provided at the request of the host country. In the event of private investors calling in the guarantee, the host country becomes liable to repay its value to the international institution. A failure to repay would provoke a costly rupture with an important international institution. Through such guarantees, the country's good standing in the international community and its continuing commitment to regulatory restraint are held hostage to each other – providing some level of safeguard against administrative expropriation.[93]

In sum, the success of a regulatory system depends on how well it fits with a country's prevailing institutions. If a country lacks the requisite institutions or erects a regulatory system that is incompatible with its institution endowment, efforts at privatization may end in disappointment, in recrimination and in the resurgence of demands for renationalization.

Notes

* Senior Economist, The World Bank; Visiting Professor of Business and Public Policy, Haas School of Business, University of California, Berkeley, respectively. This paper is part of the World Bank project on 'Institutions, Regulation and Economic Efficiency', undertaken with partial support from the World Bank Research Committee. We would like to thank Lee Alston, Hadi Esfahani, Ahmed Galal, Alice Hill, Matt McCubbins, Roger Noll, Douglass North, Mary Shirley, Ingo Vogelsang, Barry Weingast, Bjorn Wellenius, Oliver Williamson and two anonymous referees for helpful comments and suggestions, and Janet Mowery for editorial work. The opinions expressed here are entirely those of the authors, and do not represent the views of the World Bank, its Executive Directors or the countries they represent.

1. The country studies on which we base our analysis are part of the World Bank project on 'Institutions, Regulation and Economic Efficiency' funded, in part, by a grant from the World Bank Research Committee. Because of the nature of the grant, we did not include the US as one of our cases. Although we make references to the US in our analysis, applying our framework to the evolution of telecommunications regulation and performance in the US is left for future research.

2. Several studies, however, have exploited electoral changes and their repercussions on the composition of the US Congress and the executive in undertaking those tests. See, for example, Weingast and Moran (1983) and Spiller and Gely (1992).
3. For an extremely interesting analysis of the role of central government discretion in determining incentives for private sector investment, see Weingast (1993).
4. While the 'McNollgast' approach does not say it in those words, this is indeed the authors' main message concerning, for example, administrative procedures in the US. See, McCubbins, Noll and Weingast (1987).
5. Multiple, distinct regulatory episodes within individual countries do, however, provide additional 'degrees of freedom'.
6. See, among others, North (1990), Williamson (1988), Goldberg (1976) and Barzel (1989).
7. Observe that financing requirements for sunk investments are not part of the operating costs. Inability to repay debt required to pay sunk investments will only bring the utility to bankruptcy, but it will still not be worth liquidating. Asset liquidation will only take place when operating revenues fall short of operating costs, where operating costs include a return on the non-specific investments of the enterprise.
8. This does not mean that the pricing of other sectors, not characterized by large economies of scale and sunk investments, is not going to be political as well (e.g., bread prices in poor countries). What we mean is that the politicization of utilities' pricing, together with their asset characteristics, bring about unique problems.
9. Investors may limit their exposure by selecting technologies that, although implying lower quality and higher operating costs, may require lower levels of specific investments (e.g., cellular rather than fixed-link telephony).
10. Observe, though, that public enterprises are also subject to the forms of administrative expropriation we are considering here. In this case, though, systematic underfunding will be the norm.
11. For example, setting the prices of bananas below their long-run average cost will have at most a one year effect on banana prices. On the other hand, setting prices of water services below long-run average costs may imply a reduction in prices over quite a long period of time.
12. Williamson would call such constraints on regulatory decision making 'contractual governance institutions'. See Williamson (1985, p. 35).
13. Commenting on the interaction among technology (institutions), governance and price (regulatory detail) Williamson (1985, p. 36) says, '[i]nasmuch as price and governance are linked, parties to a contract should not expect to have their cake (low price) and eat it too (no safeguard)'. In other words, there is no 'free institutional lunch'.
14. For analysis of the role of separation of powers in diminishing the discretion of the executive, see Gely and Spiller (1990) and McCubbins, Noll and Weingast (1987, 1989), and references therein.
15. Non-simultaneous elections for different branches of government tend to create natural political divisions and thus electoral checks and balances. (See Jacobson 1990). For an in-depth analysis of the determinants of the relative powers of the executive, see Shugart and Carey (1992).
16. Electoral rules also have important effects on the 'effective number of parties' that will tend to result from elections, and thus the extent of governmental control over the legislative process. For example, it is widely perceived that proportional representation tends to generate a large number of parties, while first-past-the-post, with relatively small district elections, tends to create bipolar party configurations. This result has been coined Duverger's Law in political science. (See Duverger 1954). More generally, see Taagepera and Shugart (1993). For analyses of how the structure of political parties depend on the nature of electoral rules (with application to the UK), see Cain, Ferejohn and Fiorina (1987) and Cox (1987).
17. On the role of Federalism in reducing the potential for administrative discretion, see Weingast (1993) and references therein.
18. While parliamentary systems grant such powers in principle, whether they do so in practice depends upon the nature of electoral rules and the political party system. Parliamentary systems whose electoral rules bring about fragmented legislatures would not provide the executive – usually headed by a minority party with a coalition built on a very narrow set of specific common interests – with much scope for legislative initiative. By contrast, electoral rules that create strong two-party par-

liamentary systems – as well as some other kinds of non-parliamentary political institutions – would grant the executive large legislative powers. For an in-depth discussion of the difference between parliamentary and presidential systems, and the role of electoral rules in determining the relative power of the executive, see Shugart and Carey (1992).

19. In the UK, regulatory frameworks have traditionally evolved through a series of acts of Parliament. For example, major gas regulation legislation was passed in 1847, 1859, 1870, 1871,1873 and 1875. Similarly, water regulation legislation was passed in 1847, 1863, 1870, 1873, 1875 and 1887. Systematic regulation of electricity companies started in 1882, only four years after the inauguration of the first public demonstration of lighting by a public authority. The 1882 Act was followed by major legislation in 1888, 1899, 1919 and 1922, culminating with the Electricity (Supply) Act of 1926 which created the Central Electricity Board. See Dimock (1933), Hormell (1928), Keen (1925), Self and Watson (1952) and Spiller and Vogelsang (1993b) for discussions of the evolution of utility regulation in the UK.
20. This has traditionally been the way administrative discretion is restrained in the US, as regulatory statutes have tended to be quite vague. For an analysis of the choice of specificity of statutes, see Schwartz, Spiller and Urbiztondo (1993). Observe, however, that administrative law may not develop in a system where the executive has strong control over the legislative process.
21. While a corrupt judiciary may tend to side against the government on contract disputes (after all, government lawyers will have very little incentive to bribe judges, while such incentives clearly exist for private lawyers), on key issues a corrupt judiciary becomes an easy hostage to the government. Unexpected press disclosures may trigger widespread scandals, loss of legitimacy and even calls for judicial reform and sanctions. Consider the following conclusion of a World Bank report on Bolivia: ' In addition to being slow, courts are also perceived to be corrupt. In a 1991 survey of 226 litigants, 48 per cent claimed to have made illegal payments to court personnel. Confidence in the courts is also weakened by the judiciary's perceived lack of independence. Judges' independence is compromised by a history of executive supremacy, the country's tradition of political patronage, and the procedures for the selection, promotion and discipline of judges.' World Bank (1992, p. 43).
22. This is a necessary, but not a sufficient condition for strength.
23. Indeed, it is possible (although we have no examples where this is the case) that a particularly poorly designed regulatory incentive structure could in itself undermine the credibility of a regulatory system, even if the regulatory governance foundations appeared firm.
24. The discussion that follows can be interpreted as either positive or normative. It is positive in that it predicts which combinations of background institutions and regulatory systems will lead to good performance, and which will not. It is normative in that it suggest what kind of regulatory design will be credible given the background institutions of the country in question.
25. When electoral laws are designed to return the same party to power in every election, complex party decision making may provide regulatory credibility, even in the absence of dejure contractual arrangements or very precise legislation. This seems to have been the case in Japan until the 1993 elections. See Baron (1992) for an excellent discussion of how decision making in the LDP was structured so as to provide for a large number of veto points.
26. The detailed case studies on which this paper is based follow a research framework developed in Spiller and Levy (1991). That framework emphasized, as this paper does, the contracting problems endemic to utilities regulation, and required the gathering of detailed information about the regulatory structure (including information on regulatory proceedings and court cases) over time. It also required the collection of a common dossier of information concerning investments, prices and outputs.
27. Jamaica inherited British political institutions upon obtaining its independence from that country in 1962. In Jamaica, the percentage of the vote and the number of seats obtained by candidates independent of the two main parties (the PNP and the JLP) fell, respectively, from 35% and 5 (out of 35) in 1944 to 1% and zero since the 1959 election. See Stone (1981 and 1986). See also Cox (1987) and Cain, Ferejohn and Fiorina (1987) for an analysis of party politics in the UK.
28. It is not surprising that both countries have had drastic policy shifts as parties alternate in power.
29. While Jamaica's judicial institutions paralleled those of the UK, there are two important differences. First, as a former colony, Jamaica's judicial system has retained the right of final appeal of its decisions

to the Privy Council in the UK, providing an unusually strong source of credibility. Second, unlike the UK, Jamaica has combined the institution of a sovereign parliament with a written constitution.

30. For example, during the first administration of Prime Minister Michael Manley, the courts blocked Manley's attempt to expropriate landholdings by requiring the government to pay fair compensation.
31. The fact that the UK does not have a written constitution, though, has not precluded the development of a large body of constitutional law.
32. See Salzberg (1991) for a discussion of the secondary role of the UK judiciary in statutory interpretation. See Spiller and Sampson (1993) for a discussion of the judiciary in Jamaica, and Spiller and Vogelsang (1993b) on the role of the judiciary in licence enforcement until the nationalization of the electricity sector after World War II.
33. For a discussion of the development of regulatory agencies and their procedures in the UK since the beginning of the privatization process, see Veljanovski (1991).
34. For example, 'the Cable Authority is not bound to give reasons for its decisions and it may well decide not to spell out its selection criteria in any detail in an effort to retain the greatest flexibility'; Baldwin and McCrudden (1987, p. 292).
35. The Jamaican Public Utilities Commission, JPUC, did hold public hearings during the period 1966–1975 and was, in principle, subject to US-style conditions for judicial review.
36. See Baldwin and McCrudden (1987) for a discussion of procedures in various UK regulatory agencies, including the Office of Fair Trading and the Monopolies and Mergers Commission.
37. However, judicial review in the UK is becoming more frequent, in particular at the local government level, as conflict increases between local and central government. Baldwin and McCrudden (1987 p. 57), quoting from Sir Michael Kerry, the former Treasury Solicitor, observe that judicial review of administrative agencies has 'increased from a handful a year in the 60s to 50–100 in the early 70s, to a rate of about 400 a year in the first six months of [1982]'. Furthermore, 'he reported that most of these cases "come under two main heads, applications to quash planning decisions ... and immigration cases"'. See Kerry (1983, p. 168) and Young (1985).
38. Although, in the UK, judicial review may be effective in resolving disputes among branches of government. See Baldwin and McCrudden (1987, p. 59) for a discussion of this issue.
39. In the UK judicial review can be initiated on procedural grounds or if the regulator's decision has been unreasonable. A claim of unreasonableness, however, rarely wins, because the regulator is not required to provide a thorough explanation of the basis for making a particular decision (e.g. the granting of a cable licence). See Baldwin and McCrudden (1987, pp. 292–3).
40. For example, major policy changes start with an ad hoc commission that is charged with analysing the policy change which the government is interested in undertaking. The outcome of the ad hoc commission is a consultative 'green paper' which, while not representing the government's exact intentions, is nevertheless circulated for public comment. (Telecommunications reform, for example, started in 1981 with the Beesley report which recommended unrestricted resale of leased lines, BT's price flexibility on leased lines and network entry.) Following this comment period, the government may decide to drop or to continue (with or without modifications) the policy initiative. If the government decides to go ahead, it will eventually publish a white paper, which forms the basis for the cabinet's legislative initiative. This process, which is also followed in Jamaica, has the virtue of providing interest groups with warning signs about impending policy changes. Interest groups can then lobby party members and legislators in an attempt to influence the policy change in their desired direction. See Miller (1987, pp. 197–211) for a discussion of how the decision-making process in the UK provides opportunities for interested parties to participate in the legislative process. See also Spiller and Vogelsang (1993a). The role of this decision-making process is not too dissimilar from the advance warning features of the US Administrative Procedure Act. For a discussion of the latter, see McCubbins, Noll and Weingast (1987), and Spiller and Urbiztondo (1993).
41. On the role of ministerial responsibility in limiting the potential for breaks in the party's control over government, see Cox (1993). Cox's main point is that the effect of requiring joint and several ministerial responsibility 'is to increase the power of the executive body by decreasing the chance that executive decisions will be challenged in any broader arena. Indeed, the convention of collective responsibility in the United Kingdom has been so effective in preventing internal Cabinet dis-

agreement from spilling out into the Commons that many have questioned the independent importance of the legislature.' Cox (1993, p. 47).

42. To some extent, because Japan's LDP had, until recently, continuous control over government in a contestable legislative environment, it developed a formal process of government decision making prior to the submission of legislation to the Diet. This process involved the formal use of the LDP's Policy Affairs Research Committee (PARC) and of industry advisory committees, as well as of informal consultations with Zoku (*tribe*) Diet members and LDP factions. For an extremely insightful description of governmental decision making in Japan, see Baron (1992, Chapter 13). Lupia and McCubbins (1993) stress that a major function of the review of PARC committees is to provide backbenchers with information about Cabinet intentions. Because the Japanese electoral system develops a stronger personal vote in Japan than in the UK, Japanese factions are intrinsically more independent from the party leadership. As a consequence, more formal consensus-building processes are required to avoid inter-faction conflict spilling into the legislature.
43. For an interesting transaction cost discussion of the rise of the Westminster model of bureaucracy, see Palmer (1992).
44. During his first administration, Prime Minister Manley broke with political tradition and replaced many Permanent Secretaries. Since then, Permanent Secretaries have lost some of their influence and prestige, reducing the position's attractiveness to highly qualified middle-class individuals. See Stone (1986). For a discussion of the UK's bureaucracy and a comparison with that of the US, see e.g., Fesler (1983).
45. Shugart and Carey (1992, pp. 173–4) use Chile's pre-1970 political system to describe the 'archetypal presidential system'.
46. At the same time, concurrent elections provided for the development of bipolar coalitions that offered voters choices between national policies without the need to develop strong central parties (Shugart and Carey, 1992, p. 174).
47. Shugart and Carey (1992, p. 183) call the system before the constitutional changes of 1958 and 1970 the 'inefficient secret' since the regionalization of politics and the relatively weak powers of the president provided for a very dynamic legislature. Concerning the post-1970 Chilean system, they describe it (p. 200) as the strongest among presidential systems. It features a strong germaneness limitation on amendments and permits only the president to offer a budget bill. Thus, the president fully controls the budget process. That is not the case with non-budgetary issues however.
48. One may ask whether this respect for institutions persisted even during the military regime of General Pinochet. Even then signs of respect for longstanding institutions were evident. For example, during the military regime the constitution was amended by popular referendum. Similarly, the regime's decision to return the country to a democratic system followed an electoral loss.
49. See, McCubbins, Noll and Weingast (1987) for a discussion of the role of procedures in providing commitment.
50. For example, both countries have separation of powers between legislature, executive and judiciary; a written constitution limiting legislative and executive power to be enforced by the courts; two legislative houses, with weak political parties; and a federal structure of power, with strong decentralization even to local level. Although electoral rules are such that the effective number of parties contesting elections in the Philippines is 2, in Argentina it is higher than 2 and increasing, reaching 3.4 in 1989 (Shugart and Carey 1992, pp. 220–21). To a large extent, this can be explained by the importance of non-concurrent elections in Argentina. The fact that the effective number of parties in the Philippines is 2 does not mean that these are strong parties. Indeed, in the Philippines, as in the US, parties do not control nominations, nor do they use list ranks to control the order of elections or pool the votes. Thus, as in the US, Filipino legislators are quite independent of their central parties.
51. Argentina's 1853 constitutional separation of powers remained in place for almost a century, until amended in 1949 by Juan Perón in a way that substantially expanded the powers of the president. The military overthrew Perón in 1956 and restored the earlier constitution. However, two subsequent military governments came to power in 1966 and 1976. In the past, during Argentina's periods of civilian rule, governments have either been fragmented, making it difficult to enact sustained economic reforms, or have pursued zero-sum policies which rewarded the supporters of those in power. The present administration of President Menem is an important exception to this pattern of

civilian rule. Not only did his Peronist Party win control of both houses of Congress (as well as the executive) in the 1990 elections but, when Menem took office, Congress (with the active support of his opponents) ceded him special powers to deal with the economic crisis. See Hill and Abdala (1993).

52. A theory to explain why some polities develop rules of the game that defer the arbitration of interest group conflicts to the judiciary and the legislature, rather than to the army, is yet to be developed. Calvert's (1992) view of constitutions as conventions is a step forward, in that coordination games have multiple equilibria, with one equilibrium being characterized by lack of coordination. We do not attempt to provide an answer to this question here.
53. In Argentina, the disdain for constitutional legality appears even in the transfer of power following democratic elections. The transfer of power from the Radical Party to the current Peronist Party government was advanced several months before the legal date. The transfer was arranged through an agreement between the two parties that required the incumbent Congress (not yet dominated by the Peronists) to pass an Economic Emergency Law granting the future president (Carlos Menem) the power to implement a series of economic measures by decree. See Hill and Abdala (1993). Also, members of the judiciary are appointed by the country's president (and confirmed by the Senate) and serve for life, given them substantial formal independence. In practice, however, changes in government (whether constitutional or non-constitutional) have in the past been accompanied by turnover among members of the judiciary. Indeed, in 1990 the new government of President Menem, with the agreement of Congress, altered the Supreme Court by increasing the number of justices from 5 to 9, with power to name all new justices. By 1993 President Menem had been able to appoint six of the nine Supreme Court justices. The Menem 'Court' has recently been plagued by corruption scandals. See *The Miami Herald*, 12 October 1993. In the Philippines, on the other hand, while its written constitution incorporates an independent judiciary (and prior to the proclamation of martial law in 1972 the judiciary was reasonably independent), the country's press has long been filled with tales of judicial scandal. Under martial law, its independence was further constrained, with Marcos effectively empowered to remove any judge. Since 1986, the judiciary has regained some independence and influence, although corruption scandals continue. For example, in 1992 the Philippines Supreme Court blocked the entry of a competing international communications carrier (Eastern Telecom). A few months later the author of the decision (Justice Hugo Gutierrez) resigned following allegations that the opinion had been written by a PLDT lawyer (Panaligan 1993, cited in Esfahani 1993).
54. Viewed over the longer term, though, the multiplicity of parties in both countries suggests that, if the current democratic episodes represent a clear break with unconstitutional transfers of power, future authority may be weaker than at present. US-style legislative and executive institutions were reasonably effective in constraining arbitrary governmental authority in the Philippines in the first quarter-century after it obtained independence from the US in 1946 – although its constitution tilted the balance of power more sharply towards the executive than does the US model. See Abueva (1988). Ferdinand Marcos' declaration of martial law in 1972 (despite some modest reforms after 1978) further concentrated power in the executive. Since his overthrow in 1986, the country has reverted to a somewhat modified version of its pre-martial law political institutions.
55. This section is based on Spiller and Sampson (1993) and Spiller and Vogelsang (1993a).
56. While BT's licence was very specific on price setting, it was quite vague on quality regulation. Oftel, then, has spent most of its efforts and administrative discretion in implementing quality control measures. See Spiller and Vogelsang (1993a). Given BT's disastrous internal quality control systems at the time of privatization, it is not altogether clear that such efforts by Oftel were not in the interest of BT's shareholders *and* customers.
57. Jamaica's licences have traditionally been granted for 25 years. While BT's licence was granted for a similar period, its current price-cap feature expires after five years. Thus, unless BT's licence is modified before the sunset provision of its price-cap regulation, BT's pricing becomes unregulated. This sunset provision gives BT a strong bargaining position, since undertaking a licence modification against its will may take as long as a full year. See Spiller and Vogelsang (1993a).
58. Spiller and Vogelsang (1993a) report that, following the failure at the Monopolies and Mergers Commission of the Director General's proposal for licence reform concerning the marketing of 900-

type calls, the Director General was advised not to proceed with his proposal because he would be successfully challenged in court.

59. Recently, however, Mercury filed a suit against BT and Oftel, the telecommunications regulator, and won its preliminary court hearing. Mercury claims that 'Oftel had not offered it with reasonable terms for the carriage of its traffic by BT, through a *consistent misinterpretation* of BT's government licence. Mercury's victory ... means there will be a full hearing of its application for a legal interpretation of that part of the licence which deals with interconnection' (*Financial Times*, 1 March 1994, our italics).
60. Constitutional interpretation has traditionally seen independent regulatory agencies in the UK as separate entities from their respective Secretary of State. The CAA's revocation of Laker's Skytrain licence to fly to the US in 1976 following the issuance of the Secretary of States's guidance for the CAA was successfully challenged in the Court of Appeal (see *Laker Airways v Department of Trade* [1977] QB 643, cited in Baldwin and McCrudden 1987, p. 167). The Court stated that the Department of Trade's guidance 'could supplement the CAA's statutory objectives; it could not replace them. ... In issuing peremptory instructions to the CAA it constituted direction rather than guidance. ... Parliament could not have set up an elaborate licensing code, subject to limited powers of direction, only to allow the Crown to render licences useless by use of the prerogative power.' See Baldwin and McCrudden (1987, p. 167). This, however, did not preclude Ministerial influence. Indeed, since the statute provided for the appeal of CAA's decisions to the Secretary of State, subsequent to *Laker* 18 appeals to Secretary of State were successful, in whole or in part, whereas prior to *Laker* no similar appeal was successful (Baldwin and McCrudden 1987, p. 168). What *Laker* showed was that the Secretary of State may use the powers given by statute and consistent with the constitutional view of the role of independent agencies.
61. As mentioned, Jamaica's licences have traditionally been granted for 25 years. At expiration time, the drawing of a new licence agreement would also require the acquiescence of the company.
62. For example, the experience in the US with flexible competitive boundaries as a way of adapting the regulatory regime to new technologies (see Knieps and Spiller 1983) cannot be implemented in Jamaica without compensating the company for reductions in its profitability. Thus, for example, if new entrants were to be allowed, interconnection rates would necessarily have to compensate the company for its profit loss. This is not altogether different from the position taken by New Zealand's High Court in its recent *Clear Communications* decision concerning the interconnection of new entrants to New Zealand Telecom's network. See Mueller (1993).
63. As mentioned above, the politicization of the bureaucracy during the mid-1970s diminished the attractiveness of such positions in the eyes of the Jamaican middle class. Several commentators have mentioned to us that since the 1980s secretaries have tended to depend less on the advice of their permanent secretaries and more on non-civil service advisers.
64. The modern Jamaican rate of return system, though, differs in important dimensions from that common in the US or Chile (prior to the 1970s) and even from its own pre-1966 system, in that the regulator is given very little latitude to challenge capital investments. Also, the rate of return is based on stockholder's revalued assets rather than on fixed- or operating-assets (as was the case pre-1966).
65. For analyses of price-cap regulation, see, e.g., the 1989 *Rand Journal of Economics* symposium on price caps, **20** (3).
66. For a discussion of the legislative process leading to the passage of the Telecommunications Act of 1984, see Newman (1986, pp. 8–11). See also Spiller and Vogelsang (1993a).
67. Conversation with Richard Downer, Coopers & Lybrand, Jamaica, and consultant to the Jamaican government.
68. Spiller and Sampson (1993) provide evidence against the 'capture' hypothesis by computing the value of Telecommunications of Jamaica under its licence scheme, and comparing that to the price paid by private investors. They find that the price of TOJ was very close to their computation of its value as of the privatization date. In their computation they assumed a 4% dividend policy and also that the rate of return on equity would be the lower bound specified in the licence. As the discount rate, they used the real return of Jamaican bonds.
69. It is possible to say that the regulatory system in Jamaica has a de facto price-cap feature, since a freeze has been imposed on the price of local calls since privatization, while international calls have

been used to provide the necessary rate of return. However, the freeze was informally agreed at the time of privatization for a five-year period. Since then, TOJ has maintained the nominal freeze.

70. Indeed, since the elimination of the Jamaican Public Utility Commission (see below), not even one regulatory agency exists with substantial visibility and a reputation for independence.
71. A fixed price cap in perpetuity will bring widely unstable profitability outcomes, and hence is not credible.
72. We claim this to be the case in Argentina. See below.
73. Following a JPUC decision to increase rates, both the JTC and a group of users filed cases in Jamaica's Supreme Court – the former because the rate increase was too low and the latter because it was too high. The Supreme Court declined to hear either case. In 1974, the government amended the Jamaica Public Utilities Act to specify a minimum rate of return (related to the yield of the Jamaican government's foreign debt) for companies regulated under the Act. The JPUC nevertheless interpreted that amendment as not specifying a 'total entitlement' but rather a maximum. See Spiller and Sampson (1993).
74. For example, in a 1973 rate case, the JPUC rejected the company's request for a price increase. The government then imposed a tax on telecommunications and provided the company with a subsidy equal to that tax. The JPUC claimed that such action by the government was illegal, but no legal challenge was forthcoming. In consideration of the subsidy scheme, the government received a 10% share in the Jamaica Telephone Co. (JTC). Spiller and Sampson (1993).
75. This section is based mostly on Galal (1993).
76. Any return in excess of 10% would be divided equally between CTC and the government.
77. At termination of the concession, the government could either take over the company, paying the value of its assets expressed in 'pesos-gold', or could renew the concession for another 30 years.
78. In particular, we refer here to potential macroeconomic considerations arising from the Second World War and its aftermath.
79. In Latin America's presidential systems, laws may be interpreted by the administration through the issuing of regulatory decrees (*decretos reguladores*) that have the power of law. Indeed, some legislative acts have no power until such regulatory decrees are issued. As a consequence, changes in a regulatory decree may require specific new legislation, unless the regulatory decree itself left open the need for its own modification. See Shugart and Carey (1992).
80. The law requires the use of the Capital Asset Pricing Model in computing the allowed price levels. Furthermore, the law also stipulates the precise averaging procedure in recalculating the costs of the putatively efficient firm.
81. Chile imposes benchmark regulation only in those market segments that are deemed not to be contestable. It has an explicit procedure of public hearings for determining whether contestability exists in individual segments. See Galal (1993).
82. Several aspects of the regulatory regime remained to be interpreted by the antitrust commissions and the courts (e.g., interconnection agreements; also the right of Entel – a long-distance company created in the later 1960s and also privatized in the late 1980s – and CTC to enter into each other's line of business). See Galal (1993).
83. For example, in late 1992 Argentina introduced a similar regulatory regime for the electricity sector. See Spiller (1993).
84. We could even include the media, as licence renewals have always been very public affairs in both Jamaica and the UK.
85. This section is based largely on Hill and Abdala (1993) and Esfahani (1993).
86. These companies became known as Telefónica and Telecom, respectively.
87. All call prices are based on the price of a 'pulse', with more expensive calls (e.g., long distance) incurring more pulses per minute.
88. A similar disdain for rules is reflected in the fact that the exclusive licences included the service areas of the main private regional telephone company, CAT, a subsidiary of Siemens. As a consequence, the licences took away CAT's legal standing, forcing it to be sold to the new licensees. See Hill and Abdala (1993).
89. For example, the original licences specified a two-year period during which pricing was to be set on a rate-of-return basis (the rate of return being 16%, although it was unclear whether this was a

maximum or a minimum, with legislators and the president of ENTel disagreeing on that point), followed by a price-cap period with X set to zero.

90. Given that the current regulatory regime has few substantive restraints and that there are no restraints to changing the regulatory system, considering enforcement of restraints in Argentina and the Philippines is a wholly theoretical exercise. We will not tackle these issues here, except to note that although the judiciary in the Philippines has played some role in limiting regulatory discretion, even this restraining role seems to have been tainted by corruption allegations (see Esfahani 1993).
91. To a large extent, given the political impossibility of repatriating all the cash flow generated by these companies, the fact that in 1992 they quadrupled their additions to main lines may simply reflect the use of available cash flow. By reinvesting their retained earnings now, the companies hope to relax the constraints the licence investment requirements may impose in future years when cash flow reductions may require them to obtain fresh funds.
92. For example, even when the UK Labour Party denounced BT's privatization in the mid-1980s, its platform called for renationalization without 'speculative gains' rather than outright nationalization.
93. Note that a programme along these lines is different from existing programme of insurance against non-commercial risk. These shift the costs of administrative expropriation to the insurer, and thus do little to enhance the incentive of the host country to abide by its commitments.

References

Abueva, José V. (1988), 'Philippine Ideologies and National Development' in Raul P. DeGuzmán and Mila R. Reforma, *Government and Politics of the Philippines*, New York: Oxford University Press.

Baldwin, Robert and Christopher McCrudden (1987), *Regulation and Public Law*, London: Weidenfield & Nicolson.

Baron, David P. (1992), *Business and its Environment*, Englewood Cliffs, NJ: Prentice Hall.

Baron, David P. and Roger Myerson (1982), 'Regulating a Monopolist with Unknown Costs', *Econometrica*, **50**, 911–30.

Barzel, Yoram (1989), *Economic Analysis of Property Rights*, Cambridge, MA: Cambridge University Press.

Barzel, Yoram (1982), 'Measurement Cost and the Organization of Markets', *Journal of Law and Economics*, 27–48.

Cabral, Luis and Michael H. Riordan (1989), 'Incentives for Cost Reduction under Price Cap Regulation', *Journal of Regulatory Economics* **1**, 133–47.

Cain, Bruce, John Ferejohn and Morris Fiorina (1987), *The Personal Vote*, Cambridge MA: Harvard University Press.

Calvert, Randall (1992), 'a Rational Choice Theory of Social Institutions: Cooperations, Coordination and Commitment', mimeo, University of Rochester.

Cave, Martin (1991), 'Recent Developments in the Regulation of Former Nationalized Industries'.

Coase, Ronald H. (1960), 'The Nature of Social Cost', *Journal of Law and Economics*, 1–44.

Coase, Ronald H. (1988), 'R.H. Coase Lectures', *Journal of Law Economics and Organization*, Spring, 1–48.

Cox, Gary (1987), *The Efficient Secret*, New York: Cambridge University Press.

Cox, Gary (1993), 'The Development of Collective Responsibility in the United Kingdom', *Parliamentary History*, **13**, pt 1, 32–47.

Dimock, Marshall E. (1933), *British Public Utilities and National Development*, London: George Allen & Urwin, Ltd.

Duverger, Maurice (1954), *Political Parties: Their Organization and Activity in the Modern State*, New York: Wiley.

Esfahani, Hadi S. (1993), 'Regulations, Institutions and Economic Performance: The Political Economy of the Philippines' Telecommunications Sector', Washington, D.C.: The World Bank.

Fesler, James W. (1983), 'The Higher Civil Service in Europe and the Unites States' in Bruce L. Smith (ed.), *The Higher Civil Service of Europe and Canada, Lessons for the United States*, The Brookings Institution, Washington, D.C.

Fiorina, Morris (1983), 'Legislative Choice of Regulatory Forums: Legal Process or Administrative Process?', *Public Choice*, **39**, 33–66.

Galal, Ahmed (1993), 'Regulation, Commitment and Development of Telecommunications in Chile', The World Bank.

Galal, Ahmed, Leroy P. Jones, Pankaj Tandon and Ingo Vogelsang (1993), *Welfare Consequences of Selling Public Enterprises*, Washington, D.C.: World Bank.

Gely, Rafael and Pablo T. Spiller (1990), 'A Rational Choice Theory of Supreme Court Statutory Decisions, with Applications to the *State Farm* and *Grove City* Cases', *Journal of Law, Economics and Organization*, **6**, 263–301.

Goldberg, Victor (1976), 'Regulation and Administered Contracts', *Bell Journal of Economics*, 426–52.

Hill, Alice and Manuel Abdala (1993), 'Regulation, Institutions and Commitment: Privatization and Regulation in Argentine Telecommunications Sector', Washington, D.C.: The World Bank.

Hormell, Orren C. (1928), 'Electricity in Great Britain – A Study in Administration', *National Municipal Review*, **XXVII** (6), June.

Huber, Peter W., Michael K. Kellogg and James Thorne (1992), *The Geodesic Network II: 1993 Report on Competition in the Telephone Industry*, Washington D.C.: The Geodesic Company.

Jacobson, Gary C. (1990), *The Electoral Origins of Divided Government Competition in the U.S. House Elections, 1946–1988*, Boulder, CO: Westview Press.

Joskow, Paul L. (1972), 'The Determination of the Allowed Rate of Return in a Formal Regulatory Proceeding', *Bell Journal of Economics and Management Science*, **3**, 632–44.

Joskow, Paul L. (1973), 'Pricing Decisions of Regulated Firms: A Behavioral Approach', *Bell Journal of Economics and Management Science*, **4**, 118–40.

Joskow, Paul L. (1974), 'Inflation and Environmental concern: Structural Change in the Process of Public Utility Price Regulation', *Journal of Law and Economics*, 291–328.

Joskow, Paul L. and Roger G. Noll (1981), 'Regulation in Theory and Practice: An Overview', in G. Fromm (ed.), *Studies in Public Regulation*, Cambridge, MA: MIT Press.

Joskow, Paul L. and Richard Schmalensee (1983), *Markets for Power*, Cambridge, MA: MIT Press.

Keen, Frank N. (1925), *The Law Relating to Public Service Undertakings*, London: P.S. King & Sons Ltd.

Kerry, Michael (1983), 'Administrative Law and the Administrator', *Management in Government*, **38** (3), August.

Knieps, Günter and Pablo T. Spiller (1983), 'Regulating by Partial Deregulation: The Case of Telecommunications', *Administrative Law Review*, October.

Laffont, Jean Jacques and Jean Tirole (1986), 'Using Cost Observation to Regulate Firms', *Journal of Political Economy*, **94**, 614–41.

Laffont, Jean Jacques and Jean Tirole (1993), *A Theory of Incentives in Procurement and Regulation*, Cambridge, MA: MIT Press.

Loeb, Martin and Wesley Magat (1979), 'A Decentralized Method of Utility Regulation', *Journal of Law and Economics*, **22**, 399–404.

McCubbins, Matthew D., Roger G. Noll and Barry R. Weingast (1987), 'Administrative Procedures as Instruments of Political Control', *Journal of Law Economics, and Organization*, **3**, 243–77.

McCubbins, Matthew D., Roger G. Noll and Barry R. Weingast (1989), 'Structure and Process, Politics and Policy: Administrative Arrangements and the Political Control of Agencies', *Virginia Law Review*, **75**, 431–82.

Mathios, Alan and Robert Rogers (1989), 'The Impact of Alternative Forms of State Regulation of AT&T on Direct Dial, Long Distance Telephone Rates', *The Rand Journal of Economics*, **20** (3).

Miller, Charles (1987), *Lobbying Government: Understanding and Influencing the Corridors of Power*, Oxford: Basil Blackwell.

Mueller, M. (1993), 'Comments on Interconnection for European Telecommunications' presented at the 21st Annual Telecommunications Policy Research Conference, Solomon Islands, Maryland, October.

Newman, K. (1986), *The Selling of British Telecom*, London: Holt, Rinehart and Winston.

North, Douglass C. (1981), *Structure and Change in Economic History*, New York: Norton.

North, Douglass C. (1990), *Institutions, Institutional Change, and Economic Performance*, Cambridge, MA: Cambridge University Press.

North, Douglass C. and Robert P. Thomas (1973), *The Rise of the Western World: A New Economic History*, Cambridge, MA: Cambridge University Press.

Palmer, M.S.R. (1992), 'The Economics of Organization and Ministerial Responsibility: Towards a Framework of Analysis for Westminster Government', New Zealand Treasury Department.

Riordan, Michael H. (1992), 'Relevance of the New Regulatory Economics for Telecommunications', The World Bank.

Salzberg, Eli M. (1991), 'The Delegation of Legislative Powers to the Courts and the Independence of the Judiciary', University of California, Berkeley.

Schwartz, Edward, Pablo T. Spiller and Santiago Urbiztondo (1993), 'A Positive Theory of Legislative Intent', *Law and Contemporary Problems*, **57**, (1 & 2), 51–86.

Self, Henry and Elizabeth M. Watson (1952), *Electricity Supply in Great Britain: Its Development and Organization*, London: George Allen and Unwin.

Shepsle, Kenneth and Barry R. Weingast (1981), 'Structure-Induced Equilibrium and Legislative Choice', *Public Choice*, **37**, 503–19.

Shepsle, Kenneth and Barry R. Weingast (1987a), 'Institutionalizing Majority Rule: A Social Theory with Policy Implications', *AEA Papers and Proceeding*, 367–71.

Shepsle, Kenneth and Barry R. Weingast (1987b), 'The Institutional Foundations of Committee Power', *American Political Science Review*, 85–105.

Shepsle, Kenneth and Barry R. Weingast (1989), 'Penultimate Power: Conference Committees and the Legislative Process', Hoover Institution Working Paper #P–89–7, Stanford University.

Shin, Richard T. and John S. Ying (1992), 'Unnatural Monopolies in Local Telephone', *Rand Journal of Economics*, **23** (2), 171–83.

Shugart, Matthew S. and John M. Carey (1992), *Presidents and Assemblies*, New York: Cambridge University Press.

Spiller, Pablo T. (1993), 'Institutions and Regulatory Commitment in Utilities' Privatization', *Industrial and Corporate Change*, **2** (3), 387–450.

Spiller, Pablo T. and Rafael Gely (1990), 'A Rational Choice Theory of Supreme Court Statutory Decisions, with Applications to the *State Farm* and *Grove City* Cases', *Journal of Law Economics and Organization*, **6**, 263–301.

Spiller, Pablo T. and Rafael Gely (1992), 'Congressional Control or Judicial Interpretation: The Determinants of US Supreme Court Labor Decisions: 1949–1988', *Rand Journal of Economics*, **23** (4), 462–92.

Spiller, Pablo T. and Brian Levy (1991), 'Regulation, Institutions and Economic Efficiency: Promoting Regulatory Reform and Private Sector Participation in Developing Countries: A Research Proposal', mimeo, University of Illinois.

Spiller, Pablo T. and Cezley I. Sampson (1993), 'Regulation, Institutions and Commitment: The Jamaican Telecommunications Sector', The World Bank.

Spiller, Pablo T. and Santiago Urbiztondo (1993), 'Political Appointees vs. Career Civil Servants: A Multiple Principals Theory of Political Bureaucracies', *European Journal of Political Economy*.

Spiller, Pablo T. and Luis Viana (1992), 'How Not to Do It: Electricity Regulation in Argentina, Brazil, Chile, and Uruguay', mimeo, Berkeley: University of California.

Spiller, Pablo T. and Ingo Vogelsang (1993a), 'Regulation, Institutions and Commitment: The British Telecommunications Sector', The World Bank.

Spiller, Pablo T. and Ingo Vogelsang (1993b), 'Notes on Public Utility Regulation in the UK: 1850–1950', mimeo, University of Illinois.

Spulber, Daniel (1989), *Regulation and Markets*, Cambridge, MA: MIT Press.

Stone, Carl (1981), 'Party Voting in Jamaica (1959–1976)' in C. Stone and A. Brown (eds), *Perspectives on Jamaica*, Kingston: Jamaica Publishing House.

Stone, Carl (1986), *Class, State and Democracy in Jamaica*, New York: Praeger.

Taagepera, Rein and Matthew S. Shugart (1993), 'Predicting the Number of Parties: A Quantitative Model of Duverger Mechanical Effect', *American Political Science Review*, **87**, 455–64.

Veljanovski, Cento G. (1991), *Regulators and the Market: An Assessment of the Growth of Regulation in the UK*, London: Institute of Economic Affairs.
Weingast, Barry R. (1984), 'The Congressional-Bureaucratic System: A Principal Agent Perspective', *Public Choice*, 147–92.
Weingast, Barry R. (1993), 'The Economic Role of Political Institutions', mimeo, Stanford University.
Weingast, Barry R. and M. Moran (1983), 'Bureaucratic Discretion or Congressional Control: Regulatory Policy Making by the Federal Trade Commission', *Journal of Political Economy*, 765–800.
Williamson, Oliver E. (1975), *Markets and Hierarchies: Analysis and Antitrust Implications*, New York: Free Press.
Williamson, Oliver E. (1976), 'Franchise Bidding for Natural Monopolies: In General and With Respect to CATV', *Bell Journal of Economics*, 73–104.
Williamson, Oliver E. (1979), 'Transaction-Cost Economics: The Governance of Contractual Relations', *Journal of Law and Economics*, 3–61.
Williamson, Oliver E. (1985), *The Economic Institutions of Capitalism*, New York: Free Press.
Williamson, Oliver E. (1988), 'The Logic of Economic Organization', *Journal of Law, Economics and Organization*, 65–93.
Williamson, Oliver E. (1991), 'Comparative Economic Organization: The Analysis of Discrete Structural Alternative', *Administrative Science Quarterly*, 269–96.
Williamson, Oliver E. (1993), 'Public and Private Bureaus: A Transaction Cost Economics Assessment', mimeo, Berkeley: University of California.
World Bank (1992), 'Bolivia: Restructuring for Growth, Part One: The Main Report', Washington, D.C.
Young, Hugo (1985), 'Judges and the Exercise of Power', *The Guardian*, 31 October.
Zupan, Mark (1989), 'Cable Franchise Renewals: Do Incumbent Firms Behave Opportunistically?', *Rand Journal of Economics*, **20** (4), 473–82.

[19]

The Industrial Organization of Congress; or, Why Legislatures, Like Firms, Are Not Organized as Markets

Barry R. Weingast
Stanford University

William J. Marshall
Goldman, Sachs and Company

This paper provides a theory of legislative institutions that parallels the theory of the firm and the theory of contractual institutions. Like market institutions, legislative institutions reflect two key components: the goals or preferences of individuals (here, representatives seeking reelection) and the relevant transactions costs. We present three conclusions. First, we show how the legislative institutions enforce bargains among legislators. Second, we explain why, given the peculiar form of bargaining problems found in legislatures, specific forms of nonmarket exchange prove superior to market exchange. Third, our approach shows how the committee system limits the types of coalitions that may form on a particular issue.

> The organization of Congress meets remarkably well the electoral needs of its members. To put it another way, if a group of planners sat down and tried to design a pair of American national assemblies with the goal of serving members' electoral needs year in and year out,

We gratefully acknowledge the helpful comments of Lee Alston, Harold Demsetz, Thomas Gilligan, Tom Hammond, Douglass North, Michael Riordan, Brian Roberts, Kenneth Shepsle, and George Stigler. We also thank Elizabeth Case for her editorial assistance. Weingast thanks the National Science Foundation for partial support (Grant SES-8617516).

[*Journal of Political Economy*, 1988, vol. 96, no. 1]

> they would be hard pressed to improve on what exists. [MAYHEW 1974, p. 81]

The new economics of organization holds that explicit market exchange is not the universally ideal institution for a transaction. The most successful application of this approach, the theory of the firm, attempts to explain, for example, why some transactions take place within a firm under certain circumstances and across a market (e.g., between firms) under others.[1] This theory also focuses on the structure of the corporation, notably the separation of ownership and control (Alchian and Demsetz 1972; Jensen and Meckling 1976; Fama 1980; Fama and Jensen 1983; Demsetz and Lehn 1985; Grossman and Hart 1986). With few exceptions, however, it has not considered other types of organizations, such as public bureaucracies, political parties, or legislatures.[2] The purpose of this paper is to extend this theory to the study of political organizations and, in particular, to explain the pattern of institutions within the legislature that facilitates decision making.

Studies of public policy-making emphasize the dependence of political decisions on interest group and constituency participation. While this approach is consistent with outcomes in many individual policy areas, it fails to explain how so many diverse interests are provided with policy benefits simultaneously. A huge variety of interests are represented in the legislature, and almost none is represented by a majority. For most interests to gain policy benefits, representatives with different constituents must agree to exchange support. Put another way, the diversity of interests creates gains from exchange within the legislature. While the literature implicitly assumes that these gains are captured, it fails to explain how trades are accomplished and enforced. If public policy reflects a series of bargains among various interests, how are these bargains maintained over time? As we know from the modern literature on contracts, the answer to this question is not always straightforward since not all agreements are enforceable.

[1] Typical applications focus on the various forms of vertical relations (Coase 1937; Williamson 1975, 1985; Klein, Crawford, and Alchian 1978). Besides these more general treatments of vertical integration, there are excellent treatments of other forms of vertical relations such as franchising (Rubin 1978), resale price maintenance (Gilligan 1986), and long-term contracting (Joskow 1985).

[2] The exceptions include Goldberg (1976), Moe (1984), Weingast (1984), Miller and Moe (1986), Tirole (1986), Milgrom and Roberts (1987), and some of the topics in North (1981). The program for wide application of the approach is discussed in Jensen (1983). Fama and Jensen (1983) extend the analysis of market organizations to include some nonprofit ones, though their analysis only begins the study of this important category of widely different organizations.

To address these issues, we develop a theory of legislative institutions that parallels the theory of the firm and the theory of contractual institutions. Like market institutions, legislative institutions reflect two key components: the goals and preferences of individuals, here legislators seeking reelection from their constituents, and the transactions costs that are induced by imperfect information, opportunism, and other agency problems. But the enforcement mechanisms underpinning exchange in market settings are typically unavailable to or inappropriate for the legislature. Solutions to contractual problems that arise in the market (e.g., vertical integration) do not directly translate into solutions to similar problems found in legislatures. We show how the legislative institutions enforce bargains among legislators and why, given the peculiar bargaining problems found in legislatures, specific nonmarket exchange mechanisms prove superior to market exchange. From a policy perspective, these institutions have important implications. Durability of bargains leads both to the durability of policies that these bargains are designed to implement and to the coalition supporting these policies. Our model thus has important implications for coalition formation and maintenance.

Section I summarizes the new economics of organization. Section II begins the analysis by presenting several assumptions on which our approach is based. Section II describes models of the market for votes and focuses on enforcement problems. Section IV presents our theory of legislative institutions and suggests why these institutions solve problems that arise in simple markets. Section V provides empirical evidence on several propositions that follow from our model. This evidence, from a variety of contexts involving the U.S. Congress, provides significant support for the model. Section VI derives some comparative static results that provide some additional evidence for the approach and suggest some important avenues for additional tests. A discussion section, Section VII, follows in which we explore alternative explanations for enforcing legislative exchange along with possible extensions of our approach.

I. The New Economics of Organization

The theory of the firm holds that production and exchange take place through institutions (contractual patterns, organizational forms) that reflect the specific pattern of transaction costs found in trade. The emphasis of this theory is on how specific organizational or contractual forms reduce these costs. Some of the important results from this literature will prove useful in our discussion of legislatures.

The seminal paper in this tradition (Coase 1937) asserts that the firm emerges not simply to take advantage of specialization or economies of scale but to avoid the costs of using markets and the price system: "The main reason why it is profitable to establish a firm would seem to be that there is a cost of using the price mechanism. The most obvious cost of 'organising' production through the price mechanism is that of discovering what the relevant prices are" (p. 390). In other words, the firm provides a set of contractual mechanisms that substitutes for the price mechanism, in part because the price mechanism is too costly to use in certain circumstances.[3]

A major theme in the literature is that the institutions of the firm are designed, in part, to reduce the costs of assuring contractual performance. In the words of Williamson (1985, pp. 48–49), "Transactions that are subject to *ex post* opportunism will benefit if appropriate safeguards can be devised *ex ante*. Rather than reply to opportunism in kind, therefore, the wise [bargaining party] is one who seeks both to give and receive 'credible commitments.' Incentives may be realigned, and/or superior governance structures within which to organize transactions may be devised." This principle is one of the central lessons of this body of work; it underlies much of institutional and organizational design.[4]

The costs of assuring contractual performance are high in a variety of circumstances. Two settings concern us. The first centers on problems of observability (Holmstrom 1979) or measurement (Barzel 1982), for example, when it is difficult to separate out an agent's contribution from that of random events or when an agent has private information about, say, the quality of the good being sold. Imperfect observability generates well-known problems such as moral hazard, adverse selection, and shirking that plague simple spot market exchange. A large part of the literature spells out ex ante contractual forms designed to mitigate these problems. The second setting centers on incomplete contracts, for example, when it is impossible (or too costly) for contracting parties to plan for all possible contingencies. Several scholars have studied these settings and the attendant problems of ex post opportunism that arise when ex post incentives of the bargaining parties are inconsistent with performing ex ante agreements (e.g., Klein et al. 1978; Kreps 1984; Williamson 1985; Grossman and Hart 1986). Those works also study a variety of mechanisms that are used to mitigate these problems, typically some form of vertical relations.

[3] See also the discussion in Cheung (1983).

[4] Virtually every paper cited on the theory of the firm makes this argument. For particular details, see, e.g., Barzel (1982), Fama and Jensen (1983), Kreps (1984), or Williamson (1985).

We emphasize that the literature is not simply an analysis of contractual failures. As suggested by Williamson in the quote above, ex post problems lead to the design of organizational forms to mitigate these problems. The literature on vertical integration, for example, argues that this organizational form is largely an endogenous response to ex post contractual problems of the sort we have just mentioned. This example illustrates the argument that a particular form of internal organization proves superior to market exchange.

A major limitation of the new economics of organization is that it remains largely tied to market settings. Though the principles are obviously more general (as clearly articulated in Jensen [1983] or Milgrom and Roberts [1987]), applications to other settings are just beginning. Indeed, developing a general theory of organizations requires effectively applying this theory to types of organizations beyond those included in the set studied to generate it.

II. Representatives and Their Constituencies

In this paper, we take up this challenge by showing how this approach illuminates phenomena that take place in legislatures. The perspective developed in this paper rests on three assumptions.

ASSUMPTION 1. *Congressmen represent the (politically responsive) interests located within their district.*—While rational ignorance pervades the political system, that does not imply that the interests of constituents are irrelevant for representatives or that the latter are free to pursue their own interests. Rather, rational ignorance underpins interest group advantage in politics. Because most voters have only a dim awareness of an incumbent's actions, rational ignorance biases political response toward those who do form impressions. Thus interest groups, because they have greater individual stakes in particular issues, monitor congressmen and provide them with information. Groups also mobilize their members in support of friendly congressmen.

Interest groups are not uniformly distributed. They typically have concentrations of voters in particular locations. Farm organization members, for example, are concentrated in specific districts; so too are consumers of food stamps and members of welfare rights organizations. The elderly, to take another example, have a disproportionate presence in Florida and Arizona (medicare and social security) while miners are found in West Virginia, Pennsylvania, and southern Illinois (mine safety, black lung disease).

In the competition for interest group support, specific representatives have a comparative advantage. The lack of complete fungibility of votes implies that legislators are advantaged in attracting support from interest groups located in their district (see Denzau and Munger 1986). This advantage arises because service to local interests attracts both votes and organized resources for the district's representative. Service to this group by an outsider, in contrast, attracts only the latter and may lose votes.

Electoral competition induces congressmen, at least in part, to represent the interests of their constituents. Because groups are not uniformly distributed across constituencies, different legislators represent different groups.[5]

ASSUMPTION 2. *Parties place no constraints on the behavior of individual representatives.*—Parties were strong around the turn of the century when they possessed reward systems and sanction mechanisms to control the behavior of members. Specifically, party organizations determined entry into competition for the local seat, the positions of power within the legislature, and the distribution of legislative benefits (e.g., a representative obtained legislative benefits only if he supported party measures). None of these conditions now holds. In what follows, we therefore treat the individual as the decision-making unit.[6]

ASSUMPTION 3. *Majority rule is a binding constraint.*—Proposed bills (alterations in the status quo) must command the support of a majority of the entire legislature in order to become law.

III. The Gains from Exchange: The Problem to Be Solved

Legislators pursue their reelection goals by attempting to provide benefits to their constituents (assumption 1). Acting alone, they cannot succeed (assumption 3). This, in combination with the diversity of interests they represent, generates gains from exchange and cooperation among legislators. But what institutions underlie—and enforce—this cooperation?

[5] Evidence for this view abounds in the literature. For a recent summary in the political science literature, see Fiorina (1981*b*). In the economics literature, systematic evidence has been provided as part of the controversy over ideological voting in Congress. While the empirical issue concerns the degree to which representative behavior can diverge from constituents' interests, all studies provide substantial evidence that the latter systematically—though not necessarily completely—affects congressional voting (see Kau and Rubin 1979; Kalt and Zupan 1984; Peltzman 1984).

[6] Substantial evidence for this assumption is provided in the political science literature (see, e.g., Mayhew 1966). To take one example: the whip system, once a tool of the leadership to keep party members in line, now operates as a service organization providing information to the leadership and to the members. To quote one popular text on Congress, it "operates not as much as a device to coerce or even persuade members as it does simply to inform the leadership of the disposition of members toward legislation" (Polsby 1984, p. 129).

The new economics of organization suggests that institutions evolve to ensure delivery of benefits. In order to understand why one exchange mechanism survives instead of another, we need to study the potential agency and transactions cost problems faced by legislators, given the types of trades they seek to make. It is useful to begin by focusing on previous approaches to legislative exchange that explicitly rely on marketlike mechanisms. By studying the enforcement problems encountered in this setting, we can determine the characteristics a more appropriate legislative exchange mechanism must possess.

Previous work has focused on *vote trading,* also known as logrolling, centralized legislative exchange, or legislative IOUs. The major proponents of particular versions include Tullock (1967, 1981), Wilson (1969), Telser (1980), Koford (1982), and Becker (1983). While there are significant differences among these approaches, fundamental to each is an explicit or implicit market in votes. Under the most well-known logrolling version, legislators begin with proposals to benefit themselves at the expense of others, but none of these proposals commands a majority (Buchanan and Tullock 1962; Tullock 1967, 1981). Legislators therefore search out trading partners. In exchange for support, each gets his proposal passed and, on net, is better off. In the explicit market versions, votes are bought and sold for a price, with the "equilibrium" prices determining vote trades and hence the set of bills passed (see also Wilson 1969; Koford 1982).

The motivation underlying these market models is clear. By giving away votes on issues that have lower marginal impact on their district (and therefore on their electoral fortunes) in exchange for votes on issues having a larger marginal impact, legislators are better off. Whether or not they incorporate an explicit auction, models of the legislative market for votes have considerable appeal.

A careful inspection, however, reveals that this approach assumes away some of the deepest problems plaguing legislative exchange. It assumes, for example, that all bills and their payoffs are known in advance; that is, there are no random or unforeseen future events that may influence outcomes or payoffs. Either the time dimension is suppressed or enforcement of agreements over time is left exogenous. Because these models study a legislature with no future, they cannot address how legislators cope with agreements that cover more than one legislative session.

A variety of exchange problems arise because the value of today's legislation significantly depends on next year's legislative events. Members of future sessions face incentives different from those faced when the trade occurred and may seek, for example, to amend, abolish, or simply ignore previous agreements. Because current legislators typically *cannot* bind a future legislative session, problems of enforcement over time are critically important for understanding legislatures and cannot be assumed away. Moreover, as we will see, these settings inhibit the ability of noninstitutional enforcement of cooperation (e.g., reputation) as the sole means of policing bargains. In the face of uncertainty over the future status of today's bargain, therefore, legislators will devise institutions for long-term durability of agreements that ensure the flow of benefits beyond this session of the legislature.

To begin our analysis, we observe that most models of the legislative market apply to only a subset of problems faced by legislators, typically the pork barrel. Pork barrel programs are an important part of every major Western government, but they have special characteristics that do not hold for other types of legislation. For example, benefit flows are contemporaneous to different legislators (in this case, the funds financing the project), and consummation of trading is simultaneous (see, e.g., Buchanan and Tullock 1962; Tullock 1981; Koford 1982). Focusing solely on pork barrel–type programs rules out virtually all the important issues studied in the regulatory literature as well as the major U.S. redistributive programs.[7] We consider the problems generated by noncontemporaneous benefit flows and nonsimultaneity in turn.

A. *Noncontemporaneous Benefit Flows*

To see how differential patterns of benefit flows potentially inhibit trading, consider the following exchange problem. Suppose that a group of legislators seeking pork, for example, dams and bridges, attempts to find some other group of legislators with whom to exchange votes. Suppose further that one potential set of trading partners is a group of legislators who seek a flow of services from a regulatory agency. If the two sides exchange votes, the first group obtains its dams and bridges while the second obtains its regulatory agency. Once the dams are built, however, what stops the first group from reneging on the agreement, for example, from working during a future legislative session to revoke the regulatory benefits? Simple market exchange institutions do not adequately protect against this form of reneging (and, as we will see, repeated interaction alone is insufficient to prevent this problem). Rational coalition partners, therefore, discount the potential gains from a proposed trade by the probability that these benefit flows will be curtailed by reneging. Consequently, the second group of legislators might not accept the trade

[7] For several surveys in this literature, see the articles in Fromm (1981).

(e.g., if the trade yields them positive net benefits only if reneging does not occur).

B. *Nonsimultaneous Exchange*

A second exchange problem arises because many potential trades concern bills that do not come up for a vote simultaneously. In the pork barrel area, legislators are able to limit this problem by packaging all projects into an "omnibus" bill containing all elements of the trade. This simple device limits the opportunities for ex post reneging.[8] But it is not always possible for all bills in a legislative session to come up for a vote simultaneously.[9]

Consider a trade negotiation taking place just prior to a vote. In exchange for a vote, some legislator promises to support another legislator's bill that is due to come up sometime later in the session. In other words, he extends an IOU to the second party. But problems with IOUs occur in part because they are not a medium of exchange. They require that one individual rely on the future behavior of another. Were votes a medium of exchange, this reliance would not be necessary.[10]

Consequently, exchanges relying on IOUs are plagued by the two problems noted in Section I, namely, problems of observability and of the existence of contingencies too numerous (or too costly) to anticipate fully. Many events may occur between the two votes. First, public perception of the issue may change, and the electoral effect of this change is observable solely to the representative it affects. This induces a form of moral hazard. Thus the first legislator may claim that he can no longer support the bill and so attempt to renege. Since the state of the world is observed only by one legislator, it is difficult for the second legislator to verify the first's claims about whether he should be required to hold up his end of the bargain. Second, in response to changing political circumstances, the bill itself may evolve. This introduces a double-sided form of moral hazard. Since the elec-

[8] Because the omnibus mechanism for ensuring against reneging is more readily available for bargains between members of the same committee (e.g., across subcommittees), the optimal pattern of committee jurisdictions depends on the expected pattern of trading. See Ferejohn (1986) for a further discussion of this and similar issues.

[9] Nonetheless, when the volume of legislation was sufficiently low to allow all bills to be passed in a short period, legislatures in fact did so. Thus, for the U.S. Congress in the nineteenth century, it was common that a major portion of legislation was passed during the lame-duck session after the election of the next congress. This also appears to hold today for states whose legislatures meet for only short periods.

[10] As a consequence, the so-called double coincidence of wants is not satisfied by this transaction. More generally, IOUs have none of the properties of a medium of exchange: a store of value, a unit of account, and ready transferability.

toral effects of this change are observable solely by the legislator it affects, the first legislator may argue that, while he could support the original bill, he cannot support the new version. On the other hand, the drafters of the legislation, having gained additional support through trades, may opportunistically rewrite the legislation so as to increase their own benefits (and impose greater costs on others).

Trading in legislative IOUs thus poses considerable contractual problems of the sort studied in the theory of the firm. Either IOUs must be for a specific form of a bill without any alterations or they must provide for hundreds of contingencies, many of which are not observable to both parties. Neither form of IOU is likely to prove useful. The former severely limits the trading possibilities. Since most legislation is altered at several stages before it is passed, this form of IOU exchanges one vote for sure against one vote under relatively rare circumstances—an unlikely basis for a transaction.[11] Further, different contingencies are important to different legislators, and the market for specific, contingent IOUs is likely to be extremely thin, perhaps requiring a different price for each potential trade. As Coase (1937) observed, this obviates the benefits of a price system. But perhaps more important, the observability problems associated with many contingencies suggest that IOUs are unenforceable: how are the parties to agree ex post when the number of possible events is larger than the number of specified contingencies and when both parties cannot observe the outcome?

This discussion reveals that market forms of exchange are limited as a means of capturing the gains from trade. As noted in Section I, problems with observability and ex post enforceability are fundamental to understanding the motivation for internalizing a transaction with a firm. Just as these problems lead to the emergence of vertical integration to replace market exchange, they motivate the design of institutions within the legislature that substitute for explicit market exchange.

In the discussion so far, there has been little mention of the role of repeat play. Repeated interaction provides incentives for individuals to adhere to agreements this period so as to maintain a flow of benefits over time.[12] This form of endogenous cooperation surely plays a

[11] See Ferejohn (1974*b*) for a further exploration of the peculiar properties of a market in votes. This stems in part from results in the collective choice literature that show that when one set of vote trades is feasible, so are many others (e.g., Schwartz 1981). This prevents the logic of the standard arguments about supporting price systems from holding in this context.

[12] See, e.g., Axelrod (1984) and Calvert (1985). There is, of course, a growing literature in economics on this topic (e.g., Telser 1980; Klein and Leffler 1981; Kreps and Wilson 1982; Roberts 1986). A further problem limits the workability of this solution, that of legislative turnover. Even in current times when incumbents are reelected with

role in legislatures, and for some settings, it alone may be sufficient to police bargains. It is well known, however, that "the long arm of the future" is inadequate in settings in which agents have private information and in which it is impossible or too costly to specify all contingencies in advance.[13] It is precisely these problems that we have argued motivate the need for alternative legislative institutions. The importance of unanticipated contingencies in both noncontemporaneous and nonsimultaneous trading combined with private information and moral hazard in the latter suggests the need for additional mechanisms to maintain bargains.

Perhaps another way of putting the argument of this section is as follows. Repeat play alone is insufficient to prevent the breakdown of cooperation under certain circumstances. Legislators therefore have an incentive to devise institutions that reduce the circumstances in which breakdown occurs. In this sense, legislative rules are not substitutes for reputation building and trigger strategies commonly used in repeat play. Rather, rules complement the use of these strategies and, in particular, prevent the breakdown of cooperation at precisely the circumstances under which these other strategies fail.

This argument closely parallels that of vertical integration in which reputation effects are also insufficient to police cooperation between firms. In both cases, potential contractual problems lead to the design of institutions that substitute for market exchange; in so doing, they improve ex post enforceability of agreements. This does not imply that reputation building is unimportant in legislatures or in firms that are vertically tied, just that it is not the *sole* means of enforcing agreements. Indeed, the other institutions of the legislature undoubtedly facilitate its use as a means to complement other devices.

C. *Implications*

Problems concerning the durability and enforceability of bargains are ubiquitous in legislative settings, limiting the value of explicit market forms of exchange.[14] Put another way, coalitions lack durability under

high frequency, the average net turnover in Congress is 10 percent per term. Moreover, the losers are typically replaced with members with different preferences if only because the latter, in order to beat the former, had to devise a separate support constituency.

[13] The literature on the theory of the firm is built on the premise that the incentives derived from repeat dealings alone are insufficient to police incentive problems. Examples are the vertical integration or the optimal structure of financial claims. See the references in n. 2.

[14] Moreover, the problem of non–pork barrel programs and lack of simultaneity do not exhaust the situations in which a legislative market is a poor provider of durability. For example, even if two groups of legislators both seek permanent regulatory benefits,

an explicit market exchange system. In the face of these problems, legislators will devise alternative institutions that provide exchanges with a greater degree of durability (see Ferejohn 1986). We now turn to a discussion of how this is accomplished.

IV. The Legislative Committee System

This section develops a model of an idealized legislative committee system. The types of policies (i.e., legislative bargains) that emerge from this model parallel those predicted by the vote-trading models; but it is not plagued by problems of enforcement of exchanges. The legislative committee system is defined by the following three conditions.

CONDITION 1. Committees are composed of a number of seats or positions, each held by an individual legislator. Committees possess the following properties: (*a*) associated with each committee is a specific subset of policy issues over which it has jurisdiction (e.g., commerce, energy, banking, or agriculture); (*b*) within their jurisdiction, committees possess the monopoly right to bring alternatives to the status quo up for a vote before the legislature; and (*c*) committee proposals must command a majority of votes against the status quo to become public policy.

CONDITION 2. There exists a property rights system over committee seats called the "seniority system." It has the following characteristics: (*a*) a committee member holds his position as long as he chooses to remain on the committee; subject to his reelection, he cannot be forced to give it up; (*b*) leadership positions within the committee (e.g., chairmanship) are allocated by seniority, that is, the length of continuous service on the committee; (*c*) rights to committee positions cannot be sold or traded to others.

CONDITION 3. Whenever a member leaves a committee (e.g., by transfer, death, or defeat), his seat becomes vacant. There is a bidding mechanism whereby vacant seats are assigned to other congressmen.

Condition 1 defines the source of committee power and value, condition 2 defines the property rights system associated with committee positions, and condition 3 establishes an exchange mechanism over the rights established under 1 and 2.

Let us explore the consequences of the legislative committee system to determine its enforcement properties, how new policies are pro-

changing electoral fortunes may promote growth in one and shrink the other; to the extent that this change appears reasonably permanent, it provides the conditions fostering a revocation of the latter group's benefits. When the once and for all gains exceed the cost potentially imposed by the (now smaller) other side, reneging is likely to occur.

vided, its control of the agency problems that arise from the delegation of power to a particular subset of members, and the types of policies that are likely to emerge from it.

A. *Enforcement of Legislative Bargains*

The committee system provides substantial protection against opportunistic behavior, thereby providing durability to policy bargains. To see this, consider the setting described above in which one group of legislators seeks dams and bridges and the second seeks a regulatory agency benefiting its constituents. In the legislative market, this agreement is vulnerable to ex post reneging of the following form: the first group, after building its dams, might form a coalition with other legislators (perhaps the minority excluded from the original deal) to pass a new bill revoking the regulation benefiting the second group.

But now consider the same bargain assuming that it was forged under the committee system and that the first group controlled the committee with jurisdiction over pork barrel programs, the second, the committee with the jurisdiction over the relevant regulations. Under the committee system, the second group retains control over the agenda within its jurisdiction. Suppose that, once the dams and bridges are completed, the first group introduces legislation to revoke the benefits flowing to the second group, and, further, a majority supports this legislation. However, only the committee with jurisdiction can bring it to the floor for a vote. This control over the agenda within its jurisdiction implies that a committee has veto power over the proposals of others. Since this proposal would make the committee worse off (and since, by assumption, a majority will support it on the floor), the committee would not allow it to come up for a vote. In other words, the restricted access to the agenda serves as a mechanism to prevent ex post reneging.

Moreover, because exchanges in influence are institutionalized through the property rights system, the absence of simultaneity is considerably less troublesome. As long as the property rights system is maintained, the agenda power held by each committee substitutes for outstanding IOUs with uncertain contingencies. The problems associated with devising contingent claims over future events are relatively absent under the legislative committee system.

B. *Providing New Benefits (or How Committees Capture the Gains from Exchange)*

The agenda rights afford committee members considerable influence over policy choice within their jurisdiction. This follows because the set of points that command a majority against any given status quo, *W(sq)*, is generally quite large (McKelvey 1976, 1979; Shepsle and Weingast 1981). Typically, *W(sq)* includes a wide range of policy alternatives, some making committee members worse off and some making them better off. Given this range of alternatives, agenda power allows committees to bias the outcome in favor of the alternative they most prefer.[15]

The committee system institutionalizes a trade among all the legislators, policy area by policy area, for the right to select which points from *W(sq)* replace the status quo. But this is neither accomplished nor enforced by an explicit market exchange. Rather, a legislator on committee *i* gives up influence over the selection of proposals in the area of committee *j* in exchange for members of committee *j*'s giving up their rights to influence proposals in area *i*. Institutionalizing rights over agenda power—that is, control over the design and selection of proposals that arise for a vote—substitutes for purchasing the votes of others in an explicit market. Since any element of *W(sq)* will pass by definition, it is the influence over elements of this set afforded committees by agenda power that eliminates the need for explicit exchange of votes.

C. *Who Gains Influence (or How Are the Gains from Exchange Distributed)?*

This question concerns the types of policies chosen under the committee system. Since committees afford their members disproportionate influence over policy choice within their jurisdiction, it also concerns the mechanism that assigns legislators to committees.

Condition 3 provides that the legislature uses a bidding mechanism to assign members to committee positions. Since a representative's electoral fortunes depend on his obtaining benefits for his constituents and since constituent interests differ, legislators seek assignment to those committees that have the greatest marginal impact over their electoral fortunes. The real opportunity costs of bidding for committee *i* are that the representative gives up the possibility of holding a seat on committee *j*. Thus representatives from farm districts are much more likely to bid for seats on agriculture committees than they are for seats on urban, housing, or merchant marine committees. A potential problem arises, however, because some committees are valued by all (e.g., the spending or taxing committees). However, here too the bidding mechanism determines assignment. The more com-

[15] The details of this process are beyond the scope of this paper. For an in-depth analysis, see Shepsle and Weingast (1984, 1987).

petition for seats, the less likely the bid will be successful. Suppose each potential bidder for a highly valued committee (e.g., one concerning taxes) also values some specific policy committee with much less competition (e.g., housing, agriculture, or public works). The increased competition for seats on the tax committees implies that only those with the greatest differential value between the tax committee and their next-best alternative will pay the opportunity cost of bidding (i.e., giving up a higher probability of getting their policy committee).

D. *Implications for Coalition Formation*

The legislative committee system has two separate effects on coalition formation. First, agenda power held by committee members implies that successful coalitions must include the members of the relevant committee. Without these members, the bill will not reach the floor for a vote. This, in turn, implies that certain policies are unlikely to become law, for example, those that provide benefits only to a majority off the committee. In technical terms, committee veto implies that, from among the set of policies that command a majority against the status quo, only those that make the committee better off are possible (this issue is extensively explored in Shepsle and Weingast [1987]). This significantly reduces the feasible set of policies that may be implemented.

Along these lines, we also note that since committees have rights to bring a single bill to the floor, trades among committee members are more likely to succeed than those across committees. This follows because there is less chance for such a deal to fall apart. When a coalition forms between members of two committees, legislators must agree to exchange votes on two separate bills. When a coalition forms among members of the same committee, they may bring a single bill to the floor. The latter allows a single up or down vote on the package (whereas the former does not), thereby affording less chance for reneging. This suggests that drawing the jurisdictional boundaries between committees is an important strategic variable that affects the pattern of coalitions.[16] Ceteris paribus, expected trading partners are better off if they are members of the same committee so that the

[16] See Ferejohn (1986) for a discussion of this issue in the context of a trade between the urban members on the Agriculture Committee (seeking food stamps) and the farmers on this committee (seeking continued farm benefits). He argued that being on the same committee advantaged these urban members over other potential legislative partners who were part of other committees that might have brought some other form of legislation providing some subsidy for food for the poor (the latter could have easily been written by, e.g., Ways and Means).

optimal pattern of jurisdictions must in part reflect the expected pattern of trades.

The second effect on coalitions concerns durability. The durability afforded by the committee system induces some rigidities into the coalition formation process. Under a market exchange mechanism, small changes in political circumstances would lead to a small change in the optimal set of bargains and coalitions. But under the committee system, small changes in circumstances do not automatically lead to changes in policy. To see this, consider the example explored above involving dams, bridges, and regulatory benefits. We showed above that committee veto power prevents the proponents of dams from easily reneging once their dams are built or if, because of a change in political circumstances, they find a more attractive coalition partner.

This does not mean, however, that the dam-and-bridges legislators can never alter policy. Rather, it means that they must bid for seats on the committee and wait until they attain a majority. Small changes in political circumstances are not likely to make it worth the attempt. Therefore, the committee system implies that policy will respond only to large changes in political circumstances or to major shifts in the electorate.[17]

E. *Controls over Committees*

Committees are decentralized decision-making units composed of those legislators with the greatest stake in their jurisdiction. Their power to decide what proposals (if any) are brought to the floor places them in an agency relation with the rest of the legislature. As with any form of delegation, this authority provides the potential for moral hazard. What prevents the committee from extracting too much surplus at the expense of other legislators?

The committee system constrains the behavior of its subunits by restricting committee power. In particular, the majority rule condition precludes any one committee from extracting too many gains at the expense of others. Suppose, for example, that one committee attempts to extract the entire budget. The majority rule requirement implies that this proposal must get a majority of legislators to give up the opportunity to spend some of the budget in their areas. They will do so only if the value of the last dollar from this proposal to them exceeds the value of the first dollar spent within their own jurisdic-

[17] We note that this phenomenon parallels vertical integration. There, long-term agreements also induce durability and rigidities: the contract is not renegotiated with each small change in economic circumstances (e.g., prices) and therefore does not respond to changes in the way a spot market does.

tion. Since members value influence within their own jurisdictions, this situation is unlikely. Thus the voting rule plays an important constraining role over the opportunistic behavior of particular committees.[18]

F. *Summary*

Instead of trading votes, legislators in the committee system institutionalize an exchange of influence over the relevant rights. Instead of bidding for votes, legislators bid for seats on committees associated with rights to policy areas valuable for their reelection. In contrast to policy choice under a market for votes, legislative bargains institutionalized through the committee system are significantly less plagued by problems of ex post enforceability.

V. Evidence: The Distribution of Preference, Influence, and the Benefits of Committees

In what follows, we provide evidence showing that choices and decision making in the U.S. Congress are consistent with our view.[19] (Thus this is not a direct test between our model and the vote-trading approach.)

The major feature of our model is that exchange takes place via institutionalization through the committees. By far the strongest piece of evidence from the U.S. Congress in favor of our approach concerns the pattern of membership and benefit flows for the various committees (Fiorina 1981*a*). Members from farming districts dominate the agriculture committees and oversee programs that benefit farmers. Members from urban districts sit on banking, housing, and welfare committees that provide benefits to an incredible array of urban constituents. Members with large defense installations or industries dominate Armed Services committees. In each case, members mold policies in their jurisdiction to their constituents' advantage.

The model is based on a set of assertions about committee operation: (*a*) the assignment process operates as a self-selection mechanism; (*b*) committees are not representative of the entire legislature but instead are composed of "preference outliers," or those who value

[18] In most legislatures, the amendment process places additional constraints on the behavior of committees. For details of this process for the U.S. Congress, including how it qualifies this argument, see Shepsle and Weingast (1987). The problem of how this body places constraints on committees has never received systematic treatment.

[19] Congress, unlike the British Parliament, meets the conditions set out in Sec. II. We briefly compare our findings for the American case with those of the British in Sec. VII.

the position most highly; and (*c*) most centrally, committee members receive the disproportionate share of the benefits from programs within their jurisdiction. Let us survey the empirical evidence supporting these propositions.

A. *Committee Assignments*

At the beginning of each new congress, there are a number of vacant committee seats in some 25 committees and there are incoming freshmen without seats.[20] They are encouraged to request only a small number of possible positions. Then party leaders attempt to match individual assignments with their freshman requests. There is, however, a potential problem here: What prevents the system from breaking down because everyone requests seats on the best and most powerful committees? How does the bidding mechanism actually select those freshmen willing to bid the most for particular committees?

The mechanics of the assignment process are designed to work against breakdown. It turns out that there are certain committees (e.g., Post Office) that no one wants. Those who fail to get one of their requested slots are generally put on one of these committees. Requesting the most valuable slots, therefore, increases the probability of ending up with Post Office. Suppose each freshman may potentially request a particular substantive policy committee (e.g., Agriculture, Housing and Welfare, or Public Works) valuable for his district that he has a high probability of getting. Which ones will opt instead to request the more powerful committees? Since the latter option involves a lottery between the most valuable committee and one worth virtually nothing, only those freshmen who value it most highly in comparison with the sure thing of getting on their policy committee will bid for it.[21] This lottery implies that revealed preferences reflect true preferences and shows how the assignment mechanism succeeds

[20] The following description relies on Shepsle (1975, 1978). While he did not discuss the preference revelation aspects of the assignment process, it is clear that the process must rely on some means of inducing truthful requests. Since few empirical contexts that make use of these mechanisms have been studied, his data remain an untapped source for further study. In what follows, we ignore for simplicity returning members who wish to change committees. For details on how this works, see Shepsle (1978).

[21] The following table reports the frequency distribution over the lengths of request lists (i.e., how many committees each freshman requests). Three-quarters of all freshmen (87th–93d Congress) ask for three or fewer out of 25. The number of observations is 231 (source: Shepsle 1978, p. 49).

Length	1	2	3	4	5 or More
Percentage	23	16	36	15	10

TABLE 1

FRESHMAN ASSIGNMENT SUCCESS

	Proportion Receiving			
Congress	First Preference	Other Preference	No Preference	N
87th	.474	.368	.159	19
88th	.500	.306	.194	36
89th	.591	.254	.155	71
90th	.308	.308	.384	13
92d	.750	.144	.106	28
93d	.691	.166	.193	26
All	.585	.243	.172	193

SOURCE.—Shepsle (1978, p. 193).

in matching members with committees whose jurisdictions they value most highly.

The evidence supporting this interpretation is twofold. First, table 1 shows that the probability of a freshman's gaining one of his top three is above .8.[22] Second, and more important, table 2 shows that when there is no competition for a seat, the requester is virtually assured of getting his first choice (the probability is over .94); but the greater the competition, the less likely is a freshman to attain his first choice. There is also considerable evidence that freshman requests take into account competition for seats.[23] Competition of this sort appears necessary—though not sufficient—to ensure that bids reflect underlying preferences.

Overall, then, the pattern of committee assignments looks remarkably like an optimization process that maps members into those committees they value the most.

B. *Committee Membership*

To be more systematic about committee membership, we have examined indexes of member preferences over issues that correspond to

[22] Moreover, it is not clear that this frequency can be much higher because of the many accounting constraints (see Shepsle 1975) imposed on the problem (e.g., only one freshman per slot; each vacant slot must be filled).

[23] Shepsle (1978) provided one more piece of evidence for our model. Using probit analysis to predict which freshman requests particular committee slots, he estimated a set of simple demand equations. His results are consistent with our model, namely, that simple measures of constituency interest (e.g., number of agricultural workers, military employees, or housing) are good predictors of requests. Moreover, these estimates also show that freshmen rationally anticipate competition for different seats: when other factors are held constant, the estimated probability of a freshman's *requesting* a certain seat goes down as the number of competitors increases.

TABLE 2

EFFECTS OF COMPETITION ON ASSIGNMENTS

First Preference Assignment Success	Total Number of Effective Requests per Vacancy		
	Less than 1	1–2	More than 2
Yes	94.4	67.2	30.5
No	5.6	32.8	69.5

SOURCE.—Shepsle (1978, p. 201).

major committee jurisdictions. This exercise reveals that members of the relevant committee or subcommittee significantly differ from the rest of the House.[24] Most indexes are computed by an interest group with a clear stake in the policy area being considered. Because they are constructed so as to indicate which congressmen are supporters of the group, these indexes are good proxies for supporters of the group's interests. The scores computed by the AFL-CIO Committee on Political Education (COPE), for example, indicate pro- and anti-labor congressmen; the American Security Council's National Security Index (NSI) reveals supporters of a strong national defense and, apparently, opponents of foreign aid.[25]

The model predicts that representatives of particular interests gain policy benefits through membership on relevant committees. Hence we should observe that committees are composed of members who are significantly above-average supporters of the relevant interest group and, in particular, have interest group scores significantly above the mean for the entire Congress.

This pattern is borne out by the results reported in table 3. The difference in preferences between committee members and the rest of the House is highly statistically significant. For a diversity of policy areas—defense, foreign aid, consumer protection, labor, and the environment—committee members are indeed significantly above-average supporters of benefits to the relevant interest group.

Putting this evidence together with results from committee assignments reveals that legislators opt for committees relevant to their constituents' interests and that their doing so leads to committees

[24] Though this would seem to be an obvious topic for political scientists, they have never systematically collected this type of data. Instead the literature typically provides anecdotal evidence, the best of which can be found, e.g., in Jones (1962) or Fenno (1973).

[25] Foreign aid to other nations, under the jurisdiction of the Foreign Relations Committee, seems to be a (political) substitute for military spending programs. The evidence suggests that those congressmen who support this aid tend to be against defense spending, and vice versa.

TABLE 3

COMMITTEE MEMBERS ARE PREFERENCE OUTLIERS RELATIVE TO THE FULL HOUSE (1978)

	Full House Mean[a]	Committee Mean	N[b]	t-Statistic
1. Armed Services: NSI	59.1	76.8	38	17.87**
2. International Relations:				
NSI	61.7	50.2	37	11.42**
ADA[c]	37.5	46.5	37	10.23**
t-test for mean NSI difference between Armed Services and International Relations				19.40**
3. International Relations: International Economic Policy and Trade Subcommittee:				
NSI	60.8	51.3	7	4.24**
ADA	38.1	45.0	7	3.50**
4. Interstate Commerce: Consumer Protection and Finance Subcommittee:				
ADA	37.9	55.5	8	9.57**
5. Education and Labor: Economic Opportunity Subcommittee: COPE	50.4	60.0	4	3.33**
6. Environmental subcommittees: LCV[d]	46.7	58.3	28	2.08*

[a] All non–committee members.
[b] Committee or subcommittee size.
[c] Vote ratings of the Americans for Democratic Action.
[d] Includes two of the major subcommittees with oversight responsibility for the Environmental Protection Agency, the Subcommittee on Energy and the Environment (Interior Committee), and Subcommittee on Health and the Environment (Commerce Committee). LCV is the League of Conservation Voter scores for 1977.
* Significant at the .05 level.
** Significant at the .01 level.

composed of legislators with considerably higher support for policies within their jurisdiction. This pattern is precisely that expected by the view that committees institutionalize trades over influence so as to give their members greater control over policies with their jurisdiction.

C. *Committee Policy Benefits*

Do committee members receive a disproportionate share of the benefits from their committees? The evidence on preferences provides indirect support for this since committees disproportionately attract representatives seeking to provide their constituents with benefits.

Here we summarize some direct evidence in favor of this proposition.[26]

1. Ferejohn (1974*a*) in his now-classic study on the pork barrel tested a variety of hypotheses about committees. He showed that the number of new projects started in each state is a function of committee membership. His estimations imply, for example, that each member on the Public Works Committee yields an additional 0.63 new projects for his state. Further, each 10 years of service by representatives from a state yields approximately an additional project. Similar results are obtained regarding more than two dozen related hypotheses.

2. Arnold (1979) studied three areas (military base closings, water and sewage grants, and model cities grants) and provides results similar to Ferejohn's about the pattern of benefits.[27] His contingency tables provide unambiguous evidence; we reproduce two.

Table 4, part A, shows the frequency of acceptance of an application for a water and sewage grant, depending on a congressman's position in the committee system: is he a member of the relevant appropriations subcommittee? the relevant authorization committee (Banking and Currency)? of neither? The table shows that members of the relevant committees systematically fare better than nonmembers. Those on neither committee have a probability of acceptance of .176. In contrast, members of the Appropriations Subcommittee have a probability of acceptance of .313 (80 percent larger), and members of the authorizing committee have a probability of acceptance of .281 (60 percent larger). The differences are significant at the .001 level. Part B of the table shows that the same pattern holds for model cities project selection. For these projects, congressmen who are on neither relevant committee have a probability of selection of .29. The probability of acceptance for members of the Banking and Currency Subcommittee, .62, is more than double that for nonmembers; the probability for members of the Appropriations Subcommittee, .86, is nearly triple.

3. Several recent studies by economists used similar methodologies and yielded similar evidence. Malone (1982), studying defense expen-

[26] Unfortunately, by far the biggest effort to support this proposition in the political science literature comprises anecdotal or descriptive material rather than systematic data analysis. While this literature supports our proposition, it is no substitute for systematic empirical investigation.

[27] We do not reproduce his probit estimates here (nor discuss his concerns about whether congressmen manipulate bureaucrats or bureaucrats manipulate congressmen). These estimates suffer from significant econometric problems and are therefore of questionable value. Simultaneity, much like that found in estimating supply and demand equations, plagues his design.

TABLE 4

FREQUENCY OF ACCEPTANCE OF APPLICATIONS

Application Represented	Applications Accepted	Not Accepted	Total Decisions	Probability of Acceptance
	A. Water and Sewage Grant Selection (1970)			
Subcommittee of Appropriations Committee	21	46	67	.313
Banking and Currency Committee	27	69	96	.281
Neither committee	261	1,223	1,484	.176
Total	309	1,338	1,647	
	B. Model Cities Project Selection			
Subcommittee of Appropriations Committee	6	1	7	.86
Banking and Currency Committee	5	3	8	.62
Neither committee	38	78	116	.29
Total	49	82	131	

SOURCE.—Arnold (1979, pp. 139, 180).
NOTE.—For pt. A, $\chi^2 = 13.80$ and significance level is .001. For pt. B, $\chi^2 = 10.81$ and significance level is .01.

ditures, showed that members of the Armed Services committees receive a statistically significant greater share of federal expenditures in this category, though Rundquist (1973) could find none. Faith, Leavens, and Tollison (1982) studied the geographic location of firms that are the target of antitrust suits brought by the Federal Trade Commission (FTC). They showed that firms located in districts represented on the FTC oversight subcommittees were systematically underrepresented in the set of suits brought by the commission. Cohen and Noll (1986), using an innovative methodology, derived similar results for federal R & D projects.

4. Weingast and Moran (1983) studied the influence of Congress on the distribution of cases chosen by the FTC under the various statutes it administers. They found, for the Senate, that all members possess some influence but that members of the relevant subcommittee possess more influence and that the subcommittee chairman possesses even more influence (see table 5). According to their estimates for textile cases (under the Fur, Wool, and Textile Labeling acts), a member of the subcommittee had nearly three times the effect of a nonmember while the chairman had 12 times the effect of a nonmember. Their results reveal a similar pattern for the other case types studied (credit cases, Robinson-Patman cases, and merger cases).

5. The pattern of campaign donations by firms provides additional

TABLE 5

CHANGE IN THE PROBABILITY OF OPENING A TEXTILE CASE WHEN A SENATOR'S ADA SCORE INCREASES 10 POINTS

Senator's Position	Change in Probability
Not on the subcommittee	.005
On the subcommittee but not chairman	.013
Subcommittee chairman	.060

SOURCE.—Weingast and Moran (1983).

evidence. A firm's decision to donate money to a congressional campaign must pass the same test as any other investment made by the firm; namely, the expected value of the return must exceed the dollars invested. When deciding among politicians, firms must focus on those congressmen with a marginal impact on their future profitability. If committee members have a disproportionate influence over policy choice in their area, then they should attract a disproportionate share of campaign contributions from firms affected by the committee's policy jurisdiction.

This prediction is clearly borne out in Munger's (1984) study. He estimated a probit model of the probability that a certain legislator receives a donation from a given firm. He showed that political action committees are systematically more likely to donate to members of committees that affect their firms: the probability that a committee member will receive a donation is .34 higher than that of a nonmember.

VI. Comparative Statics: Predictions and Evidence

In a simple market for votes, a small change in the relative composition of interest groups leads to a small change in the demand for votes. This, in turn, leads to a small change in the equilibrium pattern of exchange and hence in the distribution of policy costs and benefits. However, our argument about the demand for durable policies and the evolution of institutions to provide them implies that policies are partially insulated from small changes in member preferences. Because committees retain a veto over policy change, we must look to how these changes affect committee members. If the change in interest groups affects only legislators who are not members of the committee, then policy change is significantly less likely. But our model also leads to an important comparative statics prediction: a sufficient condition for policy change is that there is a substantial turnover in committee membership so that the new holders of committee property rights have preferences that differ from those of their predecessors (see Weingast 1981; Weingast and Moran 1983).

While comparative statics results are a primary tool of prediction and testing in economics, few studies of political economy have used this approach to test theories of politics. Nonetheless, there exists some evidence on the prediction noted above in the empirical literature. We cite these studies and then suggest further tests.

A. *Appropriations*

Ferejohn (1974*a*) again plays an important role here. During the 1950s and early 1960s, fiscal conservatives dominated the congressional appropriations process. Further, during this period, committee leaders had nearly absolute power of assignment of members to subcommittees. One way of enforcing fiscal restraint was to assign members of the Appropriations Committee to a subcommittee only if they had no stake in the subcommittee's jurisdiction. By the mid-1960s, however, this rule had gone by the wayside so that subcommittees came to be composed of members with a high stake in their jurisdiction. Ferejohn showed that, for the Public Works Subcommittee, this led to a statistically significant increase in appropriations.

B. *Regulatory Agencies*

A host of recent studies of regulatory agencies has shown that committee members have substantial influence over agencies within their jurisdiction (Barke and Riker [1982] on the Interstate Commerce Commission, Grier [1984] on the Fed, Moe [1985] on the National Labor Relations Board, and Weingast and Moran [1983] on the FTC). In nearly all cases, these statistical studies showed that, as committee preferences change, so too does agency policy. Large swings in committee preferences lead to large swings in policy.

Weingast and Moran (1983), for example, studied the recent policy change at the FTC. In 1979 and 1980, the commission's aggressive consumer activist policies were halted by Congress. While this action was hailed as Congress's finally catching a runaway, out-of-control bureaucracy, Weingast and Moran showed that nothing of the sort happened. Instead, the FTC had been under the influence of the relevant subcommittee all along. From the late 1960s through the mid to late 1970s, this subcommittee both favored and fostered aggressive consumerist policies. However, following the 1976 election, a nearly complete turnover in membership brought to power members with substantially different preferences. Weingast and Moran interpreted the 1979–80 episode as the new committee's simply reversing the policies of their predecessors rather than catching an uncontrollable bureaucracy. Their statistical tests support this interpretation.

VII. Discussion

Representatives of different constituencies have considerable incentives to exchange support so as to provide benefits to their supporters. Because the value of today's legislative bargains depends on actions taken in future legislative sessions, legislators also have incentives to devise institutions that provide today's bargains with durability. As in all exchange settings, the institutions that evolve to support the exchange reflect the specific pattern of transaction costs underlying the potential trades. For legislatures these include the possibility of contingencies too numerous (or costly) to specify in advance and private information. This gives rise to a host of institutions underpinning a set of property rights loosely referred to as the committee system. We showed that these institutions lower the risk of ex post opportunistic behavior that would plague explicit exchanges of votes. The legislative institutions therefore lower the agency costs associated with exchange.

In addition we showed why this set of institutions is superior to a market exchange mechanism. Instead of trading votes, legislators exchange special rights affording the holder of these rights additional influence over well-defined policy jurisdictions. This influence stems from the property rights established over the agenda mechanisms, that is, the means by which alternatives arise for votes. The extra influence over particular policies institutionalizes a specific pattern of trades. When the holders of seats on committees are precisely those individuals who would bid for votes on these issues in a market for votes, policy choice under the committee system parallels that under a more explicit exchange system. Because the exchange is institutionalized, it need not be renegotiated each new legislative session, and it is subject to fewer enforcement problems.

The committee system also influences coalition formation. Committee agenda power implies that successful coalitions in the area of the committee's jurisdiction must include the committee. This rules out, for example, policies that benefit solely a coalition of members off this committee, and this holds even if this coalition contains a majority of the entire legislature. Unless a coalition of non–committee members is prepared to include or "buy out" the committee, veto power allows the committee to block access of this coalition to the floor.

We also showed that policy bargains, and hence coalitions, are more durable under the committee system. Thus the decision to enter into such an agreement is much like entering a long-term contract, and legislators will take this into account. This implies that coalitions will not always respond to small changes in political circumstances as they would under a spotlike market exchange system. Rather they tend to respond only to large shifts or major political realignments. Committee veto power combines with the property right system over seats to play an important role in maintaining a political coalition—and a particular policy—for long periods. Policy in a particular area may remain stable if committee membership is relatively stable, and this can hold even with major changes in the preferences of members off the committee. The ability to veto the proposals of others is a subtle yet powerful tool used by committees to influence policy in their jurisdiction (Weingast and Moran 1983; Shepsle and Weingast 1987).

This argument raises some interesting parallels and contrasts with those provided for vertical integration in market settings. In both cases, institutions are designed to prevent similar forms of incentive problems, for example, ex post opportunism. However, it appears that the source of these problems differs. For the case of vertical integration, it is relation-specific assets. For the legislature, however, incentive problems arise because there is no underlying medium of exchange so that trading votes requires future reliance and hence the opportunities for reneging (see n. 10). Moreover, as Ferejohn (1974*b*) has shown, it is not clear whether one can exist, given the peculiar externalities associated with vote trading.

We have pursued in this paper only one explanation for enforcing trades. It is useful, therefore, to discuss a number of potential alternatives, though a full-scale empirical investigation is beyond the scope of this paper. The first alternative is that ex post opportunism either is negligible or is handled in some other way, thereby allowing exchange to take place through trading. According to this view, the existence of committees is epiphenomenal, perhaps representing some formal (though unimportant) recognition of those legislators who have in fact "bought" influence over particular issues. An empirical test between this explanation and our model might focus on the responsiveness of policy choice to members of the committee. In an explicit exchange setting, large changes in the preferences of members off the committee should lead to changes in policy. Under the legislative committee model, committee veto rights imply that policy is more insulated from changes of this type, and hence we should observe policies to be less responsive.

A second competing explanation is perhaps more interesting. Parties, ruled out by assumption in our model, offer an obvious alternative for institutionalizing and enforcing trades. The historical evidence for the U.S. Congress suggests that strong parties and strong committees, as institutional underpinnings of legislative exchange, are substitutes. When parties were more powerful (e.g., at the turn of the century), committees, though important, did not have such clear-cut rights as in modern times. Seniority, for example, was regularly violated by party leadership in allocating the leadership positions within committees. Importantly, virtually every institutional change during this century that has made committee rights stronger has come at the expense of parties and centralized leadership.

This suggests a natural extension of our approach to the case of party government (which includes the British Parliament in addition to the House of Representatives of the past). Strong parties are characterized by control over important resources such as entry into the competition for individual seats and the positions of power within the legislature (e.g., the ministerial positions in Britain), and they wield considerable influence over the distribution of legislative (read: electorally useful) benefits. Parties, like firms, can build types of reputations different from those of the individuals who make them up (see, e.g., Kreps 1984). To the extent that they are able to influence the behavior of their members through distribution of resources, parties potentially provide an alternative means of enforcing agreements. We hope to extend our approach in the future to yield results about the institutions underpinning legislative exchange in this context.[28] An important issue of this research concerns the circumstances favoring the survival of one mechanism over the other.

One limitation of our analysis is that, while we argue that legislative rules mitigate certain contractual problems, we do not explain how the rules themselves survive. Since majorities may alter the rules, what prevents the breakdown of cooperation that takes on a slightly different form? In circumstances in which reneging, say, would occur without rules, what prevents individuals from first voting to change the rules and then reneging? An extensive investigation of this issue is beyond the scope of this paper. However, there appear a variety of circumstances under which the rules will survive a breakdown whereas cooperation without rules would not. For example, if many different policy jurisdictions are governed by the same set of rules, then a single set of rules may link behavior in one area with that in another. Hence incentives to renege in one area do not automatically result in corresponding incentives to change rules that govern many areas.[29] Since it clearly touches on issues that hold for a large variety of organizations, this question is worthy of a separate investigation.

[28] For an interesting beginning on this problem, see Leibowitz and Tollison (1980).

[29] As a second set of circumstances, we single out the notion of leadership explored by Calvert (1986) in his extension of the Kreps and Wilson (1982) model to legislatures. Calvert studied circumstances in which a particular individual is given resources by other individuals. With these resources, he then, e.g., polices the behavior of his followers. In principle, this mechanism might be used to prevent the breakdown of cooperation in certain circumstances and therefore be valuable ex ante to members.

The empirical evidence supports four implications that follow from our model of legislative institutions but do not follow from a simple market exchange mechanism. First, committees are composed of "high demanders," that is, individuals with greater than average interest in the committee's policy jurisdiction. Second, the committee assignment mechanism operates as a bidding mechanism that assigns individuals to those committees they value most highly. Third, committee members gain a disproportionate share of the benefits from their policy area. This appears to hold across widely differing policy jurisdictions. Fourth, there exists important evidence supporting a comparative statics prediction of the model, namely, that as the interests represented on the committee change, so too will policy, with the interests of non–committee members held constant. Evidence supporting this proposition exists in several regulatory areas; future tests will reveal the robustness of the results.

In sum, the institutions of Congress appear remarkably suited to legislators' reelection goals. Their specific form appears to have evolved to reduce problems that also arise in market exchange, namely, problems of measurement, moral hazard, and opportunism.

References

Alchian, Armen, and Demsetz, Harold. "Production, Information Costs, and Economic Organization." *A.E.R.* 62 (December 1972): 777–95.

Arnold, R. Douglas. *Congress and the Bureaucracy: A Theory of Influence*. New Haven, Conn.: Yale Univ. Press, 1979.

Axelrod, Robert M. *The Evolution of Cooperation*. New York: Basic Books, 1984.

Barke, Richard P., and Riker, William H. "A Political Theory of Regulation with Some Observations on Railway Abandonments." *Public Choice* 39, no. 1 (1982): 73–106.

Barzel, Yoram. "Measurement Cost and the Organization of Markets." *J. Law and Econ.* 25 (April 1982): 27–48.

Becker, Gary S. "A Theory of Competition among Pressure Groups for Political Influence." *Q.J.E.* 98 (August 1983): 371–400.

Buchanan, James M., and Tullock, Gordon. *The Calculus of Consent: Logical Foundations of Constitutional Democracy*. Ann Arbor: Univ. Michigan Press, 1962.

Calvert, Randall. "Efficiency and Equilibrium in an Infinite-Horizon Reciprocity Game." Mimeographed. St. Louis: Washington Univ., 1985.

———. "The Role of Reputation and Legislative Leadership." Mimeographed. St. Louis: Washington Univ., 1986.

Cheung, Steven N. S. "The Contractual Nature of the Firm." *J. Law and Econ.* 26 (April 1983): 1–21.

Coase, Ronald H. "The Nature of the Firm." *Economica* 4 (November 1937): 386–405.

Cohen, Linda R., and Noll, Roger G. "Political-Economy of Government Sponsored R & D." Mimeographed. Stanford, Calif.: Stanford Univ., 1986.

Demsetz, Harold, and Lehn, Kenneth. "The Structure of Corporate Ownership: Causes and Consequences." *J.P.E.* 93 (December 1985): 1155–77.

Denzau, Arthur T., and Munger, Michael C. "Legislators and Interest Groups: How Unorganized Interests Get Represented." *American Polit. Sci. Rev.* 80 (March 1986): 89–106.

Faith, Roger L.; Leavens, Donald R.; and Tollison, Robert D. "Antitrust Pork Barrel." *J. Law and Econ.* 25 (October 1982): 329–42.

Fama, Eugene F. "Agency Problems and the Theory of the Firm." *J.P.E.* 88 (April 1980): 288–307.

Fama, Eugene F., and Jensen, Michael C. "Separation of Ownership and Control." *J. Law and Econ.* 26 (June 1983): 301–25.

Fenno, Richard F. *Congressmen in Committees.* Boston: Little, Brown, 1973.

Ferejohn, John A. *Pork Barrel Politics: Rivers and Harbors Legislation, 1947–1968.* Stanford, Calif.: Stanford Univ. Press, 1974. (*a*)

———. "Sour Notes on the Theory of Vote Trading." Social Science Working Paper. Pasadena: California Inst. Tech., 1974. (*b*)

———. "Logrolling in an Institutional Context: A Case Study of Food Stamp Legislation." In *Congress and Policy Change,* edited by Gerald C. Wright, Jr., Leroy N. Rieselbach, and Lawrence C. Dodd. New York: Agathon, 1986.

Fiorina, Morris P. "Congressional Control of the Bureaucracy." In *Congress Reconsidered,* 2d ed., edited by Lawrence C. Dodd and Bruce I. Oppenheimer. Washington: Congressional Quarterly Press, 1981. (*a*)

———. *Retrospective Voting in American National Elections.* New Haven, Conn.: Yale Univ. Press, 1981. (*b*)

Fromm, Gary, ed. *Studies in Public Regulation.* Cambridge, Mass.: MIT Press, 1981.

Gilligan, Thomas W. "The Competition Effects of Resale Price Maintenance." *Rand J. Econ.* 17 (Winter 1986): 544–56.

Goldberg, Victor P. "Regulation and Administered Contracts." *Bell J. Econ.* 7 (Autumn 1976): 426–48.

Grier, Kevin. "Congressional Preferences and Fed Policy: A Principal Agent Approach." Mimeographed. St. Louis: Washington Univ., Center Study American Bus., 1984.

Grossman, Sanford J., and Hart, Oliver D. "The Costs and Benefits of Ownership: A Theory of Vertical and Lateral Integration." *J.P.E.* 94 (August 1986): 691–719.

Holmstrom, Bengt. "Moral Hazard and Observability." *Bell J. Econ.* 10 (Spring 1979): 74–91.

Jensen, Michael C. "Organization Theory and Methodology." *Accounting Rev.* 58 (April 1983): 319–39.

Jensen, Michael C., and Meckling, William H. "Theory of the Firm: Managerial Behavior, Agency Costs and Ownership Structure." *J. Financial Econ.* 3 (October 1976): 305–60.

Jones, Charles O. "The Role of the Congressional Subcommittee." *Midwest J. Polit. Sci.* 6 (November 1962): 327–44.

Joskow, Paul L. "Vertical Integration and Long-Term Contracts: The Case of Coal-burning Electric Generating Plants." *J. Law, Econ. and Organization* 1 (Fall 1985): 33–80.

Kalt, Joseph P., and Zupan, Mark A. "Capture and Ideology in the Economic Theory of Politics." *A.E.R.* 74 (June 1984): 279–300.

Kau, James B., and Rubin, Paul H. "Self-Interest, Ideology, and Logrolling in Congressional Voting." *J. Law and Econ.* 22 (October 1979): 365–84.

Klein, Benjamin; Crawford, Robert G.; and Alchian, Armen A. "Vertical Integration, Appropriable Rents, and the Competitive Contracting Process." *J. Law and Econ.* 21 (October 1978): 297–326.

Klein, Benjamin, and Leffler, Keith. "Role of Market Forces in Assuring Contractual Performance." *J.P.E.* 89 (August 1981): 615–41.

Koford, Kenneth J. "Centralized Vote-trading." *Public Choice* 39, no. 2 (1982): 245–68.

Kreps, David M. "Corporate Culture." Mimeographed. Stanford, Calif.: Stanford Univ., Grad. School Bus., 1984.

Kreps, David M., and Wilson, Robert. "Reputation and Imperfect Information." *J. Econ. Theory* 27 (August 1982): 253–79.

Leibowitz, Arleen, and Tollison, Robert D. "A Theory of Legislative Organization: Making the Most of Your Majority." *Q.J.E.* 94 (March 1980): 261–77.

McKelvey, Richard D. "Intransitivities in Multidimensional Voting: Models and Some Implications for Agenda Control." *J. Econ. Theory* 12 (June 1976): 472–82.

———. "General Conditions for Global Intransitivities in Formal Voting Models." *Econometrica* 47 (September 1979): 1085–1112.

Malone, Michael T. "The Political Determinants of the Flow of Federal Funds to States and the Impact of Federal Funds on Business Location Decisions." Paper presented at the Liberty Fund Symposium series, Government Control of Entrepreneurial Decisions, Indianapolis, November 1982.

Mayhew, David R. *Party Loyalty among Congressmen: The Difference between Democrats and Republicans, 1947–1962*. Cambridge, Mass.: Harvard Univ. Press, 1966.

———. *Congress: The Electoral Connection*. New Haven, Conn.: Yale Univ. Press, 1974.

Milgrom, Paul, and Roberts, John. "Bargaining and Influence Costs and the Organization of Economic Activity." Research Paper no. 934. Stanford, Calif.: Stanford Univ., Grad. School Bus., 1987.

Miller, Gary J., and Moe, Terry M. "The Positive Theory of Hierarchies." In *Political Science: The Science of Politics*, edited by Herbert F. Weisberg. New York: Agathon, 1986.

Moe, Terry M. "The New Economics of Organization." *American J. Polit. Sci.* 28 (November 1984): 739–77.

———. "Control and Feedback in Economic Regulation: The Case of the NLRB." *American Polit. Sci. Rev.* 79 (December 1985): 1094–1116.

Munger, Michael C. "Neoinstitutional Response to Demand Oriented Models of Public Policy: Theory and Evidence." Mimeographed. St. Louis: Washington Univ., 1984.

North, Douglass C. *Structure and Change in Economic History*. New York: Norton, 1981.

Peltzman, Sam. "Toward a More General Theory of Regulation." *J. Law and Econ.* 19 (August 1976): 211–40.

———. "Constituent Interest and Congressional Voting." *J. Law and Econ.* 27 (April 1984): 191–210.

Polsby, Nelson W. *Congress and the Presidency*. 4th ed. Englewood Cliffs, N.J.: Prentice-Hall, 1984.

Roberts, John. "Battles for Market Share." Mimeographed. Stanford, Calif.: Stanford Univ., Grad. School Bus., 1986.

Rubin, Paul H. "The Theory of the Firm and the Structure of the Franchise Contract." *J. Law and Econ.* 21 (April 1978): 223–33.

Rundquist, Barry. "Congressional Influence on the Distribution of Prime Military Contracts." Ph.D. dissertation, Stanford Univ., 1973.

Schwartz, Thomas. "The Universal-Instability Theorem." *Public Choice* 37, no. 3 (1981): 487–501.

Shepsle, Kenneth A. "Congressional Committee Assignments: An Optimization Model with Institutional Constraints." *Public Choice* 22 (Summer 1975): 55–78.

———. *The Giant Jigsaw Puzzle: Democratic Committee Assignments in the Modern House*. Chicago: Univ. Chicago Press, 1978.

Shepsle, Kenneth A., and Weingast, Barry R. "Structure-induced Equilibrium and Legislative Choice." *Public Choice* 37, no. 3 (1981): 503–19.

———. "When Do Rules of Procedure Matter?" *J. Politics* 46 (February 1984): 206–21.

———. "The Institutional Foundations of Committee Power." *American Polit. Sci. Rev.* 81 (March 1987): 85–104.

Telser, Lester G. "A Theory of Self-enforcing Agreements." *J. Bus.* 53 (January 1980): 27–44.

Tirole, Jean. "Hierarchies and Bureaucracies: On the Role of Collusion in Organizations." *J. Law, Econ. and Organization* 2, no. 2 (1986): 181–214.

Tullock, Gordon. *Towards a Mathematics of Politics*. Ann Arbor: Univ. Michigan Press, 1967.

———. "Why So Much Stability?" *Public Choice* 37, no. 2 (1981): 189–202.

Weingast, Barry R. "Regulation, Reregulation, and Deregulation: The Political Foundations of Agency Clientele Relations." *Law and Contemporary Problems* 44 (Winter 1981): 147–77.

———. "The Congressional-Bureaucratic System: A Principal-Agent Perspective (with Application to the SEC)." *Public Choice* 44, no. 1 (1984): 147–91.

Weingast, Barry R., and Moran, Mark J. "Bureaucratic Discretion or Legislative Control? Regulatory Policymaking by the Federal Trade Commission." *J.P.E.* 91 (October 1983): 765–800.

Williamson, Oliver E. *Markets and Hierarchies: Analysis and Antitrust Implications*. New York: Free Press, 1975.

———. *Economic Institutions of Capitalism: Firms, Markets, Relational Contracting*. New York: Free Press, 1985.

Wilson, Robert. "An Axiomatic Model of Logrolling." *A.E.R.* 59 (June 1969): 331–41.

A Rational Choice Theory of Supreme Court Statutory Decisions with Applications to the *State Farm* and *Grove City* Cases

RAFAEL GELY AND PABLO T. SPILLER
University of Illinois

1. INTRODUCTION

The nature and process of the main regulatory changes of the last decade represent a challenge for political economists. Not only were major deregulatory processes undertaken without the active support of the regulated industries, but the process itself by which deregulation and regulation developed through the 1970s and 1980s is puzzling. While Congress legislated regulatory and deregulatory changes in some areas (e.g., airlines, trucking, cable, oil), in many other areas regulation and deregulation were promoted and carried out by agencies and the courts, without much active legislative change (e.g., telecommunications, pollution control).

The seeming inaction of Congress in the face of rapid regulatory changes,

The authors would like to thank John Ferejohn, Jerry Mashaw, Eric Rasmusen, Roberta Romano, Tom Romer, Howard Rosenthal, Stephen Ross, Kenneth Shepsle, Harold Spaeth, Barry Weingast, Oliver Williamson, several anonymous referees, and participants at seminars at the Hoover Institution, at the Universities of Chicago, Illinois, Southern California, and California, Berkeley, for helpful comments and suggestions. Fellowship support from the Institute for Government and Public Affairs at the University of Illinois, through their Ameritech Research Fellowship Program, and from the Lilly Endowment, through the Center for the Study of the Economy and the State at the University of Chicago, to Spiller is gratefully acknowledged. Spiller also acknowledges support from the National Science Foundation, under grant SES-9008140. This paper combines two previously separated working papers by Gely and Spiller entitled "A Rational Choice Theory of the Supreme Court," and "An Economic Theory of Supreme Court Statutory Decisions: The *State Farm* and *Grove City* Cases," and parts of a working paper by Spiller entitled "Agency Discretion under Judicial Review." These working papers are available from the authors.

Journal of Law, Economics, and Organization vol. 6, no. 2 Fall 1990
 ISSN 8756-6222

introduced by regulatory agencies and the courts, has been the subject of much recent research (see, e.g., McCubbins, Noll, and Weingast, 1987, 1989; Weingast, 1981, 1984; Weingast and Moran; Ferejohn and Shipan; McCubbins and Schwartz). This research has emphasized the agency relationship among the regulatory or administrative agencies, Congress, and the President. The role of the courts, however, has been mostly unexplored in this literature, except for the work of McCubbins, Noll, and Weingast (1987, 1989) and Marks. The former develop a framework where the courts are seen as indirect agents of Congress, in charge of supporting the interests of the coalition that enacted the original legislation. Marks, on the other hand, models the impact of judicial decisions on regulatory legislation. His main insight, which we borrow heavily from, is that the bicameral nature of Congress increases the set of Court decisions that are invulnerable to legislative action. In his framework, however, the Court is unconcerned with the impact of its decisions on the legislative process. Neither Marks nor McCubbins, Noll, and Weingast (1987, 1989) consider, and explore the implications of, the conditions for the justices to behave in the way the models stipulate.

The role of the Supreme Court in the design of public policy has, on the other hand, attracted much academic attention. The emphasis, however, has been basically normative. Particular attention has been given to the normative properties of different institutional arrangements—for example, whether the Supreme Court should follow a restrained or activist policy.[1] Whether any of those institutional arrangements would actually be carried out by self-interested agents, again, has not been analyzed.

In this article we follow the recent developments of the modern theory of administrative agencies, by developing a rational choice theory of the Supreme Court. Our framework combines two of the main characteristics of this literature: namely, the rational choice modeling strategy with the notion that institutions matter in the design of public policy. We differ basically by modeling the Supreme Court as a self-interested, ideologically motivated institution, making its decisions subject not to the traditional legal rules of precedent, but to the constraints arising from the political interests of other institutions of government—namely, Congress and the President.[2]

1. There has been a long-standing debate about whether the Court must follow an "activist" or "restrained" path. For recent surveys of the different approaches to the analysis of the Supreme Court, see Rohde and Spaeth, Halpern and Lamb, and Wasby. Among the classic positive approaches to the Supreme Court is that of Dahl, who claims that, because of their recruitment, the justices are a reflection of the electorate, and they play a "legitimizing" role. Dahl's hypothesis was later expanded by Funston to reconcile short-term disagreements between the Court and Congress. An alternative view of the Supreme Court is provided in Adamany, who claims that the Court constitutes a force for instability.

2. Our Supreme Court resembles, then, in many respects the description of an "activist" court. In this sense, our Court also resembles the view of the Court held by critical legal scholars. Our approach, however, is radically different from theirs, as we develop the positive implications of such a behavioral assumption, rather than dealing with normative behavioral alternatives, not rooted in a microanalytic framework.

While we do not claim that this is the most realistic description of the actual workings of the Supreme Court, our model provides a simple positive framework that is rich enough to analyze and forecast changes over time in the behavior of the Court and in the determinants of public policy. Furthermore, many of the implications of the model are consistent with much of the current political wisdom on the role of the different political institutions, and are also empirically refutable.

We apply this approach to the analysis of two recent Supreme Court statutory decisions, the *State Farm* and *Grove City* decisions. We show that both Supreme Court decisions can be understood as the Court reacting strategically to changes in the relevant political constraints reflecting changes in both Congress and the Presidency, and not necessarily to legal precedent or to Congressional intent. Also, even though these two decisions can be seen as favoring different political tendencies, they are both consistent with a self-interested but politically moderate Supreme Court. While our analysis of these two Supreme Court decisions does not constitute an empirical test of our theory, it shows its potential usefulness to explain and forecast Supreme Court decisions.

While we argue in this article that the behavior of the Court can be understood as that of a self-interested, politically motivated actor, the justices' calculus differs from that of members of Congress. Unlike members of Congress, the Court does not necessarily have a relevant constituency whose interests it needs to consider in rendering its opinions.[3] On the other hand, the Supreme Court decisions are not taken in a political vacuum. The ability of other political actors to take actions to reverse the Supreme Court decisions is what constrains the scope and power of the Court.

While constitutional limits are important,[4] we focus here on the constraints on the Court's interpretation of statutes that result from the institutional structure of government (e.g., Congressional jurisdictional rules, the committee system, bicameralism, the President's veto power).[5]

While simple, our framework has several implications that could, in principle, be subject to empirical testing.[6] First, in our framework the Supreme Court "reads election results," as, even without changes in its composition,

3. Unlike members of Congress, or the President, who are directly elected in popular elections, the Supreme Court justices are not subject to the direct impact of electoral forces. Furthermore, interest groups do not have the same direct impact in the Court as they have in Congress. Their role in the judicial process is limited to their participation as litigants in cases where they might be directly involved, or, to the filing of "amicus briefs," in cases in which they might have interests at stake.

4. See, for example, Nowak, Rotunda, and Young, and Wasby.

5. Although these institutional arrangements have been studied within the Congressional context (e.g., Shepsle and Weingast, 1981, 1982; Weingast and Moran), few attempts have been made to analyze their effects on Supreme Court decisions. See, however, Marks, who analyzes the effect of Congress on the Supreme Court's decisions.

6. See Spiller and Gely (1990a) for an attempt to test empirically this approach using labor-relations cases.

the Court is responsive to changes in the electorate.[7] The impact of the electorate or of interest groups, however, is indirect, and it is effected through changes in the constraints faced by the Court, following changes in the composition of Congress and in the Executive. Second, our model provides an explanation for the conventional wisdom that to a large extent the most important domestic role of the President is to appoint justices to the Court. In our framework, in the absence of veto power, the Supreme Court eliminates most of the President's discretionary power. With veto power, however, the President's views carry substantially more weight in determining the equilibrium. Third, the Supreme Court, in our framework, may increase or decrease the extent of policy stability. By reducing the power of the President, the Court may increase policy stability. On the other hand, the Court may also promote policy changes, as changes in the composition of Congress open the possibility for the Supreme Court to modify the status quo.[8,9] The Court, however, will follow a more "restrained" path in periods of Congressional stability. Thus, this model of the Supreme Court, which in principle resembles an activist Court, predicts that the Court will play different roles depending on the composition of (and changes in) Congress. The Supreme Court, however, whether "restrained" or "activist," will usually follow electoral changes. Yet an "activist" Court is nothing more than a Court siding with one of the houses of Congress, or with the President.

Finally, the model predicts that Congressional inaction will follow Supreme Court decisions, as these have already taken the composition of Congress into account.

2. THE THEORY

We develop here a simple model of the Supreme Court–Congress–President relationship. We focus on statutory rather than Constitutional issues. In Gely and Spiller (1989) we expand this framework to the analysis of Constitutional interpretations.

7. This result is similar to that advocated by many political and legal scholars (e.g., Funston; Handberg and Hill, 1980, 1984). We differ, however, in providing a microanalytic foundation to that claim. Furthermore, previous positive political analyses of the Supreme Court have focused, almost exclusively, on the impact of "realigning elections" on Supreme Court decisions, suggesting that those are the times when the Court and Congress will disagree (e.g., Handberg and Hill, 1984; and Adamany). Our result, however, is different. Various degrees of changes in the political system, not only drastic electoral results, may open opportunities for the Court to become more "active," and to affect the status quo.

8. See Marks for a related analysis.

9. It is usually claimed, for example, that, so as to retain its political capital, the Court will strategically retreat from politically untenable positions. See, for example, Nagel, Adamany, and Funston. While important in principle, we do not consider here reputational considerations in Supreme Court decisions.

Our analysis is based on several simplifying assumptions concerning our four players: the House, the Senate, the President, and the Supreme Court.

Our first set of assumptions concerns Congressional and Presidential preferences. We start by assuming a bicameral legislature, with both houses of Congress having well-defined and stable preferences over the policy space (R^2), represented by strictly convex indifference contours (in particular, without loss of generality, we will assume them to be circular). The modern theory of Congressional institutions (e.g., Weingast and Marshall; Shepsle and Weingast, 1987, 1989) suggests that committees have substantial power over the issues under their jurisdiction. In particular, because of their gatekeeping and veto power (i.e., they may block legislation from being introduced, as well as kill or modify legislation in conference), committee members' preferences may dominate issue-specific legislation. Furthermore, if committee membership is not random, but rather is the result of a self-selection process (see Shepsle, and Weingast and Marshall), then committees will tend to be relatively more homogeneous in their issue-specific preferences than their respective chambers as a whole. Thus, our assumption about legislators' preferences is equivalent to assuming full control of legislature outcomes by the relevant committees.[10] Seen in this light, these assumptions may not drastically violate reality.[11] We further assume that the President also has well-defined and stable preferences over the policy space, represented by circular isopreference contours.

Our second set of assumptions concerns the preferences of the Supreme Court. We assume that the Court has well-defined and stable preferences over the policy space, which is also represented by strictly convex indifference curves. The source of the Court's preferences, however, is different from that of the legislators. While legislators "vote their district,"[12] Supreme Court justices are not subject to reelection. We assume, then, that the Court's preferences are essentially ideologically based.[13] Our assumption about the Court's preferences is similar to assuming that the Court is a single individual. This is a strong assumption as we assume multidimensional issues and, hence, the median voter theorem may not readily be applied.[14] We

10. For an extension of this framework to alternative models of Congressional decision-making, see Spiller (1990a).

11. See, however, Gilligan and Krehbiel for a different view of committee composition.

12. See Fiorina, Kalt and Zupan, Kau and Rubin, and Peltzman, for empirical tests of this proposition.

13. While the justices' monetary well-being may be unrelated to the issue in question, it is nevertheless reasonable to assume that they may have strong views about the substance of the case. Furthermore, political considerations form part of the appointment process, making it important to consider the political preferences of the justices. Thus, it is reasonable to assume that Supreme Court justices have stable preferences over the policy space.

14. For a discussion of this issue as it applies to analyses of the Court, see Easterbrook. Spiller and Gely (1990b), however, provide conditions under which the median voter result can be applied to a multidimensional bargaining game between the Court and Congress.

furthermore assume that the Court dislikes being reversed by Congress.[15] Finally, we perform our analysis under two alternative assumptions about the nature of decisions the Court can take. Most of the ensuing analysis is carried on assuming that the Court is free to make its decisions on a continuum, rather than just on a yes-or-no basis.[16] At the end of this section we extend this framework by allowing the Court only to make decisions on a yes-or-no basis.

Thus, each actor has an ideal point in R^2. We call H,S,P, and SC the ideal points of the House, the Senate, the President, and the Supreme Court, respectively.

We focus on policy-making. Policy can be made by a specific legislative act, by the actions of an administrative agency (i.e., a Presidential policy),[17] or by a Supreme Court decision. The role of the Supreme Court is to review administrative agencies' decisions, and in this way to define the policy that would take effect unless it is reversed by a joint action of the House, the Senate, and the President. The role of the President in our model is twofold: on the one hand, to interpret and implement Congressional decisions through administrative agencies; and, on the other hand, if it can and so desires, to veto Congressional decisions.

2.1. Long-Run Political Equilibria Without Presidential Veto

There are many ways of modeling the interaction among Congress, the President, and the Court. Here we consider a simple bargaining game among the House, the Senate, the President, and the Supreme Court, assuming first that the President does not have the power to sustain a veto.

15. That lower-court justices dislike being reversed is quite understandable, as their reputation may be related to how often they are reversed by superior courts. In the case of the Supreme Court, a similar rationale can be provided in a more general framework than the one we present here, one where Court legitimacy and credibility are important factors that cannot be taken for granted. In other words, a model of political institutions is needed where their relative powers are the result of some underlying game. Here, for example, we assume that what the Court says is actually the law, unless it is reversed by Congress. This assumes, for example, that the police will enforce the law. If the Court's legitimacy and credibility were extremely poor, then it is possible that their decisions will carry no weight in public decision-making, and our model would have no predictive power.

16. There are several reasons why this assumption may be proper. First, the Court is free to interpret in its own way each case that comes to it. Second, the decision to grant *cert* allows the Court to choose that case that fits its preferred outcome. Finally, it can use *dicta* to call for a particular type of case. Note, however, that, as we show below, should the Court constraint itself to decide cases on a yes-or-no basis, then the equilibrium will change.

17. We assume that administrative agencies, whether independent regulatory agencies or part of the executive branch, are fully controlled by the President. This assumption, which is counter to much of the recent literature on regulatory agencies (e.g., McCubbins and Schwartz; Weingast and Moran; McCubbins, Noll, and Weingast, 1987; Spiller, 1990b), is taken exclusively to simplify the analysis. As the analysis below will show, this assumption does not materially change the results.

We model the game in three stages with the President moving first, the Court second, and Congress last.[18] In the first stage, the President, through the administrative agencies, implements a statute. This implementation is then subject to review by the Court, which in turn determines the legal status quo. The Court's decision may leave the administrative interpretation standing, or may replace it with an alternative interpretation. In the third stage, the House and the Senate bargain. If they reach an agreement different from the current status quo (i.e., the Court's decision), then that agreement becomes the law. If they fail to reach an agreement different from the Supreme Court's decision, then the latter becomes the equilibrium.

To solve this game we work backward by first describing the bargaining problem between the House and the Senate corresponding to the final stage in the game. We assume that the outcome to the bargaining between the House and the Senate is Pareto efficient, in the sense that no other alternative outcome could improve the utility of one of the houses of Congress without reducing the utility of the other.[19] In other words, we assume that the outcome to the bargaining between the two houses of Congress is on their contract curve, which we denominate by $C(H,S)$. We also assume individual rationality, so that the bargaining process cannot make any of the two houses worse off than the status quo.

Thus, only points in $C(H,S)$ are feasible equilibria. Consider a case where the Court's initial decision was outside $C(H,S)$. Since there is always a point in $C(H,S)$ preferred by both the House and the Senate to a given point outside it, bargaining between the two will bring about a point on $C(H,S)$. Thus, the equilibrium to this game has to reside in $C(H,S)$. The Supreme Court, then, cannot force a policy outcome outside $C(H,S)$, as the House and the Senate can always agree on a point on the contract curve that will make them better off.[20] Similarly, the President cannot administratively imple-

18. Alternative sequences could easily be conceived. Games where either the Court or the President move last, however, are less interesting as, given our preference assumptions, they would always be able to implement their ideal points. Since most statutory cases deal with the Court scrutinizing administrative agencies' decisions, our assumption of the administrative agency (i.e., the President) moving first is quite realistic. One could model a four-stage game, where, in the first stage, Congress passes a law, then the agency and the Court move sequentially, and, finally, the game ends with Congress moving again. This game, however, yields exactly the same outcome as the three-stage game described in the text.

19. This is not such an unreasonable solution. First, the Nash-bargaining solution concept is efficient. Furthermore, other bargaining structures have the Nash-bargaining solution as a limit case. See Binmore.

20. If the Supreme Court would try to impose its ideal point SC as the policy outcome, it will face a reversal by Congress. If the Supreme Court tries again, after being reversed, to impose its ideal point as the policy outcome, both houses of Congress will support a constitutional amendment to limit further the power of the Court. Observe, however, that if the Supreme Court's decision changes the status quo from one point to another, both in the contract curve, no constitutional conflict would arise because one house of Congress is necessarily made

ment any policy outside *C*(H,S), as either a Court or a Congressional decision will reverse it. Given that the outcome to the third stage is in *C*(H,S), the Court's decision will take into account the correspondence between the initial status quo and the final congressional bargaining outcome. Since any point outside *C*(H,S) will be reversed by Congress, and given that the Court prefers not to be reversed, it will make its decision such that the policy outcome is on the contract curve between the House and the Senate. In this way Congress cannot agree on a different outcome, and the Court's decision becomes the law. The Court then will pick a point on *C*(H,S) that maximizes its own utility. This point will become the equilibrium.

Observe, furthermore, that if only a single point in *C*(H,S) maximizes the Court's preferences, then the President has no power, as the Court's action is independent of the initial status quo set out by the agency.[21] That is, in the absence of a Presidential veto, long-run political equilibria are determined exclusively by the preferences of the House, the Senate, and the Supreme Court. The President's current preferences, on the other hand, are inconsequential in determining long-run policies. In the bargaining game among the Court, Congress, and the President, the latter's role can simply be seen as that of providing a policy offer. If the offer is in *C*(H,S) and is the one most preferred by the Court, then that offer becomes the equilibrium. If it is not in *C*(H,S) or is not the same as the reversal point chosen by the Court, it will be reversed, by either the Court or Congress. Thus, the presence of the Supreme Court eliminates the power of the Executive.

The President, however, would have played a substantial role in determining the final equilibrium outcome in the absence of Supreme Court scrutiny. In this case, the President, through control of the executive agencies, could determine which policy point in the contract curve is actually implemented—hence, choosing that point in *C*(H,S) that maximizes his or her own utility. See point E_1 in Figure 1A. In the absence of the Supreme Court, then, the Executive seems to have actual power. As discussed above, however, this result is reversed with the introduction of the Supreme Court.

The following Proposition summarizes the determinants of long-run political equilibria.

Proposition 1. Given the preferences and bargaining structure described above, and assuming that the President does not have veto power, a long-run

better off by the Supreme Court move. See Wasby and Casper for discussions of the constitutional implications of a "ruling–response–ruling–response" sequence. See also Henschen.

21. If circular congressional preferences are assumed, then *C*(H,S) is linear and, given our assumption about the convexity of the Court's preferences, there is indeed a single point in *C*(H,S) that maximizes the Court's preferences. If, however, *C*(H,S) is not linear, and there are multiple equilibria to this game, then the President, through the administrative agencies, could actually pick that equilibrium that maximizes his or her own utility.

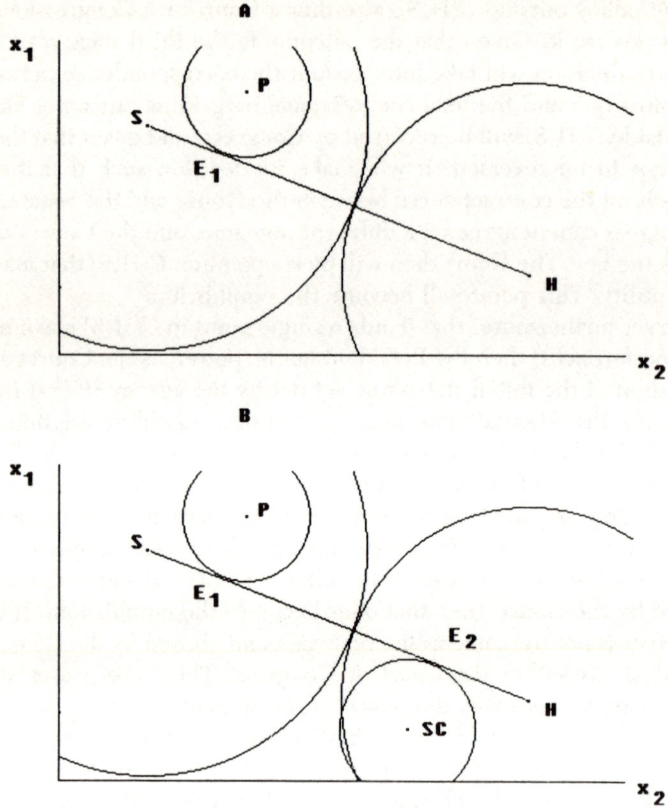

Figure 1. Political equilibrium (A) without and (B) with the Supreme Court. H: ideal point of the House; S: ideal point of the Senate; P: ideal point of the President; SC: ideal point of the Supreme Court; E_1: equilibrium without the Court; E_2: equilibrium with the Court.

political equilibrium is a feasible political outcome such that no alternative policy could make the Supreme Court better off.[22]

That is, a long-run equilibrium is that point in the contract curve between the House and the Senate that maximizes the utility of the Court (E_2 in Figure 1B).

To understand the equilibrium to the game, it may be useful to analyze an example. Consider a case where neither the Supreme Court nor the President may have substantial influence on legislative outcomes (i.e., when the

22. Formally, X^* represents a long-run political equilibrium, if $X^* = \{X|X = \text{Argmax } U^{SC}(x),$ s.t. $x \in C(\text{H,S})\}$.

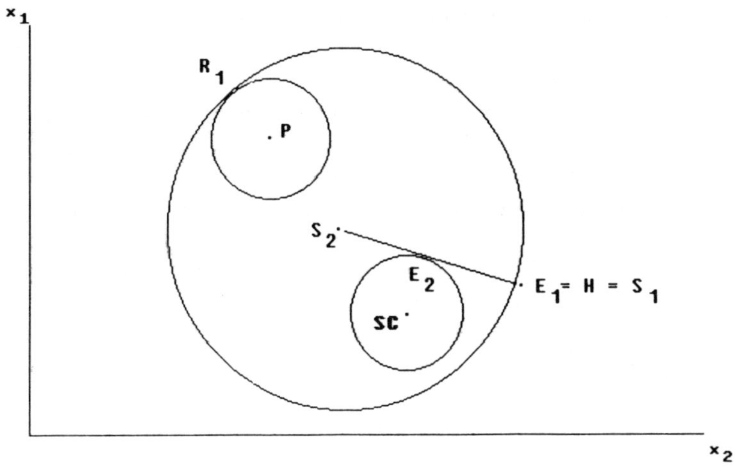

Figure 2. The Supreme Court and policy stability. H: ideal point of the House; S_1: initial ideal point of the Senate; S_2: subsequent ideal point of the Senate; P: ideal point of the President; SC: ideal point of the Supreme Court; R_1: President's most preferred point on the Senate's indifference curve through E; E_1: initial equilibrium; E_2: subsequent equilibrium.

ideal points of both the House and the Senate are the same). Then, the long-run equilibrium is represented by their ideal point (E_1), as in Figure 2. Figure 2 also depicts the positions of the President (P) and of the Supreme Court (SC). Assume now that, as the result of elections, the Senate changed drastically, with its new ideal point closer to that of the President. In the absence of any Supreme Court action, the House will block any new legislation that will change the status quo away from E_1. Thc President, however, could alter the implementation of the legislation. A policy point like R_1 leaves the Senate indifferent between the legal status quo (E_1) and the actual implementation (R_1). Since the President is better off at P, it could be undertaken by an executive agency with the Senate blocking legislation to restore the status quo.[23] The Senate, however, could offer the House to legislate S_2 as the legal standard. Such a policy would be preferred by the House to, say, P, or to any other point in the contract curve between the President and the Senate. Thus, S_2 becomes the legal standard. The President, then, shifted the equilibrium from E_1 to S_2. That is, in the absence of

23. The agency, however, may still face problems with Congress if the committee that oversees it does not support its policies. While the committee may not be able to force the agency to reverse its policy, it may try to influence the agency in different ways. Budgetary decisions as well as oversight activities may substantially disturb the agency's operations. See Spiller (1990b), and references therein.

the Supreme Court, the President could have a strong impact on public policy.

Let us now introduce the Supreme Court. In Figure 2, the position of the Supreme Court has improved following the elections, since there are points along the new contract curve between the House and the Senate that provide it with a utility level above that of E_1. Given the new location of the Senate, the Supreme Court's best choice is a point like E_2, on the new contract curve between the House and the Senate.

E_2, then, becomes the equilibrium independent of the ideal point of the President. The President, however, appoints justices to the court. To the extent that the President can appoint justices with preferences similar to his or her own, the President may have a lasting impact on public policy.[24]

2.2. Comparative Statics

The model just described can be used to understand changes in the position of the Supreme Court, even in the absence of changes in its composition. Proposition 1 implies that, in the absence of Presidential veto power, we do not have to consider the President's preferences for the purpose of analyzing the comparative statics properties of our model. Consider, for example, an initial long-run equilibrium, E_1, where the House and the Senate are as depicted in Figure 3. Let the results of an election imply a large change in the composition and preferences of the House. Since the Senate has not changed, any new legislative equilibrium (in the absence of any Supreme Court ruling) should reside in the new contact curve between the House and the Senate $[C(H_2,S_1)]$, and, in particular, in the bargaining area defined by E_1. The fact that the Senate did not change restricts the extent of policy change that can develop in the absence of Supreme Court intervention. Figure 3 shows, for example, that the new long-run equilibrium may well be outside that area, with the new long-run equilibrium, E_2, closer to the new ideal point of the House. Thus, the Supreme Court will usually follow the voters. This is, however, a qualified statement. Proposition 2, below, presents the conditions under which the Supreme Court follows the electorate.

Proposition 2. Assume that (a) preferences of the House, the Senate, and the Supreme Court are represented by circular indifference curves in R^2; (b) the initial equilibrium is in the interior of the contract curve, then moves in the electorate where either only one house moves or both houses move in

24. We do not analyze here the selection of justices to the Supreme Court. Our previous discussion, though, suggests that it is not in the interest of the Senate to ratify the President's selection without considering the preferences of the candidate at hand. A full analysis of this topic is left, however, for future research.

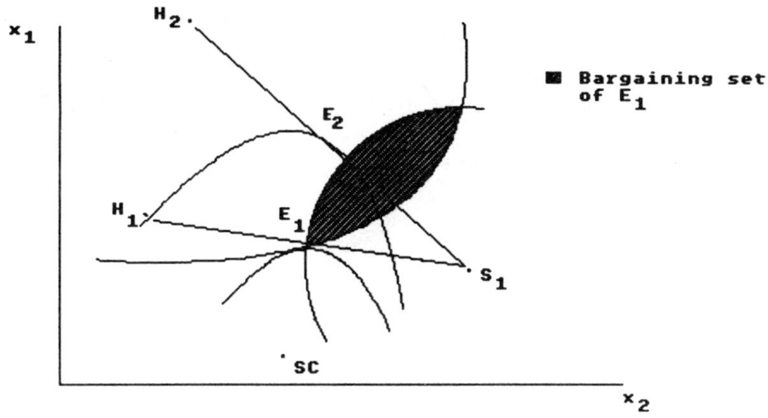

Figure 3. Comparative statics on the House's ideal point. SC: ideal point of the Supreme Court; H_1: initial ideal point of the House; H_2: subsequent ideal point of the House; S_1: ideal point of the Senate; E_1: initial equilibrium; E_2: subsequent equilibrium.

the same direction will imply changes in the long-run equilibrium which will follow the electorate, unless the change is in only one house; and (a) the dimension that changes is one that separates the House from the senate the most; and (b) the initial status quo implies a larger equilibrium value for that dimension than that of the ideal point of the Supreme Court.

Proposition 2, proved in the Appendix, shows[25] that the Supreme Court *does not* follow the electoral results only when (a) the electoral change implies a shift in, say, the House's ideal point along a dimension over which the House and the Senate were already far apart; *and* (b) the initial equilibrium value of that dimension exceeds the value for the ideal point of the Supreme Court.[26] Otherwise, the Supreme Court follows the electorate.

2.3. The Value of the Presidential Veto

The model discussed above can be expanded to account for a more active Presidential role. Here, we explore the implications to the bargaining game previously analyzed by providing the President with veto power.

Presidential veto power expands the area of feasible legislative outcomes. To model the ability of the President to veto legislation, we follow McCub-

25. The proposition assumes circular preferences, a common assumption in spatial political models.

26. The first condition relates to the steepness of the contract curve, while the second condition relates to the position of the Supreme Court's ideal point in relation to the initial contract curve.

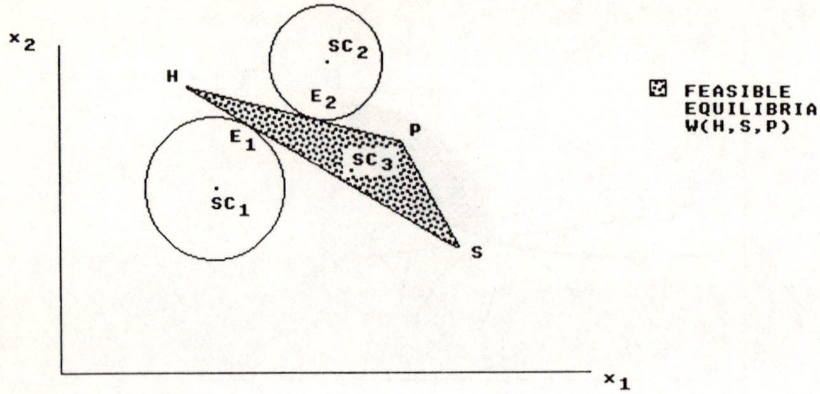

Figure 4. Feasible and long-run equilibria with Presidential veto power. H: ideal point of the House; S: ideal point of the Senate; SC: ideal points of the Supreme Court; P: ideal point of the President.

bins, Noll, and Weingast (1989) by assuming that any legislation must have the agreement of the House, the Senate, and the President.[27] In other words, any new legislation (and, in particular, any legislation to reverse the Court) cannot make any of the three actors worse off. Thus, we have to modify the third stage of the bargaining game in the previous section. Now it consists of bargaining among the House, the Senate, and the President.

We assume, again, that the outcome to the third-stage bargaining process is Pareto efficient and satisfies individual rationality constraints. Thus, all feasible legislative outcomes must reside (weakly) inside the area delineated by the three relevant contract curves [C(H,S), C(H,P), C(S,P); see Figure 4]. Call the set of feasible legislative outcomes W(H,S,P). The outcome of the three-sided bargaining game will depend on the relative bargaining positions of the three players. All we can say is that for a legislative, or administrative, action to constitute an equilibrium it must be in W(H,S,P).

The introduction of the Supreme Court provides a particular equilibrium to the game. As before, it is straightforward to see that a long-run political equilibrium is a feasible political equilibrium such that no alternative policy will make the Supreme Court better off,[28] and this is depicted in Figure 4.

27. Since we are modeling the House and the Senate as having well-specified preference orderings, we are focusing essentially on the preferences of the relevant committee with jurisdiction over the issues in question. We are, thus, not assuming that all, say, Senators have homogenous preferences. If that were the case, then Congress could overrule a Presidential veto. If Congress' preferences reflect only those of the relevant committees, they do not necessarily imply the existence of supermajorities in both houses and, hence, there is a role to the Presidential veto.

28. Formally, X^* is a long-run political equilibrium, if $X^* \in \{X | X = \text{Argmax } U^{SC}(x), \text{ s.t. } x \in W(\text{H,S,P})\}$.

Again, the initial Presidential decision in the first stage is inconsequential, as it would be reversed by the Court if it did not maximize the Court's preferences.

We can then state the following proposition.

Proposition 3. (a) If SC $\in$ *W*(H,S,P), then SC is a long-run political equilibrium.

(b) If SC $\notin$ *W*(H,S,P), then the long-run equilibrium is in the boundary of *W*(H,S,P).

The first result simply states that if the ideal point of the Supreme Court is located inside the set of feasible equilibria, then through judicial intervention, the Supreme Court will make its ideal point the long-run legislative outcome. If, however, SC is outside the set of feasible equilibria, then the long-run equilibrium is on a contract curve between any two of the three political actors.

To prove the proposition, consider first the case where the Supreme Court's ideal point is strictly inside *W*(H,S,P), as is SC_3 in Figure 4. Then by definition, any move away from SC_3 will make at least one of the three political actors worse off, and thus will be vetoed by either the President or one of the houses of Congress.

Consider now the case where the Supreme Court's ideal point is outside *W*(H,S,P). Were the Supreme Court to make a decision that falls outside *W*(·), further legislation will follow. Consider, instead a Supreme Court decision at the boundary of *W*(·). Any movement away from the point reflecting the Supreme Court decision will make at least one political actor worse off, and hence it will be vetoed. Since there is a point at the boundary of *W*(·) that makes the Supreme Court better off than at any other point strictly inside *W*(·), the long-run equilibrium must be at the boundary of *W*(·), proving the proposition.

With Proposition 3 we can analyze the power of the veto. There are two cases to consider: one where the Supreme Court decision is on the contract curve between the House and the Senate, and another where the decision is on a contract curve involving the President. Consider the former case first, represented by E_1 in Figure 4. In such a case, since the ideal points of the President and of the Supreme Court are on different sides of *C*(H,S), the Supreme Court decision will be on *C*(H,S). Thus, the veto power of the President is of no value to the President. The President cannot force a legislative outcome that moves the equilibrium outside of *C*(H,S), as such a move would imply that either the House or the Senate or both would be worse off.

Now consider a case where the ideal points of the President and of the Supreme Court are on the same side of *C*(H,S). In that case, the Supreme

Court's decision will be on a contract curve involving the President and, say, the House, represented by E_2 in Figure 4. The Senate would like to move the legislative outcome strictly inside $W(\cdot)$. To do so it has to align necessarily with the House, since aligning itself with the President is not enough to overrule a Supreme Court decision. However, any movement away from the contract curve between the House and the President that makes the House better off necessarily makes the President worse off. Thus, the President will support the Supreme Court and veto Congress' overrule of the Supreme Court decision. The power to veto, however, does not provide the President with the ability to further shift the political equilibrium closer to its ideal point. Would the President try to align with the Senate through the use of an administrative agency, the Supreme Court will reverse the President's action, and the House will veto any intent to overrule the Supreme Court action.

Thus, the power to veto provides some power to the President. In our framework, the executive power does not confer the President any particular advantage.[29] It is rather the ability to veto Congressional reversals of Supreme Court decisions that provides the power to affect the equilibrium. Thus, with Presidential veto, the Presidents' preferences matter in determining the long-run political equilibrium.

2.4. Comparative Statics

Proposition 3, then, can be used to analyze the comparative statics implications of our model. First, consider a case where the ideal point of the Supreme Court is inside $W(\cdot)$. In that case, marginal changes in the ideal points of the President, the House, or the Senate will have no impact on the legislative equilibrium and on the position of the Supreme Court. [Relatively large changes, however, that take the Supreme Court's ideal point outside $W(\cdot)$ will have an effect on the legislative equilibrium.]

Now let the ideal points of the President and of the Supreme Court be on different sides of the House–Senate contract curve. In that case, the long-run equilibrium is on $C(H,S)$, and changes in the position of the President will have no impact on the legislative equilibrium. Instead, only changes in the position of either the House or the Senate imply a change in the long-run political equilibrium.

Consider, finally, the case where the initial long-run equilibrium is on the contract curve involving the President and, say, the House (E_1 in Figure 5). Let the ideal point of the President change, say, away from the ideal point of the Supreme Court. The contract curve between the President and the House also moves away from the Supreme Court. From Proposition 3, the

29. Except in the case of multiple equilibria. See note 21.

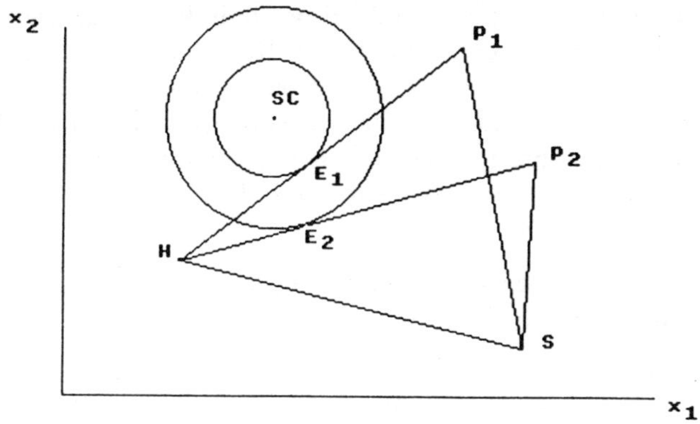

Figure 5. Comparative statics on the President's ideal point. H: ideal point of the House; S: ideal point of the Senate; SC: ideal point of the Supreme Court; P: ideal points of the President.

new long-run equilibrium has to reside on the new contract curve, with the Supreme Court following the electorate (see, however, Proposition 2 above). That is, the long-run equilibrium will follow the move in the preferences of the President.

2.5. Alternative Modes of Judicial Decisions

A basic assumption in the previous sections is that in interpreting legislative statutes, the Court is free to choose, in principle, any point in the policy space. In this framework, then, the equilibrium consists of a policy outcome such that it maximizes the Court's utility and is in the core of the bargaining game between the House, the Senate, and the President. Thus, the location in the policy space of the administrative agency is irrelevant, as is the nature of the initial legislation enacting the statute. Confronted with a case concerning a particular set of issues, the Court's choice is only a function of its current preferences and of the current political composition of Congress and the executive.

In this section we explore some of the implications of relaxing the assumption that the Court, in making its decisions, can choose any point in the policy space [for a more detailed analysis, see Spiller (1990c)]. In particular, we study the implications for agency discretion of the Court having the power only to reverse or sustain a prior agency decision. The Court, though, in making its decision behaves strategically, considering its impact on the legislative process and on the subsequent policy outcome.

The main result is that while both agency preferences and the location of the initial status quo are important in determining the equilibrium, the Court's preferences are crucial in explaining the behavior of agencies.

Agency discretion, now, is constrained not only by Congressional preferences, but by the preferences of the Court. Nevertheless, the main thrust of the previous sections remains: first, the Court will follow election results as they change the set of feasible legislative decisions; and, second, the Court, while behaving strategically, is not able to impose its preferences, but rather is constrained by the remaining institutions of government.

2.6. A Model of Agency Discretion under Judicial Review without Presidential Veto

In the previous sections we have assumed that the President has full control over the administrative agencies. We showed, nevertheless, that if the Court can make decisions on a continuum, then the President has no executive power. That is, Presidential control over the agency does not grant the President any power to affect the long-run equilibrium. In this section we relax both the assumption of full Presidential control over the agency as well as the assumption that the Court can make decisions on a continuum. Following our previous preference assumptions, we assume here that the agency also has well defined and stable preferences over the policy space, represented by strictly convex indifference curves. The agency's ideal point is represented by point A in Figure 6. We assume now that the Court can only reverse or sustain a prior administrative agency decision.

These assumptions change slightly the game analyzed in the previous sections. The game now has four stages. In the initial stage certain legislation is passed, which determines the initial status quo (represented by x_0 in Figure 6). In the second stage the agency moves by implementing the statute and choosing a point (represented by x_1). In the third stage the Court reviews the agency's decision. The Court can either reverse or sustain the agency decision. If the Court reverses the agency decision, it upholds the initial status quo, x_0. If the Court sustains the agency decision, then the new status quo becomes x_1. In the fourth stage, Congress considers the Court's decision. The Court's decision, then, determines the relevant status quo at the fourth stage. Let the Court decision be given by $Z(x_0,x_1)$. If Congress wants to reverse the Court's decision, it can do so only by making both houses of Congress better off. That is, as in the previous version, reversals of the Court decision will only be undertaken if the Court's decision, $Z(x_0,x_1)$, is not in $C(\mathrm{H,S})$. Congressional bargaining, however is not unconstrained. Let $G(x)$ represent the deterministic outcome to a bargaining process when x is the status quo. Thus, if $y \in C(\mathrm{H,S})$, then $y = G(y)$.

We solve this model backward, by analyzing first the Congressional action that will follow a previous decision by the Court. From our previous discussion, we have that if $Z(x_0,x_1)$ is in $C(\mathrm{H,S})$, then the Court's decision becomes the equilibrium. If, however, $Z(x_0,x_1))$ is not in $C(\mathrm{H,S})$, then $G(Z(x_0,x_1))$

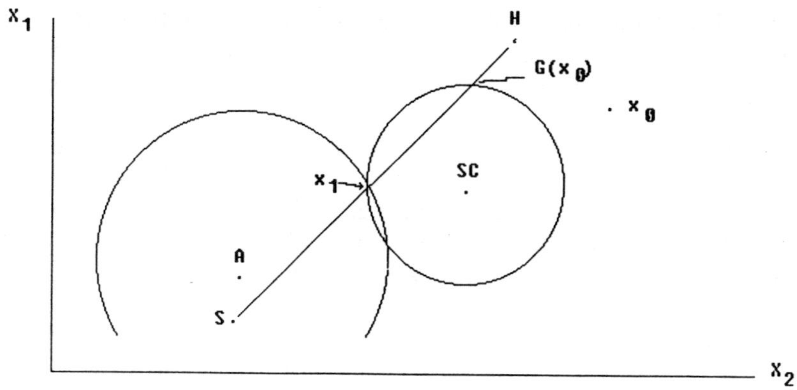

Figure 6. Agency discretion in a two-dimensional model without Presidential veto. x_0: initial status quo; x_1: agency's decision; SC: ideal point of the Court; H: ideal point of the House; S: ideal point of the Senate; $G(x_0)$: Congressional bargaining outcome starting from x_0.

becomes the equilibrium. When the Court makes its decision, it will consider the optimal response of the legislature. In analyzing the equilibrium, we have to consider two alternative cases, depending on whether the initial legislation is in $C(\mathrm{H,S})$, that is, on whether the composition of the current Congress resembles that of the enacting Congress or not. Letting $\mathrm{A}(x)$ and $\mathrm{SC}(x)$ represent those points preferred to x by the agency and the Court, respectively, the following proposition presents the basic results.

Proposition 4. (a) If $x_0 \in C(\mathrm{H,S})$, then (i) if $\mathrm{A}(x_0) \cap \mathrm{SC}(x_0) \cap C(\mathrm{H,S}) = 0$, then x_0 remains the equilibrium; and (ii) if $\mathrm{A}(x_0) \cap \mathrm{SC}(x_0) \cap C(\mathrm{H,S})$ is not empty then the equilibrium is that point in $\mathrm{SC}(x_0) \cap C(\mathrm{H,S})$ that maximizes the utility of the agency.

(b) If $x_0 \notin C(\mathrm{H,S})$, then (i) if $\mathrm{A}\,(G(x_0)) \cap \mathrm{SC}(G(x_0)) \cap C(\mathrm{H,S}) = 0$, $G(x_0)$ is the equilibrium; and (ii) if $\mathrm{A}(G(x_0)) \cap \mathrm{SC}(G(x_0)) \cap C(\mathrm{H,S})$ is not empty, then the equilibrium is the point in $\mathrm{SC}(G(x_0)) \cap C(\mathrm{H,S})$ that maximizes the utility of the agency.

Proposition 4 says that if the current Congress resembles the enacting Congress, then if the preferences of the Court and the agency are such that each prefers moving the initial status quo in different directions along $C(\mathrm{H,S})$ [i.e., $\mathrm{A}(x_0) \cap \mathrm{SC}(x_0) \cap C(\mathrm{H,S}) = 0$ means that the projection of the ideal points of the agency and the Court onto $C(\mathrm{H,S})$ are on opposite sides of x_0], then the initial status quo remains the equilibrium. If, however, both the agency and the Court prefer moving the initial status quo in the same direction along the contract curve between the House and the Senate, then the agency will pick a point, such that it will not be reversed by the Court, and such that the point will maximize the agency's utility. Finally, if the initial legislation is not in C(H,S), perhaps resulting from a change in the composition of Congress, then the same analysis can be carried out replacing x_0 by $G(x_0)$.

To prove the proposition consider the case where $x_0 \in C$(H,S) and where there are no points in the current contract curve preferred by both the Court and the agency to x_0. Assume that the agency makes a decision, x_1, which is not x_0 [it may or not be in C(H,S)], and such that it prefers $G(x_1)$ to x_0. Observe that, by assumption, x_0 is preferred by the Court to $G(x_1)$. The Court can either uphold or reject the administrative decision. If it upholds the agency's decision, then the equilibrium will become $G(x_1)$ [which could be x_1 if $x_1 \in C$(H,S)]. If, however, the Court reverses it, then the equilibrium becomes x_0. The Court's decision will depend on whether the Court prefers $G(x_1)$ to x_0 or not. In the current case, however, since there are no points on C(H,S) that make both the Court and the agency better off than x_0 does, the Court prefers x_0 to $G(x_1)$. Thus, if the agency's decision is not x_0, the Court will reverse it. Thus, the only long-run equilibrium is x_0.

If, however, there are points along the contract curve that can make both the agency and the Court better off than the initial legislation, x_0 [i.e., $A(x_0) \cap SC(x_0) \cap C$(H,S) is not empty, meaning that the projections of the ideal points of the Court and the Agency onto C(H,S) are in the same direction from x_0], then the equilibrium is given by that point along C(H,S) that will not be reversed by the Court [i.e., it belongs to $SC(x_0) \cap C$(H,S)], and that maximizes the utility of the agency. To see this point observe that the Court will not reverse any decision in C(H,S) that it prefers to x_0, nor will Congress reverse any Court decision that leaves the legal status quo in C(H,S). Thus, the agency has the discretion of choosing among those feasible policies that the Court prefers to the status quo. It will then choose that point that maximizes its own utility subject to leaving the Court at least as well off as with the original legislation, x_0. This shows the first part of Proposition 4. Similar reasoning will show the second part of the proposition. All that is needed is to understand that if x_0 is not in C(H,S), then x_0 is not a credible legislative threat. Instead, $G(x_0)$ is the credible legislative threat.

Figure 6 presents a case where x_0 is not in C(H,S). We observe that the fact that the Court can reverse the agency's decision, and thus trigger Congressional action towards $G(x_0)$, restricts the set of feasible agency decisions.

2.7. A Model of Agency Discretion under Judicial Review with Presidential Veto

In the previous section we assumed that the President cannot sustain a veto. In this section we extend this analysis to allow for a more active role by the President. We model the role of Presidential veto in the same way we did before, that is, by requiring all legislative outcomes to be the result of a bargaining game among the House, the Senate, and the President. All that can be said of this bargaining process is that it has to be efficient and that it cannot make any of the three players worse off than the initial status quo. Unconstrained bargaining, then, will imply an outcome in the area delineated by the contract curves between the three players. Again, let that area be $W(H,S,P)$.

As in the previous section, let $G(x)$ represent the equilibrium to the bargaining game when the status quo is x. thus, if $y \in W(H,S,P)$, then $y = G(y)$.

As before, the introduction of the President changes the last stage of the game. Now, it is not only Congressional action that is necessary to reverse a decision by the Court, the President's actions have to be considered as well. As before, there are two basic types of equilibria to this game, depending on whether the current political composition resembles that of the enacting Congress and President, that is, whether x_0 is in $W(H,S,P)$. Proposition 5 presents the main results.

Proposition 5. (a) If $x_0 \in W(H,S,P)$, then (i) if $A \in W(H,S,P) \cap SC(x_0)$, then A is the long-run equilibrium; and (ii) if $A \notin W(H,S,P) \cap SC(x_0)$, then the equilibrium is that point in $W(H,S,P) \cap SC(x_0)$ that maximizes the agency's utility.

(b) If $x_0 \notin W(H,S.P)$, then (i) if $A \in W(H,S,P) \cap SC(G(x_0)$, then A is the long-run equilibrium; and if (ii) $A \notin W(H,S,P) \cap SC(G(x_0))$, then the equilibrium is that point in $W(H,S,P) \cap SC(G(x_0))$ that maximizes the agency's utility.

The proof of the proposition is straightforward, following the same reasoning as that of Proposition 4; thus it is not presented here. Figure 7 shows such a case. Observe that the fact that the Court may reverse the agency restricts the policy outcomes in $W(H,S,P)$ that the agency can actually implement. In Figure 7, the agency cannot deviate too much from the status quo without triggering a reversal by the Court, which will be sustained by Congress and the President.

To summarize, when the Court can only reverse or sustain an agency decision, the agency has substantially more discretion than when the Court can choose, in principle, any point on the policy space. The Court will not support the legislative status quo in all cases, as changes away from the status quo may make the Court and the agency better off. The Court, on the other hand, will sustain the status quo when the agency's interests would move the policy away from the direction most preferred by the Court. Thus, the main thrust of the previous sections remains here as well. In particular, the Court follows election results as they change the set of feasible legislative decisions. Also, the Court, while behaving strategically, is not able to impose its preferences, but rather is constrained by the other institutions of govern-

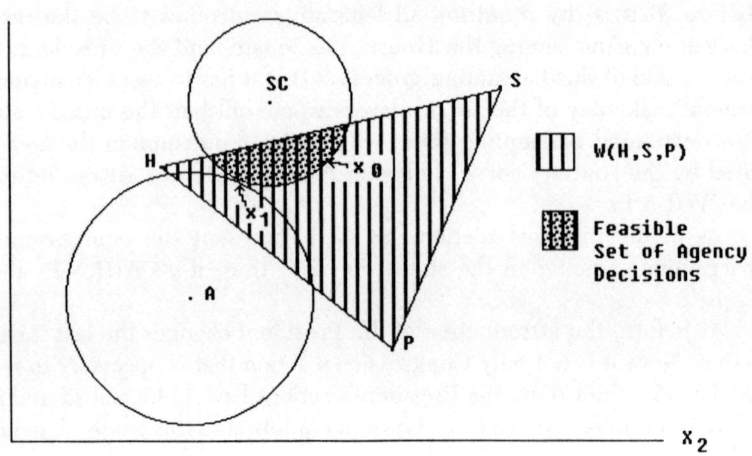

Figure 7. Agency discretion in a two-dimensional model with Presidential veto. W(H,S,P): feasible set of Congressional decisions; S: ideal point of the Senate; H: ideal point of the House; A: ideal point of the agency; SC: ideal point of the Court; x_0: inital status quo; x_1: agency's decisions.

ment. Finally, since casual observation of Supreme Court decisions shows that the Court makes decisions under both modes of behavior, the conditions for their relevance remain to be determined both theoretically and empirically.

2.8. Summary

It is worth summarizing now some of the main empirical implications of our framework concerning the rendering of statutory opinions by the Court. First, changes in Supreme Court statutory interpretations should follow changes both in the preferences of members of Congress (and in particular, of those in the relevant committees) and in the composition of the Court. Furthermore, our model implies that the Court's statutory interpretations should not be very sensitive to Presidential preferences. Finally, our theory implies that Court decisions should be followed by legislative inaction. Congressional reversals, if any, should only follow unexpected changes in the composition of Congress. Thus, our theory can be empirically refuted.

In a sense, causal empiricism has already rejected the theory, as, on occasion, Supreme Court decisions have been reversed during the same Congressional term. For example, the Court's decision in *General Electric v. Gilbert*, 429 U.S. 125 (December 7, 1976), was reversed (in 1978) by the Congress that was elected *before* the Court's actual decision. Similarly, *Zurcher v. Stanford Daily*, 436 U.S. 547 (1978), was reversed by the same Congress in 1980. As with every theory, however, ours deals with general tendencies, and thus a more appropriate test of the theory is whether most reversals develop during the same Congress or following Congressional changes. An empirical test of our approach along these lines, however, is beyond the scope of this article.

In the following sections we use the framework developed above to analyze two Supreme Court cases. Since the purpose of this exercise is not to provide a legal analysis of those cases, but rather to provide consistent self-interest rationales for these Supreme Court decisions, the ensuing analysis will be based exclusively on considerations arising from our framework, and will not take into account potentially important legal considerations. Furthermore, since the location of the Supreme Court has to be identified as part of the analysis, this exercise provides a feasible consistency test of our theory, as analyses of cases involving related issues could, in principle, imply quite different locations for the Court, providing then a refutation of the theory. While the following analyses of specific cases do not constitute a test of our theory, they are useful in showing the potential empirical relevance of this approach, and in providing new insights on two important judicial controversies.

3. THE STATE FARM CASE

This case is an example of the Court reducing the ability of the President to affect policy through administrative agencies.

Involved in this case is the extent of the National Highway Traffic Safety Administration's (NHTSA's) authority to rescind a previously issued standard. On June 24, 1983, the Supreme Court issued its opinion in *Motor Vehicle Manufacturers Association of the United States, Inc. et al. v. State Farm Mutual Automobile Insurance Co. et al.*.[30] The Court held that the NHTSA's rescission of the passive restraint requirement in Modified Standard 208 (requiring the installation of passive restraints in new vehicles) was arbitrary and capricious. The agency, according to the Court, failed to present an adequate basis and explanation for rescinding the requirement and had to either consider the matter further or adhere to or amend the Standard along the lines that its analysis supports.[31]

Let us first discuss the events that preceded the *State Farm* decision. In 1966 Congress enacted the National Traffic and Motor Vehicle Act (1966 Act), with the purpose of reducing "traffic accidents and deaths and injuries to persons resulting from traffic accidents."[32] The Act directs the Secretary of Transportation or his delegate to issue motor-safety standards that "shall be practicable, shall meet the need for motor safety, and shall be stated in

30. 463 U.S. 29 (1983).
31. Id. p. 34.
32. 15 U.S.C. § 1381.

objective terms."[33] The Secretary of Transportation delegated this authority to the NHTSA.

Under the authority of the Act, the Department of Transportation issued, in 1967, Standard 208, which at that time simply required the installation of seat belts in all automobiles.[34] Having noticed a low level of seat-belt usage, the Department started to consider the possibility of requiring "passive occupant restraint systems." After some discussion, the Department revised Standard 208 to include passive protection requirements.[35] Two years later, in 1972, the agency amended the Standard to require full passive protection for all front-seat occupants of vehicles manufactured after August 15, 1975. The two types of passive restraints considered were automatic seat belts and air bags. Vehicles built between August 1973 and August 1975 were to carry either passive restraints or lap and shoulder belts coupled with an "ignition interlock" that would prevent starting the vehicle if the belts were not connected.

The ignition interlock option proved to be very unpopular and Congress in 1974 amended the Act to prohibit a motor-vehicle safety standard from requiring or permitting compliance by means of an ignition interlock or a continuous buzzer designated to indicate that safety belts were not in use. The 1974 amendments also provided veto power to Congress for any safety standard that could be satisfied by a system other than seat belts.[36]

In 1976, the Secretary of Transportation suspended the passive restraint requirement, arguing that there would be widespread resistance to the new system.[37] Months later, however, a new Secretary issued, in 1977, a new mandatory passive restraint regulation, known as Modified Standard 208.[38] As modified, the Standard required the installation of air bags or passive seat belts. During the following three years, Modified Standard 208 survived both judicial and Congressional scrutiny.[39]

33. In issuing these standards, the Secretary or his delegate is directed to consider "relevant available motor vehicle safety data," whether the proposed standard is "reasonable, practicable, and appropriate" for the particular type of motor vehicle for which it is prescribed, and "the extent to which such standards will contribute to carrying out the purposes of the Act." 15 U.S.C. §1392(a), (1976 ed. Supp. V), and 15 U.S.C. §1392(f)(1),(3),(4).

34. 32 *Fed. Reg.* 2415.

35. 34 *Fed. Reg.* 11,148 (July 2, 1969).

36. Motor Vehicle and School Bus Safety Amendments of 1974, Pub. L. 93-492, S109, 88 Stat. 1482, 15 U.S.C. § 1410(b), and § 1410 (B)(2).

37. Rule-making opening reported at 41 *Fed. Reg.* 24,070 (June 14, 1976). Final decision reported at Department of Transportation, The Secretary's Decision Concerning Motor Vehicle Occupant Crash Protection (December 6, 1976) (Coleman decision) Joint Appendix (J.A.) 2065.

38. 42 *Fed. Reg.* 34,289 (1987); 49 C.F.R. §571-208 (1978).

39. For example, in *Pacific Legal Foundation v. Department of Transportation*, the Court of Appeals upheld Modified Standard 208 as rational, nonarbitrary regulation consistent with the agency's mandate under the act [193 U.S. App. D.C. 184, 593 F.2d. 1338, cert. denied. 444 U.S. 830 (1979)]. The Supreme Court denied certiorari of the Court's of Appeal's decision.

With the Reagan administration coming to power, a new perspective on regulatory reform was introduced. A central concern of the administration was the simplification of administrative rules implementing regulatory statutes, including the rescission of the passive restraint standard. Since it was apparent that the House of Representatives, dominated by Democrats, would not go along with the President's intent, the Administration started to implement policy changes through the administrative route.[40]

Thus, in February 1981, Secretary of Transportation Andrew Lewis reopened the rule-making and argued that a one-year delay was necessary because of the "dramatic changes in the production plans for the 1982 model fleet," and because, "the economic and other justifications for the ex isting phase-in scheduling have changed dramatically since the standard was adopted in 1977."[41] The delay was also needed, Lewis argued, to allow NHTSA officials time to reexamine the entire passive restraint issue.[42]

Shortly thereafter, the NHTSA issued a final rule (Notice 25), rescinding the passive restraint requirement as contained in Modified Standard 208. In explaining the rescission, NHTSA maintained that it was no longer able to find, as it had when the Standard was issued, that the automatic restraint requirement would produce significant safety benefits.[43]

In holding that the rescission of modified Standard 208 was arbitrary and capricious, the Supreme Court noted that the rescission of a standard must pass the same degree of scrutiny by the judiciary as would the enactment of a new regulation. The Court found that NHTSA had failed to present an adequate basis and explanation for rescinding the requirement, and ordered it to consider the matter further or to adhere to or amend the Standard along the lines which its analysis supported previously.[44] It is worth investigating,

Similarly, the Modified Standard also survived congressional scrutinity. Congress failed to exercise its authority under the legislative veto provision of the 1974 Amendments. While no action was taken by the full House of Representatives, the Senate Committee with jurisdiction over NHTSA affirmatively endorsed the Standard [S. Rep. No. 95-481 (1977)]. Several other rulings dealing with Modified Standard 208 were considered during the next several years. For example, on May 22, 1978, a notice of proposed rule-making was issued in response to a petition from General Motors requesting more flexibility in the design of emergency-release mechanisms for automatic seat belts [43 *Fed. Reg.* 21912 (May 22, 1978)]. NHTSA granted the proposal six months later [43 *Fed. Reg.* 52493 (November 13, 1978)].

40. See, for example, Thomas, Wildemann, and Brown.

41. 46 *Fed. Reg.* 53,420 (1981).

42. As part of his proposal, however, Lewis prepared three alternative amendments to the rule: (a) reversing the order of compliance, so that small cars were to be equipped first; (b) requiring all cars to comply with the standards by March 1983; or (c) rescinding the Standard altogether. See Thomas, Wildemann, and Brown.

43. In addition, given the low benefit–cost ratio arising from the analysis of this requirement, NHTSA feared that Modified Standard 208 would be regarded as an instance of ineffective regulation [46 *Fed. Reg.* 53,419 (October 29, 1981)].

44. Some legal scholars suggest that the Supreme Court decision did not simply imply the application of a standard precedent rule, as before the Supreme Court decision it may have

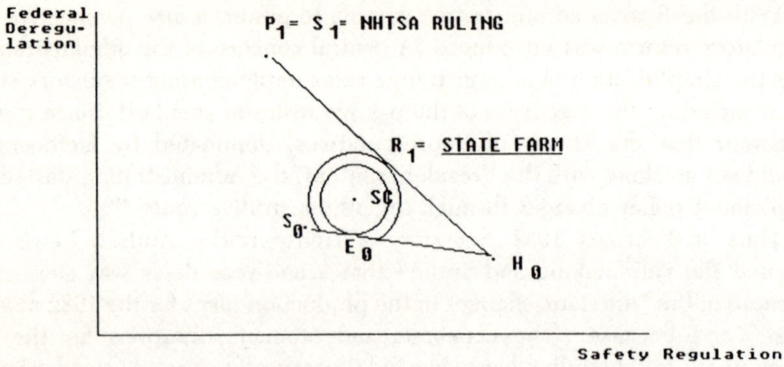

Figure 8. The *State Farm* case. E_0: initial status quo; R_1: Supreme Court's *State Farm* decision; H_0: ideal point of the House; S_0: ideal point of the Senate pre-1980; S_1: ideal point of the Senate post-1980; P_1: ideal point of the President post-1980.

however, whether there is a political-economic rationale for the decision.

Figure 8 is a graphic description of these events as they would be interpreted by the model in this article. We first identify the dimension or issues involved in the case. In *State Farm*, the Court confronted two issues. The issue of immediate attention was the validity of Modified Standard 208, and thus the extent of safety regulation in the automobile industry. A different issue was the extent by which the President can deregulate via administrative rules without the explicit consent of other branches.

Having defined the dimensions, we need next to define the relevant ideal points for the President, Congress, and the Supreme Court. The President's position is not difficult to locate, since President Reagan was very vocal about his preferences. The new Administration's preferences called for a substantial reduction in safety regulation, and also for administrative deregulatory power.

The House's and the Senate's preferences, before 1980, were in the other direction. We focus on the chairs of the committees with jurisdiction over motor-vehicle safety. In the Senate, the relevant committee was the Commerce Committee (later named the Commerce, Science, and Transportation Committee). From 1966 to 1979, the committee was controlled by Democrats. Up to 1976, Senator Magnuson (D, Washington) was the committee chair. As revealed by bills that Senator Magnuson introduced during his tenure in Congress, he was in favor of extensive government safety regula-

---

been uncertain whether the administrative elimination of a regulation should be held to the same standards as their introduction. See Garland. Others, however, see no new legal ground on *State Farm*, but rather the intent to erase a new legal ground developed in the D.C. Court of Appeals in the decision below. We thank Jerry Mashaw for suggesting this to us.

tion.[45] The preferences of the rest of the members of the Senate are expected to be at least in the same direction as those of Senator Magnuson.

In 1981, however, there was a change in the dominating preferences in the Senate. The new chairman of the Commerce Committee, Senator Packwood (R, Oregon), showed different preferences. By analyzing some of his legislative efforts during this period, we can see that Packwood supported more federal deregulation and, to some extent, less safety regulation than his predecessors.[46]

The House committee with jurisdiction over the relevant issue was the committee on Interstate and Foreign Commerce. From 1966 to 1980, R. Staggers (D, West Virginia) acted as committee chairman. In 1981, however, the jurisdiction over motor-vehicle safety was given to the committee on Energy and Commerce, under the chairmanship of R. Dingell (D, Michigan). Both, Dingell and Staggers, were supporters of government safety regulation.[47] Thus, as depicted in Figure 8, the preferences of the House, both before and after 1980, are for less federal deregulation and more extensive safety regulatory provisions than the Senate.[48] The contract curve connecting H_0 and S_0 represents the political configuration pre-1980, with E_0 representing the Modified Standard 208. Following the 1980 election, there is a new contract curve, with the Senate moving away from the House. The main change in the Senate's ideal point (and thus in the contract curve) is along the Federal Deregulation dimension.[49] Similarly, the new President moves with the Senate. For simplicity, we assume that the ideal points of the Senate and the President are the same. The change in the political configuration undermines the long-run equilibrium nature of the status quo. In the short run, however, before the Supreme Court acts, the President can try to "pull" the policy outcome toward his ideal point, even though the House will block any detrimental change to the current legislation. The opening of the rule-making by Secretary Lewis in 1981, and the rescission of Modified Standard 208, can be interpreted in this way. (P_1S_1) in Figure 8 represents

45. For example, § 1883 (1976) (directing the Secretary of Transportation to issue standards for fuel economy performance); § 1302 (1976) (to promote safety and health in the mining industry).

46. § 2038, for example, introduced in the 98th Congress, provided for the deregulation of the trucking industry.

47. While Rep. Dingell may have been an outspoken critic of motor-vehicle regulation, he was in favor of safety regulation, as his sponsoring of the 1983 seat-belt bill (H 4175, 95th Congress), providing for an extensive use of seat belts, shows. See also, H 14,256 (96th Congress) providing for an increase in consumer protection in relation to drugs and cosmetics. His support for safety regulation, however, should not imply that Rep. Dingell was not supporting his constituents (Michigan automobile companies and workers), as some have speculated that safety regulation provided advantages to the domestic car manufacturers vis-à-vis Japanese producers.

48. Since less-populated states have a relatively larger representation in the Senate than in the House, it is reasonable to predict that the Senate will usually be less supportive of regulatory measures than the House. See, McCubbins, Noll, and Weingast (1989).

49. Thus, we should expect the main change in the long-run equilibrium to be along that dimension as well.

Table 1. Bills Introduced to Amend the NTMV Act of 1966

Date and title	Sponsor	Summary
April 10, 1981; H 3237	Wirth (D)	To amend the NTMV Act of 1966 to require the installation of passive restraint systems in small new cars
October 26, 1981; S 1773	Danforth (R)	To amend the NTMV Act of 1966, to require from all car manufacturers the installation of automatic crash protection systems in new passenger cars
November 24, 1981; S 1887	Danforth (R)	To amend the Internal Revenue Code to encourage the use of air bags, allowing manufacturers to claim a refundable tax credit for the installation of air bags in 1984 and beyond, and imposing an excise tax on new cars without this technology
February 15, 1983; S 477	Danforth (R)	To amend the Internal Revenue Code of 1954 and the NTMV Act of 1966 to expedite the installation of automatic safety air bags
April 21, 1983; H 2693	Lantos (D)	To enact the Highway Safety Act of 1983
October 20, 1983; H 4175	Dingell (D)	To amend the NTMV Act of 1966 to provide for more extensive use of safety-belt systems in passenger motor vehicles, in order to assist in reducing health, disability, and other costs
June 28, 1984; S 2828	Moynihan (D)	To amend the NTMV Act of 1966 to require the provision of automatic safety air bags in all automobiles, beginning on or after September 1, 1986

the NHTSA's ruling. Since at S_1 the Senate is at its ideal point, it will block any new legislation that may alter the NHTSA's position.[50]

Several bills were introduced in Congress shortly after the February 1981 announcement and before the *State Farm* decision. As expected by our framework, however, none of those legislative initiatives were acted upon. (See Table 1.)

The NHTSA's decision, then, allowed the Senate to achieve an outcome close to its ideal point without having to get directly involved in the enactment of legislation.

At the time of the *State Farm* decision, then, the situation can be described as follows: an agency decision has modified the status quo, and has tilted the balance of power in favor of the Senate, creating a stalemate in legislative action. It is at this point that we would expect the Supreme Court to, opportunistically, enter a decision to restore a policy closer to the previous status quo.

50. Furthermore, since the NHTSA's ruling will not be supported by the House, we would not expect the Senate to promote new legislation to make the NHTSA position part of the legal standard.

For the *State Farm* decision to be in the Court's self-interest, it has to be the case that its ideal point is not to the northwest of the new ideal point of the Senate. If that would be the case, then the Supreme Court's position would be improved by the NHTSA's ruling, and hence it should have upheld it rather than reversed it. Observe, however, that a position northwest of the new ideal point of the Senate implies a very conservative court, as it would prefer very little safety regulation and substantial federal deregulatory powers. We assume, then, that the position of the Court concerning safety issues and federal deregulatory powers is in between those of the House and the new Senate.[51]

R_1, in Figure 8, represents the *State Farm* case. R_1 is more in tune with what the status quo was before 1980, since it moves the status quo away from S_1 towards H_0.

In deciding whether the NHTSA's rescission of the passive standard requirement was proper, the Court had to determine first what standard of review to apply in general to administrative rulings. As mentioned above, the Court held that a rescission of a rule is subject to the same standard of judicial review, "the arbitrary and capricious standard," as is the promulgation of a new rule. Since the NHTSA failed to supply a reasoned analysis justifying the change in policy, it did not satisfy the quasiprocedural elements of the doctrine.[52] Thus, while restraining the agency on its current deregulatory process, the Court allowed some extent of administrative deregulatory power, as long as it held to the same standards as the introduction of new administrative rules.

To summarize, in *State Farm* the Supreme Court used a procedural standard to reverse an administrative deregulatory initiative that, following a change in only one house of Congress, would have shifted public policy too far away from its most preferred point on the new contract curve between the House and the Senate.

4. THE GROVE CITY CASE[53]

The Supreme Court decision in *Grove City*, on February 28, 1984, involved the power of the Department of Education under Title IX of the Education

51. By 1983 there was already a majority, albeit narrow, of Republican-appointed justices. This narrow majority, however, was essentially the same since 1975. Observe, also, that the Court could have been located to the southeast of the ideal point of the House. But then the equilibrium would have been a corner solution, namely, the ideal point of the House.

52. Furthermore, the agency also seems to have violated the substantive elements of the doctrine in at least two respects: (a) lack of records in support of its findings of fact; and (b) failing to establish a reasonable relationship between its decision, on the one hand, and the relevant evidence, alternatives, and statutory purpose, on the other. Garland (p. 546).

53. *Grove City College v. Bell*, 465 U.S. 555 (1984). For a different political-economic analysis of this case, see Marks.

Amendments of 1972.[54] The 1972 amendments prohibit employment discrimination on the basis of sex in educational institutions receiving federal funds. The issue at hand was the determination of the appropriate scope of the Department of Education's enforcement powers under Title IX.

The two sections relevant here are Sections 901 and 902. Section 901 prohibits discrimination on the basis of sex by any education program or activity receiving federal assistance. Section 902, the enforcement provision for Section 901, provides, in its pertinent parts, that compliance may be effected by, among other alternatives, "the termination of or refusal to grant or to continue assistance under such program or activity to any recipient . . . , but such termination or refusal shall be limited in its effect to the particular program, or part thereof, in which noncompliance has been so found."[55]

The plain language of Section 902 appears to indicate a program-specific type of enforcement. However, there has been extensive debate on the meaning of Section 902. Marks (1988) argues that an examination of the legislative history of the Act points toward the conclusion that an institution-wide type of enforcement provision was intended. It has also been forcefully argued, however, that a program-specific enforcement provision is more truthful to Congressional intent.[56]

Not only has there been debate at the Congressional level on the meaning of Section 902, but courts have struggled with the issue as well. Several federal courts have decided in favor of an institution-wide enforcement provision. One such example is *Haffer v. University,* involving an athletic program that did not receive earmarked funds covered under Title IX.[57] Several other cases have followed the same approach when deciding the appropriate enforcement type for other antidiscrimination statutes.[58] On the other hand, several other courts have interpreted the enforcement provisions of antidiscrimination statutes as program-specific.[59]

54. In 1972 the Higher Education Act was enacted into law as the Education Amendments of 1972. Pub. L. 92-318, Title IX, § 902, 86 Stat. 373, 20 U.S.C. § 1682.

55. Id.

56. Garvey, for example, examines the language of several antidiscrimination statutes that used language similar to that of Title IX. He concludes that the current language of Title VI of the Civil Rights Act of 1964, Title IX, Section 504 of the Rehabilitation Act of 1973, and the Age Discrimination Act of 1975 all support a program-specific enforcement provision. Each of the statutes begin with a prohibition against discrimination in any "program or activity receiving Federal financial aid" and then proceed to make clear that the phrase "program or activity" means something less than "recipient," "educational institution," or "political entity."

57. 524 F. Supp. 531 (E.D. Pa. 1981), affirmed 688 F. 2d. 14 (3rd Cir. 1982).

58. As to § 504: *Wolff v. South Colonie School District*, 534 F.Supp. 758 (N.D.N.Y. 1982) (school trips covered). As to Title VI: *Board of Public Instruction of Taylor Co. v. Finch*, 414 F.2d. 1068 (5th Cir. 1969) (assumes institutional-wide coverage); *United States v. Jefferson Co. Board of Education*, 372 F.2d. 836 (5th Cir. 1966), affirmed en banc, 380 F.2d. 385, cert. denied subnom; *Caddo Parrish Board of Education v. United States*, 389 U.S. 840 (1967) (Title VI institution-wide desegregation order appropriate).

59. For example, *Hillsdale College v. Department of Health, Education and Welfare*, 696 F.2d. 418 (6th Cir. 1981) (the entire college as an institution was not a "program within the

Notwithstanding this debate over the interpretation of the enforcement provision, the preferences of the committees with jurisdiction over this issue in both houses can be clearly defined. Marks shows that up to 1980 the House committee on Education and Labor had stable preferences. The average mean ADA score of the Democratic committee members was relatively high (a liberal vote on the issue of enforcement is one in favor of institution-wide coverage). During this same period similar tendencies dominated the Senate committee on Labor and Human Resources. Not only did a Democratic majority control the committee, but in addition the ranking minority member of the committee, Republican Jacob Javits, was a principal sponsor of the original legislation and a supporter of institution-wide termination.[60]

Thus, until 1980, the status quo could be understood as requiring institution-wide enforcement. E_0 in Figure 9 represents this policy outcome. We assume that until 1980 the ideal points of both houses of Congress were very close in the policy space, both supporting institution-wide enforcement. E_0 is assumed to be on the contract curve $C(H,S_0)$, where H and S_0 represent the House and Senate ideal points.

In 1980 a change in the political composition of Congress opened an opportunity for the Supreme Court to alter strategically the status quo. Although the Education and Labor Committee of the House continued to be controlled by Democrats (thus, we keep the ideal point of the House at H), the Senate experienced a large change. A Republican majority now dominated the Committee on Labor and Human Resources, with the consequent change in committee preferences. Marks shows that the mean ADA legislative scores for the Senate committee under Republican domination was lower than the committee mean under Democratic domination. Furthermore, the new chairman of the Senate committee, Senator Hatch, was a strong supporter of program-specific enforcement.

This change in the political configuration is represented in Figure 9 by the new contract curve $C(H,S_1)$. The Court is now before a divided Congress.

meaning of Title IX"), vacated and remanded, 466 U.S. 901 (1984); *Rice v. President & Fellows of Harvard College*, 663 F.2d. 336 (1st Cir. 1981) (allegation that the law school at the college in question received federal funds for its work-study program, without allegation of sex discrimination in school's handling of that program, was insufficient to invoke the protection of the Education Amendments of 1972); *Dougherty County School Sys. v. Harris*, 622 F.2d 735 (5th Cir. 1980) (Title IX does not authorize Secretary to terminate all federal aid because of any discrimination in a school system if the federally assisted programs are administered impeccably); *Romeo Community Schools v. United States Department of Health, Education, and Welfare*, 600 F.2d 581 (6th Cir. 1979) (Title IX applies only to students involved in programs or activities receiving federal financial assistance and does not apply additionally to employees of educational institutions receiving such assistance), cert. denied, 444 U.S. 972 (1979).

60. Marks also analyzes the length of continuous service to show the importance of these legislators.

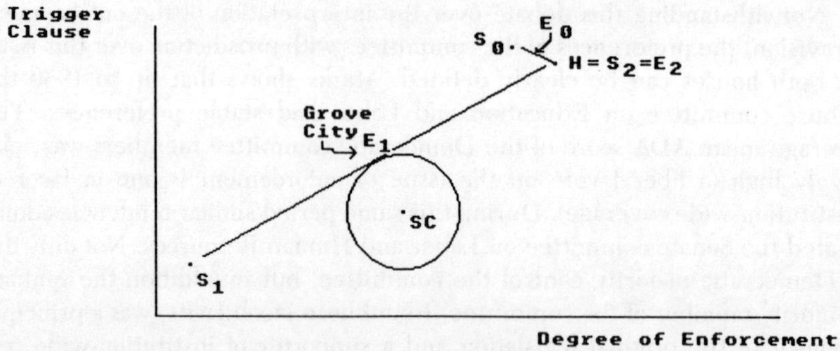

Figure 9. The *Grove City* case. SC: ideal point of the Supreme Court; E_1: *Grove City* decision; H: ideal point of the House; S_0: ideal point of the Senate pre-1981; S_1: ideal point of the Senate post-1980 elections; S_2: ideal point of the Senate post-1986 elections; E_0: pre-1980 equilibrium; E_2: post-1986 equilibrium.

Since the House has not changed, the bargaining set is very small (not depicted in Figure 9 to avoid excessive clutter). Thus, major legislation will not come out of that Congress. On the other hand, the Senate will support any change in the status quo that the Supreme Court would like to undertake.

For the Court to support changing the status quo, it cannot be the case that the Court is to the northeast of the ideal point of the House. That is, the Court cannot have a more liberal view than the House, as in that case the initial status quo would still represent the long-run equilibrium. As in *State Farm*, we will assume that the Court is located between the ideal points of the House and of the new Senate. If that is the case, then, our model would predict a change in the status quo.

Shortly after the change in the control of the Senate, in 1981, the Court granted certiorari to consider *North Haven Board of Education v. Bell.*[61] This case involved the validity of Title IX regulations promulgated by the Department of Education. These regulations prohibited federally funded education programs from employment sex discrimination. Although the issue of the enforcement provision of Title IX was not directly involved, *North Haven* gave an opportunity to the Court to signal its desire to clarify the debate, by intervening directly, if necessary. *In dicta,* the Court expressed its opinion to the fact that an examination of Title IX's language, as well as of its legislative history, corroborates a program-specific type of enforcement.[62]

While the Court was considering the interpretation of Title IX, several bills and resolutions were being introduced in Congress on the same issue.

61. 456 U.S. 511 (1982), cert. granted 450 U.S. 909 (1981).
62. *North Haven*, 456 U.S. 511, 537.

Apart from their legislative purpose, these bills may have served to communicate to the Court the different houses' preferences on this issue.[63]

In *Grove City* the Court went on to make *North Haven's dicta* the main ruling of the case. Although deciding in favor of a broad triggering clause (i.e., that any kind of financial aid even if given directly to students would trigger Title IX coverage), the Court held that the enforcement provision of Title IX was intended to be program-specific.

As argued above, following a drastic change in the preferences of one of the houses of Congress (in this case, the Senate), we would expect the Court to intervene. The intervention of the Court would bring a new policy outcome, which may well be outside the bargaining area between the Senate and the House. In fact, this is the case with *Grove City.* Program-specific enforcement had been the kind of enforcement Senator Hatch signaled to the Court as the Senate's preference. While the Court decided against a broad triggering clause, it sided with Hatch in the most relevant issue. Thus, again, the Court followed the electorate.[64]

Following *Grove City,* several other bills were introduced both in support of and against the Court's decision. As predicted by our model, no legislation came out before the new Congress.[65]

In 1986 the Democrats regained control of the Senate, while the Executive remained Republican. It is reasonable to assume that the new position of the Senate was almost identical to that of the House. Thus, the contract curve between the House and the Senate collapses to point $H = S_2$, with $H = S_2$ also becoming the new long-run equilibrium. After this drastic

63. In June 11, 1981, Senator Hatch, now Chairman of the Senate Committee on Labor and Human Resources, introduced § 1361 to reinforce the program-specific nature of Title IX, to provide for a narrow triggering clause, to restrict the scope of the Act to students, and, to include under the jurisdiction of the Act the admission process of recipients. Senator Hatch seems to have had the Court in mind: "The amendment would dispose of the issues in the Grove City College versus Harris case, currently on litigation, in which the Department of Education has contended that Federal aid to a student is sufficient by itself to subject to Title IX all the activities of whatever school he or she decides to attend." 127 *Cong. Rec.* S636 (daily ed., January 24, 1981). Two other bills were also introduced. SR 478 was introduced on September 22, 1982, and HR 190 was introduced on May 10, 1983. It reported without amendment, seemingly with the intention of signaling to the Court the House's preferences for institution-wide fund termination.

64. It has been argued that the Court's decision in Grove City was in fact the correct legal interpretation of Title IX. Garvey (1986) argues that program-specific enforcement is the standard that better fits the rationale under which Congress decided to forbid discriminatory practices by those receiving Federal aid.

65. For example, §2363 (Feb. 28, 1984: to change "program or activity" to include institution); § 2568 (April 12, 1984: to restore Title IX to its broad coverage in enforcement); § 2910 (August 7, 1984); § 3079 (October 5, 1984). § 431 and HR 700 (February 7, 1985: to restore the prior executive branch interpretation and broad, institution wide application of Title IX); § 272 (January 24, 1985, to require than in the case of educational institutions, the phrase "program or activity" shall mean the entire institution).

change in the political configuration of Congress, our model suggests that there should be an attempt by Congress to overturn *Grove City.* In fact, in 1987, Senator Kennedy introduced S. 557. The bill was similar in language and scope to S. 431. It was introduced under the findings that the Supreme Court had "unduly narrowed or cast doubt upon the broad application" of Title IX and therefore legislative action was necessary to restore the institution-wide application of Title IX.[66] On January 28, 1988 the Senate voted favorably upon S. 557. The bill was passed by a vote of 75 to 14. The House approved the bill on March 2, 1988, by a vote of 315 to 98.[67]

From Figure 9 it is clear that under the new contract curve, *Grove City,* E_1, is no longer a long-run equilibrium. The new long-run equilibrium (S. 557) is slightly broader in its enforcement guidelines than the status quo before *Grove City,* and must be located in the area to the right of E_0.[68]

To summarize, *Grove City* provides a good example of strategic behavior by the courts. In the same way as in *State Farm,* facing a divided Congress, the Court chooses to intervene by obtaining support from one of the Houses of Congress (in *State Farm,* the House; in *Grove City,* the Senate). Once Congress becomes unified again, the Court does not try to maintain the status quo, but instead allows Congress to adjust the legislative outcome. Finally, while *Grove City* seems to be a pro-conservative and *State Farm* seems to be a pro-liberal decision, both are consistent with a Court whose political preferences are at neither extreme of the political spectrum.

5. FINAL COMMENTS

This article provides a microanalytic model of Supreme Court statutory decisions. Our model combines the rational-choice modeling strategy with the notion that institutions matter in the design of public policy. We use this model to understand, in a consistent way, two major recent Supreme Court decisions. These cases show how the Supreme Court responds to political change.

In both cases the Supreme Court follows the electoral results by adjusting to the changes in the composition of Congress and the Presidency. On the one hand, in *State Farm,* the supreme Court acted to reverse an admin-

66. § 557, enacting clause, 134 *Cong. Rec.* S266 (daily ed., January 28, 1988).

67. 134 *Cong. Rec.* H 565 (daily ed., March 2, 1988).

68. The exact position of E_2 will depend on the significance attached to the Danforth amendment [§ 557, 134 *Cong. Rec.* S 266 (daily ed., Jan. 28, 1988)]. The Danforth amendment provides that institutions receiving aid are not required to provide or pay for abortions. The concern was that denial of abortion or related services would be perceived as discrimination against women. Reports in the press (e.g., *New York Times,* March 3, 1988) suggested that acceptance of the amendment led many Republicans to support the bill, giving Congress the supermajority needed to overturn a possible Presidential veto.

istrative policy that was implemented following changes in both Congress and the Presidency, which, in the absence of the Supreme Court, would have implied a drastic shift in regulatory policy. In *Grove City*, however, the Supreme Court moved to make a new policy following a change in the composition of the Senate. Such a new policy would have not, in the absence of the Supreme Court move, come out of Congress, since it would have been blocked by the House of Representatives. In both cases the Supreme Court decisions were supported by one of the houses of Congress and, thus, they could not be reversed by the then current Congress. While one is a pro-conservative and the other is a pro-liberal decision, both are consistent with a Court pursuing its own self-interest, as long as its preferences are not at either extreme of the political spectrum.

To summarize, we see in this article the dual role that the Supreme Court can play. On the one hand, it can be seen as supporting the status quo, and restraining both the President and Congress from undertaking drastic regulatory changes. On the other hand, the Supreme Court also plays an activist role, by introducing policies that change the status quo, even though Congress could not, by itself, legislate such policy changes. Thus, whether the Supreme Court is activist or restrained depends on the political circumstances. Following changes in Congress that create legislative stalemate, we would expect the Supreme Court to be activist. On the other hand, following a major change in the Presidency, we would expect the Supreme Court to follow a restrained path.

APPENDIX

Lemma 1. Assume that (a) preferences of the House, the Senate, and the Supreme Court are represented by circular indifference curves in R^2; (b) the initial equilibrium is in the interior of the contract curve; and (c) the electoral result implies a movement in the same direction of the ideal points of both the House and the Senate. Then, the long-run equilibrium moves in the same direction as the ideal points of the House and the Senate, independently of the location of the ideal point of the Supreme Court.

To prove the lemma, observe that with Euclidean preferences the contract curve is linear. Thus, there is a unique long-run equilibrium. Second, since both the House and the Senate move in the same direction, the contract curve also moves in the same direction. Thus, the set of all feasible equilibria also moves in the same direction as the House's and the Senate's ideal points. Thus, the long-run equilibrium also has to move in the same direction.

Lemma 2. Assume (a) and (b) from Lemma 1; and that (c), the electoral result, implies a movement only in the ideal point of one of the houses of Congress; (d) the movement is only in one dimension, call it x_1; and (e) the initial equilibrium level of x_1 is below the most preferred point of the Supreme Court. Then the new long-run equilibrium will follow the move in the electorate. If, however, (f) the initial equilibrium level of x_1 exceeds the most preferred point of the Supreme Court, then the new long-run equilibrium will follow the move in the electorate only if the initial contract curve implies a relatively low rate of substitution (to be specified below) between x_1 and x_2.

To prove the lemma, observe that from (a), the contract curve is linear. Thus, in a (x_1,x_2) plane, the contract curve can be represented by $x_1 = a + bx_2$, where $a = (x_{2S}x_{1H} - x_{1S}x_{2H})/(x_{2S} - x_{2H})$, and $b = (x_{1S} - x_{1H})/(x_{2S} - x_{2H})$, with x_S (x_H) representing the ideal point of the Senate (House). If we assume, say, that the House (Senate) has a higher demand for x_2 (x_1) than for x_1 (x_2), then $b < 0$, $a > 0$. Hence, the first-order condition for the Supreme Court can be represented by (where ${}^{SC}U$ represents the utility function of the Supreme Court)

$$ {}^{SC}U_1 b + {}^{SC}U_2 = 0, \qquad \Delta = {}^{SC}U_{11}b^2 + {}^{SC}U_{22} < 0. \tag{A1} $$

Assume, now, a movement in the ideal point of the Senate, such that $dx_{1S} > 0$, $dx_{2S} = 0$. Then, fully differentiating (A1), we obtain

$$ \frac{dx_1}{dx_{1S}} = \frac{2[-(a' + b'x_{20}) + bb'(x_{10} - x_{1SC})]}{{}^{SC}U_{11}b^2 + {}^{SC}U_{22}}, $$

$$ \frac{dx_2}{dx_{1S}} = \frac{2[b(a' + b'x_{20}) + b'(x_{10} - x_{1SC})]}{{}^{SC}U_{11}b^2 + {}^{SC}U_{22}}, $$

where $a' = \partial a/\partial x_{1S} = -x_{2H}/(x_{2S} - x_{2H}) > 0$, $b' = \partial b/\partial x_{1S} = 1/(x_{2S} - x_{2H}) < 0$. Thus, after substitutions, we obtain that

$$ \operatorname{sgn} \frac{dx_1}{dx_{1S}} = \operatorname{sgn}[x_{2H} - x_{20} + b(x_{10} - x_{1SC})] $$

or, from (b),

$$ \frac{dx_1}{dx_{1S}} \gtrless 0 \Leftrightarrow 1 \gtrless -b(x_{10} - x_{1SC})/(x_{2H} - x_{20}). $$

Thus, if (e) holds, so that $x_{10} - x_{1SC} < 0$, then $dx_1/dx_{1S} > 0$. If, however, (f) holds, so that $x_{10} - x_{1SC} > 0$, then the sign of dx_1/dx_{1S} depends on the value of b. Then, for very steep contract curves (high values of $-b$), increases in

x_{1S} may reduce the equilibrium value of x_1. Observe that a steep contract curve implies that the Senate's ideal point changes in the dimension that most separates the House from the Senate. Finally, observe that assumption (e) implies that the ideal point of the Supreme Court is below the contract curve, while assumption (f) implies that its ideal point is above the contract curve.

We can then state Proposition 2.

Proposition 2. Assume that (a) preferences of the House, the Senate, and the Supreme Court are represented by circular indifference curves in R^2; and (b) the initial equilibrium is in the interior of the contract curve. Then, moves in the electorate where either only one house moves or both houses move in the same direction will imply changes in the long-run equilibrium which will follow the electorate, unless the change is in only one house, and the dimension that changes is (a), one that most separates the House from the Senate, and (b) the initial status quo implying a larger equilibrium value for that dimension than that of the ideal point of the Supreme Court.

The proof of the proposition is a direct application of Lemmas 1 and 2.

REFERENCES

Adamany, D. 1973. "Legitimacy, Realigning Elections, and the Supreme Court," 3 *Wisconsin Law Review* 790–846.

Binmore, K. 1987. "Nash Bargaining Theory, I: An Introduction," in K. Binmore, and P. Dasgupta, eds., *The Economics of Bargaining*. Oxford, UK: Basil Blackwell.

Casper, J. 1976. "The Supreme Court and National Policy," 70 *American Political Science Review* 50–63.

Dahl, R. 1957. "Decision-Making in a Democracy: The Supreme Court as a National Policy-Maker," 6 *Journal of Public Policy* 279–95.

Easterbrook, F. 1982. "Ways of Criticizing the Court," 95 *Harvard Law Review* 802–32.

Ferejohn, John, and Charles Shipan. 1988. "Congressional Influence on Administrative Agencies: A Case Study of Telecommunications Policy." Mimeo, Stanford University.

Fiorina, M. 1974. *Representatives, Roll Calls and Constituencies*. Lexington, MA: Heath and Co.

Funston, R. 1975. "The Supreme Court and Critical Elections," 69 *American Political Science Review* 795–811.

Garland, M. 1985. "Deregulation and Judicial Review," 98 *Harvard Law Review* 505–91.

Garvey, J. 1986. "The Program or Activity" Rule in Antidiscrimination Law: A Comment on S. 272, H.R. 700 and S. 431," 23 *Harvard Journal on Legislation* 445–82.

Gely, R., and P. T. Spiller. 1989. "The Political Economy of Supreme Court Constitutional Decisions: The Case of the Court Packing Plan," University of Illinois; forthcoming in *International Review of Law and Economics*.

Gilligan, Thomas W., and Keith Krehbiel. 1988. "Organization of Informative Committees by a Rational Legislature," Mimeo, Hoover Institutions Working Papers in Political Science 9-88-13.

Halpern, S., and C. Lamb. 1982. *Supreme Court Activist and Restraint*. Lexington, MA: D. C. Heath.

Handberg, R., and H. Hill. 1980. "Court Curbing, Court Reversals, and Judicial Review: The Supreme Court Versus Congress," 14 *Law and Society Review* 309–22.

———, and ———. 1984. "Judicial Activism and Restraint on the United States Supreme Court: A Political-Behavioral Analysis," 20 *California Western Law Review* 173–86.

Henschen, B. 1983. "Statutory Interpretation of the Supreme Court: Congressional Response," 11 *American Political Quarterly* 441–58.

Kalt, J., and M. Zupan. 1984. "Capture and Ideology in the Economic Theory of Politics," 74 *American Economic Review* 279–300.

Kau, J. B., and P. Rubin. 1979. "Self Interest, Ideology and Logrolling in Congressional Voting," 22 *Journal of Law and Economics* 365–84.

Marks, B. 1988. "A Model of Judicial Influence on Congressional Policymaking: 'Grove City College v. Bell'," Working Paper in Political Science P-88-7, Hoover Institution.

McCubbins, M. D., and T. Schwartz. 1984. "Congressional Oversight Overlooked: Police Patrols vs. Fire Alarms," 28 *American Journal of Political Science* 165–79.

McCubbins, M., R. Noll, and B. R. Weingast. 1987. "Administrative Procedures as Instruments of Political Control," 3 *Journal of Law, Economics, and Organization* 243–77.

———, ———, and ———. 1989. "Structure and Process, Politics and Policy: Administrative Arrangements and the Political Control of Agencies," 75 *Virginia Law Review* 431–82.

Nagel, S. 1969. "Curbing the Court: The Politics of Congressional Reaction," in S. Nagel, ed., *The Legal Process from a Behavioral Perspective*. Homewood, IL: Doresy Press.

Nowak, J., R. Rotunda, and J. Young. 1983. *Constitutional Law*, 2nd ed. St. Paul, MN: West Publishing.

Peltzman, S. 1984. "Constituent Interest and Congressional Voting," 27 *Journal of Law and Economics* 181–210.

Rohde, D., and H. Spaeth. 1976. *Supreme Court Decision Making*. San Francisco: W. H. Freeman.

Shepsle, K. 1979. "Institutional Arrangements and Equilibrium in Multidimensional Voting Models," 23 *American Journal of Political Science* 27–59.

———, and B. R. Weingast. 1981. "Structure-Induced Equilibrium and Legislative Choice," 37 *Public Choice* 503–19.

———, and ———. 1982. "Institutionalizing Majority Rule: A Social Choice Theory with Policy Implications," 72 *AEA Papers and Proceedings* 367–71.

———, and ———. 1987. "The Institutional Foundations of Committee Power," 81 *American Political Sciences Review* 85–104.

———, and ———. 1989. "Penultimate Power: Conference Committees and the Legislative Process," Hoover Institution Discussion Paper no. P-89-7, Stanford University.

Spiller, P. T. 1990a. "Governmental Institutions and Regulatory Policy: A Rational Choice Analysis of Telecommunications Deregulation," University of Illinois.

———. 1990b. "Politicians, Interests Groups, and Regulators: A Multiple-Principal Agency Theory of Regulation, (or Let Them be Bribed)," 33 *Journal of Law and Economics* 65–101.

———. 1990c. "Agency Discretion under Judicial Review," University of Illinois.

———, and R. Gely. 1990a. "Congressional Control or Judicial Independence: The Determinants of US Supreme Court Labor Relations Decisions, 1949/1987," Mimeo, University of Illinois.

———, and ———. 1990b. "Understanding the Court," University of Illinois.

Thomas, L., M. Wildemann, and R. Brown. 1987. "The Courts Agency Deregulation: Limitations on the Presidential Control of Regulatory Policy," 39 *Administrative Law Review* 27–42.

Wasby, S. 1988. *The Supreme Court in the Federal Judiciary System*, 3rd ed. Chicago, IL: Nelson-Hall Publishers.

Weingast, B. R. 1981. "Regulation, Reregulation and Deregulation: The Political Foundations of Agency Clientele Relationships," 44 *Law and Contemporary Problems* 147–77.

———. 1984. "The Congressional-Bureaucratic System: A Principal Agent Perspective (with Applications to the SEC), 44 *Public Choice* 147–91.

———, and W. J. Marshall. 1987. "The Industrial Organization of Congress, (or, Why Legislatures, Like Firms, are not Organized as Markets)," 96 *Journal of Political Economy* 132–63.

———, and M. J. Moran. 1983. "Bureaucratic Discretion or Congressional Control?: Regulatory Policymaking by the Federal Trade Commission," 91 *Journal of Political Economy* 765–800.

Part IV
Antitrust

[21]

ASSESSING VERTICAL MARKET RESTRICTIONS: ANTITRUST RAMIFICATIONS OF THE TRANSACTION COST APPROACH

OLIVER E. WILLIAMSON †

Whether troublesome antitrust issues are posed when vertical restraints are placed on distributors by manufacturers has long been disputed. Although economic analysis is needed to assess the ramifications of such restraints, this analysis comes in a variety of forms and does not speak with one voice to these issues. Defective economic reasoning predictably leads to results that are inimical to economic efficiency and sound public policy. Such was the case when franchise restrictions were held anticompetitive in *United States v. Arnold, Schwinn & Co.*[1]

This Article develops the argument that failure to make express allowances for transaction cost considerations is responsible for mistaken public policy in this area.[2] The transaction cost approach applies symmetrically both to an assessment of the efficiency gains, if any, arising from vertical restraints and to an evaluation of the strategic purposes and effects, if any, that accompany such restraints. After developing the justifications for, and occasional anticompetitive effects of, vertical market restrictions, I will suggest guidelines for federal antitrust policy. Part I outlines the general transaction cost approach and concludes that antitrust enforcement agencies and the courts should assume that vertical market restrictions are efficiency-enhancing unless certain structural conditions exist within the industry. Part II discusses strategic behavior and the structural characteristics of industries needed to support strategic outcomes. Vertical restraints pose troublesome antitrust issues only when these

---

† Professor of Economics, Law, and Public Policy, University of Pennsylvania. S.B. 1955, Massachusetts Institute of Technology; M.B.A. 1960, Stanford University; Ph.D. 1963, Carnegie-Mellon University. The paper benefited from support by the Center for Advanced Study in the Behavioral Sciences, a fellowship from the Guggenheim Foundation, and support from the National Science Foundation. Comments by Eitan Muller, Chester Spatt, and David Teece are gratefully acknowledged.

1 388 U.S. 365 (1967).

2 For a discussion of the transaction cost approach, see note 5 *infra.* The transaction cost approach is especially helpful in the context of vertical market relations. *See* Phillips, Schwinn *Rules and the "New Economics" of Vertical Relations*, 44 ANTITRUST L.J. 573 (1975) (transaction cost theory is the "New Economics" of vertical market relations).

conditions exist. Part III examines the development of American distribution systems late in the nineteenth century and concludes that efforts to economize on transaction costs played a central role in the forward integration of certain manufacturers into distribution. Part IV applies my economic analysis to the facts and law of *Schwinn* and concludes that failure to recognize and make allowances for transaction costs is what led to public policy error. Part V contrasts the premises of alternative approaches to vertical restrictions with those of the transaction cost approach. The legal principles derivable from the transaction cost approach are summarized in part VI. When evaluated in light of these proposed legal principles, the Supreme Court's recent decision in *Continental T.V., Inc. v. GTE Sylvania Inc.*[3] can be seen to rest on much sounder ground than did the *Schwinn* decision.

I. Economizing on Transaction Costs

A. *Background*

The relevant unit of economic analysis differs, depending upon the behavior under examination. When the purpose is to explain alternative modes of organization, the fundamental unit of analysis is the transaction.[4] Such an approach recognizes that neither firms nor markets come in predetermined shapes. Rather, both evolve in active juxtaposition to one another. Strategic purposes aside, the object of that evolution is to reach a complementary configuration that economizes on transaction costs.[5] This elementary way of studying economic practices and institutions has only recently been introduced into antitrust economics.[6] Both major and minor errors of enforcement can be attributed to its previous neglect. Its neglect has had especially serious consequences in the area of vertical market relations.

---

[3] 433 U.S. 36 (1977).

[4] *See* Commons, *Institutional Economics*, 21 Am. Econ. Rev. 648 (1931).

[5] *See* Williamson, *Economies as an Antitrust Defense Revisited*, 125 U. Pa. L. Rev. 699, 723 (1977) [hereinafter cited as *Economies Defense*]. This oversimplifies somewhat, in that it takes technology as given. Strategic purposes aside, the more general purpose of economic organization is to devise arrangements that economize on the sum of production and transaction costs.

The basic tenets of the transaction cost approach are stated succinctly in Williamson, *The Economics of Antitrust: Transaction Cost Considerations*, 122 U. Pa. L. Rev. 1439, 1442-43 (1974) [hereinafter cited as *Transaction Cost Considerations*].

[6] *Transaction Cost Considerations*, *supra* note 5, at 1442-43.

I have examined the vertical integration of successive production stages from a transaction perspective elsewhere.[7] The argument may be summarized in the following conclusions: (1) vertical integration in production is explained primarily by transaction cost considerations rather than technological determinancy;[8] (2) although vertical integration commonly yields transaction cost savings, strategic consequences that pose antitrust concerns occasionally arise;[9] (3) antitrust enforcement ought to be more discriminating and restrict its attention to cases in which strategic effects arguably appear;[10] and (4) although vertical integration serves to overcome some of the disabilities to which interfirm trading is subject, the successive integration of additional transactions eventually engenders operating limitations of its own.[11]

This Article deals with vertical market relations between the production and distribution stages. Each of the conclusions reached in my study of the vertical integration of production holds true when the production-distribution nexus is assessed. Some specific differences should be recognized, however, and it is instructive to examine the interface between production and distribution on its own terms. Two novel problems, neither of which is present when integration occurs in intermediate product markets, arise when a firm considers forward integration into distribution.

First, final consumers are ordinarily much less well informed than industrial buyers. Specific efforts to "assist" consumers, sometimes taking the form of product differentiation, may be warranted and observed on this account. Second, but for vertical restrictions, distributors' efforts to promote local profitability objectives can sometimes impair the integrity of the distributorship system. This is often subsumed under the heading of "free rider" effects,[12] but the more general phenomenon is that of subgoal pursuit[13] with adverse systems consequences.

---

[7] *See* O. Williamson, Markets and Hierarchies: Analysis and Antitrust Implications 82-131 (1975); Williamson, *The Vertical Integration of Production: Market Failure Considerations*, 61 Am. Econ. Rev. 112 (1971).

[8] *See* O. Williamson, *supra* note 7, at 82-105; Williamson, *supra* note 7, at 112-17.

[9] *See* O. Williamson, *supra* note 7, at 106-16; Williamson, *supra* note 7, at 117-19.

[10] *See* O. Williamson, *supra* note 7, at 115-16.

[11] *See id.* 117-31.

[12] *See* note 26 *infra*.

[13] By "subgoal pursuit" I refer to efforts to promote local or individual goals to the possible detriment of global or system objectives.

To be sure, subgoal pursuit is responsible for the "ideal" outcomes attributed to competitive markets. The independent pursuit of profit by each of the parties is what the proverbial invisible hand is all about. How is it that competition between a group of distributors handling a common brand is any less valued than competition between autonomous firms selling rival brands? If competition yields social benefits in one context, why not in the other? The uncritical extension of competitive reasoning from the interfirm context to the manufacturer-distributor nexus is doubtlessly responsible for much of the confusion in the vertical restraints arena.

After setting out the principal behavioral assumptions upon which the transaction cost approach is based, I advance the argument below that organizational innovations normally indicate attempts to realize efficiency gains. This, however, is merely a presumption: it can be rebutted in individual instances when certain strategic conditions are shown.[14]

B. *Bounded Rationality and Opportunism*

Bounded rationality and opportunism are the central behavioral assumptions upon which the transaction cost approach is based. Bounded rationality, which should not be confused with irrationality, refers to a condition in which human agents are "*intendedly* rational, but only *limitedly* so." [15] Put differently, it refers to rationality in the ordinary, dictionary sense of the term—"agreeable to reason; not absurd, preposterous, extravagant, foolish, fanciful, or the like; intelligent, sensible" [16]—rather than in the hyperrational sense in which it is commonly used in microeconomics textbooks.[17] Thus, economic agents who are boundedly rational are able to receive, store, retrieve, and process only a limited amount of information. Such agents are routinely overwhelmed by the amount of information supplied to them in relation to their capacity to use it effectively. Accordingly, the economics of attention is an important but generally neglected item on the research agenda.[18]

---

[14] *See* text accompanying notes 27-31 *infra.*

[15] H. SIMON, ADMINISTRATIVE BEHAVIOR xxiv (2d ed. 1961).

[16] WEBSTER'S NEW INTERNATIONAL DICTIONARY OF THE ENGLISH LANGUAGE 2066 (2d ed. 1959).

[17] *See* Simon, *Rationality as Process and as Product of Thought,* AM. ECON. REV., May, 1978, at 1, 2-3.

[18] *See id.* 13. Simon argues that attention, *i.e.,* our capacity for considering and processing a given piece of information, is the scarce resource, not information. Calling for procedural means of focusing attention in a rational and productive way,

Opportunism extends the usual motivational assumption of self-interest to make allowance for self-interest with guile. Thus, whereas bounded rationality suggests decisionmaking less complex than the usual assumption of hyperrationality, opportunism suggests calculating behavior more sophisticated than the usual assumption of simple self-interest. Opportunism refers to "making false or empty, that is, self-disbelieved threats or promises," [19] cutting corners for undisclosed personal advantage, covering up tracks, and the like. Although it is a central assumption, it is not essential that all economic agents behave this way. What is crucial, however, is that *some* agents behave in this fashion and that it is costly to sort out those who are opportunistic from those who are not.

It has long been recognized that opportunism poses economic problems in the context of public goods,[20] in the trading of information,[21] and in insurance markets.[22] But recognition that opportunism is a pervasive economic problem has taken much longer to develop. Peter Diamond observed just seven years ago that the usual assumption is that economic agents do not lie, cheat, or steal. Instead, their actions are overt and agreements are binding.[23] Reliance upon simple self-interest, however, has been changing. More recently, Jack Hirshleifer observed that the key question "for the viability of a pattern of exchange . . . is control of cheating," [24] and

---

he notes that "[i]n a world where attention is a major scarce resource, information may be an expensive luxury, for it may turn our attention from what is important to what is unimportant." *Id.* Bounded rationality should also be distinguished from the "least reasonable man" approach, which some marketing specialists associate with the Federal Trade Commission's approach to advertising. *See* Cunningham & Cunningham, *Standards for Advertising Regulation*, J. MARKETING, October, 1977, at 92. The focus of that approach is on "'the public—that vast multitude which includes the ignorant, the unthinking, and the credulous, who in making purchases, do not stop to analyze, but are governed by appearances and general impressions.'" *Id.* (quoting Florence Mfg. Co. v. J.C. Dowd & Co., 178 F. 73, 75 (2d Cir. 1910)); *see* Charles of the Ritz Distribs. Corp. v. FTC, 143 F.2d 676, 679 (2d Cir. 1944). To be sure, when the hazards are severe and communication difficult, a cautious standard such as this has merit. Presumably, however, these are the exceptions rather than the rule: a reasonable-man standard normally ought to apply.

19 E. GOFFMAN, STRATEGIC INTERACTION 105 (1969).

20 *See, e.g.*, Samuelson, *The Pure Theory of Public Expenditure*, 36 REV. ECON. & STATISTICS 387 (1954).

21 *See, e.g.*, Arrow, *Economic Welfare and the Allocation of Resources for Invention*, in NATIONAL BUREAU OF ECONOMIC RESEARCH, THE RATE AND DIRECTION OF INVENTIVE ACTIVITY: ECONOMIC AND SOCIAL FACTORS 609, 614-16 (1962).

22 K. ARROW, ESSAYS IN THE THEORY OF RISK-BEARING 142 (1971).

23 Diamond, *Comments*, 1 FRONTIERS OF QUANTITATIVE ECONOMICS 29, 31 (M. Intriligator ed. 1971).

24 Hirshleifer, *Economics from a Biological Standpoint*, 20 J.L. & ECON. 1, 27 (1977).

Steven Salop characterizes the Rational Economic Man as one who "choose[s] to tell the truth or misrepresent according to the relative profits of the two strategies, unencumbered by any moral bounds." [25] This is a remarkable transformation in the brief span of seven years.

Given both bounded rationality and opportunism, the following organizational design problem must be faced by the firm and recognized by society: the need to organize transactions in such a way as to economize on bounded rationality while simultaneously safeguarding the transactions in question against opportunism. What is especially interesting about the production-distribution interface is that the manufacturer is concerned not only with the bounded rationality of the immediate parties, but with that of the ultimate consumer as well. Devising transactions that economize on the information needs of consumers is thus a major consideration. Opportunism is also of concern in two respects. The manufacturer is concerned both that the integrity of the distribution system be protected against free riders [26] and that the quality of his product not be debased. Although these are commonly interrelated, it is useful to address each separately. If hazards of either kind are observed, vertical market restrictions may be warranted.

C. *The Presumption that Vertical Market Restrictions Normally Enhance Efficiency*

A transaction cost analysis applies at each separate stage of activity in the production and distribution of a good or service. Whether each separate stage is autonomous or not is unimportant. In principle, each could be and market contracts could be used to bring activity at successive interfaces into adjustment. Such a proliferation of contracts can be costly, however. The basic presumption of the transaction cost approach is that successive interfaces are organized in a manner that economizes on transaction costs. Such

[25] S. Salop, Parables of Information Transmission in Markets 6-7 (April, 1978) (unpublished discussion paper no. 21, Center for the Study of Organizational Innovation, University of Pennsylvania).

[26] An example of a free rider is a retailer who sells a product promoted by one of his competitors. He benefits from the promotion, but because it has cost him nothing, he can sell the product at a lower price than the competitor who promotes it. Territorial restrictions imposed by the manufacturer may prevent this free riding, thus encouraging retailers to push the manufacturer's product. For a discussion of the free rider phenomenon in the context of resale price maintenance, see R. POSNER, ANTITRUST LAW: AN ECONOMIC PERSPECTIVE 149-50, 160, 185 (1976); Telser, *Why Should Manufacturers Want Fair Trade?*, 3 J.L. & ECON. 86 (1960).

an approach is consistent with the common law tradition for assessing economic activity.[27]

Antitrust doctrine typically maintains a more skeptical posture. Given the legal system's reliance on the adversary process, it is not surprising that a former chief of the Antitrust Division of the Justice Department should observe, "I approach territorial and customer restrictions not hospitably in the common law tradition, but inhospitably in the tradition of antitrust law." [28] The major problem with this orientation, which has been the prevailing one, is that the contestants have played the enforcement game entirely on the inhospitability tradition's turf.[29] Rather than affirmatively arguing the case in terms of transaction cost economies, defendants have mainly argued that there are no ill effects.[30] As a consequence of this preoccupation with (real or imagined) anticompetitive effects, the affirmative defenses based on the transaction cost economies underlying many vertical market restrictions have gone undeveloped. *United States v. Arnold, Schwinn & Co.*[31] is an example.

I believe that the common law tradition is based on sound premises and that, confronted with a novel organizational arrangement, the immediate reaction of antitrust enforcement agencies and the courts should not be to attribute anticompetitive purpose and

---

[27] For some recent views on the presumption of efficiency in the common law, see Rubin, *Why is the Common Law Efficient?*, 6 J. LEGAL STUD. 51 (1977); Priest, *The Common Law Process and the Selection of Efficient Rules*, 6 J. LEGAL STUD. 65 (1977). Richard Posner consistently emphasizes efficiency in his wide-ranging and influential studies of the law. *See, e.g.*, R. POSNER, ECONOMIC ANALYSIS OF LAW (1972).

[28] The quotation is attributed to Donald Turner (at a time when he was assistant attorney general in charge of the antitrust division) by Stanley Robinson. 1968 N.Y. ST. B. ASS'N, ANTITRUST LAW SYMPOSIUM 29.

[29] Robert Bork makes a similar point, noting the significance of a recent shift in the Supreme Court's orientation in Continental T.V., Inc. v. GTE Sylvania Inc., 433 U.S. 36 (1977):

> The present misshapen look of antitrust doctrine is due in large measure to the Supreme Court's habit of regarding business efficiency as either irrelevant or harmful . . . . The point is that insufficient regard for efficient methods of production and distribution meant that hardly any business practice challenged could survive. The sole benefit the practice might confer was ruled out of court, and only possible dangers were considered. . . .
>
> The Court's *Sylvania* opinion not only counted efficiencies in favor of a challenged business practice but did so in a sophisticated way . . . . This approach—concern for consumer welfare and an intelligent inquiry into the efficiency potential of challenged business practices—is capable of altering the entire corpus of antitrust jurisprudence, which now stands in considerable need of repair.

Bork, *Vertical Restraints: Schwinn Overruled*, 1977 SUP. CT. REV. 171, 172 (1978).

[30] *E.g.*, United States v. Arnold, Schwinn & Co., 388 U.S. 365 (1967).

[31] 388 U.S. 365 (1967).

intent.[32] Instead, they should inquire whether efficiency gains can plausibly be associated with the arrangement under consideration. Only when this exercise has been completed should the issue of anticompetitive abuse be raised.

The principal reason for maintaining an efficiency presumption is that this presumption accords with reality. As set out in the following section, anticompetitive effects can appear only if rather special structural conditions exist. When these are present, vigilance is warranted. Maintaining a general attitude of inhospitability, however, encourages the enforcement agencies to behave in a counterfactual way and interpret innocent and beneficial developments in a suspect and even hostile manner.

An efficiency presumption is needed to remedy the distortions that earlier traditions have introduced into the enforcement process. However, although presumptions reflect central tendencies and provide framework, they are also subject to challenge. This brings us to matters of strategic purpose and oligopolistic relations.

II. Possible Anticompetitive Effects: Strategic Behavior and Oligopolistic Interdependence

Practices that ordinarily are unobjectionable and indeed arguably are efficient should under some sets of circumstances come under further scrutiny and perhaps be proscribed. Specifically, vigilance is warranted in situations in which the behavior in question promotes strategic purposes or oligopolistic interdependence. The distinction between these two effects is this: activities of a strategic kind serve to disadvantage small rivals and potential entrants in circumstances in which actual competition is attenuated; the creation of oligopolistic interdependence, by contrast, entails efforts to maintain compliance and avoid mutually disadvantageous interfirm rivalry among established oligopolists. Thus, whereas strategic behavior is directed outward, to discipline actual and potential rivals, oligopolistic interdependence focuses inward, the concern being rivalry among major, established firms.

A. *Strategic Behavior and Impediments to Entry*

My discussion of strategic behavior is selective rather than comprehensive. It deals only with circumstances in which vertical re-

[32] An extreme example of this inventive proclivity to emphasize anticompetitive effects, even to the extent of regarding simple efficiency as an anticompetitive advantage, is the argument of the Federal Trade Commission in Foremost Dairies, Inc., 60 F.T.C. 944, 1084 (1962).

strictions can serve as impediments to entry. Predatory pricing, preemptive investment, strategic research and development, and other types of strategic behavior are neglected—although these are all members of the same family.[33]

1. The Views of Bork and Posner

Robert Bork contends, and I agree, that much antitrust mischief has resulted from loose use of the phrase "barriers to entry." [34] In order to avoid continuing abuse, Bork suggests that business practices hereafter be classified as efficiency enhancing or predatory.[35] Provided that allowance is made for the possibility that behavior that is efficient in one context can be exclusionary when used by firms with large market shares, I am prepared to accept this approach. Inasmuch as Bork expressly acknowledges that exclusionary behavior should be examined in contingent terms,[36] there would appear to be no serious conceptual differences between us. Our views do diverge, however, due to the narrowness with which he defines exclusionary practices.

Although Bork at one point concedes that a dominant firm can disadvantage a rival by disrupting optimal distribution patterns,[37] he develops the case in rather circumscribed terms and thereafter argues that there is "nothing to the notion that an established firm might integrate vertically in order deliberately to raise the capital requirements of entry."[38] The "instances of deliberate predation" [39] that expressly concern him are boycotts,[40] individual refusals to deal,[41] and predation through government processes.[42] He believes that all vertical restraints are unqualifiedly lawful.[43]

---

[33] *See* Salop, *Strategic Entry Deterrence,* 69 AM. ECON. REV. — (1979); Spence, *Entry, Capacity, Investment and Oligopolistic Pricing,* 8 BELL J. ECON. 534 (1977); Williamson, *Predatory Pricing: A Strategic and Welfare Analysis,* 87 YALE L.J. 284 (1977).

[34] R. BORK, THE ANTITRUST PARADOX 310 (1978).

[35] *Id.* 160, 329.

[36] *Id.* 156-57. Bork cites the exclusive dealing agreement as an example of a practice that manifests a very weak possibility of predation and a very strong probability of efficiency. Although his view of the lawfulness of the practice is clear, it implicitly recognizes the possibility of exceptions. "[T]he law cannot properly see predatory behavior in *all* unilaterally enforced changes in patterns of distribution." *Id.* 156 (emphasis added).

[37] *Id.* 156-58.

[38] *Id.* 323.

[39] *Id.* 329.

[40] *Id.* 330-44.

[41] *Id.* 344-46.

[42] *Id.* 347-64.

[43] *Id.* 288; Bork, *supra* note 29, at 173-80, 181-82.

Richard Posner also cautions against excessive concern with entry barrier claims. Thus he counsels that "[a] barrier to entry is commonly used . . . to mean anything which a new entrant must overcome in order to gain a foothold in the market, such as the capital costs of entering the market on an efficient scale. This is . . . meaningless . . . since it is obvious that a new entrant must incur costs to enter the market, *just as his predecessors . . . did previously.*"[44]

2. A Different View

For the reasons set out below, I am not persuaded that capital market impediments cannot arise because of vertical restraints or that the cost conditions facing early and later entrants are equal. I should make clear, however, that my differences with Bork and Posner arise only in dominant firm industries and, possibly, in collusive oligopolies. In other circumstances, efforts to behave strategically will be self-defeating. Accordingly, concern over strategic behavior vanishes in industries characterized by neither dominant firms nor tight oligopolies.

To illustrate that a capital market impediment can arise as a result of vertical integration, posit an industry with two stages, a production stage and a distribution stage. Assume that the industry is equally efficient whether or not these stages are integrated.[45] In addition, assume that manufacturing (stage I) is monopolized and that the monopolist has integrated forward into distribution (stage II). Finally, assume that a potential entrant with experience in manufacturing, but none in distribution, subsequently develops a rival product that it can manufacture at a competitive cost. The question to be addressed is whether this rival is disadvantaged by the monopolist's earlier decision to integrate.

Assessing this will be facilitated by comparing the conditions facing the potential entrant under the following nonintegrated and integrated alternatives:

> (1) [T]he monopolistic stage I producer is not integrated, in which case the prospective new entrant can enter at stage I only and utilize the facilities of stage II producers . . . (suitably expanded if necessary), [or] . . . (2) the monopolistic stage I producer is integrated into stage II so that either (a) the new entrant himself comes in at both stages or (b)

[44] R. Posner, *supra* note 26, at 59 (emphasis added).

[45] It should be noted that vertical integration could be a less efficient mode of structuring transactions but might be adopted nonetheless because of strategic incentives.

independent new entrants appear simultaneously at both stages. If Bork . . . [is] correct, the cost of capital ought to be independent of these conditions.

To contend that the terms of finance are the same under 2(a) as they are under 1 implies that the capital market has equal confidence in the new entrant's qualifications to perform stage II activities as it does in firms that are already experienced in the business. Except in circumstances where experienced firms are plainly inept, this is tantamount to saying that experience counts for nought. This, however, is implausible for transactions that involve large, discrete rather than small, but recurring commitments of funds. Although transactions of the latter type can be monitored reasonably effectively, on the basis of ex post experience, this is much less easy for transactions of the large, discrete variety—which are the kind under consideration here. Reputation, which is to say prior experience, is of special importance in establishing the terms of finance for transactions that involve large, discrete commitments of funds.[46]

The problems are worse, moreover, if the 2(b) scenario unfolds. As compared with condition 1, would-be stage II entrants are presumably penalized both for lack of experience and because nonconvergent expectations[47] pose more serious problems in the 2(b) context. The latter argument is that the flexible or expanded capacity of existing stage II processors can accommodate new entry at stage I much more easily than if simultaneous new entry by independent distributors at stage II is required. Problems with interdependent investments by new independent entities arise because of differing perceptions of the market, incentive differences, and because interfirm intentions may be difficult to signal. These hazards are presumably reflected in the cost of capital. As a consequence, neither of the type 2 scenarios is on a parity with the type 1 condition. Bork's unrestricted claim that vertical integration

[46] O. Williamson, *supra* note 7, at 111.

[47] Firms' expectations converge, creating equilibrium in a market as a whole, when every firm bases its expectations on the same set of events and signals, and comes to the same conclusions. Whether or not such market equilibrium can be achieved depends on several factors, among them the degree of interdependence among the firms, the level of certainty about the future, the number of variables to be considered, the capacity of firms to adapt to change, and the amount of information available to the firms. *See* Malmgren, *Information, Expectations and the Theory of the Firm*, 75 Q.J. Econ. 399, 405-11 (1961); Williamson, *supra* note 7, at 120.

cannot influence the cost of capital, and hence the conditions to entry, is evidently overstated.[48]

Consider now the cost issue that Posner addresses. As he puts it, the issue appears to be whether early entrants are somehow able to *avoid* costs that later entrants incur. He claims they are not, with which contention I agree. But this does not reach the question whether timing differences can give rise to differential *cost bearing* consequences. This is related to, but goes beyond, the matter of differential capital costs discussed above.

Whether potential entrants will be disadvantaged by prior integration depends on (1) the importance of learning-by-doing, (2) the degree to which learning-by-doing economies are shared by employer and employee, (3) the ease with which specialized human assets can be bid away, and (4) the degree to which prices track costs.[49] Assuming that prices track the current costs of the least-cost supplier in a fairly regular way and that it is difficult to bid specialized human assets away from current employers in effective team configurations, potential entrants will be more severely disadvantaged by prior integration the more important that learning-by-doing economies are and the less completely these learning economies are appropriated by employees.

The upshot is that decisions to integrate into activities that require investments in idiosyncratic human or physical assets can affect the subsequent ease of entry. Whether the argument has antitrust significance, however, depends on the circumstances. For one thing, the conditions of entry are relatively unimportant if actual competition is already effective. Even where this is problematical, an *additional* entry impediment because of integration can be said to exist only to the extent that access through established distribution channels is impracticable. This, in turn, depends on the size of the residual (nonintegrated) market and on whether sales through the distribution channels of integrated firms are realistic. The subset of industries warranting close antitrust scrutiny, from both actual competition and market access points of view, reduces to industries characterized by dominant firms and tight oligopolies that have comprehensively integrated into distribution.

Even here, the question whether forward integration or vertical restrictions yield net benefits should be addressed. Are the benefits

---

[48] *See* Caves & Porter, *From Entry Barriers to Mobility Barriers: Conjectural Decisions and Contrived Deterrence to New Competition*, 91 Q.J. ECON. 241, 246-47 (1977) (vertical integration may raise the capital-cost entry barrier).

[49] *See* O. WILLIAMSON, *supra* note 7, at 216-17.

great or slight in relation to the anti-competitive consequences? The results of this inquiry can vary depending on the industry's stage of development. Thus, economic benefits realized immediately after the restraint has been effected may not continue indefinitely. Put differently, although "administered distribution" may be needed to ensure viability at an early stage in an industry's development, a more mature industry may be able to support the requisite distribution system without the same need for restraints on forward integration. Thus, although forward integration may represent an effort to realize private gains with resulting economies at one stage, it may constitute an unneeded restraint at a later stage and indeed may serve strategically to disadvantage rivals if it is continued.

Although the above argument is primarily couched in terms of vertical integration, I also refer to vertical restrictions. The scope of the latter term should be qualified. Among exclusive dealing, territorial restrictions, and customer restrictions, only the first of these vertical restrictions constitutes a possible entry impediment, and this only under the special circumstances of structural dominance or tight oligopoly.[50]

More generally, except as oligopolistic interdependence is promoted,[51] I am persuaded by Bork's arguments that territorial and customer restraints should not be proscribed.[52] Manufacturers will introduce these only as they are expected to attenuate subgoal pursuit and promote efficiency.[53] But what of the possibility that exclusive dealing has objectionable effects other than that of impeding entry? If it does, under what circumstances do these effects occur and what are the ramifications for antitrust enforcement?

---

[50] I have defined a dominant firm industry as one in which the market share of the largest firm is at least sixty percent and entry into the market is not easy. Tight oligopoly is less easy to characterize. It is mainly apt to appear in mature, highly concentrated industries producing homogeneous products under uniform cost conditions and having significant barriers to entry. The reasons why oligopolistic interdependence is difficult to sustain in other circumstances is traceable to the transaction costs of reaching and policing collusive agreements. *See generally* O. WILLIAMSON, *supra* note 7, at 234-47.

[51] *See* text accompanying notes 57-62 *infra*.

[52] *See* note 40 *supra*.

[53] Preston observes that "customer-territorial restrictions considered alone . . . do not contribute to the weakening of the interbrand competition in final markets or serve as barriers to entry." Preston, *Restrictive Distribution Arrangements: Economic Analysis and Public Policy Standards*, 30 L. & CONTEMP. PROB. 506, 520 (1965). Furthermore, "[t]he case against customer-territorial restrictions where suppliers are profitable or relatively large appears to rest on an association between these restrictions and parallel limitations on the range of products marketed by a distributor, *i.e.*, exclusive dealing." *Id.* 520-21 (footnote omitted).

Suppose that entry is unaffected but that exclusive dealing benefits some customers (for example, by permitting a product to be effectively differentiated) but simultaneously disadvantages others. For instance, comparison shopping is often facilitated by side-by-side examination; exclusive dealing precludes this. Marginal customers who wish to establish whether differentiation warrants a price premium will, if confronted by exclusive dealing, be less able to make informed judgments easily. How should this be evaluated?

Or suppose that, although the restraint itself negligibly affects the condition of entry, other factors impede entry and widespread use of the restraint effectively precludes customers who *know* that they place little value on the additional services (which are not offered separately under exclusive dealing restrictions) from obtaining the product without services included.

Bork meets these types of objections with the argument that when the "technology of distribution . . . [does] not allow the preferences of both groups of customers to be met, . . . the manufacturer will choose to satisfy the larger number," which he regards as the efficient thing to do.[54] Actually, I would expect that manufacturers would service the more profitable subset—which recent scholarship discloses commonly will be, but need not be, the larger market.[55] More troublesome is the possibility that the use of a profitability calculus to decide what mix of products to offer may be at variance with welfare gains, even when the decision is to service the larger market.

However, inasmuch as such defects in the product mix calculus are difficult to ascertain in practice and since exclusive dealing does not obviously bias such choices adversely, it seems prudent to separate exclusive dealing restraints from the product variety issue. Accordingly, except as entry impediments result, a policy of permissiveness with respect to exclusive dealing restraints would normally appear to be warranted.[56]

---

[54] Bork, *supra* note 29, at 181.

[55] *See* Dixit & Stiglitz, *Monopolistic Competition and Optimum Product Diversity*, 67 AM. ECON. REV. 297 (1977); Spence, *Product Differentiation and Welfare*, 66 AM. ECON. REV. 407 (1976).

[56] Note that, directly or indirectly, all of the above issues depend on transaction-cost considerations. Thus, investors demand a premium to invest in new enterprises because (1) it is costly to assess the merits of the investment proposal (the relevant data cannot be displayed and evaluated costlessly) and (2) there are hazards of opportunism. The idiosyncrasies of human assets also reflect a condition of information impactedness in which inexperienced firms are disadvantaged. Comparison shopping has advantages because the characteristics of rival products cannot be described adequately in objective terms to allow abstract comparisons to be made. This is a reflection of bounded rationality. And nonseparable offers of product and

B. *Oligopolistic Interdependence and the Regularization of Price*

Although Posner is unconcerned with strategic (outward-directed) uses of vertical restrictions, he argues that such restrictions can be used to strengthen a dealer cartel.[57] This is worrisome, however, only when a "manufacturer ha[s] a very large market share or . . . [when] all or most of the manufacturers in the market imposed uniform restrictions on their dealers so that (in either case) the dealers had a monopoly position in a genuine economic market."[58] In all other circumstances, vertical restrictions evidently pose no antitrust concerns.

Although I agree that the issue of dealer cartels warrants antitrust scrutiny, the possibility that vertical restrictions can be used to consolidate a *manufacturer* cartel is to me more troublesome. Thus, even if, contrary to Bork, dealer cartels are not easy antitrust enforcement targets,[59] I question whether dealers are often in a position to impose restrictive terms on unwilling manufacturers. When they are not, we can be confident that manufacturers will not knowingly adopt strategies the effect of which is to transfer money from their pockets to those of their retailers.[60] Observed restrictions can thus be assumed to promote manufacturer interests.

The more troublesome possibility to which I refer—that vertical restrictions can be used to support manufacturer cartels—hinges on the proposition that regularizing exchange commonly serves to stabilize frangible associations. A crucial operating concern of a manufacturers' cartel is to devise signals whereby adherence to the cartel policy can be inferred with confidence. The elimination of false moves or ambiguous actions which, if misinterpreted, would cause the cartel to unravel, is of special importance.

---

service are made because manufacturers are unable to price-discriminate fully and cannot rely on customers to reveal true preferences accurately—manifestations of bounded rationality and opportunism, respectively.

[57] Posner, *The Rule of Reason and the Economic Approach: Reflections on the* Sylvania *Decision*, 45 U. Chi. L. Rev. 1, 17 (1977).

[58] *Id.* Posner would use a "rule of reason" approach "to isolate, and condemn, restrictions that are imposed nominally by the manufacturer but are in fact desired for monopolistic purposes by dealers using the manufacturer as their enforcement agent." *Id.*

[59] R. Bork, *supra* note 34, at 292-93. In disposing of the "dealer cartel objection" to his proposal that all vertical restraints be held lawful, Bork argues not only that dealer cartels are not difficult to uncover, but also that manufacturer-imposed restraints, affecting only intrabrand competition, are of limited, if any, use to a dealer cartel. *Id.*

[60] *See* Bork, *supra* note 29, at 188.

The avoidance of pricing ambiguity is especially critical. When retail outlets are owned or extensively controlled by manufacturers, retail price changes can normally be assumed to reflect manufacturers' intent. By contrast, the responsibility for pricing changes is less clear where dealers are fully autonomous agents. To the extent that pricing latitude among such dealers makes it more difficult for manufacturers to reach cartel agreements because ex ante confidence in the subsequent execution of agreements is lacking, efforts to remove "unwanted" degrees of freedom can be anticipated. The same is true when, despite agreement, price variability creates suspicion that cartel members are defecting, which in turn may cause the cartel to unravel.

Bork argues that the manufacturer cartel objection to vertical restrictions is "insubstantial" and "applies only to resale price maintenance." [61] I would characterize it somewhat differently. Although I agree that regularizing price is the main antitrust concern, vertical restraints other than resale price maintenance can be used to promote pricing discipline. The use of vertical restrictions to tighten oligopolistic interdependence is likely to be attractive, however, only in industries with homogenous products.[62] It is noteworthy, moreover, that an economies justification for such restrictions is difficult to provide in homogeneous product markets. Accordingly, the burden of justifying vertical restrictions in homogeneous, oligopolistic industries rests heavily on the firms employing them. The normal efficiency presumption is unwarranted in such circumstances.

III. Aspects of the Historical Development of American Distribution Systems

Alfred Chandler, Jr.'s recent monograph [63] describing marketing developments during the late nineteenth century provides strong support for the proposition that transaction costs are sufficiently significant to affect the structure of industries, sometimes motivating firms to integrate forward from manufacturing into the retail stage. In the following subsections Chandler's findings concerning effi-

---

[61] R. Bork, *supra* note 34, at 294.

[62] *See* Newman, *Strategic Groups and the Structure-Performance Relationship*, 60 Rev. Econ. & Statistics 417 (1978). For a discussion of the problems associated with effecting tight interdependence in oligopoly, see O. Williamson, *supra* note 7, at 234-47.

[63] A. Chandler, The Visible Hand: The Managerial Revolution in American Business (1977).

ciency-enhancing and strategic behavior will first be described, then analyzed from a transaction cost perspective.

A. *Efficiency and Forward Integration*

1. Chandler's Findings

Chandler's description of forward integration into distribution by American manufacturers distinguishes between the developments of infrastructure and the induced distributional response. The appearance of the railroads and the telegraph and telephone systems in the latter part of the nineteenth century permitted wider geographic areas to be served in a reliable and timely way. The "reliability and speed of the new transportation and communication" permitted greater economies of scale to be realized in factory organization.[64] These economies of scale at the factory level were latent—in the sense that the technology was there waiting to be exploited. Because it is not manufacturing cost but delivered cost that matters, however, it became profitable to realize these scale economies only when a low-cost distribution system appeared. That is, so long as transportation expenses were great, the most efficient way to serve markets was by dispersing factories.

Once the new transportation and communication infrastructure was in place, the stage was set for the distributional response. A crucial question was how to devise a *coordinated* manufacturing-distribution response. In principle, both stages could have remained autonomous: manufacturers could have remained specialized and built larger-scale plants while specialized distributors could have responded simultaneously, either on their own initiative or by contract, by assembling the requisite distribution network. In many industries, however, "existing marketers were unable to sell and distribute products in the volume they were produced . . . . Once the inadequacies of existing marketers became clear, manufacturers integrated forward into marketing." [65] An administrative override was evidently needed.[66]

Not all industries integrated forward, however, and those that did integrate forward did not do so to the same extent. Some industries linked manufacturing only with advertising and wholesaling; retail integration was not attempted. Nondurable industries that had recently adopted continuous process machinery—

[64] *Id.* 245.

[65] *Id.* 287.

[66] For an interesting treatment of vertical integration forward into distribution in the sale of gasoline, see D. TEECE, VERTICAL INTEGRATION AND VERTICAL DIVESTITURE IN THE U.S. OIL INDUSTRY 40-44 (1976).

cigarettes, matches, cereals, and canned goods are examples—were in this category.[67] More ambitious and interesting were producer and consumer durables that required "specialized marketing services—demonstration, installation, consumer credit, after-sales service and repair," services that existing middlemen "had neither the interest nor facilities to provide." [68] Examples here included sewing machines, farm machinery, office machines, and heavy electrical equipment.

2. A Transaction Cost Interpretation

The new transportation and communication infrastructure permitted manufacturers to serve larger markets in a low-cost way. The ramifications of these infrastructural developments on plant size are displayed in Figure 1.[69]

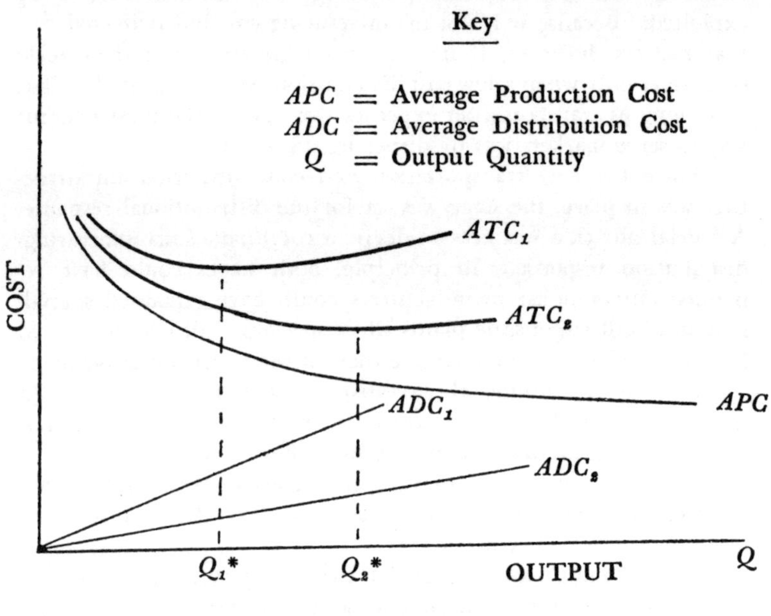

FIGURE 1

[67] "Such entrepreneurs found that the existing marketers were unable to move their goods quickly enough or to advertise them effectively enough to keep their high-volume production facilities operating steadily." A. CHANDLER, *supra* note 63, at 287.

[68] *Id.* 288.

[69] F. SCHERER, A. BECKENSTEIN, E. KAUFER, AND R. MURPHY, THE ECONOMICS OF MULTIPLANT OPERATION: AN INTERNATIONAL COMPARISON STUDY (1975).

The *APC* curve shows the average cost of production as plant size increases. These average costs decrease over a wide range due to assumed economies of scale. The curve ADC_1 shows the original average distribution cost of delivering products from a plant. This curve increases throughout because greater sales require marketing to a larger geographic region. The curve ADC_2 shows the average distribution cost after the new infrastructure is put in place. It is everywhere lower than ADC_1, but also rises throughout. ATC_1 and ATC_2 are average total cost curves: these are given by the vertical summation of *APC* with ADC_1 and ADC_2, respectively. Average total costs reach a minimum at Q_1^* *and* Q_2^*, where Q_2^* is necessarily larger the Q_1^*, given the stipulated shift in average distribution costs. An increase in plant scale and the extension of service to larger geographic markets are thus indicated.

Problems of implementation, however, are not addressed by this cost curve apparatus. How are the linkages between manufacturing and distribution to be forged? They are not created automatically. If existing middlemen respond in a slow and faltering way to the opportunities that the new transportation and communication infrastructures afford, the stage is set for someone, in this instance the manufacturers, to experiment with new organizational structures.

The issues here are of a transaction cost rather than of a production cost kind. Although a definitive analysis of the "inadequacies of existing marketers" [70] reported by Chandler would require further research, I conjecture that these distributional difficulties are due to a failure of "convergent expectations" [71] coupled with the hazards posed by small numbers supply relations between autonomous parties.[72] Convergent expectations problems are mainly attributable to bounded rationality. It was difficult for marketers who were accustomed to operating in a local market regime to perceive the opportunities that awaited them. And there was no obvious way to signal these opportunities by relying upon decentralized pricing.[73] Moreover, even if manufacturers and distributors had both perceived the opportunities that the new transportation and communication infrastructure afforded, and if each responded in-

[70] A. Chandler, *supra* note 63, at 287.

[71] *See* Malmgren, *supra* note 47, at 405-11.

[72] For a discussion of these transaction cost issues, see O. Williamson, *supra* note 7, at 86-95.

[73] *See* Malmgren, *supra* note 47.

dependently in reliance upon the other, problems of divergence would arise if each recorded or interpreted the data differently. Such divergent expectations would exist, moreover, at both an aggregate and a disaggregate level.

In principle, manufacturers could have taken the initiative and effected convergent expectations by contract. Coordination by contract is costly, however, where the two parties are bargaining in an unfamiliar situation and the hazards of contracting are great. The hazards to which I refer have been discussed elsewhere in the context of idiosyncratic exchange.[74] Such problems arise when investments in specialized human and/or physical assets are required in order that the transaction be completed in an economical way. With respect to the issues of concern to Chandler, the problems were especially severe when the mass production and sale of consumer or producer durables was contemplated. Distributors here would have to be induced to make specialized (product- and brand-specific) investments and, once made, manufacturers and distributors would thereafter often be dealing with each other in what, essentially, was a bilateral exchange arrangement.[75] Given the hazards of opportunism that arise in such circumstances, both parties were reluctant to rely on autonomous contracting to accomplish the investments and govern a continuing exchange relation.

Forward integration by manufacturers into distribution was the organizational response to these contracting difficulties. Not only were profits realized in the process, but social cost savings resulted. Absent reasons to believe otherwise, net social as well as net private gains accrue when such organizational innovations appear.

B. *Strategic Behavior and Forward Integration*

1. Chandler's Findings

Chandler assigns long-lasting entry consequences to the forward integration decisions of American manufacturers described above. Thus he observes:

> The administrative networks built to integrate the new processes of production and distribution gave the pioneer-

---

[74] O. Williamson, *supra* note 7, at 60-64; Wachter & Williamson, *Obligational Markets and the Mechanics of Inflation*, 9 Bell J. Econ. 549, 556-57 (1978).

[75] *See* O. Williamson, *supra* note 7, at 89-95.

> ing enterprises their greatest competitive advantage. Although capital intensive in terms of the ratio of capital to labor inputs, the new machinery was not that expensive. The absolute cost of entry [into manufacturing] was not high, nor in most industries were patents a barrier to entry . . . .
>
> The most imposing barrier to entry in these industries was the organization the pioneers had built to market and distribute their newly mass-produced products. A competitor who acquired the technology had to create a national and often a global organization of managers, buyers, and salesmen if he was to get the business away from the one or two enterprises that already stood astride the major marketing channels. Moreover, where the pioneer could finance the building of the first of these organizations out of cash flow, generated by high volume, the newcomer had to set up a competing network before high-volume output reduced unit costs and created a sizeable cash flow.[76]

2. A Transaction Cost Interpretation

Four things are noteworthy about Chandler's conclusions. First, entry barriers of the conventional kinds were not, in his judgment, significant. Second, the main barriers were attributable to the linking of manufacturing with distribution. Third, late entrants were at a disadvantage with respect to early entrants not because the latter were able to avoid costs but because of the differential cost-bearing consequences of later entry. This is precisely the matter of temporal cost differences discussed above.[77] Finally, although the linking of manufacturing and distribution arguably had strategic consequences, the original decisions to integrate were not motivated by a strategic purpose. Rather, the resulting entry effects appear to be unintended spillovers.

Such unintended spillovers should be contrasted with predatory pricing or predatory investment, in which a punitive or preemptive

---

[76] A. CHANDLER, *supra* note 63, at 298-99.

[77] *See* text accompanying notes 34-56 *supra*.

The essence of Chandler's argument is that a "first mover" advantage can affect the conditions of entrance later faced by others. A general discussion of this phenomenon can be found in my book *Markets and Hierarchies: Analysis and Antitrust Implications*. O. WILLIAMSON, *supra* note 7, at 34-35.

purpose is clear and an antitrust issue is sharply posed. Should the consequences of benign historical decisions also come under antitrust scrutiny? In addition, should antitrust law attempt to effect remedies for such consequences?

As to the first question, it seems clear that any development, historical or otherwise, that contributes significantly to the creation of durable dominant firms or collusive oligopolies should be identified and analyzed—lest it be unnecessarily repeated. But whether the law should attempt to undo unwanted outcomes that are attributable to once-lawful responses to business opportunities is a more difficult matter. This problem involves a tension between two fundamental values.

The affirmative case for legal intervention is based on the premise that, except when lawful patents are involved or when intervention would result in diseconomies, durable monopoly power of any kind results in direct and indirect economic losses. The direct losses include simple allocative efficiency decrements, due to the excesses of prices over costs, and the reduced vigor of intra-industry rivalry (which may impair both process and product innovation). Indirect losses are of an intergenerational kind, in which later generations find that opportunity sets are sharply circumscribed by earlier events.

The opposing argument is that penalizing winners is contrary to the spirit of an enterprise system and will impair incentives to innovate. Presumably, however, the strength of these arguments weakens as the period over which monopolistic results remain unchallenged lengthens. Whether the gains from intervention exceed the losses after only five years of uncontested dominance is perhaps doubtful. But indefinite insularity is not obviously optimal. Twelve to fifteen years of unchallenged dominance might well be reasonable,[78] though even this is subject to dispute. Dominant firm outcomes simply pose an unhappy public policy dilemma—a dilemma which is made more acute when such outcomes are attributable to preemptive signaling and investment.[79]

---

78 At a discount rate of 15 percent, the discounted values of a dollar earned 12 or 15 years in the future are 19 and 12 cents, respectively. At a twenty percent discount rate, the corresponding present values drop to 11 and 7 cents. The present value of a project that earns *K* dollars per year in perpetuity is 7.1*K* if discounted at fifteen percent and 5.5*K* if discounted at twenty percent. Eighty percent of these values are realized during the first 11½ and 9 years, respectively. Claims that investment incentives are sharply curtailed if monopoly outcomes are, at some point, subject to challenge should come to terms with this arithmetic.

79 *See* Spence, *Investment Strategy and Growth in a New Market,* 10 BELL J. ECON. _ (1979).

IV. A Transaction Cost Critique of the *Schwinn* Decision

The law of vertical restrictions appears to be tentative and unsettled.[80] Its protean character is apparent in the Supreme Court's inconsistent application of legal principles and standards in three cases: *White Motor Co. v. United States,*[81] *United States v. Arnold, Schwinn & Co.,*[82] and *Continental T.V., Inc. v. GTE Sylvania Inc.*[83] Of these, *Schwinn* best reflects the hazards of grounding legal decisions in defective economic reasoning. Although *Sylvania* made progress toward remedying some of the mischief created by *Schwinn,* I believe further progress can be made if the transaction cost attributes of vertical restriction cases are developed. The transaction cost approach to antitrust issues applies broadly,[84] and powerfully illuminates matters relating to vertical integration and vertical restraints.[85] With the expectation that systematic criticism of past mistakes aids the process of creating better antitrust law, in this section I will discuss the efficiency and strategic aspects of vertical restraints like those found in *Schwinn.* One of the reasons why inhospitable economic reasoning of the kind that prevailed in *Schwinn* has since been discredited is the growing realization that transaction cost issues that were suppressed then are central—both to *Schwinn* and to a broader understanding of economic organization.

A. *Transaction Cost Efficiencies*

Suppose that a producer has a distinctive good or service and perceives that the public, or some part thereof, will be prepared to purchase it, possibly by paying a premium above the price of substitutes, if the producer can (1) create recognition for the attributes that distinguish the item, (2) maintain quality control with respect to these attributes, and (3) maintain cost control such that the price at which the product will recover its full costs is not prohibitive.

80 *See* Bork, *supra* note 29, at 171; Goldberg, *The Law and Economics of Vertical Restrictions: A Relational Perspective* (1978) (unpublished paper on file with the University of Pennsylvania Law Review).

81 372 U.S. 253 (1963).

82 388 U.S. 253 (1967).

83 433 U.S. 36 (1977).

84 *See Transaction Cost Considerations, supra* note 5, at 1439.

85 D. Teece, *supra* note 66, at 7-25; Liebeler, *Integration and Competition,* in Vertical Integration in the Oil Industry (E. Mitchell ed. 1976); Phillips, *supra* note 2. Phenomena that other approaches regard with puzzlement, or even hostility, fall naturally into place when vertical relations issues are cast in contracting terms and the properties of alternative contracting modes are examined with respect to their transaction cost attributes.

Specifically, assume that the distinctive item in question is a bicycle, that distinctiveness takes the form of quality and service, and that the brand name of the bicycle is Schwinn.

If customers were fully knowledgeable or could be apprised without cost of all relevant attributes of all products, Schwinn could simply announce that it was supplying a bicycle that had these properties, the announcement would be registered among potential buyers, customers could verify that these conditions existed (though verification is a redundant operation in a world of complete knowledge), and those who valued the attributes could judge whether the premium was justified. Product differentiation in a world of unbounded rationality would thus proceed in a smooth and faultless manner.

Consumers, however, do not have these high-powered attributes: their capacity to receive, store, recover, and process information is limited. In the light of these limitations, not only does Schwinn face the problem of transmitting its distinctive qualities, but it faces the problem of having its image believed. Thus, if consumers are occasionally misled, in that they are sometimes told one thing and learn to their dismay that it is incorrect, and if instances of fraud or deception are not known without cost to other potential buyers, so that reputations are not instantly and accurately updated, consumers will be wary when sellers apprise them that their brand has "superior" qualities.

In a market of boundedly rational consumers, Schwinn is faced with three interrelated information problems. First, it needs to bring to the attention of consumers the distinctive attributes that it purports to supply. Second, it needs to provide an institutional infrastructure that will prevent these attributes from being degraded. Third, it needs to accomplish both of these goals in an economical fashion.

Assume that it is uneconomical for Schwinn to mount a massive advertising campaign in which to proclaim the superiority of its product. In addition, assume that, because quality and service are related attributes, Schwinn determines that the most effective way to accomplish its product differentiation objectives is to distribute through authorized dealers who agree, as a condition of franchising, to provide specified minimum services (advertising, assembly, maintaining a stock of bicycles and replacement parts, providing qualified repair personnel, and the like). Inasmuch as these services are costly to provide, Schwinn bicycles sold and serviced by authorized dealers will be priced at a premium, other things being equal.[86] Assume further that Schwinn's product differentiation efforts will be vitiated if this set of minimum services is not reliably provided.[87] Assume finally that Schwinn's franchise program is successful in that, with appropriate franchisee constraints, the image appeals to a sufficient number of customers to make it viable.

Several economic questions now arise. First, which customers will be attracted by such an image? Second, why might Schwinn want to prevent nonfranchised sales? Third, will Schwinn integrate forward into retailing if vertical restraints are not permitted? Each of these poses transaction cost issues.

With respect to customer appeal, the buyers that will be attracted by Schwinn will presumably be those for whom the opportunity cost of time is great or who are relatively inept at self-assembly and service. Thus, high-priced lawyers and other consultants who bill clients on an hourly basis will pay several times the going rate for a haircut, by patronizing barber shops that cut hair by appointment, rather than joining the queue at a wait-your-turn establishment.[88] The argument generalizes to the procurement of consumer durables. Time is economized if the customer does not have to search for a brand possessing the requisite properties and is easily able to locate and visit an outlet where the brand is stocked. And additional time is saved if the item comes pre-assembled, is reasonably trouble-free, and is reliably serviced at convenient outlets.

Such a brand of bicycle will also be attractive to customers who, though their unit opportunity cost of time may be below average, are particularly inept at self-assembly and repairs. In this situation, despite low unit costs, the total opportunity cost is great—because this is the product of unit cost and time expended. Thus, two classes of customers will respond positively to the Schwinn image: those who are inept and those who, although capable, have a high per-unit opportunity cost of time.

This merely establishes, however, that franchised sales of Schwinn bicycles will appeal to some customers. It does not reach the question whether Schwinn should sell to all comers, allowing dealers to determine whether or not to offer the set of services that

[86] Furthermore, the premium will also increase to the extent that Schwinn incurs additional expense at the manufacturing stage in order to accomplish its quality objectives.

[87] Possible causes of this problem are discussed below.

[88] *See* Becker, *A Theory of the Allocation of Time*, 75 ECON. J. 493 (1965).

would qualify them as franchisees. Were Schwinn to do this, customers who have the above-described attributes would presumably go to the franchised outlet; those who do not could go elsewhere. Because in a world of unbounded rationality more degrees of freedom—in this instance, more methods of merchandising—are necessarily better than less, the natural policy inclination would be to let consumers decide the question for themselves.

Several justifications, however, can be articulated in support of franchise restrictions: first, the Schwinn quality image may be debased without sales restraints; second, even if quality images are not impaired, the viability of franchises may hinge on sales restraints; third, the costs of enforcing the distribution contracts are increased in a mixed distribution system.[89] The quality image of Schwinn turns partly on objective considerations: Schwinn bicycles bought from authorized dealers come with an assured set of sales and service attributes. But the image may also be affected by information exchanged by word of mouth. If potential customers are told, "I bought a Schwinn bike and it was a lemon," but are not advised that the bicycle was bought from a discount house and was misassembled, and that Schwinn's guarantees were thereby vitiated, customer confidence in Schwinn is easily impaired. Put differently, quality reputation may be preserved only if goods and services are sold under conditions of constraint.[90] Note in this connection that the incentive to invest in commercial reputation, by surrounding transactions with institutional infrastructure, occurs only in a world of bounded rationality.[91]

---

[89] Although arguably not applicable to the *Schwinn* case, a fourth justification can be based on unfair allocation of demonstration costs: customers might shop for Schwinn bicycles at the franchised dealer—deciding on what model, features, etc., to buy—and then make their purchase at the discount house, where the costs of demonstration are largely avoided. This may be a more serious concern when more expensive items, such as automobiles, are being marketed.

[90] The fact that twenty percent of Schwinn's authorized sales were made by outlets—B.F. Goodrich, hardware and department stores—which did not provide service might be taken as "proof" that the above hazard is insubstantial. *See* Brief for the United States at 43-44, United States v. Arnold, Schwinn & Co., 388 U.S. 365 (1967). But there are three mitigating considerations: (1) while twenty percent nonserviced sales may be permissible, forty percent may not be; (2) the outlets described have reputation attributes rather different from discount houses, and hence may "stand behind" sales more completely; and (3) business judgment on such matters is entitled to a certain degree of undisputed respect.

[91] True attributes are presumably known or can be ascertained without cost in a world of unbounded rationality. If this boggles the mind, the reader is encouraged to examine the once-for-all time-cum-environmental bidding procedures in J.E. Meade's *The Controlled Economy*. J.E. MEADE, THE CONTROLLED ECONOMY (1971).

Even if the quality image of franchise sales is unimpaired by nonfranchise selling, the commercial viability of franchisees, which hinges on volume considerations, should be examined. Suppose that it is determined that a franchised dealer needs to sell a minimum number of bicycles in order to break even. Suppose further that Schwinn carefully locates its franchisees cognizant of these break-even needs.[92] Finally, suppose that the system is initially viable but that discount sales subsequently appear. Marginal franchise operators shortly thereafter become nonviable. As a consequence, the assurance of convenient Schwinn service outlets is jeopardized. Customer interest declines and other viable franchisees become marginal. This deterioration, taken together with the impaired quality image described above, creates the risk that the franchise mode will become nonviable, and customers for whom such differentiation yields net gains will be able to deal only in the undifferentiated market.

The third justification for franchise restrictions involves policing costs. The argument here is that it is less costly to police simple systems than it is to police more complicated ones. Causality (responsibility) is difficult to trace (attribute) in complex systems. If few "excuses" can be offered, fewer veracity checks have to be made. Although I do not suggest that this was a major consideration for Schwinn, it could be relevant to the design of other marketing systems. Again this is a problem only in a world of bounded rationality, because frictionless systems are self-policing.

Consider finally whether Schwinn will integrate forward into retailing if restrictions on sales to nonfranchised outlets are prohibited. If Schwinn's costs of integrated sales were identical with those of its franchisees, this presumably would occur. There are several reasons, however, to believe the case to be otherwise. First, franchised dealers were not exclusively engaged in the sales and service of Schwinn bicycles; other brands were also handled.[93] Also, many franchisees engaged in nonbicycle sales. Assuming that multiple brand and multiple product sales are necessary for distributors to break even, forward integration would require Schwinn

---

92 This is altogether to be expected. Franchisors will ordinarily auction off franchise locations where greater than competitive returns are expected unless such auctions are costly to run.

93 Schwinn required its franchisees to display Schwinn bicycles "with position equal to and as prominent as that of any competitive bicycle." Brief for Arnold, Schwinn & Co., Appendix 1, at 57 n.89, United States v. Arnold, Schwinn & Co., 388 U.S. 365 (1967).

to engage in unwanted and possibly unavailable sales activities.[94] Diversification into other products with which Schwinn had no expertise or familiarity is the unwanted activity. Stocking other brands, moreover, might pose difficulties of availability, as other bicycle manufacturers might suspect, with cause, that their brands would be slighted and demeaned if sold by Schwinn employees.

Furthermore, even if disabilities of these kinds did not exist, the question still remains whether Schwinn could provide incentives for managers of integrated sales outlets that prompt performance equal to that when franchising is used. Both carrot and stick considerations must be addressed. The incentive disabilities associated with bureaucratic modes of organization [95] stand as a further impediment to forward integration by Schwinn.

The upshot is that if the worst consequences obtain (namely that the franchise system collapses, Schwinn is unable to integrate forward economically, and the Schwinn brand image vanishes), prohibiting franchise restraints gives rise to real economic losses of the kind shown in Figure 2. The demand curve for Schwinn bicycles is here given by $p_2 = g(q_2;\bar{p}_1)$, where $\bar{p}_1$ is the price at which other bicycles sell (which is taken as given). The curve AC_2^f is the average cost of sales and service for franchised outlets. As drawn, franchising just breaks even (covers all of its costs, including a fair rate of return) at a price and quantity of p_2^*, q_2^*, respectively. Assuming that the costs of supplying nondifferentiated bicycles are not increased by Schwinn franchising, the net welfare gains (losses) realized by offering (withdrawing) the Schwinn brand will be given by the shaded consumer surplus region.

B. *The Absence of Strategic Effects*

Having established the transaction cost efficiencies that may be derived from a restrictive franchise arrangement, the next step of the analysis involves an inquiry whether the franchise system promotes anticompetitive effects. Specifically the question is whether Schwinn, by itself or in conjunction with other large bicycle manufacturers, introduced vertical restraints that placed rivals or cus-

---

94 Alternatively, Schwinn could run the distribution stage at a loss. However, it is doubtful that profits from manufacturing would be sufficient to cover these losses. *See* text accompanying notes 15-26 *supra*. For a discussion of the disincentives to integrate forward into distribution, see Preston, *Restrictive Distribution Arrangements: Economic Analysis and Public Policy Standards*, 30 L. & CONTEMP. PROB. 506, 512 (1965).

95 *See* O. WILLIAMSON, *supra* note 7, at 118-29.

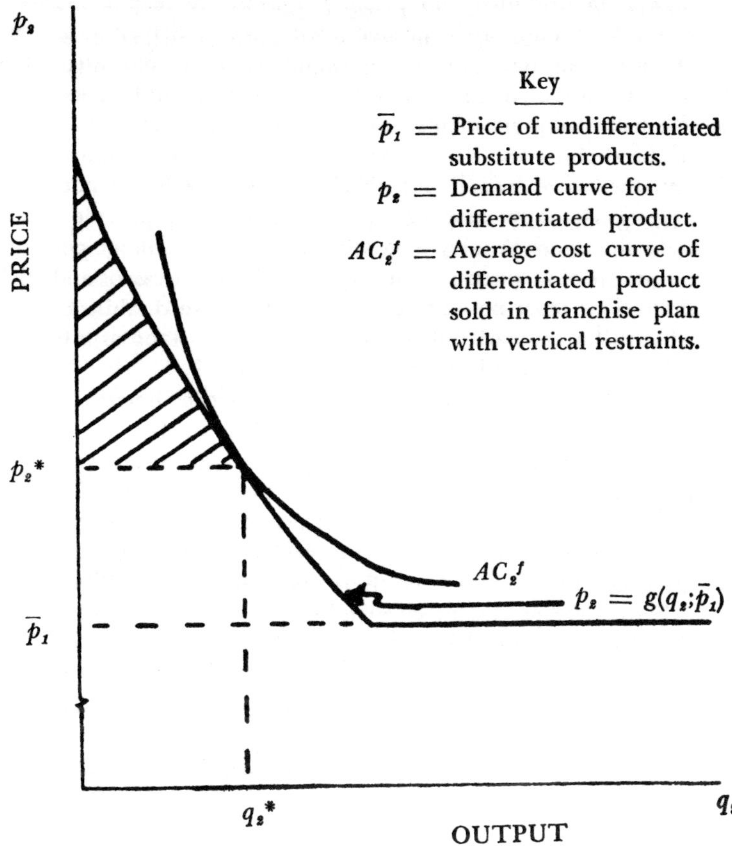

FIGURE 2

tomers at a strategic disadvantage.[96] The government plainly regarded these restraints as anticompetitive and its jurisdictional statement advanced the following theory of the case:

> In industries in which products are highly differentiated, a particular brand – like Schwinn bicycles – often has a market of its own, within which [intrabrand] competition is highly important to the consumer and should be

[96] The Supreme Court recognized the relevancy of such an inquiry in White Motor Co. v. United States, 372 U.S. 253, 263 (1963) ("economic and business stuff" out of which restraints arose and their "actual impact" are relevant to determining the existence of an antitrust violation).

> preserved . . . . Schwinn's strenuous efforts to exclude unauthorized retailers from selling its bicycles suggest that, absent these restraints, there would be a broader retail distribution of these goods with the resulting public benefits (including lower price) of retail competition.[97]

Similar views were repeated in the government's brief:

> The premise of the Schwinn franchising program is that Schwinn is a distinctive brand which commands a premium price – that it enjoys, in other words, a margin of protection from the competition of other brands. To the extent that this premise is sound, it is clear that the only fully effective control upon the retail price of Schwinn bicycles is that imposed by competition among Schwinn dealers and distributors.[98]

The government also disclosed the animosity with which it regarded product differentiation:

> Either the Schwinn bicycle is in fact a superior product for which the consumer would willingly pay more, in which event it should be unnecessary to create a quality image by the artificial device of discouraging competition in the price of distributing the product; or it is not of premium quality, and the consumer is being deceived into believing that it is by its high and uniform retail price. In neither event would the manufacturer's private interest in maintaining a high-price image justify the serious impairment on competition that results.[99]

And the government expressed its view about the merits of vertical integration as compared with vertical restraints:

> Even if the threat to integrate were not wholly lacking in credibility in the circumstances of this case, we would urge that it was not a proper defense to the restraint of trade charge. In the first place, a rule that treats manufacturers who assume the distribution function themselves more leniently than those who impose restraints on independent distributors merely reflects the fact that, although integration in distribution may sometimes benefit the econ-

[97] Jurisdictional Statement for the United States at 14, United States v. Arnold, Schwinn & Co., 388 U.S. 365 (1967).

[98] Brief for the United States at 26, United States v. Arnold, Schwinn & Co., 388 U.S. 365 (1967).

[99] *Id.* 47.

> omy by leading to cost savings, agreements to maintain resale prices or to impose territorial restrictions of unlimited duration or outlet limitations of the type involved here have never been shown to produce comparable economies.[100]

The government's views on product differentiation and franchise restraints thus can be reduced to the following three propositions: (1) differentiated products can be classed as those for which a price premium is warranted and those for which such a premium is not; (2) whether differentiation is real or contrived, intrabrand price competition is essential to the protection of consumer interests; and (3) although vertical integration sometimes yields economies, the same cannot be said for vertical restraints. Each of these premises is significantly flawed and for that reason the government's anticompetitive effect argument should have failed.[101]

The government's first premise, that it is "unnecessary to create quality images" for products that are objectively superior to those of rivals, depends upon an assumption of unbounded rationality. Plainly, however, customers are not endowed with perfect cognitive processes. Accordingly, efforts to "assist" customers and thereby economize on bounded rationality, have merit. Reliability images serve this purpose. Inasmuch as the Schwinn franchising program did not entail exclusive dealing, neither actual rivals nor potential rivals could be said to have experienced any adverse effects. Suppose, however, for purposes of argument, that exclusivity had been involved. The matter of anticompetitive effect then turns on Schwinn's market share and the conditions of entry. The government's brief, however, is devoid of any attention to market structure.

---

100 *Id.* 50.

101 Posner, who "briefed and argued the *Schwinn* case for the government," contends that his analysis of the issues at that time "reflected the then prevailing thinking of the economics profession on restricted distribution." Posner, *supra* note 57, at 3. Although I agree that there was (and is) economic thinking congenial to the views set out in the *Schwinn* brief, I would hesitate to characterize it as that of the economics profession. Inasmuch as the brief is inexplicit about the sources of its economic reasoning (Preston's is the only economics article dealing with vertical restraints that is cited in the brief, Brief for the United States at 49, United States v. Arnold, Schwinn & Co., 388 U.S. 365 (1967), and Preston expressly discusses a series of legitimate economic purposes that can be served by vertical restraints, *see* Preston, *supra* note 53, at 507-19), because Telser's work on the rationality of restraints was in the public domain at that time, *see* Telser, *supra* note 26; Telser, *Abusive Trade Practices: An Economic Analysis*, 30 L. & CONTEMP. PROB. 488 (1965), and because I expressly took exception with the brief while it was in preparation, Posner's attribution may sweep too broadly.

The simple facts are these: Schwinn's market share, which had been twenty-two percent in 1951, the year before it introduced its disputed marketing program, fell steadily in the decade that followed, dropping to thirteen percent in 1961.[102] Schwinn plainly was not a dominant firm at any time during this interval.

What then of the possible existence of a tight oligopoly in which the main firms all employed exclusive franchising? Although concentration in the bicycle industry was in the high-moderate range in 1951, the four firm concentration ratio then being sixty-three percent, the decade following was one of intense competition. Foreign imports, which accounted for eight percent of the market in 1951, rose to a high of forty percent in 1955. The escape clause to the GATT agreements was invoked in August, 1955,[103] and bicycle imports thereafter dropped—remaining in the neighborhood of thirty percent in the years that followed.[104]

Not only did the market share of the four largest firms fall sharply over this interval, but there was considerable shifting of market shares among them. Schwinn, which was the largest firm with twenty-two percent of the market in 1951, dropped to second place with thirteen percent of the market in 1961. AMF, the second place firm in 1951 with sixteen percent of the market, dropped to third with eight percent of the market in 1961. The third place firm in 1951, Columbia, dropped to fifth place in 1961, the respective market shares being twelve and five percent. However,

[102] The following table shows the market shares of the four largest firms and of foreign imports in the bicycle industry during the period of 1951 to 1961:

Market Shares of Four Largest Domestic Producers and of Foreign Imports, 1951-1961

	Four Largest Domestic Producers	Foreign Imports
	%	%
1951	63	8
1953	52	22
1955	34	40
1957	46	28
1959	49	28
1961	49	30

Source: Brief for Arnold, Schwinn & Co., Appendix 1, at 8, n.21, United States v. Arnold, Schwinn & Co., 388 U.S. 365 (1967).

[103] General Agreement on Tariffs and Trade, Oct. 30, 1947, art. XIX, 61 Stat. pts. 5 & 6, T.I.A.S. No. 1700. The escape clause was invoked by the United States on August 19, 1955, to raise the rate of duties on bicycles imported into the United States. GATT Doc. L/433 (1955), *reported in* General Agreement on Tariffs and Trade, Analytical Index 104 (2d rev. 1966).

[104] Brief for Arnold, Schwinn & Co., at 5 n.15, United States v. Arnold, Schwinn & Co., 388 U.S. 365 (1967).

Murray, the fourth place firm in 1951, jumped from a twelve percent position to a twenty-two percent position in 1961, taking over first place in the process.[105] Four established bicycle producers were acquired during the decade, two of them by AMF, a large, diversified producer of consumer and industrial products.[106] The record thus discloses active competition among extant domestic producers and with foreign rivals.

Finally, the government's third premise that intrafirm restraints (vertical integration) are less objectionable than interfirm restraints, because vertical integration often yields offsetting economies that do not accrue when interfirm relations are restrained, is simply naive. As developed above,[107] vertical market restrictions in this and other markets can often yield economies. Furthermore, vertical integration is not a cost panacea.[108] The hostility of the government to interfirm trading restrictions reflects a bias in favor of bureaucratic, as opposed to market, modes of organization that is not only unwarranted but inimical to social welfare.

In summary, the franchise restrictions which Schwinn introduced not only had a plausible efficiency justification, but, in addition, no anticompetitive effects could possibly be attributed to them. They were not part of an exclusive dealing program; Schwinn's market share was too small, by itself, to warrant antitrust concern even if exclusivity had been involved; rivals did not engage in franchising, much less exclusive dealing; and the bicycle market was characterized by active competition. Where actual competition is and arguably will continue to be effective, concern over potential competition is misplaced. The government's case against Schwinn was wholly fanciful.

V. Approaches Alternative to the Transaction Cost Approach

With the exception of the inhospitability tradition referred to above, the leading alternatives to the transaction cost approach are partly or mainly complementary to it. None, however, deals as comprehensively with the central issues posed by vertical restrictions, and hence none is an adequate substitute.

---

105 *See* note 102 *supra*.

106 Brief for Arnold, Schwinn & Co., at 2 n.5, United States v. Arnold, Schwinn & Co., 388 U.S. 365 (1967).

107 *See* text accompanying notes 12-30 & 86-94 *supra*.

108 *See* O. Williamson, *supra* note 7, at 82-131.

A. *The Inhospitability Tradition*

Proponents of the inhospitability tradition eschew reliance on common law reasoning and emphasize real or imagined effects instead.[109] Not only is there no presumption that business practices are ordinarily motivated by efficiency purposes, but this possibility is not even actively considered. Instead, attention is focused on the possibility that some anticompetitive effect, however remote, might be connected with the practice in question. This type of orientation and reasoning is hostile to an enterprise mode of organization and commonly results in bad public policy arguments and outcomes.[110]

B. *The Populist Approach*

The populist approach favors attention to fairness and relies little on economic analysis. Some of those who advocate the populist approach seem to regard economic analysis as not merely unhelpful but ill-advised. Thus the populist approach has been characterized by Professor Sullivan as one that regards allocative efficiency as "useless as a guide to antitrust policy." [111] Values other than efficiency are instead assigned a decisive role:

> During the eighty-odd years that antitrust has been with us, there have been ebbs and flows of interest in enforcement, all correlated with other developments in national life. The values which, until very recently, have shown themselves most strongly in the expression of policy have been populist in origin, and have had such aims as the transfer of wealth and power from industrial interests to agrarian ones, the decentralization and dispersion of economic and related political power, the preservation of a commerce and industry open to entry by small entrepreneurs, the reduction of prices, and the prohibition of unfair competitive tactics.[112]

Sullivan's argument against the use of partial equilibrium welfare economics is that considerations of "second best" demonstrate that efficiency claims are pointless.[113] The reduction of price

109 *See* text accompanying note 28 *supra.*

110 *See, e.g.,* United States v. Arnold, Schwinn & Co., 388 U.S. 365 (1967); Brown Shoe Co. v. United States, 270 U.S. 294 (1962).

111 Sullivan, Book Review, 75 COLUM. L. REV. 1214 (1975).

112 *Id.*

113 Sullivan's premise is that "[t]he standard theoretical demonstration of the allocative efficiency of a competitive market as contrasted to a monopolized market . . . has no welfare implications except as part of a general equilibrium analysis." Sullivan, *supra* note 111, at 1219 (footnote omitted). Thus, "[t]he theoretical

distortions in one sector when they remain in others is "just as likely to . . . make allocations worse—or to leave allocations as bad as they are" as it is to yield an efficiency gain.[114]

Although this is a common interpretation of the second best literature,[115] it is not a correct one. To demonstrate that a local correction can yield a global loss in the face of distortions elsewhere is an existence argument. It says nothing about likelihood, which is a much stronger statement. Sullivan's leap from an existence to a likelihood claim is unwarranted. As Baumol points out, the policy importance of second best qualifications turns on the strength of interdependence: "[A] great many interrelationships within the economy are weak enough to be ignored. Thus, for all practical purposes, the demand for most goods is likely to be dependent only on the demands for a few other items. . . . It may, then, be possible to partition the economy more effectively than some might have suspected."[116] Strong interaction effects then can be taken expressly into account, and elsewhere the second best qualification deserves the weight that lawyers label "de minimis."

Additionally, Sullivan's comments appear to be restricted entirely to price distortions (due to "monopolies, cartels, tariffs, and distorting taxes"[117]). But allocative inefficiency is more apt to arise with respect to cost concerns, such as diseconomies of scale, failure to operate assets in a least cost way, and the incurring of

conclusion that consumer welfare (as measured by the aggregate amounts consumers will pay for goods and services) will be improved when a monopoly market is converted (without loss of scale economies) into a competitive one is warranted only if it is presupposed, first, that all other industries are already competitively organized, and, second, that there exist no other deviations from optimality . . . ." *Id.* 1219. From this premise Sullivan reasons that

> [a]bsent the simultaneous fulfillment of all conditions of optimum allocation . . . *economic theory tells us nothing about how to improve resources allocations. . . .* Economics simply provides no basis on which to say, for example, that ending monopoly in the shoe industry or ending a price cartel in the electrical equipment industry (or doing both of these things) will improve resource allocations and increase aggregate welfare. Given the persistence of other deviations (other monopolies, cartels, tariffs, and distorting taxes), there is no basis for assuming that doing away with any one or more deviations from optimality would improve efficiency at all.

Id. 1220 (emphasis in original).

114 Sullivan, *supra* note 111, at 1220 (emphasis added).

115 As Bork notes, the theory of second best "does not address itself to the probability of the bad result, but merely states it as a possible outcome." R. Bork, *supra* note 34, at 113. Consequently, to take the "possibility of second best as destroying the rationality of the consumer welfare basis of the law (which it does not) and therefore freeing the courts to evolve new rules on other social and political values . . . is little short of preposterous." *Id.* 114.

116 Baumol, *Informed Judgment, Rigorous Theory and Public Policy,* 32 S. Econ. J. 137, 144 (1965).

117 Zeckhauser, *Procedures for Valuing Lives,* 23 Pub. Pol'y 419, 446 (1975).

significant transaction costs. Organizational changes that give rise to cost savings in any of these respects will, if not accompanied by offsetting price distortions, invariably yield social gains. Thus Sullivan both overstates the weight to be assigned to second best arguments in evaluating relative price distortions and makes no allowance for allocative efficiency analysis in the matter of cost savings.

A further problem with this approach is that it easily links up with the inhospitability tradition, in which anticompetitive purpose is found lurking behind every business initiative. The populist approach has the advantage, however, of calling attention to the merits of process in a way that other approaches do not. Although this last is often disregarded, it is the distinctive strength of the populist orientation. As Richard Zeckhauser observes in his discussion of "The Importance of Process," "[m]any analysts dismiss too quickly the significance of having an equitable and widely accepted process." [118] For many societal decisions, "the procedure by which the decision is made may be as important as the actual dollar numbers employed. . . . [Consequently] monies available for other goods may give a wholly unrealistic impression of welfare. How people feel about the society in which they are living matters a tremendous amount." [119]

To be sure, process values are not easily quantified and even the qualitative aspect may be disputed. When one is close to the margin, however, process considerations can frequently be used to break ties. Moreover, in circumstances in which fairness is thought to be a central issue, process values ought to be assigned even greater weight. Lest arguments in favor of dispersed economic power be used or manipulated irresponsibly, however, claims of this kind ought to be reserved for circumstances in which they are plainly important. Again, *Brown Shoe Co. v. United States* illustrates the hazards of relying on such arguments when the facts of a case are inapposite.[120]

C. *The Structure-Conduct-Performance Approach*

The structure-conduct-performance approach also complements the transaction cost approach. Recall that although the transaction cost approach employs an efficiency presumption, this

[118] *Id.*

[119] *Id.* 459.

[120] 370 U.S. 294 (1962).

can be rebutted by a showing of strategic purpose and effect.[121] The latter showing requires a demonstration that the industry in question is characterized by a dominant firm or collusive oligopoly. This entails an examination of conventional structure and conduct relations.

The preoccupation of the structure-conduct-performance paradigm with technological features, however, has been self-limiting. Vertical integration, which is principally a transaction cost phenomenon, remained a puzzle for so long precisely because of this technological orientation.[122] For this reason, the structure-conduct-performance paradigm served to reinforce the orientation of the inhospitability tradition—because if transaction cost economies are unimportant, the suspicion that novel business practices are motivated by anticompetitive purposes is easy, indeed natural, to entertain. Recent contributions to this approach,[123] however, have moved away from this technological orientation.

D. *New Modeling Approaches*

Opportunism was, until recently,[124] mainly disregarded in formal models of economic processes, but this has been changing. A convergence between the transaction cost issues that I emphasize and formal strategic analysis seems to be developing. How far this convergence will go remains to be seen. My sense accords with Simon, who argues that "qualitative institutional analysis, in which discrete structural alternatives are compared" can frequently proceed by relying on "only rather modest and simple applications of mathematical analysis." [125] At the same time, however, I am both encouraged and greatly impressed by the quality of rigorous modeling that is being done on the matter of strategic behavior. Even if formal analysis merely confirms qualitative institutional arguments, it is useful to express the same arguments in different languages. And frequently I expect that formal models will yield sharper and sometimes additional implications.[126]

121 *See* text accompanying notes 27 & 28 *supra.*

122 *See* Liebeler, *supra* note 85.

123 *See, e.g.*, Caves & Porter, *supra* note 48.

124 *See* text accompanying note 19 *supra.*

125 Simon, *supra* note 17, at 6-7.

126 *See, e.g.*, Dixit & Norman, *Advertising and Welfare*, 9 BELL J. ECON. 1 (1978); Nelson & Winter, *Forces Generating and Limiting Concentration Under Schumpeterian Competition*, 9 BELL J. ECON. 524 (1978); Schmalensee, *Entry Deterrence in the Ready-to-Eat Breakfast Cereal Industry*, 9 BELL J. ECON. 305 (1978).

E. *The Nonstrategic Tradition*

What I refer to as the nonstrategic tradition is the important stream of antitrust research that traces its origins to Aaron Director's teaching and research at the University of Chicago. Prominent examples are Bork and Bowman and, more recently, Posner. As I have indicated elsewhere, antitrust specialists in law and economics owe an everlasting debt to this tradition, which has insisted that complex policy matters be assessed in a tough-minded economic fashion in which the rudimentary issues are stated in stark microeconomic terms. Logical errors of less rigorous antitrust reasoning have been exposed in the process and a deeper appreciation for the economic benefits of purportedly anticompetitive practices has been manifested.

The principal problems that I find in this approach are that its proponents often disregard transaction costs and rarely concede that strategic considerations sometimes operate. These are clearly interrelated: if transaction costs are zero or negligible, strategic intentions are beside the point, because they can have no effect, and the simple microtheory model applies. Examples of this "friction-free" approach are Bowman's views on price discrimination [127] and Bork's views on vertical market restrictions.[128]

With respect to price discrimination, the friction-free view is that, perverse elasticity conditions excepted, allocative efficiency gains will result if a monopolist is permitted to price discriminate.[129] The argument depends on the assumption that discrimination, in whatever degree attempted, is costless to effectuate. Once allowance is made for the transaction costs of discovering differential valuations among customers and enforcing restrictions against resale (so that there can be no arbitrage), however, this allocative efficiency claim is much more problematical.[130] Simple sensitivity to bounded rationality (which explains the inability of the monopolist to assess differing customer valuations without cost) and the hazards of opportunism (whence the need to police against resale) are the missing ingredients in the friction-free tradition.

The possibility that vertical restraints and strategic objectives are linked is also resisted by the nonstrategic tradition.[131] Although

[127] *See generally* W. Bowman, Patents and Antitrust Law: A Legal and Economic Appraisal (1973).

[128] R. Bork, *supra* note 34, at 280-98.

[129] *See* W. Bowman, *supra* note 127, at 111-13.

[130] For an elaboration, see O. Williamson, *supra* note 7, at 113.

[131] *See* text accompanying notes 34-44 *supra.*

Bork acknowledges that exclusionary purposes occasionally operate, his discussion of these matters reduces them to insignificance.[132] A broader view in which transaction costs are expressly acknowledged demonstrates that strategic behavior may occur in a wider range of circumstances than his discussion discloses. If the logic of this broader view is adopted—under which the possibilities of human asset and capital market frictions of the kinds that I describe are admitted—the question then is whether Bork's position on the lawfulness of vertical restrictions ought to prevail because the frictions that I describe are quantitatively unimportant and too insubstantial to influence the enforcement of the law on vertical restrictions. My response to this is as follows: (1) I have attempted to delimit the objectionable subset of restrictive practices more carefully than had been done previously; (2) as a consequence, Bork and I differ in a serious way only with respect to the use of exclusive dealing in dominant firm industries; (3) I am not persuaded that the effects of the frictions that I discuss are insubstantial in this context, and Chandler's historical survey suggests otherwise; and (4) until the transaction cost attributes of these markets are studied more fully and the basis for my concerns and Chandler's are expressly allayed, the discriminating application of the law along the lines that I propose is the prudent posture to take.

VI. Conclusion

Antitrust is an interdisciplinary field that is best served by acknowledging that a deeper understanding of the issues will result by addressing the subject from several points of view. The economic approach that I favor, especially for dealing with vertical market relations, is the transaction cost approach. The principal points of this Article and the legal principles that result from the systematic application of transaction cost analysis to vertical restraints are summarized below.

A. *Economic Implications of the Transaction Cost Approach*

1. As with the integration of successive intermediate product market stages, vertical restrictions between manufacturing and distribution are primarily to be understood in transaction cost terms.

2. Despite striking similarities, there are also important differences between these two types of vertical relationships. The dif-

132 R. Bork, *supra* note 34, at 320-24.

ferences arise because the interests of final consumers as well as those of distributors have to be considered in designing the interface between manufacturing and distribution.

3. Contrary to the inhospitability tradition, contractual constraints can and often do serve legitimate economic purposes. Specifically, vertical constraints may be needed lest subgoal pursuit by the individual parts destroy the viability of the system.

4. Contrary to the inhospitability tradition, product differentiation can and often does promote consumer welfare. The feasibility of differentiation, moreover, may depend on the use of constraints at the manufacturer-distributor nexus.

5. The principal hazard that should concern the antitrust enforcement agencies in enforcing the law on vertical restrictions is if restraints are introduced with the strategic purpose and effect of disadvantaging rivals. Exclusive dealing restraints by dominant firms or tight oligopolies can have this effect.

6. Economies defenses should be entertained before exclusive dealing restrictions are prohibited.

7. Whether one is interested in assessing the vertical relations that govern a specific interface, as in *Schwinn,* or in understanding the historical evolution of vertical relations, such as the transformation that occurred in response to infrastructural changes late in the nineteenth century, the same microanalytic approach in which transaction costs are featured should apply.

That the errors that appeared in the government's jurisdictional statement and brief in *Schwinn* are not repeated today suggests to me that antitrust law has made real progress. I submit, moreover, that this is partly because there is now a greater sensitivity to transaction cost considerations.[183]

B. *Legal Implications of the Transaction Cost Approach*

Federal agencies charged with enforcing antitrust law should rely on the foregoing economic principles when implementing en-

[183] Turner and Posner were both instrumental in persuading the Supreme Court to reverse itself in Continental T.V., Inc. v. GTE Sylvania Inc., 433 U.S. 36 (1977). Posner's reservations with the *Schwinn* doctrine appeared in 1977. *See* Posner, *supra* note 57. Turner participated in an amicus brief with attorneys for the Motor Vehicle Manufacturers Association. The brief argues, among other things, the "the 'new economics of vertical relations' is increasingly illuminating the economies that can be achieved by manufacturer influence on dealer practices." Motion for Leave

forcement policy. Vertical market restrictions should be assumed to be efficiency-enhancing unless specific structural characteristics exist within the industry. Exclusive dealing is the only vertical restraint posing the threat of strategic hazards. Absent the existence of a dominant firm or a tight oligopoly within an industry,[134] vertical restrictions of all kinds, exclusive dealing included, should be assumed to promote transaction costs economies.

When the industry is characterized by a dominant firm or tight oligopoly, antitrust agencies and courts should subject exclusive dealing constraints, but not other vertical restrictions, to close scrutiny to ascertain whether they create barriers to entry. A firm in such a situation should not be charged with nor found to have committed an antitrust violation if it can affirmatively show that nontrivial transaction cost economies are created by the vertical restraint under scrutiny.[135]

Finally, uniform reliance on vertical restrictions of any kind—on price, territories, customers, or exclusive dealing—in industries marked by tight oligopolies should be subject to close scrutiny to determine whether the restriction regularizes trade and promotes greater interdependence. Again, firms in such a situation should not be charged with nor found to have committed an antitrust violation if they can affirmatively demonstrate that nontrivial transaction cost economies are achieved by the vertical restraint under scrutiny.

---

to File Brief and Brief for Motor Vehicle Manufacturers Association as Amicus Curiae, at 24, Continental T.V., Inc. v. GTE Sylvania Inc., 433 U.S. 36 (1977) (quoting Phillips, *supra* note 2, at 574) (footnote omitted).

134 *See* note 50 *supra.*

135 A rigorous demonstration of these economies is not apt to be feasible. But more than a showing that some economies are plausibly realized should be required. For a discussion of economies as an antitrust defense, see generally Williamson, *Economies Defense, supra* note 5.

Note that Posner proposes an output test—"did the manufacturer's output increase or decrease after imposing the restriction?"—to get at these issues. Posner, *supra* note 57, at 19. (An equivalent test would be to examine the effect on price.) Ordinarily, however, I would expect that output and price effects would be distributed over time and confounded by many other factors. The elaborate econometric investigation that Posner contemplates to sort these out does not appear to me to be feasible.

The basic issues, if exclusive dealing is to be prohibited, are what transaction cost economies does exclusive dealing promote and whether the sacrifice of these will be significant. These matters ought ordinarily to be amenable to examination in qualitative and crude quantitative terms.

[22]

THE ECONOMICS OF BLOCK BOOKING*

ROY W. KENNEY *and* *BENJAMIN KLEIN*
California State University, Northridge
University of California, Los Angeles

I. Introduction

Block booking involves "the practice of licensing, or offering for license, one feature or group of features on the condition that the exhibitor will also license another feature or group of features released by distributors during a given period."[1] This contractual arrangement, common in the American motion picture industry from as early as 1916,[2] was declared illegal in two Supreme Court decisions, *Paramount Pictures,*[3] where blocks of films were rented for theatrical exhibition, and *Loew's*,[4] where blocks of films were rented for television exhibition.

The primary legal objection to block booking is that the practice "extends monopoly power." In *Paramount* the Supreme Court stated that block booking "adds to the monopoly of a single copyrighted picture that of another copyrighted picture."[5] Similarly, in *Loew's*, the Court asserted that a distributor cannot use the market power granted by the copyright in a "desirable" film to force exhibitors to license a second "undesirable" film, stating that "the antitrust laws do not permit a compounding of

*We gratefully acknowledge research support from the University of Chicago Law School Antitrust Project and from the Sloan Foundation Grant to UCLA for the study of contractual arrangements. We are indebted to Armen Alchian, Frank Easterbrook, Robert Hansen, William Jennings, George Miron, Kevin M. Murphy, John Sawyer, Finis Welch, and participants at Industrial Organization workshops at UCLA and the University of Chicago for useful comments on previous drafts and to Elizabeth Granitz and Robert Hansen for research assistance.

[1] United States v. Paramount Pictures, Inc., 334 U.S. 131, 156 (1948).

[2] Terry Ramsaye, A Million and One Nights: A History of the Motion Picture 750–51 (1926).

[3] United States v. Paramount Pictures, Inc., 344 U.S. 131 (1948).

[4] United States v. Loew's, Inc., 371 U.S. 38 (1962).

[5] Paramount, 334 U.S. at 156–57, quoting the district court.

[*Journal of Law & Economics*, vol. XXVI (October 1983)]

the statutorily conferred monopoly."[6] George Stigler has trenchantly criticized this extension-of-monopoly argument by asking the obvious economic question: Why can the distributor not collect just as much revenue by using his "market power" to set the price of the desirable film?[7] If the undesirable film is "overpriced," then the desirable film must be "underpriced."

Although the monopoly extension analysis makes no sense, a satisfactory alternative economic explanation has not been developed. The commonly accepted analysis is that block booking is a subtle form of price discrimination. This explanation dates back to the Aaron Director "oral tradition" at Chicago, where the block booking practiced in *Paramount* was considered similar to IBM's "tie" of tabulating machines and cards.[8] In 1956 Director published the hypothesis that block booking was a "method of charging different prices to different customers,"[9] but he did not formalize or test it. In 1963 Stigler applied the hypothesis to the Loew's case, presenting the theoretical argument in more detail together with some apparently confirming evidence.[10] Director and Stigler's price discrimination explanation for block booking has been widely, if uncritically, accepted[11] and has led to the general acceptance of price discrimination as a major economic motivation for "bundling."[12]

The price discrimination hypothesis assumes that films vary in their relative appeal across market areas. A distributor may find it difficult to

[6] Loew's, 371 U.S. at 52. Justice Goldberg also based his objection to block booking on a "market foreclosure" argument, stating that "[t]elevision stations forced by appellants to take unwanted films were denied access to films marketed by other distributors who, in turn, were foreclosed from selling to the stations." *Id.* at 48–49. This argument is clearly inapplicable to the Loew's case where the blocks together accounted for a small fraction of total television station programming. At the time of the case feature films constituted less than 8 percent of a typical station's programming. *Id.* at 47. In addition, since we are dealing in the Loew's case with films that had already been produced, the marginal cost of extending their use to TV stations was a very small portion of the total license fee. With such cost conditions it is difficult to see how one distributor could possibly set up a "barrier to entry" to another distributor.

[7] George J. Stigler, United States v. Loew's, Inc.: A Note on Block Booking, 1963 Supreme Court Review 152.

[8] International Business Machine Corp. v. United States, 298 U.S. 131 (1936).

[9] See Aaron Director & Edward H. Levi, Law and the Future: Trade Regulation, 51 Nw. U. L. Rev. 281, 292 (1956).

[10] Stigler, *supra* note 7.

[11] See, for example, Ward S. Bowman, Jr., Tying Arrangements and the Leverage Problem, 67 Yale L. J. 19 (1957); Lester G. Telser, Abusive Trade Practices: An Economic Analysis, 30 Law & Contemp. Prob. 488 (1965); and Robert H. Bork, The Antitrust Paradox: A Policy at War with Itself 377–78 (1978).

[12] See William J. Adams & Janet L. Yellen, Commodity Bundling and the Burden of Monopoly, 90 Q. J. Econ. 475 (1976).

gauge this variation as closely as the buyers can and therefore sets uniform prices across markets for each film. If, however, films that are more highly valued in some markets are the less highly valued ones in other markets, distributors may increase their revenue by assembling films into blocks, which are priced uniformly. The prices set are "discriminatory" because, although there is only one price per block, the implicit price paid for individual films will vary across markets.

This simple price discrimination explanation for block booking, although ingenious, is inconsistent with the facts of *Paramount* and *Loew's*, for the prices of the blocks varied a great deal across markets. For example, evidence in *Loew's* indicates that an eighty-five-film package distributed to television stations by National Telefilm Associates sold for $700,000 in New York City and $1,600 in Lake Charles, Louisiana.[13] There were similar price differences in the theatrical exhibition contracts in the Paramount litigation, with a possible first-run exclusive showing rental fee of $150,000 and a last-run rental fee on the same film of only $10.[14] This large price variation undermines the uniform price assumption of the simple price discrimination hypothesis.[15]

One could rescue the price discrimination hypothesis by recasting it in terms of a uniform pricing formula rather than a uniform price per block.[16] If buyers' relative values on individual films vary across markets, and the distributor sets prices in each market according to a general "average value" pricing formula (for example, in the television case a price based on the advertising rates of stations in the different markets), then he will underprice some films in some markets and other films in other markets. However, if the demand for a block of films is more closely related to the factors in the distributor's pricing formula than are the demands for the individual films in the block, the distributor can capture a larger total revenue by block pricing. Block booking then appears to be a device which aids in the distributor's pricing decision and implies price discrimi-

[13] National Telefilm Associates, Exhibit 11, "Dream Features," Record at Exhibits 778, 803–06, Loew's 371 U.S. 38 (1962).

[14] Michael Conant, Antitrust in the Motion Picture Industry 72 (1960).

[15] Telser, *supra* note 11, at 493, notes that "[i]t takes a somewhat complicated mathematical analysis to state precisely the conditions that would make block booking more profitable than single pricing. Roughly speaking, block booking is more profitable if the variation of the revenue for the combination among cities is not too large." In a more recent article, Lester G. Telser, A Theory of Monopoly of Complementary Goods, 52 J. Bus. 211 (1979), he presents a formal analysis of the demand conditions under which tie-ins of complementary goods can be used by a monopolist to increase its return. But once again he assumes that prices are identical across markets, which makes the analysis inapplicable to the block booking cases.

[16] See Stigler, *supra* note 7.

nation across markets in terms of deviations of implicit individual film values from what would be given by the distributor's pricing formula.

Even this more subtle statement of the price discrimination hypothesis is inconsistent with the facts of *Loew's* and *Paramount*. The analysis implicitly assumes that prices are "set" by distributors rather than determined competitively. Yet in most markets there was more than one potential buyer of the distributor's product. The contract employed by distributors in *Loew's* granted one television station an exclusive right to broadcast the given group of films in each market area. In negotiating this contract distributors could and did in fact rely on competitive bidding among stations in each market to determine price. If, as Stigler assumed, the stations have more information about individual films values than the distributor, the distributor could just let this information be revealed by competitive auctions in multiple station markets. There is no reason for the distributor to set imperfect prices on the basis of estimated demand and hence no reason for block sales. Similarly, during the period covered by the Paramount litigation most cities had more than one theater that could potentially exhibit any individual film. These theaters could, in principle, compete with one another for exhibition rights to a film. There does not appear to be any reason for distributors to set uniform or formulaic rental fees.

To develop an explanation for block booking that *is* consistent with the facts of *Loew's* and *Paramount,* we first consider the arrangement employed by De Beers to market gem-quality rough diamonds. The basic economic forces are identical in all three cases. To economize on transaction costs a group of goods of individually uncertain and difficult-to-measure quality are average priced. Such block packaging can operate only if sufficiently high brand-name capital exists. Sellers are shown to choose the particular contractual arrangement that minimizes these brand-name costs in addition to other transaction costs.

II. De Beers

A. *The CSO Marketing Arrangement*

The Central Selling Organization (CSO) of the De Beers group markets most of the world's gem-quality uncut diamonds. Its share in 1980 was estimated at 80–85 percent, with total sales of approximately $3 billion.[17] However, only about 40 percent of the gems sold by the CSO come from

[17] Timothy Green, The World of Diamonds 65 (1981). Apparently much of the approximately 20 percent of gem-quality diamonds that are not marketed through the CSO is stolen merchandise. Michael Szenberg, The Economics of the Israeli Diamond Industry 14 (1973).

the seventeen mines owned or leased by De Beers.[18] The rest are purchased from independent mine owners under long-term (five to ten year) exclusive-dealing, monthly quota production contracts. If an independent producer's monthly output is higher than the particular quota fixed by De Beers for the month, the producer is required to stockpile the excess.[19]

Why do independent mine owners market through De Beers when it appears to be more profitable for them individually to expand production and sell their output on the open market? We suggest that the cartel enforcement mechanism that has prevented the deterioration of the CSO's dominance in wholesale diamond marketing is the efficiency of the CSO's selling practices. These cost savings, related to the minimization of buyer "oversearching" for information, appear to exceed any potential extra revenue to a diamond producer from marketing outside the CSO arrangement.

The details of the CSO marketing arrangement are important for understanding our analysis. Several million rough diamonds from all sources pass through the CSO's selling office each year. The CSO sorts these stones first by shape (six categories), then by quality (about seven categories), by color (about eight categories), and, finally, by weight, resulting in more than two thousand categories.[20] The variance in the value of stones within each category is nonetheless substantial. Independent producers are paid according to the number of stones of each category they provide, with the price of the stones in each category determined by the actual selling price received by the CSO during a representative period.[21] The long-term exclusive sales requirement, in addition to controlling total supply, prevents mines from searching through their output and selecting the best stones within each category for sale on the open market rather than through De Beers.[22]

The CSO's customers consist of approximately three hundred invited diamond traders and cutters. These customers are of two types: manufac-

[18] Green, *supra* note 17, at 64.

[19] Godehard Lenzen, The History of Diamond Production and the Diamond Trade 190 (F. Bradley trans. 1970).

[20] De Beers Consolidated Mines, The Diamond Mines of the De Beers Group 33 (1963); and Paul Gibson, De Beers: Can a Cartel Be Forever? 123 Forbes 45 (1939).

[21] Lenzen, *supra* note 19, at 190.

[22] Such selection would result in a negative externality on all other producers of stones in the particular category because compensation is related to average quality supplied by all. In addition to preventing such free-riding distribution effects, exclusive dealing saves the real resource costs of such "cherry picking." For a further examination of exclusive dealing as a mechanism to prevent wasteful preselection in a nonmonopsony context, see Edward C. Gallick & Benjamin Klein, Exclusive Dealing, Specialized Assets, and Joint Ownership: A Study of Tuna Fishing Contracts (Working Paper, UCLA, Dep't Econ. 1983).

turers who have their own cutting and polishing facilities and a few dealers in each cutting center in the world who supply small manufacturers.[23] Each customer is expected to buy regularly and, since average annual sales per customer are approximately $10 million, is screened to be financially sound.[24]

Each of the CSO's customers periodically informs the CSO of the kinds and quantities of diamonds it wishes to purchase. The CSO then assembles a single box (or "sight") of diamonds for the customer. Each box contains a number of folded, envelope-like packets called papers. The gems within each paper are similar and correspond to one of the CSO's classifications. The composition of any sight may differ slightly from that specified by the buyer because the supply of diamonds in each category is limited.

Once every five weeks, primarily at the CSO's offices in London, the diamond buyers are invited to inspect their sights.[25] Each box is marked with the buyer's name and a price. A single box may carry a price of up to several million pounds.[26] Each buyer examines his sight before deciding whether to buy. Each buyer may spend as long as he wishes, examining his sight to see that each stone is graded correctly (that is, fits the description marked on each parcel). There is no negotiation over the price or composition of the sight. In rare cases where a buyer claims that a stone has been miscategorized by the CSO, and the sales staff agrees, the sight will be adjusted.[27] If a buyer rejects the sight, he is offered no alternative box. Rejection is extremely rare, however, because buyers who reject the diamonds offered them are deleted from the list of invited customers.[28]

Thus stones (*a*) are sorted by De Beers into imperfectly homogeneous categories, (*b*) to be sold in preselected blocks, (*c*) to preselected buyers, (*d*) at nonnegotiable prices, with (*e*) buyers' rejection of the sales offer leading to the withdrawal by De Beers of future invitations to purchase stones.

B. Oversearching

Because the De Beers sorting procedure implies a substantial variance in the value of stones within each quality category, stones within such

[23] Green, *supra* note 17, at 148. Given the fixed cost of traveling to London, it will not be economic for small manufacturers located in the cutting centers to deal directly with the CSO. In addition, as we shall see, it is economic for the CSO to limit the number and therefore the minimum size of customers.

[24] *Id.*

[25] Gibson, *supra* note 20, at 46.

[26] H. L. Van der Laan, The Sierra Leone Diamonds 95–96 (1965); and Gibson, *supra* note 20, at 49.

[27] Green, *supra* note 17, at 151.

[28] Szenberg, *supra* note 17, at 14.

categories therefore can be said to be average priced. Consumers faced with such a situation will have an incentive to search for undervalued goods and to find the exceptional values first. For example, consider a bin of oranges. If the oranges vary in quality but sell for a uniform price, each potential buyer has an incentive to inspect more oranges than he wants to buy, hoping to find those of unusually high quality (which are therefore undervalued). The problem is that the prices set by the seller for different qualities of oranges are not equal to market clearing prices and consumers will search out the higher quality oranges and leave the poorer quality oranges behind. A Gresham's Law type of phenomenon is created.[29]

The average price set by the seller is determined by his knowledge. Unless he is omniscient and costlessly knows the exact market value of each stone, we can expect buyers to search for the underpriced stones. While such prepurchase inspections consume real resources, they can be assumed to lead only to wealth transfers between consumers and the seller with no allocative effects.[30] The attempt by buyers to obtain an informational advantage over the seller can thus be labeled "oversearching."[31]

[29] Gresham's Law was originally applied to full-bodied metallic currency. The law stated that when both good (full weight) and bad (light, clipped, or sweated) coins circulate at par, the "bad coins will drive out the good." People will remove the "undervalued" fullbodied coins from circulation and use the metal for nonmonetary purposes (including foreign trade). This same effect occurs with the oranges. Early arriving shoppers will expend real resources to find the most undervalued oranges, and shoppers arriving late will find that the average quality of the remaining oranges has fallen. Note, however, that if consumers differ in their ability to search out different qualities and this ability is related to elasticity of demand, the bunching of different qualities together by the seller may be intentional price discrimination.

[30] We are assuming that price-adjusted high- and low-quality units of the good are perfect substitutes. For example, the quality of oranges may be measured solely in terms of amount of juice, and an average high-quality orange may yield twice as much juice as an average low-quality orange and sell for double the price. However, if one type of orange is preferred for a particular use (for example, juicing), some search would be socially valuable.

[31] Our analysis of excess search for quality information is equivalent to the Hirshleifer analysis of speculative oversearch, Jack Hirshleifer, The Private and Social Value of Information and the Reward to Inventive Activity, 61 Am. Econ. Rev. 561 (1971); to the analysis regarding the overinvestment in education as a screening device, Michael Spence, Job Market Signaling, 87 Q. J. Econ. 355 (1973); and, more generally, to the competition for the establishment of property rights, see Don Gordon, The Economic Theory of a Common-Property Resource: The Fishery, 62 J. Pol. Econ. 124 (1954): Steven Cheung, The Structure of a Contract and the Theory of a Nonexclusive Resource, 13 J. Law & Econ. 49 (1970); and Edmund Kitch, The Nature and Function of the Patent System, 20 J. Law & Econ. 265 (1977). In these cases, as in ours, the return to an investment is assumed to be purely distributive. Barzel has noted, in the spirit of our analysis, "The fact that many information situations have the potential for waste does not necessarily mean that waste actually occurs. If, in the aggregate, these actions produce a negative product, arrangements that successfully restrain them or reduce their impact will generate a positive return." Yoram Barzel, Some Fallacies in the Interpretation of Information Costs, 20 J. Law & Econ. 291, 292 (1977). In this context he discusses briefly the De Beers's selling practices and the supposed

Since buyers will have to examine the stones before they are cut (the exact placement of each flaw, chip, and inclusion must be discovered to determine the size of the largest finished gem that can be cut from each diamond), it may seem as if buyer inspection is necessary and hence Gresham's Law oversearching is costless. However, buyer search produces two costly effects: duplicative buyer inspections and induced increases in seller sorting.

The search for underpriced stones within a quality classification implies that some stones will be inspected and not purchased. Whether there is a social cost associated with persons' examining the quality of goods they do not then buy depends on the goods and buyers in question. When buyers have different tastes, duplicate inspections are necessary for each buyer to acquire the particular units that most closely satisfy his particular desires. Tastes vary considerably among people considering, for example, the purchase of a diamond engagement ring, and duplicate inspections are necessary for allocative efficiency.

In contrast, we may assume that each wholesale buyer places essentially the same value on rough uncut stones offered for sale by De Beers within the various quality categories. With a reasonable amount of search, all would agree very closely on the relative value of the different stones; they would agree on how to cut and set the stones and how long it would probably take to sell them (that is, on the inventory costs).[32] Because wholesale search is not necessary for the stones to go to the highest valuing ultimate user, and because whoever purchases the stones must inspect each closely no matter how much prepurchase inspection was done in the aggregate by other potential buyers, duplicate inspections in such a situation waste real resources.

On the other hand, very large stones weighing more than 14.8 carats, where presumably estimates of value vary considerably among buyers, are not included in the CSO sights. Instead of being sold on a fixed average-price basis, they are offered to particular buyers on an individual stone, negotiated-price basis. The buyers offered large stones are free to reject them without endangering their relationship with the CSO.[33]

gains which result from prepackaging of gems, *id.* at 304. Our analysis, which emphasizes the importance of prespecified buyers earning rents within a repeat-sale/brand-name enforcement mechanism, builds on his insightful work.

[32] Since the sight holders are purchasing stones for resale in fairly thick markets, the presumption that each values the same stones equally is reasonable. The hypothesis that the De Beers scheme is a method of interbuyer price discrimination, see, for example, Kenneth W. Clarkson & Roger L. Miller, Industrial Organization: Theory Evidence and Public Policy 244 (1982), is therefore highly unlikely to be correct. De Beers can neither take advantage of different consumer surpluses between buyers nor, in the long-run, appropriate the quasi rents between different-skilled cutters.

[33] Until his death in 1978, Harry Winston, a New York diamond dealer, was usually given the first opportunity to examine and purchase these stones. Green, *supra* note 17, at 152.

The attempt by buyers to discover underpriced stones would lead to lower total revenue to De Beers. After the buyer search, if underpriced stones within a classification were purchased and overpriced stones rejected, the CSO would be forced to lower its price to sell any of the remaining stones of lower than average quality—and buyer oversearching would begin again. To prevent this costly adverse selection process, the CSO could be expected to increase their initial classification effort. Increased expenditures on the quality sorting process would result in more accurate average prices, that is, a reduced variance in the value of stones within each quality classification, and hence higher total revenue received in the face of oversearching.

Oversearching will be eliminated entirely only if the seller is omniscient and can perfectly set the correct (market-clearing) price and buyers learn this. With any finite expenditure of resources by the diamond seller, gems will not be valued perfectly. Rather, gems will be categorized, with some remaining variance of quality within each classification. Therefore, some units of detectably different qualities will be offered at the same price and the potential for buyer oversearch remains.

More important, much of the quality search conducted by De Beers in attempting to set prices very accurately would be duplicative. Because the specific information required by the cutter to cut each stone optimally cannot be costlessly communicated by De Beers, we can reasonably assume that the cutter will have to examine the stone more closely no matter how much information De Beers collects in setting prices. Rather than engage in excessive quality search necessary to price each stone accurately, we can expect the CSO to adopt an alternative arrangement to minimize buyer oversearch. A marketing arrangement that prevented oversearching could increase the profitability of De Beers by the real resources they and their buyers expend on duplicate inspections.

C. *Preselected Buyers Earning a Premium Stream*

The CSO does not sell diamonds in average-priced quality classification bins through which buyers are permitted to search. Rather, the CSO assigns each sight of diamonds to a particular preselected buyer. However, if buyers could "freely" reject the sights they were assigned, they would accept only those they considered undervalued. The rejected sights would presumably have to be repriced at a lower level and assigned once again to another buyer, implying duplicative oversearch. In addition, De Beers would receive a lower price for its diamonds than the average of the value of all stones represented within each of its classifications.

Given that it is not economic for De Beers to spend the large amount of money that would be necessary to price sights perfectly, they must devise an alternative way to discourage buyers from rejecting their assigned sights. The CSO accomplishes this by pricing in such a way that buyers on average are earning rents the present discounted value of which is greater in almost all cases than the short-run profit that can be achieved by rejecting the sights of lower than average quality. Since these rents are lost if the buyer decides to reject a sight and is terminated from the list of invited buyers, a wealth-maximizing buyer will not generally reject sights, with the implied duplicative search, but will examine and purchase his own allotted sight.

This is analytically identical (but the transactors are reversed) to the Klein-Leffler case of a seller with a valuable reputation who is prevented from cheating a buyer.[34] In that case the seller receives a premium stream for the continued provision of high-quality goods to the buyer. In this case, the seller (the CSO) "pays" a premium to its buyers by selling diamonds at less than (costless-search) market-clearing prices. This premium serves to encourage the buyer to take low-quality goods occasionally. The payment of the premium is offset by savings in marketing costs, that is, the avoidance of oversearching, made possible by encouraging buyers to go along with the CSO's marketing scheme. The right to be on the CSO's list of invited buyers appears to be a valuable asset, the capital value of which is greater than any short-run incentive for buyers to search and reject overpriced sights.[35]

The CSO can minimize the costs of this arrangement by reducing the number of buyers on their list of invitees. This can be seen by assuming that the CSO intends to sell m stones each period forever. Let X_i equal the quality of the ith stone, measured in dollars. Assume further that the qualities of the stones marketed each period are identically, independently, and normally distributed random variables with means μ and variances σ^2:

$$X_1, \ldots, X_m \sim N(\mu, \sigma^2). \qquad (1)$$

[34] See Benjamin Klein & Keith Leffler, The Role of Market Forces in Assuring Contractual Performance, 89 J. Pol. Econ. 615 (1981).

[35] Our argument is analogous to the economic rationalization for a manufacturer to have retailers earn a profit premium with the use of resale price maintenance and entry restrictions. See Benjamin Klein, Andrew McLaughlin, & Kevin M. Murphy, The Economics of Resale Price Maintenance: The Coors Case (Working Paper, UCLA, Dep't Econ. 1983). The existence of excess demand to be on the CSO list of invited buyers is evidence that presence on the list is a valuable asset. A number of qualified dealers have stated that they would like to be able to buy directly from the CSO. Van der Laan, *supra* note 26, at 98. De Beers does not sell this right to be an invited buyer for an initial lump-sum payment because of the additional "seller cheating" incentives that are created. (Intentional supply of low quality stones with buyer termination and resale of purchase rights by De Beers.) For further discussion of seller cheating see Section *E infra*.

Let P_i equal the price set by the CSO on the ith stone, such that

$$P_i = X_i - c + \epsilon, \tag{2}$$

where X_i equals the quality or "true" value of the ith stone to a buyer, determined after buyer inspection; c is a constant; and ϵ is a random variable distributed $N(0, \sigma_\epsilon^2)$. The expected premium to the buyer from acceptance of the CSO sale offer of the ith stone is $X_i - P_i$, or c.[36]

Consider two alternative marketing arrangements: (1) the CSO offers the m diamonds per period to m different buyers, that is, one stone per buyer, and (2) the CSO sells the m diamonds per period by offering $n(>1)$ stones per period to each of $j(<n)$ buyers, where $n = m/j$.[37] In arrangement 1, where each buyer is assumed to purchase one stone per period forever, the expected present discounted value to a buyer of remaining on the CSO list of invited buyers is

$$PV_1 = \frac{E(X_i - P_i)}{r} = \frac{E(c - \epsilon)}{r} = \frac{c}{r}. \tag{3}$$

The capital cost to a buyer of rejecting an individual stone after examination and being blacklisted by the CSO is therefore c/r. Hence, a buyer will reject an individual stone if and only if

$$P_i - X_i > \frac{c}{r}. \tag{4}$$

Under arrangement 2, where each buyer is offered n stones per period forever, the expected present discounted value to the buyer of remaining on the CSO list of invited buyers is

$$PV_2 = \frac{nE(X_i - P_i)}{r} = \frac{nE(c - \epsilon)}{r} = \frac{nc}{r}; \tag{5}$$

[36] Note that, more realistically, the expected premium is not a constant but is determined by past CSO behavior. Therefore, for example, if the buyer receives a stone where P_i is greater than X_i, the anticipated premium can be expected to fall. This will be discussed further in Section E *infra* when we consider the possibility of intentional deception by the CSO.

[37] We are not assuming here that the n stones are offered to the buyer on a "block" (single price, take it or leave it) basis. We want to consider only the effect of decreasing the number of buyers or, equivalently, the repurchase period. Section D *infra* considers the "blocking" question.

and a buyer will reject an individual stone if and only if[38]

$$P_i - X_i > \frac{nc}{r}. \tag{6}$$

It is therefore obvious that the expected number of stones rejected will be different for the two arrangements. The probability that a buyer in arrangement 1 will reject an individual stone is

$$\begin{aligned} P_r(1) &= P_r\left(P_i - X_i > \frac{c}{r}\right) \\ &= P_r\left(\epsilon - c > \frac{c}{r}\right) \\ &= P_r\left(\epsilon > c + \frac{c}{r}\right). \end{aligned} \tag{7}$$

The probability that a buyer in arrangement 2 will reject an individual stone is

$$\begin{aligned} P_r(2) &= P_r\left(P_i - X_i > \frac{nc}{r}\right) \\ &= P_r\left(\epsilon - c > \frac{nc}{r}\right) \\ &= P_r\left(\epsilon > c + \frac{nc}{r}\right). \end{aligned} \tag{8}$$

These rejection probabilities are represented by the cross-hatched areas in Figure 1. The CSO can decrease the probability that stones will be rejected (and hence duplicative quality inspection will occur) by (i) increasing expenditure on presale classification, and thereby decreasing σ_ϵ; (ii) by increasing the share of the marketing cost savings, the premium per stone, c, going to buyers; or (iii) by increasing the number of stones offered to each buyer per period n.

Decreasing the number of buyers (and hence increasing the number of stones each buyer receives per period) while keeping the expected premium per stone constant, raises the capital value to each buyer of remain-

[38] Expression (6) actually underestimates how much an individual stone must be overpriced in order for the buyer to reject it, since it excludes the lost premium on additional stones offered "this" period. It should more properly be considered the rejection point for the "last" stone offered in the current period. In addition, it underestimates the necessary overprice for rejection, because the expected value to a buyer of playing this game is greater than nc/r. Even if c equaled zero, buyers would obtain an expected return from the ability to reject, that is, from the ability to determine the last period. The expected value would be an average of the underpriced and slightly overpriced stones accepted before rejection; nc/r represents the total expected return given the absence of any rejection, which turns out to be our equilibrium condition.

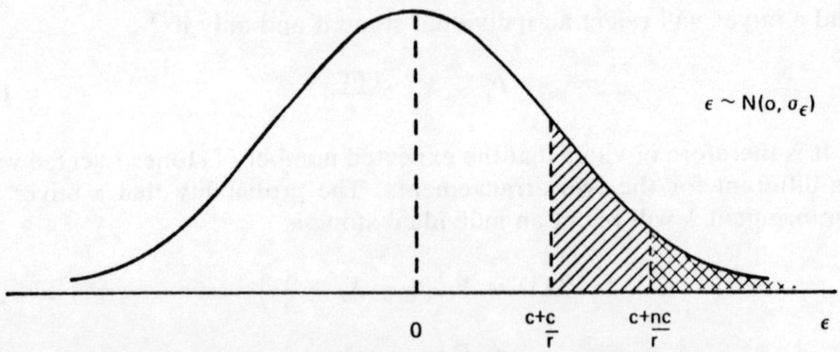

FIGURE 1.—Rejection probabilities, one versus *n* stones per period

ing on the CSO list of invited buyers. He is therefore less likely to reject any individual stone. Alternatively, for any given rejection probability the CSO can decrease the premium per stone as the number of buyers is also decreased. What limits this economizing process short of one or a few buyers the diseconomies of scale in cutting the stones. Given the fairly small scale of manufacture,[39] limiting the sale of rough diamonds to a few buyers would imply reselling of the stones before they are cut and hence oversearching.

Given the number of continuing buyers, the CSO wealth maximizing decisions concern (*a*) how much should be spent on categorizing and evaluating stones, thereby affecting the distribution of the actual values of stones around anticipated values,[40] and (*b*) how much of the total marketing cost savings should be shared with buyers by pricing stones at less than anticipated values. Given a particular sharing decision (that is, a given expected premium stream received by buyers), a greater categorization expenditure will reduce the variance of the value of stones and hence the number of stones rejected (and therefore the extent of duplicative searching). On the other hand, given a particular categorization expenditure and hence quality variance of price standardized stones, a greater share of the marketing cost saving that is passed on to buyers (that is, a greater price premium stream) will also imply fewer rejections and less duplicative searching.[41]

[39] For example, in 1961 the majority of people employed in the Israeli diamond cutting industry, which accounts for 30 percent of the world's output, worked in firms with thirty to ninety-nine employees. Szenberg, *supra* note 17, at 17, 60.

[40] The CSO "warranty" that gross classification "mistakes" will be corrected can be seen as a means of economizing on categorization expenditures in producing the desired underlying variance in stone quality within each stated classification.

[41] The premium per stone necessary to prevent rejection is quite small. Given the CSO physical classification process and the fact that mistakes are adjusted by the CSO, the

D. *Block Selling*

If the qualities of the individual stones within a classification are assumed to be independent, as seems reasonable, block selling does not generally decrease the incentive of buyers, each of whom is assumed to be receiving a given total number of stones per unit time and hence a given future premium stream, to reject stones. This can best be seen by continuing to assume that the CSO wishes to sell n stones per period forever to each of j buyers and, from equation (5), the present value to a buyer of remaining on the CSO list of invited buyers is nc/r, where c is the expected premium per stone. As we have seen, if an individual buyer is offered an individual stone, he will reject it only if it is overpriced by more than nc/r (eq. [6]) and the probability of this occurring is given by equation (8).

Alternatively, if the individual buyer is offered n stones this period at a block price of P_B, take it or leave it, the buyer will reject the package if and only if

$$P_B - n\bar{X}_B > \frac{nc}{r}, \tag{9}$$

where $\bar{X}_B$ is the average quality of a stone in the block. That is, once again a buyer will reject the package if and only if its price exceeds its total value by more than the present discounted value of the expected premium stream of remaining on the list of invited buyers. Since

$$P_B = n\bar{X}_B - nc + \Sigma\epsilon_i, \tag{10}$$

the probability that the block will be rejected by a buyer, pr (B), is equal to

$$\begin{aligned} \text{pr}\,(B) &= \text{pr}\left(\Sigma\epsilon_i - nc > \frac{nc}{r}\right) \\ &= \text{pr}\left(\Sigma\epsilon_i > nc + \frac{nc}{r}\right). \end{aligned} \tag{11}$$

That is, in order for rejection to occur, the total error of the n stones in the block must exceed n times the expected premium per stone plus the same critical capital value of the future premium stream value.

distribution of the value of stones within a category is not likely to be approximated by a normal distribution but rather by a distribution with much smaller tails and possibly a finite range. If, for example, the underlying distribution of an average value sight of $1 million is uniform between $.5 million and $1.5 million and there are ten sights a year, a premium per sight of only $5,000, or .5 percent of the average value, would be sufficient to prevent rejection of any sight if the interest rate were 10 percent. Only if a buyer underestimates the future expected premium stream or overestimates the quality deviation relative to the CSO estimates will a sight be rejected and the buyer be terminated by the CSO. We have not been able to find any examples of such buyer behavior and CSO punishment.

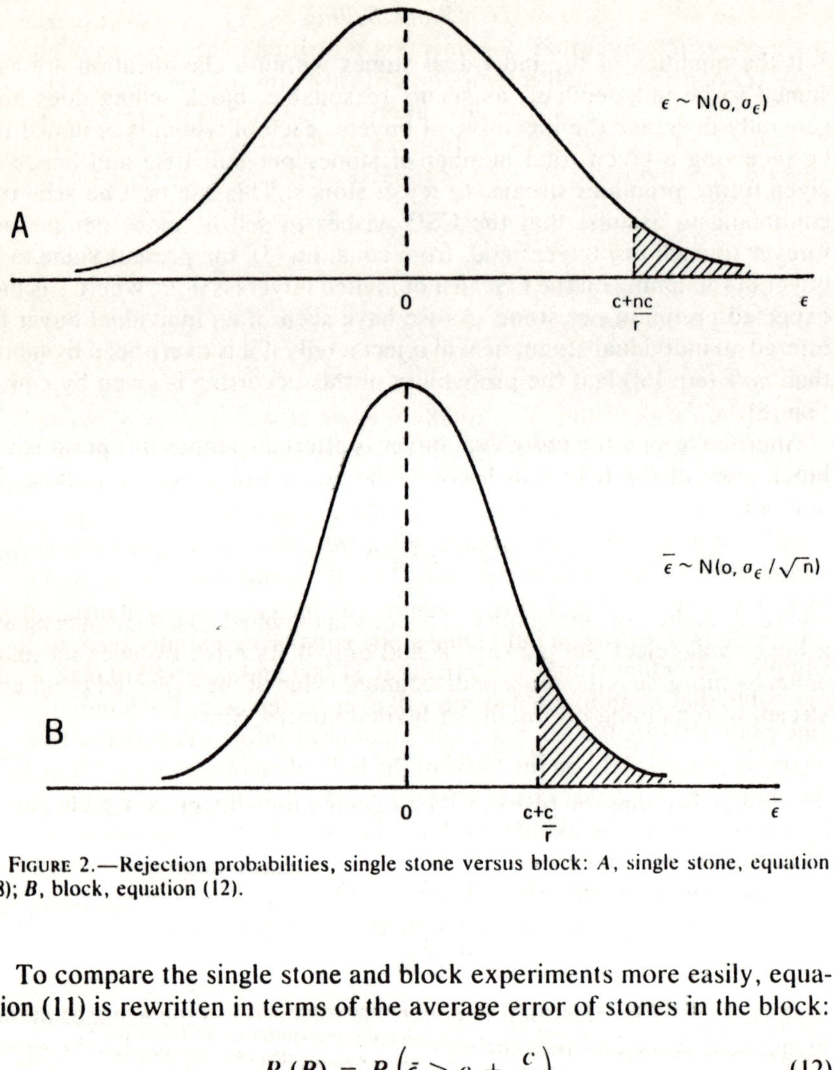

FIGURE 2.—Rejection probabilities, single stone versus block: *A*, single stone, equation (8); *B*, block, equation (12).

To compare the single stone and block experiments more easily, equation (11) is rewritten in terms of the average error of stones in the block:

$$P_r(B) = P_r\left(\bar{\epsilon} > c + \frac{c}{r}\right), \tag{12}$$

and the rejection probabilities given by equations (8) and (12) are represented by the shaded areas in Figure 2.

Whether the block will be rejected more or less frequently is not obvious from examination of Figure 2. Although the standard error of the average random error of the stones included in the block is less than the standard error of the random error of an individual stone, the critical rejection value for the average error is less than that for the individual stone error. The question is whether $c + c/r$ in Figure 2*B* is more or fewer standard deviations from zero than $c + nc/r$ in Figure 2A. Because $\sigma_{\bar{\epsilon}} = \sigma_\epsilon/\sqrt{n}$, we can standardize our rejection probability expressions in equations (12) and (8) by multiplying the critical point for the block case by $\sqrt{n}$. That is, the block will be less likely to be rejected [$\text{pr}(1) > P_r(B)$] if and only if $c(r + n)/r$, the critical value from equation (8), is fewer standard deviations away from zero than $c(r + 1)/r$, the critical value from equation (12), or

$$\frac{c(r + n)}{r} < \frac{c(r + 1)\sqrt{n}}{r}, \tag{13}$$

or, equivalently, when

$$r > \sqrt{n}. \tag{14}$$

Since the rate of interest is unlikely to be greater than $\sqrt{n}$, equation (14) indicates that it is generally not the case that the block will be less likely to be rejected. It is generally much more likely that a buyer will reject a block than an individual stone. The intuitiveness of this result can be seen as follows. We have assumed that the value of the future premium stream, nc/r, is the same in the case of both the individual stone and the block.[42] It follows that if this premium stream value is substantial, the probability of rejecting an individual stone must be essentially zero. If, for example, individual stones are priced at $1,000 and nc/r is $10,000, it is impossible that an individual stone will ever be rejected. Each individual stone by itself supplies such a small amount of information that a buyer will never reject solely on the basis of the individual observation.[43] On the other hand, because the variance of the *total* value of stones in a block is necessarily larger, the likelihood that a block will be overpriced by nc/r, and hence the probability of rejection, is necessarily larger.

Although not blocking appears to reduce the probability of rejection, it is far from obvious what such a selling arrangement would consist of.

[42] As we noted above, see note 38 *supra*, the lost premium stream resulting from rejection is identical in the two cases only if we consider the individual stone to be the last stone offered in the current period. However, we want to assume that the buyers in the two cases are offered the same number of stones each period to avoid the effect that increasing the number of stones per period, whether blocked priced or not, has on decreasing rejection probabilities. Therefore, in general, the value of the lost premium stream will be greater in the individual stone case than indicated in the text. (For example, if the stone is the first stone of the period we must add $(n - 1)c$ as the lost premium this period to the nc/r lost in the future.) Hence, modifying our analysis in this manner would reinforce our results—it would be even less likely that an "average" individual stone will ever be rejected.

[43] It appears that the CSO can continue to supply low quality stones without any danger of rejection. However, if the expected premium per stone is assumed more realistically not to be a constant but to be endogenously determined by past CSO behavior, the expected premium stream and critical rejection value will decrease over time.

Presumably, rather than one price being given for the entire sight, each stone would be individually priced. However, since there are thousands of very small diamond chips in many sights, in terms of increased transaction costs this would be analogous to putting a price tag on each kernel in a can of corn. As an alternative, at very little additional transaction cost we could certainly imagine separate prices on each individual diamond packet ("paper") in the sight.

How are the individually priced stones or packets in the sight to be offered to nonblock buyers? One obvious alternative would be a sequential presentation of the stones with rejection of any individual stone leading to immediate termination of additional sales in this and future periods. This arrangement is similar to what we have analyzed above and implies that an individual stone will be less likely to be rejected. For that reason sequential presentation increases the seller's potential to cheat buyers by supplying a nonrandom (overpriced) sample of stones. As opposed to block pricing, or the presentation of all of this period's stones before the buyer purchases any stones, buyers do not see the entire period's supply. A cheating seller can assume that buyers who would reject an entire period's package of stones if it were made available for them to inspect would initially accept some overpriced stones when they are offered and examined sequentially. As an extreme case, if the buyer's entire promised lifetime supply were sold in a block this period, then seller cheating would not be possible. With sequential pricing buyers are, in a sense, locked into past decisions regarding acceptance.

Although a theoretical framework of sequential search is "natural" to an economist familiar with the standard models of, for example, labor market search,[44] such a framework is difficult to consider as a realistic marketing alternative. The transaction costs of instituting such a sequential arrangement generally would be prohibitive. The idea of a produce man in a grocery store handing each customer individually priced oranges one at a time, or the CSO salesman's presenting a sight to each buyer one individually priced stone or paper at a time, is extremely counterintuitive. The marketing costs of such an arrangement would be so high as to make the suggestion close to nonsense.

A reasonable alternative definition of nonblock sales may be the presentation to the buyer of a package of *n* individually priced stones, where the buyer is not forced to accept the entire package on a take it or leave it basis. Buyers could be told that if they rejected any individual stone in the package they would not be invited in the future to purchase stones, but in

[44] S. A. Lippman & J. J. McCall, The Economics of Job Search (pts. 1,2), 14 Econ. Inquiry 153, 347 (1976).

principle they would not be facing a blocked marketing arrangement this period. Yet such a marketing alternative implies greatly increased costs of oversearching. If CSO priced each of the stones in a sight individually and let buyers search through their sights and reject any individual stones they wished to, such a nonblocked arrangement would increase the last period gains to a buyer rejecting stones and substantially increase rejection probabilities.

In terms of our previous framework, a buyer will reject a block if and only if it is overpriced by more than the future expected premium, or, rewriting equation (9),

$$\sum_i (P_i - X_i) > \frac{nc}{r}. \tag{15}$$

With separate prices a buyer will reject some stones if equation (15) holds, but also more generally, if

$$\sum_{(X_i - P_i) > 0} (X_i - P_i) > \frac{nc}{r}. \tag{16}$$

That is, even if equation (15) does not hold, if the sum of the deviations of all underpriced stones in the package is greater than the capital value of the future expected premium stream, it will pay for the buyer to search through and separate out these stones and take his return now by rejecting the remaining stones in the package. Rather than increasing its categorization expenditures or the premium per stone it pays to buyers, the CSO prevents such increased rejection by demanding purchase or rejection of the entire sight.[45]

More generally, the exact manner in which this period's n stones are priced is not as important as the fact that this period's transaction is not isolated but rather is part of a long-term continuing relationship. The crucial element of the De Beers marketing arrangement is not the block price in the current period but the large block sale over time to prespecified buyers. A limited number of repeat buyers are promised n stones per period forever, on which they expect to earn a valuable premium per stone. These rents and the termination provisions established by the CSO encourage buyers not to search and reject any particular sight, whether the sight consists of an individual stone or of a larger

[45] Even if eq. (15) held and stones would be rejected whether block priced or not, there is no reason to permit a buyer who determined his entire sight was so significantly overpriced as to reject it then to select out and purchase the most underpriced stones in the package. This would merely transfer wealth from the CSO to last-period buyers before they are terminated.

subset of the promised total "lifetime" supply. While separate pricing of the *n* stones supplied in any period eliminates the conditional tie-in sale within that period, it is the temporal conditional tie-in sale between periods of seller selected stones that is essential for the marketing arrangement.

E. "Blind" Selling and Seller Brand Names

The CSO could prevent buyer rejection of sights and hence oversearching without any rent sharing (buyer premium) merely by prohibiting buyer search, that is, by completing the contracting process and demanding payment before the buyer has an opportunity to examine the stones. Although this may seem unusual, it is a fairly common marketing practice. For example, a seller of potatoes may prepackage and sell them in opaque bags. Because hiding the quality information eliminates the incentive for buyers to search, such a policy by the seller may be both profit maximizing and socially efficient.[46] More generally, some element of blindness is present in all transactions where buyers do not know fully every characteristic of the product being sold or where contract specification and enforcement is not perfect, that is, every transaction where buyers rely on seller brand names to some extent.

The problem involved in prohibiting all consumer prepurchase inspection is that it creates an increased incentive for the seller to cheat buyers and hence the necessity for increased brand-name capital. If goods are sold blindly, sellers can intentionally supply a very low quality product and earn an extra short-run profit. This extra profit occurs only for a short period of time because buyers that are so cheated will refuse to purchase on such terms from the seller in the future.

The "seller cheating" problem in the case of the marketing of diamonds is the intentional supply by the CSO of low-quality (overpriced) gems. When such cheating is detected, buyers will refuse to purchase from the CSO on the same basis. Therefore, cheating is prevented if the extra

[46] An example where a producer deliberately made prepurchase quality inspection more difficult can be found in FTC v. Adolph Coors Co., 83 FTC 32 (1973). Coors, a producer of beer with a limited shelf life, resisted a suggestion by the FTC that it open-date its product by marking each can with a packaging date. The additional cost of open-dating would be small, since each can was already marked with the packaging date in code. Coors's resistance may be rational because the open-dating would encourage inefficient search by prospective purchasers and the necessity for a sliding scale of prices or a costly dispensing mechanism. With the dates in code, purchasers are forced to take a "random" sample from the seller's shelves. In addition, open dating would "advertise" the beer's limited shelf life and possibly decrease consumer demand. See Klein, McLaughlin, & Murphy, *supra* note 35. In addition to preventing inefficient oversearch, blind packaging reduces search and hence the uncompensated damage to goods that occurs in the process.

short-run profit that could be earned by the CSO is less than the present discounted value of the cost savings of their marketing arrangement.[47]

Under blindness the capital value of short-run profit from intentionally supplying stones of a lower quality than anticipated is likely to be greater than the discounted value of the lost marketing cost savings after the selling arrangement collapses. While extreme forms of cheating, for example, placing gravel in packets and selling it as diamonds, could be prevented by explicit contractual specification of sale terms, the remaining short-run cheating potential is enormous. Given the CSO's imperfect classification process and somewhat subjective categories, the CSO's ability for short-run deception of blind purchasers of contractually specified grades of diamonds appears to be sufficiently high to prevent the use of blindness without some additional costly, firm-specific, nonsalvageable investments by the CSO.

Permitting prepurchase inspections reduces the CSO's short-run cheating potential but, as we have seen, makes it necessary to share the marketing cost savings of the CSO selling arrangement with buyers to prevent rejection of sights. For the CSO this is cheaper than the increased brand-name capital investment required under blindness. In equilibrium the present discounted value of the marketing cost savings net of the premium paid to buyers is greater than the lower short-run cheating potential under a system of buyer inspection.

The CSO can be thought of as possessing two distinct "brand names"—the expected discounted value of the net marketing cost efficiencies associated with their selling arrangement, which assures buyers that they will not cheat, and a reputation that it will share these marketing cost savings with buyers in the future, which prevents buyers from "cheating" them. De Beers's "monopolistic" return can be thought of as a normal return on these brand-name assets, and the likely economies of scale in creating these assets explain the stability of the marketing arrangement.

III. The Paramount Case

A. *The Economic and Legal Setting*

During the 1930s and 1940s, before the introduction and growth of television, movie attendance in the United States was substantially

[47] This is analogous to the mechanism used to prevent reverse franchisor cheating on franchisees by unfair termination. See Benjamin Klein, The Borderlines of Law and Economic Theory: Transaction Cost Determinants of "Unfair" Contractual Arrangements, 70 Am. Econ. Rev. Papers & Proc. 356 (1980).

greater than it is today.[48] On average, about five hundred feature films were produced yearly, with each of the eight largest motion picture distributors releasing between twenty-five and sixty films a year. The five "majors" named in the Paramount suit accounted for 73.3 percent of domestic film rentals in the 1943–44 season.[49] Distributors were fully integrated backward into production and partially integrated forward into theatrical exhibition.

Exhibition consisted of a series of separate runs over time, with contractually specified clearance periods between each run within designated geographical zones. First-run exhibition accounted for between 30 and 50 percent of total receipts, with later runs accounting for smaller and smaller fractions of revenues.[50] The last-run or neighborhood theater was the closest thing to television viewership today. While first-run theaters generally supplied a single feature program in elaborate surroundings for a variable period of time, often a few weeks, neighborhood theaters catered more to families and usually offered a program of double bills, shorts, and newsreels, changing their programs frequently, often twice a week. Of the approximately 18,075 theaters in operation in 1945, the eight largest distributors had an interest in 3,137, or 17 percent. However, their representation in first-run exhibition was large, controlling more than 70 percent of the first-run theaters in the nation's ninety-two largest cities.[51]

First-run admission prices were higher than later-run prices, with film licensing contracts specifying minimum admission prices for each exhibitor and run. Distributor-set prices combined with the geographically and chronologically separated exhibition schedules implied by distributor-set run and clearance terms created a fairly transparent marketing arrangement to facilitate price discrimination among consumers.

Film rental terms generally were stated in contingent form, that is, percentage of gross revenues for earlier run showings and flat fee per time for later runs. Percentage rental terms were generally stated as a simple fraction of admissions revenue until some dollar amount, or splitting point, after which the rental percentage would be increased. (Sliding per-

[48] Average weekly movie attendance peaked during the immediate postwar period (1945–48) at 90 million, a figure greater than half of the total U.S. population. By 1953, weekly attendance had dropped nearly 50 percent to 46 million, clearly reflecting the growth of television ownership. Recently the market has become even more limited in size and also in the age of customers. Weekly attendance in 1976 was about 18 million people, 74 percent of whom were under thirty years of age. Cobbett S. Steinberg, Film Facts 45–46 (1980).

[49] Conant, *supra* note 14, at 36. Current annual U.S. production is approximately two hundred films, Steinberg, *supra* note 48, at 43, and distribution is less concentrated.

[50] The actual number of runs depended on size of city, with, for example, eleven runs in the 1930s in Chicago and fewer runs in smaller cities. Conant, *supra* note 14, at 69–70, 155.

[51] *Id.* at 48–50.

centages of gross as a positive function of revenues—that is, multiple splitting points—sometimes existed.) Films were generally grouped in four or five categories or "classes" (determined largely by budgetary considerations) with different rental terms for each category. Percentage rental terms also declined with length of run and were sometimes specified to be lower for midnight shows.[52] Percentage rentals generally ranged up to a maximum of 50 percent, after the split point, for the first week and first run of the best films.[53]

Contracts between distributors and theaters for the exhibition rights to films typically covered a group or block of several different films. Since these "block-booked" contracts were made prior to the films' production, they were also said to be "blind sold." It is important to recognize that a common description of the usual block booking contract as an arrangement where "an independent exhibitor had to agree to license the distributor's entire yearly output of features or he could license none,"[54] is clearly an inaccurate description of the practice. Only in the case of the small, late-run neighborhood theaters was demand sufficiently large for the exhibitor to choose to license the entire annual stock of several distributors. More generally, early-run theaters, including those owned by producer-distributors, contracted on a block basis for the "best" films available from various distributors to fill out their annual schedules. Contracting for a distributor's entire schedule was therefore relatively rare.[55]

[52] See *id.* at 70; Howard Lewis, The Motion Picture Industry 191–200 (1933); and Brief for the United States, app. United States v. Paramount, for a description of the contracts.

[53] See Brief for the United States, app. United States v. Paramount. Gone With The Wind was licensed at the very unusual rate of 70 percent. See Motion Picture Films (Compulsory Block Booking and Blind Selling): Hearings on S. 280 Before the House Comm. on Interstate and Foreign Commerce, 76th Cong., 3d Sess. 542 (1940) (hereinafter cited as 1940 Congressional Hearings) (statement of William F. Rodgers). Today, film rental terms range up to 90 percent of gross, after deducting a contractually specified amount to cover exhibition costs (that is, the "house nut"). However, average film rental fees remain quite similar, with a 34 percent average rate paid currently (Steinberg, *supra* note 48, at 40); the average rate paid by the affiliated theaters to the eight distributor defendants was 27 percent, Brief of the Warner Defendants to the Supreme Court at 138, U.S. v. Paramount.

[54] Conant, *supra* note 14, at 77.

[55] Twentieth Century–Fox sold its entire output of fifty-two films in 1938–39 to less than 20 percent of their accounts. The bookings for the fifty-two films distributed by Paramount during the 1938–39 season ranged from 14,261 to 4,408 with a median of 7,855 (1940 Congressional Hearings, *supra* note 53, at 469, 584 (testimony of Charles C. Pettijohn and Hammond Woober, respectively). The Famous Players–Lasky Corp. (predecessor of Paramount) licensed their entire annual film output to only 4.6, 2.6, and 4.7 percent of the exhibitors they dealt with in 1922, 1923, and 1924, respectively. Lewis, *supra* note 52, at 158–59. Part of the confusion regarding the nature of the practice may be due to the fact that the original "trust" method of distributing films pre-1920 appears to have involved complete "program booking"; that is, the distributor's films were rented on an all or nothing basis. See Ralph Cassady, The Impact of the Paramount Decision on Motion Picture Distribution

Most exhibitors dealt with too many different distributors to exhibit all of each distributor's films, shorts, and newsreels.[56]

After an unsuccessful earlier attempt by the Federal Trade Commission to outlaw block booking,[57] in 1938 the Department of Justice brought a monopolization case against the industry and certain of its trade practices. In 1940 the government and the five major film distributors agreed to a consent decree that ostensibly eliminated block booking and blind selling. It required, among other things, that exhibition contracts be limited to five or fewer films and that every film be shown to exhibitors in each district prior to licensing.[58] Although the distributors followed the terms of the decree, the marketing of films remained largely unchanged. Exhibitors kept their designated runs, rented approximately the same number of films from each distributor as they had previously,[59] and almost never attended trade showings.[60]

The government reactivated the Paramount case in 1944 in an attempt to modify the decree. The district court's opinion, issued in 1946, required an end to minimum admission prices, "unreasonable" runs and clearances, and block booking and the institution of a system of competitive bidding film by film in each run, open to all theaters regardless of past

and Price Making, 31 S. Cal. L. Rev. 150, 154 n.30, 155 n.46 (1958). This "full-line forcing" method of distribution had vanished by the time of the Paramount litigation.

[56] The fact that exhibitors almost universally licensed films from more than one distributor is inconsistent with the hypothesis that block booking served the purpose of preventing exhibitors' free riding on the brand name of the distributor. While it is true that the brand name of the distributor was relatively more important to consumers than it is today, block booking does not appear to have served a purpose similar to the use by a franchisor of an exclusive requirements contract on an important input. Neighborhood theaters, changing their double bill programs twice a week, demanded more than two hundred films a year, or more than three times the annual output of the largest distributor. Hence exclusive input supply was impossible. However, this "brand name" analysis of block booking can explain the use of block-booking-type contracts by the television networks. Free riding on the audience flows between programs in the absence of block booking is demonstrated by the supply of substantially lower-quality programming by the affiliates (that is, lower audience ratings) when the block was broken by the FCC prime time access rule. See William Jennings, The Economic Effects of the Prime Time Access Rule (1983) (unpublished manuscript, Cal. State Univ., Northridge, Dep't Econ. 1983).

[57] FTC v. Paramount Famous-Lasky Corp., 57 F.2d 152 (2d Cir. 1932).

[58] United States v. Paramount Pictures Inc., [1940–43] Trade Reg. Rep. (CCH) at S56,072 (S.D.N.Y. 1940).

[59] For example, prior to 1940 the State Theater in Norfolk, Virginia rented almost all its films from Loew's and United Artists. After the decree in the 1943–44 season the same theater rented thirty-six of its thirty-eight films from the same two distributors. See Loew's Brief to the Supreme Court, app. 2 at xii, Paramount, 334 U.S. 131.

[60] See testimony of William J. Kemper, general sales manager, Twentieth Century–Fox, Supreme Court Briefs & Records, Paramount Trial record at 1178–79, 334 U.S. 131 United States v. Paramount, 66 F. Supp. 323 (S.D.N.Y. 1946).

status or affiliation. Blind selling was permitted, but exhibitors were given the right to reject 20 percent of films licensed if distributors chose not to offer prior trade showings.[61]

The Supreme Court affirmed in 1948 the lower court rulings on the illegality of the trade practices, including block booking, but reversed the lower court's competitive bidding requirement. The Court maintained that competitive bidding would necessitate detailed regulation of the industry to evaluate and monitor essentially incomparable bid terms. Instead, the Court directed the lower court to reconsider divestiture of theaters as a more workable remedy.[62] On remand the district court ordered the distributors to sell their theaters and, while not requiring a system of open competitive bidding, prohibited discrimination against small independent exhibitors in the licensing of films.

B. Prespecified Blind Buyers

Potential exhibitors during the period of the Paramount litigation contracted for their films blindly. Although they had some information about production budget estimates, likely writers, actors, and directors of each film title and the past year's gross rentals of the studio's films, they could not view the product they were purchasing. This is similar to the De Beers marketing arrangement where stones are ordered blindly. A major difference between De Beers and *Paramount* is that to economize on brand-name costs sight holders are permitted to check the quality of the diamonds they order before paying the CSO. Diamond buyers are, in principle, permitted to reject what they order while film exhibitors were not. Film rentals are fully blind, thereby increasing the short-run cheating potential and required brand-name capital of the distributor.[63] However,

[61] United States v. Paramount Pictures, 66 F. Supp. (S.D.N.Y. 1946). Paramount, 334 U.S. at 163.

[62] The Supreme Court also rejected competitive bidding on the grounds that such a system would place those exhibitors with "the longest purse," namely the defendants and the large circuits, at an advantage. Paramount, 334 U.S. at 164.

[63] Hammond Woober, general manager of Twentieth Century–Fox, recognized the brand-name mechanism when he testified at the 1940 Congressional Hearings in opposition to legislation that would have prohibited "blind" selling. He stated that "[t]here is a belief that we sell, as it is commonly expressed, a pig in a poke. In reality that is not the way pictures are sold. We sell pictures the same as other articles of merchandise are sold. If you are the owner of a Buick car and you paid a certain price for it, and the time comes to repurchase a car, you either place your confidence in the machine you own or you change the type of machine that you are going to buy and this is the way motion pictures are negotiated for." 1940 Congressional Hearings, *supra* note 53, at 585. The necessity for brand-name capital explains one of the sources of the apparent relative economies of scale in current film distribution, namely, that small independent producers generally distribute through a "major," and the fact that blind selling currently is utilized only by the majors. See David Lees & Stan Berkowitz, The Movie Business 135 (1981).

the fact that the film rental payment is contingent on quality supplied, that is, stated as a share of gross, reduces the distributor's short-run cheating profit and his necessary brand-name capital.

Film licensing in the 1930s was similar to the CSO marketing arrangement in another respect. Distributors did not conduct a competitive auction among exhibitors for blind films, but rather dealt with de facto prespecified buyers. Given the elaborate discriminatory marketing arrangement of runs, zones, and clearances, theaters in particular geographical locations were predesignated in terms of run and all theaters could not freely bid on all films without creating an extremely complex scheduling problem. During the selling season, which began each fall and continued over the next few months, hundreds of unproduced films were fitted into the schedules of thousands of theaters. Each theater generally dealt with the same distributors each year, contracting in advance for the following exhibition season, for approximately the same number of films rented in the current season. The rental of films by theaters, very far from a competitive auction, was closer to a continuing franchise relationship.[64]

Within this franchising environment it is unlikely that blind selling was employed to prevent prespecified exhibitors from searching to obtain an informational advantage over distributors. While films are average priced, oversearching does not appear to be important because distributors are much more likely than exhibitors to have information on the marketability of individual films. Prerelease screenings are not likely to supply much valuable information to an exhibitor. (If they did, the exhibitor would have a comparative advantage in production-distribution and should change his line of business.) In fact, as we have noted, when presale trade showings were required by court decree for a brief period of time, exhibitors did not attend them.[65]

Rather than preventing the buyer from taking advantage of an informational asymmetry, the primary purpose of blind selling appears to be substantial inventory-cost savings. Given the necessity of scheduling exhibitors months in advance of release, trade showings, while supplying little or no valuable information, would increase distribution costs substantially.[66] The main impact of the 1940 decree requiring such trade

[64] Explicit franchise agreements giving the exhibitor exclusive rights to license the distributor's films over a period of time, usually more than one year, were entered into with affiliated circuits. See Brief for Plaintiff, app. at 50–58, United States v. Paramount 334 U.S. 131 (1948); and 1940 Congressional Hearings, *supra* note 53, at 645 (Statement of R. H. Poole).

[65] Nonattendance may have been due also to exhibitors' fear of losing their valuable run designation if they attended such showings. But we have not been able to find any evidence to support the existence of such a threat by distributors.

[66] Hammond Woober testified at the 1940 Hearings that "each producing company would have to increase its inventory 50 to 100 percent to meet the requirements of the bill and that

showings appears to have been an increase in the inventory cost to distributors and an increase in the number of visits and hence the number of salesmen required to service exhibitor accounts.[67]

C. *Block Booking*

The *Paramount* marketing arrangement appears to differ from the De Beers arrangement in the absence of search by buyers for an informational advantage over the seller. Although films are average-priced, rejection of individual films from the group ordered and supplied does not appear possible. Sales are blind, and even if they were not, prerelease search, such as attendance at a trade showing, yields little valuable information. However, one point in the transaction process is completely analogous to the De Beers arrangement in terms of the ability and incentive of buyers to take advantage of an informational asymmetry.

After initial first-run results become available, the limited information conditions under which the licensing agreements had been made are altered drastically and a significant exhibitor contract-reneging problem is created. In particular, after the initial marketing results are available, the films are no longer blind and exhibitors have a potential informational advantage over distributors. Exhibitors could increase their return if they could select a subset of the originally licensed films to exhibit. This would be equivalent to the rejection after examination of overpriced diamonds in the De Beers marketing case. Rejection by an exhibitor of films contracted for creates scheduling problems, entails a costly recontracting process and rearrangement of the planned run scheme, and leads to lower average license fees on the distributor's total film output. Blocking was used solely as a way to prevent exhibitors from engaging in this postcontractual rejection of overpriced films.[68]

---

would require at least $100,000,000 to $200,000,000 of new capital. . . ." 1940 Congressional Hearings, *supra* 53, at 585.

[67] H. Huetting, Economic Control of the Motion Picture Industry: A Study in Industrial Organization 122–23 (1944 repr. 1971). Our analysis of blind bidding implies that both distributors and exhibitors would generally favor the practice. This appears to be consistent with the available evidence at the time. At the 1940 Congressional Hearings numerous independent theater representatives and owners voiced strong opposition to a proposed legislative end to blind bidding (and block booking). Support for the legislation primarily came from "disinterested" civic and religious consumer groups concerned about theater owners being "forced" to exhibit "immoral" films. The recent state legislative movement to outlaw blind-bidding arangements, on the other hand, has been supported by exhibitor trade associations and is more difficult to explain.

[68] Postcontractual substitution of films by theaters within a zone also could prevent group and distributor maximization. For example, if two theaters in a particular zone are showing different films, say A and B, with weekly revenues of $1,000 and $200, individual exhibitor maximization may lead the second theater to substitute to film A from film B. This substitu-

Block booking existed as a means of enforcing contractual commitments and thereby preventing exhibitors from rejecting films after initial run results became available. If a theater owner attempted to refuse to exhibit a film licensed on a percentage of gross basis, the block contract defined the liquidated damages. Once an exhibitor contracted for a particular group of films within a category and a total price was agreed on, the blocked contract stated that refusal by an exhibitor to accept a particular previously agreed-on film would require the exhibitor to pay 1/*n*th of the total agreed-on block price to the distributor.[69] Since the film of unanticipated low quality that the exhibitor would choose to reject will likely have a true value of less than 1/*n*th of the package price, the liquidated damage block-booking clause can be viewed as a disguised penalty clause. Block booking, or the intentional overpricing of ex post unexpectedly poor quality films, can be thought of in this context as a way of enforcing blindness, effectively preventing exhibitors from searching out and rejecting the poorest-quality films after their first-run results become available.[70]

Block booking existed also in the sense of average pricing. Observers have generally described block booking as a practice where distributors systematically underpriced their good movies and overpriced their poor movies.[71] This ex post result occurs whenever anticipated quality within a

tion may lead to a reduction in joint weekly revenue below $1,200—say $1,000 ($500 at each theater). Distributors and consumers alike would seek ways to prevent this. If the contract were with an exhibitor in a one-theater town, postcontractual substitution would not be disruptive and hence would be permitted as long as rental fees were not reduced. 1940 Congressional Hearings, *supra* note 53, at 553 (statement of William F. Rodgers).

[69] Lewis, *supra* note 52, at 196; 1940 Congressional Hearings, *supra* note 53, at 430, 585 (Twentieth Century–Fox License Agreement and statement of Hammond Woober, respectively).

[70] In addition to this contractual mechanism distributors could have used a quasi-rent stream mechanism similar to that employed by De Beers to prevent rejection. By reclassifying the theater's run designation, distributors could reward or punish exhibitors. See Conant, *supra* note 14, at 61–69; and The American Film Industry 164 (Tino Balio ed. 1976). The magnitude of the theater owners' investment was dependent on run and, given the complex scheduling arrangement, generally not costlessly and immediately transferable to another distributor. See, for example, 1940 Congressional Hearings, *supra* note 53, at 714 (statement of William G. Ripley), at 643 (statement of R. H. Poole), and at 600–601 (testimony of Roy L. Walker), for evidence that an exhibitor's run assignment was considered a valuable right. It is interesting to note that of the 450 arbitration cases filed between 1941 and 1946 under the terms of the 1940 Paramount decree (which established a system of arbitration tribunals where independent exhibitors were permitted to bring complaints against distributors) more than 400 were related to clearance or run designation disputes rather than to contract disputes. See Conant, *supra* note 14, at 96; and Paramount, 334 U.S. 131, 1860 (1948).

[71] See, for example, Lewis, *supra* note 52, at 163; Bertrand Daniel, The Motion Picture Industry: A Pattern of Control 5–6 (1941). Conant, mirroring the explanation given by the court, notes that "[b]lock booking involved the transfer of monopoly power from popular

group cannot be measured perfectly ex ante and average pricing is employed. However, since most rental terms were set on the basis of actual performance of individual films ex post, why were more accurate pricing formulas not devised to minimize the extent of the average pricing present? The answer appears to hinge on the creation of optimal incentives for the supply of exhibition services.

D. Optimal Incentives

Flat lump-sum film rental fees appear to be the most efficient. The alternative, percentage rental contracts, entails two distinct costs—the costs of checking reported box office receipts and the costs of inducing exhibitors to supply optimum cooperative input levels. Since the costs of monitoring to assure accurate revenue reports by exhibitors are somewhat invariant to theater gross, flat rental fee contracts were generally used for the small, low-grossing, later-run theaters.[72] Flat rental fees maximize exhibitors' incentive to supply cooperative inputs such as local advertising, cleanliness of physical facilities, competent ushers and projectionists, the number of shows, length of run, and program design.[73] Many of these exhibition services have a significant but not easily measurable effect on total attendance. Even if the optimum level of services were known ex ante, their supply could not be contractually specified in a precise, enforceable manner.

Flat rental fees can solve the exhibitor incentive problem only if the fee is totally independent of performance. The lump sum cannot be determined ex post on the film's results, since knowledge of the formula on which such a payment is to be made would defeat its purpose of not influencing marginal incentives. The lump sum cannot even be a particu-

pictures and actors of great public preference to inferior pictures and unknown actors. Distributors charged less than the highest possible price for superior films and more for inferior films than if sold singly." Conant, *supra* note 14, at 79.

[72] See Conant, *supra* note 14, at 71; and Lewis, *supra* note 52, at 193–95 for a discussion of the magnitude of the monitoring of revenue receipts problem, including the problem of monitoring the monitors. Lewis concludes that "the rentals involved in many theaters were not large enough to warrant the expense involved in checking." *Id.* at 195.

[73] If the first or A film of a double feature bill was rented on a percentage of gross basis, the second or B film selected by the theater was required to be contracted for on a flat fee basis. Frank H. Ricketson, The Management of Motion Picture Theaters 194 (1938). To eliminate the incentive by exhibitors to rent lower than optimal quality B films, their flat rental fee was generally deducted from the gross before the sharing percentage was applied. This created an obvious contrary incentive on the part of the exhibitor to rent higher than optimal quality B films. Therefore some contracts contained a limit on the rental that could be deducted for the second feature. See, for example, Brief for the United States, app. at 127, United States v. Paramount.

lar amount per day because it would then distort incentives regarding length of run. The lump sum must be a one-time payment based ex ante on anticipated quality, related, say, to the film's production budget. Because film quality is so unpredictable, we would have a substantial variance within each anticipated quality/initial lump-sum payment classification. With such extreme ex ante average pricing, exhibitors would have the same desire to renege on contractual commitments by selecting individual films and rejecting others after initial results became available. However, since payment would presumably already have been made, reneging would not be possible.

Although flat rental fees maximize exhibitor incentives and minimize monitoring costs, they may not be optimal for two reasons. First, such an arrangement would require an increased amount of distributor brand-name capital. Given blindness, exhibitors must rely on the brand name of distributors to supply the optimum type and magnitude of film quality and promotional services. A distributor's ability to increase in the future the average lump-sum rental fees on its films if it supplies an exceptionally high level of services in the current period (and the necessity to lower its rental terms when supply is lower than anticipated) is an expensive policing mechanism. The brand-name capital required for the mechanism to work is large, because the short-run cheating potential on the part of the distributor is substantial. Quality is not easy to specify contractually ex ante, and there is a large random element in audience acceptance. Thus the exhibitor cannot know cheaply, even ex post, whether low quality has been supplied intentionally. A contingent payment arrangement, by decreasing the distributor's short-run cheating potential, economizes on the required brand-name capital costs.

The producer-distributor's incentive problem is completely analogous to the exhibitors' incentive problem. The distributor could rely on the brand name of the exhibitor alone to supply the optimum levels of cooperating inputs in the production process, but presumably the required exhibitor premium stream and specific capital investment are too large, and a contingent payment economizes on the required brand-name capital.

When both parties to a transaction must supply important inputs that cannot be prespecified cheaply by contract and when brand name costs are nontrivial, a sharing arrangement, while it creates potential moral hazard problems, may be the most efficient solution. In a world of imperfect foresight, measurement, and enforcement, some combination of specification, brand name, and disincentive costs will be associated with any contractual arrangement. The efficient solution entails choosing the particular arrangement that minimizes the sum of these transaction costs.[74]

A second factor, in addition to increased distributor brand-name costs, that may make a flat-fee arrangement nonoptimal is that exhibitor disincentives (and hence required exhibitor brand-name capital) do not vanish under lump-sum rental fees. Given the elaborate distribution system of multiple runs, early-run exhibitors renting films for a flat fee will have an incentive to exhibit the film for too long a period and interfere with profit-maximizing price discrimination. Theoretically, flat fees produce no distortions only when property rights are fully defined. In this case they are not; a theater owner deciding to exhibit a film for a longer period of time produces an externality on later-run theater owners who have purchased exhibition rights.[75]

An ingenious solution to this problem was the distribution contract with the large theater circuits. These circuits consisted of up to several hundred theaters under common ownership. The contract specified payment for licensed films based upon a percentage of the film's national gross (so-called formula deals). The circuit's actual success with the film did not affect the price paid,[76] so that the decreased average pricing of an accu-

[74] The contractual form and the particular share settled on will depend on the relative importance and contractual specifiability and enforceability of the cooperating inputs involved. When particular services are extremely large and not easily contracted for, flat fees may be the full-cost-minimizing solution (including transaction costs). For example, although first-run theaters generally rented films on a sharing basis, when the exhibitors supplied live entertainment, the films were often rented on a flat-fee basis. See 1940 Congressional Hearings, *supra* note 53, at 983 (statement of Austin C. Keough). Alternatively, theaters were sometimes able to deduct the cost of a stage show, up to some maximum amount, from the gross in calculating percentage rental fees. Brief for the United States, app. at 131. Exhibitor risk aversion, rather than transaction-cost minimization, is an alternative, not mutually exclusive, hypothesis for the presence of sharing arrangements. However, one should in general be hesitant to accept risk-aversion explanations for contractual terms. Risk explanations are logically equivalent to relying on tastes to explain behavior. They ignore the separate insurance market that may develop in response to such tastes and the fact that many similar sharing contracts are observed in situations where risk considerations alone would appear to imply lump-sum payments (for example, royalty contracts made by publishers with authors). If both parties to a contract can shirk, a partial sharing arrangement may be shown to be optimal under fairly general measurement and transaction-cost conditions within a risk-neutral environment. See Benjamin Klein, Kevin M. Murphy, & Ben T. Yu, Measurement Costs and Sharing Contracts (1983) (unpublished manuscript, UCLA, Dep't Econ.).

[75] Vertical integration of first-run exhibition may possibly be explained by the fact that it had the largest variability of run length, in addition to the largest amounts of other cooperating inputs. The distributors could have been expected to use their reciprocal transacting positions with one another to assure exhibitor performance in all first-run theaters. See Benjamin Klein, Robert G. Crawford, & Armen A. Alchian, Vertical Integration, Appropriable Rents, and the Competitive Contracting Process, 21 J. Law & Econ. 297, 305 (1978).

[76] Conant, *supra* note 14, at 74.

rate ex post contract was combined with the incentive structure of a lump-sum contract. Since these circuits had theaters in various runs, the problem of unnecessary holdovers between runs would be solved. Contractual arrangements similar to these formula deals are still used with the large circuits in England.[77]

Because these forces are likely to imply the use of a percentage of gross licensing arrangement, accurate ex post rental terms, as opposed to more approximate individual film average pricing (or blocking), would create severe exhibitor incentive problems. In particular, as the quality of an individual film increases, it is unlikely that the marginal rental percentage can likewise rise without disturbing exhibitor incentives. For example, consider a hypothetical case where it costs ten cents for the exhibitor to clean a theater seat and that it is worth twenty cents to the consumer to have the seat cleaned. If the film rental licensing fee is 50 percent (or lower) the seat will be cleaned. But if the rental fee of a higher-grossing film is raised beyond 50 percent the exhibitor will not clean the seat. Only if exhibitor services are supplied solely by a fixed cost, with no variable costs related to audience size, can the distributor increase the marginal rental percentage for higher-quality films without creating additional disincentives regarding the supply of exhibition services.

That block booking in the sense of ex post average pricing is related to exhibitor incentives is consistent with the fact that United Artists, which distributed films supplied by many independent producers and therefore required accurate measures of individual film values, licensed each film separately and extensively employed complex contracts with sliding rental percentages.[78] All distributors have now adopted similarly precise rental agreements. However, film licensing in England, which does not have the legal legacy of the Paramount decree, continues to have relatively simple contract terms with the maximum rate at 50 percent.[79]

E. *Product Splitting*

If the Paramount litigation was designed to encourage allocation of films by competitive bidding, it was unsuccessful. In the period immediately following the final decree, open competition occurred in perhaps several hundred cases out of approximately 15,000 or more potential

[77] U.K., House of Commons, Monopolies Commission, Films: A Report on the Supply of Films for Exhibition in Cinemas 12 (1966).

[78] Brief on Appeal of Appellant United Artists Corporation to the Supreme Court at 25, United States v. Paramount; and Brief for the United States, app.

[79] U.K., House of Commons, *supra* note 77, at 8.

selling transactions,[80] and these instances were arranged so that the distributors would avoid the risk of suit by disgruntled exhibitors.[81] Whenever possible distributors divided their films among competing theaters, either by assigning the films of a particular distributor or by assigning shares of the films of a particular distributor to competing exhibitors, with one exhibitor breaking the distributor's films into groups and the other distributor choosing first.[82]

This "product splitting" instituted by the distributors strongly supports our analysis. It was a natural reaction to the final decree, representing an obvious attempt by distributors to continue the de facto franchise relationship that existed with exhibitors during the 1930s and 1940s. However, given the radical changes that occurred in the film industry in the 1950s, it is difficult to understand why the practice persisted and remains fairly common today. In particular, the multiple-run scheduling considerations that required long-term exhibitor relationships largely disappeared with the introduction and growth of television. Film attendance, the number of theatrical films, especially B films, the number of theaters, and the number of runs declined dramatically. Price discrimination via second- and later-run exhibition is accomplished today primarily with cable and then network television release.

In addition, as we have noted, during the postdecree period, pricing of films moved from an average block regime to one where individual films

[80] Cassady, *supra* note 55, at 161. One general sales manager of a large distributor stated in 1956 that competitive bidding occurred in only 3.2 percent of the selling situations. Motion Picture Distribution Trade Practices, Hearings Before a Subcomm. of the Select Comm. on Small Business, U.S. Senate, 84th Cong., 2d Sess. 372 (1956) (hereinafter cited as 1956 Senate Hearings) (statement of Charles M. Reagan).

[81] As one company official stated, "The plain fact was that . . . [we] lawyers felt very keenly that the only way we could eliminate these endless legal disputes . . . was to have some system like competitive bidding which will afford the company an immunity. . . ." Problems of Independent Motion Picture Exhibitors relating to Trade Distribution Practices, Hearings Before a Subcomm. of the Select Committee on Small Business, U.S. Senate, 83d Cong., 1st Sess. 582 (1953) (statement of William Zimmerman). An antitrust division spokesman stated in 1953 that there were more than one hundred private antitrust suits pending against the major distributors, *id.* at 655 (statement of Philip Marcus). One company stated that it used competitive bidding only at the "specific request of one or more competing exhibitors or at the request of an exhibitor that he be licensed pictures on a run which had been formally licensed by his competitor." 1956 Senate Hearings, *supra* note 79, at 372 (statement of Charles M. Reagan).

[82] Cassady, *supra* note 55, at 164; James Gordon, Horizontal and Vertical Restraints of Trade: The Legality of Motion Picture Splits under the Antitrust Laws, 75 Yale L. J. 239, 240 (1965); Cassady at 165 and Gordon at 241 n.5 make extremely weak attempts to rationalize this practice. Film licensing in England consists of quite explicit product-splitting arrangements in the form of right of first refusal agreements by the two major exhibition circuits, ABC and Rank, each accounting for approximately one half of all first-run releases. U.K. House of Commons, *supra* note 77, at 15.

were priced more accurately by complex sliding percentages. Interfilm variances in the length of run and in grosses increased, and the predictability of the value of a given studio's annual output decreased. In this period exhibitors complained less frequently that they were forced to rent overpriced bad films in order to rent (presumably underpriced) good films and more frequently that distributors demanded excessive amounts for their better films.[83]

Yet as the industry and marketing arrangements have changed, product splitting has mysteriously survived. It is unlikely that a monopsonistic exhibition industry has imposed product splitting on reluctant distributors. Distributors initiated, and acquiesced in, the arrangement as an attempt to imitate the essential conditions, namely prespecified buyers, prohibited by the Paramount decree; and distributors could terminate it as easily by playing one exhibitor against another. Some exhibitors within each city are outside the split, and most split agreements include a provision for competition among alternative exhibitors if the distributor rejects the split designee. Alternatively, the distributor could bring suit against exhibitors who persisted against their desires for competitive bidding.[84] In cities where product splits are present, such distributor behavior is totally absent.[85]

Instead of monopsony, a likely rationale for product splitting is as a substitute for average block pricing in creating correct marginal exhibitor

[83] Conant, *supra* note 14, at 150.

[84] The argument that distributors might be reluctant to bring suit against exhibitors and damage their good will in continuing relationships makes little sense. There already exists a substantial amount of litigation between these parties concerning underreporting of receipts and other claims regarding contractual breach, and a large number of private antitrust actions. See Ralph Cassady, Jr. & Ralph Cassady III, The Private Antitrust Suit in American Business Competition: A Motion Picture Industry Case Analysis (Occasional Paper No. 4, UCLA Bur. Business & Economic Research 1964).

[85] Most litigation with regard to splitting has involved suits by exhibitors excluded from the split. See, for example, Viking Theater Corp. v. Paramount Film Distribution Corp., 320 F.2d 285 (3d Cir. 1963). There are a number of cases where distributors have claimed the illegality of product splits, but, as far as we know, these represent counteractions. For example, General Cinema Corp. v. Buena Vista Distribution Co., Inc., 532 F. Supp. 1244 (C.D. Cal. 1982) represents a counterclaim by Buena Vista against General Cinema's original claim that a minimum film rental based on a per capita charge represented illegal price fixing. (This contractual term appears to be designed to prevent exhibitors from underpricing admission and overpricing a complementary input, such as popcorn, on which no licensing fee is paid.) The court dismissed the original complaint and ruled on the counterclaim that General Cinema's participation in split agreements was per se illegal. This decision is contrary to most recent opinions. See, for example, Greenbrier Cinemas, Inc. v. Attorney General of the United States, 511 F. Supp. 1046 (W.D. Va. 1981), which represented an exhibitor's challenge to the Department of Justice April 1, 1977, change in policy regarding the legality of splits. Distributors are, however, cooperating with the Department of Justice in their most recent attack on the practice of splitting in Milwaukee, United States v. Capitol Service, Inc. Civil Action no. 80-C-407 (E.D. Wisc).

incentives. In nonbidding situations, including cities where product splits occur, distributors engage in renegotiation, that is, adjust rental terms downward if the film performs poorly.[86] This behavior would be extremely unlikely if distributors were facing exhibitors imposing an artificially low monopsonistic price. Renegotiation serves the purpose of mitigating the increased marginal disincentives regarding the supply of exhibition services created by the accurate, single-film, complex pricing schedule. Although the supply of exhibition services cannot be specified fully in an ex ante contractual manner, the distributor will presumably know ex post if the exhibitor "did a good job" and this will be reflected in the final adjustment.[87] Such renegotiation is not possible in bidding situations without violating the terms of the auction that the film go to the highest bidder, thus opening the distributor up to a discrimination suit by an exhibitor that submitted a failed bid.

Although the evidence is unclear whether the existence of a split depresses rental terms,[88] it appears to have an unambiguous effect on lowering guarantees—minimum, nonrenegotiable, up-front rental payments for the film run. Although complex sliding-percentage rental terms now price individual films more accurately, they do not set prices perfectly. Therefore, given the absence of block booking, guarantees are an alternative means of preventing exhibitors from reneging on contracts after initial poor attendance results become available. Money payments up front create the correct marginal exhibitor incentives regarding the supply of cooperating inputs, including run length and number of shows. The de facto long-term franchise arrangements with particular exhibitors implied

[86] See Cassady, *supra* note 55, at 176–77. Renegotiation only goes one way, namely, noncontractually required payments made by distributors to exhibitors.

[87] During the 1930s, renegotiation, although rarer and of a smaller magnitude, did occur when an entire block was, ex post, priced "unjustly." See Loew's Inc., 20 Fortune Magazine 25, 110 (August 1939); and 1940 Congressional Hearings, *supra* note 53, at 547. Contracts also contained provisions for reducing the percentages of gross in each price quality class if the aggregate receipts from films within that class fell below a contractually determined level. For example, for each film in the two highest percentage categories, if the theater did not earn a profit equal to at least one-third of the total film rental paid, the film automatically reverted to the next lowest category. Ricketsen, *supra* note 73, at 32–33; and Brief for the United States, app. at 131, United States v. Paramount.

[88] We would expect that a split would be accepted by a distributor only if rental terms are not lower. Charles M. Reagan, general sales manager and vice president of Loew's Inc., stated that ". . . we have indicated a willingness to eliminate competitive bidding whenever possible in situations where returns from the theaters are comparable by licensing our pictures on a split basis, that is, dividing our product between or among competitors," 1956 Senate Hearings, *supra* note 81, at 373 (statement of Charles M. Reagan). The evidence presented in United States v. Capital Service, Civil Action no. 80-C-407, indicates an unambiguously sharp decline in guarantees after the establishment of the split in Milwaukee (see exhibit GX9 and GX) but disagreement regarding the effect of the split on film rentals (see trial testimony of Ben Marcus and Irving Palace and exhibit DX509).

by product splitting with the possibility of distributor renegotiation reduce the necessity for such guarantees.[89]

IV. The Loew's Case

A. *The Economic and Legal Setting*

Many of the films produced during the 1930s and 1940s, covered by the theatrical exhibition contracts declared illegal in *Paramount* became the subject of new litigation as they were released by the major motion picture producers for television exhibition. Among the approximately 2,500 feature films made available for television by 1956 were major portions of the pre-1948 film libraries of MGM, RKO–Radio Pictures, Columbia, United Artists, and Warner Brothers.[90]

Distributors licensed feature films directly to local television stations. Each station renting a film received the exclusive right to air that film in its market area for some stipulated period of time. After a distributor announced the availability of a well-known library of films through advertisements in trade magazines (such as *Variety*) and direct mail advertising to local stations, the distributor's salesmen visited the stations offering a number of blocks of films. The contents of each block were named by the distributor, with each block consisting of a fairly representative subdivision of the entire library, and were uniform in composition throughout the country. Prices for the blocks were established by salesman negotiations with the stations in each market area, with the negotiating process often consuming several months.[91]

Not all license agreements covered distributor-selected blocks. Some stations were allowed to choose films from the entire library, cutting across the blocks. For example, only 113 of the 203 contracts made by Loew's and television stations between June 1956 (when they decided to release for television distribution their pre-1948 feature film library) and

[89] The common argument that guarantees are used as a means of reducing distributor's risk (see, for example, Film Studios Theater Retaliation against States Banning Blind Bids, Los Angeles Times, June 1, 1981, § 4, at 1, 3, 5) makes little intuitive sense given the relative asset positions of distributors and exhibitors, the ready access of distributors to more generalized capital and insurance markets, and the fact that they are used much less frequently in product splitting situations.

[90] United States v. Loew's Inc., 189 F. Supp. 373, 382 (S.D.N.Y. 1960).

[91] The description of a "typical" contracting sequence is a composite of testimony from the trial court case Civil Action no. 119–24, reproduced in Court Records and Briefs, Loew's, 371 U.S. 38. In particular see the testimony of Oliver A. Under, president of National Telefilm Associates Inc., *id.* at 5825–944.

March 1960 involved preselected packages of films or block booking.[92] Nevertheless, in 1957 the government brought six separate civil antitrust actions against the six major distributors of motion picture films for television (Loew's, C&C Super Corporation, Screen Gems, Associated Artists, National Telefilm Associates, and United Artists) alleging that refusal to license films on other than a block-booking basis violated the Sherman Act. As opposed to the Paramount litigation, there were no allegations of conspiracy.

The suits were consolidated and tried beginning in March 1960. The government demanded that the defendants be required to license feature films to television picture by picture and station by station. The district judge ruled that even one instance of refusal to license motion picture films other than by block-booking was a violation and granted injunctive relief.[93] The Supreme Court upheld the decision and imposed the government's desired remedy, although it permitted a distributor to refuse to offer for sale to one station an individual film that was part of a block of films over which negotiations were currently in progress with a competing station.[94] The effect of this reservation was to allow the distributors to continue their existing selling practices: trying to negotiate block sales but permitting deviations.

B. Contractual Cheating

One possible explanation for block sales is contractual cheating. Many films are made with contracts requiring compensation of actors, directors, writers, and investors out of the film's profits. When a block of films is rented, the distributor may attempt to hide profits on an individual film by allocating the rental receipts for the block arbitrarily among the individual films. If some films in the block are not profitable or do not contain profit-sharing clauses, producers and distributors could attempt to assign them the lion's share of the proceeds from the block's price and thereby reduce the contractually obligated profit-sharing compensation they must pay on the successful films.[95] However, this form of contractual cheating is

[92] The 113 block licenses included sixty-three contracts for the entire 723-film library, nine contracts for either preselected half of the library, thirty-six contracts for one or more of the three preselected groups of one hundred films, and five contracts for a group of sixty-seven films preselected by Loew's. Information about the Loew's contracts is from Court Record, Exhibits 626, Loew's Exhibit 21, Civil Action No. 119-24, Loew's, 371 U.S. 38. The information about the relative quantities of the various Loew's packages is found in Court Record at 675, 4869.

[93] Loew's, 189 F. Supp. 373 (1960).

[94] Loew's, 371 U.S. at 55.

[95] This may explain Twentieth Century–Fox's alleged violation of the Paramount decree in 1978 by forcing theaters to exhibit the unsuccessful film The Other Side of Midnight in

likely only if some unanticipated contingency occurs, not easily avoided contractually. If the potential cheating is anticipated, actors and investors would negotiate for an allocation device.[96] The Loew's case involved movies made in the 1930s and 1940s, when the possibility of future television sales must have seemed quite remote. Therefore explicit contractual protection against this form of opportunism must have been rare.

Although this explanation is appealing, it is not consistent with the facts of *Loew's*. The pre-1948 films in question were made under the "studio system." The actors, writers, and directors were on long term exclusive employment contracts and were paid a flat weekly salary.[97] Executive compensation for some of the producers and others employed by the studio was based in part on total studio profit and an agreement was reached by the distributors and the guild not to claim royalties on these television sales. All the evidence indicates that the distributors had, or acquired, full and exclusive rights to the films licensed for television use.[98]

C. *Price Discrimination*

The most commonly accepted theoretical explanation for block booking is that it is a subtle form of price discrimination, where distributors use a block to set prices on films that unpredictably vary in relative value across geographical markets. This theory is intuitively appealing. Stigler found that first-run theatrical grosses of several different movies released during 1946–47 varied significantly across different U.S. cities. He hypothesized that the aggregate value of a group of films was more predictable and related to general factors of the particular market.[99] In fact, block-sale prices in *Loew's* appear to be fairly predictable across markets.

---

order to rent the highly successful film Star Wars, in which George Lucas had a 40 percent share of net revenues.

[96] An example of a contractual solution to an anticipated cheating opportunity can be found in United States v. Columbia Pictures Corp. 189 F. Supp. 153 (S.D.N.Y. 1960). The government challenged an agreement between Universal Pictures and Screen Gems, a wholly owned subsidiary of Columbia Pictures, in which Universal granted to Screen Gems a fourteen-year exclusive license to distribute for television exhibition approximately six hundred pre-1948 Universal feature films. Since Screen Gems also distributed for television substantially all of Columbia's pre-1948 films, the agreement further required that films in the two libraries would be classified before distribution into categories of comparable quality and that the Universal films would not be sublicensed to TV stations by Screen Gems for less than the Columbia films of comparable quality. The court recognized that without such an agreement it would have been possible for Screen Gems to shift profit from Universal to Columbia by offering TV stations Universal films at lower prices if they also rented Columbia films at correspondingly higher prices. See Robert H. Bork, The Rule of Reason and the Per Se Concept: Price Fixing and Market Division, 75 Yale L. J. 373, 461–64 (1966).

[97] See Balio, *supra* note 70, at 376–77.

[98] For example, Oliver A. Unger testified that both Loew's and Columbia owned their negatives fully. Court Record at 5840, Loew's, 371 U.S. 38.

[99] See Stigler, *supra* note 7, app.

The variation in prices paid for a single package of eighty-five films sold by National Telefilm Associates across seventy-six different television markets between July 1, 1946, and April 23, 1960, can be explained largely on the basis of a few economic factors.[100]

Once prices for a block are determined in a few markets—that is, quality is estimated—prices in other markets can be predicted and set accurately by such factors as income and population. If Stigler is correct, individual film prices cannot be set accurately across markets on the basis of such similar limited information, since each market area is characterized by people whose tastes differ significantly from those of people in other market areas. Therefore, although the total demand for a group of films may be highly predictable across markets, the relative values of the individual films in the block vary unpredictably between markets. However, as we noted in the introduction, there is no reason for a distributor selling films in a multiple television station market on an exclusive exhibition basis not to let the competitive market operate to reveal buyers' demand prices. Since there is no need for distributors to set prices, there is no need for blocks as a means for distributors to ameliorate the informational advantage assumed to be possessed by buyers.[101]

Stigler's price discrimination explanation makes some sense only in

[100] Oliver A. Unger of National Telefilm Associates, when asked at trial about the factors influencing price replied: "Well, the rate card of the station is a factor as to how much time costs in that area. The competitive situation is another important factor to establish value. The set circulation is an important factor, the number of television sets in the area, and of course the quality of the merchandise that is being offered at that time is also a big factor." Court Record at 5856, Loew's, 371 U.S. 38. Our estimated equation is

$$\log(\text{price}) = -7.0 + \underset{(6.4)}{.58} \log(\text{circulation}) + \underset{(9.7)}{2.1} \log(\text{income}) + \underset{(3.8)}{.83} (\text{number}),$$

$R^2 = .82$. The price of the block is taken from Court Record, National Telefilm Associates Exhibit 11, Exhibits at 778, 803–06, Loew's, 371 U.S. 38. Circulation is taken from Broadcast Information Bureau, TV Factbook no. 33, Metropolitan Markets, 249–289 (1962) and is a measure of potential audience. Income is the per family median income by SMSA for 1960, Country and City Data Book, item 28 (where data by SMSA were unavailable, county data were used) and is a measure of the value of advertising messages per viewer reached. Number of stations refers to the number of commercial stations within a fifty-mile radius in each market area, from TV Factbook no. 33. The positive significance of number on price may reflect demand variables unaccounted for by circulation and income or the net positive theoretical effect of number of buyers on price within a Nash equilibrium framework.

[101] If the relative demand for individual films varied significantly and unpredictably among television stations within a market, it would generally pay for a distributor to break the block and sell the individual films separately in a competitive bidding manner. As in all discontinuous markets the distributor would only receive the value of the second highest valuing station. However, the within-market interstation variation is unlikely to be very important because viewers can switch stations to watch a particular movie on whatever station it appears.

TABLE 1
LOEW'S TELEVISION LICENSING CONTRACTS, JUNE 1956–MARCH 1960

	Loew's Selected Block Sales	Customer Selected Nonblock Sales	Total
One-station markets	*a*) 21 (29)	*b*) 31 (23)	52
Multiple-station markets	*c*) 92 (84)	*d*) 59 (67)	151
Total	113	90	203

SOURCE.—Data from Court Record, Exhibits 626, Loew's exhibit 21, Civil Action No. 119-24, Loew's, 371 U.S.; and Quigley Publications, International Television Almanac (1960).

one-station markets. In such a situation, which obtained in many regional markets in the late 1950s, distributors face monopsonistic buyers of their films. Therefore they obviously cannot leave it to competition to determine the final price of their films. The distributors must bargain, and superior knowledge of the value of a block of films compared with the value of each individual film separately may produce a relative bargaining advantage for them.[102]

The evidence from the *Loew's* record indicates that the exact opposite occurred. Distributors were less likely to break preselected blocks in multiple-station markets, where interstation competition could be used to reveal valuations, than in single-station markets, where the supposed increased predictability in the valuation of the block was necessary for the distributor to counteract the superior information possessed by the monopsonistic buyer on the valuations of individual films.

Table 1 presents a two-way classification of each of the 203 Loew's contracts, reflecting whether the transaction involved a Loew's-selected

[102] This assumes that buyers have better information than sellers about the relative appeal of individual movies. Otherwise buyers will also want to depend on their knowledge of the value of the block in striking a bargain. The existence of such asymmetrical information seems unlikely. Monopsonistic buyers in one-station markets may appear to be able to bargain price down to the seller's marginal cost, which in this case of previously produced films with essentially no alternative use is essentially zero. However, the seller can be assumed to make a firm commitment not to sell unless he receives his asking price, which he sets equal to the market-clearing price given by the estimated equation in note 100 *supra*. Such a commitment will be credible because the various regional markets are tied together by the exchange of price information and therefore an individual transaction is not isolated. As opposed to the standard bilateral bargaining problem, a seller who cuts the price below his commitment price in one single-station market loses revenues in other single-station markets as other monopsonistic buyers adjust their estimates of the seller's ability to keep his commitment. This potential loss in revenues in other markets serves as an incentive for the seller to maintain his commitment in any one market. The single station observation residuals in our estimated equation are not generally negative or very large.

block or a customer-selected film or group of films and whether the transaction was with a television station in a multiple station or single station market. Our restatement of Stigler's price discrimination theory predicts that cell *a* (Loew's "block" sales, one-station markets) and cell *d* (customer selected sales, multiple-station markets) would show more than the chance number of contracts. The chance numbers (in parentheses) are calculated on the assumption that there is no relation between the number of stations in a market and Loew's behavior. Since 56 percent of all Loew's transactions were block sales (113/203), we would naively expect 56 percent, or 29 of the 52 sales in one-station markets and 84 of the 151 sales in multiple-station markets also to be blocks. If the Stigler price discrimination hypothesis were correct, we would expect more than 56 percent of sales in one-station markets and fewer than 56 percent of sales in multiple-station markets to be blocks. Instead, only 40 percent of the sales in one-station markets (21/52) and 61 percent of the sales in multiple-station markets were blocks. The evidence indicates a significantly nonrandom distribution of transactions in the *opposite* direction one would expect from the price discrimination hypothesis.[103]

D. Product Standardization

The films licensed to television stations in *Loew's* generally were of relatively low individual value. Although Justice Goldberg used *Gone with the Wind* in his decision as the hypothetical example of a desirable film with monopoly power to which sellers would tie less desirable films,[104] such exceptional films were not part of these agreements. The average three-year rental price for films in the National Telefilm Associates block discussed above was less than $200 and in some markets it was less than $20.[105] The films were generally "time fillers," randomly used by the stations at the end of the program day in, for example, the 11:30 P.M. time slot.

These films were of highly uncertain individual value. Potential purchasers could not merely check the original theatrical gross in the particular market of the individual film in question (reported in trade magazines such as *Variety*) and hope to obtain with some simple conversion formula an accurate estimate of the film's current TV license value. Very dramatic demographic changes had occurred in particular markets over the years

[103] Using a χ^2 test, the null hypothesis that there is no relation between single or multiple stations in a market and the presence of block sales can be rejected at a .05 level of significance ($\chi^2 = 5.807$).

[104] Loew's, 371 U.S. at 52.

[105] Court Record at 803–06, Exhibits 778, Loew's, 371 U.S. 38.

since original release and the values of the films had depreciated at widely different rates.[106] In addition, they could not rent the films on an ex post contingency basis, such as for a share of advertising revenue, because audience flows and the need to standardize for the presence of competitive programming made quality measurements difficult.

However, individual film values were not economically important. The station owners often programmed by choosing individual films randomly from the block, and advertisers purchased blocks of time without knowing during which film their ads would appear. As opposed to the De Beers case—where seller search for individual product quality information was duplicative because buyers would eventually have to determine value accurately when cutting the stone—in this case neither the distributor nor the station owner requires the information for any allocative purpose. All quality search, by both buyers and sellers, would be wasteful.

Information regarding the average value of films is economically relevant in determining price, and blocking can be expected to reduce these information costs. If Director's and Stigler's insight is correct, films' values are individually highly uncertain but are predictable in the aggregate. Distributors packaged films in a manner similar to De Beers's random selection of stones for sights, attempting to give buyers an average representation of the quality of the distributor's library. For example, Associated Artists Productions divided its entire library of 754 pre-1948 Warner Brothers films into thirteen groups of fifty-eight films each, with each group intended to be of the same overall quality and to be "balanced" to contain a similar mix of musicals, comedies, dramas, and westerns.[107] As a result, any buyer with an estimate of the overall quality of the Warner Brothers library also had an estimate of the "value" of each of the thirteen groups.

As opposed to the De Beers and Paramount situations, there may not appear to be a seller brand-name repeat-sale mechanism present to assure buyers that the films in the block are selected randomly. Some of the distribution companies in this case were formed solely for the one-time sale of the old film libraries to television stations. However, because we are dealing with a standardized product and therefore information collected from one transaction can be transmitted cheaply across markets, a

[106] George Hartford, vice president and general manager of Station WTOP testified that some older films, particularly musicals, were badly dated and would no longer be well received by the audience, Court Record at 391, Loew's, 371, U.S. 38. However, many of these musicals were later edited, spliced together and rereleased theatrically by MGM with great success as "That's Entertainment."

[107] See the testimony of Eliot Hyman, president of Associated Artists Production, Court Record at 5581, Loew's, 371 U.S. 38.

repeat-sale mechanism is present. If a nonrandom selection of films were made by the distributor, such information could be expected to be discovered after the first few sales and to be reflected in prices paid for the same block in other markets over time.[108]

Films within these distributor-created packages were average priced. If buyers searched through these randomly created blocks and purchased individual films selectively, a negative externality would be created on the buyers of the remaining films in the block. In addition to knowing about the average value of a distributor's quality, buyers are familiar with the transaction price of the block in other markets and hence have information about the particular block's value. Given the predictability of block values across markets, we are dealing with a product that is standardized intermarket. Attempts by individual buyers to find exceptional values within the average-priced block destroy the standardization and create increased uncertainty about the value of the remaining films in the block.

Because Loew's had a fixed supply of films available for license and the marginal cost of licensing a film to an additional station was low, the license fee was almost a pure rent. Buyers' inspection costs would be borne almost entirely by the seller, who would have the incentive to choose selling practices that reduced search costs. Since breaking a block destroys valuable information and could be expected to induce increased buyer search, distributors would resist buyers' offers to purchase a part of a prepackaged block.

This information-cost theory of block booking is consistent with the evidence presented in Table 1. We would expect significantly more blocks to be broken in one-station markets than in multiple-station markets, because when a block is broken other buyers in the same market area can no longer use the knowledge of the average quality of the distributor's library and the price information generated on sales of the particular standardized package in other markets. Buyers in single-station markets, on the other hand, do not impose such externalities.

V. Conclusion

Although it is generally the case that there are many different economic reasons for the existence of any particular marketing practice, the essen-

[108] There is some indication that buyers in the various markets were in contact with one another. For example, Oliver A. Unger (of National Telefilm Associates, Inc.) testified that "[t]his is a business of so few people that you [as a film distributor] can do something in New York at 8 o'clock in the morning and you will hear about it in Seattle at 3 that afternoon. This is the fastest underground there ever was." Trial Record at 5870, Loew's, 371 U.S. 38. Since the stations in each of the 240 regional TV markets were not in competition with each other, they may have shared information with one another. In addition, transactions for the various standardized blocks and transaction prices were regularly reported in trade journals such as Variety.

tial rationale for block booking is the same in all three of the cases we have examined. Blocking serves to prevent buyers from rejecting parts of a package of products that has been average-priced. In the De Beers case, if stones in each sight were individually priced and buyers were permitted to search through and select the particular stones they wished, the probability of rejection would increase and De Beers would be able to sell the remaining stones in each quality category group only at a lower price. Similarly, in the Paramount case buyers cannot be permitted, after the initial exhibition results become available, to pick through the group of films originally contracted for at a particular average price per film and select the subset they wish. And similarly, in the Loew's case buyers must be discouraged from searching for exceptional individual film values within randomly selected groups of films that are priced on the basis of a fairly well-known average value.

The extent of average pricing required in these cases is substantial because of the degree of the underlying quality variance. The goods we have examined are unique in that the quality of the particular good is not easily known or cheaply controlled by the supplier. A precise estimate of the value of individual rough diamonds would require costly, duplicative examination costs. Similarly, the values of films are notoriously variable and not related very predictably to production costs, and accurate presale measures of individual product quality are costly and wasteful.

Average pricing could be eliminated, in principle, by the use of an ex post contractual mechanism such that the value of the good and hence its price would be determined only after final sale of the product to consumers. Even in the presence of substantial ex ante uncertainty regarding values of individual goods, there would presumably be no uncertainty ex post. However, all ex post contracts entail measurement costs in separating out the effects on final value of cooperating inputs in the production process. These costs of accurate ex post pricing are prohibitive in De Beers and *Loew's* and entail substantial incentive problems in *Paramount*.

Finally, in our cases, buyers must rely on the brand name of the supplier. This is not unusual in itself; for almost any good it is prohibitively costly to know before purchase or to specify in an enforceable way every element of quality. However, in the usual case it is generally assumed that sellers know the quality of the goods they are selling and their brand name assures the buyers that this quality will not be less than anticipated.[109] In our cases, sellers do not know very accurately individual product quality before sale, and their brand names assure performance in the sense that buyers have confidence that they have selected a random sample of goods

[109] See Klein & Leffler, *supra* note 34.

from the underlying quality distribution on which the average price is based. Seller brand names then prevent buyers from taking advantage of the informational asymmetries present within such average-pricing schemes.

The particular contractual arrangements chosen by the parties in the various cases are designed in part to minimize these brand name costs. To economize on brand-name capital De Beers has chosen to share their marketing cost savings with buyers, the distributors in *Paramount* have chosen an ex post pricing mechanism, and the distributors in *Loew's* have standardized their products. Sellers are optimizing so as to minimize transaction costs, recognizing that performance called for in every transaction is partially guaranteed by costly private brand-name capital mechanisms and partially guaranteed by costly government-enforced contractual mechanisms.[110] The results of our analysis demonstrate that difficult-to-explain contractual terms can be analyzed rigorously rather than merely labeled as "noncompetitive." Although the contractual arrangements examined are incompatible with the perfectly competitive model, they provide us with an opportunity to improve our understanding of the competitive economy.

[110] See Klein, *supra* note 47; and Oliver E. Williamson, Transaction Cost Economics: The Governance of Contractual Relations, 22 J. Law & Econ. 233 (1979).

[23]

UNITED STATES VERSUS UNITED SHOE MACHINERY CORPORATION: ON THE MERITS*

SCOTT E. MASTEN and EDWARD A. SNYDER
University of Michigan

I. Introduction

Although *United States v. United Shoe Machinery Corporation* ranks among the most famous of antitrust cases, the economic principles involved in the dispute have remained obscure.[1] The most prominent economic issues have been (i) the role of leasing as a solution to the durable-goods-monopoly problem and (ii) the exclusionary potential of specific lease provisions. Of these, the durable-goods-monopoly rationale appears to have gained the greater acceptance among economists—an occurrence due in no small part to Chicago School arguments that challenged the logic of anticompetitive exclusion.[2]

* We would like to extend our thanks for helpful comments to Ian Ayers, Patrick DeGraba, Victor Goldberg, D. Bruce Johnsen, James Meehan, Michael Meurer, Eric Rasmusen, Alan Schwartz, Richard Zerbe, participants at seminars at the Department of Justice, Antitrust Division and at Boston University, the University of Chicago, Columbia University, the University of Connecticut, Cornell University, George Mason University, the University of Michigan, Massachusetts Institute of Technology, North Carolina State University, the University of California, Los Angeles, the University of Southern California, Washington University, Yale University, and at the National Bureau of Economic Research's "Program in Industrial Organization" conference. We gratefully acknowledge the financial support of the Lynde and Harry Bradley Foundation, the RGK Foundation, and the Office for the Study of Public and Private Institutions. We would also like to express our gratitude to the United Shoe Machinery Corp. and especially John Meuse, Nick Gelsomini, and George Armstead for providing access to their files and records, to Edward McCarthy for additional data and consultations, and to Justice Department officials for their help in obtaining records from the case. James Bohn provided excellent research assistance. Parts of this research were completed while Masten was a John M. Olin Faculty Research Fellow at Yale Law School.

[1] United States v. United Shoe Machinery Corporation, 110 F. Supp. 295 (D. Mass. 1953), aff'd; 347 U.S. 521 (1954) (hereafter cited as District Court Opinion).

[2] The Chicago views were developed by Aaron Director and Edward Levi, Ward Bowman, Richard Posner, and Robert Bork. Director and Levi argued in 1956 that exclusionary

[*Journal of Law & Economics*, vol. XXXVI (April 1993)]

Two developments, however, have stimulated renewed interest in United's motives and the overall merits of the case. The first was the realization that the duration of United's leases was inconsistent with the durable-goods-monopoly argument. Whereas short-term leasing facilitates monopoly pricing of durable goods by curbing the monopolist's temptation to cut prices to successive customers, United's leases were originally seventeen years in duration and were subsequently shortened (first to ten and later to five years) only at court direction.[3] Second, new theoretical models have overcome the logical hurdle to exclusionary claims by demonstrating that exclusion may indeed be profitable despite the need to compensate customers or suppliers for the resulting loss of competition.[4] If claims of anticompetitive exclusion cannot be rejected a priori, then lease terms and other contractual provisions that limit rivals' access to markets must be evaluated on their merits.

In this article, we offer what we believe to be a tenable efficiency defense of United's practices against the charge of anticompetitive exclu-

---

practices tended to be unprofitable because it is costly "to impose additional coercive restrictions on . . . suppliers." Aaron Director & Edward Levi, Law and the Future: Trade Regulation, 51 Nw. U. L. Rev. 281, 292 (1956). Bowman argued in the same year that Kaysen's analysis of *United* was flawed because, if customers preferred leases of shorter duration and with less restrictive elements, they would have been willing to pay a premium. Ward S. Bowman, Review of "*United States v. United Shoe Machinery Corporation*, An Economic Analysis" by Carl Kaysen. 66 Yale L. J. 303 (1956). Posner cited *United Shoe* to illustrate his claim that suppliers must compensate customers for exclusionary contract provisions: "[C]ustomers of United would be unlikely to participate in a campaign to strengthen United's monopoly position without insisting on being compensated." Richard A. Posner, Antitrust Law: An Economic Perspective 203 (1976). Bork criticized the court's reasoning that United's practices could be anticompetitive without being predatory and concluded conversely that, in the absence of predatory behavior, the presumption must favor efficiency. Robert H. Bork, The Antitrust Paradox (1978). Bork, like the others, did not attempt to provide an affirmative efficiency explanation for the practices, however.

[3] As originally expounded by Ronald Coase, buyers of durable goods will be reluctant to pay monopoly prices initially without a guarantee that prices will not be lowered in the future. R. H. Coase, Durability and Monopoly, 15 J. Law & Econ. 143 (1972). Leasing offers such an assurance insofar as the manufacturer, by retaining ownership rights to the existing stock of capital, will bear some of the losses from additional production and distribution. The size of the manufacturer's losses, however, is inversely related to the length of the lease contract. Hence, shorter-term leases offer more effective guarantees to buyers than do longer-term leases. The inconsistency between the theory and the duration of United's leases has been previously noted by Victor P. Goldberg, The United Shoe Machinery Leases (unpublished manuscript, Columbia Univ. Law School 1990); and John S. Wiley, Eric Rasmusen, & J. Mark Ramseyer, The Monopolist That Leases, 37 UCLA L. Rev. 693 (1990).

[4] Specifically, Phillipe Aghion and Patrick Bolton show how a firm can profit from exclusionary practices despite the need to compensate customers for agreeing to exclusionary terms if the contract can be structured to extract economic rents from third parties, either potential rivals or future customers. Phillipe Aghion & Patrick Bolton, Contracts as a Barrier to Entry, 77 Am. Econ. Rev. 388 (1987).

sion. Specifically, we argue that leasing served as an alternative to contractual warranties for assuring the quality of machines and as a way to foster the provision of a range of manufacturer services and information in support of the productive use of that equipment. Shoe machines were remarkably complex and heterogeneous instruments, costly to develop and prone to failure. The efficient operation of a shoe factory required a large number of these complex devices and an assortment of services that included guidance on the selection and configuration of shoe machines, training in their operation, timely and effective repairs, and the dissemination of technical advice on shoes and shoe manufacturing generally. The complexity of shoe machines and of related services would have left conventional contractual arrangements hopelessly incomplete and susceptible to conflicts. By making the proceeds from machinery transactions contingent on the retention and use of machines, leasing promoted the supply of quality machines and the generation and dissemination of nonpatentable innovations and know-how without the need for comprehensive contracting.

The importance of innovation and know-how to sustaining efficient production in the shoe industry also underlay the long-term and exclusionary features of United's leases that were the central component of the government's complaint. Specifically, the government cited three provisions of United's leases for their exclusionary effect: (i) return charges due upon termination of a lease, (ii) minimum monthly usage charges on machines subject to per-unit payments, and (iii) the "full-capacity" clause that required lessees to "use the machine to its full capacity upon all shoes upon which the machine is capable of being used."[5] Combined with the long term of the leases, these provisions can be justly interpreted as impeding adoption of competitor machines. The relevant question, however, is whether the impediments they created were excessive in relation to organizational problems encountered in the industry. We argue, to the contrary, that the duration and restrictive features of United's leases established appropriate incentives to retain and use machines and, in particular, were necessary to prevent customers from attempting to escape paying for information and services from which they had already benefited and that could be profitably used with competitors' machines. We more broadly contend that the structure of United's leases reflected the desire of transactors generally to economize on the costs associated with governing exchange and resolving disputes.

[5] Civil No. 7198 (D. Mass. filed December 15, 1947, at 30) (hereafter cited as Complaint). The government also objected to United's practice of providing repair services without separate charges.

Our investigation has two advantages over recent studies by Victor Goldberg and by John Wiley, Eric Rasmusen, and Mark Ramseyer that also explore efficiency rationales for United's practices.[6] First, although each suggests plausible efficiency justifications for leasing durable goods, neither attempts to reconcile their rationales for leasing with the specific provisions of United's leases. Second, these studies also fail to account for United's selective use of leasing and pricing arrangements. Of the 343 machines United offered at the time of the case, only half were available on lease-only terms. Of those, half levied charges on a per-operation basis while the balance relied exclusively on monthly rental fees. A satisfactory theory should generate testable hypotheses regarding United's pricing and leasing policies as well as explain the important elements of the overall structure of its leases.

We begin in Section II with a description of the nature of the intermediate market for shoe machines. Then, in Section III, we present two efficiency motives for leasing in such circumstances, discuss what form such leases should take, and present testable hypotheses regarding the use and structure of United's leases. Section IV contains econometric evidence that United systematically selected the terms under which it offered its machines to reflect these incentive considerations. A more thorough examination of the details of United's leases and their implementation shows United's practices to be broadly consistent with the efficiency arguments we present. Sections V and VI offer brief discussions of the practices of United's predecessors and competitors and of the aftermath of the case. We conclude with some observations on the implications of the *United* decision and on public policies toward exclusionary contracts generally.

II. An Industry Primer

The organizational problems encountered in the market for shoe machines trace ultimately to the nature of shoes and of shoe demand.[7] From a mechanical standpoint, the most distinctive features of shoes are their complex shape and extreme heterogeneity. To accommodate the intricate curves and irregular surfaces of shoes, shoe machines had to perform

[6] Goldberg, *supra* note 3; and Wiley, Rasmusen, & Ramseyer, *supra* note 3.

[7] The court record provides considerable detail on the nature of shoe production and the services provided by shoe machinery manufacturers. Following an extensive review of these facts, Judge Charles Wyzanski questioned "not the accuracy, but the relevance of the generalizations." District Court Opinion, *supra* note 1, at 300–302, 329–32. See also Carl Kaysen, *United States v. United Shoe Machinery Corporation:* An Economic Analysis of an Antitrust Case (1956).

complex motions in multiple spatial planes—actions that required major advances in machine technologies. At the same time, these machines had to be easily adjustable to the variety of styles, sizes, materials, and constructions in or of which shoes were made. There were at least eighteen principal methods of producing a shoe,[8] each of which entailed between one hundred fifty and two hundred operations.[9] Although wood, fabrics, and later rubber were also employed, the principal raw material remained leather, which varied almost continuously in its thickness, strength, and flexibility. To provide an approximate fit to feet of varying dimensions, shoe manufacturers normally produced over one hundred and often over two hundred size-width combinations for each shoe design, the attributes of which varied in turn with both function and fashion.[10] Accordingly, shoe machines, unlike other manufacturing equipment of the period, could not be designed for repetitive operations on large, homogeneous lots. Rather, "[t]he machine-type performing each operation, though a special tool from the point of view of the operation performed, [had to] be a general tool in relation to each shoe in process requiring the operation."[11]

The reliability of these complex devices was a critical concern to shoemakers. Shoe fashions were inherently unpredictable and transient. As a result, retailers initially placed orders for new styles in small volumes. Shoemakers then were expected to deliver repeat orders of successful styles on short order.[12] Delays in delivery implied missed sales opportunities and could lead to cancellations of orders. In addition, the failure of one machine could disrupt operations throughout a plant, idling both labor and other machinery.[13]

Surmounting the technical problems associated with designing machines capable of reliably performing the varied and intricate operations of producing a shoe required "advanced engineering skill, familiarity with the problems of shoe-making, and generally, prolonged expensive re-

[8] Request for Findings of Fact of the United Shoe Machinery Corporation in the District Court of the United States for the District of Massachusetts, 24 (January 1952) (hereafter cited as United Facts).

[9] On Their Toes, Baron's, September 28, 1959, at 3; Footwear's Desperate Drive for Productivity, Bus. Week, June 10, 1972, at 68. Approximately half of the operations to produce a shoe were performed by hand.

[10] United Facts, *supra* note 8, at 37.

[11] *Id.* at 47.

[12] *Id.* at 38.

[13] According to United, production interruptions often led to "cancellations of orders, tying up of inventories, and strained labor relations." *Id.* at 48. Also see District Court Opinion, *supra* note 1, at 302.

search,"[14] endeavors to which United devoted considerable resources. At the beginning of 1950, United had 572 employees engaged in research on shoes, materials, machines, and processes and had spent approximately $4.3 million on research during the preceding year. The only machinery manufacturer with a larger research laboratory was General Motors.[15] Over the fifteen years or so leading up to the case, moreover, United had trained all of its own inventive talent.[16] Its research and development efforts made it one of the five largest patent holders in the United States.[17]

The result of those efforts was the development of a large number of complex and interdependent machines, the productive use of which depended heavily on the initial provision and continued flow of a range of supplementary services. In 1948, United offered 343 types of machines, of which a shoe manufacturer would need from thirty-seven to one hundred to perform the operations required to produce a shoe.[18] The efficient combination and arrangement of those machines varied depending on the manufacturing process adopted, the type and quality of shoes being produced, the scale of production, and the skills and experience of employees.[19] Identifying the best techniques and most productive combination and configuration of machines and training the work force in their proper use and maintenance demanded extensive knowledge of both shoe machines and manufacturing.

Once in operation, shoemakers were also in frequent need of advice on problems encountered during the course of production. This advice, which often had "little or nothing to do with any individual machine," included "the application of broad know-how along shoe making and manufacturing lines" and involved, in addition to technical advice on machine operations, "the analyzing of problems, whether arising from styles, materials, constructions, labor skills or any one of many factors and the giving of expert advice and assistance to help the manufacturer to make more and better shoes at lower cost."[20]

[14] District Court Opinion, *supra* note 1, at 302.

[15] Kaysen, *supra* note 7, at 152.

[16] District Court Opinion, *supra* note 1, at 330.

[17] In addition, United devoted much of its research effort to improvements in existing machines, many of which were not patentable. Kaysen, *supra* note 7, at 171–76.

[18] District Court Opinion, *supra* note 1, at 314; and United Facts, *supra* note 8, at 42.

[19] United Facts, *supra* note 8, at 25.

[20] Brief for Appellant, Appeal from the United States District Court for the District of Massachusetts to the Supreme Court of the United States, 191 (October 1953) (hereafter cited as Appeal). United divided its services into four general categories. In addition to the application of general shoemaking know-how, United listed three types of service "essen-

Finally, despite extensive efforts to improve reliability, the tasks expected of many shoe machines were so complicated that malfunctions were inevitable.[21] When a breakdown did occur—the incidence of which increased during peak demand periods when machines were most intensively used—shoemakers wanted rapid and effective repair services. To meet those demands, a servicer had to have a comprehensive knowledge of both shoe machines and their interactions. Although malfunctions were often the consequence of parts wear or breakage on a particular machine, failures also resulted from defective materials or work performed by a machine or operator earlier in the manufacturing process. Repairs that did not treat the ultimate source of the breakdown would lead to recurrent failures and repeated delays.[22]

The parties best situated to provide the services auxiliary to shoe machinery were the machine manufacturers themselves. Much of the expertise needed to use and repair machines arose as a by-product of their engineering and manufacture.[23] Repair activities, in turn, provided an important source of feedback on machine and manufacturing problems and on developments in shoe styles and constructions that aided in the improvement of existing machines as well as in the development of new machines and shoe production processes.[24] Hence, the production of shoe machinery and associated services exhibited significant scope economies grounded in the knowledge necessary to design, manufacture, and support machines.[25]

In both the scope of services it offered and its size, United dominated

---

tially related to specific machines" that consisted of "the installation of new United machines, the instruction of operatives in their use, and their subsequent repair, maintenance, and adjustment" *Id.* at 192. Note that, while installation and repair are specific to individual machines, machine layouts and training in the operation of a machine provides knowledge generalizable to similar equipment of other manufacturers.

[21] "No matter how skillfully designed, these complicated machine types will require frequent service." District Court Opinion, *supra* note 1, at 302.

[22] United called its ability to trace the source of failures throughout the shoe manufacturing process its "most important service." United Facts, *supra* note 8, at 49.

[23] United discussed at length the sources of its expertise and the advantages of its breadth of experience relative to shoemakers in developing and maintaining a stock of knowledge on the manufacturing of shoes. Appeal, *supra* note 20, at 204–6.

[24] United kept extensive records of machine breakdowns and problems. See District Court Opinion, *supra* note 1, at 323.

[25] There also appeared to be economies of convenience for shoemakers in dealing with a single provider of a wide range of related products and services. See District Court Opinion, *supra* note 1, at 340. As David Teece has noted, problems in the transfer of know-how rather than joint-production economies per se determine whether production should occur within a single organization. David Teece, Economics of Scope and the Scope of the Enterprise, 1 J. Econ. Behav. & Org. 223 (1980).

the industry. To satisfy shoemakers' needs for information and service, United developed and maintained, in addition to its machine-engineering personnel, a sizable staff of experts on the problems of shoe production. Its planning department offered assistance "to shoe manufacturers desiring engineering surveys on production methods, on costs, on factory layouts, and other matters,"[26] while its "Shoe Ex" department existed solely to tackle difficult shoemaking problems encountered by its customers. To meet repair needs, United kept an inventory of 107,000 types of spare parts[27] and maintained a staff of 1,500 employees in sixteen branch and twenty-nine suboffices in seventeen states, who were responsible for keeping its machines in good working order.[28] Of these, 828 were "roadmen" who, in addition to repairing machines, installed new machines, instructed operators in their use, and, when asked, would "give expert advice on how to improve the quality of shoe production, give help in various technical shoemaking and shoe factory problems, and, in general, [be] available for all sorts of counsel and cooperation."[29]

United was also the only manufacturer offering a full line of shoe machines. Yet, despite an average market share of machines outstanding of approximately 85 percent, potential competition plus a sizable group of active competitors limited United's ability to exercise market power. In 1947, United faced a competitive fringe consisting of more than eighty firms, including twenty-two known competitors for its major machines.[30] Competitor machines, moreover, were available for all essential steps in the shoe-manufacturing process.[31] An indication of the depth of United's concern about competition from rival machinery was its efforts to keep track of that machinery; at the time of the case, United had about 76,000 "Outside Machine Reports" in its files, detailing the installation, use, and removal of non-United machines in its customers factories.[32] Evidence that this competition prevented United from exercising market power is its apparent failure to capture the substantial value created by shoe machines. Although labor savings from the mechanization of shoe

[26] District Court Opinion, *supra* note 1, at 322. Also see United Facts, *supra* note 8, at 238–41.

[27] United Facts, *supra* note 8, at 313–14.

[28] District Court Opinion, *supra* note 1, at 322.

[29] *Id.* at 322.

[30] Kaysen, *supra* note 7, at 52–53.

[31] District Court Opinion, *supra* note 1, at 339. Of the 1,460 shoe firms operating 1,650 factories in the United States, approximately 1,220 were United customers. Hence, at least 240 firms produced shoes in the United States without United equipment. Kaysen, *supra* note 7, at 27; District Court Opinion, *supra* note 1, at 322.

[32] District Court Opinion, *supra* note 1, at 303–4, 332.

production were enormous, shoe machinery costs represented only about 2 percent of the wholesale price of a shoe.[33] Consistent with this, the court found "no evidence that United has secured a monopoly profit on its total operations, or on the machinery branch as a whole."[34]

In sum, the shoe-machinery industry was one in which research, information, and service were paramount.[35] Despite United's conspicuous dominance of the market, the availability of numerous complex yet dependable machines and the efficient provision of a range of supplier services—rather than United's monopoly power—were shoemakers' foremost concerns.[36] Testifying in court, an officer of Compo, United's main rival, stated, "The shoe machinery manufacturing industry is really a service industry. . . . When a shoe manufacturer leases a Compo machine, he becomes the beneficiary of a service system which is made up of the skills, 'know-how,' knowledge and experience of the whole Compo organization whose primary business is to see to it that he is successful in making cemented shoes."[37] The organizational problem confronting the industry was how best to assure that that know-how and experience would be efficiently applied to the development, manufacture, and support of shoe machinery.

III. A Belated Defense

As stated in Section I, a satisfactory explanation of United's leasing practices should account for both United's selective use of leasing and the overall structure of its leases. We begin this section with a discussion of leasing's dual roles in fostering the provision of quality machinery

[33] *Id.* at 340. To produce a thousand men's welt shoes a day without the aid of shoe machinery would have required roughly a thousand skilled craftsmen. With a full line of shoe machines, the same number of shoes could have been produced with between fifty and sixty workers. Since United's formation in 1899, improvements in shoe machinery alone were estimated to have reduced the number of workers needed to produce a given number of shoes by 35 percent. United Facts, *supra* note 8, at 428. Labor costs, in comparison to shoe machinery costs, accounted for approximately 25 percent of the wholesale price of a shoe at the time of the case. *Id.* at 35.

[34] *Id.* at 325.

[35] Less than 20 percent of United's machinery expenses reflected manufacturing costs, with research, service, distribution, and administrative activities accounting for approximately equal shares of the remainder. Kaysen, *supra* note 7, at 118.

[36] "As seen by the shoe manufacturer, United's activities are clearly benevolent. The testimony of 15 shoe manufacturers, representing a wide variety of firms in terms of size, location, types and price of shoe manufactured, and general history, leaves no doubt of this. The testimony occupied some 900 pages of the transcript, and nearly the whole of it shows that the shoe manufacturers consider themselves well and cheaply served by United." *Id.* at 202. Also, see testimony cited in United Facts, *supra* note 8, at 230–41.

[37] Appeal, *supra* note 20, at 224.

and the dissemination of know-how and then consider how these leasing functions interact with the design and restrictiveness of lease agreements.

A. *A Comparative Analysis of Leasing*

Leasing offers two distinct, albeit related, benefits.

Assuring Machine Quality. When the prospective reliability and other performance attributes of complex, durable goods are difficult to discern at the time of purchase, outright sales pose well-known moral-hazard problems. Receiving payment up-front, a manufacturer has no interest, beyond its reputation, in the ultimate performance of its product.[38] A common solution to the durable-goods-quality problem is for the manufacturer to warrant the product.[39] But warranties are fundamentally contractual obligations and, as such, face the same obstacles in formation and enforcement as contracts generally.[40] Again aside from reputational considerations, a manufacturer's only incentive to honor its warranty is the legal sanctions a dissatisfied customer can bring to bear. The larger the cost of meeting its contractual obligations, the greater the incentive to evade performance. Where the product and its associated environment are complex, the difficulty of exploring contingencies, allocating responsibilities, adjudicating disputes, and crafting effective remedies is likely to undermine the utility of contractual guarantees.

Leasing offers an alternative to the durable-goods-quality problem that avoids many of the practical limitations associated with contractual warranties. In particular, by affording the customer the threat of terminating

[38] On the role of reputation in contracts generally, see Benjamin Klein & Keith B. Leffler, The Role of Market Forces in Assuring Contractual Performance, 89 J. Pol. Econ. 615 (1981). As we argue below, fault for shoe machine failures was difficult for third parties to assess. To the extent that other customers had difficulty ascribing blame for a particular customer's misfortunes, the strength of the reputation deterrent to cheating is diminished. Moreover, the combination of machine durability and fallibility may itself combine to undermine the reputation function. While the cost of supporting existing machinery is proportional to the stock of machines in use, the incentive to continue that support is related to the flow of new machine sales. As the stock of machines outstanding rises relative to the level of sales, the cost of supporting existing machines may eventually exceed the loss of the reputation premium on future sales. In 1947, the total number of United machines outstanding was 115,787 (District Court Opinion, *supra* note 1, at 304–5); by comparison, in 1950 United's expected shipments for 1951 were 11,355 machines (Kaysen, *supra* note 7, at 37).

[39] On the theory of warranties, see George L. Priest, A Theory of the Consumer Product Warranty, 90 Yale L. J. 1297 (1981); and Russell Cooper & Thomas W. Ross, Product Warranties and Double Moral Hazard, 16 Rand J. Econ. 103 (1985).

[40] For a discussion of remedies for breach of warranties, see Kenneth Chapman & Michael J. Meurer, Efficient Remedies for Breach of Warranty, 52 L. & Contemp. Prob. 107 (1989).

the exchange, leasing makes the proceeds from machinery transactions contingent on the realized value of machines. The prospective loss of revenues on current (as well as future) transactions provides manufacturers the incentive to keep machines operational ex post and, knowing this, to develop quality machines ex ante.[41] More important, leasing makes the incentives to develop and support quality machinery largely self-enforcing and thus avoids the practical limitations of contractual guarantees. As long as nothing in either the contract or the nature of the transaction prevents it, a customer can respond unilaterally to interruptions or decreases in the value of machine services by returning the machine.[42] In effect, leasing transforms the transaction from the discrete sale of durable machines to the continuous sale of instantaneous machine services.[43]

[41] This motive was noted by Kaysen, *supra* note 7, at 190: "Since United is paid on performance . . . the design of rugged, high-performance machines is stimulated. Every improvement in an existing machine which increases its production rate, or decreases the repair time . . . benefits the manufacturer. . . . By contrast, in a sales market, United would profit only once and thus would have no stimulus to continue improvements of existing machines." Wiley, Rasmusen, & Ramseyer, *supra* note 3, also include a product-quality motive as one of six potential efficiency rationales for leasing generally. Their brief discussion, however, does not apply this reasoning to the circumstances in *United* in a systematic way and, as the discussion below reveals, is incomplete in several important respects. The warranting function of leasing has also been noted previously by David Flath, The Economics of Short-Term Leasing, 18 Econ. Inquiry 247 (1980); and David T. Levy, Short-Term Leasing and Monopoly Power: The Case of IBM, 144 J. Inst. & Theoretical Econ. 611 (1988).

[42] Leases would have to leave the right to terminate the lease largely unconditional to avoid introducing the prospect of litigation. Generally, the fewer the restrictions on returns and the shorter the lease term, the stronger the incentives to produce quality products. On the length and structure of United's leases, see below.

[43] The advantages of leasing, moreover, could not be replicated by selling machines with service contracts that made payments for service contingent on the performance of machines. Examples are service contracts for copiers and laser printers that charge for service on a per copy rather than per visit basis. Specifically, service calls are made free of charge for the duration of the contract, which is specified in terms of a total number of copies. The contract is more likely to be renewed and will be renewed sooner if the service firm promptly and effectively repairs machines so that machine output is not interrupted.

Sales with service contracts and leasing differ in evasion incentives, however. To replicate fully the incentives of leases, manufacturers would have to provide machines (virtually) free and collect compensation exclusively through cancelable charges for service. Under such terms, however, a customer who discovers that he has received a high-quality machine will wish to cancel the contingent payments to avoid paying for the machine, to which the manufacturer would have no effective recourse. Alternatively, a sale that capitalized a large part of the expected value of a machine in an initial payment (with correspondingly lower contingent payments) would invite the manufacturer to produce poor-quality equipment and either deteriorate service or contrive cancellation of the contract by claiming customer mistreatment of the assets. Whereas the only recourse available to disputants under a service contract is litigation, leasing relies on self-help. Specifically, under leasing, the manufacturer has the unilateral option of retrieving and the customer of returning the ma-

Contracting for Knowledge. Leasing may also serve as a practical means of motivating the development and provision of expert advice where direct contracting for the transfer of information is infeasible. The problems of selling information where the customer does not know the value of the information beforehand are well known.[44] But even where the *potential* value of a supplier's information is understood, the customer may be unable to determine whether the information and advice actually obtained was the best the supplier had to offer and almost surely would be unable to prove the contrary in court. Answers to questions such as, "Was the instruction of operators as conscientious as it should have been?" and "Were engineering surveys thorough and machine layouts the best feasible?" are known ultimately only to the provider of the information. As a result, contractual assurances may do little to guarantee a machine manufacturer's complete and enthusiastic conveyance of its expertise and know-how.

If the value of information received is correlated with some measurable index such as the output of the firm, then compensating suppliers for the provision of information as a function of that index has desirable properties.[45] Thus, to the extent information contributes to the success of machinery users, attaching an "information premium" to the rental price of machines would establish an incentive for a manufacturer to supply such information. The more machines employed, the longer each machine is retained, and, if usage-based charges are assessed, the more intensively a machine is used, the larger will be the total implicit payment.

Circumstances in the intermediate market for shoe machines supported leasing for both its warranting and information-transfer purposes. As the record reviewed in Section II makes clear, shoemakers cared about the supply and quality of a wide range of services and information as well as about the quality of the machines themselves. Shoe machines and the tasks they were designed to perform, meanwhile, were often so compli-

---

chine if the other behaves opportunistically. Attempts to structure installment-contract sales to mimic leases would pose similar problems. It is possible that the existence of sale- and service-contract arrangements are at least partly the byproduct of antitrust challenges to manufacturer leasing of durable goods.

[44] See Kenneth Arrow, Essays in the Theory of Risk Bearing 152 (1971); Oliver E. Williamson, Markets and Hierarchies 31–33 (1975); and Teece, *supra* note 25.

[45] See William P. Rogerson, Profit Regulation of Defense Contractors and Prizes for Innovation, 97 J. Pol. Econ. 1284 (1989). Rogerson applies this argument to awarding prizes for innovation to defense contractors. The discussion below shows that Rogerson's analysis extends beyond regulatory settings to anywhere the quality of information cannot be judicially verified but is correlated with a verifiable index. Parallels also can be drawn to the role of royalty payments in motivating the supply of manufacturer services such as national advertising in franchise arrangements.

cated that complete specification of their performance attributes would have been infeasible, leaving ambiguity as to the expectations of the parties and abundant scope for opportunistic efforts to shift responsibility or contrive cancellation of contractual guarantees.[46] Even where blame lay clearly with the manufacturer, problems securing the timely repair of defective or broken equipment would have diminished the value of contractual warranties. Optimal response time to a call for repairs varied as a function of both when the breakdown occurred (peak versus nonpeak periods, for instance) and the opportunity cost of allocating repair personnel and parts across customers. On the one hand, the complex and variable nature of servicing needs across factories and individual machines would have precluded comprehensive specification of timing requirements and damages for delays. Relying on court interpretations of contract stipulations for "timely" or "prompt" repairs, on the other hand, would have been unpredictable and expensive where legitimate delays were likely to be indistinguishable from strategic ones.[47]

Lease versus Sale. The features common to the warranting and information-transfer functions of leasing are, first, the limitations of contracting that make explicit stipulation and direct compensation for the desired commodity impractical, and, second, the contingent nature of the payment stream that motivates performance of any activity that increases the demand for the services of the leased good. Against leasing's advantages, however, must be weighed its limitations. First, under leasing, residual rights of control and claims on the residual value of assets do not reside with the party that actually uses the equipment, diminishing the high-powered incentives to maintain and use machines with appropriate care.[48] Although a lessor may discipline a lessee for misuse or abuse of

[46] With performance expectations imprecisely defined, determining the optimal allocation of responsibility for individual failures would, in a large number of cases, have been virtually impossible. Operator errors and the use of faulty materials, for instance, were common sources of machinery malfunctions. Whether responsibility for a failure rested ultimately on the shoemaker, however, would have been unclear given that machine versatility, particularly its adaptability to varying sizes, styles, and materials, was a valued but largely unspecifiable aspect of machine design.

[47] Legitimate delays might result from temporary shortages of spare parts, employee turnover or illness, or the precedence of customers with greater urgency of demand. The frequency and potentially high cost of machine failures exposed shoe machine users to the threat of holdups on repairs. The ability to provide prompt repairs required a stock of spare parts and a ready, proximate, and knowledgeable repair staff. By threatening to delay repairs, an opportunistic supplier could attempt to extract a premium on repairs. Scott E. Masten, James W. Meehan, and Edward A. Snyder, The Costs of Organization, 7 J. L. Econ. & Org. 1 (1991), refer to the source of holdups that derive from the need for precise timing of performance as *temporal specificity*.

[48] Thus, the transfer of ownership under leasing relative to sales raises many of the same issues and trade-offs involved in the analysis of integration decisions. Obviously, if

machinery by refusing to renew a lease or, depending on the terms of the lease, by repossessing machines, detecting abuse requires active monitoring by the lessor, which can be accomplished, obviously, only at additional cost. Second, rewarding information supply via machine transactions distorts machine-usage incentives. Because information charges attached to machines must exceed the cost of transferring the information to motivate its supply, paying for information indirectly through lease charges inefficiently discourages use of machines at the margin.[49]

Where information is of a type that can be priced and sold independently and where the attributes of assets are sufficiently simple so that quality can be adequately discerned or described at the outset of the transaction and responsibilities for breakdowns assigned ex post, sales will generally be preferred.[50] As assets become more complex and their quality more important, however, the costs of writing and enforcing contractual warranties are likely to grow relative to the benefits of customer ownership, raising the likelihood that leasing will become the favored organizational arrangement. Similarly, the more important and complex the information to be transferred, the more difficult it will be to sell information directly, and the greater the advantage of charging implicitly for information through machine rentals.[51]

B. Lease Design

Lease Duration, Termination, and Exclusion. The arguments of the preceding subsections suggest that leases should generally allow both customers and manufacturers broad scope to terminate the transaction.

---

transactors could contract over all possible actions affecting the value of the machine, ownership would be irrelevant. Typically, however, some actions are left unspecified, wherein ownership allocates all residual rights over the asset in question. See Sanford J. Grossman & Oliver D. Hart, The Costs and Benefits of Ownership: A Theory of Vertical and Lateral Integration, 94 J. Pol. Econ. 691 (1986). In the analogy to integration decisions, sales, which are dependent on contractual assurances of quality, correspond to the contractual or market mode and leasing to integration. On the relationship between ownership and high-powered and low-powered incentives, see Oliver E. Williamson, The Economic Institutions of Capitalism (1985).

[49] Another, more mundane, drawback of leasing is simply the additional bookkeeping costs that must be incurred collecting and recording periodic payments under leases compared with one-time sales.

[50] Also, a customer is more likely to be able to accomplish repairs of simple machines personally. ("[M]achines . . . of simpler construction [are] not likely to develop troubles too complicated to be attended to by the operator or the shoe manufacturer's own mechanics." United Facts, *supra* note 8, at 229.)

[51] An alternative to leasing would have been forward integration into shoe manufacturing. Forward integration would have forfeited the high-powered incentives of the large number of independent shoemakers and would likely have posed antitrust problems of its own.

For leases to warrant quality, the lessee must be able to curtail payments if quality or service decline. The quicker the response, the greater the discipline customers exercise over manufacturers. Similarly, leasing will only serve its information-transfer function if the lessor's revenue varies with the quality of the information provided. The longer and more restrictive the lease, the more closely leasing resembles sales. Hence, these functions of leasing require that leases should be short-term, readily terminable, or, in the case of usage-based charges, that usage levels should be freely and continuously variable.[52] Finally, leases should also afford manufacturers wide discretion to repossess machines. To the extent leasing reduces customer incentives to operate machines with appropriate levels of care, manufacturers would want to monitor machine use and retrieve abused equipment, thereby terminating the stream of quasi rents accruing to the customer's use of the machine.[53] The power of that threat will be greatest in leases that facilitate detection of abuse and retrieval of equipment.

The advantages of unrestricted, unilateral termination may be reduced, however, where circumstances enable either party to act opportunistically. Generally, transactors enter long-term contracts either to limit costly haggling over appropriable quasi rents or to control free riding on services and information that one of them provides. Thus, if shoe machines were specially designed for particular shoe factories, a lessee or lessor might have been tempted to exploit his termination authority strategically, subverting leasing's critical self-enforcing character.[54] In actuality, however, shoe machines were neither specialized to particular customers nor expensive to relocate.

Free riding, in contrast, was a genuine concern. First, most of United's machinery improvements, though important, were not patentable.[55] As

[52] Although Wiley, Rasmusen, & Ramseyer, *supra* note 3, noted the inconsistency between the duration of United's leases and the durable-goods-*monopoly* rationale, they apparently did not recognize the same inconsistency in the durable-goods-*quality* explanation.

[53] Compare Benjamin Klein & Kevin M. Murphy, Vertical Restraints as Contract Enforcement Mechanisms, 31 J. Law & Econ. 265 (1988).

[54] If such opportunistic terminations were difficult to distinguish from legitimate ones, the self-enforcement advantages of leasing over warranties would disappear. An untested prediction of our theory is that sale (customer ownership) is likely to be preferred to leasing where durable goods are customer specific.

[55] The court cited "United's practice of continuing improvement of existing machine types and models by so-called blue-bulletin changes, representing both patented and unpatented improvements, the advantages of which are made available to lessees through installation of the parts required by each change." Appeal, *supra* note 20, at 247. The vast majority of United's machinery improvements were not patentable; on average, machinery research resulted in approximately eight patentable and 192 nonpatentable (blue-bulletin) improvements over the life of a machine. Kaysen, *supra* note 7, at 171–74.

the court acknowledged, elimination of United's ability to exclude would "confer upon United's competitors the unearned opportunity to copy the unpatented features of United's machines. These competitors get a free ride."[56] Second, the implicit pricing of information and services gave shoemakers an incentive to free ride on United's investments in shoemaking know-how. As the description of United's services in Section II indicates, much of the information United provided was, in fact, of a type that could be profitably used with competitors' equipment. Although installation and repairs were wholly specific to individual machines, the selection and layout of machines, operator training, and general shoemaking know-how all provided knowledge that was in varying degrees generalizable to similar equipment from other manufacturers. Where the benefits of information accrue over an extended period but are not specific to a particular manufacturer's product, customers may seek to avoid implicit information charges embodied in the price of a full-service supplier by switching to alternative suppliers for some portion of their needs. Having acquired that knowledge, shoemakers had an incentive to return or reduce usage on the machine or machines to which implicit information premia had been attached and substitute similar equipment from a "no-frills" supplier.

To prevent free riding from undermining the supply of free-ridable services, transactors would want to restrict in some way lessees' ability to substitute competitors' equipment.[57] Stipulation of monetary deterrents to switching within long-term agreements would serve this purpose. In addition, transactors would want to attach information premia to machines most crucial to the production process and for which hand labor is a poor substitute to hinder a lessee's ability to escape paying implicit charges by bypassing machines. Finally, offering machines on lease-only terms would prevent the direct substitution of nonlease equipment and the development of a market in secondhand machines that could substitute for leased machines. To preserve the benefits that motivated leasing in the first place, however, deterrents to returning machines should be

[56] District Court Opinion, *supra* note 1, at 350. Also see Kaysen, *supra* note 7, at 76.

[57] Howard Marvel has cited free riding on manufacturer promotional efforts to justify the use of exclusive dealing arrangements in the context of retail sales. Howard P. Marvel, Exclusive Dealing, 25 J. Law & Econ. 1 (1982). Prior to 1918, some of United's leases contained a set of "exclusive-use" clauses limiting the ability of customers to use competitor machines on certain operations. See Kaysen, *supra* note 7, at 13–16. In that year, the Supreme Court upheld a lower court ruling that these clauses violated § 3 of the recently enacted Clayton Act. The practice of leasing, the then-seventeen-year duration, and other terms (including return charges and the full-capacity clause) were held to be reasonable and lawful at the time. Appeal, *supra* note 20, at 25; Kaysen, *supra* note 7, at 15.

conditional on machines being abandoned opportunistically to escape paying for information received. Customer returns or usage reductions for other reasons should be afforded far more latitude.

Lease Pricing. Both the warranty and information functions of leasing described above depend on manufacturer revenues correlating with machine performance, a correlation established whether flat rental rates or usage-based charges are imposed. The greater sensitivity of usage-based charges to variations in demand and machine performance, however, may, under certain conditions, justify the added cost of monitoring machine operations.[58] With flat rental fees, revenue fluctuations occur only if a customer returns or leases an additional machine, whereas receipts from "unit charges" vary continuously with intensity of machine usage. Where the number of machines adopted varies little with the success of a factory, for instance, changes in revenue under monthly-rental leases may be too discrete to motivate machine improvements or the supply of information and services on the margin. Consequently, unit charges would be more desirable where the capacity of a machine dictates the use of only one or a small number of machines of a particular type.

The adoption of unit charges is also likely to be related to the expected cost of machine failures. The higher the expected cost of failures, the greater is the need for prompt repairs and for ongoing improvements to avert breakdowns in the first place. The probability and cost of breakdowns, in turn, are likely to be related to the complexity of a machine and its importance to the production process. More complex machines would tend to be less tolerant of errors and thus more likely to malfunction, have more components subject to wear and breakage, and be more difficult to repair, while the failure of machines central to the production process could impede production throughout the factory.[59] Tying the manufacturer's revenues to the continued operation of these machines through unit charges effectively internalizes to the manufacturer the costs to customers of production interruptions. Indeed, by comparing the reduction of unit-charge revenues from various factories, a machinery man-

[58] Unit charges would also tend to discourage use of machines on the margin. The costs of metering usage would have been essentially the same on all shoe machines with moving parts. Note that policing usage was not a major problem given that roadmen made frequent visits to factories and that discrepancies in factory output or in usage rates across machines would have been detectable.

[59] The opportunity for machine improvements was also likely to be greater on more complex machines. Indeed, the number of blue bulletins (which documented improvements; see note 55 *supra*) issued on a machine correlated positively with the measure of machine complexity described below.

ufacturer would have had approximately the correct incentives to allocate repair services and parts across customers.[60]

C. *Summary*

The preceding analysis provides several specific predictions about United's practices and the structure of its leases.

1. The merits of leasing relative to sales are likely to be greatest where (i) the need for assurances about the quality and reliability of durable goods and the costs of specifying and enforcing performance of contractual warranties are great or (ii) productive use of machinery requires the development and dissemination of manufacturer-supplied information. The importance of reliability is likely to be greatest on machines critical to the production process, while the difficulty of contracting for machine quality, the need for repairs and technical advice on machine operations, and the opportunity for machine improvements will tend to be higher on more complex machines.
2. For leasing to serve its warranting function, primary responsibility and the expense of repairs must rest with the manufacturer.
3. To motivate the provision of information and repair services, these services should be priced implicitly in the rental price of machines.
4. To discourage free riding on manufacturers' investments on nonpatentable innovations and general know-how, (i) information premia should be attached to the most important and widely adopted machines, (ii) such machines should be offered for "lease only," and (iii) those leases should be long-term and penalize inefficient switching. Because customers must be able to return machines to discipline the manufacturer's supply of quality and services, however, return or usage penalties should apply discriminatorily against returns to substitute competitors' machines.
5. To deter lessee misuse of borrowed equipment, lease agreements should authorize the lessor to monitor use and to repossess abused machines.

[60] In fact, United sometimes "borrowed" parts from underutilized machines in the factory of one shoe firm to use in another firm's equipment when replacement parts were temporarily unavailable. United Facts, *supra* note 8, at 235. The argument with regard to the role of unit charges is not an "as if" one; United explicitly asserted this function in its defense: "It is obviously to United's interest to give the best possible service to its lessees. Its revenue depends on keeping machines in efficient running order." *Id.* at 247. This role of unit charges has also been noted by Wiley, Rasmusen, & Ramseyer, *supra* note 3, and Goldberg, *supra* note 3, and by Kaysen, *supra* note 7, at 191. The metering of machine output is also consistent with traditional price discrimination explanations for such practices. Price discrimination, however, fails to explain the choice between sale and monthly rental leases as well as many important elements of United's lease structure.

6. Finally, unit charges should be preferred to flat rental rates (i) where the expected cost of breakdowns and the opportunity for ongoing improvements are greatest (that is, for machines that are most complex and critical to the production process) and (ii) where variations across factories in the number of machines adopted is small.

IV. United's Practices

In this section, we consider United's actual distribution practices in light of the preceding analysis. We begin by examining evidence regarding United's selective use of leasing and pricing arrangements. We then discuss the nature and implementation of United's standard lease provisions.

A. *Evidence*

At the time of the case, United distributed shoe machines under five types of arrangements. Those arrangements and the number of machine types offered under each were: sale only, 42; optional sale or lease, 122; lease with monthly rental charges only (no unit charges), 88; lease with monthly rental plus unit charges, 85; and lease with unit charges only (no monthly rental), 6.[61] Hence, almost half (164 out of 343) of United's machine offerings were available for purchase. Moreover, 35 percent or 9,472 out of the 27,140 optional sale-or-lease machines outstanding in 1947 had been sold, indicating that sale was a real alternative for these machines, contrary to the government's complaint.[62]

Analytically, United faced a two-tiered sequence of decisions consisting of, first, whether to sell or lease machines, and, second, the method by which to price machines if it chose to lease. The analysis of the preceding sections predicts that United should have offered the most complex and important machines for lease only. Simpler, less important machines pose fewer of the incentive problems discussed earlier and therefore should have been more likely to have been offered for sale. Of those machines that United offered for lease, unit charges should have been most common on machines for which adoption rates varied little

[61] Exhibits B, C, D1, D2, and D3, annexed to the Defendant's Answer to the Complaint, May 27, 1948. Each machine type was offered exclusively under one of these five arrangements. Optional-sale-or-lease machines were let under monthly rental but no unit charges. Most optional-sale-or-lease machines and a few lease-only machines also required an initial payment.

[62] Exhibits G-446 and S-59. The sales figure includes only machines sold over the period 1931–47. Since many machines sold prior to 1931 would still have been in operation, these figures understate the true number of sale machines outstanding in 1947.

with the size of the factory and for which the expected cost of breakdowns and opportunity for machine improvements were greatest—again, on the most complex machines and those most critical to the production process.

To test these propositions, we assembled data from the trial record and from information obtained directly from United. Definitions of variables and descriptive statistics for the sample are provided in Table 1. To gauge the complexity of machines offered by United, we constructed a variable, PARTS, consisting of the number of parts listed in parts manuals for the original machines. We were able to locate manuals for 193 of the 343 machines United offered at the time of the case.[63]

As a measure of the importance of a machine in the shoe-production process, we employed a classification adopted by the government in the case. Specifically, the government divided machines into two categories: major and minor. Major machines were those that performed "[t]he principal procedures involved in the manufacture of shoes, including upper cutting, upper fitting, stock fitting, lasting, bottoming, and making."[64] Minor machines, in contrast, were "either auxiliary to major machines in the sense that their functions [were] immediately related to those of major machines, or they perform[ed] work independent of that done by major machines but of somewhat less importance in the shoemaking process."[65] A failure in one of these machines, though still disruptive, could often be mitigated by deferring the task or substituting hand labor.

Finally, the theory predicts that the need for unit charges would be less where the number of machines employed within a given factory would adequately meter the quality of machines and information received. The

[63] The distribution of those 193 machines by terms were: sale only, thirteen; optional sale or lease, seventy-four; lease with monthly rental only, forty-eight; lease with monthly rental and unit charges, fifty-four; and lease with unit charges only, four. Hence, data were obtained on more than half of the machines in each category except sale only. Consistent with our hypothesis, United claimed that "those [machines] which are offered for sale only are generally simple machines such as gearless sole cutters, tools and grinders." United Facts, *supra* note 8, at 182. Manuals for machines of this type were less likely to have been preserved. Another variable of obvious importance to lease-versus-sale decisions generally is the durability of machines. According to United officials, the basic structure of United's machines were made to last indefinitely with the replacement or reconditioning of moving parts. Some machines manufactured in the early part of the century are still in operation today.

[64] Complaint, *supra* note 5, at paras. 11, 16.

[65] *Id.* at para. 16. Although failures of an auxiliary machine were more likely to disrupt operations on associated major machines than were failures of independent minor machines, the resulting interruption in unit-charge flows from the major machine reduced the need for separate unit charges on the auxiliary unit. The government's classification did not distinguish between "related" and "independent" minor machines.

TABLE 1

DESCRIPTIVE STATISTICS

Variable	Description	No. of Observations			
A. Categorical variables:					
LEASEONLY	= 1, if lease-only machine	106			
	= 0, if machine is for sale	87			
UC	= 1, if leased with unit charges	58			
	= 0 otherwise	48			
MAJOR	= 1, if major machine	48			
	= 0, if minor machine	145			
		Mean	SD	Minimum	Maximum
B. Continuous variables:					
PARTS	= number of machine parts	542	521	28	2,880
MACH/FACT	= (number of machines outstanding within class)/1.220	1.07	1.78	.01	13.40
YEAR	= year machine was introduced (N = 171)	1.923	12	1.899	1,944

TABLE 2

LOGIT UNIT CHARGE VERSUS MONTHLY RENTAL-ONLY ESTIMATIONS

	(1)	(2)	(3)
CONSTANT	−1.480	−1.504	2,105.3
	(−3.421)	(−3.202)	(.262)
PARTS	.0020	.0025	.0026
	(2.947)	(3.118)	(3.029)
MAJOR	1.052	1.702	1.664
	(1.989)	(2.756)	(2.644)
MACH/FACT		−.4213	−.4323
		(−2.023)	(−2.062)
YEAR	−2.164		
			(−.259)
$YEAR^2$	.0006		
			(.255)
N	106	106	100
Log-likelihood	−57.348	−52.151	−47.563

NOTE.—The dependent variable is UC; *t*-statistics are in parentheses.

failure of one among many machines in a given factory may also reduce the urgency of repairs and, hence, the motive for both leasing and unit charges. Although existing records do not contain information on the number of machines of each type employed in each of the 1,220 shoe factories United served (from which a measure of differences in factory adoption rates across machines could be constructed), the record does indicate the total number of machines of each type outstanding, permitting us to calculate the average number of machines per factory (MACH/FACT).[66] Because shoemakers are more likely to need at least one machine within a functional class than a particular model within such a class, we used the average number of machines outstanding within a machine class rather than the number of machines of a particular model.

Table 2 presents logit results on the decision of whether or not to employ unit charges on lease-only machines. The coefficients on both PARTS and MAJOR are positive and significant, as expected, while the

[66] A disadvantage of this measure relative to variations in machine adoption rates is that it is impossible to distinguish whether a high average is the result of a few factories adopting many machines or many factories adopting a small number of machines. Only the former correlates with the success of a specific factory and could form the basis for rewarding the provision of quality machines and information. United's leases restricted the ability of a shoemaker to hold more machines than were necessary to perform the available work. District Court Opinion, *supra* note 1, at 317. To the extent this limits a shoemaker's ability to hold machines as a means of insuring against breakdowns, variations in MACH/FACT would tend to reflect relatively exogenous technological and scale factors. The lack of exogenous variables prevents correcting for potential endogeneity by instrumental methods.

TABLE 3

LOGIT AND NESTED LOGIT LEASE VERSUS SALE ESTIMATIONS

	(1)	(2)	(3)	(4)	(5)
CONSTANT	−1.576	7,817.30	−1.344	9,035.8	6,384.1
	(−4.695)	(1.355)	(−3.720)	(1.449)	(1.108)
PARTS	.0042	.0033	.0028	.0043	.0018
	(5.143)	(3.824)	(2.708)	(2.557)	(1.844)
MAJOR	1.449	2.622	1.503	3.593	1.161
	(2.495)	(3.103)	(1.656)	(2.238)	(1.460)
MACH/FACT	−2.478	−.2724	...	−.4175	...
	(−2.253)	(−2.344)		(−1.805)	
YEAR	...	−8.179	...	−9.438	−6.698
		(−1.362)		(1.505)	(−1.117)
YEAR^2	...	.0021	...	.0025	.0018
		(1.369)		(1.511)	(1.126)
INCLU	...	...	.3321	−1.029	1.352
			(.413)	(−.757)	(1.571)
N	193	171	171	171	171
Log-likelihood	−98.231	−83.887	−88.713	−82.640	−84.098

NOTE.—The dependent variable is LEASEONLY; *t*-statistics are in parentheses.

coefficients on MACH/FACT are negative and significant. Hence, conditional on a machine being offered for lease only, unit charges were more likely to be adopted on major, complex machines and where the number of machines per factory was smaller. We also estimated the model employing a quadratic of the year in which the machine was introduced in order to control for the possibility that the observed correlation between leasing practices and variations in the number of machines outstanding reflected machinery life-cycle considerations.[67] The results suggest that United's use of unit charges on its leased machines did not vary systemically over time.

Table 3 reports the results on the lease-versus-sale decision. Columns 1 and 2 contain results from standard logit estimations. Columns 3–5 present nested logit estimates where the "inclusive value," INCLU, was calculated using the coefficients in column 3 of Table 2.[68] The coefficients

[67] Older machines that are becoming obsolete and newer machines that have only recently been introduced are likely to have fewer machines outstanding, other things being the same. United rarely altered its distribution arrangements for particular machine models after their introduction. Hence, the year variables capture trends over time in the decision to lease or employ unit charges on new models.

[68] The nested logit estimation of the lease-versus-sale decision accounts for the option to lease with or without unit charges. Unlike multinomial logit, nested logit avoids the assumption of independence of irrelevant alternatives. See G. S. Maddala, Limited Dependent and

on PARTS are positive and significant under all five specifications, indicating that more complex machines are less likely to be offered for sale; MAJOR is positive and is significant in all but column 5. In addition, the results indicate that machines adopted in large numbers were more likely to be sold. The results also suggest a modest trend in favor of leasing.

Finally, we regressed the frequency of leasing and sales among the optional term machines on the characteristics of those machines. The mean number of leased machines for the sixty-seven optional term machines for which we had data was 63 percent, with a minimum of 5 percent and maximum of 95 percent. The results indicate that the tendency for more important and complex machines to be leased remained even when customers were given a choice between purchasing and leasing:

$$\text{PCTLEASED} = \underset{(-.676)}{-.21635} + \underset{(2.857)}{1.7868} \cdot \text{MAJOR} + \underset{(3.749)}{.00314} \cdot \text{PARTS}$$

$$\underset{(-1.208)}{-.23991} \cdot \text{MACH/FACT}, \quad R^2 = .235.$$

(The dependent variable is defined as − log[(100/percent of machines leased) − 1] and t-statistics are in parentheses.)

Thus, overall, United's choice of leasing and pricing arrangements is consistent with the efficiency motives identified above. In particular, minor machines with fewer parts were more likely to be offered for sale, while, among leased machines, complex, major machines were more likely to be offered for lease with unit charges. The average number of machines outstanding also reduced the likelihood of using unit charges and increased the probability of a machine being sold.[69]

B. *The Structure and Implementation of United's Leases*

Although the uniform construction of United's leases precludes formal tests of each of our predictions regarding their structure, a more detailed

---

Qualitative Variables in Econometrics 68–69 (1983). For comparison purposes, we estimated the choice of lease, sale, and pricing alternatives using multinomial logit and ordered probit models. The results were consistent with those presented. In particular, the choice categories "ordered" correctly in both models.

[69] We ran the regressions in Tables 2 and 3 including market share and found that leasing and unit charge adoption were both positively correlated with market share. Other qualitative results were unaffected. Given the endogeneity of market share, correlations between market share and distribution arrangements have no clear interpretation. Regression of market share on PARTS, MAJOR, YEAR, and YEARSQ revealed a positive but weak correlation of market share to PARTS and MAJOR, with all four variables explaining less than 10 percent of the variation in market share.

examination of United's lease provisions—and of some significant departures in the way United implemented those provisions—is nevertheless illuminating. Even where United's nominal lease provisions and the hypothesized structure appear to deviate, United's *actual* practices are consistent with the theory. Moreover, the anomalous lease provisions can be fairly interpreted to have supported the interests of the parties in effecting low-cost, efficient adaptations by establishing contractual fallbacks that facilitated "self-help" responses to opportunistic behavior.

Exclusionary Features. As already noted, United's leases at the time of the case were ten years in duration (having been shortened at court direction from seventeen years) and contained three allegedly exclusionary provisions: (i) return charges, or "deferred payments," due on return of leased machines;[70] (ii) minimum-usage charges for operation of unit-charge machines below a specified level; and (iii) a full-capacity clause obligating lessees of unit-charge machines to "use the leased machinery to its full capacity upon all boots, shoes or other footwear or parts thereof made by . . . the lessee in the manufacture or preparation of which such machinery is capable of being used."[71] In addition to these express terms, United assessed a commutation charge of 25 percent of monthly rentals or 50 percent of minimum-usage charges on the balance of the lease term for machines returned prior to the expiration of the lease.[72]

Although the application of these terms was nominally uniform, United discriminatorily applied the commutation charges and full-capacity clause in practice. Specifically, United waived the monthly rental and minimum-usage balances due on unexpired leases when machinery returns were made for reasons other than the substitution of a competitor's machine.[73] Similarly, failure to employ a machine at full capacity violated the full-capacity clause only if "the lessee fail[ed] to use the machine on work for which the machine [was] capable of being used, and instead perform[ed] such work by using a competitor's machine."[74] Penalties were not assessed, however, where machine use was attenuated as the result

[70] With the exception of three minor machine types, all leased machines were subject to this provision. District Court Opinion, *supra* note 1, at 320. Note that return charges were assessed even upon returns at the expiration of the lease and were thus not conditional on premature termination. In effect, return charges were deferred initial payments and, with the exception of interest considerations, were equivalent to lump-sum transfers.

[71] *Id.* at 316. Violations of the full capacity clause were remedied by billing the customer for use of the machine to its appraised capacity.

[72] *Id.* at 320.

[73] *Id.*

[74] *Id.*

of demand shifts, product abandonment, conversion to manual operations, or replacement with another United machine.[75]

Both the existence and discriminatory application of return and usage restrictions in United's leases are consistent with efficiency motives. Even in the absence of free-rider considerations, efficient lease incentives would justify return charges in proportion to the expenses associated with repossessing and re-leasing returned machines.[76] Where rental prices also include premia for the provision of information that is potentially free ridable, the need to counter customer incentives to circumvent those premia by substituting competitor machines warrants additional deterrents applied in a discriminatory fashion.

The congruity between United's practices and efficiency concerns does not, however, preclude anticompetitive motives and effects. The profitability of exclusion, for instance, was conceivably greatest on the most complex and important machines. An excluding monopolist, moreover, would want to exclude efficiently.[77] Consequently, the question of whether particular contractual arrangements are anticompetitive turns on the magnitude of the switching costs they create. Specifically, to be anticompetitive, a contract restriction must deter efficient switching. In the absence of free-rider considerations, this means that the incremental price (conditional on retention or use) of a machine must be below the lessor's opportunity cost of leaving the machine with the lessee or, equiv-

[75] *Id.* The government cited eighty-eight instances between 1932 and 1948 involving twenty companies in which United invoked provisions of its leases to discourage substitution of a non-United for a United machine. Plaintiff's Request for Findings of Fact and Conclusions of Law, January 29, 1953, at 125–65 (hereafter Plaintiff's Request).

[76] In general, optimal return fees or damages for breach of lease may also include the lessor's profits on the unexpired portion of the lease. Ignoring incidental costs associated with the return, it is efficient to return a machine only if the value to the lessee of retaining it falls below the manufacturer's opportunity cost of leaving it with the lessee. Without return fees, however, a lessee would wish to return a machine whenever his valuation fell below the stream of payments required to retain it. To the extent a lessor earned economic rents on the transaction, the alternative value to him of a leased machine is its marginal revenue—equated (in expected terms) to its marginal cost—rather than the rental price. In legal terms, the manufacturer is a "lost-volume" seller and is entitled to the difference between price and cost. U.C.C. § 2-708, comment 2. See also § 2A-528(2) of the proposed U.C.C. article dealing with leases. Awarding lost profits, however, would remove the contingent nature of the seller's profits that was argued earlier to support the provision of quality goods and information. Hence, where leasing has been adopted for these purposes, damages should be limited to incidental costs connected with the return.

[77] The optimal barrier to switching in Aghion and Bolton's model, *supra* note 4, of strategic contracting is a function of the efficient level of damages as well as strategic factors. See Scott Masten & Edward Snyder, The Design and Duration of Contracts: Strategic and Efficiency Considerations, 52 L. & Contemp. Prob. 63, 68 (1989).

alently, that the size of the damage stipulated in the contract exceed the actual damages caused by the termination.[78] Hence, a contract restriction cannot be exclusionary unless it would constitute a penalty under common law.[79]

By this standard, the nondiscriminatory restrictions contained in United's leases do not appear unreasonable. On unit-charge machines, which accounted for over 80 percent of United's lease revenues,[80] return charges amounted to approximately one to two month's rent.[81] Hence, over 98 percent of prospective revenues from United's most complex and important machines were contingent on the use and retention of the equipment. Even on monthly rental machines, where return charges ranged more typically between five and ten month's rentals, over 92 percent of potential lease revenue reflected contingent payments.[82] Stated differently, the fixed component of United's lease revenues averaged

[78] Masten & Snyder, *supra* note 77. The desired incentives can be established in either of two ways: by stipulating a price, p, and damages, d; or through a two-part price schedule with fixed component, F, and incremental price, p'. Using the first form, the buyer pays p if he keeps the machine (or accepts delivery) and d if he returns it, making the cost to the buyer of keeping the machine $p - d$. Under the two-part price contract, the buyer pays $F + p'$ if he keeps the machine and F if he returns it, the cost of retaining the machine being simply p'. The incentives created by the two contracts are equivalent if $p = F + p'$ and $d = F$. Efficiency requires that the cost to the buyer of retaining the machine equal the value or savings to the seller of the buyer's retention, say c. This can be accomplished by setting either $d = p - c$ or $p' = c$. A contract is exclusionary only if $d > p - c$ or $p' < c$.

[79] Specifically, the common law requires that damages stipulated in a contract be "reasonable in light of the anticipated or actual loss caused by the breach"; terms that fix damages in excess of that amount are considered penalties and unenforceable. Restatement (Second) of Contracts § 356 (1979). See also § 2A-504(1) of the proposed U.C.C. article dealing with leases.

[80] Kaysen, *supra* note 7, at 139.

[81] These estimates are based on normal machine-usage rates and on predecree price information contained in Report of United Shoe Machinery Corporation under Decree, para. 18, app. D, filed December 15, 1964 (hereafter United Report). Goldberg arrives at a similar estimate using a smaller sample of lease terms reported in the District Court Opinion, *supra* note 1, at 314. See Goldberg, *supra* note 3, at 4.

[82] The average was approximately eight months. Optional sale-or-lease machines had somewhat higher return charges and also required initial (or up-front) payments. Hence, optional lease machines had terms that made them closer in nature to sales. Although return charges were larger on monthly rental than on unit-charge machines in percentage terms, the dollar amount averaged approximately $67 on monthly rental equipment compared to $247 on unit-charge machines. The percentage figures reported in the text represent total undiscounted lease revenues minus the fraction of that total represented by the return charges. Since the return charges are deferred to the end of the lease, the appropriately discounted fraction of prospective lease revenue represented by the monthly charges would be even smaller.

across leased machines was equivalent to liquidated damages of less than 3 percent of the price of a machine.[83]

The size of the switching deterrent was, of course, larger where a machine was being returned for the purpose of substituting competitors' equipment. As already noted, lessees who replaced a United machine with a competitor's machine were required to pay 25 percent of monthly rentals on monthly-rental only machines and 50 percent of minimum-usage charges on unit-charge machines due on the unexpired balance of the lease. Since minimum-usage charges represented about 10 percent of revenues expected from unit-charge machines used at full capacity and unit-charge machines accounted for over 80 percent of lease revenue, these additional charges were compatible with a value of free-ridable information equal to approximately 8 or 9 percent of total lease revenue. Although the record does not permit a precise estimate of the cost of providing those services, United's expenditures on all research and service activities accounted for over 40 percent of its machinery expenses.[84] Hence, if even a quarter of United's research and service efforts reflected expenditures on nonpatentable machinery improvements or free-ridable know-how, its commutation charges would have fallen well within the range of reasonable values for damages caused by the return of machines in order to to free ride on those investments. Moreover, note that, because the commutation charge applied to the unexpired portion of the lease, the size of this deterrent declined linearly over the course of the lease. Whereas exclusionary motives provide no basis to expect the strategic component of lease restrictions to decrease over time, a declining schedule of damages is consistent with the desire to adjust deterrents to free riding in proportion to the benefits of information accrued but not paid for.

The minimum-usage provisions implied a similarly small deterrent. Under United's formula, a lessee who used a machine at a level (q) less than the minimum number of pairs designated in the lease (q_m) was obligated to pay, in addition to unit charges on that output, a proportion of a

[83] The court in this case did not address the reasonableness of United's return fees relative to the common-law standard. An appeals court did address this issue in an earlier case, however, and concluded that deferred fees in United's earlier leases were "not unreasonable compensation for the costs to [United] of replacing the machines in use after the end of a prior lease" and therefore did not constitute penalties. In re Diana Shoe Corporation, 80 F.2d 827, 829 (1936). United's practice was to salvage parts from returned machines for use in the manufacture of new machines. United Facts, *supra* note 8, at 484. Parts accounted for approximately 90 percent and assembly 10 percent of United's manufacturing costs. *Id.* at 483.

[84] Kaysen, *supra* note 7, at 118. Also see note 55 *supra*.

stipulated minimum monthly payment (M) equal to the ratio of the deficiency to the minimum number of pairs, or $pq + M(q_m - q)/q_m$.[85] The effect was to reduce by M/q_m the marginal cost of producing an additional pair of shoes at output rates below q_m. In practice, the minimum quantity was typically set at approximately 25 percent of machine capacity and the minimum payment at 40 percent of the unit charges for that quantity.[86] As a result, the incremental cost of an additional operation over the first 25 percent of capacity equalled approximately 60 percent of the nominal unit charge. Hence, in contrast to standard minimum bill provisions, United's restriction implied a substantial incremental cost of use below the minimum.[87] Moreover, the implied reduction in unit charges at low production levels established incentives that are consistent with the fact that machines that were being used less intensively needed to be repaired with less haste.

Finally, United's implementation of its lease provisions deviated from their formal terms in ways that increased flexibility. For example, although the formal provisions provided for their uniform application, United waived the minimum-usage charge for four months each year to lessen their burden during periods of slack demand.[88] More significant, United also established what it called a "Right of Deduction Fund" under which 4 percent of all unit and rental charges was credited to an account that lessees in good standing could use to pay return, minimum-usage, and commutation charges.[89] A lessee who had leased a large number of United machines over an extended period gained substantial flexibility to return or reduce usage of United equipment.[90]

In sum, the size, nature, and implementation of United's exclusionary-

[85] United Facts, *supra* note 8, at 196.

[86] *Id.* at 197; and District Court Opinion, *supra* note 1, at 320.

[87] For a discussion of minimum-bill provisions, see Scott E. Masten, Minimum Bill Contracts: Theory and Policy, 37 J. Indus. Econ. 85 (1988). For an opinion (written by Judge Richard Posner) interpreting minimum-bill provisions as creating penalties, see Lake River Corp. v. Carborundum Co., 769 F.2d 1284 (7th Cir. 1985).

[88] District Court Opinion, *supra* note 1, at 321. The application of this waiver was automatic. If the lessee failed to select which four months he wanted waived, United would select those most favorable to him. The waiver also applied to the calculation of commutation charges. In addition, United made available "peak-load" machines and offered thirty-day-trial-period installations on its machines. *Id.*

[89] *Id.* at 320. Balances in the Right of Deduction Fund could be applied to any leased machine.

[90] The government acknowledged that the accumulated credits were generally "adequate to take care of current returns of a factory which is in operation, having a large number of United machines." Plaintiff's Request, *supra* note 75, at 117. See also Hanover Shoe Inc. v. United Shoe Machinery Corp., 245 F. Supp. 258 (1965).

lease provisions are hard to reconcile with anticompetitive motives. The monetary deterrents to returning or ceasing to use United's machines were small relative to the total value of the lease and appear to have been proportionate to the harm caused United. Even ignoring the moderating effects of the Right of Deduction Fund, the discriminatory charges applied to returns or usage reductions for the purpose of substituting a rival's equipment were modest and declined as the term of the lease progressed, suggesting that United's objective was not to discourage efficient returns but only large-scale free riding on the advice and technical information it provided.[91]

Lessor Monitoring and Termination. To police against machine abuse and to detect tampering with usage indicators, a shoe manufacturer would want easy access to its machines and the ability to observe their operation. United's leases provided explicitly for such access, reserving to United the right "at all times [to] have free access to the leased machinery for the purpose of inspecting it or watching its use and operation, or of altering, repairing, improving, or adding to it, or determining the nature or extent of its use."[92] United also required lessees to keep records and file reports on the use of its equipment.[93] Where a "breach or default in the performance of any of the conditions contained in the lease" was detected, United reserved the right to terminate the lease "forthwith,"[94] whereupon United was authorized to enter the customer's premises and repossess machines.[95] Hence, United's leases sought to lower the costs of detecting and punishing lessee misconduct.

Maintenance and Repairs. Contrary to our prediction (and the representations of many commentators), the responsibility and expense of maintaining and repairing machines under the lease rested with the lessee and not with United. Specifically, United required the lessee "at all times and at his own expense [to] keep the leased machinery in good and efficient working order and condition."[96] Should the lessee fail to maintain machinery in a satisfactory manner, United reserved the right to make

[91] Returns, in fact, occurred in significant numbers; the district court estimated that between 20 and 25 percent of leased machines were returned within five years. District Court Opinion, *supra* note 1, at 319. Turnover among shoe manufacturers, meanwhile, was 10–12 percent a year. See Kaysen, *supra* note 7, at 55. Also see Posner, *supra* note 2, at 203.

[92] District Court Opinion, *supra* note 1, at 315.

[93] *Id.* at 317.

[94] *Id.*

[95] *Id.* at 318. Leased machinery remained the property of United, and neither the machinery nor the lease could be transferred to another firm.

[96] *Id.* at 315.

any necessary repairs itself and to bill the lessee accordingly.[97] In practice, however, United consistently assumed the burden of repairing its leased machines and charged only for the cost of replacement parts.[98]

This discrepancy between the de jure and de facto responsibility for repairs under United's leases is consistent with a desire to avoid costly legal disputes by reducing the scope for contract evasion. As long as a machine was not abused or its indicator tampered with, United had no incentive to terminate a lease and, moreover, had substantial incentives given the contingent nature of payment under leasing to maintain and repair its machinery. Formal assignment of the obligation to maintain machines to United would have done nothing to augment those incentives and could have provided the lessee with an avenue to contrive cancellation of the lease by claiming unsatisfactory performance on the part of United. Given the difficulty of defining satisfactory performance contractually and the high incidence of breakdowns on even the highest-quality and best-maintained machines, an opportunistic lessee wishing to return a machine to avoid the implicit charges for information would likely have been able to construct a credible claim of dissatisfaction and thereby evade performance.

Legal assignment of the material and financial burden of caring for machines to the lessee, in contrast, reinforced United's legal authority to punish a customer's tampering and abuse by repossessing machines. Lessees were, in effect, always in gross violation of the lease's maintenance requirements and would thus have found it difficult to challenge a termination by United. Moreover, since United had nothing to gain from prematurely terminating a lease to a productive shoemaker, United could not exploit its termination authority opportunistically. Thus, again, the formal structure of United's leases appear to support desired performance with minimum risk of costly adjudication.

V. Competitor and Predecessor Practices

The leasing of shoe machines did not originate with United but was a common practice among both United's predecessors and competitors. The practice of leasing shoe machinery had begun as early as the Civil War with the McKay Sewing Machine.[99] Gordon McKay, the industry's most renowned figure, developed a leasing system with royalty charges

[97] *Id.*

[98] *Id.* at 322.

[99] *Id.* at 314; United Facts, *supra* note 8, at 192.

to overcome resistance to the adoption of his machines.[100] In addition, the four companies that merged to form United in 1899 had all offered machines for lease only with lease provisions similar to United's, including return fees, minimum-usage charges, and the full-capacity clause.[101] Like United, these companies provided service and training in the use of machines; "McKay's corps of repairmen kept machines in top condition and taught operators and shoe manufacturers this wholly different system of shoemaking."[102]

Although detailed information on the terms under which United's rivals supplied machines is not available, leasing was clearly the predominant mode of distribution.[103] The record does indicate, moreover, that Compo, a full-service shoe-machinery supplier[104] and United's largest competitor with roughly 2 percent of the market,[105] also offered its most important machines for lease only[106] and that its leases contained return charges.[107] That shoe machine manufacturers in substantially different market positions responded to the underlying organizational problems in a like manner is additional support for an efficiency interpretation of United's practices.

VI. The Aftermath

In February 1953, Judge Charles Wyzanski ruled that United had illegally monopolized the shoe-machinery market and that United's leasing practices were the means by which it had done so. Rejecting the government's call for dissolution, he issued a decree having three central features. First, he required that United make all of its machines available for sale under terms that "do not make it substantially more advanta-

[100] Martin L. Lindahl and William A. Carter, Corporate Concentration and Public Policy 226 (1959).

[101] U.S. vs. United Shoe Machinery Co., 222 Fed. Rep. 349, at 385–86 (1915); U.S. v. United Shoe Machinery Co., 247 U.S. 32, at 62 (1911); Brief for United Shoe Machinery Corporation 278 (January 1952).

[102] A Legend and How It Began, 1 United Shoe Machinery Today 4 (1974). The level of services provided by United's predecessors, however, was not as high as United's, nor were repair services as prompt. U.S. v. United Shoe Machinery Co. (1915), *supra* note 101, at 369–72.

[103] See District Court Opinion, *supra* note 1, at 314; United Facts, *supra* note 8, at 193.

[104] See text at note 37 *supra*.

[105] Kaysen, *supra* note 7, at 52–53.

[106] Reply of United Shoe Machinery Corporation to Brief of the United States on Relief, April 11, 1952, at 27.

[107] United Facts, *supra* note 8, at 201.

geous for a shoe factory to lease rather than to buy a machine." Second, he directed that United's leases be shortened to five years and "be purged of their restrictive features." In particular, the full capacity and minimum-usage requirements were completely prohibited, while return fees were sharply restricted and their discriminatory application forbidden. Finally, the decree allowed United to provide instruction and repair services free of charge for thirty days following installation but required that United charge separately for all services, including repairs, rendered thereafter. Thus, the decree circumscribed both United's ability to lease and the structure of its leases.[108]

As a result of the decree, United lost several of the principal instruments through which it fashioned incentives and governed the exchange of machines and services. In particular, the court's restrictions on the size and implementation of switching penalties reduced United's ability to curb free riding and, thereby, its incentive to invest in generating nonpatentable know-how. The requirement that machines be sold on favorable terms (about half of the machines previously leased were purchased between 1953 and 1963)[109] (i) limited the ability of United and its customers to realize leasing's advantages in warranting machines and in safeguarding information transfers and (ii) aggravated the free-riding problem by creating a new alternative to United's leased machines in the form of sale and secondhand machines. Finally, segregating repair charges undermined United's incentive to provide prompt repairs and interfered with the warranting function of leasing by weakening the link between machine performance and United's profits.

As might be expected, United sought to mitigate the harm caused by the ruling by adjusting the terms of its leases within the constraints of the decree. Thus, for instance, one effect of the ruling was to alter the relative merits of monthly rental and unit charges. Whereas the court condoned limited return charges on monthly rentals[110] by voiding the minimum-usage and full-capacity provisions, the decree abolished all deterrents to free riding through reductions in machine usage. In response, United eliminated unit charges on eight of the eighty-eight unit-charge machines it offered in 1954 and reduced them on all but one of the remain-

[108] The decree did not limit the leasing practices of other shoe machinery manufacturers. District Court Opinion, *supra* note 1, at 349.

[109] Brief for Respondent United Shoe Machinery Corp., June 3, 1968, at 10.

[110] The decree limited the size of return fees to three monthly rental payments. Final Decree, February 18, 1953, para. 6, as modified by orders of the Court, July 12, 1954, and September 17, 1954, as reported in the District Court Opinion, *supra* note 1, at 351–54.

TABLE 4

CHANGES IN UNITED'S ROADMEN AND MACHINES OUTSTANDING

Year	Roadmen	Leased Machines	Total Machines	Ratio of Leased to Total	Ratio of Roadmen to Total Machines
1920	700*	95,595†	108,631†	.880	.00644
1955	846‡	100,525§	113,928§	.882	.00743
1964	349‡	28,819§	94,355§	.305	.00370

* Source.—United States v. United Shoe Machinery Co., 264 Fed. Rep. 138, 143–44 (1920).

† Estimate based on Carl Kaysen, *United Shoe v. United Shoe Machinery Corporation:* An Economic Analysis of an Antitrust Case 28 (1956); and United States v. United Shoe Machinery Co., 264 Fed. Rep. 138, 163 (1920).

‡ Source.—Report of United Shoe Machinery Corporation under Decree Paragraph 18, December 15, 1964, at 41.

§ Source.—Report of United Shoe Machinery Corporation under Decce Paragraph 18, December 15, 1964, at 8, 10, 18.

der, while increasing the size of both monthly rentals and initial payments on these machines.[111]

But the more important consequence of the decree, and one harder to quantify, was its effect on real variables, such as the quality of United's machinery and services and its research effort to develop new techniques and other shoemaking know-how. One measure of United's service was its employment of roadmen, its principal conduit for machine repairs and day-to-day advice on shoemaking problems. As Table 4 reveals, the number of roadmen declined precipitously, both in absolute terms (col. 2) and relative to machines outstanding (col. 6), following the loss of the appeal to the Supreme Court in 1954[112] and implementation of the decree beginning in 1955. To the extent this reduction is indicative of an overall decline in United's support for its machines, it implies a major deterioration in United's performance.

Finally, although attributing the decline of the U.S. shoe industry to the decision in *United Shoe* would be overly heroic, it is true nevertheless that the industry went into a sharp decline in the decades following the decree. The share of imported shoes rose from a tiny fraction prior to

[111] The decrease in unit charges averaged 30 percent. Kaysen, *supra* note 7, at 326, estimated repair costs to average 13.3 percent of total lease costs prior to the decree. Monthly rentals on unit charge machines rose from an average of $5.73 to $29.19 and initial payments from $2.27 to $65.98, compared to average increases from $8.07 to $18.68 in monthly rentals and from $90.36 to $170.08 in initial payments on all leased machinery. Pre- and postdecree lease terms are reported in United Report, *supra* note 81, app. D. Note that the segregation of repair charges might also have led to a reduction in unit charges but would not by itself have dictated increases in other lease charges.

[112] The Supreme Court issued a per curium opinion on May 17, 1954. 347 U.S. 521 (1954).

1950 to 25 percent by 1964 and continued to rise thereafter. Furthermore, United's decline definitely preceded that of the domestic shoe industry. Despite the increasing growth of imports, domestic shoe production rose 32 percent during the 1950s and remained at around 725 million pairs during much of the 1960s. By contrast, United had lost over a third of its predecision market share by 1963.[113]

VII. Concluding Remarks

A reexamination of *United States v. United Shoe Machinery Corp.* is of more than historical interest. First, equipment leasing is an important organizational form, accounting for $36.8 billion worth of transactions in the United States in 1988.[114] Its growing significance is evidenced by the recent creation of a separate Uniform Commercial Code article concerned exclusively with leasing. Understanding the role that leasing plays in commercial transactions is fundamental to assessing the quality of such legal rules and can help inform judges as to their appropriate application in individual cases. Second, judges are repeatedly asked to rule on charges of anticompetitive exclusion, a contemporary example being the litigation over the contract terms governing airline computer-reservation systems.[115] If recently developed theories of strategic exclusion were to stimulate widespread antitrust challenges of contracting practices, *United Shoe* would furnish the legal precedent for courts to dictate the details of commercial dealings. Not only did the case target a variety of specific lease terms, but the court, after ruling against United, entered a judgment that essentially rewrote United's contracts. What limited evidence is available suggests that external interference in the incentive provisions of contracts can seriously diminish the efficiency of contractual exchange.[116]

[113] United Report, *supra* note 81, at 19.

[114] Aviation Daily, November 7, 1989, at 251. Interestingly, the three largest categories of leased equipment—computers, aircraft, and telecommunications equipment—are, like shoe machinery, complex, durable, and redeployable. IBM lawyers apparently represented a sizable and attentive section of the audience at United's trial. Conversation with John Meuse, chairman of United Shoe Machinery Corp., December 18, 1990. IBM's leasing practices were themselves the subject of private antitrust charges in the 1970s. See Masten and Snyder, *supra* note 77, at 74, 82–83, and cites therein.

[115] See, for instance, United Airlines, Inc., v. Austin Travel Corporation, 867 F.2d 737 (1989) (defendant claimed that liquidated damages in computer-reservation-system agreements were unreasonable and violated antitrust statutes). See also the federal carrier-owned computer-reservation-system regulations codified at 14 C.F.R. 255 (1989). The Federal Trade Commission's current investigation of Microsoft's pricing of its software may raise similar issues insofar as the pricing scheme, while discouraging customers from purchasing rivals' products, may encourage the transfer of nonpatentable know-how.

[116] See Keith J. Crocker & Scott E. Masten, Mitigating Contractual Hazards: Unilateral Options and Contract Length, 19 Rand J. Econ. 327 (1988).

We have argued here that United's leasing practices represented a coherent and measured response to the incentive and governance problems encountered in these transactions. Specifically, leasing performed two distinct but related functions. First, leasing served as an alternative to contractual warranties in motivating the development, production, and servicing of a large number of complex machines. Second, leasing provided a means of indirectly rewarding shoe machine manufacturers for the provision of a wide range of technical advice and shoe-manufacturing know-how and thus offered a partial solution to now-familiar information transfer problems.

United appears, moreover, to have framed its leases, within the practical limitations on contracting, to promote the efficient provision and use of its machines and services. The long-term and "exclusionary" features of United's leases, for instance, were necessary to prevent customers from reneging on implied promises to pay for United's information and advice through the use of machines. Even United's discriminatory application of return and usage restrictions is consistent with efficiency; to preserve the benefits of leasing while deterring free riding, the magnitude of switching costs should be conditional on machines being returned to substitute competitor equipment. On a broader level, the assignment of powers and responsibilities within United's leases was consistent with a goal of minimizing costly court adjudication in favor of unilateral responses to lease violations.

Finally, data on United's leasing and pricing practices provide evidence that United chose distribution arrangements systematically to reflect the incentive and transaction-cost considerations identified in this article. While it is true, as the prosecution claimed, that United offered its most important machines for lease only, the efficiency advantages of leasing relative to sales were greatest on the most important and complex machines where the limitations of contractual warranties and the hazards of free riding were most acute. The fact that service-oriented shoe-machine manufacturers both preceding and following United's formation leased machines under similar terms further supports the view that leasing was a solution to fundamental organizational problems in the industry.

Evidence that contracting practices were sensitive to efficiency concerns does not preclude anticompetitive motives. Doing so requires a showing either that the conditions necessary to sustain anticompetitive behavior are absent or that the restrictions imposed by the contract are insufficient to have an anticompetitive effect. The conditions required for strategic behavior in the few models that explore the exclusionary potential of contracts have not been adequately enumerated and scrutinized.

What efforts have been made in that regard suggest either that the circumstances in which contractual exclusion can occur are limited[117] or that distinguishing between strategic and efficiency motives using market screens is difficult.[118] As a result, it will often be necessary to assess the reasonableness of specific restrictions on a case-by-case basis. One's willingness to subject widely used contractual terms to antitrust review will depend in part on one's confidence in the ability of judges to recognize the many legitimate purposes served by contract restrictions in diverse and multifaceted business transactions. In our view, the decision in *United Shoe* stands as an illustration of the hazards inherent in such a policy.

Bibliography

Aghion, Patrick, and Bolton, Phillipe. "Contracts as a Barrier to Entry." *American Economic Review* 77 (1987): 388–401.

Arrow, Kenneth J. *Essays in the Theory of Risk-bearing*. Chicago: Markham, 1971.

Bork, Robert H. *The Antitrust Paradox*. New York: Basic Books, 1978.

Bowman, Ward S. "Review of '*United States v. United Shoe Machinery Corporation*, An Economic Analysis' by Carl Kaysen." *Yale Law Journal* 66 (1956): 303–14.

Chapman, Kenneth, and Meurer, Michael J. "Efficient Remedies for Breach of Warranty." *Law and Contemporary Problems* 52 (1989): 107–31.

Coase, R. H. "Durability and Monopoly." *Journal of Law and Economics* 15 (1972): 143–49.

Cooper, Russell, and Ross, Thomas W. "Product Warranties and Double Moral Hazard." *Rand Journal of Economics* 16 (1985): 103–13.

Crocker, Keith J., and Masten, Scott E. "Mitigating Contractual Hazards: Unilateral Options and Contract Length." *Rand Journal of Economics* 19 (1988): 327–43.

Director, Aaron, and Levi, Edward. "Law and the Future: Trade Regulation." *Northwestern University Law Review* 51 (1956): 281–96.

Flath, David. "The Economics of Short-Term Leasing." *Economic Inquiry* 18 (1980): 247–59.

Goldberg, Victor P. "The United Shoe Machinery Leases." Unpublished manuscript. New York: Columbia University Law School, 1990.

Grossman, Sanford J., and Hart, Oliver D. "The Costs and Benefits of Owner-

[117] See Masten & Snyder, *supra* note 77; and Eric Rasmusen, Recent Developments in the Economics of Exclusionary Contracts, in Canadian Competition Law and Policy at the Centenary (R. S. Khemani & W. T. Stanbury eds. 1991).

[118] Edward A. Snyder & Thomas E. Kauper, Misuse of the Antitrust Laws: The Competitor Plaintiff, 90 Mich. L. Rev. 551 (1991).

ship: A Theory of Vertical and Lateral Integration." *Journal of Political Economy* 94 (1986): 691–719.

Kaysen, Carl. *"United States v. United Shoe Machinery Corporation": An Economic Analysis of an Antitrust Case*. Cambridge, Mass.: Harvard University Press, 1956.

Klein, Benjamin, and Leffler, Keith B. "The Role of Market Forces in Assuring Contractual Performance." *Journal of Political Economy* 89 (1981): 615–41.

Klein, Benjamin, and Murphy, Kevin M. "Vertical Restraints as Contract Enforcement Mechanisms." *Journal of Law and Economics* 31 (1988): 265–97.

Levy, David T. "Short-Term Leasing and Monopoly Power: The Case of IBM." *Journal of Institutional and Theoretical Economics* 144 (1988): 611–34.

Lindahl, Martin L., and Carter, William A. *Corporate Concentration and Public Policy*. Englewood Cliffs, N.J.: Prentice Hall, 1959.

Maddala, G. S. *Limited Dependent and Qualitative Variables in Econometrics*. Cambridge: Cambridge University Press, 1983.

Marvel, Howard P. "Exclusive Dealing." *Journal of Law and Economics* 25 (1982): 1–25.

Masten, Scott E. "Minimum Bill Contracts: Theory and Policy." *Journal of Industrial Economics* 37 (1988): 85–97.

Masten, Scott E.; Meehan, James W.; and Snyder, Edward A. "The Costs of Organization." *Journal of Law, Economics, and Organization* 7 (1991): 1–25.

Masten, Scott E., and Snyder, Edward A. "The Design and Duration of Contracts: Strategic and Efficiency Considerations." *Law and Contemporary Problems* 52 (1989): 63–85.

Posner, Richard A. *Antitrust Law: An Economic Perspective*. Chicago: University of Chicago Press, 1979.

Priest, George L. "A Theory of the Consumer Product Warranty." *Yale Law Journal* 90 (1981): 1297–1352.

Rasmusen, Eric. "Recent Developments in the Economics of Exclusionary Contracts." In *Canadian Competition Law and Policy at the Centenary*. Edited by R. S. Khemani and W. T. Stanbury. Halifax, Nova Scotia: Institute for Research on Public Policy, 1991.

Rogerson, William P. "Profit Regulation of Defense Contractors and Prizes for Innovation." *Journal of Political Economy* 97 (1989): 1284–1305.

Snyder, Edward A., and Kauper, Thomas E. "Misuse of the Antitrust Laws: The Competitor Plaintiff." *Michigan Law Review* 90 (1991): 551–603.

Teece, David. "Economies of Scope and the Scope of the Enterprise." *Journal of Economic Behavior and Organization* 1 (1980): 223–45.

Wiley, John S.; Rasmusen, Eric; and Ramseyer J. Mark. "The Monopolist That Leases." *University of California Law Review* 37 (1990): 693–731.

Williamson, Oliver E. *Markets and Hierarchies*. New York: Free Press, 1975.

Williamson, Oliver E. *The Economic Institutions of Capitalism*. New York: Free Press, 1985.

Name Index

The International Library of Critical Writings in Economics

1. Multinational Corporations
   Mark Casson
2. The Economics of Innovation
   Christopher Freeman
3. Entrepreneurship
   Mark Casson
4. International Investment
   Peter J. Buckley
5. Game Theory in Economics
   Ariel Rubinstein
6. The History of Economic Thought
   Mark Blaug
7. Monetary Theory
   Thomas Mayer
8. Joint Production of Commodities
   Neri Salvadori and Ian Steedman
9. Industrial Organization
   Oliver E. Williamson
10. Growth Theory (Volumes I, II and III)
    R. Becker and E. Burmeister
11. Microeconomics: Theoretical and Applied (Volumes I, II and III)
    Robert E. Kuenne
12. The Economics of Health (Volumes I and II)
    A.J. Culyer
13. Recent Developments in Macroeconomics (Volumes I, II and III)
    Edmund S. Phelps
14. Urban and Regional Economics
    Paul C. Cheshire and Alan W. Evans
15. Modern Public Finance (Volumes I and II)
    A.B. Atkinson
16. Exchange Rate Economics (Volumes I and II)
    Ronald MacDonald and Mark P. Taylor

17. The Economic Value of Education: Studies in the Economics of Education
Mark Blaug

18. Development Economics (Volumes I, II, III and IV)
Deepak Lal

19. The New Classical Macroeconomics (Volumes I, II and III)
Kevin D. Hoover

20. The Economics of the Environment
Wallace E. Oates

21. Post Keynesian Theory of Growth and Distribution
Carlo Panico and Neri Salvadori

22. Dynamic Labor Demand and Adjustment Costs
Giorgio Galeazzi and Daniel S. Hamermesh

23. The Philosophy and Methodology of Economics (Volumes I, II and III)
Bruce J. Caldwell

24. Public Choice Theory (Volumes I, II and III)
Charles K. Rowley

25. Evolutionary Economics
Ulrich Witt

26. Economics and Psychology
Shlomo Maital and Sharone L. Maital

27. Social Choice Theory (Volumes I, II and III)
Charles K. Rowley

28. Non-Linear Dynamics in Economic Theory
Marc Jarsulic

29. Recent Developments in Experimental Economics (Volumes I and II)
John D. Hey and Graham Loomes

30. Monopoly and Competition Policy (Volumes I and II)
F.M. Scherer

31. The Economics of Technical Change
Edwin Mansfield and Elizabeth Mansfield

32. The Economics of Exhaustible Resources
Geoffrey Heal

33. The Economics of Institutions
Geoffrey M. Hodgson

34. The Economics of Transport (Volumes I and II)
Herbert Mohring

35. Implicit Contract Theory
Sherwin Rosen

36. Foundations of Analytical Marxism (Volumes I and II)
John E. Roemer

37. The Economics of Product Differentiation (Volumes I and II)
Jacques-François Thisse and George Norman

38. Economic Growth in Theory and Practice: A Kaldorian Perspective
John E. King

39. Markets and Socialism
Alec Nove and Ian D. Thatcher

40. Recent Developments in the Economics of Education
Elchanan Cohn and Geraint Johnes

41. The Theory of Inflation
Michael Parkin

42. The Economics of Location (Volumes I, II and III)
Melvin L. Greenhut and George Norman

43. Financial Intermediaries
Mervyn K. Lewis

44. The Political Economy of Privatization and Deregulation
Elizabeth E. Bailey and Janet Rothenberg Pack

45. Gender and Economics
Jane Humphries

46. Macroeconomics and Imperfect Competition
Jean-Pascal Bénassy

47. Labor Economics (Volumes I, II, III and IV)
Orley C. Ashenfelter and Kevin F. Hallock

48. The Economics of Altruism
Stefano Zamagni

49. The Economic Analysis of Rent Seeking
Robert D. Tollison and Roger D. Congleton

50. Economics and Biology
Geoffrey M. Hodgson

51. The Economics of Ageing
John Creedy

52. Fiscal and Monetary Policy (Volumes I and II)
Thomas Mayer and Steven M. Sheffrin

53. The Economics of Information (Volumes I and II)
David K. Levine and Steven A. Lippman

54. Transaction Cost Economics (Volumes I and II)
Oliver E. Williamson and Scott E. Masten

Future titles will include:

Economics and Discrimination
William A. Darity, Jr

Long Wave Theory
Christopher Freeman

International Trade
J. Peter Neary

Agricultural Economics
G.H. Peters

International Debt
Graham Bird and P.N. Snowden

Small Firms and Economic Growth
Zoltan Acs

Business Cycle Theory
Finn E. Kydland

General Equilibrium Theory
Gerard Debreu

The Money Supply in the Economic Process
Marco Musella and Carlo Panico

Producer Cooperatives and Labor-Managed Systems
David L. Prychitko and Jaroslav Vanek

The Foundations of Public Finance
Peter Jackson

Ethics and Economics
Alan Hamlin

The Economics of Training
Robert J. LaLonde and Orley Ashenfelter

The Economics of the Family
Nancy Folbre

The New Growth Theory
Gene M. Grossman

Chaotic Dynamics in Economics
W. Davis Dechert

The Economics of Communication and Innovation
Donald M. Lamberton

International Finance
Robert Z. Aliber

Welfare Economics
William J. Baumol and Janusz A. Ordover

The Theory of the Firm
Mark Casson

The Economics of Inequality and Poverty
A.B. Atkinson

The Economics of Housing
John M. Quigley

Population Economics
Julian L. Simon

The Economics of Crime
Isaac Ehrlich

The Economics of Integration
Willem Molle

The Rhetoric of Economics
Donald McCloskey

Migration
Oded Stark

Economic Forecasting
Paul Ormerod

The Economics of Defence
Keith Hartley and Nicholas Hooper

Consumer Theory
Kelvin Lancaster

Law and Economics
Judge Richard A. Posner

The Economics of Business Policy
John Kay

Microeconomic Theories of Imperfect Competition
Jacques Thisse and Jean Gabszewicz

The Economics of Increasing Returns
Geoffrey Heal

The Balance of Payments
Michael J. Artis

Cost-Benefit Analysis
Arnold Harberger and Glenn P. Jenkins

The Economics of Unemployment
P.N. Junankar

Mathematical Economics
Graciela Chichilnisky

Economic Growth in the Long Run
Bart van Ark

Gender in Economic and Social History
K.J. Humphries and J. Lewis

The Economics of Uncertainty
John D. Hey